CENTRE FOR EDUCATIONAL RESEARCH
AND INNOVATION
INDICATORS OF EDUCATION SYSTEMS

EDUCATION AT A GLANCE
OECD Indicators

ORGANISATION FOR ECONOMIC CO-OPERATION AND DEVELOPMENT

ORGANISATION FOR ECONOMIC CO-OPERATION AND DEVELOPMENT

Pursuant to Article 1 of the Convention signed in Paris on 14th December 1960, and which came into force on 30th September 1961, the Organisation for Economic Co-operation and Development (OECD) shall promote policies designed:
- to achieve the highest sustainable economic growth and employment and a rising standard of living in Member countries, while maintaining financial stability, and thus to contribute to the development of the world economy;
- to contribute to sound economic expansion in Member as well as non-member countries in the process of economic development; and
- to contribute to the expansion of world trade on a multilateral, non-discriminatory basis in accordance with international obligations.

The original Member countries of the OECD are Austria, Belgium, Canada, Denmark, France, Germany, Greece, Iceland, Ireland, Italy, Luxembourg, the Netherlands, Norway, Portugal, Spain, Sweden, Switzerland, Turkey, the United Kingdom and the United States. The following countries became Members subsequently through accession at the dates indicated hereafter: Japan (28th April 1964), Finland (28th January 1969), Australia (7th June 1971), New Zealand (29th May 1973), Mexico (18th May 1994), the Czech Republic (21st December 1995) and Hungary (7th May 1996). The Commission of the European Communities takes part in the work of the OECD (Article 13 of the OECD Convention).

The Centre for Educational Research and Innovation was created in June 1968 by the Council of the Organisation for Economic Co-operation and Development and all Member countries of the OECD are participants.

The main objectives of the Centre are as follows:
- *to promote and support the development of research activities in education and undertake such research activities where appropriate;*
- *to promote and support pilot experiments with a view to introducing and testing innovations in the educational system;*
- *to promote the development of co-operation between Member countries in the field of educational research and innovation.*

The Centre functions within the Organisation for Economic Co-operation and Development in accordance with the decisions of the Council of the Organisation, under the authority of the Secretary-General. It is supervised by a Governing Board composed of one national expert in its field of competence from each of the countries participating in its programme of work.

Publié en français sous le titre :
REGARDS SUR L'ÉDUCATION
Les indicateurs de l'OCDE

© OECD 1996
Applications for permission to reproduce or translate all or part of this
publication should be made to:
Head of Publications Service, OECD
2, rue André-Pascal, 75775 PARIS CEDEX 16, France.

Foreword

The first edition of *Education at a Glance* appeared in September 1992. This fourth edition presents an updated set of the OECD education indicators that covers a wider range of educational domains and is more internationally comparable.

Like its predecessors, the publication is the fruit of the collective effort of policy officials, civil servants, researchers and statisticians from 30 countries. The indicators have been prepared and discussed by the INES Technical Group and by four Networks of countries which co-operate with the OECD Secretariat in developing indicators of common interest in accordance with the policy priorities of the Member countries and the conceptual framework prepared by the OECD-INES project.

The publication was prepared by the Statistics and Indicators Division of the OECD Directorate for Education, Employment, Labour and Social Affairs. This work was facilitated by the financial and material support of the four countries responsible for co-ordinating the INES Networks – the Netherlands, Sweden, the United Kingdom (Scotland) and the United States. In addition, work on the publication has been aided by a grant from the National Center for Education Statistics (NCES) in the United States. *Education at a Glance – Indicators* is published on the responsibility of the Secretary General of the OECD.

ALSO AVAILABLE

Education at a Glance – Analysis
ISBN 92-64-15357-8   FF 50   £6   US$10   DM15

Employment Outlook
ISBN 92-64-14900-7   France: FF 230   Other countries: FF 305   £39   US$60   DM89

Lifelong Learning for All
ISBN 92-64-14815-9   France: FF 195   Other countries: FF 255   £33   US$50   DM74

Literacy, Economy and Society –
Results of the First International Adult Literacy Survey
(OECD and Statistics Canada)
ISBN 92-64-14655-5   France: FF 160   Other countries: FF 210   £26   US$40   DM60

Prices charged at the OECD Bookshop.
The OECD CATALOGUE OF PUBLICATIONS and supplements will be sent free of charge
on request addressed either to OECD Publications Service,
or to the OECD Distributor in your country.

Table of contents

		Present page number	Page number in the 1995 edition of *Education at a Glance*
INTRODUCTION		9	
A SELECTION OF INDICATORS		14	
A GUIDE THROUGH THE 1996 OECD INDICATORS		16	
READER'S GUIDE		29	

Chapter 1: DEMOGRAPHIC, SOCIAL AND ECONOMIC CONTEXT OF EDUCATION

C1	Educational attainment of the adult population	32	(19)
C2	Gender differences in educational attainment of the adult population	38	(24)
C3	The relative size of the young population	43	(30)
C11	Rates of labour force participation by level of educational attainment	46	(32)

Chapter 2: COSTS OF EDUCATION AND HUMAN AND FINANCIAL RESOURCES

F1	Educational expenditure relative to Gross Domestic Product	54	(71)
F3	Expenditure on educational services per student	64	(86)
F3-R	Inter-regional disparities in expenditure on educational services per student	74	
F5	Educational expenditure by resource category	77	(102)
F12	Public funds by level of government	82	(115)
F13	Proportion of public expenditure spent on education	88	(121)
P31	Staff employed in education	94	(174)
P32	Ratio of students to teaching staff	100	(178)

Chapter 3: ACCESS TO EDUCATION, PARTICIPATION AND PROGRESSION

P1	Participation in formal education	107	(124)
P2	Participation by young children	114	(129)
P3	Participation in education towards the end of compulsory schooling and beyond	119	(134)
P6	Participation in tertiary education	125	(152)
P8	Job-related continuing education and training for the adult labour force	131	(157)

Chapter 4: SCHOOL ENVIRONMENT AND SCHOOL/CLASSROOM PROCESSES

P11	Total intended instruction time for students at the lower secondary level	137	(164)
P33	Teaching time	142	(181)

Table of contents

P35	Statutory salaries of teachers in public primary and lower secondary schools	145	(187)
P22(A)	Stability in educational staff at the primary level	150	
P22(B)	School leadership at the primary level	153	
P22(C)	Staff co-operation	156	
P22(D)	Monitoring and evaluation at the primary level	158	
P22(E)	Differentiation at the primary level	161	
P22(F)	Achievement orientation at the primary level	164	
P22(G)	Parental involvement in schools at the primary level	167	

Chapter 5: GRADUATE OUTPUT OF EDUCATIONAL INSTITUTIONS

R11	Graduates at upper secondary level	172	(213)
R12	Graduates at the tertiary level	177	(217)
R14	Tertiary qualifications by field of study	184	(220)
R15	Supply of high-level qualifications in science-related fields	189	(224)

Chapter 6: STUDENT ACHIEVEMENT AND ADULT LITERACY

R6	Student achievement in mathematics and science	198	
R7	Student differences in mathematics and science achievement	202	
R9	Difference in achievement between two grades in mathematics and science	210	
R10	Gender differences in mathematics and science	214	
R30	Literacy and the adult population	218	
R31	Adult literacy by level of educational attainment	221	
R32	Literacy skills of younger versus older persons	224	
R33	Adult literacy by gender	227	

Chapter 7: LABOUR MARKET OUTCOMES OF EDUCATION

R21(A)	Unemployment and education	232	(227)
R21(B)	Youth unemployment and education	235	
R22	Education and earnings from employment	239	(239)
R24	Unemployment rates of persons leaving education	244	(247)

Table of contents

ANNOTATED ORGANISATION CHARTS OF EDUCATION SYSTEMS

Australia	250	Korea	297
Austria	253	Mexico	300
Belgium (Flemish and French Communities)	256	Netherlands	303
Canada	260	New Zealand	306
Czech Republic	263	Norway	309
Denmark	266	Poland	312
Finland	269	Portugal	313
France	273	Russian Federation	316
Germany	277	Spain	319
Greece	281	Sweden	322
Hungary	284	Switzerland	325
Ireland	287	Turkey	328
Italy	291	United Kingdom (England and Wales)	332
Japan	294	United States	335

ANNEX 1 – TYPICAL AGES AND REFERENCE YEARS 340

ANNEX 2 – BASIC REFERENCE STATISTICS 346

ANNEX 3 – SOURCES, METHODS AND TECHNICAL NOTES 348

GLOSSARY 385

PARTICIPANTS IN THE INES PROJECT 392

Introduction

The OECD education indicators

Throughout OECD countries, governments are seeking effective policies for enhancing economic productivity through education, employing incentives to promote the efficiency of the administration of schooling, and searching for additional resources to meet increasing demands for education.

Education is an investment that can help foster economic growth, contribute to personal and social development and reduce social inequality. Like any investment, it involves both costs and returns. Some of the returns are monetary and directly related to the labour market, while others are personal, social, cultural and more broadly economic. Some returns accrue to the individual while others benefit society in general, for example, in the form of a more literate and productive population.

The OECD education indicators provide an insight into the comparative functioning of education systems – reflecting both on the resources invested as well as on the returns. The illumination of the relative qualities of education systems provides an opportunity for countries to learn more about themselves, to recognise weaknesses in their education systems, but also to identify their strengths which may, at times, be overlooked in the domestic debate. The OECD education indicators can assist policy-makers in evaluating student and school performance, monitoring the functioning of education systems, and planning and managing resources and educational services. Directly and indirectly they can influence the process of policy formation and contribute to the public accountability of education systems.

The indicators are the product of a continuing process of conceptual development and data collection, the objective of which is to link a broad range of policy needs with the best data internationally available. Through extensive co-operation, Member countries and the OECD Secretariat are seeking answers to questions such as: What phenomena at the heart of current policy debates are to be measured? How can they be made amenable to quantitative assessment? Are the proposed measures cross-nationally valid and feasible in the field, and will they yield comparable data? Discussion and the search for consensus in the development of indicators focus on their conceptual and policy relevance, methodology, data collection and reporting. Political, educational and practical considerations are involved.

The 1996 edition of *Education at a Glance*

The 1996 edition of *Education at a Glance - Indicators* provides a richer and more comparable and up-to-date array of indicators than ever before. The 43 indicators that are included here represent the consensus of professional thinking on how best to measure the current state of education internationally, tempered by the availability of valid, reliable and comparable information.

The thematic organisation of this new volume, together with the additional information provided on the analytical context and the interpretation of the indicators, make this publication a valuable resource for anyone with an interest in analysing education systems across countries.

The OECD education indicators are published simultaneously with the volume *Education at a Glance - Analysis*, which takes up selected themes of key importance for governments and presents the implications for educational policy. In addition, most of the data underlying the OECD education indicators are now accessible via the INTERNET (URL http://www.oecd.org/els/els_stat.htm).

Introduction

New developments

A wider range of educational domains is covered.

To respond to increasing public and government concern with the outcomes of education, more than one-third of the indicators in this edition have been devoted to individual and labour market outcomes of education, and to the evaluation of school effectiveness. Indicators drawing on the first International Adult Literacy Survey offer an insight, for the first time, into levels of adult literacy skills and their relationship to key educational variables. In addition, the publication includes a comprehensive set of indicators on student achievement in mathematics and science which covers almost all OECD countries, based on the Third International Mathematics and Science Study. Indicators drawing on the first INES school survey extend the knowledge base on school effectiveness.

Improved coverage of the private sector of education – with respect to both participation rates and sources of funds – together with wider coverage of school-based adult education and training, provide a more complete picture of costs and resources in education and overall participation in education.

Methodological advances have made the indicators more comparable.

In 1995, UNESCO, OECD and EUROSTAT introduced a new set of instruments through which they now jointly collect data on key aspects of education. The result of this collaboration, which was led by the OECD and carried out in close consultation with the OECD-INES Technical Group, has been substantial progress in the collection, organisation and quality of international education statistics as well as a reduction in the time taken to publish the indicators. The application of common definitions, use of criteria for quality control and improved data documentation have improved the international comparability of education statistics and led to an expansion of the knowledge base on which the OECD indicators on costs and resources, participation and graduation are based.

Furthermore, significant methodological developments have enhanced the consistency and international comparability of the indicators.

Finally, for many indicators a significantly larger number of countries are now providing data. Among these are Korea and Mexico, which joined the OECD education indicators programme in 1995.

Trend data offer an insight into developments in the supply of and demand for learning opportunities.

The premise that current education and training systems must adapt to new conditions is based on an analysis of broad shifts in OECD economies and societies. That analysis, as well as a review of options and strategies for change, must be informed by an understanding of how education and training systems have evolved.

To this end, the new edition of *Education at a Glance – Indicators* complements its review of cross-sectional variation with a first set of trend indicators which examine how the demand for learning opportunities has evolved, and who the main beneficiaries of public and private provision have been. However, these trend indicators must be interpreted with great care because the dynamic nature of education and training systems sometimes impairs the validity of comparisons over time. Many national changes in definitions and methodology have occurred, especially in the allocation of national educational programmes to the levels defined in the International Standard Classification of Education (ISCED). Not all of these inconsistencies have been resolved, despite a careful review and update of all time-series data by Member countries.

Information on variation within countries offers a new perspective on disparities.

A major policy concern in many countries is to ensure that all children have access to a fair share of educational resources, no matter where they live within a country. Many countries have developed policies to reduce disparities in regional resources in order to equalise educational opportunities, by providing additional resources to poor regions, for example, or to

Introduction

regions with large numbers of poor or disadvantaged children. This new edition includes selected information on regional resource disparities.

The indicators will yield their maximum value for education policy when viewed within a comprehensive framework and an appropriate analytical context. The new thematic organisation of this volume is intended to meet this requirement.

The structure of national education systems exerts a major influence on a large number of indicators. More contextual information provided by diagrams and descriptions of national education systems has therefore been added to the quantitative indicators and their interpretations.

Lastly, the indicator set is more up-to-date. The data on adult literacy and student achievement refer to the school year 1994/95, the data on school effectiveness to the school year 1995/96 and the remainder to the financial year 1993 and the school year 1993/94.

A new thematic organisation, additional contextual information and more up-to-date statistics are significant improvements to this year's edition.

Future priorities

The four editions of *Education at a Glance* have demonstrated that it is possible to produce a limited set of up-to-date and internationally comparable indicators on education.

However, there are still deficiencies in the current management of comparative educational data and the progress accomplished has made clear how much further improvement is needed in terms of the coverage, validity, comparability, accuracy and timeliness of the indicators.

Most importantly, there is a critical absence of quantitative information on lifelong learning and its impact on society and the economy. Since economies can no longer rely solely on a gradual expansion of initial schooling to meet the demands for new and high-level skills, other indicators are needed that will help policy-makers to improve the foundations for lifelong learning. This will require development of data sources on enterprise-based training, continuing education and training for adults as well as other forms of learning outside school. Understanding the factors that influence patterns of learning throughout the life-cycle will be a challenge. The adult literacy data reported in Indicators R30 to R33 are a first step in this direction, providing information on the links between the school curriculum and the skills needed by adults, and between learning and work for people of all ages.

New indicators are needed that will help policy-makers to improve the foundations for lifelong learning.

Changing information needs also call for a further expansion of the knowledge base on outcomes, particularly student and school outcomes. Data sources here will have to go beyond diagnostic measures of relative country performance and must attempt to identify those factors that influence performance. Some schools achieve higher standards than others even though they may operate under similar socio-economic conditions. Such schools may be well equipped or have good teachers who excel in their subject matter, know how to structure the material to be learned, demand much from their students, obtain systematic feedback from students on what objectives have been mastered, and give help to those who are having particular problems. Some schools may be particularly well managed or have principals who stimulate teachers through enthusiastic and creative leadership in teaching methodology and foster an educational and social climate conducive to learning. A significant expansion and analysis of the current knowledge base on student and school outcomes will be needed to explore these questions.

The knowledge base on student and school outcomes needs to be expanded.

Finally, further methodological development is needed. The diversity of education systems and differences in the structure of the governance of education provide a challenge for international educational comparisons. Even where data are reasonably accurate and adequate

Further methodological development is needed.

Introduction

for the needs of national information systems, they may, nevertheless, be inadequate for certain types of international comparison. Furthermore, a number of significant comparability problems need to be resolved:

- One major constraint for the comparability of international education indicators is the International Standard Classification of Education (ISCED). ISCED, in its present form, is ill adapted to current needs and imposes limitations on international comparisons of education statistics as well as on the analytical use and interpretation of the indicators. A conceptually adequate and operationalised definition of the levels of education is required.
- Although substantial progress has been made in reducing double-counting, problems remain in particular with the indicators on graduates. For the statistics on tertiary graduates a consistent classification of tertiary qualifications will need to be developed. It will also be important to develop better estimates of the number of transfers between different levels and types of tertiary education.
- A consistent classification of types of educational programmes is not yet available. The current distinction between general and vocational programmes poses problems of validity as it mainly draws on national institutional structures, which differ significantly from country to country.
- Most countries cover participation in educational programmes outside the formal school sector to a limited extent only, even if the content of these programmes is similar to the content of ordinary school-based programmes.
- Many countries cover educational expenditure by households and other private entities only partially in their data submissions. In particular, many countries with major apprenticeship systems have not reported the costs incurred by private firms for training in the work place. As a result, their expenditure may be understated in comparison with those countries that rely largely on school-based modes of training.
- Consistency has not been achieved in the coverage of expenditure for ancillary services, such as student lodgings, meals and transportation. There are also problems in comparing subsidies for students' living expenses among countries.
- Problems connected with research funding still hamper expenditure comparisons at the tertiary level. On the one hand, countries differ in the extent to which they include research outlays by educational institutions in their expenditure figures; on the other hand, no satisfactory method has been found for consistently estimating the research component of spending on education.
- The methods for estimating full-time-equivalent participation have been improved. However, the comparison of expenditure per tertiary student is still impaired by problems in quantifying full-time-equivalent tertiary enrolment, particularly in countries which do not recognise the concept of part-time attendance.
- A problem affecting comparisons at all levels is the incomplete or inconsistent measurement of expenditure on the retirement (pensions) of education personnel. The magnitude of the potential impact on comparability makes this a high priority for future development.

A selection of indicators

	Upper secondary attainment (25-64 year-olds) (per cent)	Upper secondary graduation rate	Tertiary attainment (25-64 year-olds) (per cent)	First time university graduation rate	Expenditure for educational institutions as a percentage of GDP	Expenditure per student in equivalent U.S. dollars – primary level	Expenditure per student in equivalent U.S. dollars – secondary level	Expenditure per student in equivalent U.S. dollars – tertiary level
Australia	27	m	23	32 *	6.0	2 985	4 871	9 036
Austria	60	82	8	9 **	5.4	4 291	6 721	8 642
Belgium	27	97	22	14 **	5.6	2 953	5 373	6 380
Canada	28	71	46	30 *	7.3	m	m	11 132
Czech Republic	63	78	10	14 **	5.0	1 506	1 903	4 788
Denmark	40	82	20	26 *	7.2	4 745	6 175	8 045
Finland	44	93	19	21 **	7.3	4 095	4 769	7 295
France	50	81	17	14 **	6.1	3 154	5 685	6 033
Germany	62	89	22	13 **	5.9	2 815	6 481	7 902
Greece	27	75	18	12 **	3.4	m	1 578	2 502
Hungary	m	81	m	16 **	6.6	1 607	1 685	5 189
Iceland	m	m	m	m	5.3	2 645	3 258	5 059
Ireland	27	98	19	23 *	5.8	1 882	3 031	7 076
Italy	26	76	8	11 **	5.1	4 107	5 235	5 169
Japan	m	92	m	23 *	4.9	3 960	4 356	7 556
Mexico	m	25	m	7 **	4.1	741	1 477	4 264
Netherlands	38	69	21	27 *	5.0	2 793	3 979	8 665
New Zealand	34	64	23	22 *	6.4	2 659	3 951	7 337
Norway	53	102	27	23 *	7.6	m	m	8 343
Portugal	8	m	11	14 **	5.4	2 581	2 491	5 667
Spain	11	68	15	21 **	5.3	2 293	3 033	3 835
Sweden	46	75	26	13 **	6.9	4 917	5 651	12 693
Switzerland	61	82	21	9 **	5.7	5 835	7 024	15 731
Turkey	13	38	7	7 *	3.3	832	587	2 696
United Kingdom	54	m	21	27 *	5.0	3 295	4 494	8 241
United States	53	74	32	32 *	6.8	5 492	6 541	14 607
Korea	m	91	m	23 *	5.7	1 715	2 026	2 589
Poland	m	90	m	12 *	m	m	m	m
Russian Federation	m	91	m	23 *	m	m	m	m

m = missing data

* Mostly short first university programmes
** Mostly long first university programmes

Indicator	C1	R11	C1	R12	F1	F3	F3	F3
Page	32	172	32	177	54	64	64	64

14

A selection of indicators

Ratio of students to teaching staff — primary level	Ratio of students to teaching staff — secondary level	Annual intended instruction hours for 12 to 14 year-olds	TIMSS mathematics achievement score	Unemployment rate (25-29 year-olds), university-level	Ratio of unemployment rates (25-29 year-olds), university to upper secondary	Index of earning differentials, university to upper secondary — men	Index of earning differentials, university to upper secondary — women	
18,5	m	m	530	5.4	0.7	144	152	Australia
11.9	8.1	1 084	539	4.6	1.6	146	134	Austria
13.3	8.5	m	548 *	8.7	0.8	149	164	Belgium
16.5	19.1	m	527	6.4	0.5	152	162	Canada
19.7	13.1	m	564	m	m	m	m	Czech Republic
11.0	9.0	890	502	10.3	0.9	142	133	Denmark
m	m	851	m	12.0	0.6	192	175	Finland
19.6	13.7	954	538	11.0	0.7	187	165	France
20.5	14.4	950	509	5.8	0.7	167	162	Germany
16.5	12.1	927	484	19.9	1.3	m	m	Greece
10.2	11.5	m	537	m	m	m	m	Hungary
m	m	m	487	m	m	m	m	Iceland
24.3	16.1	935	527	5.1	0.5	171	187	Ireland
10.2	8.5	1 020	m	28.4	1.7	141	112	Italy
19.2	16.0	m	605	m	m	m	m	Japan
29.1	16.4	m	m	m	m	m	m	Mexico
22.4	16.7	1 067	541	7.4	1.4	136	141	Netherlands
20.2	15.0	918	508	m	m	157	155	New Zealand
m	m	823	503	4.5	0.7	158	156	Norway
12.2	13.1	949	454	6.3	0.6	179	188	Portugal
19.2	16.0	900	487	32.5	1.1	148	139	Spain
12.5	12.7	828	519	5.6	0.5	164	158	Sweden
m	m	m	545	m	m	142	160	Switzerland
27.4	23.7	712	m	11.1	0.8	m	m	Turkey
20.7	15.8	m	505	4.3	0.4	164	204	United Kingdom
m	m	m	500 **	3.1	0.4	168	175	United States
33.2	24.6	m	607	m	m	m	m	Korea
m	m	m	m	m	m	m	m	Poland
m	m	m	536	m	m	m	m	Russian Federation

Note: The student/teaching staff ratio cannot be equated with the class size

* Weighted average of the French and Flemish communities in Belgium
** Weighted average of England and Scotland

Indicator	P32	P32	P11	R6	R21(B)	R21(B)	R22	R22
Page	100	100	137	198	235	235	239	239

A guide through the 1996 OECD indicators

This guide summarises key results and guides the reader through the 1996 edition of *Education at a Glance - Indicators*. The 43 indicators in this volume are organised into seven chapters:
- Chapter 1: Demographic, social and economic context of education
- Chapter 2: Costs of education and human and financial resources
- Chapter 3: Access to education, participation and progression
- Chapter 4: School environment and school/classroom processes
- Chapter 5: Graduate output of educational institutions
- Chapter 6: Student achievement and adult literacy
- Chapter 7: Labour market outcomes of education

Each of the chapters begins with a brief synopsis that explains the choice and context of the indicators. This is followed by the indicators, which are numbered consistently with earlier editions of *Education at a Glance*. The three annexes provide basic demographic and financial reference statistics that can help the reader to translate some of the indicators back into the national context, as well as information on the coverage of the indicators and on methods, sources and interpretation of national data.

Demographic, social and economic context of education

Education systems and the results they produce do not exist in a vacuum; they are the product of a complex historical process and are embedded in a demographic, social and economic context. The four indicators in the first chapter present data on the educational attainment of the population and on the demographic conditions under which education systems operate.

On average, less than 60 per cent of adults in OECD countries have completed upper secondary education ...

Educational attainment and, by extension, labour force qualifications, are important factors in determining economic outcomes and the quality of life for both individuals and society as a whole. Indicator C1 shows that there are marked differences in the levels of educational attainment of the adult population among OECD countries. In Belgium, Greece, Ireland, Italy, Portugal, Spain and Turkey, more than half of the population aged 25-64 years have not completed upper secondary education, with the figures for Portugal and Turkey equal to or above 80 per cent (see Chart C1.1). With increasing skill requirements of jobs in today's economies, persons with low attainment levels find themselves at a distinct disadvantage in the labour market (see also Indicators R21, R22 and R24). Since the attainment of the population aged 25-64 years is mainly the result of historical patterns of participation in education and most 25 to 64 year-olds have already left initial education and training, the various forms of continuing education and training provide important means of enhancing the attainment of the adult population.

... but upper secondary education is now becoming the norm and the attainment gap between countries is closing.

A comparison of the attainment of the population aged 25 to 34 years with the attainment of the population aged 55 to 64 years (see Chart C1.2) shows that the gap among countries with respect to persons having completed upper secondary education is rapidly closing, particularly in Southern Europe. A look at the upper secondary graduation rates presented in Indicator R11 confirms that completion of upper secondary education is becoming the norm. The proportion of students completing a first upper secondary programme is on average 77 per cent across OECD countries and exceeds 80 per cent in more than half of the countries for which data are reported (see Chart R11).

A guide through the 1996 OECD indicators

The rising skill requirements of labour markets and the higher expectations of individuals and society have also led to a marked increase in the proportion of young people who have attained a qualification at the tertiary level of education (see Chart C1.1).

Among persons 25 to 64 years old, women constitute the majority of those who have completed only primary or lower secondary education and men are in a majority among those who have completed university-level tertiary education (see Chart C2).

Among older age groups women have lower levels of education than men ...

However, these differences are mostly attributable to the large gender differences in the attainment of older age groups and have been significantly reduced or reversed among younger age groups. In over half of the countries reporting upper secondary graduation rates for first programmes by gender, graduation rates for women exceed those of men (see Indicator R11); in Belgium, Denmark, Finland, Ireland and Spain this is by more than 10 per cent. Only in Austria, the Czech Republic, Norway, Switzerland and Turkey does the graduation rate for men exceed that for women by more than 5 per cent.

... but for younger persons the pattern is now reversing in over half of the countries.

Data on the number of university degrees conferred also demonstrate clearly the educational progress of women relative to men. Graduation rates from first university programmes are higher among women in most countries (see Table R12.1). Only in Germany, Japan, Korea, Switzerland and Turkey are they significantly lower. For second university degrees, graduation rates for men are slightly higher than those for women in most countries.

Young women are also overtaking men in tertiary graduation rates...

However, despite these gains in educational attainment, women still earn less than men with similar levels of education (see Chart R22). In all countries and at all attainment levels, the earnings of women are on average approximately one-half to three-quarters of the earnings of men. In addition, there is only a relatively weak tendency for earnings differences between men and women to decrease in line with educational attainment. Differences in progression rates, types of course and fields of study, and the relative incidence of part-time work may all affect the labour market opportunities of women relative to men.

... but women still earn less than men with similar levels of education.

As populations age, the number of persons in the labour force relative to the total population will fall in many countries. However, this may be partly offset by higher attainment levels which tend to result in increased participation in the labour force (see Table C11.1). Differences in labour force participation rates between persons with different educational levels are much larger among women than among men. Men have higher participation rates than women at all educational levels (see Chart C11). The difference between the genders is on average around 10 percentage points among those with university education but more than three times as much at levels below upper secondary.

Labour force participation is higher for more highly educated persons – and the differences relative to lower attainment levels are particularly high for women.

Costs of education and human and financial resources

At a time of austerity in public budgets, the questions of access to educational opportunities and of the distribution of available resources between the various levels and types of education and training are objects of considerable debate.

The indicators in the second chapter examine cost patterns and resource utilisation in OECD countries. Structural variation in spending patterns between countries can suggest potential alternatives for policy-makers seeking better value for money.

A guide through the 1996 OECD indicators

Educational services are a major factor in national economies.

Indicators F1, F13, P31 and P32 show that OECD countries invest a substantial amount of human and financial resources in education. At the combined primary and secondary level of education, the teaching force accounts, on average, for 2.8 per cent of the whole labour force and at the tertiary level for 0.5 per cent (see Chart P31.1). Including educational and administrative personnel and other support staff in the education sector, this percentage rises, on average, to 5.5 per cent across OECD countries. This percentage is as high as, or in some countries even higher than the percentage of workers in a traditional economic sector such as agriculture.

The economic weight of education is also reflected in the amount of financial resources invested. Taking into account both public and private sources of funds, OECD countries as a whole spend 6.1 per cent of GDP in support of their educational institutions (see Chart F1.2). Most of this (4.9 per cent) is accounted for by direct public expenditure on educational institutions. Public subsidies to households and other private entities for educational institutions comprise for another 0.1 per cent and expenditure by households and other private institutions accounts for 1.1 per cent of the overall GDP of OECD countries.

Expenditure on institutions at the primary and secondary level (including private expenditure and public subsidies that are channelled through the private sector) amounts to 3.9 per cent of GDP for the OECD as a whole, varying between 2.4 and 4.7 per cent among countries (see Table F1.2). At the tertiary level, expenditure accounts for 1.6 per cent of GDP for the OECD as a whole but varies from 0.7 to 2.6 per cent among countries.

Since the mid-1970s, the proportion of GDP spent by the public sector on education has stabilised or fallen slightly in most countries and the indicator suggests a trend towards the convergence of public education expenditure in OECD countries (see Table F1t). Rising participation, changing curricular provision and increases in teachers' salaries have exerted upward pressure on educational spending, while a declining school-age population (see Indicator C3) and general public spending restraint have tended to reduce spending.

Another way to benchmark the national resources invested in education is to examine expenditure on education in relation to total public expenditure. Indicator F13 shows that, on average, OECD countries devote 12.3 per cent of total government outlays to educational institutions, with the values for individual countries ranging between 8.7 and 18 per cent (see Chart F13.1). Between 5.7 and 14.5 per cent of total public expenditure is allocated to primary and secondary education and between 1.1 and 4.7 per cent to tertiary education. Most of the public funds are spent on supporting public educational institutions but some countries spend more than 2 per cent of public funds on subsidies to the private sector for education.

The fewer young people in the population, the more a country can afford to spend on each of them.

While Indicators F1 and F13 provide a broad indication of the national resources devoted to education, they need to be interpreted in the light of a number of inter-related supply and demand factors, such as the demographic structure of the population (Indicator C3), enrolment rates (Indicator P1), the size of the economy, the level of income per capita and national price levels for educational resources. The relative size of the youth population, for example, shapes the potential demand for initial education and training in a country [see Chart F1.2(B) and Chart F13.1(B)]. The fewer students of school age, the less a country needs to spend on initial education. Similarly, participation rates affect expenditure on education: the higher the enrolment rates, the more financial resources will be required, other things being equal [see Chart F1.2(C)]. It is important to look at the different factors that affect spending on education together. Belgium, Denmark, Finland and Sweden, for example, are countries in which a smaller proportion of young people in the population is, in part, offset by comparatively high participation rates. Austria, Germany and Switzerland, on

A guide through the 1996 OECD indicators

the other hand, are countries with both a comparatively small proportion of young people in the population and a comparatively low enrolment rate. With a high national income, these countries are able to spend more per student than OECD countries on average (Indicator F3), although spending on education remains a moderate proportion of GDP.

The relative size of the public budget influences the difference between countries in the proportion of total public expenditure on education (see Chart F13.2). If total public expenditure is low, then education's share of it, other things being equal, will tend to be high. This, for example, is the case in Hungary and Switzerland. On the other hand, in countries such as Italy or the Netherlands which tend to have relatively large public budgets, education accounts for a smaller proportion of total public spending.

Where public spending budgets are smaller overall, spending on education figures more prominently.

The contribution of the private sector to the financing of education also helps to explain the variation among countries in the proportion of total public spending devoted to education (see Chart F13.3). The question of whether or to what extent the costs of education should be borne by the individuals who benefit from education or by society as a whole is answered differently in different countries. While in Finland, Italy and Turkey less than 1 per cent of expenditure on educational institutions is found in the private sector, the figure is over 20 per cent in Germany, Japan, Korea and the United States.

Countries differ in the extent to which the costs of education are borne by the beneficiaries of education or by society as a whole.

All of these factors explain how national financial resources spent on education translate into the amount of money that is ultimately spent per student (Indicator F3). As a whole, OECD countries spend about US$ 4 760 per student each year (all levels of education combined). US$ 3 320 are spent per student at the primary level, US$ 4 730 per student at the secondary level and US$ 9 670 per student at the tertiary level (see Table F3.1). Expenditure per student, for the OECD as a whole, averages 18 per cent of per capita GDP at the primary level, 26 per cent at the secondary level and 49 per cent at the tertiary level (see Table F3.2).

Expenditure per student varies widely from one country to another.

These OECD averages mask a broad range of expenditure per student across countries. Even excluding the two highest and lowest-spending countries, the range in expenditure per student is wide: from about US$ 1 500 to more than US$ 4 900 at the primary level, from about US$ 1 600 to more than US$ 6 000 at the secondary level, and from less than US$ 2 700 to more than US$ 12 600 at the tertiary level (see Chart F3.1).

Despite wide differences in absolute amounts, expenditure per student exhibits a common pattern throughout the OECD: in each country it rises sharply with the level of education, it is dominated by staff costs (see Indicator F5), and it has a tendency to rise over time. This pattern can be understood by looking at the determinants of expenditure, particularly the place and mode of educational provision. Education still takes place predominantly in traditional school and university settings with, despite some differences, similar organisation, curriculum, teaching style and management. The labour intensiveness of traditional education accounts for the predominance of teachers' salaries in overall costs. Differences in student/teaching staff ratios and staffing patterns (Indicator P32), teachers' salaries (Indicator P35), and teaching materials and facilities largely account for the cost differences among levels of education, types of programme and types of school.

Expenditure per student rises sharply with the level of education, it is dominated by staff costs and has a built-in tendency to rise over time.

Although there is a general tendency for expenditure per student to rise with the level of education, differentials in unit expenditure by level vary markedly among countries, particularly at the tertiary level of education. At this level, expenditure per student is, on average, 153 per cent higher than at the primary level, varying from 26 per cent in Italy to more than 200 per cent in Australia, the Czech Republic, Hungary, Ireland, Mexico, the Netherlands and Turkey (see Chart F3.2).

The higher the level of education, the more countries differ in per-student spending.

A guide through the 1996 OECD indicators

Low annual expenditure can translate into high costs if the duration of studies is long.

Differences among countries in the annual expenditure per tertiary student shown in Indicator F3, however, do not necessarily reflect the total cost incurred for students over the duration of tertiary studies. This is primarily because countries differ significantly both in the length of tertiary studies (see also Indicator R12 and Annex 1) and in the intensity with which students participate in educational programmes. Comparatively low annual expenditure per student may nonetheless translate into comparatively high overall costs of tertiary education if the typical duration of tertiary studies is very long. Annual tertiary expenditure in the United Kingdom (US$ 8 241) is, for example, higher than in Germany (US$ 7 902). However, because of differences in the university degree structure (see Indicator R12), the average duration of tertiary studies is almost twice as long in Germany (6.4 years) as in the United Kingdom (3.4 years). As a consequence, expenditure on a tertiary student over the duration of studies is on average significantly higher in Germany than in the United Kingdom (see Chart F3.4).

OECD average student/ teaching staff ratios are 18 : 1 (primary), 16 : 1 (lower secondary) and 13 : 1 (upper secondary education).

In addition to expenditure per student, student/teaching staff ratios are an important indicator of educational resources (see Indicator P32). Because teachers' salaries are the main component of educational spending, these ratios indirectly reflect the financial resources that countries need to devote to education. There is a potential trade-off between low student/teaching staff ratios, which increase educational costs but are generally thought to contribute to learning, and salary levels sufficient to attract qualified teachers (see also Indicator P35). In most countries the ratio of students to teaching staff decreases with the level of education; that is, the higher the level of education, the more teachers there are relative to the number of students. Canada, Sweden and Turkey are the only notable exceptions. For public and private institutions the OECD average ratio of students to teaching staff is 18 : 1 at the early childhood and primary level, 16 : 1 at the lower secondary level, and 13 : 1 at the upper secondary level (see Chart P32) (note, however, that student/teaching staff ratios can not be equated with class sizes). Declining birth rates in OECD countries since the early 1960s (see Indicator C3) have provided an opportunity of improving students' access to teachers.

In some countries, there are considerable regional disparities in educational resources.

In some countries, geographical variation in educational resources is relatively small. In Sweden, for example, expenditure per student in the highest-spending region is only 1.4 times as high as in the lowest-spending region for the combined primary and secondary levels (see Chart F3-R). In other countries, the variation in resources is considerably higher, particularly in the United States, where expenditure in the highest-spending state is about 2.7 times that in the lowest-spending state. Because educational needs in different geographical or socio-economic settings may differ and thus require differential treatment, such measured disparities may be difficult to interpret. Still, such disparities can reflect inequities in access to educational resources.

Access to education, participation and progression

Lifelong learning needs to be built on a solid foundation. Modern manufacturing and service industry techniques demand a labour force capable of adjusting to new technologies and making informed decisions. Education and skills are widely viewed as important economic resources. The improvement of the quality of initial education and the extension of the benefits of tertiary education and of continuing education and training to a larger share of the population have been given high priority in most countries. The indicators on enrolment rates and the expected duration of schooling that are shown in the third chapter of this volume provide a broad picture of the size and structure of education systems, and of access to formal education and training.

A guide through the 1996 OECD indicators

Virtually everyone participates in formal education at some stage of his or her life. In more than half of OECD countries, over 60 per cent of the population aged 5 to 29 years are enrolled in education (see Chart P1.1). The variation across countries is largely explained by the uneven weight of tertiary enrolment: from less than 3 tertiary education students per 100 persons in the population aged 5 to 29 in Mexico to more than 15 in Canada and the United States (see Table P1.1). In some countries, particularly in Australia, Belgium, Sweden and the United States, a significant portion of the population aged 30 to 39 years is also enrolled in formal education (see Table P1.2).

In more than half of OECD countries, over 60 per cent of the population aged 5 to 29 are enrolled in education.

Full-time participation of the population aged 5 to 29 years was higher in 1994 in most countries than it was in the mid-1970s – although there are some exceptions (see Table P1t). In some countries, such as Canada, New Zealand, Norway, the United Kingdom and the United States, the increase has occurred only since the late 1980s or early 1990s. In compulsory education, enrolment has tended to follow the decline in birth rates (see also Indicator C3). However, in the post-compulsory phase, increases in enrolments have outweighed the impact of lower birth rates since the mid-1970s.

Higher participation in post-compulsory education outweighs lower birth-rates.

Another way of looking at participation in education is to estimate the number of years of education a 5 year-old child can expect to receive up to the age of 29 under current conditions (see Chart P1.2). This varies from just over 9 years in Turkey to around 17 years in Belgium and the Netherlands. Typically, school expectancy is in the range of 14.5 to 16.5 years. Expectancy of formal schooling has increased in recent years in almost all countries for which data are available, in many by more than one year since 1985 (see Chart P1.2). The longer duration of schooling is another factor that contributes to the observed rise in enrolment rates over recent decades.

The number of years spent in initial education has risen in almost all countries since 1985.

A range of factors, among them an increasing risk of unemployment and other forms of exclusion for young people with insufficient education, has increased the incentives for young people to stay in school beyond the end of compulsory schooling (see Indicator P3). In all but six countries, more than 94 per cent of 15 year-olds participate in education. By age 17 enrolment rates have, on average, dropped to 78 per cent and at age 19 to 47 per cent, with no country having enrolment rates at this age exceeding 75 per cent. The countries which appear to retain students longer at the secondary level are generally those in which a majority of upper secondary students follow vocational courses — particularly those which involve an element of work-based education (see Table P3.2).

Early childhood education and early intervention programmes in primary schooling are important aspects of a strategy aimed at ensuring equal opportunity in foundation learning and at helping children and young people at risk. Thirteen out of 25 countries report enrolment rates of at least 30 per cent in early childhood education at age 3; 18 countries report enrolment rates of at least 50 per cent for 4 year-olds (see Chart P2.1). At age 6, over 90 per cent of children in all but four countries are enrolled in either early childhood or primary education.

Early childhood education now accommodates on average more than 60 per cent of 4 year-olds.

Sixteen per cent of 18 to 21 year-olds, 12 per cent of 22 to 25 year-olds, and 5 per cent of 26 to 29 year-olds participate, on average, in university-level tertiary programmes in OECD countries (see Chart P6). The corresponding averages for participation in non-university level programmes are 6, 3 and 2 per cent. The highest enrolment rates in tertiary education are, in most countries, reported for 18 to 21 year-olds (see Chart P6.3) although in a few (especially in Austria, Germany, Iceland, the Nordic countries and Switzerland) participation

Sixteen per cent of 18-21 year-olds take part, on average, in university-level tertiary education, and 6 per cent in non-university tertiary education.

A guide through the 1996 OECD indicators

is higher among the 22 to 25 year-olds. This reflects, in part, a relatively late entry into tertiary studies and a significantly longer duration of tertiary studies in these countries (see Indicator R12). In general, the age profile for women is younger than that for men.

All countries have seen a marked increase in tertiary enrolment rates.

All countries for which trend data are available have seen a marked increase in tertiary enrolment rates over the last decade, in virtually all age groups (Table P6t). In Canada, Ireland, New Zealand and Portugal enrolment rates for men and women have more than doubled over the last decade, at least for some age groups. In Canada, Denmark and the United States, the increase in participation has largely occurred in the older age groups while in France, the Netherlands, Portugal and Sweden the increase has been more pronounced for younger age groups. The enrolment rates in the three age bands reflect both the total number of individuals participating in tertiary education and the duration of tertiary programmes. A longer duration of studies (see also Indicator R12) tends to increase the stock of enrolments, and thus the level of required resources, all other things being equal. Longer tertiary studies also explain, in part, why some countries that report high tertiary enrolment rates show comparatively low graduation rates (Indicator R12).

Differences in educational attainment are amplified by subsequent training decisions by employers and employees.

Finally, participation in job-related continuing education and training (Indicator P8) provides information on participation in education beyond the formal school system. Participation in job-related continuing education and training appears to be closely linked to the previously attained level of education. In all countries, those with the lowest levels of education also have the lowest levels of participation in job-related continuing education and training while those with tertiary education attain the highest levels of participation in such programmes (see Chart P8). These findings apply to both the employed and the unemployed. Initial skill differences are thus amplified by subsequent training decisions of employers and employees. A second result is that among the employed, a larger proportion of women than of men participate in job-related continuing education and training in most countries.

School environment and school/classroom processes

Indicators F3 (on expenditure per student) and P32 (on student/teaching staff ratios) are sometimes used as a proxy for the quality of education. But what can be said directly about the quality of schools? Are schools providing a safe and supportive environment that allows students to devote their energies to learning? Does the way in which instruction is organised and delivered reflect national goals and intentions and live up to best practices?

Because of the diverse and complex nature of the activities within schools, many of these questions are not as easily addressed as enrolments, expenditure or examination results. Nonetheless, a certain number of national, regional, school and classroom-level characteristics can be assessed, using data reported by those involved or data drawn from policy statements.

The effectiveness of schooling is not only reflected in curricular variables but also in the instructional environment which schools provide and in the importance attached to education outside school.

Intended instruction time for 12 year-olds averages 908 hours per year.

Indicator P11 compares the amount of intended instruction time for students at the lower secondary level, and the relative emphasis on different fields of study in the curriculum, as measured by the apportionment of instruction time over subject areas. The intended number of instructional hours per year is on average 908 for 12 year-olds, 931 for 13 year-olds and 935 for 14 year-olds (see Table P11.1). Reading and writing in the mother tongue, together

A guide through the 1996 OECD indicators

with modern foreign languages, typically account for 28 per cent of the intended instruction time for 12-14 year-olds, followed by mathematics and science with about 24 per cent (see Chart P11.1). Countries differ both with respect to the overall amount of instruction time that students at different ages receive – for 14 year-olds this ranges from under 700 hours to more than 1 000 hours per year – as well as with respect to its allocation over the different subject areas (see Chart P11.2).

Good teachers are a key to improved education. Ensuring that there will be enough skilled teachers to educate all children is an important concern in all OECD countries. Key determinants of the supply of teachers are the salaries and working conditions of teachers as well as the costs incurred by individuals in becoming teachers, as compared to salaries and costs for other occupations. Both affect the career decisions of potential teachers and the type of persons countries will be able to attract into the teaching profession. Differences between starting and maximum salary levels and in the design of pay-scales can affect career decisions as well.

Salaries and working conditions are key determinants of the supply of teachers – and they differ considerably among countries.

The desire to improve the quality of education and to expand access to education is subject to increasing fiscal constraints, and teachers' salaries represent the most important component of educational spending (see Indicator F5). There are considerable differences in annual salaries for teachers in OECD countries, with starting salaries ranging from less than US$ 8 500 to more than US$ 30 000 at the primary level of education; and from less than US$ 7 000 to more than US$ 36 000 at the lower secondary level of education (see Chart P35.1).

Also, the structure of pay-scales differs significantly between countries: after 15 years of experience a lower secondary teacher in Spain or Turkey can expect to earn less than 1.2 times his or her starting salary while in Portugal the salary level will have almost doubled over the same period (see Chart P35.1). The number of years it takes teachers in public primary and lower secondary education to progress from their minimum to their maximum salary varies across countries from 8 to 42 years. The average number of years is 25 for primary and lower secondary education.

Starting salaries of teachers are comparable in level to per capita GDP in most countries and after 15 years of experience, they are generally above per capita GDP (see Chart P35.1). While in some countries teachers are well paid relative to the average earnings of wage and salary workers, in other countries their salaries lag behind (see Chart P35.2). Note, however, that in countries with lower average levels of education, teachers are often among the most educated workers and are therefore being compared to persons with, on average, lower formal qualifications. Conversely, in countries with more highly qualified workers, teachers tend to fare worse.

Starting salaries of teachers are comparable to per capita GDP in most countries.

Other aspects of working conditions for teachers need to be taken into account as well, such as the working time of teachers compared to that of other professions. At the primary level the annual teaching load is 818 hours on average, but it is over 40 per cent lower for Swedish teachers, at one extreme, than for Swiss teachers, at the other (see Chart P33). At the lower and upper secondary levels, there are fewer teaching hours on average (760 hours at the lower secondary level, 688 and 722 hours at the general and vocational upper secondary levels, respectively). The pattern across levels of education is similar for most countries. However, these figures do not include non-teaching hours within the school or work in the community or at home.

Teaching loads differ significantly among OECD countries.

Given the amount of educational reform introduced recently in many of the 12 countries covered by indicators P22(A)-(G) there is a surprisingly high rate of stability – measured by the percentage of teachers staying at the same school for at least five years – in educational

Overall, there is high stability in the teaching staff in schools.

A guide through the 1996 OECD indicators

staff at the primary level [see Chart P22(A).2]. In some instances, the impact of reform policies may have been counterbalanced by circumstances which discourage teacher mobility, such as an oversupply of teachers or contractual conditions which encourage teachers to remain in the same school.

Measuring the progress of students is common practice in primary schools.

The frequency with which students' progress is assessed during the school year is an indicator of interest. The registering of marks and test scores in a way that makes them accessible for inspection by headteachers and other teachers enables this information to be used for the proper guidance of individual students and school self-evaluation. Indicator P22(D) shows that qualitative monitoring of progress by teachers is common practice in primary schools, although the frequency of such practices differs considerably. Methods developed more recently, such as the administration of standardised tests to all students, occur less frequently at the primary level. In some countries, the preference for qualitative rather than quantitative evaluation is a deliberate choice.

The practice whereby schools designate a time for parents to meet their child's teacher to discuss his or her performance is a further indication of the use made of student evaluation. [See Table P22(D).1].

Parental involvement conforms to the traditional division of roles between parents and schools.

There is a general tendency to follow the traditional division of roles between parents and schools. In practically every country, most primary schools inform parents regularly on the performance of their children. There is much more variation among countries in the percentage of schools which provide structures for the involvement of parents in decision-making at school. Wherever these structures exist, they are used less frequently for sensitive educational domains such as curriculum and staffing. Only a fairly small percentage of parents are engaged in the teaching and learning process inside the classroom [see Indicator P22(G)].

Achievement standards are commonly set for students but less frequently for schools.

The setting of achievement standards for individual students is quite a common practice in countries. Achievement standards for primary schools, however, are less commonly found [see Indicator P22(F)]. In almost all countries, the majority of primary students are in schools that provide public recognition of progress by students, irrespective of their level of performance.

On average, 80 per cent of students are exposed to some form of differentiation.

The picture of the frequent use of various forms of differentiation between students is possibly the most telling sign of attempts to make learning in school more effective. According to the findings, about 80 per cent of students (averaged across countries) are exposed to some form of differentiation [see Chart P22(E)]. Differentiation within classrooms may be a sign of a more individualised, flexible approach to teaching.

Graduate output of educational institutions

Unlike measures of educational attainment, which relate to the stock of knowledge and skills in the population, tertiary graduation rates are an indicator of the current production rate of high-level knowledge by each country's education system. Countries with high graduation rates at the tertiary level are the most likely to be building or maintaining a highly-skilled labour force.

Between 1 and 47 per cent of the typical age cohort obtain a non-tertiary university qualification.

For the purpose of this publication, tertiary qualifications are divided into those equivalent and those not equivalent to a university qualification. The tertiary programmes leading to the latter qualifications are typically shorter in duration than the former and are often focused on a specific area of the labour market. At the non-university tertiary level, the highest graduation rates per 100 people at the most common graduation age are in Japan, Norway and the Russian Federation (see Table R12.1). In these countries, graduation rates are equal to or exceed 26 for every 100 people at the typical graduation age.

A guide through the 1996 OECD indicators

Tertiary graduation rates are affected by the way in which the degree and qualification structures are organised within countries (see also Annex 3). University-level programmes vary greatly in structure and scope by country. The duration of programmes leading to the award of a first university-level qualification ranges from 3 years (e.g. the Bachelor's degree in the United Kingdom in most fields of study) to over 5 years (e.g. the *Diplom* in Germany and the *Doctorandus* in the Netherlands). In countries that offer short first university degrees, such as the Bachelor's in the United States, graduation rates average around 16 per cent across OECD countries (see Chart R12). However, in Denmark, Ireland, Japan, Korea, New Zealand, the Russian Federation and the United Kingdom, more than 20 per cent of persons at the theoretical age group obtain such a degree and in Australia, Canada, and the United States, more than 30 per cent. Students tend to graduate around the age of 23 from these programmes. For long first university degrees, such as the German *Diplom* or the Italian *Laurea*, many of which are often considered equivalent in academic level to second university degrees in countries such as Australia or the United States, graduation rates average 10 per cent across countries.

Graduation rates for short first university programmes average 16 per cent; for long first degree courses, 10 per cent.

Indicator R12 suggests that countries whose tertiary education systems offer only long first university-level programmes have, in general, lower overall university graduation rates than those that offer university programmes of shorter duration as well. A longer duration of studies also tends to increase both the measured enrolment stock and the level of required resources because turnover rates are lower, all other things being equal.

Graduation rates for second university degrees, such as the Master's in the United States, range from less than 1 per cent to 12 per cent, with an OECD average of 4 per cent. About 1 per cent of the typical age cohort on average obtain an advanced research degree such as a Ph.D.

Indicator R12 shows striking variation across countries in the ages at which students graduate from university programmes and, potentially, become available for the labour market. Of the 10 countries included in this comparison, Denmark, Finland and Sweden show more than 75 per cent of university students completing their studies at 25 years or older. The typical university graduation age ranges from 21 years in Australia, New Zealand, Portugal, Spain and the United Kingdom (short university programmes) to 26 years in Germany and Switzerland (long university programmes).

The typical university graduation age varies from 21 to 26 years.

Student achievement and adult literacy

The achievement of students in basic disciplines such as mathematics, science, reading and in cross-curricular domains is one of the key criteria for an assessment of the performance of education systems. Competencies in mathematics and science are of particular importance in modern economies, which depend increasingly on scientific discoveries and technological innovation.

Indicators R6 and R7 reveal substantial differences among countries in students' achievement in mathematics and science. The difference in mathematics achievement between Japan and Korea, on the one hand, and the OECD average, on the other, exceeds more than twice the typical difference in achievement between students in the seventh and eighth grades in OECD countries (see Chart R6.1). High performance is also shown by students in Austria, the Flemish Community of Belgium, the Czech Republic and the Netherlands.

Countries differ widely in the achievement of their students – in mathematics, eighth-graders in Japan and Korea are more than twice a school year ahead of the OECD average.

A guide through the 1996 OECD indicators

The high performance standards in the Czech Republic, Japan and Korea are all the more impressive as the financial resources which these countries devote to their educational institutions appear moderate when compared with those of other OECD countries (see Indicator F3).

Results and country rankings are broadly similar in mathematics and in science, but some countries do show substantially higher performance in one discipline than in the other, relative to the other countries. English children, for example, perform better in science than in mathematics, while in France the picture is reversed. The fact that countries vary in their performance in the two disciplines suggests that variation cannot be explained entirely in terms of the demographic or socio-economic context but may reflect, in part, differences in factors susceptible to policy influence, such as curriculum and instruction.

Disparities in student achievement within countries present a challenge to education systems.

Mean achievement is often used as an outcome measure to assess classrooms, schools, school types and education systems as a whole. An examination of overall performance relative to a standard can be equally revealing. For example, over three-quarters of students in the eighth grade in Japan and Korea show mathematics achievement scores above the OECD average (see Chart R7.1). At the other end of the scale, some of the 25 per cent best performing students in Portugal fail to reach the OECD average.

Disparities in student achievement in mathematics and science within countries present a challenge to almost all education systems (see Charts R7.1 and R7.2). The variation in achievement that exists within classes, within schools and within a country as a whole can result from disparities in resources and in the socio-economic background of students and schools, as well as from curricular differences and the way in which instruction is organised and delivered. Some education systems attempt to deal with this variation explicitly by forming homogeneous student groups through selection either within or between classes and schools, while others leave it as an individual challenge for teachers and students.

Boys consistently outperform girls in science.

In mathematics, the gender gap in achievement is moderate – with a slight advantage for boys. In science, however, it is considerable. Boys outperform girls in all 26 education systems, with score differences ranging from around 10 points in Australia, Canada, the Russian Federation and the United States to more than 30 points – almost one grade-year equivalent – in Denmark (see Chart R10.2). Are the gender differences observed at this age predictive for later ages and future career choices? Although this question cannot be answered directly, in almost all countries women are currently far less likely to obtain a scientific university degree than are men (see Indicator R14).

There is no close and uniform connection between educational attainment and adult literacy performance.

Knowledge and skills need to be acquired and updated beyond the initial stage of education and throughout an individual's life. Indicators R30 to R33 therefore broaden the picture of educational outcomes by examining literacy skills among adults of working age. To the extent that education aims to equip children for adult life, testing adult skill in relation to everyday tasks is, in part, a measure of how successful education systems have been in carrying out this function.

In European countries, literacy levels tend to be more homogeneous than in North America, whether these levels are relatively high (Sweden), relatively low (Poland) or mid-range (Germany, the Netherlands and Switzerland) (see Chart R30). By contrast, in Canada and the United States, there are significant proportions of persons at all literacy levels and thus a much wider dispersion in literacy and numeracy ability.

One might expect educational attainment and literacy skills to be closely linked. However, literacy as measured by the International Adult Literacy Survey is not curriculum-based but

A guide through the 1996 OECD indicators

reflects the ability to perform literacy tasks encountered in everyday life, including the work place. The extent to which education systems adequately prepare young people for the wider world has traditionally been a question of significant interest to educational policy-makers. As one might expect, in all countries high prose literacy levels are associated with high levels of educational attainment (see Chart R31). However, the correspondence between the two is far from perfect. There are significant proportions of persons with low attainment who achieve relatively high literacy levels and, likewise, not insignificant proportions of persons with high attainment who score lower than one might expect on the basis of their formal qualifications. Similarly, for a given level of educational attainment, adults in some countries achieve higher literacy scores on average than persons at the same level in other countries.

Generally, the literacy levels of the young (16-24) are higher than those of older persons (25-65) (see Chart R32). In all countries there is a smaller proportion of young persons at the lowest literacy level relative to the older population, and in almost all cases, a larger proportion of young persons at the highest three levels. However, signs of convergence among countries in the literacy skills of the youth population are mixed if cross-country differences for youth are compared to those observed for their elders.

Literacy performance among the young is generally higher than among older people.

Labour market outcomes of education

The final chapter of this volume focuses on interdependencies between attainment levels and labour market outcomes.

Unemployment rates in OECD countries generally decrease as the level of educational attainment of workers increases [see Chart R21(A)]. This is a result that appears to hold generally across countries with widely different distributions of educational attainment in their populations (see Table C1 for background) and with labour markets subject to varying degrees of governmental regulation and rates of job creation. A second result is that, with the exception of one country, the range of unemployment rates across OECD countries for persons with university-level attainment is relatively narrow. Indeed, what distinguishes countries from one another is the ability of their economies to provide employment opportunities for persons at the other end of the spectrum, namely those with relatively low educational attainment.

Persons with low attainment are at a distinct disadvantage in the labour market.

In most OECD countries, educational policy has aimed at encouraging young people to complete secondary education. With the continuing upskilling of jobs, persons with low attainment are at a distinct disadvantage in the labour market. Even with increasing educational attainment, unemployment among young people is high in many countries [see Chart R21(B)]. This is a waste of human resources and can pose a risk to both the individual and to society at large. The unemployment rates of young people are consistently higher in OECD countries than those of older age groups, often twice as high, and sometimes three or more times. Nowhere is the handicap of low educational attainment more evident in the labour market than among the young, who cannot compensate for this through work experience and skills learned on the job. With some exceptions, each increment in the formal qualifications of young people results in a lower unemployment rate in the early stages of working life. In a number of countries, young workers with even tertiary level attainment have high unemployment rates.

Unemployment among the young can be three times as high as among older people.

The transition from school to work is a gradual one, with the unemployment rates of young persons one year after leaving school slowly decreasing as more and more of them find suitable jobs. Five years after leaving school, rates have nearly reached the levels characteristic of adult workers (see Chart R24).

The handicap of low educational attainment makes itself felt very quickly in the labour market, with exceedingly high unemployment rates one year after leaving school, and persistent unemployment even five years later. This situation improves as one moves up the attainment ladder. Indeed, highly-educated young people are in general more fully integrated into the labour force in the first year after leaving school than are their less educated counterparts after five years.

Reader's guide

Coverage of the statistics

Although a lack of data still limits the scope of the indicators in many countries, the coverage extends, in principle, to the entire national education system regardless of the ownership or sponsorship of the institutions concerned and regardless of the institutional context in which instruction is delivered. With one exception described below, all types of students and all age groups are meant to be included: children (including those classified as exceptional), adults, nationals, foreigners, as well as students in open distance learning, in special education programmes or in educational programmes organised by ministries other than the Ministry of Education, provided the main aim of the programme is the educational development of the individual. However, vocational and technical training in the work place, with the exception of combined school and work-based programmes that are explicitly deemed to be parts of the education system, is not included.

Educational activities classified as "adult" or "non-regular" are covered, provided that the activities involve studies or have a subject-matter content similar to "regular" education studies or that the underlying programmes lead to qualifications similar to regular educational programmes. Courses for adults that are primarily for general interest, personal enrichment, leisure or recreation are excluded.

Regional groups of countries

The categories "OECD" and "European Union" in the tables refer to the respective membership as of September 1996, when this publication went to print. Data in tables and charts were produced before Poland's entry into the OECD.

Calculation of international means

For many indicators a country mean is presented, and for some an OECD total.

The *country mean* is calculated as the unweighted mean of the data values of all OECD countries for which data are available or can be estimated. The country mean therefore refers to an average of data values at the level of the national systems and can be used to see how an indicator value for a given country compares with the value for a typical or average country. It does not take into account the absolute size of the education system in each country.

The *OECD total* is calculated as a weighted mean of the data values of all countries for which data are available or can be estimated. It reflects the value for a given indicator when the OECD area is considered as a whole. This approach is taken for the purpose of comparing, for example, expenditure figures for individual countries with those of the entire OECD area for which valid data are available, with this area considered as a single entity.

Note that both the country mean and the OECD total can be significantly biased by missing data. Given the relatively small number of countries, no statistical methods are used to compensate for this. In cases where a category is not applicable in a country or where the data value is negligible for the corresponding calculation, the value *zero* is imputed for the purpose of calculating means.

ISCED levels of education

The classification of the levels of education is based on the International Standard Classification of Education (ISCED). ISCED is an instrument for compiling statistics on education internationally and distinguishes between seven levels of education. The Glossary describes the ISCED levels of education and Annex 1 shows corresponding theoretical durations and the typical starting and ending ages of the main educational programmes by ISCED level.

Main data sources

Data sources are described in Annex 3. The main sources are as follows:

• Data for Indicators C1, C2, C11, P8, R21(A), R21(B), R22 and R24 are derived from household and labour force surveys conducted by the countries.

• Data for Indicator C3 are derived from the OECD Demographic Database.

• Data for Indicators F1, F3, F5, F12, F13, P31, P32, P1, P2, P3, P6, R11, R12, R14 and R15 are derived from the 1995 UNESCO/OECD/EUROSTAT data collection on statistics of education.

Reader's guide

• Indicators P22(A) to (G) are based on the 1995 OECD School Survey conducted by the OECD-INES Network C during the school year 1995/96.

• Indicators P11, P33 and P35 are based on a special survey conducted during 1995 by the OECD-INES Network C and refer to the school year 1993/94.

• Indicators R6, R7, R9 and R10 are based on the Third International Mathematics and Science Study conducted during 1994/95 by the International Association for the Evaluation of Educational Achievement.

• Indicators R30, R31, R32 and R33 are based on the International Adult Literacy Survey conducted during 1994 by Statistics Canada.

• Data on regional resource disparities were collected through a special survey conducted by the OECD-INES Technical Group.

• Supporting data on the size of the labour force are derived from household and labour force surveys conducted by the countries. Supporting data on GDP, purchasing power parities and total public expenditure are derived from the OECD National Accounts Database. Supporting data on gross average earnings are taken from the OECD Earnings Distribution Database.

For information on reference periods for the indicators, refer to Annex 3. Note that, by convention, indicators that refer to the school year 1993/94 are referred to as 1994 indicators. For information on the beginning and end of national school/academic years, refer to Annex 1.

Missing data

Four symbols are employed in the tables to denote missing data:

- *n*   Magnitude is either negligible or zero.
- *x*   Data included in another category of the question, or in another question.
- *a*   Data not applicable because the question does not apply.
- *m*   Data not available, either because they were not collected in the country, or because of non-response.

Rounding of data

Data may not always add up to the totals indicated because of rounding.

Country abbreviations

Australia	AUS
Austria	OST
Belgium	BEL
Canada	CAN
Czech Republic	CZC
Denmark	DEN
Finland	FIN
France	FRA
Germany	GER
Greece	GRE
Hungary	HUN
Iceland	ICE
Ireland	IRE
Italy	ITA
Japan	JPN
Korea	KOR
Luxembourg	LUX
Mexico	MEX
Netherlands	NET
New Zealand	NZL
Norway	NOR
Poland	POL
Portugal	POR
Russian Federation	RUS
Spain	SPA
Sweden	SWE
Switzerland	SWI
Turkey	TUR
United Kingdom	UKM
United States	USA

Chapter 1

DEMOGRAPHIC, SOCIAL AND ECONOMIC CONTEXT OF EDUCATION

Education and training systems both shape and respond to broad social and economic changes. In order to interpret differences in educational structures, processes and outcomes among countries, the conditions under which education systems operate need to be taken into account. Such conditions include the demand for education at the different levels and in the various sectors of education, and the attainment profiles of different sections of the population.

Demographic characteristics, for example, are an important factor in the design and implementation of education policies. The number of children and young persons in a population (see **Indicator C3**) determines the demand for schooling and hence the targets for the supply of learning opportunities, and influences the educational resources that will be required.

Similarly, educational attainment – and, by extension, the level of qualification of the labour force – is an important factor shaping economic outcomes and the quality of life for both individuals and society as a whole. The indicators presented in this chapter, which compare populations on the basis of completed levels of education, provide a broad and indirect measure of the stock of human capital in a country, of its evolution over time (through an examination of differences between younger and older persons), and of differences between men and women (see **Indicators C1 and C2**).

With ageing populations, the number of persons in the labour force relative to the total population will fall in many countries. **Indicator C11** shows how labour force participation varies with educational attainment and suggests that higher levels of educational attainment may help to offset this effect.

Indicators R21, R22 and R24 in Chapter 7 take the analysis of attainment profiles further and point to interdependences between attainment levels and economic outcomes.

Since the values of the indicators shown in this chapter are largely a reflection of the history of participation in education, it is instructive to look at them alongside the indicators on the current output of educational institutions (particularly Indicators R11 and R12). Such a comparison will reveal the progress that virtually all countries have achieved in recent decades in raising the educational attainment of their populations and in reducing the gender gap.

C1: Educational attainment of the adult population

C1: EDUCATIONAL ATTAINMENT OF THE ADULT POPULATION

This indicator shows a profile of the educational attainment of the adult population and provides a proxy for assessing the level of qualification of the labour force.

POLICY CONTEXT

A well-educated and well-trained labour force is important for the social and economic well-being of countries. Education plays a role in expanding scientific knowledge and transforming it into productivity-enhancing technology, as well as in raising the skills and competencies of the population, thereby improving the capacity of people to live, work and learn well. Educational attainment – and, by extension, labour force qualifications – are important factors in determining economic outcomes and the quality of life for individuals and society as a whole. Yet rising levels of educational attainment entail increasing costs for both governments and households and, as education systems emphasise initial school-based education, a later entry into the labour market.

The attainment of the population aged 25-64 is mainly the result of historical patterns of participation in education. The various forms of continuing education and training therefore provide important means whereby policy-makers can enhance the attainment of the adult population.

KEY RESULTS

OECD countries differ widely in the levels of educational attainment of their populations (see Chart C1.1). In most OECD countries more than 60 per cent of the population aged 25 to 64 have completed at least upper secondary education and in four countries – Germany, Norway, Switzerland and the United States – this proportion exceeds 80 per cent. In other countries, especially in Southern Europe, the educational structure of the adult population shows a different profile. In Belgium, Greece, Ireland, Italy, Portugal, Spain and Turkey, more than half of the population aged 25-64 years have not completed upper secondary education, with the figures for Portugal and Turkey equal to or above 80 per cent. With the increasing skill requirements of jobs in today's economies, persons with low attainment levels may find themselves at a distinct disadvantage in the labour market [see also Indicators R21(A), R21(B) and R22]. Similarly, countries with a relatively high proportion of persons with low attainment may find themselves disadvantaged internationally in attracting investment in high-technology sectors.

DESCRIPTION AND INTERPRETATION

This indicator is often used as a proxy for measuring the quality or level of skills in the labour force. It is an indirect measure which is largely based on formal educational qualifications and only partially captures the skills and competencies that are acquired through adult, or continuing education or training, or other non-formal ways of learning at home and in the work place. Therefore, formal educational attainment reflects only partially the actual stock of knowledge and skills available in the labour force. Furthermore, there is not always a close correspondence between educational attainment and the skill requirements of jobs, which are more difficult to identify and measure. By comparing the results of this indicator with indicators R30 and R31 – which provide a direct measure of functional adult literacy – it can be seen that, although higher levels of adult literacy are generally associated with higher educational attainment, there is considerable variation in reported skill levels among persons with the same level of formal educational attainment.

Of key interest is the flexibility with which education systems have adapted to changes in labour markets and socio-economic conditions. One way of looking at differences in educational attainment over time is to examine the attainment levels of different age cohorts.

A comparison of the attainment of the population aged 25 to 34 years with the attainment of the population aged 55 to 64 years (see Chart C1.2) shows that the proportion of persons completing less than upper secondary education has been shrinking in all OECD countries. Also the attainment gap between countries is becoming smaller, with younger generations obtaining more education than their elders. In Finland and France, the difference in attainment of upper secondary education is 43 percentage points or more between 25-34 year-olds and 55-64 year-olds. In Austria, Belgium, the Czech Republic, Greece, Ireland, Italy, Spain and Sweden this difference between generations still exceeds 30 per cent. However, the changes in educational attainment have been uneven in OECD countries and substantial differences in educational

C1: Educational attainment of the adult population

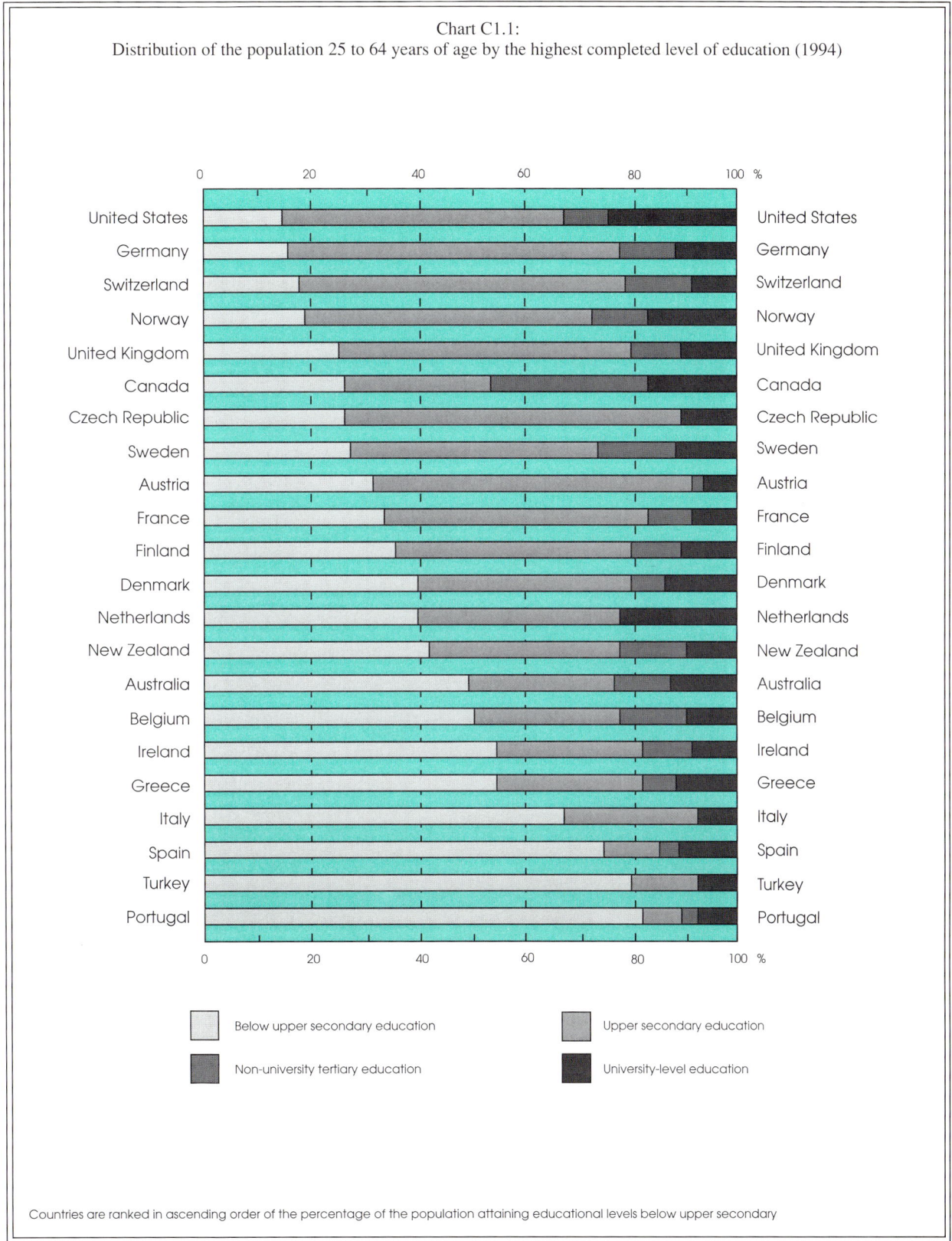

C1: Educational attainment of the adult population

attainment still remain. Older persons may increasingly find their comparatively low levels of skills and competencies overtaken by rising qualification requirements, and may find their limited basic educational competencies a hindrance in updating their qualifications through retraining.

Differences in educational attainment at the tertiary level are even more pronounced (see Table C1.3). In Canada 46 per cent of the population aged 25 to 64 years have attained a tertiary level of education – with the greater part at the non-university level. In Norway, Sweden and the United States more than 25 per cent of the population have attained tertiary education, whereas in Austria, Italy, Portugal and Turkey the figure is 10 per cent or less. However, it should be noted that countries such as Austria, Germany, the Netherlands and Switzerland classify many advanced vocational programmes at the upper secondary level. These programmes may be more similar in content, orientation and qualifications awarded to programmes that are classified at the tertiary level in, for example, Canada and the United States.

The rising skill requirements of labour markets, the increase in unemployment during recent years, and the higher expectations of individuals and society have led to a marked increase in the proportion of young people who have attained a qualification at the non-university or university tertiary level of education. This is also reflected in the comparatively higher literacy skills of the young population shown in Indicator R30. In Belgium, Canada, France, Greece and Spain the proportion of persons who have attained tertiary level is 16 to 20 percentage points higher among 25-34 year-olds than among 55-64 year-olds (see also Indicator P6 on current enrolment in tertiary educational programmes). In Austria, Germany, Italy, New Zealand, Switzerland and Turkey this difference is only 5 percentage points or less (see Table C1.3). The smaller increase in tertiary attainment between 25-34 and 55-64 year-olds in Austria, Denmark, Germany, Italy and Switzerland may, in part, be due to the relatively late completion of the tertiary level of education (see Annex 1) in these countries.

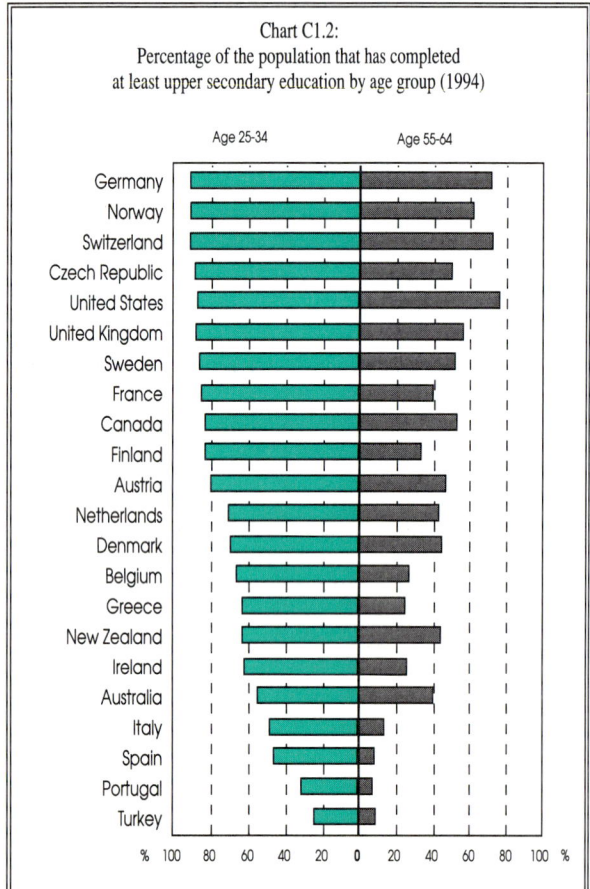

Chart C1.2:
Percentage of the population that has completed at least upper secondary education by age group (1994)

DEFINITIONS

The attainment profiles shown here are based on the percentage of the population in a specified age group that has completed a specified highest level of education, defined according to the International Standard Classification of Education (ISCED). However, the education systems of many countries have changed considerably since the ISCED classification was adopted. As a result, many educational programmes now in existence cannot be easily classified and the contents of a specific ISCED level may differ among countries. Countries may not always classify diplomas and qualifications at the same ISCED levels, even if they are received at roughly the same age or after a similar number of years of schooling. Annex 1, which shows the average number of years of schooling corresponding to each completed level of education in each country, sheds some light on this question.

C1: Educational attainment of the adult population

Table C1.1:
Percentage of the population 25 to 64 years of age
by the highest completed level of education (1994)

	Early childhood, primary and lower secondary education	Upper secondary education	Non-university tertiary education	University-level education	Total
North America					
Canada	26	28	29	17	100
United States	15	53	8	24	100
Pacific Area					
Australia	50	27	10	13	100
New Zealand	43	34	14	9	100
European Union					
Austria	32	60	2	6	100
Belgium	51	27	12	10	100
Denmark	40	40	6	14	100
Finland	36	44	9	11	100
France	33	50	8	9	100
Germany	16	62	10	13	100
Greece	55	27	6	12	100
Ireland	55	27	10	9	100
Italy	67	26	a	8	100
Netherlands	40	38	a	21	100
Portugal	81	8	3	7	100
Spain	74	11	4	11	100
Sweden	28	46	14	12	100
United Kingdom	26	54	9	12	100
Other OECD countries					
Czech Republic	27	63	x	10	100
Norway	19	53	11	16	100
Switzerland	18	61	13	8	100
Turkey	80	13	a	7	100
Country mean	**41**	**39**	**8**	**12**	**100**

Source: OECD Database. See Annex 3 for notes

C1: Educational attainment of the adult population

Table C1.2: Percentage of the population that has completed at least upper secondary education, by age group (1994)

	Age groups				Difference in attainment between age groups			
	25-34 (a)	35-44 (b)	45-54 (c)	55-64 (d)	(a)–(b) *	(b)–(c) *	(c)–(d) *	(a)–(d) *
North America								
Canada	82	79	70	53	3	9	17	29
United States	86	89	85	76	–2	4	10	11
Pacific Area								
Australia	54	54	47	41	1	6	7	14
New Zealand	62	60	56	45	2	4	11	16
European Union								
Austria	79	72	64	48	7	8	16	31
Belgium	65	54	43	28	12	11	15	37
Denmark	68	62	59	46	6	2	13	22
Finland	82	72	56	34	10	16	22	48
France	84	73	60	41	12	12	19	43
Germany	90	88	84	72	1	5	11	17
Greece	62	50	35	26	13	15	9	37
Ireland	61	47	35	27	14	12	8	34
Italy	47	41	26	14	6	15	12	33
Netherlands	69	64	54	44	6	10	10	25
Portugal	30	22	15	8	8	8	7	22
Spain	45	29	16	9	16	13	7	36
Sweden	85	78	69	52	7	9	17	33
United Kingdom	86	78	69	57	8	9	12	29
Other OECD countries								
Czech Republic	87	79	68	51	8	11	17	36
Norway	89	85	78	63	4	7	14	25
Switzerland	89	84	79	73	4	5	7	16
Turkey	24	20	16	10	4	3	6	13
Country mean	**69**	**63**	**54**	**42**	**7**	**9**	**12**	**28**

* The figures may differ from figures calculated from the percentages in the preceding columns due to rounding
Source: OECD Database. See Annex 3 for notes

C1: Educational attainment of the adult population

Table C1.3:
Percentage of the population that has completed tertiary education, by age group (1994)

	Age groups				Difference in attainment between age groups			
	25-34 (a)	35-44 (b)	45-54 (c)	55-64 (d)	(a)–(b) *	(b)–(c) *	(c)–(d) *	(a)–(d) *
North America								
Canada	51	49	45	31	2	3	14	19
United States	32	36	33	24	-4	3	10	8
Pacific Area								
Australia	24	28	22	15	-4	6	7	9
New Zealand	21	26	26	18	-5	0	8	3
European Union								
Austria	9	10	7	4	-1	4	3	5
Belgium	30	24	20	11	6	4	9	19
Denmark	20	24	19	13	-5	5	6	7
Finland	22	22	19	12	-1	3	6	9
France	24	18	16	8	6	2	8	16
Germany	20	27	24	17	-6	3	6	3
Greece	25	21	14	9	4	7	5	16
Ireland	24	19	15	11	5	4	4	13
Italy	8	10	7	4	-2	3	3	4
Netherlands	24	25	19	14	-1	5	5	10
Portugal	13	14	9	6	-1	4	4	8
Spain	25	16	10	6	9	6	5	20
Sweden	27	30	26	17	-3	4	9	10
United Kingdom	23	24	20	15	-1	4	5	8
Other OECD countries								
Norway	31	31	25	18	-1	6	8	13
Switzerland	22	23	22	17	-1	1	5	5
Turkey	7	8	8	4	-1	0	4	2
Country mean	**23**	**23**	**19**	**13**	**0**	**4**	**6**	**10**

* The figures may differ from figures calculated from the percentages in the preceding columns due to rounding
Source: OECD Database. See Annex 3 for notes

C2: GENDER DIFFERENCES IN EDUCATIONAL ATTAINMENT OF THE ADULT POPULATION

This indicator compares the levels of educational attainment of men and women. It also shows the difference in the mean number of years of schooling between men and women.

POLICY CONTEXT

The pattern of the educational attainment of men and women in the adult population is uneven in most OECD countries, suggesting that women did not have sufficient opportunities and/or incentives to reach the same level of educational attainment as men. Although the attainment gap between men and women is closing in most OECD countries – as current graduation rates suggest – this still represents a challenge for the various forms of continuing education and training.

KEY RESULTS

Women form the majority of those who have completed only primary or lower secondary education. Men are in a clear majority among those who have completed university-level education. In Austria, Belgium, the Czech Republic, Germany, Switzerland, Turkey and the United Kingdom, the proportion of women among university graduates is 40 per cent or below. However, with the exception of Turkey, the under-representation of women is mostly attributable to large gender differences in the attainment of older age groups, suggesting that there has been significant progress towards greater equality in opportunities between the genders. Furthermore, current university graduation rates show that the gender gap has either been significantly reduced or even that the trend has reversed (see Indicator R12).

DESCRIPTION AND INTERPRETATION

Women are generally over-represented among those ending their education at a level below upper secondary. In Australia, Austria, the Czech Republic, Germany, Switzerland and the United Kingdom 60 per cent or more of those who have not attained the upper secondary level of education are women. In around half of the countries there is also a clear dominance of women in tertiary programmes that do not lead to a university degree or equivalent. Programmes at this level are often of shorter duration than university courses, and often lead to occupations with a traditionally strong female presence. The over-representation of women at the non-university tertiary level is particularly pronounced in Austria, Belgium, Denmark, New Zealand, Portugal and the United Kingdom. On the other hand, there is a striking over-representation of men at the university tertiary level in many countries. Indicator R32, which compares adult literacy skills between the genders, shows that this attainment profile is also reflected in adult literacy outcomes.

In addition to these overall gender differences in attainment, men and women often choose different fields of study, a tendency that leads them to different points of the labour market, even when they have received the same level of education and training.

However, the data also suggest a trend towards greater equality in the attainment of men and women in most OECD countries. Differences in attainment between men and women are much more pronounced among older age groups; specifically, the proportion of women having attained only primary or lower secondary education is as a rule much greater among 55 to 64 year-olds than among 25 to 34 year-olds. It should also be noted that upper secondary graduation rates no longer show significant differences between men and women (see Indicator R11).

Similarly, among university graduates, the average proportion of women is 32 per cent in the age group 55-64, whereas this proportion is 48 per cent for those aged 25-34. Furthermore, a comparison of university graduation rates for men and women (see Indicator R12) suggests that, in most OECD countries, the attainment gap between men and women is also disappearing at the university level.

Although the number of years of schooling of the total population varies greatly across countries, differences between men and women in each country are often small. In most countries, men have more years of schooling than women in the age group 25-64 years (see Table C2.2). The largest differences can be observed in Austria, Germany, Greece, Italy and Switzerland, and to a lesser degree in Australia, France, the Netherlands, New Zealand, Turkey and the United Kingdom, where men have, on average, at least half a year more schooling. However, in Ireland and Sweden women aged 25-64 have had more years of schooling then men. In the age group 25-34 years this is the case in many countries.

C2: Gender differences in educational attainment of the adult population

DEFINITIONS

The indicator shows the percentage of women in a specific age group having completed a specified highest level of education. As with Indicator C1, caution must be exercised because of problems with the classification of the levels of education. The indicator also shows the difference in the mean number of years of schooling between men and women. The number of schooling is obtained by converting the attainment levels into years of schooling on the basis of the theoretical cumulative duration of the respective levels of education (see Annex 1 for details).

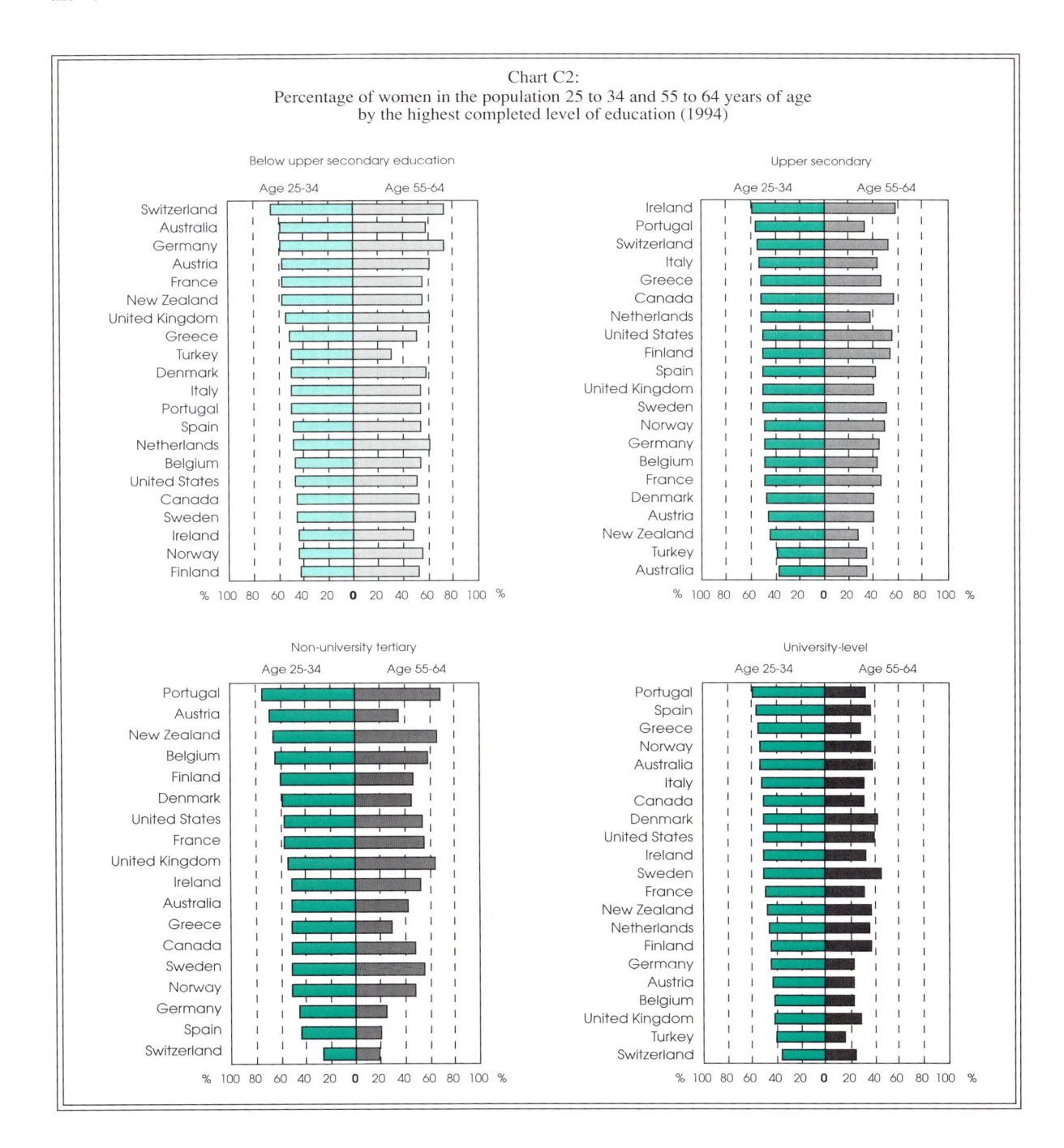

Chart C2:
Percentage of women in the population 25 to 34 and 55 to 64 years of age by the highest completed level of education (1994)

C2: Gender differences in educational attainment of the adult population

Table C2.1.1:
Percentage of women in the population 25 to 64 years of age by the highest completed level of education (1994)

	Early childhood, primary and lower secondary education	Upper secondary education	Non-university tertiary education	University-level education	Total
North America					
Canada	49	54	50	45	50
United States	49	53	55	46	51
Pacific Area					
Australia	60	34	47	47	50
New Zealand	57	38	66	43	50
European Union					
Austria	61	44	59	36	50
Belgium	51	47	62	36	50
Denmark	55	44	57	47	49
Finland	49	52	54	42	50
France	57	47	56	43	51
Germany	69	49	35	36	49
Greece	52	51	44	44	51
Ireland	47	58	53	42	50
Italy	52	49	a	44	51
Netherlands	56	46	a	42	49
Portugal	52	49	74	49	53
Spain	52	47	36	50	51
Sweden	46	50	55	48	49
United Kingdom	61	46	58	37	50
Other OECD countries					
Czech Republic	66	46	x	40	51
Norway	50	50	48	47	49
Switzerland	69	53	23	31	50
Turkey	43	35	a	31	41
Country mean	**55**	**47**	**44**	**42**	**50**

Source: OECD Database. See Annex 3 for notes

C2: Gender differences in educational attainment of the adult population

Table C2.1.2:
Percentage of women in the population 25 to 34 and 55 to 64 years of age by the highest completed level of education (1994)

	Age group	Early childhood, primary and lower secondary education	Upper secondary education	Non-university tertiary education	University-level education	Total
North America						
Canada	25 - 34	45	51	51	51	50
	55 - 64	52	57	49	32	51
United States	25 - 34	46	50	57	50	50
	55 - 64	52	56	54	40	52
Pacific Area						
Australia	25 - 34	59	37	51	53	50
	55 - 64	59	35	43	39	50
New Zealand	25 - 34	56	43	66	48	51
	55 - 64	56	28	66	38	49
European Union						
Austria	25 - 34	57	46	69	43	48
	55 - 64	63	41	35	24	52
Belgium	25 - 34	46	47	64	42	49
	55 - 64	55	45	59	22	52
Denmark	25 - 34	49	47	58	51	49
	55 - 64	59	42	46	43	51
Finland	25 - 34	41	50	60	45	49
	55 - 64	53	55	48	37	52
France	25 - 34	57	47	57	49	50
	55 - 64	56	47	56	31	52
Germany	25 - 34	58	48	44	44	48
	55 - 64	74	46	25	23	50
Greece	25 - 34	52	52	51	54	52
	55 - 64	51	47	30	28	49
Ireland	25 - 34	44	58	51	50	51
	55 - 64	49	59	54	33	50
Italy	25 - 34	49	52	a	52	50
	55 - 64	54	45	a	31	52
Netherlands	25 - 34	48	50	a	47	49
	55 - 64	61	38	a	36	51
Portugal	25 - 34	49	55	74	59	52
	55 - 64	54	34	70	33	54
Spain	25 - 34	49	50	44	56	50
	55 - 64	54	42	22	38	52
Sweden	25 - 34	45	49	51	50	49
	55 - 64	51	51	55	46	51
United Kingdom	25 - 34	54	50	54	42	49
	55 - 64	62	42	65	29	52
Other OECD countries						
Norway	25 - 34	43	49	51	54	49
	55 - 64	56	50	48	38	51
Switzerland	25 - 34	65	54	26	36	50
	55 - 64	73	54	20	24	53
Turkey	25 - 34	49	38	a	40	47
	55 - 64	32	36	a	15	31
Country mean	25 - 34	50	49	47	48	50
	55 - 64	57	45	46	32	51

Source: OECD Database. See Annex 3 for notes

C2: Gender differences in educational attainment of the adult population

Table C2.2:
Cumulative years of schooling in the population aged 25 to 64 and 25 to 34 by gender (1994)

	Age group 25 - 64			Age group 25 - 34		
	Men	Women	Difference between men and women	Men	Women	Difference between men and women
North America						
Canada	12.5	12.4	0.1	13.0	13.2	–0.2
United States	12.7	12.6	0.1	12.7	12.8	–0.1
Pacific Area						
Australia *	12.8	12.4	0.5	12.8	12.6	0.2
New Zealand	11.3	10.8	0.5	11.5	11.3	0.2
European Union						
Austria *	12.5	11.7	0.8	12.8	12.4	0.3
Belgium	10.5	10.2	0.3	11.4	11.5	–0.1
Denmark	12.3	12.0	0.4	12.4	12.5	–0.1
Finland	11.5	11.5	0.1	12.0	12.2	–0.2
France	10.9	10.4	0.5	12.1	12.0	0.1
Germany *	13.9	13.0	0.9	13.7	13.4	0.3
Greece	10.8	10.1	0.7	12.0	12.1	–0.1
Ireland	10.7	10.9	–0.2	11.8	12.1	–0.3
Italy	9.2	8.5	0.7	10.5	10.7	–0.2
Netherlands	11.8	11.1	0.6	12.0	12.0	0.1
Portugal	7.7	7.7	0.0	8.3	8.9	–0.6
Spain	9.1	8.8	0.4	10.9	11.2	–0.3
Sweden	11.5	11.7	–0.2	12.2	12.3	–0.1
United Kingdom *	12.8	12.2	0.6	13.1	12.9	0.2
Other OECD countries						
Norway	12.3	12.2	0.1	12.5	12.7	–0.2
Switzerland *	13.9	12.5	1.3	13.9	13.0	1.0
Turkey	7.7	7.2	0.5	8.0	7.4	0.6
Country mean	**11.4**	**11.0**	**0.4**	**11.9**	**11.9**	**0.0**

* For all persons, minimum completion of the lower secondary level of education is assumed
Source: OECD Database. See Annex 3 for notes

C3: The relative size of the young population

C3: THE RELATIVE SIZE OF THE YOUNG POPULATION

This indicator shows the percentage of 5-14 year-olds in the total population.

POLICY CONTEXT

The number of young people in a population influences both the rate of renewal of labour force qualifications and the amount of resources and organisational effort a country must invest in its education system. Countries with a larger proportion of young people in the population must allocate a greater portion of their national income to initial education and training than countries with smaller young populations but similar participation rates.

KEY RESULTS

The proportion of young people aged 5 to 14 has gone through a cycle of modest increase and decline in all OECD regions over the last quarter of a century. Differences among countries in the relative size of the youth population have diminished since 1970, but the proportion of people aged 5 to 14 years still varies widely, ranging from just over 10 per cent in Italy to more than 20 per cent in Mexico and Turkey.

DESCRIPTION AND INTERPRETATION

The proportion of 5-14 year-olds in the total population lies between 11 and 14 per cent in most OECD countries; the proportion of 15-24 year-olds is slightly larger (see Table C3). Although differences among countries in the relative size of the youth population have diminished since 1970 (see Chart C3.2), there are still remarkable contrasts. In Mexico and Turkey, more than 20 per cent of the population are aged between 5 and 14. Thus, the least prosperous countries have both fewer resources to allocate to education and more students over whom to distribute these resources (see also Indicators F1 and F3). Mexico and Turkey are closely followed by Iceland, Ireland, Korea and Poland, in which more than 16 per cent of the population are aged 5 to 14. At the other end of the spectrum are Austria, Belgium, Denmark, Germany, Italy, Japan, the Netherlands, Sweden and Switzerland, where the proportion of 5 to 14 year-olds is between 10 and 12 per cent.

In all countries, the proportion of young people aged 5 to 14 years in the total population has declined between 1984 and 1994, in the Czech Republic, Italy, Japan, Mexico, Portugal and Spain by more than 3 per cent. The decline in the number of young people, which reflects a reduced birth rate, has somewhat eased the pressure on expanding school systems at the lower levels of education. However, this long-term decline in birth rates has significant implications for the rate of renewal of labour force qualifications, which will reveal their full impact in the years to come. It should also be noted that in most, although not all, countries higher participation in post-compulsory schooling has outweighed lower birth rates, resulting in higher net enrolments (see Indicators P3 and P6).

During recent years the decline in the proportion of young people has slowed down in many OECD countries – the Czech Republic, Greece, Ireland, Italy, Portugal and Spain are the exceptions.

Population forecasts suggest (see Table C3) that over the next decade the proportion of the 5 to 14 year-old population will stabilise in most countries; the exceptions are the Czech Republic, Greece, Ireland, Mexico and Spain, where this proportion is expected to decrease by more than 2 percentage points – and, on the other hand, Denmark, Norway and Sweden, where it is expected to increase by around 1 percentage point. The forecasts also indicate that overall differences among countries in the relative size of the youth population will continue to diminish.

DEFINITIONS

The indicator shows the size of the population in a specified age group per 100 people in the population. The statistics cover all persons residing in the country, regardless of citizenship, educational or labour market status.

C3: The relative size of the young population

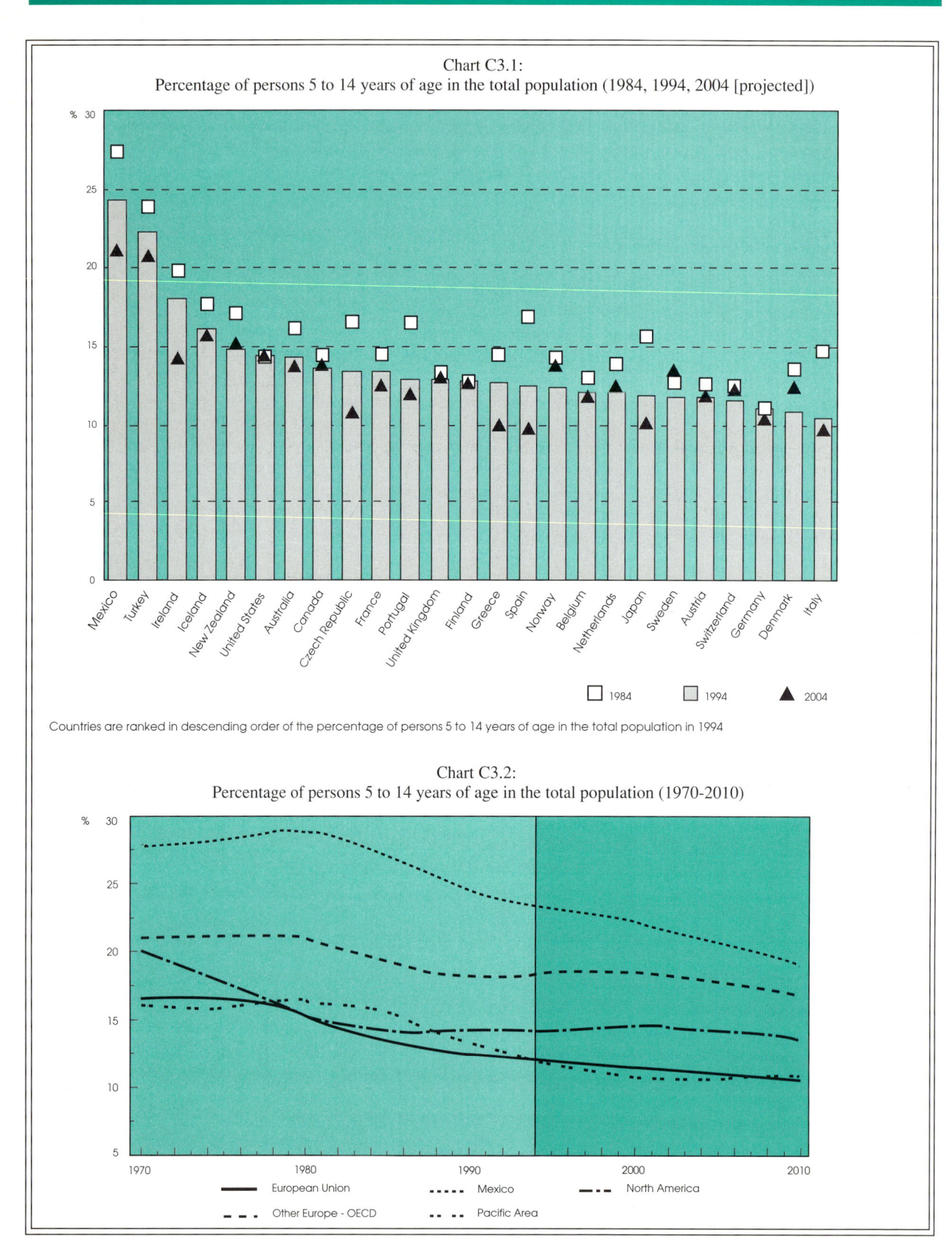

Chart C3.1:
Percentage of persons 5 to 14 years of age in the total population (1984, 1994, 2004 [projected])

□ 1984   ■ 1994   ▲ 2004

Countries are ranked in descending order of the percentage of persons 5 to 14 years of age in the total population in 1994

Chart C3.2:
Percentage of persons 5 to 14 years of age in the total population (1970-2010)

— European Union   ⋯⋯ Mexico   —·— North America
--- Other Europe - OECD   —··— Pacific Area

44

C3: The relative size of the young population

Table C3:
Percentage of persons 5 to 29 years of age in the total population (1984, 1994, 2004)

	Age groups					
	1994	1984	1994	2004	1994	1994
	5 - 29	5 - 14	5 - 14	5 - 14	15 - 24	25 - 29
North America						
Canada	35.5	14.3	13.6	13.7	13.8	8.1
Mexico	54.5	27.6	24.3	21.1	21.5	8.7
United States	35.8	14.3	14.4	14.4	13.9	7.5
Pacific Area						
Australia	37.5	16.1	14.3	13.7	15.4	7.7
Japan	33.9	15.7	11.8	10.0	15.3	6.8
New Zealand	37.8	17.1	14.8	15.4	15.5	7.5
European Union						
Austria	34.1	12.6	11.7	11.7	13.4	9.0
Belgium	32.7	12.9	12.0	11.7	13.0	7.7
Denmark	32.6	13.6	10.8	12.3	13.7	8.0
Finland	32.4	12.8	12.7	12.5	12.4	7.3
France	35.0	14.5	13.4	12.4	14.2	7.5
Germany	31.6	11.3	11.0	10.0	11.8	8.7
Greece	35.1	14.5	12.6	9.8	15.0	7.6
Ireland	42.1	19.8	18.0	14.2	17.2	7.0
Italy	33.3	14.7	10.4	9.7	14.7	8.3
Luxembourg	m	11.8	m	11.3	m	m
Netherlands	34.4	13.9	12.0	12.3	14.0	8.5
Portugal	36.9	16.5	12.8	11.8	16.6	7.5
Spain	37.3	16.9	12.4	9.7	16.5	8.4
Sweden	31.7	12.7	11.7	13.5	12.6	7.4
United Kingdom	34.1	13.2	12.8	13.0	13.2	8.2
Other OECD countries						
Czech Republic	36.4	16.5	13.4	10.7	16.2	6.7
Hungary	34.7		12.7		15.7	6.3
Iceland	39.8	17.6	16.1	15.7	15.6	8.0
Norway	34.3	14.3	12.3	13.7	14.1	7.9
Switzerland	32.3	12.2	11.5	12.1	12.5	8.3
Turkey	51.0	23.9	22.3	20.6	20.2	8.5
Country mean	**36.4**	**15.4**	**13.7**	**13.0**	**14.9**	**7.8**
Other non-OECD countries						
Korea	45.1		16.6		19.2	9.3
Poland	38.4		16.9		15.1	6.4
Russian Federation	36.1		15.7		13.6	6.8

Source: OECD Database. See Annex 3 for notes

C11: Rates of labour force participation by level of educational attainment

C11: RATES OF LABOUR FORCE PARTICIPATION BY LEVEL OF EDUCATIONAL ATTAINMENT

This indicator shows the labour force participation rate by level of educational attainment and the overall attainment profile of the labour force.

POLICY CONTEXT

The level of educational attainment is an important factor, influencing both participation rates in the labour force as well as the relative position of different educational groups in the labour market.

KEY RESULTS

Although overall labour force participation rates vary substantially across countries, there is a strong relationship between the level of educational attainment and labour force participation rates in all countries. Differences in participation rates across groups with different educational levels are much larger among women than among men. Men have higher participation rates than women at all educational levels. This difference between the genders is on average around 10 percentage points among those with university education but more than three times as much at levels below upper secondary.

DESCRIPTION AND INTERPRETATION

The overall labour force participation rate varies substantially across countries. It ranges from around 65 per cent of the population 25 to 64 years of age in Ireland and Southern Europe (except Portugal) to around 80 or 90 per cent of this population in Switzerland and the Nordic countries (except Norway). These large differences in the overall participation rate, which embrace both genders, are mostly due to differences in participation rates for women, which in turn are highly correlated with the educational attainment of women. Sweden has the highest (88 per cent) and Turkey the lowest (32 per cent) participation rate for women. For men, Switzerland has the highest (95 per cent) and Belgium the lowest participation rate (81 per cent), the range being much smaller than for women. However, it should be noted that gender differences in labour force participation rates are insignificant in most countries for younger age groups, particularly if the focus is on the tertiary level.

A similar pattern can be seen at each educational level. The variation in labour force participation rates across countries is much larger for women than for men. The variation in participation rates between the educational levels in each country is also much larger for women than for men. In Ireland, Italy and Turkey, female university graduates have participation rates around 50 percentage points higher than the rates for those at levels below upper secondary. Among men the corresponding difference is 22 percentage points in the United States, and almost as much in Austria, Belgium, Finland, France, Norway and the United Kingdom.

All things being equal, one would expect from the preceding results that overall participation rates would be higher in countries where the educational attainment of the labour force is high (see Table C11.3). However, the actual relationship is far from exact. Although lower attainment levels tend to be associated with lower participation rates, Portugal shows low attainment levels of the labour force but an overall participation rate in the mid-range, and the Netherlands has relatively high attainment levels but a participation rate only slightly higher than that of the countries with low educational attainment.

DEFINITIONS

The labour force participation rate is calculated as the percentage of the population in different age groups that is in the labour force. The labour force is defined as all persons who are economically active, either employed or unemployed according to ILO definitions.

C11: Rates of labour force participation by level of educational attainment

Chart C11: Rates of labour force participation by level of educational attainment for men and women 25 to 64 years of age (1994)

Below upper secondary education

University-level education

Men ■ Women ☐

C11: Rates of labour force participation by level of educational attainment

Table C11.1:
Rates of labour force participation by level of educational attainment for the population 25 to 64 years of age (1994)

	Early childhood, primary and lower secondary education	Upper secondary education	Non-university tertiary education	University-level education	Total
North America					
Canada	62	80	85	89	78
United States	58	79	86	88	79
Pacific Area					
Australia	66	80	84	88	75
New Zealand	66	84	83	88	77
European Union					
Austria	59	78	90	90	73
Belgium	55	78	85	89	68
Denmark	73	89	93	94	83
Finland	68	85	85	92	80
France	61	83	87	87	76
Germany	56	76	85	88	75
Greece	62	67	84	87	67
Ireland	58	73	85	89	67
Italy	54	77	a	88	63
Netherlands	56	77	a	86	70
Portugal	72	84	87	95	75
Spain	58	80	88	87	65
Sweden	86	90	92	93	90
United Kingdom	64	82	87	91	79
Other OECD countries					
Czech Republic	67	90	x	96	85
Norway	64	83	87	93	82
Switzerland	72	81	92	89	82
Turkey	63	73	a	89	66
Country mean	**64**	**80**	**74**	**90**	**75**

Source: OECD Database. See Annex 3 for notes

C11: Rates of labour force participation by level of educational attainment

Table C11.2:
Rates of labour force participation by level of educational attainment
for the population 25 to 64 years of age, by gender (1994)

	Gender	Early childhood, primary and lower secondary education	Upper secondary education	Non-university tertiary education	University-level education	Total
North America						
Canada	Men	75	89	91	92	87
	Women	48	72	79	85	70
United States	Men	72	88	92	93	87
	Women	45	72	81	82	71
Pacific Area						
Australia	Men	83	90	91	94	88
	Women	55	61	76	82	62
New Zealand	Men	80	91	94	94	88
	Women	56	72	77	81	66
European Union						
Austria	Men	73	86	93	93	84
	Women	49	68	87	86	62
Belgium	Men	71	88	92	91	81
	Women	39	68	81	85	56
Denmark	Men	78	90	94	95	87
	Women	68	86	93	92	79
Finland	Men	72	89	87	93	83
	Women	64	81	83	89	76
France	Men	72	90	93	91	85
	Women	52	74	83	81	67
Germany	Men	79	85	89	92	86
	Women	45	67	80	81	64
Greece	Men	86	88	91	91	88
	Women	40	47	74	81	48
Ireland	Men	82	93	94	94	87
	Women	31	58	77	81	48
Italy	Men	77	88	a	92	81
	Women	33	66	a	83	44
Netherlands	Men	76	87	a	90	84
	Women	40	66	a	79	56
Portugal	Men	86	89	90	95	87
	Women	59	80	86	95	64
Spain	Men	82	91	94	91	85
	Women	37	68	77	83	46
Sweden	Men	91	92	91	94	92
	Women	81	89	92	93	88
United Kingdom	Men	75	90	93	94	88
	Women	57	73	82	88	70
Other OECD countries						
Norway	Men	75	89	90	95	87
	Women	55	77	83	90	75
Switzerland	Men	93	95	96	94	95
	Women	62	69	77	78	68
Turkey	Men	88	91	a	93	89
	Women	28	39	a	81	32
Country mean	**Men**	**79**	**89**	**79**	**93**	**86**
	Women	**50**	**69**	**70**	**85**	**63**

Source: OECD Database. See Annex 3 for notes

C11: Rates of labour force participation by level of educational attainment

Table C11.3:
Percentage of the labour force 25 to 64 years of age by the highest completed level of education (1994)

	Men					Women				
	Early childhood, primary and lower secondary education	Upper secondary education	Non-university tertiary education	University-level education	Total	Early childhood, primary and lower secondary education	Upper secondary education	Non-university tertiary education	University-level education	Total
North America										
Canada	23	27	31	20	100	17	31	33	19	100
United States	13	51	7	29	100	9	55	10	26	100
Pacific Area										
Australia	38	37	11	15	100	54	18	11	17	100
New Zealand	34	44	10	11	100	39	27	20	9	100
European Union										
Austria	22	69	2	8	100	31	59	3	6	100
Belgium	43	31	11	15	100	36	31	22	11	100
Denmark	32	47	5	16	100	38	39	8	15	100
Finland	32	45	8	14	100	30	49	10	11	100
France	24	56	8	11	100	29	51	11	9	100
Germany	8	54	11	15	100	14	57	8	10	100
Greece	53	26	7	14	100	48	26	8	18	100
Ireland	55	24	10	11	100	33	38	16	13	100
Italy	62	29	a	10	100	51	37	a	12	100
Netherlands	31	42	a	26	100	33	42	a	26	100
Portugal	80	9	2	9	100	74	10	7	10	100
Spain	69	13	6	12	100	61	15	5	19	100
Sweden	28	45	12	15	100	23	47	16	13	100
United Kingdom	17	59	8	16	100	25	52	12	11	100
Other OECD countries										
Norway	16	54	11	19	100	14	55	12	19	100
Switzerland	11	56	20	11	100	21	63	6	6	100
Turkey	77	14	a	9	100	74	13	a	13	100
Country mean	**37**	**40**	**10**	**14**	**100**	**36**	**39**	**12**	**14**	**100**

Source: OECD Database. See Annex 3 for notes

Chapter 2

COSTS OF EDUCATION AND HUMAN AND FINANCIAL RESOURCES

Education is an investment in human skills that can help foster economic growth and enhance productivity, that can contribute to personal and social development, and that has the potential to reduce social inequality. Like any investment, it involves both costs and returns.

Some of the returns are monetary, while others are personal, social, cultural and more broadly economic. Some returns accrue to the individual while others benefit society in general, for example in the form of a more literate and productive nation. Some returns are directly related to the labour market [see Indicators R21(A), R21(B), R22 and R24] while others may include greater interest and participation in civic affairs and lower rates of welfare dependency.

However, public education budgets are under pressure in many OECD countries. The questions of access to educational opportunities and of the distribution of available resources across the various levels and types of education and training are objects of considerable debate. Also under scrutiny are issues of institutional diversity and the relative proportions of educational expenditure that are channelled to education through the public and private sectors.

The indicators presented in this chapter can assist in the comparative analysis of cost patterns and resource utilisation. Such analyses can help in improving the efficiency of educational investment, for example in determining the distribution of resources across levels or types of education, in making better use of existing personnel and facilities, and in adopting alternative technologies of education.

Although the prime concern of governments generally relates to expenditure of public origin, a broader understanding of the economic value of the inputs used in education needs to take private expenditure into account as well. This includes direct private costs (such as tuition and other education-related fees and the costs of textbooks, uniforms and transportation) but also indirect private costs (such as foregone earnings). However, some of this private expenditure is difficult to measure and to compare internationally. The indicators in this chapter therefore focus on public and private expenditure on educational institutions, because it is easier to obtain comparable data for these components of educational spending. Although the proportion of private expenditure on educational institutions shown in this chapter may appear comparatively low, it should be borne in mind that the overall costs which families incur for the education of their children usually well exceed the private payments to educational institutions captured in these indicators.

Indicator F1 examines the proportion of national resources devoted to educational institutions, the sources of these funds and the levels of education to which they are directed. The nature of the expenditure, in particular the proportion of current expenditure that is accounted for by the compensation of staff (including both salary and non-salary compensation) is shown in **Indicator F5**.

Indicator F13 provides another way of comparing the national resources invested in education by examining the proportion of total national public expenditure that is spent on education.

While Indicators F1 and F13 provide a broad picture of the resources devoted to education, they need to be interpreted in the light of a number of inter-related supply and demand factors, such as the demographic structure of the population (Indicator C3), enrolment rates (Indicator P1), the size of the economy, the level of income per capita and, last but not least, national price levels for educational resources. The relative size of the youth population, for example, shapes the potential demand for initial education and training in a country. The greater this proportion, the more resources need to be devoted to education, other things being equal. Similarly, participation rates affect expenditure on education: the higher the enrolment rates, the more financial resources will be required, again other things being equal.

The data for Indicator F13 are also affected by various patterns of public spending. The proportion of total public expenditure devoted to education is affected by the overall size of public budgets, and by the degree to which the private sector is involved in the financing of education. For example, countries that require students to pay tuition fees and/or to fund most or all of their living expenses are likely to devote a smaller percentage of public funds to tertiary education, other things being equal, than countries that provide "free" tertiary education and/or generous public subsidies to tertiary students. Similarly, countries in which private enterprises contribute significantly to the education of students (as is the case in countries which have adopted the dual system) can be expected to devote a comparatively lower share of public expenditure to education.

The various financial resources spent on education taken together translate eventually into a more amenable statistic, the amount of funds ultimately spent per student (**Indicator F3**). Policy-makers must balance the need to improve the quality of educational services against the need to expand access to educational opportunities. They must also decide how to apportion expenditure per student among the different levels of education – including continuing education and training – and among different types of educational programmes. For example, some countries emphasise broad access to higher education while others invest in near-universal education for children as young as two or three. Since there are no absolute standards for the resources per student needed to ensure optimal returns for both the participant and society as a whole, international comparisons of national investment in education provide an important insight. Spending per student is examined in this chapter both in absolute terms and in relation to national levels of GDP per capita.

A comparison of countries' annual expenditure on educational services per student reflects the total expenditure incurred for each student over the average duration of tertiary studies to a varying extent. This is primarily because countries differ significantly both in the length of tertiary studies (see also Indicator R12) and in the intensity with which students participate in educational programmes. For example, annual expenditure per student is affected, especially at the tertiary level, by differences in how countries define full-time, part-time and full-time-equivalent enrolment. Some countries count every participant at the tertiary level as a full-time student while others determine a student's intensity of participation by the credits he or she obtains for successful completion of specific course units during a certain reference period. Moreover, comparatively low annual expenditure per student may actually translate into comparatively high overall costs of tertiary education if the typical duration of tertiary studies is very long. To shed light on this, Indicator F3 compares countries with respect to the average expenditure that is incurred per student throughout the course of studies.

Finally, **Indicator F3-R** provides an overview of regional disparities in expenditure per student. While it is striking that the variation of expenditure per student within a country often exceeds typical differences among countries, regional disparities in unit expenditure may reflect the fact that education in different geographical or socio-economic settings has different needs to meet and thus requires different treatment. Nonetheless, disparities may reflect inequities in access to educational resources, and reducing such inequities may be a desirable objective.

In addition to financial resources, the intangible qualities of dedicated teachers are of utmost importance. **Indicator P31** shows the percentage of the labour force employed in education and **Indicator P32** shows the ratio of students enrolled to teaching staff by level of education. There is a potential trade-off between low student/teacher ratios on the one hand, which are generally considered to contribute to educational quality, and salary levels sufficient to attract qualified teachers, on the other (see Indicator P35).

F1: Educational expenditure relative to Gross Domestic Product

F1: EDUCATIONAL EXPENDITURE RELATIVE TO GROSS DOMESTIC PRODUCT

This indicator examines the proportion of national resources devoted to educational institutions, the sources from which this expenditure originates and the levels of education to which it is directed.

POLICY CONTEXT

Expenditure on education is a productive investment that can help foster economic growth, enhance productivity, contribute to personal and social development and, potentially, reduce social inequality.

However, public education budgets are under pressure in many OECD countries and the share of total financial resources to be devoted to education is one of the key choices that each country must make, implicitly or explicitly. This has led to debate over the questions of access to educational opportunities and of the allocation of available resources among the various levels and types of education and training. Also at stake are issues of institutional diversity and the proportions of educational expenditure to be channelled to education through the public and private sectors respectively. A question of special concern in some countries is whether or to what extent the costs of education should be borne by the individuals who benefit from education or by society as a whole.

This indicator sheds some light on these issues by examining the share of national financial resources devoted to educational institutions, the sources of funds spent on education and the levels of education to which they are directed.

KEY RESULTS

In all OECD countries, education consumes a significant proportion of national resources. Taking into account both public and private sources of funds, OECD countries as a whole spend 6.1 per cent of GDP in support of their educational institutions (all levels of education combined). Most of that, 4.9 per cent, is accounted for by direct public expenditure on educational institutions. Public subsidies to households and other private entities for educational institutions comprise another 0.1 per cent and expenditure by households and other private institutions accounts for 1.1 per cent of the overall GDP of OECD countries (see Table F1.1a and Chart F1.1).

However, there are considerable differences in the percentage of GDP which countries devote to their educational institutions. This ranges from 3.3 per cent in Turkey to 7.2 per cent or more in Canada, Denmark, Finland and Norway [see Chart F1.2(A)]. This variability is mainly a function of national differences in expenditure per student, participation rates and GDP.

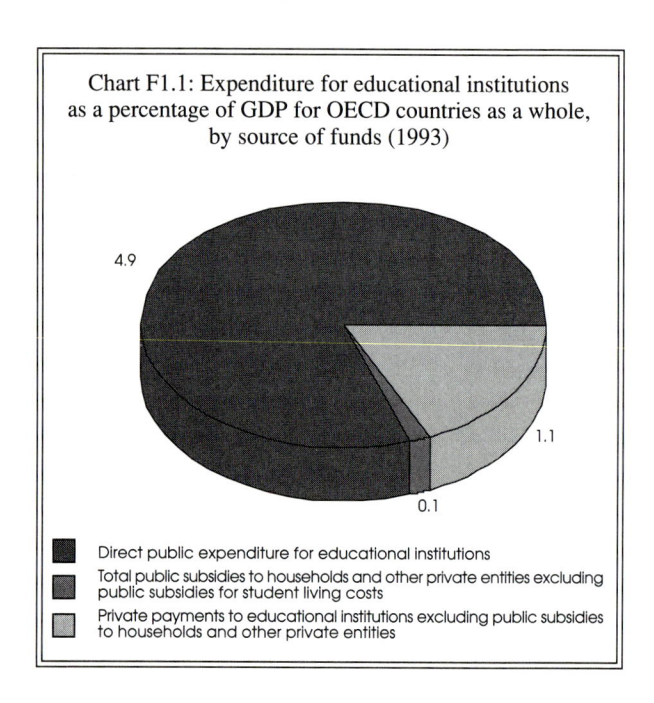

Chart F1.1: Expenditure for educational institutions as a percentage of GDP for OECD countries as a whole, by source of funds (1993)

- Direct public expenditure for educational institutions: 4.9
- Total public subsidies to households and other private entities excluding public subsidies for student living costs: 0.1
- Private payments to educational institutions excluding public subsidies to households and other private entities: 1.1

Expenditure on institutions at the primary and secondary level (including private expenditure and public subsidies that are channelled to educational institutions through the private sector) amount to 3.9 per cent of GDP for the OECD as a whole, varying between 2.4 and 4.7 per cent across countries. At the tertiary level, expenditure accounts for 1.6 per cent of GDP for the OECD as a whole but varies from 0.7 to 2.6 per cent across countries [see Chart F1.2(A)].

Since the mid-1970s, the proportion of GDP spent by the public sector on education has stabilised or fallen slightly in most countries and the indicator suggests a trend towards convergence of public education expenditure in OECD countries (see Table F1t). Rising participation, changing curricular provision and increases in teachers' salaries have exerted upward pressure on education spending, while a declining school-age population

F1: Educational expenditure relative to Gross Domestic Product

and general public spending restraint have created pressure to reduce spending.

DESCRIPTION AND INTERPRETATION

Expenditure on education by source of funds

The percentage of GDP devoted to public expenditure on educational institutions varies by more than a factor of two across OECD countries (see Table F1.1a). The percentage exceeds 6.6 per cent in the Nordic countries (Denmark, Finland, Norway, Sweden) and is 3.8 per cent or less in Greece, Japan, Korea and Turkey. Inclusion of public subsidies to households and other private entities for educational institutions increases the percentage by more than 0.3 per cent in Canada, the Netherlands, New Zealand and the United Kingdom.

Although the primary concern of governments generally relates to expenditure of public origin, a broader understanding of the economic value of the inputs used in education needs to take private expenditure into account as well. This includes direct private costs (such as tuition and other education-related fees and the costs of textbooks, uniforms and transportation) as well as indirect private costs (such as earnings foregone). However, some of these private costs are difficult to measure and to compare internationally. This indicator therefore focuses on public and private expenditure on educational institutions. Although the proportion of private expenditure on educational institutions as shown in this indicator may appear comparatively low, it should be borne in mind that the overall costs which families incur for the education of their children usually well exceed the private payments to educational institutions captured in this indicator. It should also be noted that the coverage of private sources of funds is not complete in many countries.

In OECD countries, the average proportion of funds for educational institutions that are generated by the private sector amounts to 1.1 per cent of GDP. However, countries differ significantly in the degree to which expenditure on educational institutions is borne by the beneficiaries of education as compared to society as a whole. Out of the 18 countries for which such data are available, private payments to educational institutions (net of public subsidies) exceed 1.2 per cent of GDP in Germany, Japan, Korea and United States. In these countries, more than 22 per cent of initial funds for educational institutions originate in the private sector (see also Chart F13.3). Whereas in Japan, Korea, and the United States most of this expenditure comes from households, in countries like Germany business enterprises provide and support the work-based component of the dual apprenticeship system. For Australia, Canada, Denmark, France, Hungary, Iceland, Ireland and Spain, the private share of expenditure still lies between 0.5 and 0.8 per cent of GDP, which corresponds to a relative share of private funds for educational institutions of between 7 and 14 per cent.

If the indicator is broadened to include funds from international sources as well as all public subsidies to students and households, then the proportion of educational expenditure rises to more than 7.6 per cent of GDP in Canada and the Nordic countries, and to between 6 and 7 per cent in Australia, France, Germany, Hungary, Ireland and the United States, while it remains below 5 per cent in Japan and Turkey. However, the coverage of public subsidies to households by this indicator is still uneven across countries.

Expenditure on educational institutions by level of education

The percentage of GDP devoted to the primary and secondary levels follows by and large the overall spending pattern. Deviations from this overall pattern can be explained largely by differences in enrolment rates and in institutional structures (see the organisation charts of education systems), and by demographic factors. Most of the funding for these levels comes from public sources (see Table F1.1b).

At the tertiary level there are significant differences in funding patterns among countries (see Table F1.1c). While OECD countries as a whole devote 1.6 per cent of their GDP to the funding of tertiary education, Canada and the United States spend significantly larger fractions of their GDP on tertiary education (2.4 per cent of GDP or more). At the other end of the scale are Iceland, Italy, Japan, Portugal, Spain, Turkey and the United Kingdom, which devote less than 1 per cent of their GDP to the funding of tertiary institutions. Differences depend, however, in part on the extent to which expenditure on research has been included by countries.

Full or near-full public funding of education is less common at the tertiary than at the primary and secondary levels. In many countries, selective user fees are charged at higher levels and subsidies are reduced for services that are deemed to have higher private returns. The share of tertiary spending that originates in the private sector

F1: Educational expenditure relative to Gross Domestic Product

Chart F1.2

A) Expenditure for educational institutions as a percentage of GDP, by source of funds (1993)

Primary and secondary level

Tertiary level

All levels of education combined

- ■ Direct public expenditure for educational institutions
- ▨ Total public subsidies to households and other private entities excluding public subsidies for student living costs
- □ Private payments to educational institutions excluding public subsidies to households and other private entities

Impact of demography and enrolment on expenditure for educational institutions as a percentage of GDP (1993)

B) Estimated increase/decrease in expenditure for educational institutions as a percentage of GDP, if the proportion of the population 5 to 29 years of age in each country were at the OECD average level

C) Estimated increase/decrease in expenditure for educational institutions as a percentage of GDP, if the full-time-equivalent enrolment rate for the population 5 to 29 years of age in each country were at the OECD average level

Countries are ranked in descending order of total educational expenditure
* Figures on public subsidies to households and other private entities are not included
** Figures on private payments to educational institutions are not included

F1: Educational expenditure relative to Gross Domestic Product

ranges from 0.01 per cent or less of GDP in Austria, Denmark, Finland and Turkey to more than 0.6 per cent in Japan, Korea and the United States (see Table F1.1c), where the private share in initial funds is between 48 and 81 per cent.

Important factors influencing national expenditure on education

The national resources devoted to education depend on a number of inter-related supply and demand factors, such as the demographic structure of the population, enrolment rates, the size of the economy, the level of income per capita, and national price levels for educational resources. Many of these factors lie beyond the control of governments and institution administrators.

To provide an insight into how national resources devoted to education (expressed by Indicator F1) translate into the resources that are ultimately available per student (shown in Indicator F3), the following paragraphs examine the extent to which deviations from the OECD average in the results of F1 are related to two key indicators in this publication: the age structure of the population (Indicator C3) and the rate of enrolment of the youth population (Indicator P1).

The overall wealth of a country, as measured by GDP per capita, obviously has a significant influence over the resources that can be devoted to education. National GDP levels are taken as the benchmark against which educational expenditure is compared in Indicator F1.

The size of the youth population shapes the potential demand for initial education and training in a country. The greater this population is, the greater is the potential demand for educational services and thus the smaller the relative effect of a given proportion of the GDP that is devoted to education, other things being equal. In other words, the fewer students there are of an age relevant to initial education, the less a country needs to spend on education. Chart F1.2(B) shows the shifts in Indicator F1 that would be expected if the proportion of the population aged 5-29 years were equal in OECD countries, other things being constant. In Germany and Sweden, for example, less than 32 per cent of the population is in the age group 5 to 29 years as compared to an OECD average of 36 per cent (see Indicator C3). Other things being equal, these two countries would therefore not be expected to devote as much of their national resources to educational institutions as other countries with a larger proportion of the youth population. Or expressed differently, the expected amount of educational expenditure as a percentage of GDP would be 1.2 per cent higher in Sweden and 0.9 per cent higher in Germany if the relative size of the youth population in these countries were at the OECD average (other things being equal). In contrast, in Turkey and Mexico more than 50 per cent of the population is in the age group 5 to 29 years. As shown in Chart F1.2(B), expenditure on education could be expected to be lower by 1.3 per cent of GDP in Mexico and by 1.0 per cent of GDP in Turkey if the share of the youth population in these two countries were at the OECD average (other things being equal).

Participation rates also affect expenditure on education: the higher the enrolment rate, the more financial resources will be required, other things being equal. Indicator P1 shows that the proportion of persons aged 5-29 years who are either enrolled full-time or part-time in early childhood, primary, secondary or tertiary education ranges from less than 55 per cent in the Czech Republic, Greece, Mexico and Turkey to more than 67 per cent in Australia, Belgium, Canada and New Zealand. If participation rates of 5 to 29 year-olds were equal across countries (in terms of full-time equivalent enrolment), expenditure for educational institutions would be expected to rise by more than 1 per cent of GDP in Austria, Italy and Turkey, while it would fall by around 1 per cent in Belgium, Denmark, Finland and France [see Chart F1.2(B)], other things being equal.

It is important to look at the different factors that affect spending on education in combination. Belgium, Denmark, Finland and Sweden, for example, are countries in which a smaller share of the youth population is, in part, balanced off by comparatively high participation rates. Austria, Germany and Switzerland, on the other hand, are countries with both a comparatively small share of the youth population and a comparatively low enrolment rate. Taking into account also the high national income in these countries, this enables them to spend more per student than OECD countries on average (see Indicator F3) even though their expenditure on education as a percentage of GDP is either below (in the case of Austria and Germany) or just slightly above (in the case of Switzerland) the OECD average. For a further analysis of this matter, see *Education at a Glance – Analysis*.

Trends in public expenditure on education

Table F1t indicates changes over time in public educational expenditure as a percentage of GDP for selected countries. These changes are influenced both by changes in supply factors (such as the growth rate of the

F1: Educational expenditure relative to Gross Domestic Product

national economy or competing demands of other public services) as well as by changes in demand, particularly changing demographic conditions.

In 1970, public expenditure on education as a percentage of GDP ranged from 2.4 per cent in Mexico to 10.2 per cent in Canada. In the majority of Member countries, public expenditure was 5 per cent of GDP or more. In the early 1970s, the dominant position of education in publicly-financed social programmes began to change as a consequence of two factors: slowing economic growth and decreasing enrolments, with the drop in birth rates beginning to influence the size of the school-age population. At the same time a number of factors, such as rising participation rates at higher levels and changes in teachers' pay, began to exert an upward pressure on education spending.

Overall, as a proportion of GDP, public educational expenditure roughly held its ground, but the data suggest a trend towards convergence of public educational expenditure among OECD countries.

Table F1t would ideally have shown trends in the proportion of GDP devoted to education from both public and private sources. However, comparable trend data for expenditure on education from private sources are not available. Note that, unlike the data shown in Charts F1.1 and F1.2, the expenditure shown in Table F1t do not only include public expenditure for educational institutions but, to a varying extent, also public subsidies for student living expenses. It should also be noted that the broadened statistical coverage of education spending in recent years contributes to a rise over time in the figures on the proportions of GDP spent on education in some countries.

DEFINITIONS

In this indicator, expenditure on education is expressed as a percentage of GDP and presented by source of funds and by level of education. The distinction by source of funds is based on the initial source of funds and does not reflect subsequent public-to-private or private-to-public transfers.

Direct public expenditure on educational institutions (see column 1 of Tables F1.1a, b and c) can take either the form of purchases by the government agency itself of educational resources to be used by educational institutions, or of payments by the government agency to educational institutions that have responsibility for purchasing educational resources themselves.

Public subsidies to households and other private entities for educational institutions (see column 2 of Tables F1.1a, b and c) are composed of government transfers and certain other payments to students/households, in so far as these translate into payments to educational institutions for educational services, for example fellowships, awards or student loans (on a gross basis). They also include government transfers and certain other payments (mainly subsidies) to other private entities, for example subsidies to firms or labour organisations that operate apprenticeship programmes, subsidies to non-profit organisations that provide student housing, interest subsidies to private financial institutions that provide student loans, etc.

Payments from households and other private entities to educational institutions (see column 3 of Tables F1.1a, b and c) include tuition fees and other fees, net of offsetting public subsidies.

Public subsidies to households that are not attributable to payments to educational institutions (which are included in column 5 of Tables F1.1a, b and c) include subsidies for student living expenditure or the value of special subsidies provided to students, either in cash or in kind, such as free or reduced-price travel on public transport or family allowances that are contingent on student status.

Private payments other than to educational institutions (see column 6 of Tables F1.1a, b and c) include direct purchases of personal items used in education or subsidised expenditure on student living expenses.

The data do not include benefits provided to students or households in the form of tax reductions, tax subsidies or other special tax provisions. Note also that the coverage of expenditure from private sources is still uneven across countries.

The methodology that was used for the calculation of the estimates in Charts F1.2(B) and F1.2(C) is described in Annex 3.

The *country mean* is calculated as the simple average over all OECD countries for which data are available. The *OECD total* reflects the value of the indicator when the OECD region is considered as a whole (for details see *Reader's Guide* p. 29).

F1: Educational expenditure relative to Gross Domestic Product

Table F1.1a:
Educational expenditure as a percentage of GDP for all levels of education combined, by source of funds (1993)

	Direct public expenditure for educational institutions	Total public subsidies to households and other private entities excluding public subsidies for student living costs	Private payments to educational institutions excluding public subsidies to households and other private entities	Total expenditure from both public and private sources for educational institutions	Total expenditure from public, private and international sources for educational institutions **plus** public subsidies to households	Private payments other than to educational institutions
North America						
Canada	6.2	0.5	0.7	7.3	7.6	0.3
Mexico	4.1	m	m	m	m	m
United States	5.1	0.1	1.6	6.8	6.9	0.2
Pacific Area						
Australia	4.9	0.2	0.8	6.0	6.5	0.5
Japan	3.7	m	1.2	4.9	4.9	m
New Zealand	6.0	0.4	m	m	m	m
European Union						
Austria	5.3	0.01	0.1	5.4	5.6	0.1
Belgium	5.6	n	m	m	m	m
Denmark	6.7	n	0.5	7.2	8.8	1.6
Finland	7.3	m	0.03	7.3	7.9	0.6
France	5.6	n	0.5	6.1	6.3	0.2
Germany	4.5	0.01	1.4	5.9	6.1	m
Greece	3.4	n	m	m	m	m
Ireland	5.2	0.1	0.5	5.8	6.2	0.3
Italy	5.0	0.1	0.03	5.1	5.2	m
Luxembourg	m	m	m	m	m	m
Netherlands	4.6	0.3	0.1	5.0	5.5	0.7
Portugal	5.3	n	0.1	5.4	5.6	0.1
Spain	4.5	n	0.8	5.3	5.4	0.6
Sweden	6.7	n	0.1	6.9	8.0	1.1
United Kingdom	4.7	0.3	m	m	m	m
Other OECD countries						
Czech Republic	5.0	n	m	m	m	m
Hungary	5.9	n	0.7	6.6	6.8	0.2
Iceland	4.6	n	0.6	5.3	5.9	0.2
Norway	7.6	n	m	m	m	m
Switzerland	5.6	0.1	m	m	m	m
Turkey	3.3	a	a	3.3	3.4	0.1
Country mean	**5.3**	**0.1**	**0.5**	**5.9**	**6.3**	**0.5**
OECD total	**4.9**	**0.1**	**1.1**	**6.1**	**6.2**	**0.2**
Other non-OECD countries						
Korea	3.7	0.05	1.9	5.7	5.7	0.01
Poland	m	m	m	m	m	m
Russian Federation	m	m	m	m	m	m

Source: OECD Database. See Annex 3 for notes

F1: Educational expenditure relative to Gross Domestic Product

Table F1.1b:
Educational expenditure as a percentage of GDP for primary and secondary education, by source of funds (1993)

	Direct public expenditure for educational institutions	Total public subsidies to households and other private entities excluding public subsidies for student living costs	Private payments to educational institutions excluding public subsidies to households and other private entities	Total expenditure from both public and private sources for educational institutions	Total expenditure from public, private and international sources for educational institutions **plus** public subsidies to households	Private payments other than to educational institutions
North America						
Canada	4.3	x	0.3	4.5	4.5	x
Mexico	3.0	m	m	m	m	m
United States	3.8	x	0.4	4.1	4.1	0.02
Pacific Area						
Australia	3.6	0.03	0.4	4.1	4.4	0.3
Japan	3.0	m	0.3	3.2	3.2	m
New Zealand	4.4	0.1	m	m	m	m
European Union						
Austria	3.5	0.01	0.02	3.6	3.6	0.02
Belgium	3.7	n	m	m	m	m
Denmark	4.5	n	0.1	4.5	5.1	0.6
Finland	4.7	m	0.02	4.7	4.9	0.2
France	4.0	n	0.3	4.4	4.4	0.1
Germany	3.0	n	0.9	3.9	4.1	m
Greece	2.6	n	m	m	m	m
Ireland	3.7	n	0.2	3.8	4.0	0.1
Italy	3.5	0.1	n	3.5	3.5	m
Luxembourg	m	m	m	m	m	m
Netherlands	3.0	0.1	0.1	3.2	3.4	0.3
Portugal	3.8	n	0.1	3.9	3.9	0.1
Spain	3.4	n	0.5	3.8	3.9	0.3
Sweden	4.7	n	0.01	4.7	5.1	0.4
United Kingdom	3.9	0.04	m	m	m	0.03
Other OECD countries						
Czech Republic	3.4	n	m	m	m	m
Hungary	4.1	n	0.4	4.5	4.5	n
Iceland	3.5	n	x	3.5	3.6	0.1
Norway	4.5	n	m	m	m	m
Switzerland	4.2	0.1	m	m	m	m
Turkey	2.4	a	a	2.4	2.5	0.04
Country mean	**3.7**	**0.02**	**0.2**	**3.9**	**4.0**	**0.2**
OECD total	**3.5**	**0.02**	**0.4**	**3.9**	**3.9**	**0.1**
Other non-OECD countries						
Korea	3.0	n	0.8	3.8	3.9	n
Poland	m	m	m	m	m	m
Russian Federation	m	m	m	m	m	m

Source: OECD Database. See Annex 3 for notes

F1: Educational expenditure relative to Gross Domestic Product

Table F1.1c:
Educational expenditure as a percentage of GDP for tertiary education, by source of funds (1993)

	Direct public expenditure for educational institutions	Total public subsidies to households and other private entities excluding public subsidies for student living costs	Private payments to educational institutions excluding public subsidies to households and other private entities	Total expenditure from both public and private sources for educational institutions	Total expenditure from public, private and international sources for educational institutions **plus** public subsidies to households	Private payments other than to educational institutions
North America						
Canada	1.7	0.5	0.4	2.6	2.8	0.4
Mexico	0.7	m	m	m	m	m
United States	1.2	0.1	1.2	2.4	2.5	0.1
Pacific Area						
Australia	1.1	0.1	0.4	1.7	1.9	0.2
Japan	0.4	m	0.6	0.9	0.9	m
New Zealand	1.2	0.3	m	m	m	m
European Union						
Austria	1.1	n	0.01	1.1	1.1	0.1
Belgium	1.0	n	m	m	m	m
Denmark	1.3	n	n	1.3	2.2	0.8
Finland	1.8	m	0.01	1.8	2.2	0.5
France	0.9	n	0.2	1.1	1.1	0.1
Germany	0.9	0.01	0.1	1.1	1.2	m
Greece	0.8	n	m	m	m	m
Ireland	1.0	0.1	0.3	1.4	1.6	0.2
Italy	0.8	0.02	0.1	0.9	1.1	m
Luxembourg	m	m	m	m	m	m
Netherlands	1.3	0.1	0.04	1.4	1.8	0.4
Portugal	0.8	n	0.1	0.9	1.0	0.1
Spain	0.8	n	0.2	0.9	1.0	0.1
Sweden	1.5	n	0.1	1.6	2.3	0.7
United Kingdom	0.7	0.2	n	0.9	1.2	0.2
Other OECD countries						
Czech Republic	0.8	n	m	m	m	m
Hungary	0.9	n	0.2	1.1	1.3	0.2
Iceland	0.7	n	0.05	0.7	1.2	0.5
Norway	1.5	n	m	m	m	m
Switzerland	1.2	0.01	m	m	m	m
Turkey	0.8	a	a	0.8	0.9	0.1
Country mean	**1.0**	**0.1**	**0.2**	**1.3**	**1.5**	**0.3**
OECD total	**1.0**	**0.1**	**0.6**	**1.6**	**1.7**	**0.2**
Other non-OECD countries						
Korea	0.3	0.01	1.1	1.4	1.4	0.01
Poland	m	m	m	m	m	m
Russian Federation	m	m	m	m	m	m

Source: OECD Database. See Annex 3 for notes

F1: Educational expenditure relative to Gross Domestic Product

Table F1.2:
Educational expenditure from public and private sources for educational institutions as a percentage of GDP by level of education (1993)

	Primary and secondary education			Tertiary education			All levels of education combined (including pre-primary and undistributed)
	All	Primary	Secondary	All	Non-university	University-level	
North America							
Canada	4.5	x	x	2.6	1.0	1.6	7.3
Mexico	m	m	m	m	m	m	m
United States	4.1	x	x	2.4	x	x	6.8
Pacific Area							
Australia	4.1	1.7	2.4	1.7	0.3	1.4	6.0
Japan	3.2	1.4	1.8	0.9	0.1	0.8	4.9
New Zealand	m	m	m	m	m	m	m
European Union							
Austria	3.6	1.0	2.6	1.1	0.1	1.0	5.4
Belgium	m	m	m	m	m	m	m
Denmark	4.5	1.6	3.0	1.3	x	x	7.2
Finland	4.7	2.0	2.7	1.8	0.4	1.4	7.3
France	4.4	1.2	3.1	1.1	x	x	6.1
Germany	3.9	x	x	1.1	0.03	1.0	5.9
Greece	m	m	m	m	m	m	m
Ireland	3.8	1.5	2.3	1.4	x	x	5.8
Italy	3.5	1.1	2.4	0.9	0.1	0.8	5.1
Luxembourg	m	m	m	m	m	m	m
Netherlands	3.2	1.2	2.0	1.4	a	1.4	5.0
Portugal	3.9	1.9	1.9	0.9	x	x	5.4
Spain	3.8	1.2	2.7	0.9	x	x	5.3
Sweden	4.7	2.0	2.7	1.6	x	x	6.9
United Kingdom	m	m	m	0.9	x	x	m
Other OECD countries							
Czech Republic	m	m	m	m	m	m	m
Hungary	4.5	1.3	3.2	1.1	n	1.1	6.6
Iceland	3.5	1.5	2.0	0.7	0.04	0.6	5.3
Norway	m	m	m	m	m	m	m
Switzerland	m	m	m	m	m	m	m
Turkey	2.4	1.7	0.8	0.8	a	0.8	3.3
Country mean	**3.9**	**1.5**	**2.4**	**1.3**	**0.2**	**1.1**	**5.9**
OECD total	**3.9**	**1.6**	**2.4**	**1.6**	**0.2**	**1.0**	**6.1**
Other non-OECD countries							
Korea	3.8	1.7	2.1	1.4	0.3	1.1	5.7
Poland	m	m	m	m	m	m	m
Russian Federation	m	m	m	m	m	m	m

Source: OECD Database. See Annex 3 for notes

F1: Educational expenditure relative to Gross Domestic Product

Table F1t:
Public expenditure on education as a percentage of GDP, including public subsidies to households, 1970 - 1993

	1970	1975	1980	1985	1990	1993
North America						
Canada	10.2	8.5	7.7	6.9	6.2	6.9
Mexico	2.4	3.9	4.6	3.8	4.0	4.1
United States	6.0	5.7	4.9	4.6	5.2	5.2
Pacific Area						
Australia	4.6	6.2	5.6	5.4	4.6	5.6
Japan	m	m	m	m	3.6	3.6
New Zealand	m	6.5	6.7	5.1	m	6.7
European Union						
Austria	4.6	5.7	5.7	5.8	5.4	5.5
Denmark	m	6.9	7.4	6.2	6.3	6.6
Finland	m	m	5.8	5.7	6.0	7.9
France	m	5.6	5.1	5.7	5.1	5.7
Germany	3.7	5.1	4.8	4.6	4.1	4.8
Greece	2.8	3.4	3.2	4.0	m	3.5
Ireland	6.2	6.5	6.4	6.0	5.0	5.6
Italy	m	4.8	4.5	5.0	5.2	5.1
Netherlands	7.5	7.4	7.1	6.6	5.7	5.4
Portugal	m	3.3	3.7	4.0	4.3	5.4
Spain	m	m	m	3.6	4.4	4.7
Sweden	7.9	7.1	8.5	7.0	5.6	7.7
United Kingdom	6.2	6.8	5.7	4.9	4.9	5.1
Other OECD countries						
Czech Republic	m	m	m	m	4.2	6.0
Norway	m	6.4	5.8	5.6	m	9.0
Switzerland	3.9	5.3	5.2	5.1	5.2	5.8

Vertical bars indicate breaks in series which may affect the comparability over time
Source: OECD Database. See Annex 3 for notes

F3: Expenditure on educational services per student

F3: EXPENDITURE ON EDUCATIONAL SERVICES PER STUDENT

This indicator provides information on annual expenditure per student in absolute terms (in equivalent U.S. dollars converted at purchasing power parities). It also compares per-student expenditure in relative terms – with per capita GDP, as a broad measure of a country's standard of living, taken as the basis for comparisons.

POLICY CONTEXT

OECD countries face a continuing debate on whether the amount spent on each student's education is too high, too low, or "just right" given the demand for high-quality education, on the one hand, and the need to avoid an undue burden on taxpayers, on the other. Policy-makers must balance the need to improve the quality of educational services with the need to expand access to educational opportunities. They must also decide how to allocate per-student expenditure over the different levels of education – including continuing education and training – and over different types of educational programmes. For example, some countries emphasise broad access to higher education while others invest in near-universal education for children as young as two or three.

Since there are no absolute standards for the resources per student needed to ensure optimal returns for both the participant and society as a whole, international comparisons of national investment in education provide an important source of insight.

KEY RESULTS

OECD countries as a whole spend about US$ 4 760 per student each year (all levels of education combined). US$ 3 320 are spent per student at the primary level, US$ 4 730 per student at the secondary level and US$ 9 670 per student at the tertiary level. However, these OECD-wide totals are heavily influenced by the high expenditure levels in the United States. The levels per student in the "typical" OECD country, as represented by the simple mean across all countries, are US$ 3 140 at the primary level, US$ 4 180 at the secondary level and US$ 7 460 at the tertiary level of education.

These averages mask a broad range of expenditure per student across countries. Even excluding the two highest and lowest-spending countries, the range in expenditure per student is wide: from about US$ 1 500 to more than US$ 4 900 at the primary level, from about US$ 1 600 to more than US$ 6 000 at the secondary level, and from less than US$ 2 700 to more than US$ 12 600 at the tertiary level (see Chart F3.1). The range in reported spending per pre-primary student – from under US$ 1 000 to more than US$ 5 200 – reflects variations in the types of early childhood services provided in the different countries.

Per-student expenditure not only differs substantially in absolute terms across countries, but also the differentials in unit expenditure between the levels of education vary markedly among countries.

For the OECD as a whole, expenditure per student averages 18.3 per cent of per capita GDP at the primary level, 25.8 per cent at the secondary level and 49.0 per cent at the tertiary level.

DESCRIPTION AND INTERPRETATION

Expenditure per student in equivalent U.S. dollars

The data used in calculating expenditure per student include only the expenditure for educational institutions. Public subsidies for students' living expenses are excluded. Unless indicated otherwise, the figures include expenditure per student in public and private institutions. This represents a departure from *Education at a Glance* in previous years which, for most countries, covered only expenditure for public institutions.

Of the 24 countries for which data on expenditure per primary student are available, five spend about US$ 1 700 or less per primary student (the Czech Republic, Hungary, Korea, Mexico and Turkey) and seven countries spend more than US$ 4 000 (Austria, Denmark, Finland, Italy, Sweden, Switzerland and the United States).

At the secondary level, the Czech Republic, Greece, Hungary, Mexico and Turkey spend less than US$ 2 000 per student, whereas Austria, Belgium, Denmark, France, Germany, Sweden, Switzerland and the United States spend between US$ 5 300 and about US$ 7 000 per secondary student (see Table F3.1).

At the tertiary level, expenditure per student varies by more than a factor of six, with Greece and Switzerland constituting the extremes among the 26 countries for which such data are available (see Table F3.1). While Greece, Korea, Spain and Turkey report per-student expenditure

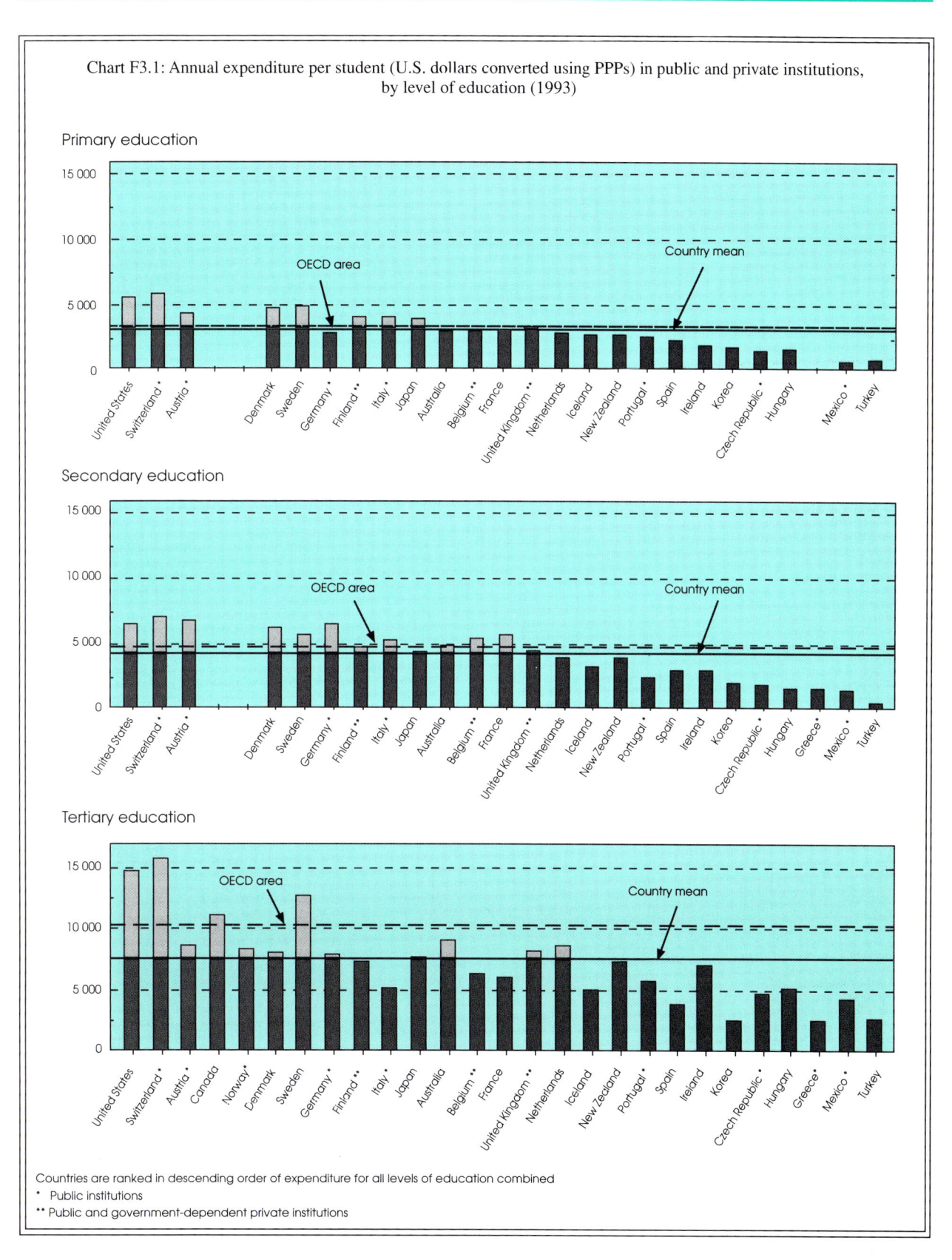

F3: Expenditure on educational services per student

Chart F3.1: Annual expenditure per student (U.S. dollars converted using PPPs) in public and private institutions, by level of education (1993)

Primary education

Secondary education

Tertiary education

Countries are ranked in descending order of expenditure for all levels of education combined
* Public institutions
** Public and government-dependent private institutions

F3: Expenditure on educational services per student

of less than US$ 4 400, Canada, Sweden, Switzerland and the United States report expenditure between US$ 11 000 and almost US$ 16 000 per year.

To interpret the figures on early childhood education spending per student, one must consider the differences between the Nordic countries and all the others. Early childhood institutions in the Nordic countries often provide extended day and evening care for young children, the costs of which are included in the spending per student reported for Finland and Norway.

Expenditure per student exhibits a common pattern throughout the OECD: in each country it rises sharply with the level of education, it is dominated by personnel costs (see Indicator F5), and it has a built-in tendency to rise over time. This pattern can be understood by looking at the determinants of expenditure, particularly the place and mode of educational provision. Education still takes place predominantly in traditional school and university settings with – despite some differences – similar organisation, curriculum, teaching style and management. These commonalities are undoubtedly the most important reason for the similar patterns of unit expenditure. The labour intensiveness of traditional education accounts for the predominance of teachers' salaries in overall costs. Differences in student/teaching staff ratios (see Indicator P32), staffing patterns, teachers' salaries (see Indicator P35), teaching materials and facilities largely account for the cost differences among levels of education, types of programmes, and types of schools. Furthermore, pay scales based on qualifications and automatic increases make personnel costs rise over time.

Institutional arrangements often adapt to changing demographic conditions with a considerable time lag. Also, this can influence unit expenditure. For example, a declining number of students at the primary level may lead to higher unit costs at that level if school facilities and teaching resources do not follow this trend. Finally, differences in national price levels for educational services, in so far as they deviate from overall price levels accounted for in the purchasing power parities, impact on the differences in unit expenditure across countries.

It would be misleading to equate lower unit expenditure generally with a lower quality of educational services and lower outcomes. The Czech Republic, Japan and Korea, for example, which report comparatively

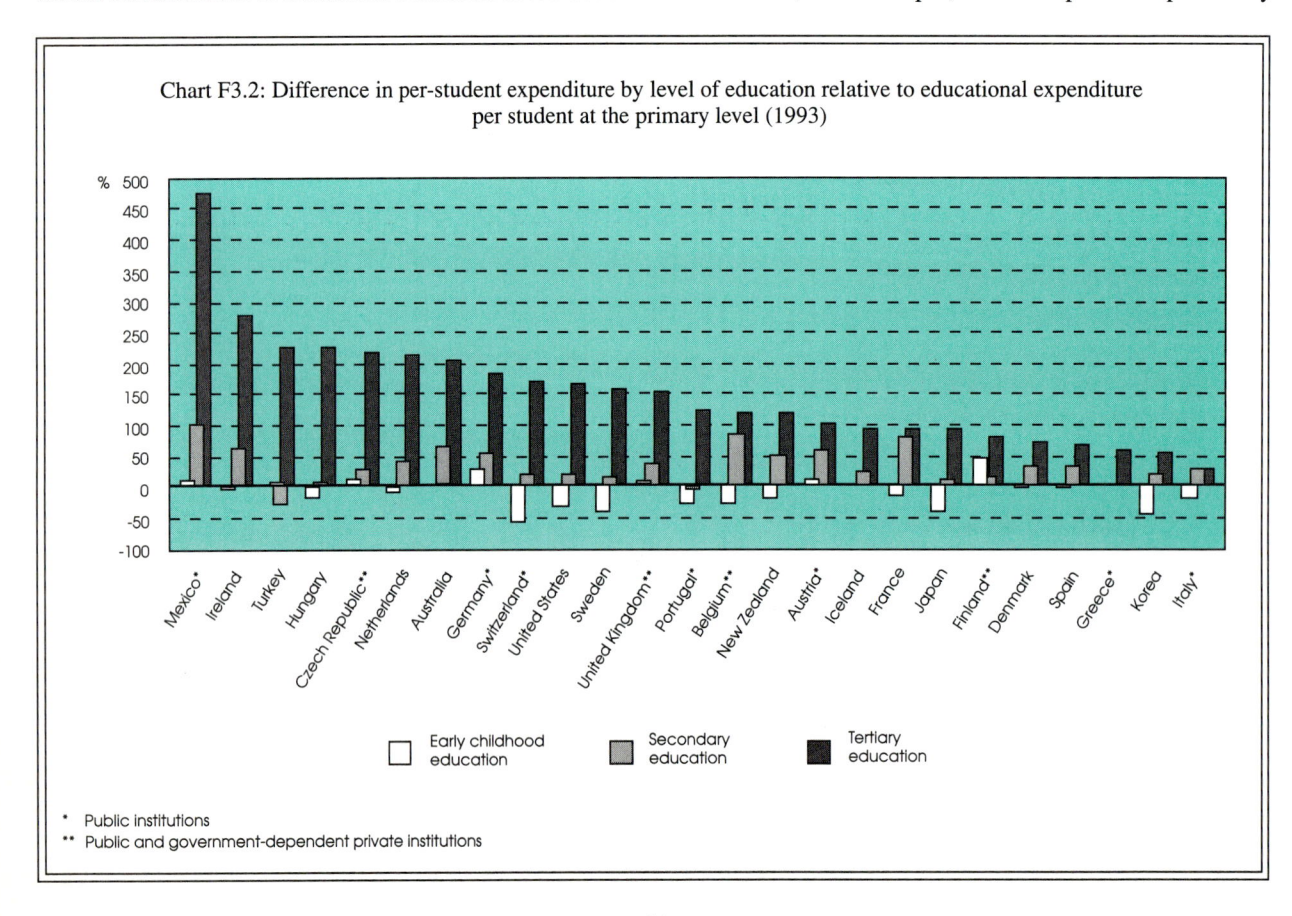

Chart F3.2: Difference in per-student expenditure by level of education relative to educational expenditure per student at the primary level (1993)

* Public institutions
** Public and government-dependent private institutions

66

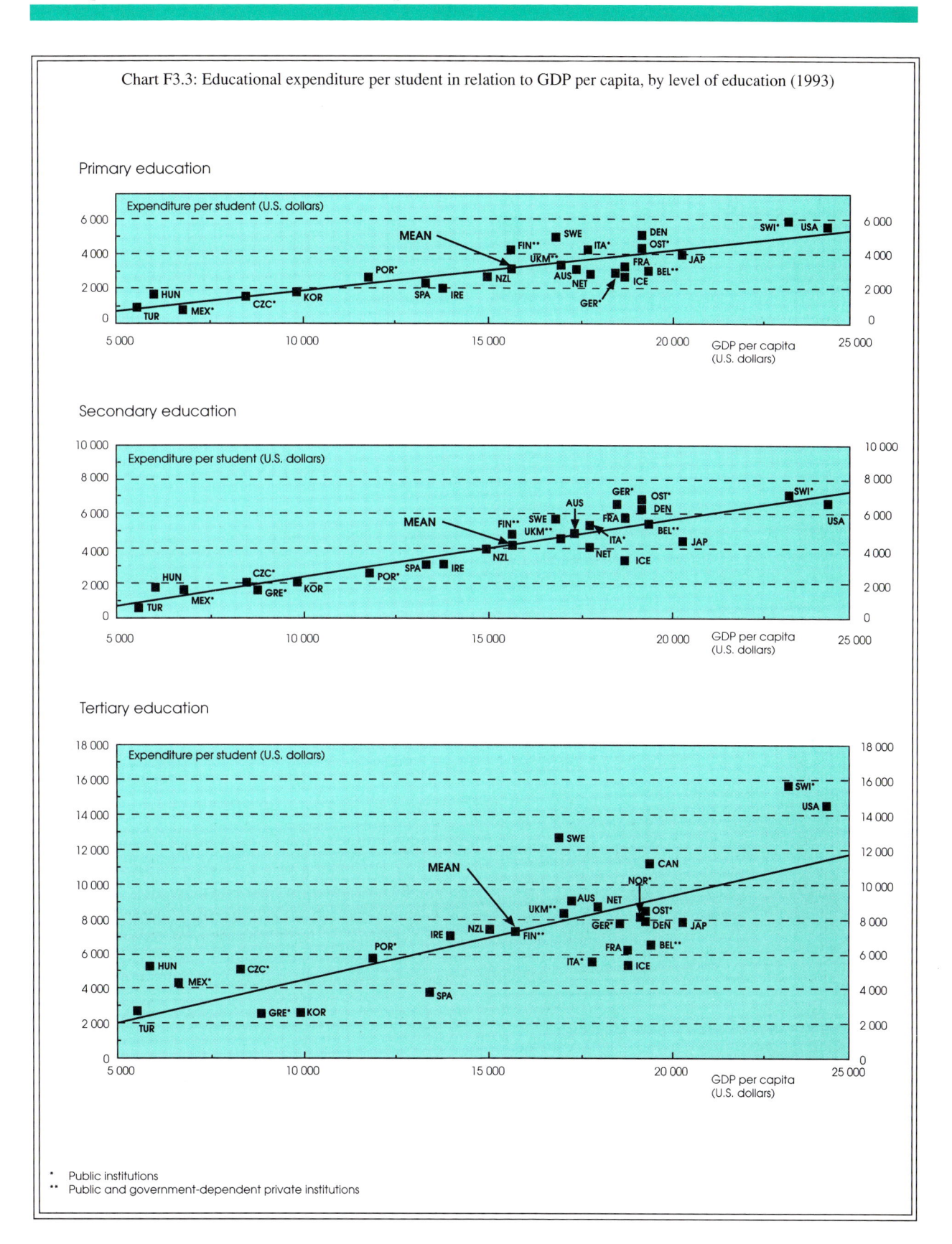

F3: Expenditure on educational services per student

Chart F3.3: Educational expenditure per student in relation to GDP per capita, by level of education (1993)

Primary education

Secondary education

Tertiary education

* Public institutions
** Public and government-dependent private institutions

F3: Expenditure on educational services per student

moderate expenditure per student, are the countries with the highest level of performance by students in mathematics and science around age 13 (see Indicator R6).

Differentials in educational expenditure per student across levels of education

Chart F3.2 compares per-student expenditure at the pre-primary, secondary and tertiary levels of education with those at the primary level of education. Although in all countries per-student expenditure rises with the levels of education, the differentials in unit expenditure across the levels of education vary markedly across countries.

Unit expenditure at the pre-primary level of education varies from 40 per cent of that at the primary level in Switzerland to 144 per cent in Finland. While, on average, unit expenditure at the pre-primary level reaches only 90 per cent of that at the primary level, seven countries spend more per child at the pre-primary level than at the primary level.

At the secondary level, per-student expenditure is, on average, 34 per cent higher than that at the primary level but the variation here ranges from 71 per cent of expenditure per primary student in Turkey to more than 180 per cent in Belgium, France and Mexico. More than three-quarters of the countries fall into the range 105 to 165 per cent of the unit expenditure at the primary level.

The most significant differentials occur at the tertiary level. Here, per-student expenditure is, on average, 153 per cent higher than at the primary level but differentials vary from merely 26 per cent in Italy to more than 200 per cent in Australia, the Czech Republic, Hungary, Ireland, Mexico, the Netherlands and Turkey. These differentials for the tertiary level may even underestimate real cost differences. This is because in some countries private sources are excluded and because foregone earnings of students have not been taken into account. Both factors could be expected to have a much larger impact at the tertiary level.

Educational expenditure per student in relation to national GDP levels

As one might expect, per-student expenditure is broadly related to national levels of GDP per capita. However, although the relationship is generally positive (see Chart F3.3), there is considerable variation in per-student spending among both richer and poorer countries.

Educational expenditure per student over the average duration of tertiary studies

The annual expenditure for educational services per student shown in Tables F3.1 and F3.2 reflects the costs incurred for each student over the average duration of tertiary studies to a varying extent. This is primarily because countries differ significantly both in the length of tertiary studies (see also Indicator R12) and in the intensity with which students participate in educational programmes.

For example, the indicator is strongly affected, especially at the tertiary level, by differences in how countries define full-time, part-time and full-time-equivalent enrolment. Some countries count every participant at the tertiary level as a full-time student while others determine a student's intensity of participation by the credits he or she obtains for successful completion of specific course units during a specified reference period.

Similarly, comparatively low annual expenditure per student may result in comparatively high overall costs of tertiary education if the typical duration of tertiary studies is very long. Chart F3.4 examines the average expenditure that is incurred per student throughout the course of studies for 13 countries. The figures account for all students for which expenditure is incurred, including those who do not finish their studies. Although the calculations are based on a number of simplifying assumptions (see Annex 3) and therefore need to be treated with some caution, significant shifts in the rank order of countries can be noted. Annual tertiary expenditure in the United Kingdom is, for example, higher than in Germany (US$ 8 241 in the United Kingdom as compared to US$ 7 902 in Germany). However, due to differences in the degree structure at the tertiary level (see Indicator R12), the average duration of tertiary studies is almost twice as long in Germany as in the United Kingdom (6.4 years in Germany, which provides only "long university programmes", as compared to 3.4 years in the United Kingdom, which provides both "short" and "long" university programmes). As a consequence of this, the overall expenditure on a tertiary student appears to be significantly higher in Germany than in the United Kingdom.

Important notes on interpretation

When interpreting differences among countries in expenditure per student, the following factors should be taken into account:

F3: Expenditure on educational services per student

The data used in calculating expenditure per student include only public and private expenditure on educational institutions. Public subsidies for students' living expenses have been excluded to ensure the international comparability of the data. For some countries, expenditure data for students in private educational institutions were not available (indicated by one or two asterisks in the table). However, many of the countries that do not have data on independent private institutions have a very small number of those institutions.

The variation in expenditure per student does not always reflect variation in real resources provided to students (e.g. variations in student/teacher ratios). In some cases, it reflects variation in relative prices. For example, a country may appear to spend an above-average amount because the salaries of its teachers are high relative to the country's general price level.

The figures on spending per student are affected by reporting and comparability problems in the expenditure data. For example, countries differ in whether, or to what extent, they have reported funds from private sources; whether they have included amounts spent by business enterprises to train apprentices; and how they measure the cost of pensions for educational personnel.

An important comparability problem at the tertiary level is that the expenditure of some countries includes essentially all spending on research in institutions of higher education, whereas the data from other countries exclude separately funded or separately budgeted research.

DEFINITIONS

Expenditure per student for a particular level of education is calculated by dividing the total expenditure at that level by the corresponding full-time equivalent enrolment. Only those types of educational institutions and programmes are taken into account for which both enrolment and expenditure data are available. The enrolment data are adjusted by interpolation so as to match either the financial year or the calendar year of each country (for details see Annex 3). The result in national currency is then converted to U.S. dollars by dividing by the purchasing power parity (PPP) exchange rate between the national currency and the U.S. dollar. The PPP exchange rates used pertain to GDP and were derived from the OECD National Accounts Database (see Annex 2). The PPP exchange rate gives the amount of a national currency that will buy the same basket of goods and services in a country as the U.S. dollar will in the United States. The PPP exchange rate is used because the market exchange rate is affected by many factors (interest rates, trade policies, expectations of economic growth, etc.) that have little to do with current, relative domestic purchasing power in different countries.

The *country mean* is calculated as the simple average over all OECD countries for which data are available. The *OECD total* reflects the value of the indicator when the OECD region is considered as a whole (for details see *Reader's Guide* p. 29).

Expenditure per student relative to per capita GDP is calculated by expressing expenditure per student in units of national currency as a percentage of per capita GDP, also in national currency. In cases where the educational expenditure data and the GDP data pertain to different reference periods, the expenditure data are adjusted to the same reference period as the GDP data, using inflation rates for the country in question (see Annex 2).

Expected expenditure over the average duration of tertiary studies is calculated by multiplying current annual expenditure with the typical duration of tertiary studies. The methodology used for the estimation of the typical duration of tertiary studies is described in Annex 3.

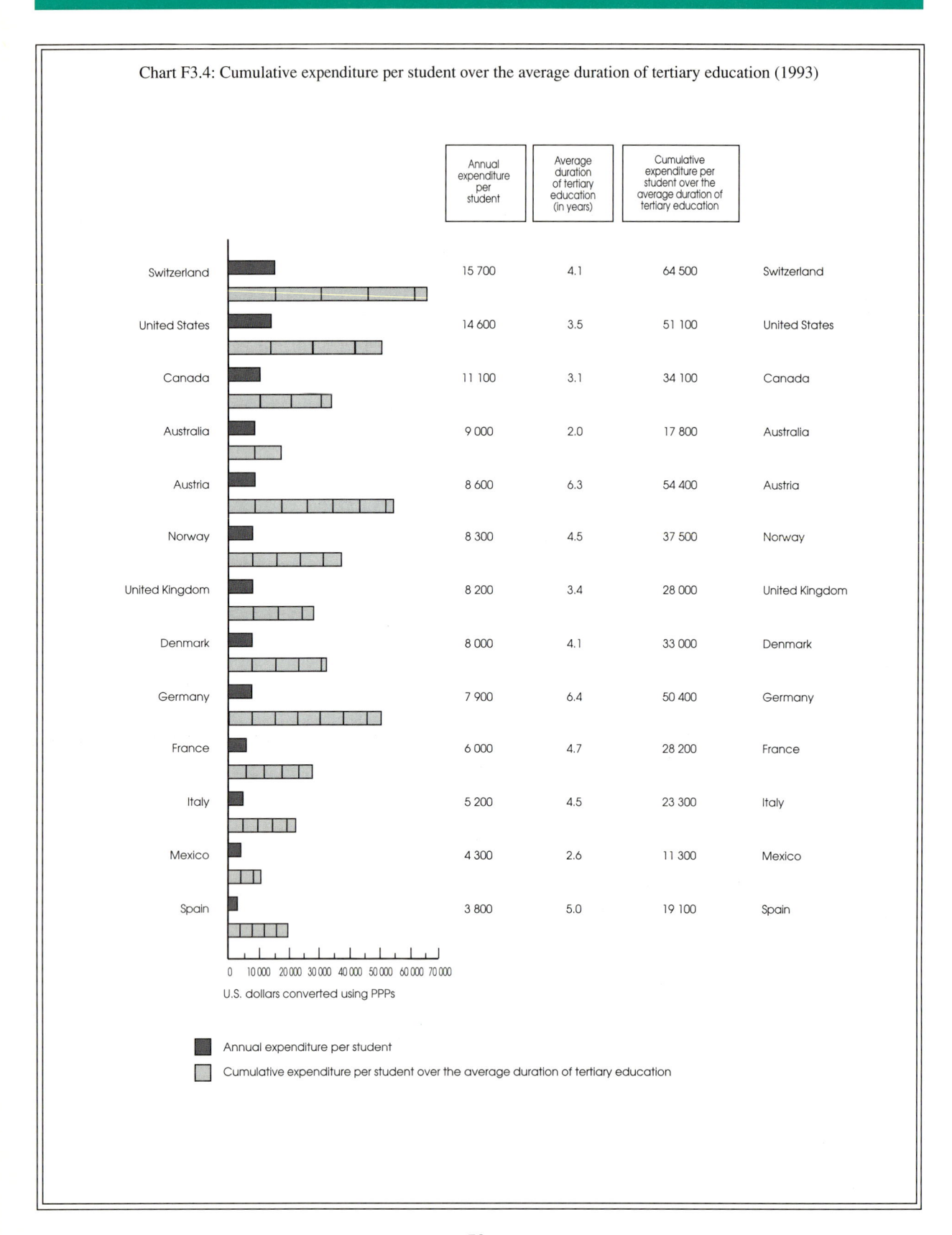

F3: Expenditure on educational services per student

Chart F3.4: Cumulative expenditure per student over the average duration of tertiary education (1993)

Country	Annual expenditure per student	Average duration of tertiary education (in years)	Cumulative expenditure per student over the average duration of tertiary education
Switzerland	15 700	4.1	64 500
United States	14 600	3.5	51 100
Canada	11 100	3.1	34 100
Australia	9 000	2.0	17 800
Austria	8 600	6.3	54 400
Norway	8 300	4.5	37 500
United Kingdom	8 200	3.4	28 000
Denmark	8 000	4.1	33 000
Germany	7 900	6.4	50 400
France	6 000	4.7	28 200
Italy	5 200	4.5	23 300
Mexico	4 300	2.6	11 300
Spain	3 800	5.0	19 100

U.S. dollars converted using PPPs

■ Annual expenditure per student
□ Cumulative expenditure per student over the average duration of tertiary education

F3: Expenditure on educational services per student

Table F3.1:
Expenditure per student (U.S. dollars converted using PPPs) in public and private institutions by level of education (1993)

	Early childhood	Primary	Secondary	Tertiary All	Tertiary Non-university	Tertiary University-level	All levels of education combined
North America							
Canada	5 270	m	m	11 132	11 163	11 112	6 466
Mexico *	817	741	1 477	4 264	5 471	4 158	1 102
United States	3 551	5 492	6 541	14 607	x	x	7 341
Pacific Area							
Australia	m	2 985	4 871	9 036	5 903	10 257	4 628
Japan	2 294	3 960	4 356	7 556	5 925	7 945	4 727
New Zealand	2 180	2 659	3 951	7 337	7 301	7 348	3 681
European Union							
Austria *	4 712	4 291	6 721	8 642	11 466	8 492	6 565
Belgium **	2 152	2 953	5 373	6 380	x	x	4 616
Denmark	4 584	4 745	6 175	8 045	x	x	5 902
Finland **	5 891	4 095	4 769	7 295	7 058	7 369	5 167
France	2 678	3 154	5 685	6 033	x	x	4 548
Germany *	3 611	2 815	6 481	7 902	3 564	8 143	5 450
Greece *	m	m	1 578	2 502	1 976	2 712	1 616
Ireland	1 866	1 882	3 031	7 076	x	x	2 881
Italy *	3 299	4 107	5 235	5 169	4 857	5 195	5 021
Luxembourg	m	m	m	m	m	m	m
Netherlands	2 635	2 793	3 979	8 665	a	8 665	4 048
Portugal *	1 794	2 581	2 491	5 667	x	x	3 131
Spain	2 210	2 293	3 033	3 835	x	x	2 916
Sweden	2 942	4 917	5 651	12 693	x	x	5 702
United Kingdom **	3 508	3 295	4 494	8 241	x	x	4 339
Other OECD countries							
Czech Republic *	1 676	1 506	1 903	4 788	1 824	5 400	2 081
Hungary	1 376	1 607	1 685	5 189	a	5 189	1 849
Iceland	m	2 645	3 258	5 059	1 474	5 919	3 932
Norway *	6 451	m	m	8 343	12 994	6 543	6 010
Switzerland *	2 335	5 835	7 024	15 731	8 947	17 807	7 011
Turkey	871	832	587	2 696	x	x	897
Country mean	2 987	3 138	4 181	7 457			4 293
OECD total	2 706	3 315	4 730	9 665			4 762
Other non-OECD countries							
Korea	935	1 715	2 026	2 589	2 412	2 634	2 132
Poland	m	m	m	m	m	m	m
Russian Federation	m	m	m	m	m	m	m

* Public institutions
** Public and government-dependent private institutions
Source: OECD Database. See Annex 3 for notes

F3: Expenditure on educational services per student

Table F3.2:
Expenditure per student relative to per capita GDP in public and private institutions by level of education (1993)

	Early childhood	Primary	Secondary	Tertiary All	Tertiary Non-university	Tertiary University-level	All levels of education combined
North America							
Canada	27.3	m	m	57.6	57.8	57.5	33.5
Mexico *	12.0	10.9	21.7	62.8	80.5	61.2	16.2
United States	14.6	22.6	27.0	60.2	x	x	30.3
Pacific Area							
Australia	m	17.2	28.1	52.0	34.0	59.1	26.7
Japan	11.3	19.5	21.5	37.3	29.2	39.2	23.3
New Zealand	14.6	17.8	26.4	49.0	48.7	49.1	24.6
European Union							
Austria *	24.6	22.4	35.1	45.1	59.8	44.3	34.3
Belgium **	11.1	15.3	27.8	33.0	x	x	23.9
Denmark	23.9	24.8	32.2	42.0	x	x	30.8
Finland **	37.7	26.2	30.5	46.6	45.1	47.1	33.0
France	14.3	16.9	30.4	32.3	x	x	24.3
Germany *	19.5	15.2	35.1	42.8	19.3	44.1	29.5
Greece *	m	m	18.0	28.5	22.5	30.9	18.4
Ireland	13.5	13.6	22.0	51.3	x	x	20.9
Italy *	18.6	23.2	29.6	29.2	27.4	29.3	28.4
Luxembourg	m	m	m	m	m	m	m
Netherlands	14.8	15.7	22.4	48.8	a	48.8	22.8
Portugal *	15.2	21.9	21.1	48.0	x	x	26.5
Spain	16.6	17.2	22.8	28.8	x	x	21.9
Sweden	17.5	29.2	33.6	75.4	x	x	33.9
United Kingdom **	20.7	19.4	26.5	48.6	x	x	25.6
Other OECD countries							
Czech Republic *	19.8	17.8	22.4	56.5	21.5	63.7	24.5
Hungary	22.9	26.7	28.0	86.4	a	86.4	30.8
Iceland	m	14.1	17.4	27.1	7.9	31.7	21.0
Norway *	33.9	m	m	43.8	68.2	34.3	31.5
Switzerland *	10.1	25.2	30.3	67.9	38.6	76.8	30.2
Turkey	15.7	15.0	10.5	48.5	x	x	16.1
Country mean	**18.7**	**19.5**	**25.9**	**48.1**			**26.3**
OECD total	**15.5**	**18.3**	**25.8**	**49.0**			**25.6**
Other non-OECD countries							
Korea	9.5	17.4	20.6	26.3	24.5	26.7	21.6
Poland	m	m	m	m	m	m	m
Russian Federation	m	m	m	m	m	m	m

*   Public institutions
** Public and government-dependent private institutions
Source: OECD Database. See Annex 3 for notes

F3: Expenditure on educational services per student

Table F3.3:
Educational expenditure per student by level of education relative to educational expenditure per student at the primary level (1993)

	Early childhood education	Primary education	Secondary education	Tertiary education
North America				
Canada	m	m	m	m
Mexico *	110	100	199	575
United States	65	100	119	266
Pacific Area				
Australia	m	100	163	303
Japan	58	100	110	191
New Zealand	82	100	149	216
European Union				
Austria *	110	100	157	201
Belgium **	73	100	182	216
Denmark	97	100	130	170
Finland **	144	100	116	178
France	85	100	180	191
Germany *	128	100	153	281
Greece *	m	100	100	159
Ireland	99	100	161	376
Italy *	80	100	127	126
Luxembourg	m	m	m	m
Netherlands	94	100	142	310
Portugal *	70	100	97	220
Spain	96	100	132	167
Sweden	60	100	115	258
United Kingdom **	106	100	136	250
Other OECD countries				
Czech Republic *	111	100	126	318
Hungary	86	100	105	323
Iceland	m	100	123	191
Norway *	m	m	m	m
Switzerland *	40	100	120	270
Turkey	105	100	71	324
Country mean	**90**	**100**	**134**	**253**
OECD total	**85**	**100**	**135**	**277**
Other non-OECD countries				
Korea	55	100	118	151
Poland	m	m	m	m
Russian Federation	m	m	m	m

*   Public institutions
** Public and government-dependent private institutions
Source: OECD Database. See Annex 3 for notes

F3-R: Inter-regional disparities in expenditure on educational services per student

F3-R: INTER-REGIONAL DISPARITIES IN EXPENDITURE ON EDUCATIONAL SERVICES PER STUDENT

This indicator illustrates the variation in expenditure per student across regions at the primary and secondary levels.

POLICY CONTEXT

A major policy concern is to ensure that all children have access to a fair share of educational resources, no matter where they live within a country. Many countries have developed policies to reduce regional resource disparities. These policies include the provision of additional resources to regions with large numbers of poor or disadvantaged children in order to equalise educational opportunities.

Regional disparities in unit expenditure as shown in this indicator have varied policy implications because education in different geographical or socio-economic settings may have different needs to meet that require different treatment. Still, these disparities can reflect inequities in access to educational resources, and reducing such inequities can be a desirable policy objective.

KEY RESULTS

In some countries, geographical variation in educational resources is relatively small. In Sweden, for example, expenditure per student in the highest-spending region is just 1.4 times as high as expenditure in the lowest-spending region at primary and secondary level combined. Children living in one region or locality therefore receive about the same financial resources as children living in others. In other countries, the variation in resources is considerably higher, particularly in the United States where expenditure in the highest-spending state exceeds 2.7 times that in the lowest-spending state.

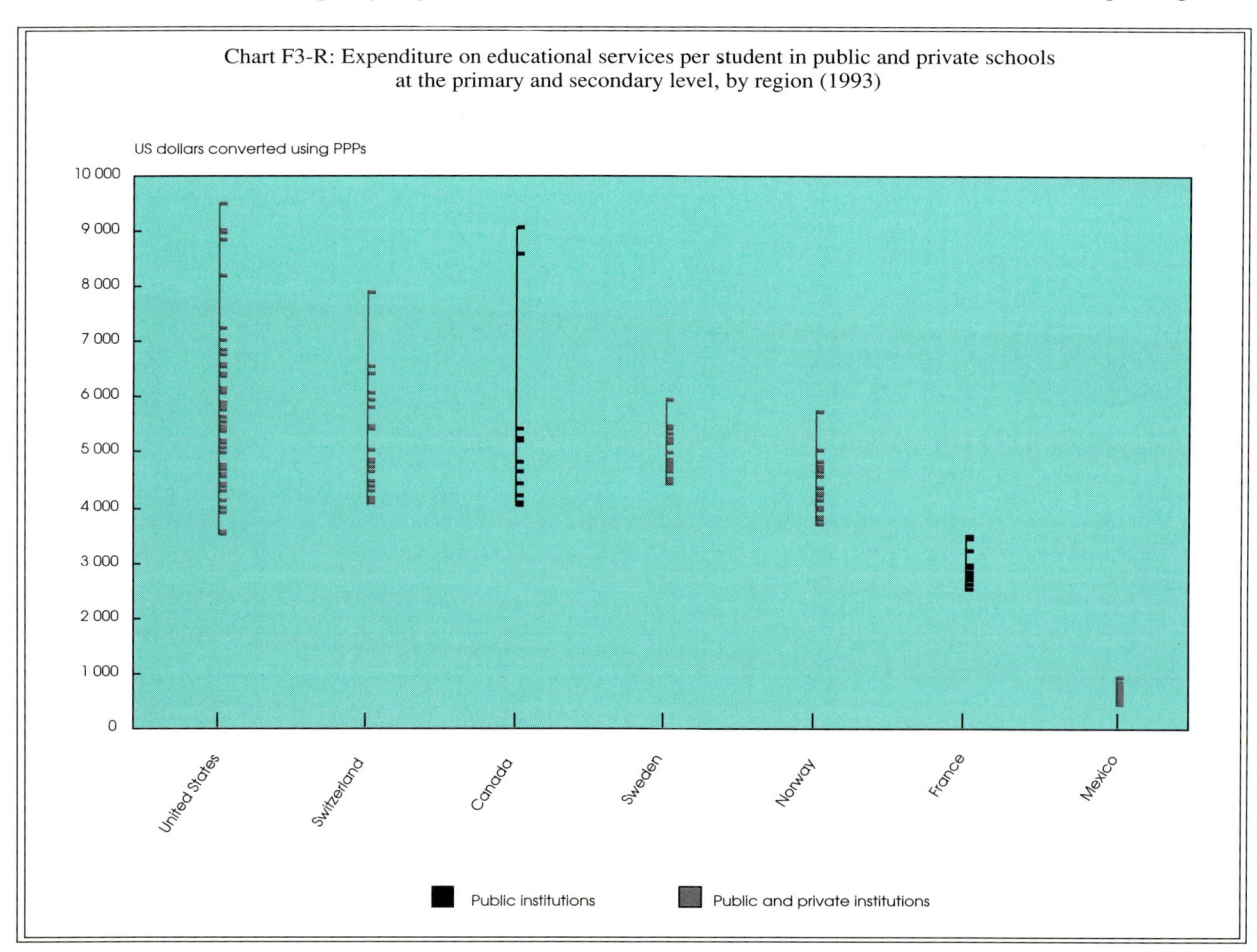

Chart F3-R: Expenditure on educational services per student in public and private schools at the primary and secondary level, by region (1993)

F3-R: Inter-regional disparities in expenditure on educational services per student

For the seven countries included in this indicator the within-country differences exceed the differences in unit costs at the primary and secondary level that exist across countries. However, the data presented are developmental and need to be interpreted with care in the context of the description that follows.

DESCRIPTION AND INTERPRETATION

While Indicator F3 provides a perspective on how countries draw on national resources for education, with the implication that resource levels are relatively uniform across the country, the supplementary Indicator F3-R illustrates the variation in expenditure per student across regions within countries for schools at the primary and secondary level.

Financial resources are often provided by the central government to regional governments in order to equalise the regions' ability to finance education; funds may also be provided by regional governments to local authorities to reduce disparities in educational expenditure. Policies can therefore involve the provision of additional resources to poor regions or to regions with large numbers of poor or disadvantaged children in order to equalise educational opportunities.

However, it needs to be taken into account that there are varied and compound factors that influence regional differences in expenditure per student, including differences in the cost of education across regions or local authorities. In countries such as the United States, indicators of inter-state differences in expenditure per student have been calculated that attempt to take these cost differences into account. Cost adjustments do tend to reduce expenditure disparities across states, but substantial inter-state variation still remains even after cost adjustments have been incorporated into the indicators.

Regional variation in expenditure per student tends to be higher than variation in student/teaching staff ratios in the small number of countries that provided regional data on both resource measures. However, there is also a high level of correspondence between the two indicators: countries that show wide regional variation in expenditure per student also tend to show wide variation in student/teaching staff ratios. Regional variation in expenditure per student can result from variation in staff salaries as well as differences in student/teaching staff ratios among regions.

The interpretation of these data requires caution since the regions that are appropriate units for comparisons in one country may not have a counterpart in other countries. Chart F3-R does not therefore attempt to express the disparities in the form of a single summative measure but merely illustrates the dispersion. Note that no account is taken of the size of the regions. Of particular importance is the fact that the extent to which the regional units chosen for this exercise control their own resources differs significantly among countries (see Table F3-R). Canada, Mexico, Switzerland and the United States are federal systems or confederations, in which the chosen regions are political entities whose governments have at least some authority to establish educational policy and to finance education. In France, Norway and Sweden the chosen units are governmental units created for administrative purposes to implement educational policies. The size of the disparities can depend significantly on whether the units chosen as regions are in fact the entities which have control over the resources or are sub-units or aggregates of those entities. Furthermore, the chosen regions differ substantially in size, population and other characteristics (both within and among countries) (see Table F3-R). Finally, the relative size of the regions can influence the magnitude of the disparities, with countries divided into a large number of small regions tending to show greater variation than countries subdivided into a small number of larger regions.

DEFINITIONS

See definitions for Indicator F3. Note that regional expenditure data can differ from the national aggregates shown in Indicator F3 because of differences in the coverage of sources of funds at the regional and national level. However, consistent definitions of expenditure are used within each country. For Canada, France, Norway, Mexico, Sweden and the United States, the combined expenditure on primary and secondary institutions is presented, while expenditure on compulsory education is presented in the case of Switzerland. With the exception of Canada and France, the data cover only expenditure on public institutions.

A brief description of the regions that have been employed as well as their size in terms of population are shown in Table F3-R.

F3-R: Inter-regional disparities in expenditure on educational services per student

Table F3-R:
Characteristics of regions used for tables and charts on regional differences in educational expenditure (1993)

	Names of regions	Number of regions	Role in school administration	Role in school financing	Population of largest region	Popupation of smallest region
North America						
Canada	Provinces/Territories	12	Yes	Yes	10 085 000	26 000
Mexico	Estados	32	Yes	Yes	9 815 795	317 764
United States	States	51	Yes	Yes	31 211 000	470 000
Pacific Area						
Australia	States/Territories	8	Yes	Yes	6 008 578	168 266
European Union						
Austria	Länder	9	Yes	Yes	1 539 848	331 472
Belgium	Communautés/ Gemeenschappen	3	Yes	Yes	5 967 178	68 471
France	Régions / Académies	22/26	Some levels	Some levels	7 037 618	176 038
Germany	Länder	16	Yes	Yes	17 679 000	686 000
Greece	Periféria	13		Yes	3 494 134	188 107
Italy	Regioni	20	Some levels	Yes	8 856 074	115 938
Netherlands	Provincies	12	No	No	3 258 000	227 000
Spain	Comunidades Autónomas	17	Yes	Yes	7 040 627	267 943
Sweden	Län	24	Upper secondary and tertiary education only	Tertiary education only	1 686 230	57 751
Other OECD countries						
Norway	Fylke	19	Yes	Upper secondary education only	477 515	76 442
Switzerland	Cantons	26	Yes	Yes	1 164 500	14 800
Other non-OECD countries						
Korea	Do	15	Yes	Yes	10 926 000	511 000

Source: OECD Database. See Annex 3 for notes

F5: Educational expenditure by resource category

F5: EDUCATIONAL EXPENDITURE BY RESOURCE CATEGORY

This indicator compares countries with respect to, first, the division of spending between current and capital outlays and, second, the distribution of current expenditure between compensation of teaching and non-teaching staff, and current spending on non-personnel resources.

POLICY CONTEXT

Educational expenditure can be divided into capital expenditure incurred in providing school plants and facilities, and current expenditure, which refers to financial outlays for school resources that are used each year in the operation of schools. The amount allocated to each will depend in part on changes in enrolment, in salaries of educational personnel and in costs for the maintenance of school buildings and teaching facilities.

KEY RESULTS

At the combined primary and secondary level, current expenditure accounts, on average, for almost 93 per cent of total outlays on educational institutions across OECD countries. In most countries, over 80 per cent of current expenditure is accounted for by expenditure on the compensation of staff (including both salary and non-salary compensation). At the tertiary level, the proportion of capital expenditure is generally larger. Current expenditure at this level represents on average 88 per cent of the total outlays on educational institutions in OECD countries. Furthermore, at the tertiary level almost all countries devote a significantly smaller amount of current expenditure to the compensation of staff than at the primary-secondary level.

DESCRIPTION AND INTERPRETATION

Education takes place mostly in school and university settings, and the labour-intensive technology of education explains the large proportion of current spending in total educational expenditure. Nevertheless, there is still wide variation across countries with respect to the relative proportions of current and capital spending: at the primary-secondary level, the capital proportion ranges from less than 5 per cent in Belgium, Canada, Ireland, Italy, Portugal and the United Kingdom to more than 10 per cent in Austria, the Czech Republic, Iceland, Japan, Korea and Switzerland (see Chart F5). In 16 out of the 25 countries for which data are available, more than 80 per cent of current expenditure is accounted for by the compensation of educational staff and in Greece, Italy, Portugal and Turkey, this percentage exceeds 90 per cent.

At the tertiary level, the proportion of capital expenditure is higher reflecting, among other things, more differentiated and advanced teaching facilities. In 14 out of 24 countries, the capital proportion is above 11 per cent, and in Greece, Italy, Japan, Korea and Turkey, it lies between 20 and 28 per cent (see Chart F5). At the same time the proportion of staff compensation in current expenditure is significantly lower at the tertiary level: all countries for which data are available spend more than 14 per cent of current expenditure on purposes other than the compensation of educational staff, and in more than half of the countries the figure is above 30 per cent.

The distribution of expenditure by resource category and, in particular, the share of expenditure accounted for by the compensation of educational staff depends among other things on the ratio of students to teaching staff (see Indicator P32), the level of teachers' salaries (see Indicator P35), the number of instructional hours for teachers and the division of the teacher's time between teaching and other duties (see Indicators P11 and P33).

In practice, the allocation of staff compensation expenditure between teaching and non-teaching staff is not clear-cut. Some countries define "teachers" narrowly as persons who teach students in the classroom while others include heads of schools and other professional personnel. Because of these (and other) definitional differences, as well as differences among countries in the coverage of non-teaching staff, the variation observed in the reported percentages of expenditure on non-teaching staff should be viewed with caution.

DEFINITIONS

The current and capital portions of expenditure are the percentages of total expenditure reported as current expenditure and capital expenditure, respectively. Only expenditure on educational institutions is considered. Subsidies for students' living expenses are excluded.

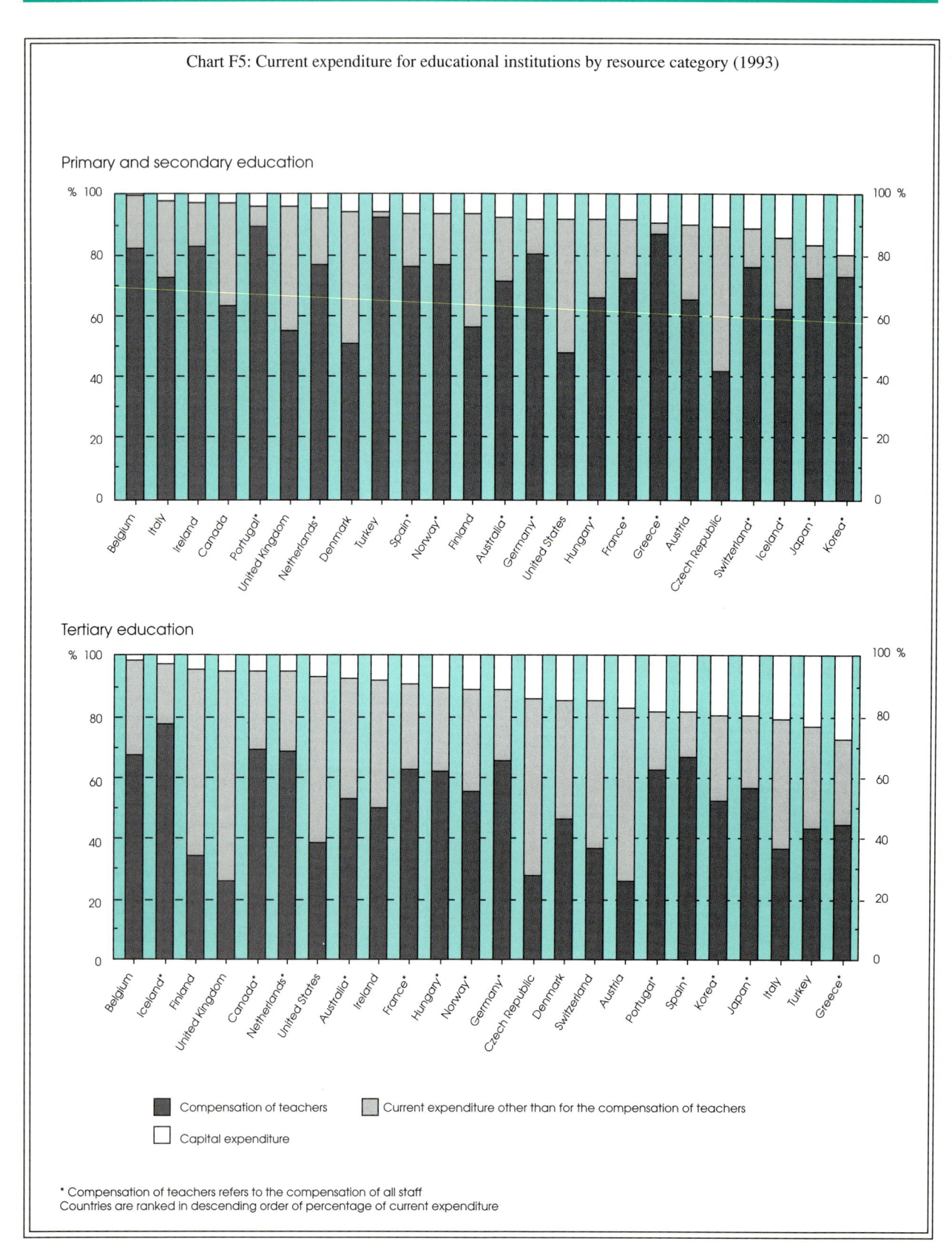

F5: Educational expenditure by resource category

Chart F5: Current expenditure for educational institutions by resource category (1993)

Primary and secondary education

Countries (left to right): Belgium, Italy, Ireland, Canada, Portugal*, United Kingdom, Netherlands*, Denmark, Turkey, Spain*, Norway, Finland, Australia, Germany*, United States, Hungary, France*, Greece*, Austria, Czech Republic, Switzerland*, Iceland*, Japan*, Korea*

Tertiary education

Countries (left to right): Belgium, Iceland*, Finland, United Kingdom, Canada*, Netherlands*, United States, Australia, Ireland, France*, Hungary*, Norway*, Germany*, Czech Republic, Denmark, Switzerland, Austria, Portugal*, Spain*, Korea*, Japan*, Italy, Turkey, Greece*

Legend:
- Compensation of teachers
- Current expenditure other than for the compensation of teachers
- Capital expenditure

* Compensation of teachers refers to the compensation of all staff
Countries are ranked in descending order of percentage of current expenditure

F5: Educational expenditure by resource category

Calculations cover expenditure by public institutions or, where available, those of public and private institutions combined. The proportions of current expenditure allocated to compensation of teachers, compensation of other staff, total staff compensation, and other (non-personnel) current outlays are calculated by expressing the respective amounts as percentages of total current expenditure. In some cases, compensation of teaching staff means compensation of classroom teachers only, but in others it includes that of heads of schools and other professional educators. The average teacher and staff compensation per student is calculated by multiplying expenditure per student as shown in Indicator F3, with the respective proportions of teacher and staff compensation in total expenditure on educational institutions. Current expenditure other than on compensation of personnel includes expenditure on contracted and purchased services such as expenditure on support services (e.g. for the maintenance of school buildings), ancillary services (e.g. for the preparation of meals for students) and rents paid for school buildings and other facilities. These services are obtained from outside providers as opposed to services produced by the education authorities or educational institutions themselves using their own personnel.

The *country mean* is calculated as the simple average over all OECD countries for which data are available. The *OECD total* reflects the value of the indicator when the OECD region is considered as a whole (for details see *Reader's Guide* p. 29).

F5: Educational expenditure by resource category

Table F5.1:
Educational expenditure on primary and secondary education by resource category for public and private institutions (1993)

	Percentage of total expenditure		Percentage of current expenditure				Average teacher compensation per student (in equivalent U.S. dollars)	Average staff compensation per student (in equivalent U.S. dollars)
	Current	Capital	Compensation of teachers	Compensation of other staff	Compensation of all staff	Other current expenditure		
North America								
Canada	96.2	3.8	65.0	15.4	80.5	19.5	3 291	4 073
Mexico	m	m	m	m	m	m	m	m
United States	91.3	8.7	56.2	23.3	79.5	20.5	2 849	4 028
Pacific Area								
Australia	91.9	8.1	x	x	76.9	23.1	m	2 714
Japan	83.0	17.0	x	x	87.0	13.0	m	3 016
New Zealand	m	m	m	m	m	m	m	m
European Union								
Austria *	89.8	10.2	72.2	8.3	80.6	19.4	3 767	4 202
Belgium **	99.7	0.3	81.9	2.3	84.1	15.9	3 514	3 612
Denmark	94.0	6.0	54.1	27.2	81.3	18.7	2 848	4 277
Finland **	92.9	7.1	60.1	12.5	72.6	27.4	2 488	3 004
France	90.7	9.3	x	x	78.6	21.4	m	3 312
Germany *	91.5	8.5	x	x	87.2	12.8	m	3 052
Greece *	90.2	9.8	x	x	95.4	4.6	m	1 353
Ireland *	96.4	3.6	84.8	3.9	88.7	11.3	1 993	2 086
Italy *	97.3	2.7	74.1	17.4	91.5	8.5	3 482	4 297
Luxembourg	m	m	m	m	m	m	m	m
Netherlands	94.8	5.2	x	x	80.5	19.5	m	2 619
Portugal *	95.6	4.4	x	x	92.4	7.6	m	2 239
Spain	93.4	6.6	x	x	81.0	19.0	m	2 097
Sweden *	100.0	x	47.9	15.1	62.9	37.1	2 540	3 340
United Kingdom **	95.3	4.7	57.9	14.8	72.7	27.3	2 162	2 715
Other OECD countries								
Czech Republic *	89.0	11.0	47.1	17.1	64.2	35.8	745	1 016
Hungary *	91.1	8.9	x	x	72.0	28.0	m	1 090
Iceland	85.4	14.6	x	x	72.7	27.3	m	1 836
Norway *	92.9	7.1	x	x	81.7	18.3	m	3 823
Switzerland *	88.3	11.7	x	x	85.7	14.3	m	m
Turkey	93.6	6.4	97.3	0.6	97.9	2.1	669	673
Country mean	**92.7**	**7.6**			**81.2**	**18.8**		
OECD total	**91.0**	**9.1**			**81.8**	**18.2**		
Other non-OECD countries								
Korea *	79.9	20.1	x	x	89.8	10.2	m	1 344
Poland	m	m	m	m	m	m	m	m
Russian Federation	m	m	m	m	m	m	m	m

* Public institutions only
** Public and government-dependent private institutions
Source: OECD Database. See Annex 3 for notes

F5: Educational expenditure by resource category

Table F5.2:
Educational expenditure on tertiary education by resource category for public and private institutions (1993)

	Percentage of total expenditure		Percentage of current expenditure				Average teacher compensation per student (in equivalent U.S. dollars)	Average staff compensation per student (in equivalent U.S. dollars)
	Current	Capital	Compensation of teachers	Compensation of other staff	Compensation of all staff	Other current expenditure		
North America								
Canada	93.8	6.2	x	x	72.8	27.2	m	7 600
Mexico	m	m	m	m	m	m	m	m
United States	92.4	7.6	49.1	24.0	73.2	26.8	5 540	8 250
Pacific Area								
Australia	91.8	8.2	x	x	56.7	43.3	m	4 703
Japan	79.9	20.1	x	x	69.6	30.4	m	4 199
New Zealand	m	m	m	m	m	m	m	m
European Union								
Austria *	82.0	18.0	31.5	20.0	51.5	48.5	2 235	3 649
Belgium **	97.5	2.5	68.0	0.9	68.9	31.1	4 230	4 288
Denmark	84.7	15.3	53.8	26.2	80.0	20.0	3 669	5 452
Finland **	94.3	5.7	36.2	23.5	59.6	40.4	2 487	4 102
France	90.1	9.9	x	x	68.7	31.3	m	3 732
Germany *	88.1	11.9	x	x	73.2	26.8	m	5 109
Greece *	72.0	28.0	x	x	61.2	38.8	m	1 102
Ireland *	90.8	9.2	54.4	31.3	85.8	14.2	3 495	5 508
Italy *	78.8	21.2	45.9	25.2	71.1	28.9	1 871	2 896
Luxembourg	m	m	m	m	m	m	m	m
Netherlands	93.7	6.3	x	x	71.9	28.1	m	5 836
Portugal *	80.8	19.2	x	x	76.6	23.4	m	3 508
Spain	80.8	19.2	x	x	81.3	18.7	m	2 519
Sweden *	100.0	x	x	x	54.9	45.1	m	6 967
United Kingdom **	93.9	6.1	27.3	17.5	44.8	55.2	2 110	3 468
Other OECD countries								
Czech Republic *	85.3	14.7	32.4	29.8	62.2	37.8	1 325	2 541
Hungary *	88.9	11.1	x	x	68.7	31.3	m	3 166
Iceland	96.3	3.7	x	x	79.4	20.6	m	3 869
Norway *	88.2	11.8	x	x	61.8	38.2	m	4 549
Switzerland *	84.6	15.4	50.7	28.1	78.8	21.2	m	m
Turkey	76.1	23.9	56.4	26.9	83.3	16.7	1 157	1 708
Country mean	**87.7**	**12.8**			**69.0**	**31.0**		
OECD total	**88.8**	**11.4**			**70.3**	**29.7**		
Other non-OECD countries								
Korea *	80.0	20.0	x	x	64.6	35.4	m	1 338
Poland	m	m	m	m	m	m	m	m
Russian Federation	m	m	m	m	m	m	m	m

* Public institutions only
** Public and government-dependent private institutions
Source: OECD Database. See Annex 3 for notes

F12: PUBLIC FUNDS BY LEVEL OF GOVERNMENT

This indicator shows the initial sources of public educational funds and the final purchasers of educational resources by level of government

POLICY CONTEXT

The locus of decision-making in educational matters can be either central, regional or local, with the balance among the levels of government being a matter of national choice. The range of possibilities includes complete centralisation and complete decentralisation, with each of these having certain advantages and disadvantages. Complete centralisation can lead to delays in decisions and a failure to take proper account of changes in local needs and desired practices. Under complete decentralisation, on the other hand, funding for education may be determined solely by locally available resources and can lead to inequity of educational opportunity and insufficient attention to long-term national needs.

An important factor in educational policy is the division of responsibility for, and control over, the funding of education among national, regional and local authorities.

KEY RESULTS

Countries differ significantly in how they allocate responsibility for financing education among the levels of government. Four basic patterns are observed:
- the central government is both the main initial source of funds and the main final spender on education;
- the central government is the main initial source but funds are transferred to regional or local authorities, who are the main direct purchasers of educational resources;
- regional authorities are both the main initial sources and the main final purchasers;
- funding responsibilities are shared between regional and local authorities.

DESCRIPTION AND INTERPRETATION

Countries can be grouped according to the percentage of public funds generated and spent by central, regional and local governments.

In Ireland, the Netherlands, New Zealand, Portugal and Turkey, the central government is both the initial source of more than 95 per cent of educational funds and the final spender of at least 80 per cent of these funds. In Austria, the Czech Republic, France, Greece, Iceland and Italy, the central government is still the source of the majority of initial funds and the main final spender. By contrast, in Canada, Germany, Switzerland and the United States, the central government generates less than 20 per cent of educational funds and in the same four countries as well as in Australia, Japan, Korea and the United Kingdom, less than 20 per cent of final educational funds are spent by the central government.

The central government is the main initial source of funds, but regional or local authorities are the main final purchasers of educational services, in Austria, Finland, Hungary, Korea and Norway.

Regional governments are both the main initial sources and the main final spenders of educational funds in Australia, Belgium, Germany, Japan, Spain and Switzerland; although in Australia and Spain some 40 per cent of funds are generated by the central government.

In Canada and the United States, regional governments are the main initial source of funds, but in these countries local authorities are the main final purchasers of educational services (with the regional governments spending only 29 and 15 per cent of funds, respectively).

For many countries, differences can be observed between the funding for primary and secondary and that for the tertiary level of education. With some notable exceptions, responsibility for financing tertiary education is more centralised and, in most countries for which data are available, the central government has the dominant role as both initial source and final spender at this level.

Note that this indicator does not take into account flows of general-purpose funds – that is, funds not specially earmarked for education – from central to regional or local governments, or in some cases from regional to local governments. If appropriate proportions of these general-purpose transfers were attributed to education, the central government's role as the initial

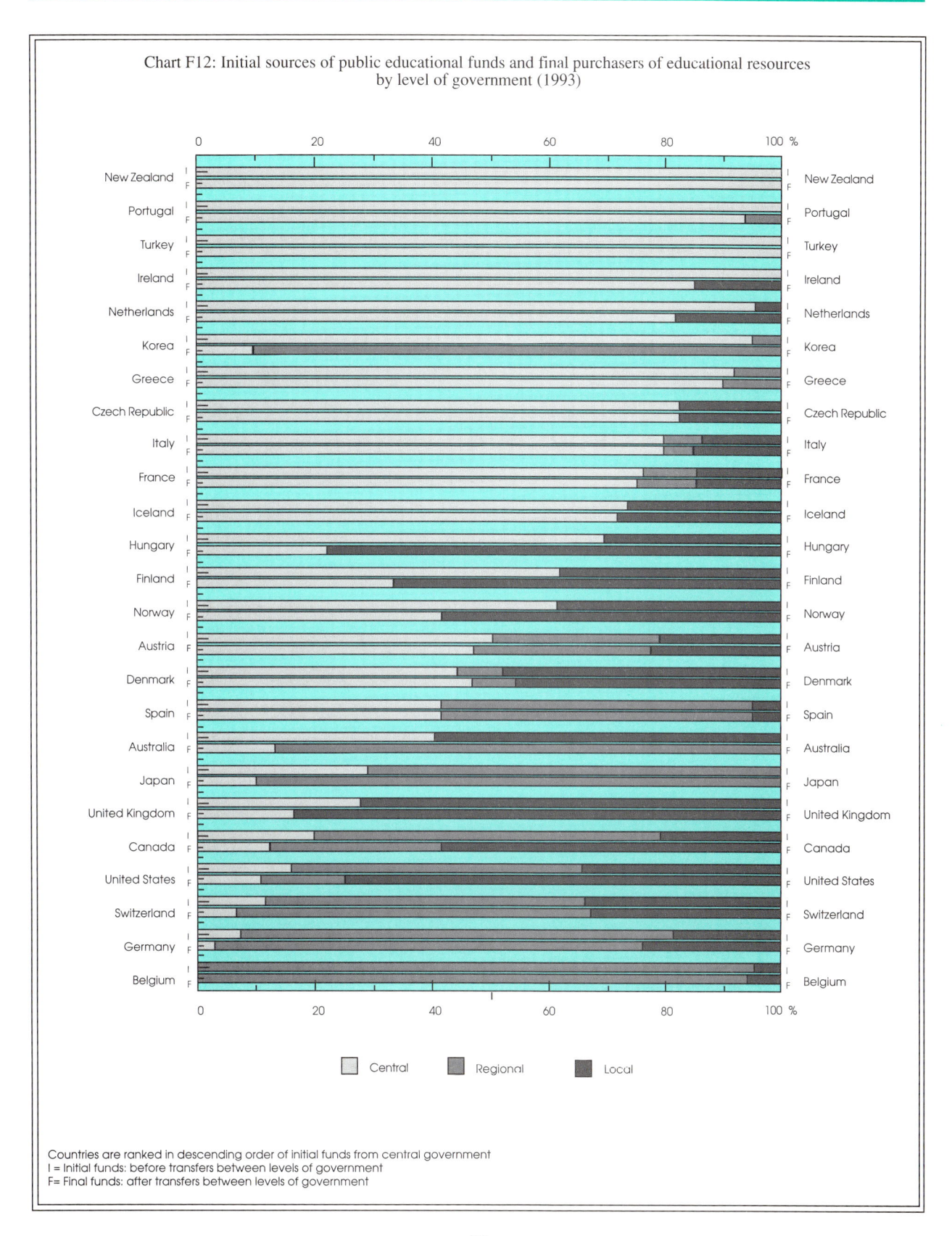

F12: Public funds by level of government

Chart F12: Initial sources of public educational funds and final purchasers of educational resources by level of government (1993)

Countries are ranked in descending order of initial funds from central government
I = Initial funds: before transfers between levels of government
F = Final funds: after transfers between levels of government

Legend: Central, Regional, Local

Countries (top to bottom): New Zealand, Portugal, Turkey, Ireland, Netherlands, Korea, Greece, Czech Republic, Italy, France, Iceland, Hungary, Finland, Norway, Austria, Denmark, Spain, Australia, Japan, United Kingdom, Canada, United States, Switzerland, Germany, Belgium

F12: Public funds by level of government

provider of funds would appear significantly larger in many countries, particularly in Australia, Austria, Belgium, Canada, Germany and Spain.

Two special cases deserve mention. First, the local authorities responsible for operating schools in the United Kingdom are financed mainly by central government funds. Although these consist mainly of general-purpose grants and shared revenue, it seems appropriate in this comparison to count the United Kingdom as one of the countries in which the central government is the main source of educational funds. Secondly, the main responsibility for financing education in Belgium is borne by the language-based communities. Because the Belgian authorities classify the communities as regional governments, Belgium has been included among the countries that assign primary responsibility to regional units.

DEFINITIONS

The initial educational expenditure of each level of government – also referred to as the expenditure originating at that level – is the total educational expenditure of all public authorities at the level in question (direct expenditure plus transfers to other levels of government and to the private sector), less the transfers received from governments at other levels. The share of initial expenditure by a particular level of government is calculated as a percentage of the total, consolidated expenditure of all three levels. Funds received from international sources have been excluded. Only expenditure specifically designated for education is taken into account in determining the share of initial expenditure borne by a particular level. General-purpose transfers between levels of government, which provide much of the revenue of regional and local governments in some countries, have been excluded from the calculations.

The final expenditure of each level of government is the amount spent directly on educational services by all public authorities at that level. It does not include transfers to other levels of government or to households or other private entities. The share of final expenditure by a particular level of government is calculated as the percentage of total direct expenditure on educational services of all levels of government combined. For the public sector as a whole, final expenditure is less than initial expenditure because some funds generated in the public sector are transferred to, and ultimately used by, households and other private parties.

The *country mean* is calculated as the simple average over all OECD countries for which data are available. The *OECD total* reflects the value of the indicator when the OECD region is considered as a whole (for details see *Reader's Guide* p. 29).

F12: Public funds by level of government

Table F12.1:
Initial sources of public educational funds and final purchasers of educational resources by level of government for all levels of education combined (1993)

	Initial funds (before transfers between levels of government)				Final funds (after transfers between levels of government)			
	Central	Regional	Local	Total	Central	Regional	Local	Total
North America								
Canada	19.3	59.6	21.1	100	12.5	29.3	58.2	100
Mexico	m	m	m	m	m	m	m	m
United States	16.3	49.3	34.4	100	11.1	14.6	74.3	100
Pacific Area								
Australia	41.0	58.9	0.1	100	13.6	86.2	0.2	100
Japan	29.4	70.6	x	100	10.3	89.7	x	100
New Zealand	100	a	a	100	100	a	a	100
European Union								
Austria	50.1	28.7	21.2	100	46.9	30.4	22.7	100
Belgium	a	94.6	5.4	100	a	93.4	6.6	100
Denmark	44.5	7.7	47.8	100	46.6	7.7	45.7	100
Finland	61.5	a	38.5	100	33.3	a	66.7	100
France	75.8	9.3	14.9	100	74.8	10.3	15.0	100
Germany	7.6	73.6	18.9	100	3.3	72.4	24.2	100
Greece	91.5	8.5	a	100	89.2	10.8	a	100
Ireland	99.9	a	0.1	100	84.5	a	15.5	100
Italy	79.5	6.5	14.4	100	79.5	5.0	16.0	100
Luxembourg	m	m	m	m	m	m	m	m
Netherlands	95.1	0.1	4.8	100	81.3	0.1	18.6	100
Portugal	100	a	a	100	93.5	6.5	a	100
Spain	41.6	53.0	5.4	100	41.6	53.0	5.4	100
Sweden	m	m	m	m	m	m	m	m
United Kingdom	28.1	a	71.9	100	16.7	a	83.3	100
Other OECD countries								
Czech Republic	82.0	a	18.0	100	82.0	a	18.0	100
Hungary	69.1	x	30.9	100	22.0	x	78.0	100
Iceland	73.0	n	27.0	100	71.4	n	28.6	100
Norway	60.9	a	39.1	100	41.4	a	58.6	100
Switzerland	11.9	53.9	34.2	100	7.0	59.9	33.0	100
Turkey	100	a	a	100	100	a	a	100
Country mean	**57.4**	**25.0**	**19.5**	**100**	**48.4**	**24.8**	**29.1**	**100**
Other non-OECD countries								
Korea	94.6	5.4	a	100	10.0	90.0	a	100
Poland	m	m	m	m	m	m	m	m
Russian Federation	m	m	m	m	m	m	m	m

Source: OECD Database. See Annex 3 for notes

F12: Public funds by level of government

Table F12.2:
Initial sources of public educational funds and final purchasers of educational resources by level of government for primary and secondary education (1993)

	\multicolumn{4}{c	}{Initial funds (before transfers between levels of government)}	\multicolumn{4}{c	}{Final funds (after transfers between levels of government)}
	Central	Regional	Local	Total	Central	Regional	Local	Total
North America								
Canada	3.5	63.9	32.6	100	2.5	7.7	89.8	100
Mexico	m	m	m	m	m	m	m	m
United States	7.9	47.7	44.3	100	0.8	0.9	98.3	100
Pacific Area								
Australia	25.0	75.1	a	100	5.6	94.5	a	100
Japan	24.1	75.9	x	100	0.8	99.2	x	100
New Zealand	100	a	a	100	100	a	a	100
European Union								
Austria	33.5	43.7	22.8	100	31.9	44.4	23.7	100
Belgium	a	94.3	5.7	100	a	93.1	6.9	100
Denmark	31.6	11.3	57.1	100	34.8	11.3	53.9	100
Finland	53.3	a	46.7	100	15.0	a	85.0	100
France	75.7	11.3	13.0	100	74.4	12.7	13.0	100
Germany	3.5	76.9	19.6	100	2.8	72.9	24.2	100
Greece	88.5	11.5	a	100	85.4	14.6	a	100
Ireland	99.9	a	0.1	100	83.9	a	16.1	100
Italy	83.1	3.6	13.2	100	83.1	2.5	14.3	100
Luxembourg	m	m	m	m	m	m	m	m
Netherlands	93.6	0.1	6.2	100	75.1	0.1	24.8	100
Portugal	100	a	a	100	100	a	a	100
Spain	40.9	53.0	6.1	100	40.9	53.0	6.1	100
Sweden	m	m	m	m	m	m	m	m
United Kingdom	7.5	a	92.5	100	4.4	a	95.6	100
Other OECD countries								
Czech Republic	80.5	a	19.5	100	80.5	a	19.5	100
Hungary	67.1	x	32.9	100	5.1	x	94.9	100
Iceland	64.8	n	35.2	100	62.6	n	37.4	100
Norway	47.0	a	53.0	100	14.7	a	85.3	100
Switzerland	3.7	53.2	43.1	100	0.8	57.9	41.3	100
Turkey	100	a	a	100	100	a	a	100
Country mean	51.4	27.0	23.6	100	41.9	24.6	36.1	100
Other non-OECD countries								
Korea	m	m	m	m	m	m	m	m
Poland	m	m	m	m	m	m	m	m
Russian Federation	m	m	m	m	m	m	m	m

Source: OECD Database. See Annex 3 for notes

F12: Public funds by level of government

Table F12.3:
Initial sources of public educational funds and final purchasers of educational resources by level of government for tertiary education (1993)

	\multicolumn{4}{c}{Initial funds (before transfers between levels of government)}	\multicolumn{4}{c}{Final funds (after transfers between levels of government)}
	Central	Regional	Local	Total	Central	Regional	Local	Total
North America								
Canada	48.3	51.7	0.05	100	30.8	69.1	0.05	100
Mexico	m	m	m	m	m	m	m	m
United States	38.7	55.5	5.9	100	38.7	55.5	5.9	100
Pacific Area								
Australia	84.1	15.9	a	100	32.9	67.1	a	100
Japan	88.0	12.0	x	100	87.7	12.3	x	100
New Zealand	100	a	a	100	100	a	a	100
European Union								
Austria	m	m	m	m	99.2	0.3	0.5	100
Belgium	a	98.8	1.2	100	a	98.0	2.0	100
Denmark	89.2	1.4	9.5	100	89.2	1.4	9.5	100
Finland	87.3	a	12.7	100	82.7	a	17.3	100
France	91.2	5.4	3.4	100	91.1	5.4	3.4	100
Germany	18.5	80.8	0.6	100	3.0	96.3	0.8	100
Greece	100	n	a	100	100	n	a	100
Ireland	100	a	n	100	78.9	a	21.1	100
Italy	85.8	13.9	0.3	100	85.8	11.4	2.8	100
Luxembourg	m	m	m	m	m	m	m	m
Netherlands	99.7	n	0.3	100	98.1	n	1.9	100
Portugal	100	a	a	100	100	a	a	100
Spain	48.6	50.5	0.9	100	48.6	50.5	0.9	100
Sweden	96.1	3.2	0.7	100	95.4	3.9	0.7	100
United Kingdom	100	a	n	100	59.4	a	40.6	100
Other OECD countries								
Czech Republic	99.0	a	1.0	100	99.0	a	1.0	100
Hungary	100	a	a	100	100	a	a	100
Iceland	100	n	n	100	100	n	n	100
Norway	100	a	a	100	100	a	a	100
Switzerland	43.6	56.0	0.5	100	30.1	69.4	0.5	100
Turkey	100	a	a	100	100	a	a	100
Country mean	**79.9**	**18.5**	**1.6**	**100**	**74.0**	**21.6**	**4.5**	**100**
Other non-OECD countries								
Korea	98.4	1.6	a	100	98.4	1.6	a	100
Poland	m	m	m	m	m	m	m	m
Russian Federation	m	m	m	m	m	m	m	m

Source: OECD Database. See Annex 3 for notes

F13: Proportion of public expenditure spent on education

F13: PROPORTION OF PUBLIC EXPENDITURE SPENT ON EDUCATION

This indicator shows direct public expenditure on educational services, public subsidies to the private sector and total educational expenditure as a percentage of total public expenditure.

POLICY CONTEXT

Education competes for public financial support against a wide range of other areas covered in government budgets. The relative level of government spending on education is a function of its perceived role in this area, as well as of the extent of its involvement in other related areas, such as health, employment and social affairs, and of the involvement of private sources in expenditure on education.

KEY RESULTS

On average, OECD countries devote 12.3 per cent of total government outlays to supporting educational institutions, with the values for individual countries ranging between 8.7 and 18 per cent. Between 5.7 and 14.5 per cent of total public expenditure is allocated to primary and secondary education and between 1.1 and 4.7 per cent to tertiary education. Most of the public funds are spent on supporting educational institutions but some countries spend more than 2 per cent on subsidies to the private sector for education.

DESCRIPTION AND INTERPRETATION

The education share of the public sector budget is lowest (below 10 per cent) in Germany, Greece, Italy and the Netherlands. Those countries also devote the smallest share of the public budget to primary and secondary education. By contrast, the highest percentages of total public spending allocated to education (15 per cent or more) are in Hungary, Korea, New Zealand, Norway and Switzerland. Canada and New Zealand devote the largest fraction of public spending to tertiary education (4.7 and 4.4 per cent respectively). Japan's low public spending on tertiary education (1.1 per cent of the total) is explained in part by its heavy reliance on private funding of tertiary education. Other countries that spend relatively small shares of public funds on tertiary education (1.8 per cent or less) are Belgium, France, Italy and Korea.

The relative size of the youth population shapes the potential demand for initial education and training in a country. The greater this proportion, the more resources need to be devoted to education or, in other words, the fewer students are at the age relevant for initial education, the less a country needs to spend on education. Chart F13.1(B) indicates the change in the share of educational expenditure in total government outlays that would be expected if the relative size of the population aged 5-29 were at the OECD average in each country, other things being equal. In countries such as Belgium, Denmark, Finland, Germany, Sweden and Switzerland, where the proportion of the youth population is relatively small, public spending on education would be some 10 per cent higher if the youth share of the total population were at the level of the OECD average. On the other hand, the effective expenditure share of Korea would be 20 per cent lower and that of Ireland 14 per cent lower if the proportion of young people in these countries were at the OECD average.

The overall size of public budgets (see Chart F13.2) also affects the relative share of educational expenditure in public spending. For example, the relatively high public spending on education in Hungary and Switzerland must be seen together with comparatively small public budgets relative to GDP. Likewise, countries such as Italy or the Netherlands, where education accounts for a low share of total public spending, tend to have relatively large public budgets.

Another factor that contributes to the variation among countries in the proportion of total public spending devoted to education is the involvement of the private sector in the financing of education. For example, countries that require students to pay tuition fees and/or to fund most or all of their living expenses are likely to devote a smaller percentage of public funds to tertiary education, other things being equal, than countries that provide "free" tertiary education and/or generous public subsidies to tertiary students. Similarly, countries in which private enterprises contribute significantly to the education of students (as is the case in countries with the dual system) can be expected to devote a comparatively lower share of public expenditure to education. Chart F13.3 shows the relative proportions of funds for educational institutions that are generated from public and private sources (taken before transfers between levels of government and before transfers from the public to the private sector). As can be seen, while in Finland, Italy and Turkey less than 1 per cent of expenditure on educational institutions originates in the private sector, it

F13: Proportion of public expenditure spent on education

Chart F13.1

A) Public expenditure on education as a percentage of total public expenditure (1993)

Primary and secondary

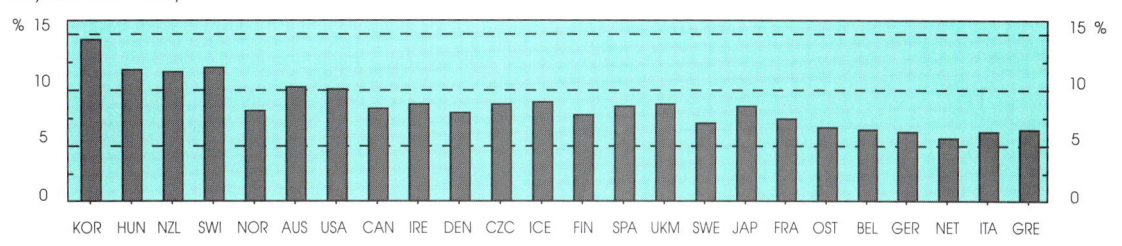

Tertiary

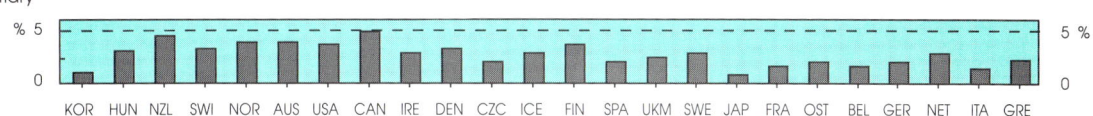

All levels of education combined

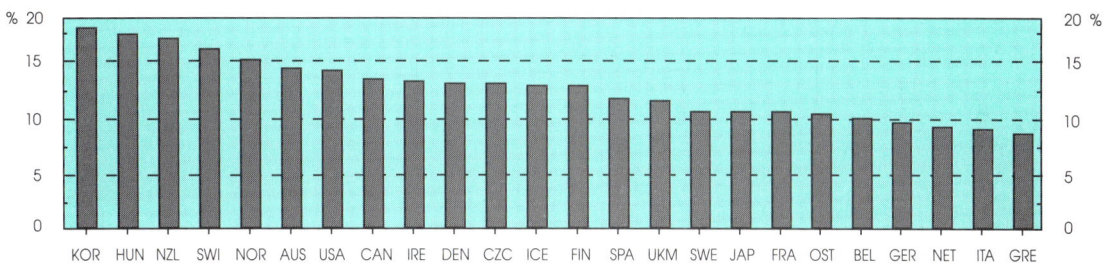

B) Estimated increase/decrease in public expenditure on education as a percentage of total public expenditure, if the proportion of the population 5 to 29 years of age in each country were at the OECD average level

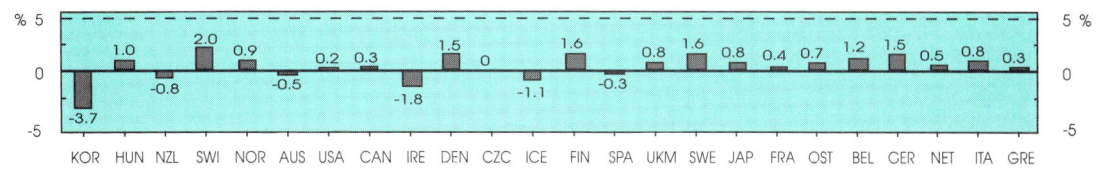

Countries are ranked in descending order of public expenditure on education for all levels of education combined

F13: Proportion of public expenditure spent on education

Chart F13.2: Total public expenditure as a percentage of GDP (1993)

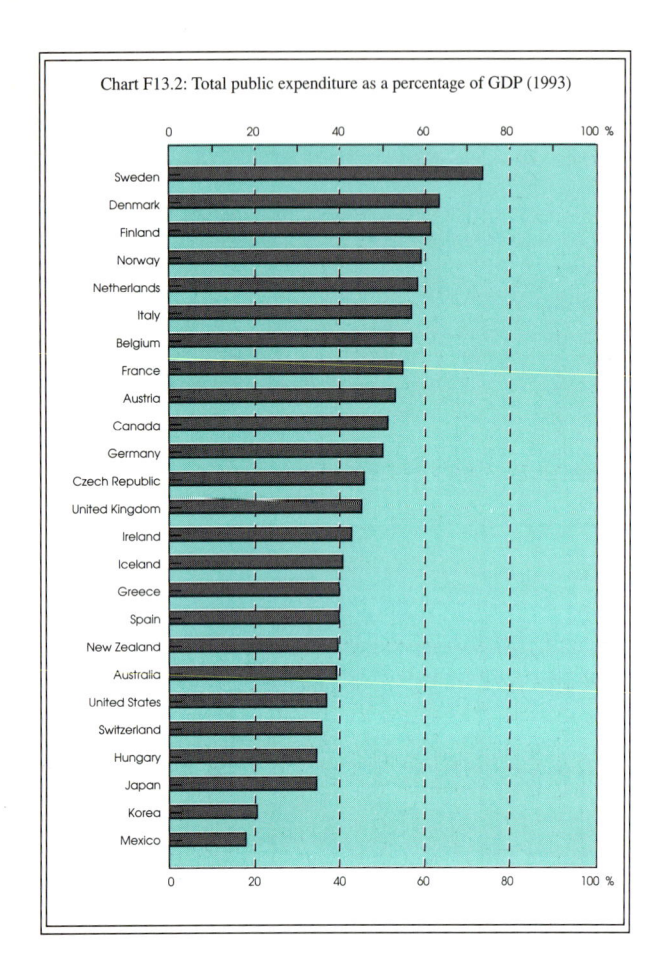

Sweden
Denmark
Finland
Norway
Netherlands
Italy
Belgium
France
Austria
Canada
Germany
Czech Republic
United Kingdom
Ireland
Iceland
Greece
Spain
New Zealand
Australia
United States
Switzerland
Hungary
Japan
Korea
Mexico

is over 22 per cent in Germany, Japan, Korea and the United States.

Finally, variations in the education share of total public spending can also reflect differences in the scope of the education sector among countries as well as differences in the breadth and depth of the public sector's involvement in areas outside education. For example, countries that spend relatively large amounts on their social security and national health care systems (such as Austria, Denmark, France, Germany and Sweden) may appear to be spending relatively smaller percentages on education even though educational institutions and participants in education may still benefit directly or indirectly from, for example, funds spent on social security or health matters. Furthermore, some countries provide benefits to students/households in the form of tax reductions, tax subsidies or other special tax provisions which are not accounted for in the educational expenditure shown in this indicator.

Over the last decade, the proportion of public expenditure spent on education has been fairly constant in most countries, the notable exception being Mexico, where it has risen by almost 10 per cent (see Table F13t).

DEFINITIONS

In this indicator each of the following three expenditure variables is expressed as a percentage of a country's total public sector expenditure: *i)* direct public expenditure on educational services; *ii)* public subsidies to the private sector; and *iii)* total educational expenditure. The percentages are calculated separately for primary-secondary education, tertiary education, and all levels combined.

Direct public expenditure on educational services includes both amounts spent directly by governments to hire educational personnel and to procure other resources, and amounts provided by governments to public or private institutions for use by the institutions themselves to acquire educational resources. Public subsidies include scholarships and other financial aid to students plus certain subsidies to other private entities, but exclude payments to institutions. The data on total public expenditure for all purposes (the denominator in all percentage calculations) have been taken from the OECD National Accounts Database (see Annex 2).

The methodology that was used for the calculation of the estimates in Charts F13.1(B) is explained in Annex 3.

The *country mean* is calculated as the simple average over all OECD countries for which data are available. The *OECD total* reflects the value of the indicator when the OECD region is considered as a whole (for details see *Reader's Guide* p. 29).

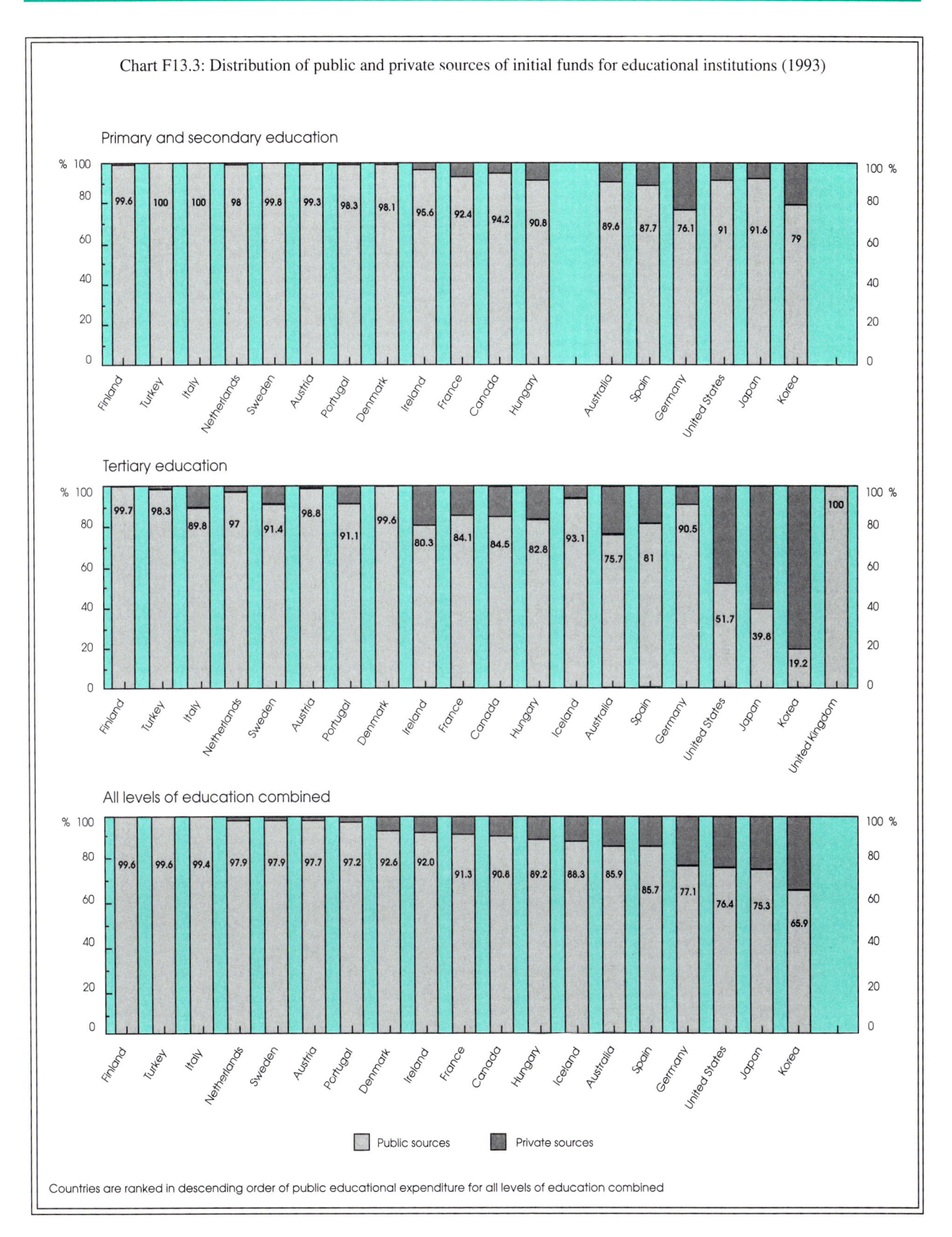

F13: Proportion of public expenditure spent on education

Chart F13.3: Distribution of public and private sources of initial funds for educational institutions (1993)

Primary and secondary education

Country	Public sources (%)
Finland	99.6
Turkey	100
Italy	100
Netherlands	98
Sweden	99.8
Austria	99.3
Portugal	98.3
Denmark	98.1
Ireland	95.6
France	92.4
Canada	94.2
Hungary	90.8
Australia	89.6
Spain	87.7
Germany	76.1
United States	91
Japan	91.6
Korea	79

Tertiary education

Country	Public sources (%)
Finland	99.7
Turkey	98.3
Italy	89.8
Netherlands	97
Sweden	91.4
Austria	98.8
Portugal	91.1
Denmark	99.6
Ireland	80.3
France	84.1
Canada	84.5
Hungary	82.8
Iceland	93.1
Australia	75.7
Spain	81
Germany	90.5
United States	51.7
Japan	39.8
Korea	19.2
United Kingdom	100

All levels of education combined

Country	Public sources (%)
Finland	99.6
Turkey	99.6
Italy	99.4
Netherlands	97.9
Sweden	97.9
Austria	97.7
Portugal	97.2
Denmark	92.6
Ireland	92.0
France	91.3
Canada	90.8
Hungary	89.2
Iceland	88.3
Australia	85.9
Spain	85.7
Germany	77.1
United States	76.4
Japan	75.3
Korea	65.9

Countries are ranked in descending order of public educational expenditure for all levels of education combined

F13: Proportion of public expenditure spent on education

Table F13:
Public expenditure on education as a percentage of total public expenditure (1993)

	Total: direct expenditure plus public subsidies to the private sector			Direct public expenditure for educational services			Public subsidies to the private sector		
	Primary and secondary education	Tertiary education	All levels of education	Primary and secondary education	Tertiary education	All levels of education	Primary and secondary education	Tertiary education	All levels of education
North America									
Canada	8.3	4.7	13.4	8.3	3.4	12.1	x	1.4	1.4
Mexico	m	m	m	16.3	3.9	22.3	m	m	m
United States	10.1	3.6	14.2	10.1	3.2	13.8	x	0.4	0.4
Pacific Area									
Australia	10.1	3.8	14.3	9.2	2.9	12.4	0.9	0.9	1.9
Japan	8.5	1.1	10.5	8.5	1.1	10.5	m	m	m
New Zealand	11.5	4.4	17.0	10.9	3.0	15.0	0.5	1.3	2.0
European Union									
Austria	6.7	2.1	10.2	6.7	2.0	10.0	0.1	0.1	0.3
Belgium	6.5	1.7	10.0	6.5	1.7	9.9	0.01	0.04	0.1
Denmark	7.9	3.4	13.0	7.0	2.1	10.5	0.9	1.3	2.4
Finland	7.8	3.6	12.8	7.6	2.8	11.8	0.2	0.8	1.0
France	7.4	1.8	10.4	7.3	1.6	10.2	0.1	0.2	0.3
Germany	6.2	2.1	9.5	5.9	1.9	9.0	0.2	0.2	0.5
Greece	6.4	2.3	8.7	6.4	2.1	8.5	0.04	0.2	0.2
Ireland	8.8	2.9	13.1	8.5	2.3	12.1	0.3	0.6	0.9
Italy	6.2	1.5	8.9	6.1	1.4	8.7	0.1	0.1	0.2
Luxembourg	m	m	m	m	m	m	m	m	m
Netherlands	5.7	2.9	9.2	5.2	2.1	7.9	0.5	0.8	1.3
Portugal	m	m	m	m	m	m	m	m	m
Spain	8.5	2.1	11.6	8.4	1.9	11.3	0.1	0.2	0.3
Sweden	6.9	2.9	10.6	6.3	2.0	9.1	0.6	0.9	1.5
United Kingdom	8.7	2.6	11.5	8.6	1.5	10.3	0.2	1.1	1.3
Other OECD countries									
Czech Republic	8.8	2.1	12.9	7.3	1.7	10.9	1.5	0.4	2.1
Hungary	11.8	3.0	17.3	11.7	2.6	16.8	0.0	0.5	0.5
Iceland	8.9	2.9	12.8	8.6	1.6	11.3	0.3	1.2	1.5
Norway	8.1	3.9	15.0	7.5	2.5	12.7	0.6	1.4	2.3
Switzerland	11.9	3.3	16.1	11.6	3.2	15.7	0.3	0.2	0.5
Turkey	m	m	m	m	m	m	m	m	m
Country mean	**8.3**	**2.8**	**12.3**	**8.3**	**2.3**	**11.8**	**0.4**	**0.6**	**1.0**
Other non-OECD countries									
Korea	14.5	1.3	18.0	14.5	1.2	17.7	0.01	0.1	0.3
Poland	m	m	m	m	m	m	m	m	m
Russian Federation	m	m	m	m	m	m	m	m	m

Source: OECD Database. See Annex 3 for notes

F13: Proportion of public expenditure spent on education

Table F13t:
Public expenditure on education as a percentage of total public expenditure (1985-93)

	1985	1990	1993
North America			
Canada	13.7	13.6	13.4
Mexico	12.8	15.7	22.3
United States	13.1	14.3	14.2
Pacific Area			
Australia	15.5	12.2	14.3
Japan	m	11.3	10.5
European Union			
Austria	11.0	10.6	10.2
Belgium	10.3	9.5	10.0
Denmark	11.6	10.6	13.0
Finland	12.9	12.9	12.8
France	m	10.3	10.4
Germany	9.6	m	9.5
Ireland	m	12.2	13.1
Italy	9.1	9.6	8.9
Netherlands	10.2	9.9	9.2
Portugal	m	m	m
Spain	8.6	10.1	11.6
Sweden	m	9.3	10.6
United Kingdom	11.1	11.9	11.5
Other OECD countries			
Norway	13.2	m	15.0
Switzerland	15.0	15.4	16.1
Other non-OECD countries			
Korea	20.3	22.3	18.0

Vertical bars indicate breaks in series which may affect the comparability over time
Source: OECD Database. See Annex 3 for notes

P31: STAFF EMPLOYED IN EDUCATION

This indicator shows the percentage of the labour force employed in education.

POLICY CONTEXT

The percentage of the labour force employed in education is an indicator of the proportion of total economic resources that are tied up in education. The number of persons employed as either teachers or educational support personnel is one of the two main factors – the other being the level of compensation for educational staff (see Indicator P35) – that determine the financial resources that countries must commit to education. The extent to which teachers work on a part-time basis can be an indication of the relative flexibility of the specialised education labour market, which is largely within the public sector.

KEY RESULTS

Overall, the teaching force comprises a significant proportion of the labour force in all OECD countries. At the combined primary and secondary level of education, teaching personnel accounts, on average, for 2.8 per cent of the labour force and at the tertiary level for 0.5 per cent. However, there is substantial variation among countries. Including educational and administrative personnel as well as other support staff in the education sector, the percentage of the labour force employed at all levels of education rises, on average, to 5.5 per cent across OECD countries.

In almost half of the countries, administrative and support staff represent between 30 and 40 per cent of persons employed in education, with a high of more than 50 per cent in the United States and a low of 8 per cent in Turkey.

Whereas women outnumber men as teachers at the primary and lower secondary level of education in most OECD countries, at the upper secondary and especially at the tertiary level there is generally a significantly larger proportion of male teachers.

DESCRIPTION AND INTERPRETATION

The number of teachers employed either full- or part-time in primary and secondary education combined ranges from less than 1.8 per cent of the total labour force in Japan and Korea to over 3.5 per cent in Belgium, Hungary and Italy. At the tertiary level this percentage ranges from less than 0.4 per cent in Denmark, Italy, the Netherlands, Turkey and the United Kingdom to more than 0.7 per cent in Belgium and Canada (see Chart P31.1).

The variation among countries cannot be accounted for solely by differences in the size of the school-age population, but is also affected by the average size of classes, the number of hours that students attend class each day, the length of a teacher's working day, the number of classes or students for which a teacher is responsible and the division of the teacher's time between teaching and other duties.

In all countries for which such a distinction is available, the majority of teaching staff are under full-time contracts. In Italy, Mexico and Turkey all teachers are employed full-time, and in countries such as Finland, Korea and Spain the proportion of teachers employed part-time is still less than 10 per cent. At the other end of the scale are Belgium, Canada, Denmark, Germany, the Netherlands and New Zealand, where between 25.2 and 48.2 per cent of all teachers are employed part-time.

With the exception of the Netherlands and Turkey, women outnumber men at the primary and lower secondary level of education in all countries (see Chart P31.2). In the Czech Republic, Hungary and Italy the percentage of female teachers exceeds 80 per cent. At the upper secondary level the percentage of female teachers ranges from less than 25 per cent in Germany, Japan, Korea and the Netherlands to between 50 and 65 per cent in Canada, the Czech Republic, Hungary, Ireland, Italy and the United States. At the tertiary level, male teachers form the majority in all countries for which such data are available, with the proportion of female teachers ranging from between less than 20 per cent in Japan, the Netherlands and the United Kingdom to just 40 per cent in Iceland. Women are thus under-represented in the better paid teaching jobs at the higher levels of education.

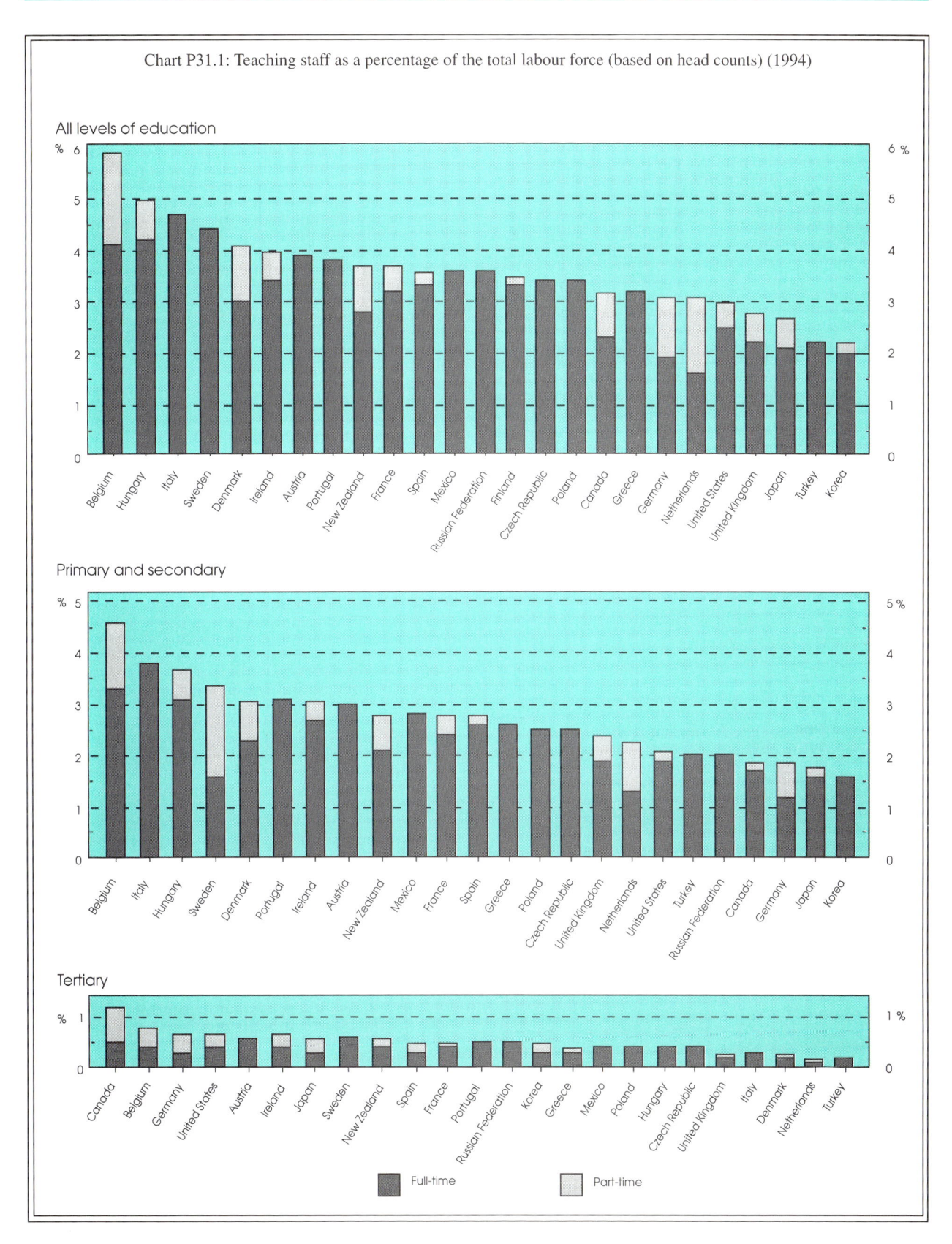

P31: Staff employed in education

Chart P31.1: Teaching staff as a percentage of the total labour force (based on head counts) (1994)

All levels of education

Countries (left to right): Belgium, Hungary, Italy, Sweden, Denmark, Ireland, Austria, Portugal, New Zealand, France, Spain, Mexico, Russian Federation, Finland, Czech Republic, Poland, Canada, Greece, Germany, Netherlands, United States, United Kingdom, Japan, Turkey, Korea.

Primary and secondary

Countries (left to right): Belgium, Italy, Hungary, Sweden, Denmark, Portugal, Ireland, Austria, New Zealand, Mexico, France, Spain, Greece, Poland, Czech Republic, United Kingdom, Netherlands, United States, Turkey, Russian Federation, Canada, Germany, Japan, Korea.

Tertiary

Countries (left to right): Canada, Belgium, Germany, United States, Austria, Ireland, Japan, Sweden, New Zealand, Spain, France, Portugal, Russian Federation, Korea, Greece, Mexico, Poland, Hungary, Czech Republic, United Kingdom, Italy, Denmark, Netherlands, Turkey.

Legend: Full-time, Part-time

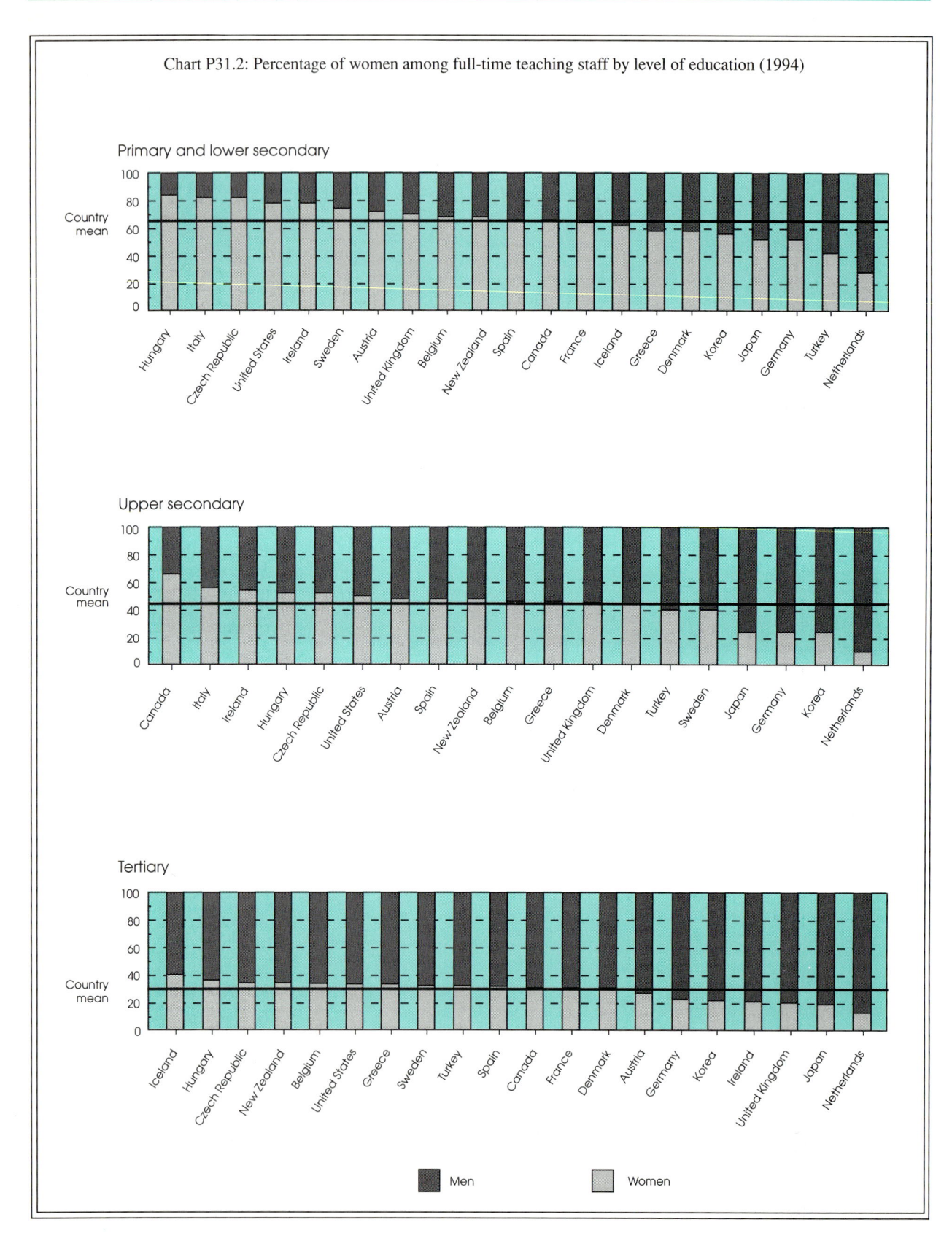

P31: Staff employed in education

Chart P31.2: Percentage of women among full-time teaching staff by level of education (1994)

Primary and lower secondary

Countries (left to right): Hungary, Italy, Czech Republic, United States, Ireland, Sweden, Austria, United Kingdom, Belgium, New Zealand, Spain, Canada, France, Iceland, Greece, Denmark, Korea, Japan, Germany, Turkey, Netherlands

Upper secondary

Countries (left to right): Canada, Italy, Ireland, Hungary, Czech Republic, United States, Austria, Spain, New Zealand, Belgium, Greece, United Kingdom, Denmark, Turkey, Sweden, Japan, Germany, Korea, Netherlands

Tertiary

Countries (left to right): Iceland, Hungary, Czech Republic, New Zealand, Belgium, United States, Greece, Sweden, Turkey, Spain, Canada, France, Denmark, Austria, Germany, Korea, Ireland, United Kingdom, Japan, Netherlands

■ Men   □ Women

P31: Staff employed in education

In most countries the proportion of support staff is comparatively low. However, in Canada, Denmark, France, Hungary and the United States, educational and administrative personnel and other support staff in the education sector represent between 2.4 and 3.7 per cent of the labour force. In these countries the percentage of all educational staff in the labour force ranges from 5.6 to 7.3 per cent.

DEFINITIONS

This indicator gives the numbers of full-time and part-time teaching staff, non-teaching staff and all educational personnel as percentages of the total labour force in each country. The figures include staff employed in primary, secondary and tertiary education in both public and private schools and other institutions. Teachers are defined as persons whose professional activity involves the transmitting of knowledge, attitudes and skills that are stipulated in a formal curriculum to students enrolled in a formal educational institution (see also the Glossary). Non-teaching staff includes two categories: *i)* other pedagogical staff such as principals, supervisors, counsellors, psychologists, librarians, etc.; and *ii)* support staff such as clerical personnel, building and maintenance personnel, food service workers, etc. The figures on the size of the total labour force are taken from OECD's *Labour Force Statistics*. The stipulation of full-time employment is generally based on "statutory hours", or "normal or statutory working hours" (as opposed to actual or total working time or actual teaching time). Part-time employment (see column 4 in Table P31.1) generally refers to persons who have been employed to perform less than 90 per cent of the number of statutory working hours required of a full-time employee.

P31: Staff employed in education

Table P31.1:
Staff employed in public and private education as a percentage of the total labour force (1994) (based on head counts)

	Teaching staff: Primary and secondary education	Teaching staff: Tertiary education	Teaching staff: All levels of education combined (including early childhood education)	Percentage of part-time teachers for all levels of education combined	Educational, Administrative/Professional support personnel and other support staff	All staff (teaching, educational, administrative, support)	Student enrolments as a percentage of labour force
North America							
Canada	1.9	1.2	3.2	27.5	2.4	5.6	48.0
Mexico	2.8	0.4	3.6	a	1.3	4.9	77.6
United States	2.1	0.7	3.0	15.5	3.7	6.8	49.8
Pacific Area							
Australia	m	m	m	m	m	m	54.8
Japan	1.7	0.6	2.6	21.1	0.7	3.3	39.7
New Zealand	2.8	0.5	3.8	25.2	m	m	61.1
European Union							
Austria	3.0	0.6	3.9	m	m	m	41.2
Belgium	4.5	0.8	5.9	31.0	1.4	7.3	61.1
Denmark	3.1	0.3	4.1	27.0	2.9	7.0	41.2
Finland	x	x	3.5	5.0	1.3	4.9	45.4
France	2.8	0.5	3.7	12.8	2.4	6.1	59.1
Germany	1.9	0.7	3.1	38.7	m	m	42.4
Greece	2.6	0.4	3.2	m	m	m	48.7
Ireland	3.1	0.6	4.1	15.4	m	m	74.6
Italy	3.8	0.3	4.7	a	m	m	49.4
Luxembourg	m	m	m	m	m	m	m
Netherlands	2.3	0.3	3.1	48.2	m	m	52.2
Portugal	3.1	0.5	3.8	m	1.3	5.1	48.9
Spain	2.8	0.5	3.6	9.3	m	m	63.7
Sweden	3.4	0.6	4.4	x	m	m	44.6
United Kingdom	2.4	0.3	2.8	22.6	m	m	49.2
Other OECD countries							
Czech Republic	2.5	0.4	3.4	x	1.6	5.0	42.5
Hungary	3.7	0.4	5.0	15.4	2.4	7.3	49.7
Iceland	m	m	m	m	m	m	m
Norway	m	m	m	m	m	m	49.0
Switzerland	m	m	m	m	m	m	35.8
Turkey	2.0	0.2	2.2	a	0.2	2.4	57.4
Country mean	**2.8**	**0.5**	**3.7**	**18.5**	**1.8**	**5.5**	**51.5**
Other non-OECD countries							
Korea	1.6	0.5	2.2	9.7	0.6	2.8	57.1
Poland	2.5	0.4	3.4	m	m	m	54.7
Russian Federation	2.0	0.5	3.6	m	0.4	4.0	47.9

Source: OECD Database. See Annex 3 for notes

P31: Staff employed in education

Table P31.2:
Percentage of women among full-time teaching staff by level of education (1994)

	Primary and lower secondary education	Upper secondary education	Tertiary education
North America			
Canada	64.8	64.9	30.4
Mexico	m	m	m
United States	78.0	50.1	33.4
Pacific Area			
Australia	m	m	m
Japan	52.0	24.6	18.9
New Zealand	67.8	47.6	34.0
European Union			
Austria	71.2	48.6	27.3
Belgium	68.2	45.9	33.6
Denmark	58.0	44.6	30.3
Finland	m	m	m
France	62.7	x	30.4
Germany	51.1	23.7	22.3
Greece	58.2	45.8	33.3
Ireland	77.2	53.7	21.3
Italy	83.0	56.4	m
Luxembourg	m	m	m
Netherlands	27.1	10.5	12.3
Portugal	m	m	m
Spain	65.3	47.7	31.9
Sweden	72.6	38.7	32.4
United Kingdom	69.5	45.5	19.9
Other OECD countries			
Czech Republic	81.7	50.3	34.7
Hungary	83.1	51.6	36.9
Iceland	60.8	m	39.7
Norway	m	m	m
Switzerland	m	m	m
Turkey	42.0	40.4	32.4
Country mean	**64.7**	**43.9**	**29.2**
Other non-OECD countries			
Korea	55.2	23.7	21.6
Poland	m	m	m
Russian Federation	m	m	m

Source: OECD Database. See Annex 3 for notes

P32: Ratio of students to teaching staff

P32: RATIO OF STUDENTS TO TEACHING STAFF

This indicator shows the ratio of students to teaching staff by level of education.

POLICY CONTEXT

Teachers are the single most important resource in education. The amount of this resource that is available per student is therefore an important indicator. The ratio of students to teaching staff is also a determinant of the financial resources that countries need to devote to education. There is a potential trade-off between low student/teaching staff ratios, on the one hand, and salary levels sufficient to attract qualified teachers, on the other (see also Indicator P35). This trade-off is constrained by many factors, among them inflexibilities in adapting the teacher supply to changing demographic conditions, collective bargaining agreements and the geography of the country. The optimal balance may also be different at different levels of education.

KEY RESULTS

In most countries the ratio of students to teaching staff decreases with the level of education, that is, the higher the level of education, the more teachers there are in comparison to the number of students enrolled. Canada, Sweden and Turkey are the only notable exceptions. For public and private institutions the OECD average ratio of students to teaching staff is 18 : 1 at the early childhood and primary level, 16 : 1 at the lower secondary level, and 13 : 1 at the upper secondary level (as explained below, this student/teaching staff ratio can not be interpreted as a measure of class size).

Declining birth rates in OECD countries since the early 1960s (see Indicator C3) have provided an opportunity of improving students' access to teachers, which is reflected in the overall decline in student/teaching staff ratios.

DESCRIPTION AND INTERPRETATION

Austria, Denmark, Hungary, and Italy report the most favourable student/teaching staff ratios for students in public and private primary schools with less than twelve students for each teacher whereas Germany, Ireland, Korea, Mexico, the Netherlands, New Zealand, Turkey and the United Kingdom, report ratios that exceed 20 : 1 (see Chart P32). At the lower secondary level Austria, Denmark and Italy report ratios of less than 10 : 1 whereas the ratios in Canada, Korea and Turkey exceed 19 : 1. The pattern at the upper secondary level is similar although the ratios tend to be slightly smaller. An exception is Turkey, where the ratio at the upper secondary level is substantially lower (about 14 : 1); this must be seen in the context of a significant decrease in participation rates at the upper secondary level (see also Indicator P1).

At the early childhood level the ratio of children to teaching staff is less than 13 : 1 in the Czech Republic, Denmark, Hungary, Italy, New Zealand and the Russian Federation, whereas it is larger than 24 : 1 in France, Ireland, Korea and Mexico. However, the number of statutory hours for full-time attendance differs widely between countries at the early childhood level. In some countries children attend early childhood programmes for only a few hours a day and thus use less teaching time than in other countries where children participate on a full-day basis. To a lesser extent this qualification applies also to the primary level of education.

It must be emphasised that the ratio of students to teaching staff is not an indicator of class size. The fact that one country has a lower ratio of students to teaching staff than another does not necessarily imply that classes are smaller in the first country or that students in the first country receive more instruction. The relationship between the student/teaching staff ratio and both average class size and the amount of instruction per student is complicated, for example by differences among countries in the length of the school year, the number of hours that a student attends class each day, the length of a teacher's working day, the number of classes or students for which a teacher is responsible, and the division of the teacher's time between teaching and other duties.

In most OECD countries there has been a significant decrease in student/teaching staff ratios since 1985 at both the primary and secondary levels of education (see Table P32t), most markedly in Denmark, Germany, Ireland (for both primary and secondary levels combined), Italy, Spain and Turkey (for primary level only). This trend is influenced both by the desire of teachers and parents to improve student access to teaching resources by means of smaller classes, and by the political difficulty of reducing teacher numbers in proportion to falling enrolments caused by demographic decline.

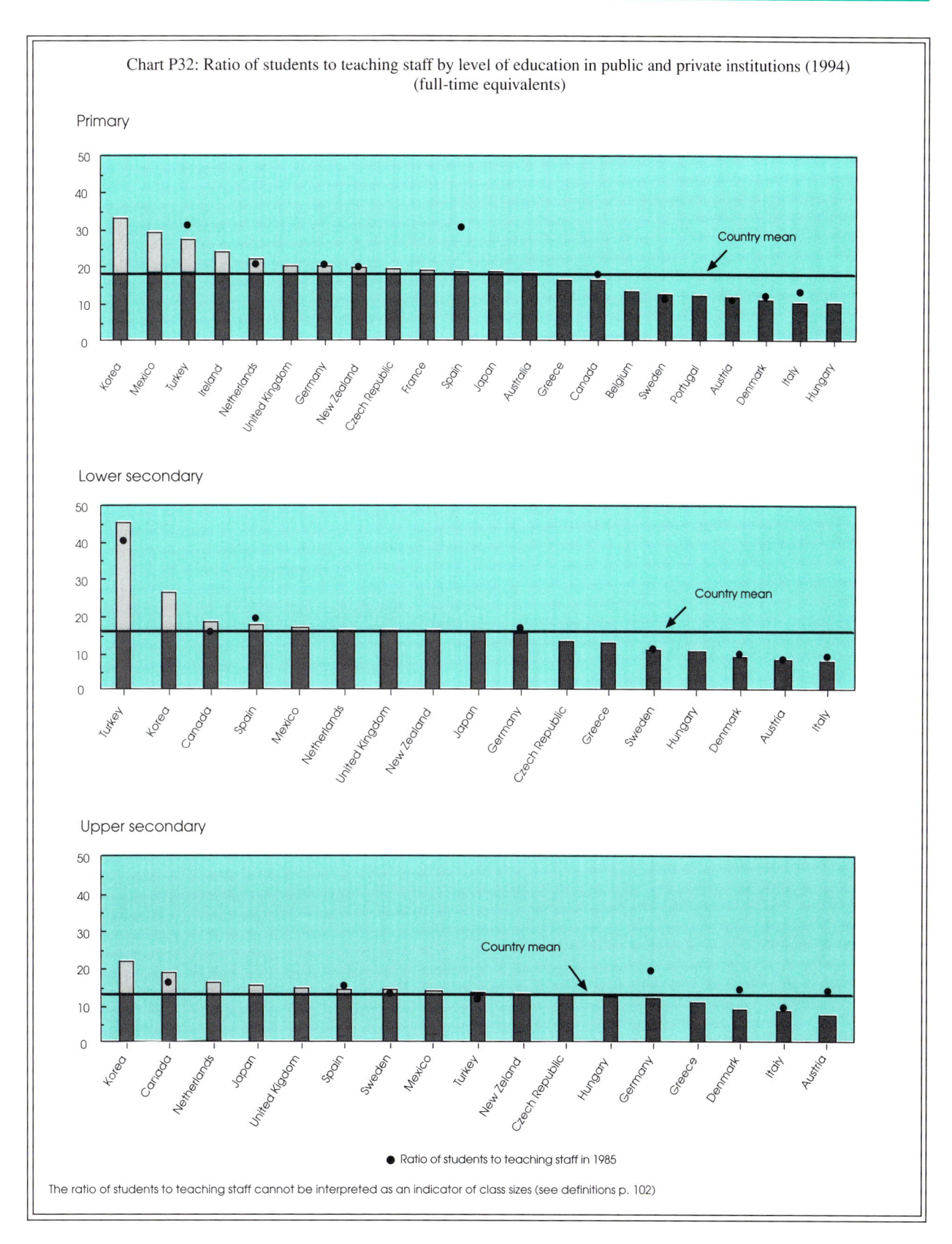

P32: Ratio of students to teaching staff

Chart P32: Ratio of students to teaching staff by level of education in public and private institutions (1994) (full-time equivalents)

Primary

Korea	~33
Mexico	~30
Turkey	~28
Ireland	~25
Netherlands	~22
United Kingdom	~21
Germany	~21
New Zealand	~20
Czech Republic	~20
France	~20
Spain	~19
Japan	~19
Australia	~19
Greece	~17
Canada	~17
Belgium	~14
Sweden	~13
Portugal	~13
Austria	~12
Denmark	~11
Italy	~10
Hungary	~10

Lower secondary

Turkey	~46
Korea	~27
Canada	~19
Spain	~18
Mexico	~17
Netherlands	~17
United Kingdom	~17
New Zealand	~17
Japan	~17
Germany	~17
Czech Republic	~14
Greece	~13
Sweden	~11
Hungary	~11
Denmark	~9
Austria	~9
Italy	~8

Upper secondary

Korea	~22
Canada	~19
Netherlands	~17
Japan	~16
United Kingdom	~15
Spain	~15
Sweden	~15
Mexico	~14
Turkey	~14
New Zealand	~14
Czech Republic	~14
Hungary	~13
Germany	~13
Greece	~11
Denmark	~9
Italy	~8
Austria	~7

● Ratio of students to teaching staff in 1985

The ratio of students to teaching staff cannot be interpreted as an indicator of class sizes (see definitions p. 102)

P32: Ratio of students to teaching staff

While the national average student/teaching staff ratio is an important benchmark, not all students in a country may have the same access to educational resources. Chart P32-R shows that the student/teaching staff ratio differs significantly between regions within the twelve countries reporting such data.

In public primary schools, the regions with the highest and lowest student/teaching staff ratios differ merely by a factor of 1.1 in the Netherlands, whereas in Switzerland the highest regional student/teaching staff ratio for such schools is more than twice the lowest. In public secondary schools, the disparities are often greater, ranging from a factor of 1.1 in the Netherlands to more than a factor of 3 in the United States. Regional differences of this kind may have a number of causes. Education in different geographic or socio-economic settings may have different needs to meet and thus requires different treatment. The results need to be treated with caution because the regions depicted in the chart do not always correspond to the locus of decision-making where student/teacher ratios are determined (see also Table F3-R).

DEFINITIONS

This indicator shows the ratio of students to teaching staff, obtained by dividing the number of full-time-equivalent students at a given level of education by the number of full-time-equivalent teachers at the same level and for the same type of institutions. The definitions that were applied to obtain regional student/teaching staff ratios may not be fully comparable across countries even though they are internally consistent within each country.

A brief description of the regions that have been employed as well as their size in terms of population and enrolment are shown in Table F3-R.

Table P32t:
Ratio of students to teaching staff in primary and secondary education (1985-94) (calculations based on full-time equivalents)

	1985	1990	1994
North America			
Canada	16.9	15.9	17.7
Mexico	29.4	26.6	25.1
Pacific Area			
New Zealand	m	m	17.1
European Union			
Austria	11.4	10.2	9.1
Denmark	12.2	11.0	9.8
Germany	17.2	15.6	16.0
Ireland	21.5	21.6	19.5
Italy	11.1	10.1	9.0
Netherlands	16.3	m	19.1
Spain	21.7	19.0	17.0
Sweden	11.7	10.8	12.6
United Kingdom	m	17.3	17.8
Other OECD countries			
Turkey	27.1	27.3	25.8
Other non-OECD countries			
Korea	36.8	29.5	28.0

Vertical bars indicate breaks in series which may affect the comparability over time
The ratio of students to teaching staff can not be interpreted as an indicator of class sizes (see definitions)
Source: OECD Database. See Annex 3 for notes

P32: Ratio of students to teaching staff

Chart P32-R: Ratio of students to teaching staff in public and private institutions at the primary and secondary level, by region (1994) (calculations based on full-time equivalents)

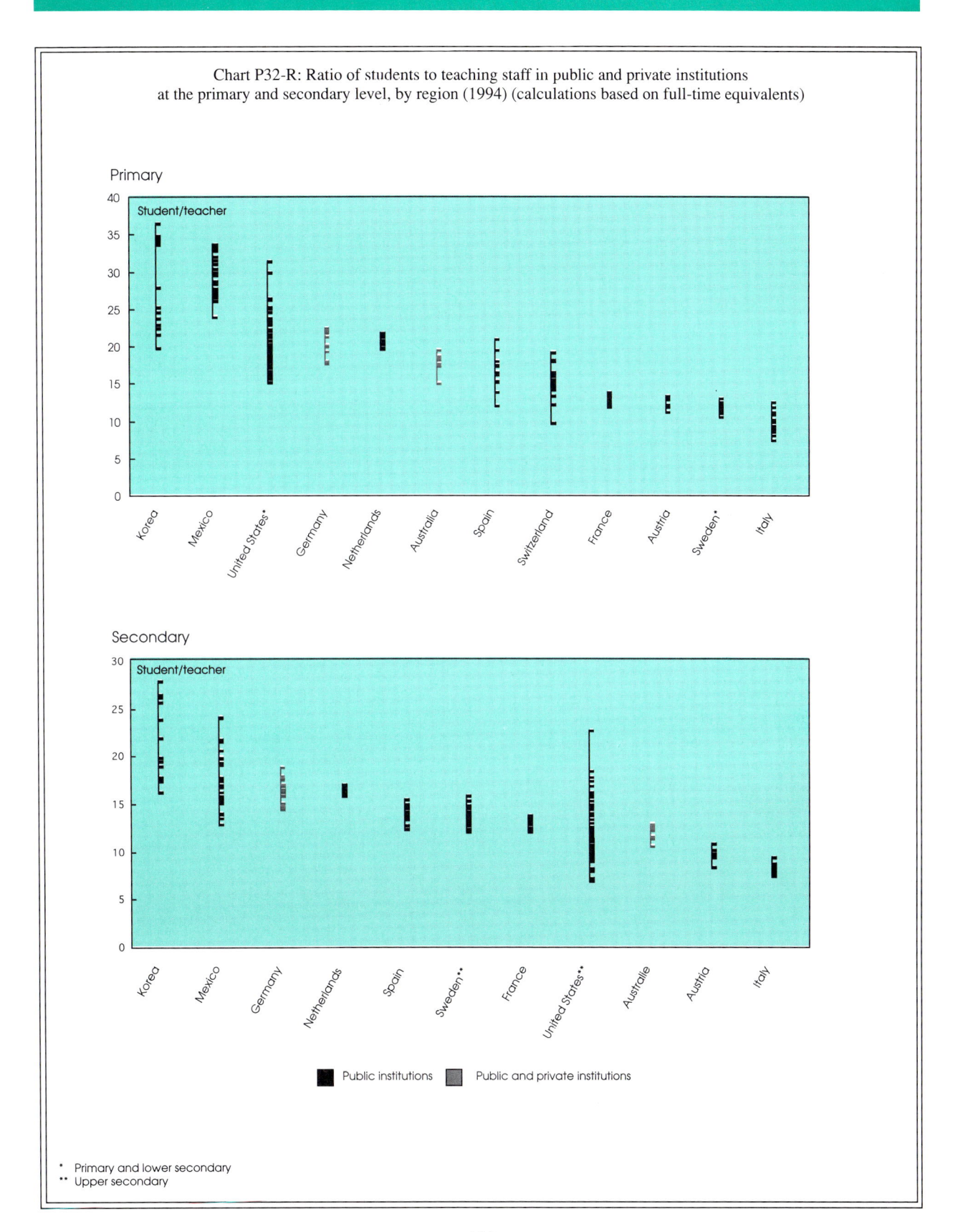

Primary

Secondary

Public institutions   Public and private institutions

* Primary and lower secondary
** Upper secondary

103

P32: Ratio of students to teaching staff

Table P32:
Ratio of students to teaching staff by level of education (1994) (calculations based on full-time equivalents)

| | \multicolumn{5}{c|}{Public education} | \multicolumn{5}{c|}{Public and private education} |
	Early childhood education	Primary education	Lower secondary education	Upper secondary education	All secondary education	Early childhood education	Primary education	Lower secondary education	Upper secondary education	All secondary education
North America										
Canada	20.7	16.7	18.9	19.1	19.0	20.5	16.5	19.1	19.1	19.1
Mexico	25.2	29.2	19.1	16.6	18.3	24.5	29.1	17.6	14.3	16.4
United States	m	m	m	m	m	m	m	m	m	m
Pacific Area										
Australia	m	18.3	m	m	m	m	18.5	m	m	m
Japan	13.5	19.2	16.3	14.9	15.6	17.6	19.2	16.2	15.8	16.0
New Zealand	11.3	20.5	16.9	13.1	15.0	9.6	20.2	16.7	13.2	15.0
European Union										
Austria	17.4	11.8	8.2	7.8	8.0	18.2	11.9	8.3	7.8	8.1
Belgium	16.1	13.2	x	x	7.4	19.3	13.3	x	x	8.5
Denmark	12.4	11.2	9.2	9.2	9.2	12.4	11.0	9.0	9.1	9.0
Finland	m	m	m	m	m	m	m	m	m	m
France	24.7	19.3	x	x	13.2	24.8	19.6	x	x	13.7
Germany	19.0	20.4	15.7	12.4	14.6	23.1	20.5	15.7	12.0	14.4
Greece	15.6	16.5	13.3	11.4	12.3	15.8	16.5	13.1	11.1	12.1
Ireland	25.7	24.4	x	x	16.4	25.4	24.3	x	x	16.1
Italy	11.7	9.9	8.0	9.2	8.6	13.0	10.2	8.0	8.9	8.5
Luxembourg	m	m	m	m	m	m	m	m	m	m
Netherlands	m	m	m	m	m	21.1	22.4	16.9	16.5	16.7
Portugal	17.1	12.1	x	x	13.0	19.0	12.2	x	x	13.1
Spain	18.8	17.6	17.1	13.7	14.8	19.8	19.2	18.2	14.8	16.0
Sweden	m	12.4	10.8	14.7	12.7	m	12.5	10.9	14.6	12.7
United Kingdom	21.6	21.7	17.8	12.9	15.2	21.6	20.7	16.9	15.1	15.8
Other OECD countries										
Czech Republic	11.5	19.6	13.4	12.4	12.9	11.5	19.7	13.4	12.8	13.1
Hungary	11.3	10.2	10.7	11.8	11.2	11.2	10.2	10.7	12.4	11.5
Iceland	m	m	m	m	m	m	m	m	m	m
Norway	m	m	m	m	m	m	m	m	m	m
Switzerland	18.7	15.3	12.8	m	m	m	m	m	m	m
Turkey	16.2	27.6	44.5	14.6	24.2	16.1	27.4	45.6	14.1	23.7
Country mean	**17.3**	**17.5**	**15.8**	**12.9**	**13.8**	**18.1**	**17.9**	**16.0**	**13.2**	**14.0**
Other non-OECD countries										
Korea	21.0	33.0	26.2	19.8	23.9	26.0	33.2	26.8	22.4	24.6
Poland	m	m	m	m	m	m	m	m	m	m
Russian Federation	9.1	m	m	m	m	9.1	m	m	m	m

The ratio of students to teaching staff cannot be interpreted as an indicator of class sizes (see definitions p. 102)
Source: OECD Database. See Annex 3 for notes

Chapter 3
ACCESS TO EDUCATION, PARTICIPATION AND PROGRESSION

National economies are now global in their competitive outlook and crucially dependent upon the availability of human talent. Reliance upon a narrow intellectual elite appears increasingly outmoded. Modern manufacturing and service industry techniques demand a labour force capable of adjusting to new technologies and making informed decisions. Educated and highly-skilled workers are increasingly viewed as one of the most important economic resources. In this context, societies have an interest in ensuring broad access to educational opportunities. Information on enrolment rates at the different levels of education and the expected duration of schooling can provide a picture of the size and structure of education systems as well as of access to education.

Indicator P1 gives a broad comparison of enrolment rates in school-based education and training in both public and private educational institutions, and compares the expected duration of schooling for 5 to 29 year-olds among countries. This information not only is important in itself but also provides important background information for the interpretation of Indicators F1, F13 and P31 that deal with national resources invested in education. Finally, Indicator P1 shows how enrolment rates have evolved since the mid-1970s and, in particular, how higher enrolment rates in the post-compulsory phase have generally outweighed the impact of lower birth rates, leading to an overall increase in the number of full-time participants in formal education.

While Indicator P1 provides an overall picture of the size of education systems, the remaining indicators in this chapter provide more detail on access, participation and progression at the different levels of education.

Early childhood education and initial programmes in primary schooling are important aspects of a strategy aimed at ensuring equal opportunity in foundation learning and at helping children and young people at risk. **Indicator P2** describes the participation of very young children in pre-primary and primary programmes and examines the average duration of education for children up to the age of six.

A range of factors, among them the increased risk of unemployment and other forms of exclusion for young people with insufficient education, have strengthened the incentive for young people to stay enrolled beyond the end of compulsory schooling. Patterns of participation towards the end of compulsory education and beyond are examined in **Indicator P3**. This indicator shows the age boundaries in the transition from secondary to tertiary education, and compares the relative size of enrolments in general education and both school-based and combined school and work-based vocational education at the upper secondary level across countries.

Indicator P6 examines participation in non-university and university-level tertiary education.

Finally, **Indicator P8** presents data on participation in job-related continuing education and training, that is, participation in education beyond the formal school system. This indicator is of particular importance at a time when governments can no longer solely rely on a policy of gradually expanding initial schooling to meet the demands for new and high-level competencies generated by the economy. Continuing education and training gives individuals an opportunity to upgrade and/or complement previously received education and training. It allows employers to maintain a productive workforce and is a means used by governments to stimulate the economy and to promote equity.

P1: Participation in formal education

P1: PARTICIPATION IN FORMAL EDUCATION

This indicator shows enrolment rates at the different levels of education and the expected duration of schooling.

POLICY CONTEXT

A well-educated population is critical for the current and future economic and social development of a country. Virtually everyone participates in formal education during some stage of his or her life. Information on enrolment rates at the different levels of education and the expected duration of schooling can provide an overall picture of the level of participation in the formal education system. Indicator P1 should be seen together with Indicator P8 on job-related continuing education and training which provides some indication on participation in education beyond the formal school system.

KEY RESULTS

In more than half of OECD countries, over 60 per cent of the population aged 5 to 29 years are enrolled in education. Naturally, there is considerably more variation in enrolment rates among countries at pre-primary and tertiary levels than at primary and secondary levels. At the tertiary level enrolment rates range from less than 3 to more than 15 per cent of the population aged 5 to 29. Students are predominantly enrolled in public institutions, particularly at the lower levels of education.

In almost all countries higher enrolment rates in the post-compulsory phase have outweighed lower birth rates, so that the number of full-time participants in formal education has generally increased since the mid-1970s.

A 5 year-old child in the OECD is typically expected to attend school for between 14.5 and 16.5 years but there are considerable differences among countries. School expectancy has increased since the mid-1980s, in many countries by more than a year.

DESCRIPTION AND INTERPRETATION

Overall participation of 5-29 year-olds in education

In most OECD countries, virtually all 5 to 14 year-olds are enrolled in education (see Chart P1.1). In countries where lower rates (below 95 per cent) are reported, compulsory schooling either begins late or ends early.

Participation beyond the age of 14 varies much more – from less than 20 per cent in the population aged 15 to 29 in Japan, Mexico and Turkey to over 40 per cent in Australia, Belgium, Canada, Denmark, Finland, Iceland, the Netherlands and Norway.

In some countries, particularly in Australia, Belgium, Sweden and the United States, a significant portion of the population aged 30 to 39 years is enrolled in formal education.

The variation in enrolment rates among countries in the population aged 5 to 29 years is largely explained by the uneven weight of tertiary enrolments: from less than 3 tertiary education students per 100 persons in the population aged 5 to 29 in Mexico to more than 15 in Canada and the United States.

Full-time participation of the population aged 5 to 29 years was higher in 1994 in most countries than it was in the mid-1970s – although there are some exceptions. In some countries, such as Canada, New Zealand, Norway, the United Kingdom and the United States, expansion has occurred only since the late 1980s or early 1990s. While in compulsory education enrolment tends to follow the decline in birth rates, in the post-compulsory phase higher enrolment rates appear to have a balancing effect. In some countries, for example, enrolment rates in tertiary education have doubled over the last decade (see Table P1t). Note that Table P1t covers only full-time enrolments while the remaining tables in this indicator extend to both part-time and full-time participation.

School expectancy

Another way of looking at participation in education is to estimate the number of years of education a 5 year-old child might expect to receive up to the age of 29 (see Chart P1.2). This varies from just over 9 years in Turkey to around 17 years in Belgium and the Netherlands. Typically, school expectancy is in the range of 14.5 to 16.5 years.

School expectancy has increased in recent years in almost all countries for which data are available. The increase since 1985 exceeds more than one year in many countries, and in the Nordic countries it is even more than 18 months. Longer duration of schooling is another

P1: Participation in formal education

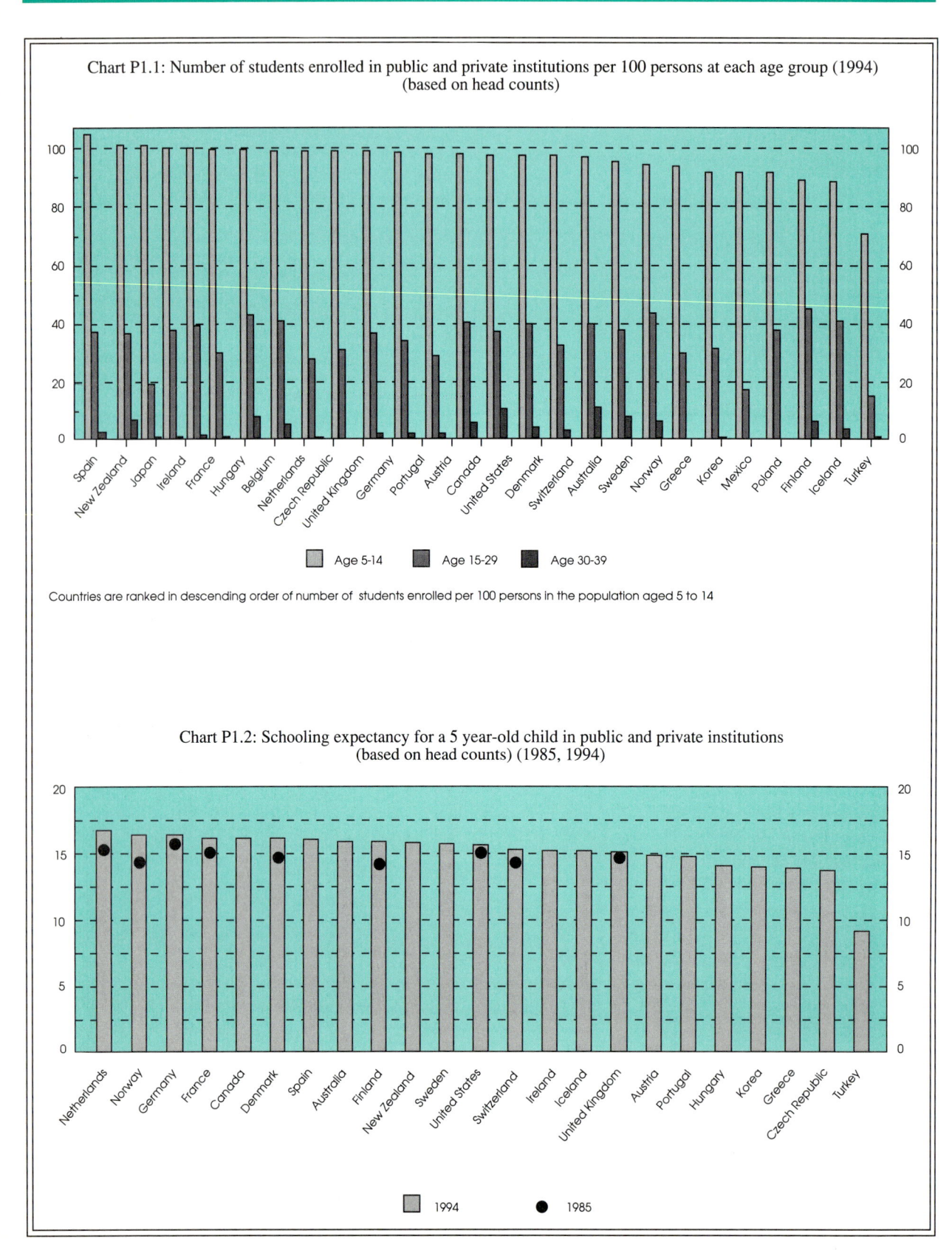

Chart P1.1: Number of students enrolled in public and private institutions per 100 persons at each age group (1994) (based on head counts)

Age 5-14 ■ Age 15-29 ■ Age 30-39

Countries are ranked in descending order of number of students enrolled per 100 persons in the population aged 5 to 14

Chart P1.2: Schooling expectancy for a 5 year-old child in public and private institutions (based on head counts) (1985, 1994)

□ 1994   ● 1985

P1: Participation in formal education

factor that contributes to the observed rise in enrolment rates over recent decades.

Participation by level of education

In all countries the majority of participants are enrolled in the lower levels of education – typically the compulsory or pre-compulsory phases (see Chart P1.3). In Australia, Ireland and New Zealand, enrolments in primary and lower secondary education represent over 40 per cent of the 5 to 29 year-olds – compared with enrolment rates of less than 30 per cent in Austria, Hungary, Italy, Spain, and Turkey. Variations in enrolment rates at these levels among countries are heavily influenced by the proportion of the population who are actually in the relevant age bracket, as well as by the variable lengths of primary and lower secondary programmes (between 8 and 10 years).

In the countries reporting data, enrolments in upper secondary education represent, on average, 14 per cent of the population aged 5 to 29. Mexico is at the lower end of the scale with an enrolment rate of less than 5 per cent. This compares with Belgium, Spain and the United Kingdom where enrolment rates exceed 20 per cent.

At the tertiary level in the Czech Republic, Hungary, Mexico and Turkey enrolment rates in formal education are less than 5 per cent. By contrast, in Canada and the United States, enrolment rates in tertiary education are highest – representing more than 15 per cent of the population aged 5 to 29. Canada, the Russian Federation and the United States show higher enrolment rates at the tertiary level than at the upper secondary level. This reflects partly the longer course lengths at the tertiary level as well as the comparatively high tertiary

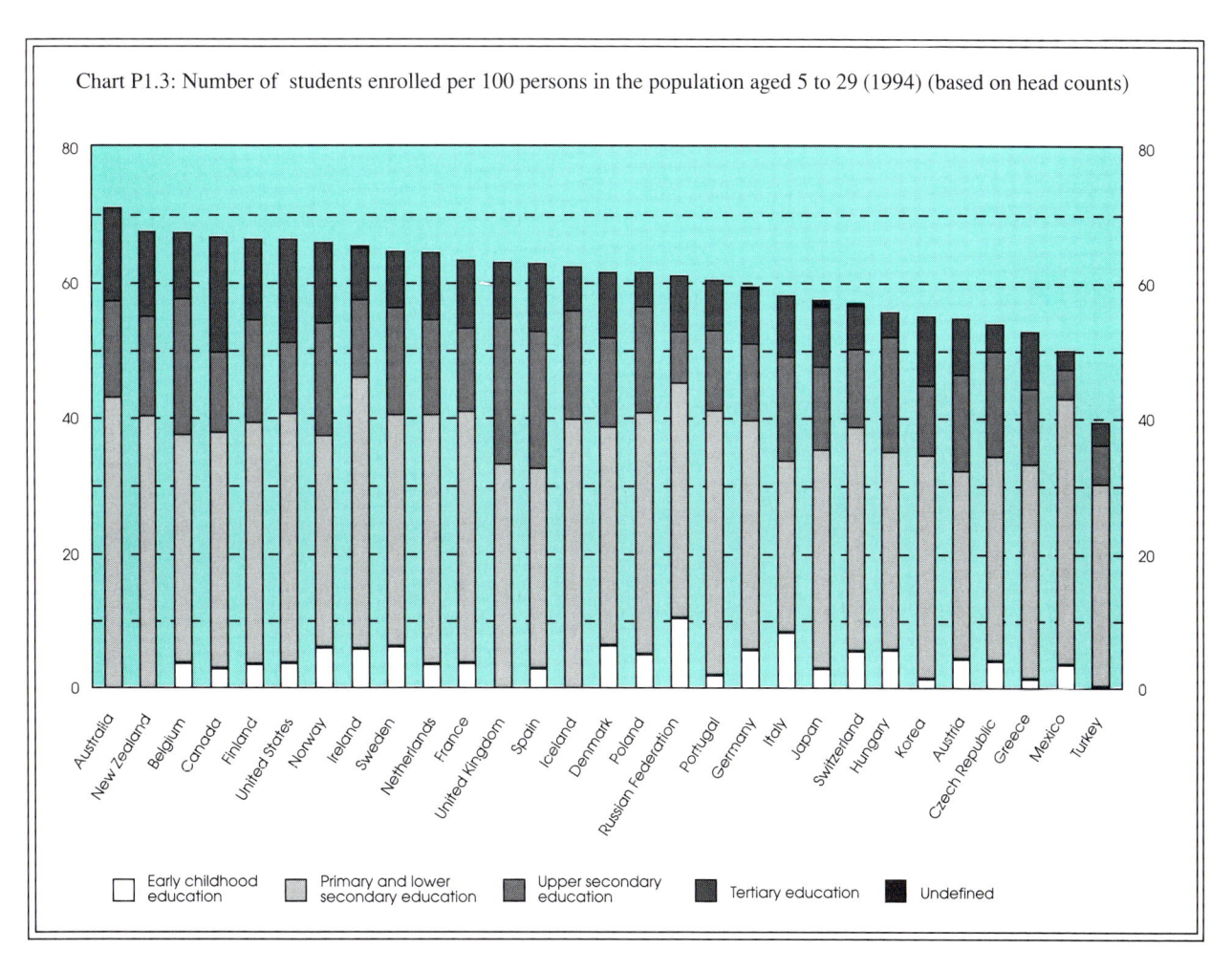

Chart P1.3: Number of students enrolled per 100 persons in the population aged 5 to 29 (1994) (based on head counts)

P1: Participation in formal education

net enrolment rates in these countries. It should, however, be noted that countries differ in the organisation and allocation of programmes to the different levels of education. Countries such as Canada and the United States offer technical and vocational programmes at the tertiary level that are similar in content to programmes offered in other countries at the upper secondary level of education.

Participation by type of institution

All OECD countries have both public and private provision of education. Public institutions account for the large majority of provision except in two countries – Belgium and the Netherlands – where government-dependent private institutions predominate. The independent private sector is a fairly important provider in Korea, Portugal and the United States whereas it is almost non-existent in many others.

Participation by gender

In about two-thirds of OECD countries women can expect to receive more years of education than men (see Table P1.2) although in most cases the differences are fairly small – less than 5 months (except in Finland, Spain and Sweden).

DEFINITIONS

This indicator shows the number of students enrolled at the early childhood, primary, secondary and tertiary levels of education per 100 individuals 5 to 29 years of age.

These figures are based on head counts, that is, they do not distinguish between full- and part-time participants. A standardised distinction between full-time and part-time participants is very difficult since many countries do not recognise the concept of part-time study, although in practice at least some of their students would be classified part-time by other countries.

School expectancy under current conditions relative to the 1993/94 school year is obtained by adding the net enrolment rates for each year of age from 5 to 29, and dividing by 100. Should there be a tendency to lengthen (or shorten) studies during the ensuing years, the actual average duration of schooling for the cohort will be higher (or lower). Caution is required when comparing data on school expectancies. Neither the length of the school year nor the quality of education is necessarily the same in each country. Furthermore, the expected number of years also does not necessarily coincide with the expected number of grades of education completed, due to repeating and late entry. It should also be noted that the estimates do not account for many types of continuing education and training.

P1: Participation in formal education

Table P1.1:
Number of students enrolled per 100 persons in the population aged 5 to 29 (1994) (based on head counts)

	Early childhood education	Primary and lower secondary education	Upper secondary education	Tertiary education	Undefined	All levels of education combined	Public institutions	Government-dependent private institutions	Independent private institutions
North America									
Canada	2.9	35.1	11.9	17.2	n	67.2	64.4	1.2	1.5
Mexico	3.5	39.5	4.6	2.8	n	50.4	45.5	a	4.9
United States	3.7	37.0	10.7	15.4	n	66.8	57.7	a	9.2
Pacific Area									
Australia	m	43.2	14.4	14.0	n	71.6	58.3	13.3	0.04
Japan	3.0	32.3	12.6	9.1	1.0	57.9	m	a	m
New Zealand	0.1	40.4	14.9	12.7	n	68.1	63.7	2.7	1.7
European Union									
Austria	4.3	28.0	14.5	8.3	n	55.1	50.2	4.9	x
Belgium	3.8	33.9	20.3	9.8	n	67.8	27.9	39.9	m
Denmark	6.3	32.5	13.2	10.0	n	62.0	57.8	4.1	a
Finland	3.5	35.9	15.5	12.0	n	66.9	64.2	2.7	a
France	3.8	37.3	12.4	10.3	n	63.8	52.6	10.4	0.8
Germany	5.6	34.1	11.5	8.4	0.2	59.7	53.3	6.4	x
Greece	1.5	31.8	11.3	8.6	n	53.1	50.4	n	2.7
Ireland	5.9	40.1	11.8	7.8	0.3	65.9	64.7	a	1.0
Italy	8.3	25.5	15.5	9.3	n	58.6	53.0	a	5.6
Luxembourg	m	m	m	m	m	m	m	m	m
Netherlands	3.5	37.1	14.2	10.1	n	64.9	16.1	48.1	0.6
Portugal	2.0	39.2	12.0	7.6	n	60.8	49.2	2.4	9.2
Spain	2.9	29.7	20.5	10.1	n	63.1	45.8	17.3	x
Sweden	6.1	34.5	16.1	8.4	n	65.2	63.7	1.5	0.1
United Kingdom	0.004	33.3	21.7	8.4	n	63.4	41.4	19.3	2.8
Other OECD countries									
Czech Republic	4.1	30.3	15.7	4.3	n	54.5	52.9	1.6	a
Hungary	5.6	29.5	17.1	4.0	n	56.3	54.9	1.4	a
Iceland	m	39.9	16.2	6.7	n	62.8	m	m	m
Norway	6.0	31.4	17.0	11.9	n	66.3	59.6	6.6	x
Switzerland	5.5	33.3	11.7	6.6	0.3	57.4	52.8	1.9	2.7
Turkey	0.4	29.9	6.0	3.7	n	40.0	39.5	a	0.6
Country mean	**3.8**	**34.4**	**14.0**	**9.1**	**0.1**	**61.1**	**51.5**	**7.4**	**2.3**
Other non-OECD countries									
Korea	1.4	33.2	10.6	10.3	n	55.6	36.7	9.4	9.4
Poland	5.1	35.8	15.9	5.1	n	61.9	61.0	a	0.9
Russian Federation	10.4	34.8	7.9	8.4	n	61.5	61.2	a	0.3

Source: OECD Database. See Annex 3 for notes

P1: Participation in formal education

Table P1.2:
Enrolment rates and school expectancy in public and private institutions (1994) (based on head counts)

	Students aged 5-14 as a percentage of the population aged 5-14	Students aged 15-29 as a percentage of the population aged 15-29	Students aged 30-39 as a percentage of the population aged 30-39	School expectancy for a 5 year-old child M+W 1985	M+W 1994	Men 1994	Women 1994
North America							
Canada	97.8	40.4	5.9	m	16.2	16.1	16.3
Mexico	91.6	17.4	m	m	m	m	m
United States	97.7	37.6	10.7	15.0	15.6	15.5	15.7
Pacific Area							
Australia	97.1	40.0	11.4	m	15.9	15.9	15.8
Japan	101.2	19.3	0.3	m	m	m	m
New Zealand	101.3	37.0	7.0	m	15.8	15.7	15.9
European Union							
Austria	98.0	29.2	2.5	m	14.9	15.2	14.6
Belgium	99.4	43.1	8.2	m	16.9	16.9	17.0
Denmark	97.5	40.0	4.3	14.5	16.2	16.1	16.3
Finland	89.2	45.4	6.3	14.0	15.9	15.4	16.4
France	100.2	39.5	1.7	14.8	16.2	16.1	16.4
Germany	98.8	36.8	2.1	15.6	16.4	16.7	16.1
Greece	93.8	30.2	0.3	m	13.9	14.1	13.7
Ireland	100.3	38.1	1.5	m	15.2	15.1	15.3
Italy	m	m	m	m	m	m	m
Luxembourg	m	m	m	m	m	m	m
Netherlands	99.1	41.0	5.4	15.2	16.8	17.2	16.3
Portugal	98.7	34.0	2.5	m	14.8	14.7	15.0
Spain	104.7	37.5	2.8	m	16.1	15.9	16.5
Sweden	95.3	37.8	8.1	13.4	15.7	15.4	16.0
United Kingdom	98.9	31.0	m	14.8	15.1	15.0	15.3
Other OECD countries							
Czech Republic	98.9	28.2	0.5	m	13.7	13.7	13.7
Hungary	99.7	30.3	1.3	m	14.1	m	m
Iceland	88.6	41.2	3.7	m	15.2	15.1	15.3
Norway	94.4	43.7	6.3	14.0	16.4	16.4	16.5
Switzerland	97.4	32.7	3.3	14.3	15.3	15.9	14.8
Turkey	71.0	15.2	1.4	m	9.2	10.2	8.2
Country mean	**96.4**	**34.7**	**4.2**	**14.6**	**15.3**	**15.4**	**15.3**
Other non-OECD countries							
Korea	91.8	31.6	0.5	m	14.0	14.6	13.4
Poland	91.5	37.9	m	m	m	m	m
Russian Federation	m	m	m	m	m	m	m

Source: OECD Database. See Annex 3 for notes

P1: Participation in formal education

Table P1t: Number of full-time students enrolled in public and private institutions per 100 persons in the population aged 5 to 29 (1975-94)

	All levels of education combined (except early childhood education)				Upper secondary education				Tertiary education			
	1975	1985	1990	1994	1975	1985	1990	1994	1975	1985	1990	1994
North America												
Canada	54.5	52.7	55.6	57.9	12.5	10.6	10.9	11.9	6.7	8.6	9.3	10.8
Mexico	m	m	49.1	46.9	m	m	4.6	4.6	m	m	2.7	2.8
United States	55.6	50.2	52.6	56.5	7.3	10.3	9.7	10.7	6.6	7.4	8.2	8.8
Pacific Area												
Australia	m	m	m	53.7	6.9	6.5	m	6.5	4.5	m	m	6.2
Japan	47.6	m	57.1	53.0	9.7	12.0	13.5	12.2	4.3	m	7.1	8.5
New Zealand	55.1	50.9	53.5	59.7	6.6	7.5	9.5	12.0	2.5	3.0	4.8	7.3
European Union												
Austria	53.0	48.9	49.0	50.2	13.4	16.3	15.0	13.9	2.9	6.5	8.3	8.3
Denmark	53.2	55.6	55.2	55.6	7.4	12.1	12.8	13.2	6.1	6.8	8.2	10.0
Finland	49.2	53.2	58.3	63.4	9.4	13.2	13.2	15.5	5.0	7.3	9.8	12.0
France	51.3	55.1	57.1	60.0	8.7	9.6	12.0	12.4	4.9	6.4	7.7	10.3
Germany	57.2	53.0	49.6	53.7	11.0	15.2	13.0	11.4	4.4	7.1	8.2	8.2
Greece	m	m	m	m	6.8	m	m	10.9	3.4	m	m	8.6
Ireland	51.1	52.4	55.9	57.0	6.1	8.5	10.1	10.7	2.4	3.3	4.4	6.2
Italy	50.8	48.4	48.9	50.3	10.0	11.8	15.5	15.5	4.6	5.5	6.6	9.3
Netherlands	51.0	52.3	51.1	55.8	5.1	8.7	9.3	12.3	4.9	5.5	6.5	7.5
Spain	m	53.9	56.4	57.9	9.0	12.4	15.7	18.2	3.7	5.4	7.5	10.1
Sweden	m	52.2	49.8	50.5	7.4	11.1	10.4	12.0	5.6	6.5	6.7	5.7
United Kingdom	m	48.5	47.1	54.7	11.2	12.7	11.7	12.9	2.5	2.9	3.4	5.3
Other OECD countries												
Norway	m	52.7	53.6	57.5	m	12.7	15.1	16.6	m	4.7	7.6	9.5
Switzerland	41.2	49.4	48.0	50.0	3.2	13.9	13.2	11.5	3.1	4.0	4.7	5.2
Turkey	36.1	37.7	38.8	39.6	3.3	3.8	4.6	6.0	1.5	1.6	2.4	3.7
Other non-OECD countries												
Korea	m	52.1	52.4	52.3	10.2	10.1	11.0	10.4	m	6.0	7.2	8.7

Source: OECD Database. See Annex 3 for notes

P2: Participation by young children

P2: PARTICIPATION BY YOUNG CHILDREN

This indicator shows net enrolment rates of young children in pre-primary and primary programmes.

POLICY CONTEXT

Early childhood education and initial programmes in primary schooling are important aspects of a strategy aimed at ensuring equal opportunity in foundation learning and at assisting children and young people at risk. It is widely recognised that the early years of education play an important role in a child's future, because they shape attitudes to learning and provide basic social skills. Research also indicates that attainments during later years of schooling are related to the cognitive ability of young children. At what age should early childhood education begin? What factors and conditions can make early intervention programmes successful?

KEY RESULTS

Thirteen out of 25 countries report enrolment rates of at least 30 per cent in early childhood education at age 3; 18 countries report enrolment rates of at least 50 per cent for 4 year-olds. At age 6, over 90 per cent of children in all countries listed but four are enrolled in either early childhood or primary education. The transition from early childhood education to primary education takes place at age 5 in a few countries, but occurs in most countries at age 6. By age 7, the vast majority of children are enrolled in primary education.

DESCRIPTION AND INTERPRETATION

This indicator shows rates of participation in early childhood and primary education at each age from age 3 to 6 (Chart P2.1). Participation by young children in education – even in the pre-compulsory years – is becoming increasingly important in OECD countries, and in a few countries it is virtually universal from age 3 (in Belgium and France) or 4 (in the Netherlands, New Zealand and Spain).

Overall, rates of participation increase for each succeeding year of age. At age 3, nine out of 25 countries report enrolment rates of over 50 per cent. Rates vary widely among countries, however, ranging from under 10 per cent in Canada, Ireland, Korea, Mexico, the Netherlands, Switzerland and Turkey to over 90 per cent in Belgium and France. At age 4, enrolment rates rise sharply in several countries. Still, there is significant variation among countries at age 4, with rates ranging from less than 30 per cent in Finland, Korea, Poland, Switzerland and Turkey to over 90 per cent in Belgium, France, Japan, the Netherlands, New Zealand, Spain and the United Kingdom.

Enrolment at age 5 continues to increase, and begins to divide into early childhood and primary education. The vast majority of children in most countries still attend early childhood education institutions, but in two countries (New Zealand and the United Kingdom), the majority of 5 year-olds are enrolled in primary education. At age 6, participation in early childhood and primary education is nearly universal (90 per cent or more) in all but four countries (Finland, Korea, Norway and Turkey). Also at this stage, the balance in enrolments shifts further to primary education, with a majority being enrolled at this level in over half of the countries. In Germany, Hungary, Ireland, Poland, Switzerland and the Nordic countries, on the other hand, the majority of children are still enrolled in early childhood education.

In practice, there is not a clear boundary between the type of education offered in early childhood and primary programmes at these ages. The distinction may be more relevant within a country than among countries, especially if the two programmes take place in different types of institutions or are funded or staffed differently. Typically, the distinction is between pre-compulsory and compulsory schooling. Primary programmes are generally those offered to children in their first years of compulsory schooling (even if some participants are below compulsory school age).

Enrolment rates for young children are affected by differences in reporting practices, for example by the extent to which child-care programmes that mainly offer custodial care have been included in the statistics. Especially for the very youngest children, for whom the natural pace of development limits the pedagogical possibilities, the distinction between early childhood education and organised child care is difficult to operationalise in an internationally consistent way. Countries also differ widely in their approaches to early childhood education. Some approaches focus on

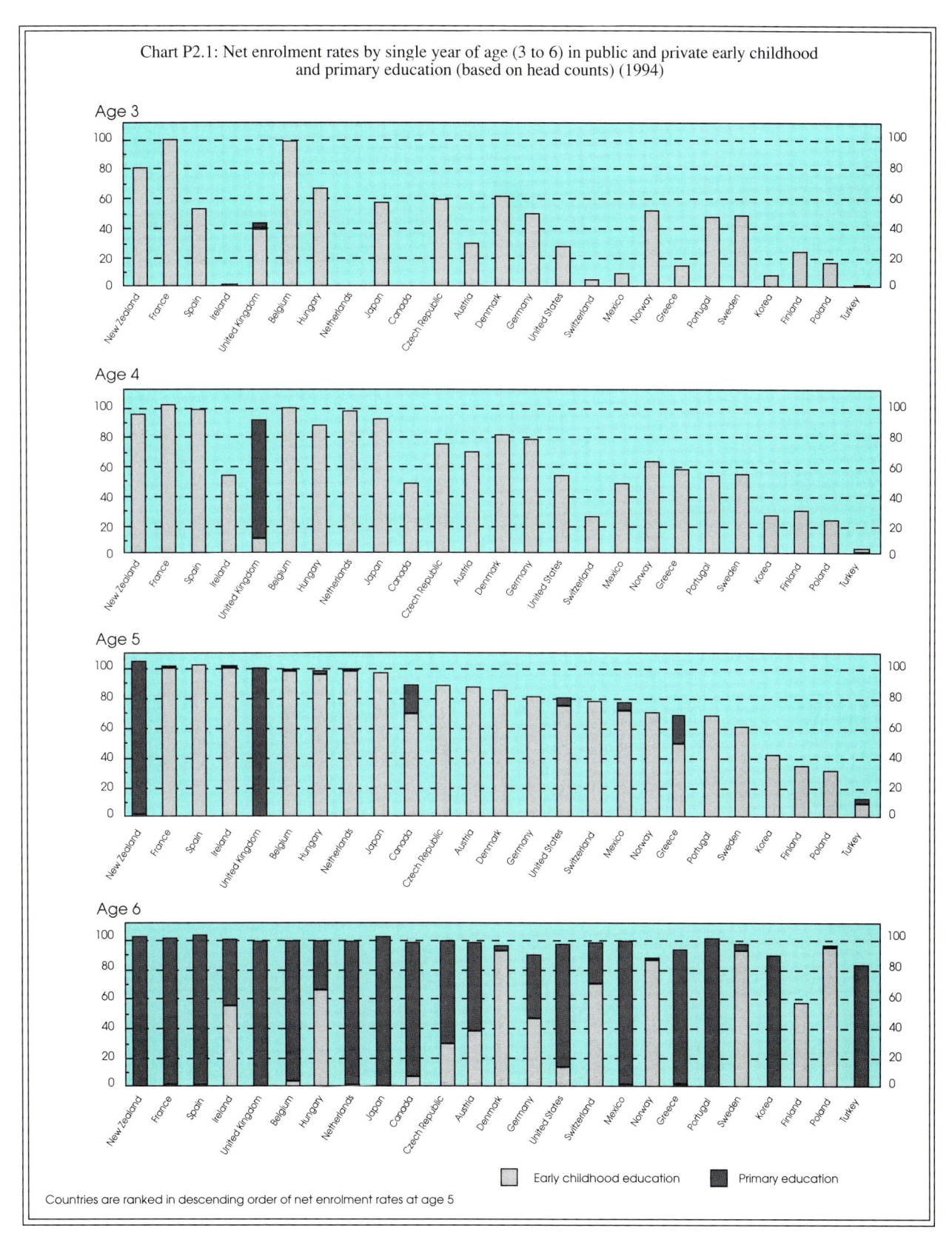

P2: Participation by young children

Chart P2.1: Net enrolment rates by single year of age (3 to 6) in public and private early childhood and primary education (based on head counts) (1994)

Age 3

Age 4

Age 5

Age 6

■ Early childhood education ■ Primary education

Countries are ranked in descending order of net enrolment rates at age 5

P2: Participation by young children

experiential education while others emphasise skill development, academic development, the visual arts or a particular religious faith. In addition, there is great variation in the cost and quality of private day care and pre-school education.

Another way of looking at participation by young children is to measure the expected number of years of education up to the age of 6 (see Chart P2.2). In three countries (Belgium, France and New Zealand) young children receive, on average, more than four years of education before the age of 7, and in a further seven countries (including Denmark, where compulsory schooling does not begin until 7 years of age) children average more than three years of education by age 7.

DEFINITIONS

This indicator shows the number of children enrolled in early childhood and primary programmes from age 3 to age 6 as a percentage of the population of the respective age group.

For this indicator, all children enrolled are counted equally to reflect the number of children participating in early childhood education, regardless of the number of daily hours they participate in programmes.

The expected number of years of early childhood education, primary education, and both levels combined is calculated by adding the net enrolment rates for each single age from 0 to 6 years and dividing the total by 100.

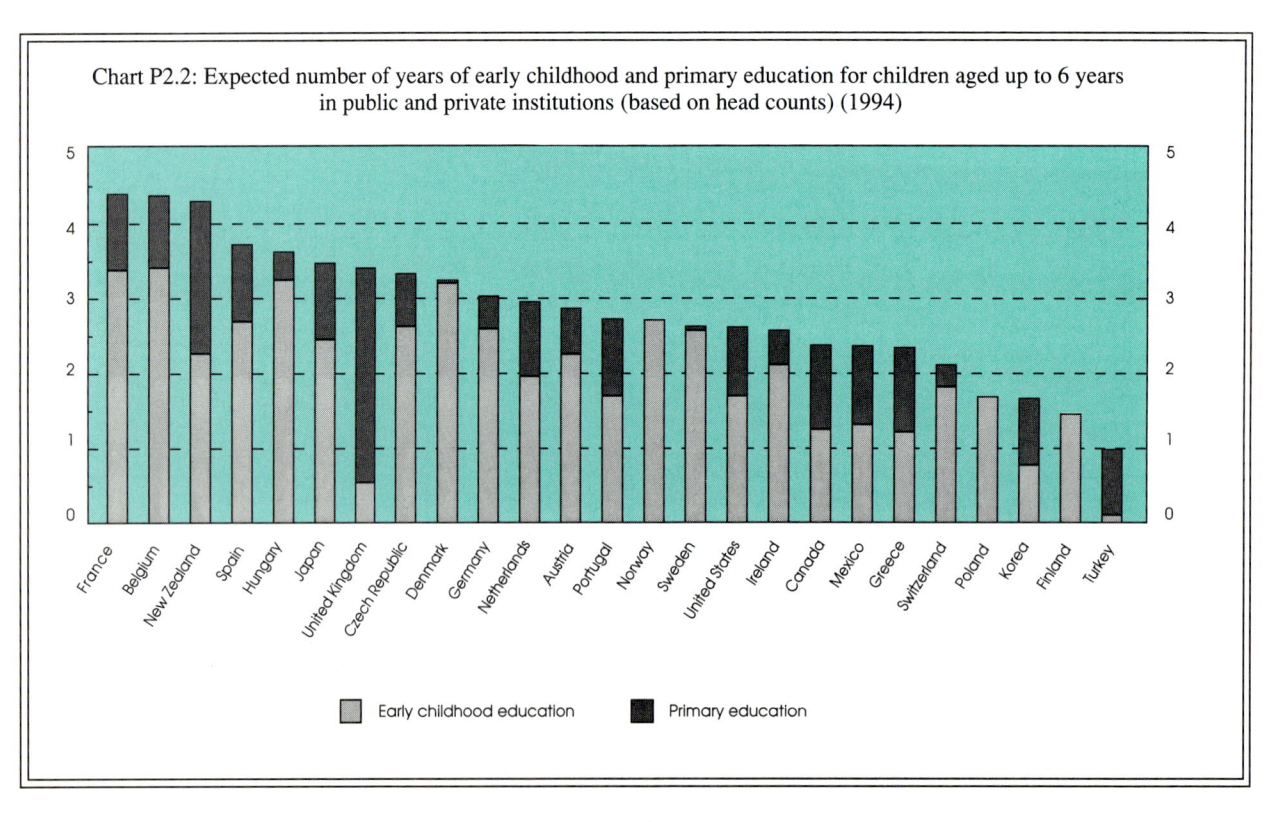

Chart P2.2: Expected number of years of early childhood and primary education for children aged up to 6 years in public and private institutions (based on head counts) (1994)

P2: Participation by young children

Table P2.1:
Net enrolment rates by single year of age (3 to 6) in public and private early childhood and primary education (1994) (based on head counts)

	Age 3 Early childhood education	Age 3 Primary	Age 3 All levels of education combined	Age 4 Early childhood education	Age 4 Primary	Age 4 All levels of education combined	Age 5 Early childhood education	Age 5 Primary	Age 5 All levels of education combined	Age 6 Early childhood education	Age 6 Primary	Age 6 All levels of education combined
North America												
Canada	n	n	n	48.2	n	48.2	69.1	20.4	89.5	7.2	92.2	99.3
Mexico	9.7	a	9.7	48.4	a	48.4	71.8	5.5	77.3	1.7	98.8	100.6
United States	27.6	n	27.6	54.1	n	54.1	74.8	6.1	81.0	13.3	84.6	98.0
Pacific Area												
Australia	m	n	m	m	n	m	m	74.6	m	m	99.2	m
Japan	57.0	a	57.0	91.8	a	91.8	96.2	a	96.2	a	101.9	101.9
New Zealand	80.4	n	80.4	95.7	0.2	95.9	2.4	102.3	104.6	n	101.8	101.8
European Union												
Austria	29.5	n	29.5	69.3	n	69.3	87.0	n	87.0	37.9	61.2	99.1
Belgium	98.2	n	98.2	99.7	n	99.7	98.0	1.4	99.4	4.2	95.6	99.8
Denmark	61.0	n	61.0	81.7	n	81.7	84.7	n	84.7	92.7	3.8	96.5
Finland	24.4	n	24.4	29.9	n	29.9	34.8	n	34.8	56.8	0.8	57.6
France	99.3	n	99.3	101.4	n	101.4	99.9	2.1	102.0	1.1	100.1	101.2
Germany	49.8	n	49.8	78.3	n	78.3	81.2	n	81.2	46.8	43.8	90.7
Greece	14.4	n	14.4	57.6	n	57.6	49.2	20.0	69.2	1.1	91.6	92.6
Ireland	1.0	n	1.0	54.2	n	54.2	100.1	0.3	100.4	55.5	45.3	100.8
Italy	m	m	m	m	m	m	m	m	m	m	m	m
Luxembourg	m	m	m	m	m	m	m	m	m	m	m	m
Netherlands	n	0.1	0.1	97.1	0.4	97.5	98.0	0.6	98.7	0.9	98.2	99.1
Portugal	47.6	n	47.6	54.2	n	54.2	68.6	n	68.6	n	101.6	101.6
Spain	52.7	n	52.7	98.5	n	98.5	102.0	n	102.0	0.2	103.3	103.5
Sweden	48.6	n	48.6	54.5	n	54.5	61.2	n	61.2	92.8	5.3	98.1
United Kingdom	39.6	4.1	43.7	10.9	81.7	92.6	0.1	99.4	99.5	n	99.3	99.3
Other OECD countries												
Czech Republic	59.3	n	59.3	74.7	n	74.7	88.4	n	88.4	29.4	70.6	100.0
Hungary	66.7	n	66.7	87.9	n	87.9	95.5	3.7	99.2	65.4	34.4	99.8
Iceland	m	n	m	m	n	m	m	0.3	m	m	98.4	m
Norway	51.4	n	51.4	62.9	n	62.9	69.8	n	69.8	86.5	0.9	87.5
Switzerland	5.4	n	5.4	26.5	n	26.6	77.7	0.2	78.0	70.0	28.7	99.1
Turkey	0.3	n	0.3	1.7	n	1.7	9.0	4.3	13.2	n	83.1	83.1
Country mean	**40.2**	**0.2**	**40.4**	**64.3**	**3.3**	**67.9**	**70.4**	**13.6**	**82.0**	**28.9**	**69.8**	**96.1**
Other non-OECD countries												
Korea	8.7	n	8.7	26.8	n	26.8	42.2	n	42.2	0.1	89.4	89.5
Poland	17.1	a	17.1	24.3	a	24.3	31.2	a	31.2	94.4	1.3	95.7
Russian Federation	m	m	m	m	m	m	m	m	m	m	m	m

Source: OECD Database. See Annex 3 for notes

P2: Participation by young children

Table P2.2:
Expected number of years of early childhood and primary education for children aged up to 6 years in public and private institutions (1994) (based on head counts)

	Early childhood education		Primary education		Total (i.e. both levels)
	Typical starting age	Expected number of years	Typical starting age	Expected number of years	Expected number of years
North America					
Canada	4	1.2	6	1.1	2.4
Mexico	3	1.3	6	1.0	2.4
United States	3	1.7	6	0.9	2.6
Pacific Area					
Australia	m	m	m	1.7	m
Japan	3	2.5	6	1.0	3.5
New Zealand	2	2.3	5	2.0	4.3
European Union					
Austria	3	2.2	6	0.6	2.9
Belgium	2.5	3.4	6	1.0	4.4
Denmark	3	3.2	7	0.04	3.2
Finland	3 to 6	1.5	7	0.01	1.5
France	2	3.4	6	1.0	4.4
Germany	3	2.6	6	0.4	3.0
Greece	3.5	1.2	5.5	1.1	2.3
Ireland	4 to 5	2.1	6 to 7	0.5	2.6
Italy	3	m	6	m	m
Luxembourg	m	m	m	m	m
Netherlands	4	2.0	6	1.0	3.0
Portugal	3	1.7	6	1.0	2.7
Spain	2	2.7	6	1.0	3.7
Sweden	3	2.6	6 to 7	0.1	2.6
United Kingdom	2	0.6	5	2.9	3.4
Other OECD countries					
Czech Republic	3	2.6	6	0.7	3.3
Hungary	3	3.2	6	0.4	3.6
Iceland	2	m	6	1.0	m
Norway	3	2.7	7	0.01	2.7
Switzerland	4 to 5	1.8	6 to 7	0.3	2.1
Turkey	3	0.1	6	0.9	1.0
Country mean		2.1		0.9	2.9
Other non-OECD countries					
Korea	5	0.8	6	0.9	1.7
Poland	3	1.7	7	0.01	1.7
Russian Federation	3	m	6	m	m

Source: OECD Database. See Annex 3 for notes

P3: PARTICIPATION IN EDUCATION TOWARDS THE END OF COMPULSORY SCHOOLING AND BEYOND

This indicator shows net enrolment rates at the secondary and tertiary levels of education.

POLICY CONTEXT

A range of factors, among them an increasing risk of unemployment and other forms of exclusion for young people with insufficient education, influence the decision to stay at school beyond the end of compulsory schooling. A longer and more complex transition from education to employment than in the past provides opportunities for combining learning and work. Recent years have also seen the dissolving of age boundaries in the transition from secondary to tertiary education with the process now occurring largely in the age range from 15 to 24 years. This provides an opportunity for countries to explore new organisational frameworks for learning both outside as well as inside the classroom.

KEY RESULTS

Compulsory schooling ends in OECD countries between the ages of 14 and 17 – in most cases at ages 15 or 16. Up to the end of compulsory schooling, virtually all young people are enrolled in school but once the compulsory phase is over, enrolment rates begin to fall. The decline is more rapid in some countries than in others. In all but six countries, more than 94 per cent of 15 year-olds participate in education. By age 17 enrolment rates have, on average, dropped to 78 per cent and at age 19 to 47 per cent, with no country having enrolment rates exceeding 75 per cent.

Some countries offer students who have completed upper secondary education the opportunity to re-enrol and pursue additional qualifications. The percentage of 20 year-olds who choose this option instead of entry into tertiary education is significant.

The tertiary level of education is designed to begin in most countries at age 18 or 19 although younger and older students are not uncommon. The transition from secondary to tertiary education occurs usually between the ages of 17 and 20.

DESCRIPTION AND INTERPRETATION

Participation towards the end of compulsory schooling and beyond

Table P3.1 shows net enrolment rates of students from age 15 to 24. In some countries (Australia, Austria, Finland, France, Ireland, Japan, the Netherlands, Norway and Sweden) virtually all students (more than 90 per cent) stay in school for at least a year beyond the end of compulsory education and in about one-third of the countries at least three-quarters of young people stay on for two years after the end of compulsory schooling (Austria, Finland, France, Japan, the Netherlands, Norway and Sweden). In most countries, secondary education is still compulsory at age 15.

By age 19 no country has enrolment rates exceeding 75 per cent and by age 21 none is over 50 per cent. Only four countries report enrolment rates of 24 year-olds of more than 25 per cent (Denmark, Finland, Iceland and Norway).

Between the ages of 15 and 24, young people in OECD countries receive between 1.5 and 6.5 years of education. In about two-thirds of countries, young people receive five or more years of education between these ages – the majority of them (over 70 per cent) concentrated between the ages of 15 and 20.

The countries which appear to retain students at the secondary level for longer are generally those in which a majority of upper secondary students follow vocational courses – particularly those which involve an element of work-based education (see Table P3.2). They also tend to be countries where men can expect to receive more years of education than women between the ages 5 and 29 (Germany, the Netherlands and Switzerland) or where the advantage in favour of women is not very marked (Belgium, Denmark, France and Norway) (see also Indicator P1).

Participation in vocational education

In more than half of the OECD countries, the majority of upper secondary students attend vocational or apprenticeship programmes. In countries with dual-system apprenticeship programmes (such as Austria, Belgium, Germany, the Netherlands and Switzerland) but also in the Czech Republic, Hungary, Italy and Poland, around 70 per cent or more of upper secondary students

P3: Participation in education towards the end of compulsory schooling and beyond

Chart P3: Net enrolment rates at ages 17 to 20 by level of education (head counts) in public and private institutions (1994)

Age 17

Age 18

Age 19

Age 20

☐ Secondary education   ■ Non-university tertiary education   ▨ University-level education

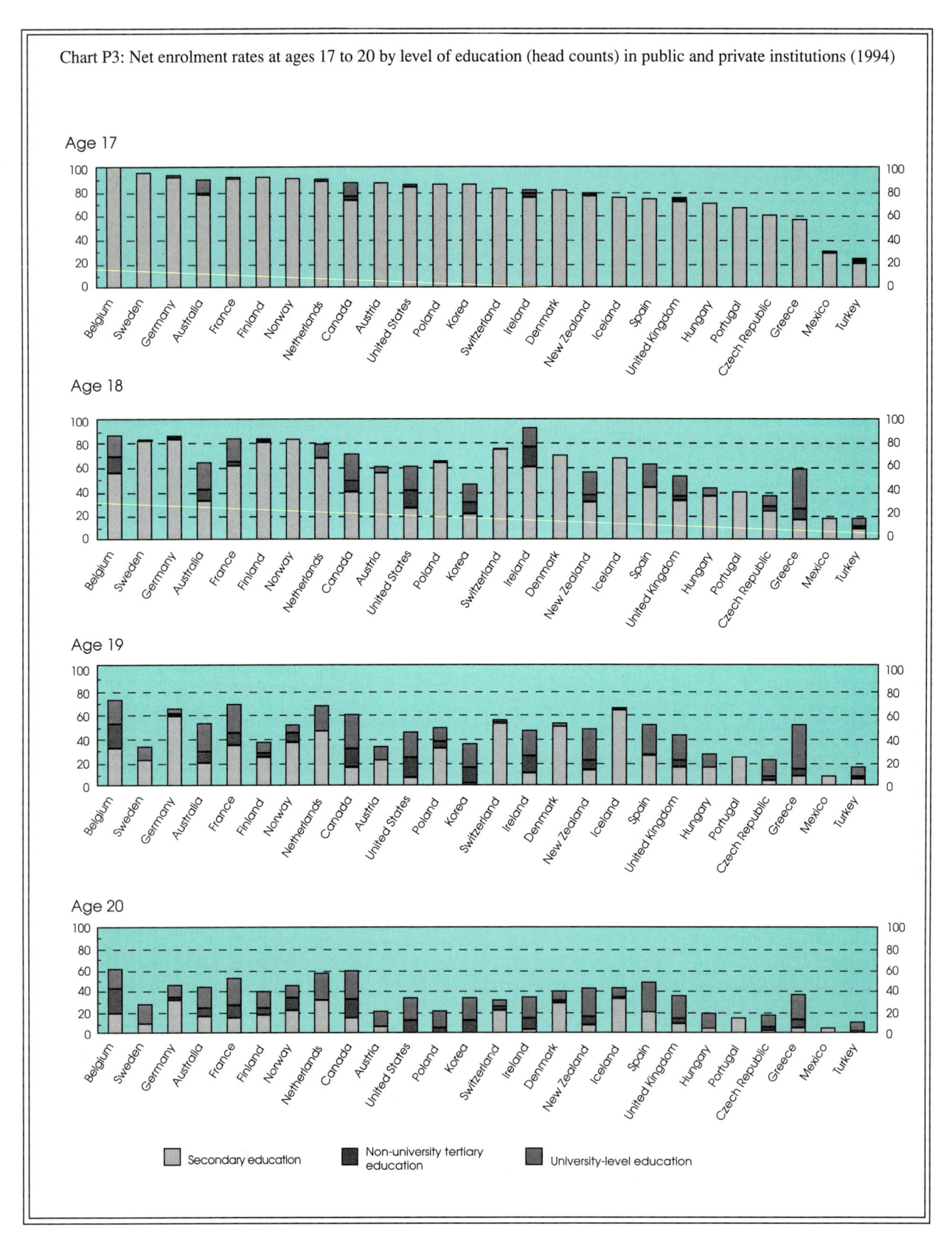

P3: Participation in education towards the end of compulsory schooling and beyond

are enrolled in vocational programmes. Among countries of the European Union only Greece, Ireland, Portugal and Spain have a minority of upper secondary students in vocational or apprenticeship programmes. In most countries vocational education is school-based but in the Czech Republic, Denmark, Germany and Switzerland, programmes that have both school-based and work-based elements are the most common form of vocational education and training.

In seven European countries, a significant number of students complete upper secondary education and then enrol in a second or subsequent secondary programme. In two countries – Germany and Spain – more than 20 per cent of upper secondary students are enrolled in second or subsequent programmes in the age group most commonly attending this level of education. Virtually all of these students pursue vocational education or an apprenticeship.

Women in upper secondary education are generally less likely to be in vocational programmes than men, and in some countries the differences are substantial.

The transition to tertiary education

Chart P3 shows net rates of participation in secondary, non-university tertiary and university education at each year of age from 17 to 20. The transition from secondary education to tertiary education occurs at different ages in different countries. At age 17, most students are still enrolled in secondary education. At age 19 about half of the countries have more students in tertiary education than in secondary education and by age 20 only six countries (Denmark, Germany, Iceland, Mexico, the Netherlands and Switzerland) have more students in secondary education than in tertiary education. However, some countries classify certain types of programmes as upper secondary which are similar in content to programmes classified as tertiary in other countries. Differences in such practice will clearly affect the relative proportion of students of a particular age enrolled at a particular level.

DEFINITIONS

Net enrolment rates in Table P3.1 are calculated by dividing the number of students of a particular age group enrolled in all levels of education by the number of persons in the population in that age group (times 100). Figures in bold in Table P3.1 indicate enrolment in compulsory schooling. Net enrolment rates in Table P3.3 are calculated by dividing the number of students of a particular age group enrolled in a specific level of education by the number of persons in the population in that age group (times 100).

These figures are based on head counts, that is, they do not distinguish between full- and part-time study. This represents a departure from earlier editions of *Education at a Glance*. A standardised distinction between full-time and part-time participants is very difficult since many countries do not recognise the concept of part-time study, although in practice at least some of their students would be classified part-time by other countries. Note that in some countries part-time education is not completely covered by the data reported.

Vocational and technical programmes include both school-based programmes and combined school and work-based programmes that are explicitly deemed to be parts of the education system. Entirely work-based education and training of which no formal education authority has oversight is not taken into account.

P3: Participation in education towards the end of compulsory schooling and beyond

Table P3.1:
Total participation (net enrolment in all levels of education) for ages 15 to 24 in public and private institutions (1994)
(based on head counts)

	Ending age of compulsory schooling	\multicolumn{10}{c}{Net enrolment rates by single year of age (in %)}
		15	16	17	18	19	20	21	22	23	24
North America											
Canada	16	**96.3**	94.2	88.1	72.2	60.6	59.6	39.8	33.2	23.5	20.4
Mexico	15	**50.7**	38.9	30.1	18.3	9.3	6.1	4.1	2.7	2.0	1.8
United States	17	**97.1**	**95.4**	**85.9**	61.2	45.4	34.9	33.6	28.0	22.3	19.2
Pacific Area											
Australia	15	**97.5**	95.8	92.3	64.7	52.8	45.1	32.5	25.0	21.1	18.6
Japan	15	**99.8**	96.4	93.4	m	m	m	m	m	m	m
New Zealand	16	**104.8**	**94.3**	78.7	56.8	48.5	42.8	33.7	24.5	17.9	13.8
European Union											
Austria	15	**95.3**	92.2	86.4	60.9	33.6	22.6	19.2	15.7	14.9	13.1
Belgium	18	**103.3**	**103.5**	**101.4**	**86.8**	72.4	61.1	45.2	34.5	24.3	18.1
Denmark	16	**98.0**	**93.7**	81.0	69.6	53.2	40.9	37.0	34.1	30.9	26.9
Finland	16	**99.6**	**96.1**	91.8	82.5	37.3	40.3	46.0	46.0	39.3	32.7
France	16	**97.8**	**96.1**	92.2	84.1	68.6	53.6	40.1	29.2	19.5	12.3
Germany	18	**98.3**	**96.3**	**92.5**	**85.2**	65.8	46.2	33.8	38.6	20.6	18.4
Greece	15	**81.3**	81.6	57.0	58.7	52.6	38.7	32.6	17.1	13.3	8.2
Ireland	15	**94.8**	93.2	83.2	93.4	47.7	35.2	28.4	13.2	7.9	5.4
Italy	14	m	m	m	m	m	m	m	m	m	m
Luxembourg	15	m	m	m	m	m	m	m	m	m	m
Netherlands	16	**98.9**	**97.5**	90.6	79.8	67.3	57.1	45.6	36.2	28.9	22.2
Portugal	14	84.8	74.2	66.8	54.6	44.1	36.8	31.4	26.5	20.4	15.4
Spain	16	**94.4**	**81.9**	74.5	62.8	52.2	49.1	40.1	33.6	23.7	17.8
Sweden	16	**96.6**	**96.2**	94.8	82.7	34.3	28.3	27.8	28.0	25.5	22.3
United Kingdom	16	**98.7**	**87.1**	73.6	52.7	43.9	36.5	28.1	20.2	15.8	13.5
Other OECD countries											
Czech Republic	15	**98.3**	88.0	61.0	35.6	22.9	18.2	18.7	17.6	10.2	4.2
Hungary	16	**91.9**	**86.1**	70.2	43.1	28.4	20.2	17.6	14.4	11.4	8.4
Iceland	m	99.2	86.4	74.5	66.8	63.6	43.3	39.6	35.7	31.4	26.3
Norway	16	**99.2**	**93.9**	90.6	83.0	51.6	45.9	43.9	41.2	35.9	29.7
Switzerland	15	**96.7**	87.3	83.3	76.2	56.3	33.1	23.5	20.8	18.8	16.1
Turkey	15	**46.2**	40.9	24.2	17.8	17.1	11.4	10.8	9.4	7.8	6.1
Country mean		92.8	87.5	78.3	64.6	47.1	37.8	31.4	26.1	20.3	16.3
Other non-OECD countries											
Korea	14	86.3	93.4	85.2	47.5	37.0	34.7	29.0	22.8	17.7	15.9
Poland	15	m	m	m	m	m	21.9	20.1	17.1	14.9	10.6
Russian Federation	m	m	m	m	m	m	m	m	m	m	m

Figures in bold indicate ages at which schooling is compulsory
Source: OECD Database. See Annex 3 for notes

P3: Participation in education towards the end of compulsory schooling and beyond

Table P3.2:
Percentage of upper secondary students enrolled in public and private general and vocational education (1994)
(based on head counts)

	Men and women – All programmes					Of which: Second educational programmes		Women		
	General programmes	Vocational and technical programmes	of which: school-based	of which: combined school and worked-based	Total	General programmes	Vocational and technical programmes	General programmes	Vocational and technical programmes	Total
North America										
Canada	x	x	x	x	100	a	a	x	x	100
Mexico	81.9	18.1	18.1	a	100	a	a	79.3	20.7	100
United States	x	x	x	x	100	a	a	x	x	100
Pacific Area										
Australia	40.1	59.9	x	x	100	x	x	43.2	56.8	100
Japan	72.2	27.8	27.8	a	100	a	a	74.4	25.6	100
New Zealand	68.0	32.0	32.0	a	100	a	m	69.9	30.1	100
European Union										
Austria	22.2	77.8	41.3	36.5	100	a	4.7	24.2	75.8	100
Belgium	32.3	67.7	64.3	3.4	100	a	a	35.0	65.0	100
Denmark	45.9	54.1	a	54.1	100	2.8	3.9	52.4	47.6	100
Finland	46.4	53.6	49.6	3.9	100	m	m	48.8	51.2	100
France	47.5	52.5	43.6	8.9	100	x	x	53.4	46.6	100
Germany	22.5	77.5	22.8	54.7	100	1.2	20.7	26.1	73.9	100
Greece	66.6	33.4	33.4	a	100	a	a	88.3	11.7	100
Ireland	76.9	23.1	18.0	5.2	100	a	14.7	77.6	22.4	100
Italy	26.9	73.1	73.1	a	100	a	11.3	30.6	69.4	100
Luxembourg	m	m	m	m	m	m	m	m	m	m
Netherlands	29.8	70.2	44.7	25.4	100	m	m	35.0	65.0	100
Portugal	77.3	22.7	22.7	a	100	m	m	80.5	19.5	100
Spain	59.1	40.9	39.6	1.3	100	a	22.7	59.9	40.1	100
Sweden	36.6	63.4	x	x	100	a	a	25.4	74.6	100
United Kingdom	42.3	57.7	x	x	100	m	m	38.9	61.1	100
Other OECD countries										
Czech Republic	15.7	84.3	33.3	51.0	100	a	3.1	19.3	80.7	100
Hungary	26.3	73.7	45.2	28.5	100	x	x	33.0	67.0	100
Iceland	60.6	39.4	x	x	100	x	x	71.6	28.4	100
Norway	41.6	58.4	x	x	100	a	a	48.7	51.3	100
Switzerland	29.8	70.2	8.9	61.3	100	a	m	37.5	62.5	100
Turkey	58.6	41.4	x	x	100	a	a	62.1	37.9	100
Country mean	**47.0**	**53.0**	**34.4**	**18.6**	**100**	**0.2**	**5.1**	**50.6**	**49.4**	**100**
Other non-OECD countries										
Korea	57.3	42.7	40.1	2.7	100	n	n	52.9	47.1	100
Poland	28.1	71.9	x	x	100	m	m	39.8	60.2	100
Russian Federation	60.8	39.2	x	x	100	m	m	m	m	m

Source: OECD Database. See Annex 3 for notes

P3: Participation in education towards the end of compulsory schooling and beyond

Table P3.3:
Transition characteristics at each year of age from 17 to 20: net enrolment rates by level of education in public and private institutions (1994) (based on head counts)

	Age 17 Secondary education	Age 17 Non-university tertiary education	Age 17 University-level education	Age 18 Secondary education	Age 18 Non-university tertiary education	Age 18 University-level education	Age 19 Secondary education	Age 19 Non-university tertiary education	Age 19 University-level education	Age 20 Secondary education	Age 20 Non-university tertiary education	Age 20 University-level education
North America												
Canada	72.0	4.1	11.9	40.2	9.3	22.7	16.3	15.4	29.0	14.6	17.7	27.4
Mexico	29.9	0.2	x	17.8	0.5	x	8.5	0.7	x	5.2	0.9	x
United States	82.9	1.2	1.7	26.3	14.4	20.5	7.1	17.5	20.8	1.4	12.1	21.4
Pacific Area												
Australia	76.7	2.9	12.6	32.1	9.6	23.0	19.6	9.9	23.3	16.1	8.6	20.3
Japan	93.4	n	n	2.0	m	m	0.5	m	m	m	m	m
New Zealand	75.7	1.6	1.5	30.8	6.2	19.9	13.8	8.2	26.4	8.6	7.7	26.5
European Union												
Austria	86.4	n	n	55.5	n	5.3	21.5	n	12.0	7.8	n	14.7
Belgium	100.5	0.2	0.6	55.7	12.2	18.9	31.5	20.6	20.3	19.3	23.4	18.4
Denmark	80.9	n	0.01	69.3	0.0	0.2	49.1	0.7	3.4	28.8	2.0	10.2
Finland	91.3	0.5	0.02	80.3	1.7	0.5	23.9	4.0	9.3	17.5	7.0	15.7
France	90.0	0.2	2.0	60.9	4.5	18.6	34.1	10.5	24.0	14.7	13.1	25.7
Germany	91.6	0.8	0.02	82.3	1.8	1.0	57.6	2.6	5.5	31.6	2.9	11.7
Greece	57.0	n	n	17.5	8.7	32.4	8.4	6.7	37.5	6.1	7.8	24.8
Ireland	74.8	3.6	3.9	60.4	15.9	16.8	11.0	14.7	22.0	3.9	11.6	19.7
Italy	m	m	m	m	m	m	m	m	m	m	m	m
Luxembourg	m	m	m	m	m	m	m	m	m	m	m	m
Netherlands	88.4	a	2.0	67.5	a	12.2	45.8	a	21.5	30.8	a	26.3
Portugal	66.4	x	x	39.1	x	x	24.1	x	x	15.2	x	x
Spain	74.3	n	0.02	43.3	0.4	18.9	25.9	0.5	25.6	20.1	1.0	28.0
Sweden	94.7	x	0.01	81.7	x	0.8	22.4	x	11.7	10.3	x	17.8
United Kingdom	71.7	0.6	1.3	32.1	4.0	16.7	16.0	6.1	21.8	10.2	5.3	21.0
Other OECD countries												
Czech Republic	61.0	n	n	24.2	3.2	8.2	4.6	4.7	13.6	2.9	2.8	12.5
Hungary	70.2	a	n	36.3	a	6.8	16.5	a	11.8	6.4	a	13.8
Iceland	74.5	n	n	66.8	n	0.02	62.8	0.2	0.6	33.1	0.9	9.2
Norway	90.6	n	n	82.6	0.3	0.2	36.5	8.7	6.4	22.2	11.5	12.2
Switzerland	82.2	0.2	0.02	74.6	0.5	0.5	51.7	1.3	2.9	22.6	3.0	7.1
Turkey	20.6	1.0	2.6	9.4	2.1	6.3	5.8	2.6	8.7	n	2.3	9.1
Country mean	**75.9**	**0.7**	**1.7**	**47.6**	**4.3**	**11.4**	**24.6**	**6.2**	**16.3**	**14.6**	**6.4**	**17.9**
Other non-OECD countries												
Korea	85.2	n	n	22.1	9.8	15.6	2.6	13.6	20.7	0.3	12.3	22.1
Poland	85.4	a	a	63.8	0.1	0.4	31.9	5.1	12.2	x	5.6	16.3
Russian Federation	m	m	m	m	m	m	m	m	m	m	m	m

Source: OECD Database. See Annex 3 for notes

P6: PARTICIPATION IN TERTIARY EDUCATION

This indicator shows the percentage of people aged 18 to 29 participating in university-level and non-university tertiary education.

POLICY CONTEXT

OECD economies are more strongly dependent on the production, distribution and use of knowledge and skills than ever before. Output and employment are expanding fastest in high-technology industries as well as in knowledge-intensive service sectors. It is highly-skilled labour that is in greatest demand in OECD countries [see also Indicators R21(A), R21(B) and R22]. At the same time, greater participation at the tertiary level of education, where unit costs tend to be significantly higher than at lower levels of education (see Indicator F3), puts an additional financial burden on public authorities and households.

A wide range of university and non-university tertiary programmes offer different options for improving links between education and the labour market.

KEY RESULTS

Sixteen per cent of 18 to 21 year-olds, 12 per cent of 22 to 25 year-olds, and 5 per cent of 26 to 29 year-olds participate, on average across OECD countries, in university-level programmes. The corresponding averages for participation in non-university level programmes are 6, 3 and 2 per cent. However, these averages mask wide differences between countries in tertiary enrolment rates.

The highest enrolment rates in tertiary education are, in most countries, reported for the 18-21 year-olds (see Chart P6) although in a few countries (especially in Austria, Germany, Iceland, the Nordic countries and Switzerland) participation is higher among the 22 to 25 year-olds, reflecting, in part, a relatively late entry into tertiary studies and a significantly longer duration of such studies in these countries (see Indicator R12).

In general, the age profile for women is younger than for men. In only four countries (the Czech Republic, Korea, Switzerland and Turkey) are enrolment rates higher for men than for women in the 18-21 age group whereas in the 26-29 age group the opposite is true.

All countries for which trend data are available have seen a marked increase in tertiary enrolment rates over the last decade in virtually all age groups. In Canada, Ireland, New Zealand and Portugal enrolment rates for men and women have more than doubled over the last decade, at least for some age groups. In Canada, Denmark and the United States, the increase in participation has largely occurred in the older age groups while in France, the Netherlands, Portugal and Sweden, the increase has been more pronounced for younger age groups.

DESCRIPTION AND INTERPRETATION

The enrolment rates in the three age bands reflect both the total number of individuals participating in tertiary education and the duration of tertiary programmes. Longer duration of studies (see also Indicator R12) tends to increase the stock of enrolments, and thus the level of required resources, all other things being equal. This also explains, in part, why some countries that report high tertiary enrolment rates still show comparatively low graduation rates (see Indicator R12).

Gender differences are significant for both non-university tertiary education and university-level education: enrolment rates for women aged 18-21 years are generally higher than those for men except in Korea, Switzerland and Turkey; in Belgium and the Czech Republic for university-level education; and in Greece, Ireland, Korea, Turkey and the United Kingdom for non-university tertiary education. In tertiary education the largest differences are observed in Belgium, Canada, France, Portugal and the United States. This partly reflects the fact that, in many countries, entry rates to tertiary education for women are now higher than for men although fewer women stay on for second or higher degree programmes (especially doctoral studies) than men. Compulsory national service for men also plays a part in some countries.

Differences among countries in enrolment rates at the non-university level of education need to be interpreted with caution. For example, Canada and the United States, which show comparatively high non-university tertiary-level enrolment rates, classify certain programmes as non-university tertiary education which are similar in content to programmes that other countries, such as Austria, Germany or Switzerland, classify as upper secondary programmes.

P6: Participation in tertiary education

DEFINITIONS

This indicator is based on net enrolment rates for students in three age groups: 18-21, 22-25 and 26-29. Net enrolments for each age group are obtained by dividing the number of tertiary education students in the age group by the total population in that age group.

The figures are based on head counts, that is, they do not distinguish between full- and part-time participants. A standardised distinction between full-time and part-time participants at the tertiary level is very difficult since many countries do not recognise the concept of part-time study, although in practice at least some of their students would be classified part-time by other countries.

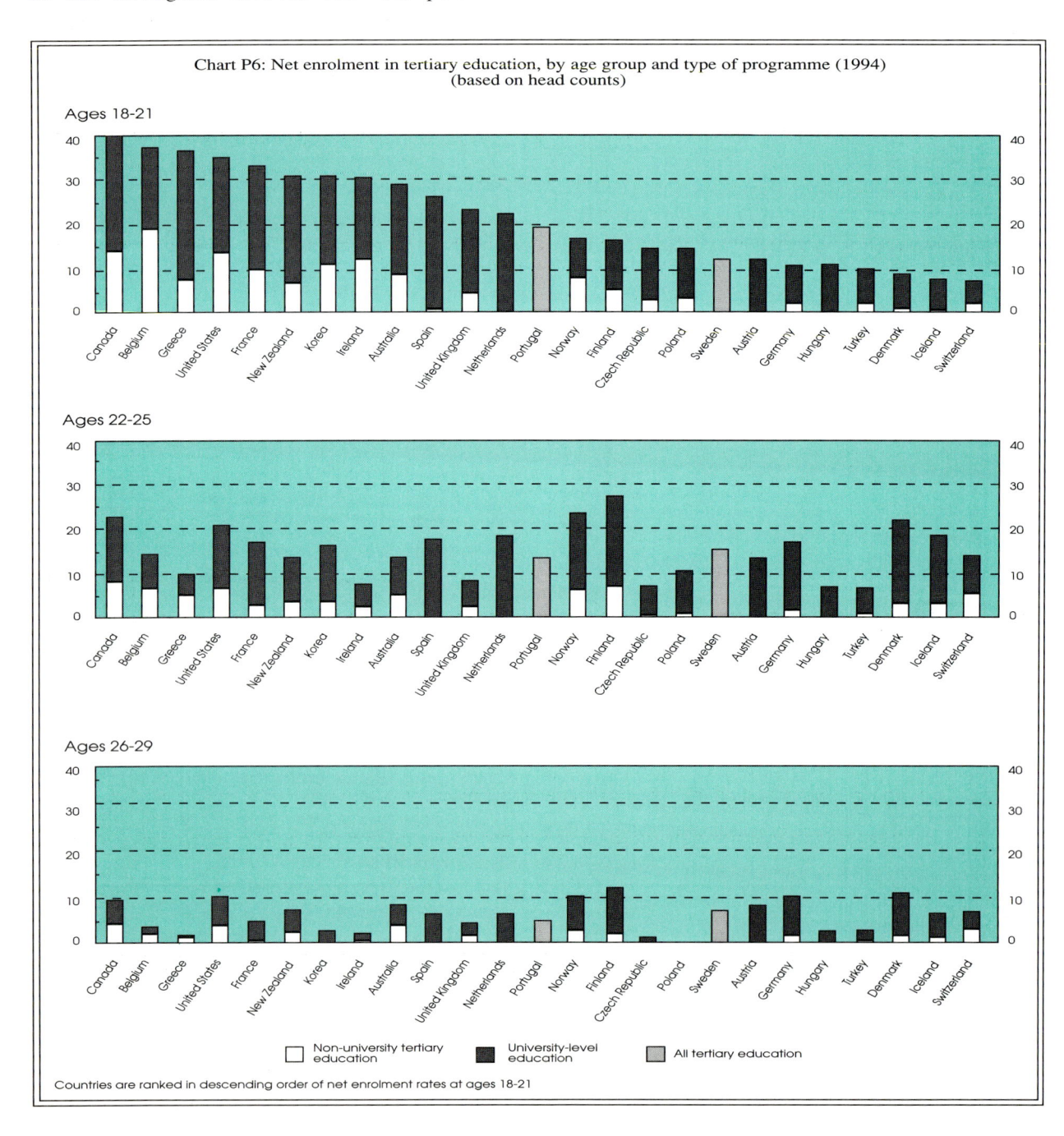

Chart P6: Net enrolment in tertiary education, by age group and type of programme (1994)
(based on head counts)

Legend: Non-university tertiary education / University-level education / All tertiary education

Countries are ranked in descending order of net enrolment rates at ages 18-21

P6: Participation in tertiary education

Table P6.1:
Net enrolment in public and private tertiary education for persons 18 to 21 years of age, by type of programme (1994)
(based on head counts)

	\multicolumn{9}{c}{Ages 18-21}
	\multicolumn{3}{c}{Non-university tertiary education}	\multicolumn{3}{c}{University-level education}	\multicolumn{3}{c}{Total}
	M + W	Men	Women	M + W	Men	Women	M + W	Men	Women
North America									
Canada	14.0	12.8	15.4	26.2	22.2	30.4	40.3	35.0	45.8
Mexico	0.7	m	m	m	m	m	m	m	m
United States	13.6	12.7	14.5	21.3	18.8	24.0	34.9	31.5	38.5
Pacific Area									
Australia	8.7	8.9	8.6	20.5	18.0	23.2	29.3	26.8	31.8
Japan	m	m	m	m	m	m	m	m	m
New Zealand	7.1	6.1	8.1	23.8	21.7	26.0	30.9	27.8	34.1
European Union									
Austria	n	n	n	12.0	11.2	12.8	12.0	11.2	12.8
Belgium	18.9	14.3	23.7	18.5	19.2	17.8	37.4	33.5	41.5
Denmark	1.5	1.5	1.4	7.6	7.3	8.0	9.1	8.9	9.4
Finland	5.4	3.3	7.5	11.2	10.3	12.1	16.6	13.7	19.6
France	9.9	9.5	10.3	23.3	19.5	27.3	33.2	29.0	37.6
Germany	2.4	0.8	4.2	8.7	7.7	9.8	11.2	8.5	14.0
Greece	7.8	9.2	6.3	28.9	26.6	31.4	36.7	35.7	37.7
Ireland	12.2	13.1	11.3	18.3	17.0	19.6	30.5	30.1	30.9
Italy	m	m	m	m	m	m	m	m	m
Luxembourg	m	m	m	m	m	m	m	m	m
Netherlands	a	a	a	22.1	21.3	23.0	22.1	21.3	23.0
Portugal	m	m	m	m	m	m	19.3	15.7	23.0
Spain	0.6	0.6	0.5	24.9	21.7	28.2	25.4	22.2	28.8
Sweden	x	x	x	12.3	10.3	14.4	12.3	10.3	14.4
United Kingdom	4.8	5.2	4.4	18.7	18.2	19.4	23.6	23.3	23.8
Other OECD countries									
Czech Republic	3.2	2.4	4.1	11.6	12.8	10.3	14.8	15.2	14.4
Hungary	a	a	a	11.0	m	m	11.0	m	m
Iceland	1.0	1.0	1.0	6.9	6.3	7.4	7.9	7.3	8.5
Norway	7.9	6.6	9.2	9.3	8.1	10.6	17.1	14.6	19.8
Switzerland	2.4	2.6	2.3	5.2	5.5	4.9	7.6	8.0	7.2
Turkey	2.3	2.6	1.9	8.2	9.7	6.7	10.5	12.3	8.6
Country mean	**5.6**	**5.4**	**6.4**	**15.9**	**14.9**	**17.5**	**21.5**	**20.1**	**23.9**
Other non-OECD countries									
Korea	11.0	12.3	9.7	19.8	22.8	16.6	30.8	35.1	26.3
Poland	3.6	1.5	5.6	11.1	9.9	12.3	14.6	11.5	17.9
Russian Federation	m	m	m	m	m	m	m	m	m

Source: OECD Database. See Annex 3 for notes

P6: Participation in tertiary education

Table P6.2:
Net enrolment in public and private tertiary education for persons 22 to 25 years of age, by type of programme (1994)
(based on head counts)

	Ages 22-25							
	Non-university tertiary education			University-level education			Total		
	M + W	Men	Women	M + W	Men	Women	M + W	Men	Women
North America									
Canada	8.2	8.9	7.4	14.6	14.2	15.1	22.8	23.1	22.6
Mexico	0.9	m	m	m	m	m	m	m	m
United States	6.6	6.4	6.7	14.4	14.7	14.1	20.9	21.1	20.8
Pacific Area									
Australia	5.2	5.9	4.5	8.4	8.4	8.4	13.6	14.3	12.9
Japan	m	m	m	m	m	m	m	m	m
New Zealand	3.8	3.7	3.8	10.1	10.2	10.0	13.9	13.9	13.8
European Union									
Austria	n	n	n	13.3	14.3	12.3	13.3	14.3	12.3
Belgium	6.6	7.0	6.1	8.1	9.1	7.1	14.7	16.1	13.2
Denmark	3.1	3.5	2.6	19.0	16.9	21.2	22.1	20.5	23.8
Finland	6.9	5.3	8.6	20.4	21.3	19.4	27.3	26.6	28.0
France	2.9	2.7	3.0	14.1	12.6	15.7	17.0	15.3	18.7
Germany	1.7	1.8	1.5	15.5	18.4	12.5	17.2	20.2	14.0
Greece	5.2	6.7	3.7	4.8	5.6	4.0	10.1	12.3	7.7
Ireland	2.6	2.9	2.3	5.3	5.8	4.8	7.9	8.7	7.1
Italy	m	m	m	m	m	m	m	m	m
Luxembourg	m	m	m	m	m	m	m	m	m
Netherlands	a	a	a	18.4	20.4	16.3	18.4	20.4	16.3
Portugal	m	m	m	m	m	m	13.4	11.6	15.2
Spain	0.1	0.1	0.1	17.4	17.0	17.7	17.5	17.1	17.8
Sweden	x	x	x	15.3	15.0	15.6	15.3	15.0	15.6
United Kingdom	2.6	2.4	2.8	5.8	6.5	5.2	8.4	8.8	8.0
Other OECD countries									
Czech Republic	0.5	0.3	0.7	7.1	7.4	6.8	7.6	7.7	7.4
Hungary	a	a	a	6.9	m	m	6.9	m	m
Iceland	3.3	3.1	3.6	15.4	13.6	17.3	18.8	16.7	20.9
Norway	6.2	6.2	6.2	17.4	16.6	18.2	23.6	22.8	24.5
Switzerland	5.7	8.2	3.3	8.5	10.4	6.7	14.2	18.5	10.0
Turkey	1.2	1.3	1.0	6.0	8.1	3.8	7.2	9.4	4.9
Country mean	3.3	3.6	3.2	12.1	12.7	12.0	15.3	16.1	15.2
Other non-OECD countries									
Korea	3.6	5.6	1.5	12.7	19.3	5.7	16.3	24.9	7.2
Poland	0.9	0.8	1.1	9.9	9.7	10.1	10.8	10.5	11.2
Russian Federation	m	m	m	m	m	m	m	m	m

Source: OECD Database. See Annex 3 for notes

P6: Participation in tertiary education

Table P6.3:
Net enrolment in public and private tertiary education for persons 26 to 29 years of age, by type of programme (1994)
(based on head counts)

	\multicolumn{9}{c}{Ages 26-29}
	\multicolumn{3}{c}{Non-university tertiary education}	\multicolumn{3}{c}{University-level education}	\multicolumn{3}{c}{Total}
	M + W	Men	Women	M + W	Men	Women	M + W	Men	Women
North America									
Canada	4.2	5.0	3.4	5.4	5.4	5.5	9.6	10.4	8.8
Mexico	x	m	m	m	m	m	m	m	m
United States	3.9	2.6	5.2	6.5	6.6	6.4	10.4	9.2	11.6
Pacific Area									
Australia	3.8	4.6	3.0	4.7	4.7	4.6	8.5	9.3	7.7
Japan	m	m	m	m	m	m	m	m	m
New Zealand	2.5	2.5	2.5	4.8	4.6	4.9	7.2	7.1	7.4
European Union									
Austria	n	n	n	8.0	9.2	6.8	8.0	9.2	6.8
Belgium	2.2	2.4	1.9	1.7	2.1	1.3	3.8	4.5	3.1
Denmark	1.6	1.8	1.3	9.4	9.1	9.6	10.9	10.9	10.9
Finland	2.2	1.4	3.0	10.0	10.7	9.3	12.2	12.1	12.3
France	0.4	0.2	0.6	4.2	4.2	4.2	4.6	4.4	4.8
Germany	1.7	1.9	1.5	8.6	10.8	6.2	10.3	12.8	7.6
Greece	1.3	1.5	1.1	0.9	1.0	0.8	2.2	2.5	1.9
Ireland	0.6	0.8	0.4	1.8	2.1	1.5	2.4	2.8	2.0
Italy	m	m	m	m	m	m	m	m	m
Luxembourg	m	m	m	m	m	m	m	m	m
Netherlands	a	a	a	6.2	7.3	5.1	6.2	7.3	5.1
Portugal	m	m	m	m	m	m	4.8	4.5	5.1
Spain	n	n	n	6.2	6.6	5.8	6.2	6.6	5.8
Sweden	x	x	x	7.2	7.5	6.9	7.2	7.5	6.9
United Kingdom	1.6	1.4	1.9	2.8	3.0	2.5	4.4	4.4	4.4
Other OECD countries									
Czech Republic	n	n	n	1.5	1.7	1.3	1.5	1.7	1.3
Hungary	a	a	a	2.9	m	m	2.9	m	m
Iceland	1.5	1.4	1.6	5.3	4.4	6.1	6.8	5.8	7.7
Norway	2.7	2.8	2.7	7.6	7.8	7.5	10.4	10.5	10.2
Switzerland	3.2	4.8	1.6	3.9	5.0	2.8	7.1	9.8	4.4
Turkey	0.7	0.7	0.7	2.4	3.4	1.4	3.2	4.1	2.1
Country mean	**1.6**	**1.7**	**1.5**	**5.1**	**5.6**	**4.8**	**6.6**	**7.2**	**6.3**
Other non-OECD countries									
Korea	n	n	n	2.7	4.5	0.9	2.7	4.5	0.9
Poland	x	x	x	x	x	x	x	x	x
Russian Federation	m	m	m	m	m	m	m	m	m

Source: OECD Database. See Annex 3 for notes

P6: Participation in tertiary education

Table P6t:
Net enrolment in public and private tertiary education by age group (1985-94) (based on head counts)

	Ages 18-21			Ages 22-25			Ages 26-29		
	1985	1990	1994	1985	1990	1994	1985	1990	1994
North America									
Canada	25.5	28.9	40.3	9.5	11.4	22.8	3.0	3.4	9.6
United States	33.0	36.2	34.9	14.5	17.1	20.9	8.2	8.5	10.4
Pacific Area									
New Zealand	14.9	20.8	30.9	9.6	13.8	13.9	m	m	7.2
European Union									
Denmark	7.4	7.4	9.1	16.3	17.9	22.1	8.2	9.3	10.9
Finland	9.3	13.6	16.6	17.3	20.7	27.3	7.9	10.2	12.2
France	19.4	24.6	33.2	10.0	11.8	17.0	4.3	3.9	4.6
Germany	8.8	8.5	11.2	15.5	15.9	17.2	8.9	10.4	10.3
Ireland	15.2	20.3	30.5	2.8	4.3	7.9	m	m	2.4
Netherlands	14.4	17.9	22.1	11.9	13.4	18.4	5.7	4.7	6.2
Portugal	5.8	m	19.3	5.4	m	13.4	2.3	m	4.8
Spain	14.9	21.2	25.4	10.6	13.5	17.5	4.0	4.5	6.2
Sweden	7.9	8.7	12.3	11.3	11.4	15.3	6.5	6.1	7.2
United Kingdom	m	16.1	23.6	m	4.7	8.4	m	m	4.4
Other OECD countries									
Norway	8.8	14.4	17.1	13.2	18.9	23.6	5.7	8.2	10.4
Switzerland	5.7	6.4	7.6	10.6	12.1	14.2	5.2	6.4	7.1
Turkey	m	7.4	10.5	m	4.6	7.2	m	2.3	3.2

Vertical bars indicate breaks in series which may affect the comparability over time
Source: OECD Database. See Annex 3 for notes

P8: Job-related continuing education and training for the adult labour force

P8: JOB-RELATED CONTINUING EDUCATION AND TRAINING FOR THE ADULT LABOUR FORCE

This indicator shows the percentage of employed and unemployed persons who have, in a specified period, participated in job-related or career-related continuing education and training.

POLICY CONTEXT

A skilled labour force is a prerequisite for economic success, and reducing the relative supply of unskilled labour through job-related continuing education and training can be an effective policy to combat unemployment. Moreover, because skills are increasingly important for both social and economic success, the lack of skills is also a potential source of inequality.

Skills not only depend on initial education. There is some indication that, when not used, they tend to decline over time. Continuing education and training therefore serves multiple purposes. It gives individuals an opportunity to repair and/or complement previously received education and training, it allows employers to maintain a productive workforce, and it allows governments to stimulate the economy and to promote equity.

KEY RESULTS

Two results stand out. First, participation in job-related continuing education and training (CET) is closely linked to the previously attained level of education. In all countries, those with the lowest levels of education also have the lowest levels of participation in CET, while those with tertiary education attain the

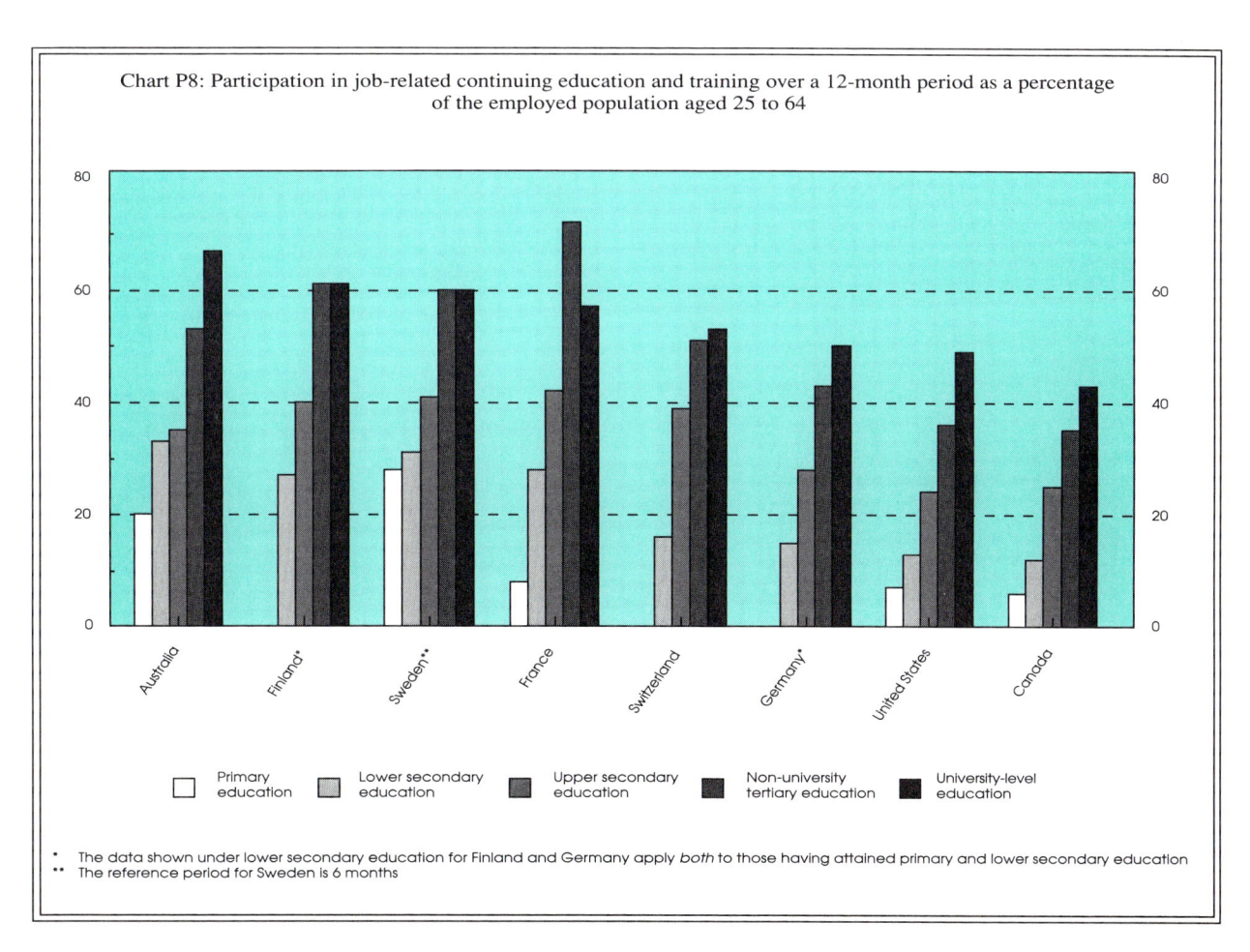

Chart P8: Participation in job-related continuing education and training over a 12-month period as a percentage of the employed population aged 25 to 64

Categories: Primary education; Lower secondary education; Upper secondary education; Non-university tertiary education; University-level education

* The data shown under lower secondary education for Finland and Germany apply *both* to those having attained primary and lower secondary education
** The reference period for Sweden is 6 months

P8: Job-related continuing education and training for the adult labour force

highest levels of participation in CET. These findings apply to both the employed and the unemployed. Initial skill differences are thus amplified by subsequent training decisions by employers and employees. The second result is that among the employed a larger proportion of women than of men participate in job-related CET in most countries.

DESCRIPTION AND INTERPRETATION

The indicator shows the percentage of employed and unemployed persons who have participated in job-related CET. It does not show the volume in hours or days. Most countries measure the amount of participation in CET over a period of either twelve months or four weeks. For Sweden, the reference period is six months. Figures pertaining to different reference periods are not comparable.

Around 40 per cent of the employed in Finland, France and Switzerland participated in CET during a 12-month period in the reference period. In Canada and the United States the rate was around 30 per cent. In Sweden the participation was the highest, 44 per cent, despite the fact that participation was measured over a 6-month period only. Naturally the reported participation rates were much lower in countries measuring the participation in CET during a 4-week period. In Denmark and the United Kingdom, the participation rate was, however, as high as about 15 per cent over that short period.

The degree of participation in job-related or career-related CET is in general smaller among the unemployed than among the employed (see Table P8.2). In Germany, the United Kingdom and the United States the rate was twice as high for the employed as for the unemployed. The same pattern holds for Ireland, where relatively few take part in job-related CET. Also in Australia and Canada participation rates were considerably higher for the employed than for the unemployed. The opposite was true in Belgium and Spain. Caution must, however, be exercised when analysing the data for the unemployed because the participation rates for the unemployed may be imprecise as a result of small sample sizes.

As with the employed, the proportion of those who participated in some form of job-related CET increases with the previous level of educational attainment. Those with the highest formal qualifications – whether they are employed or not – are most likely to receive such training. In virtually all countries, those with university degrees are at least twice as likely (and often much more) to receive job-related training than those with only primary or lower secondary qualifications. Of the countries reporting data with a 12-month reference period, each additional level of education adds on average about 10 per cent to the proportion who received training. However, there are some exceptions to this general observation. In Australia, for example, those who have attained lower secondary education are as likely to receive training as those who have obtained an upper secondary qualification. The CET figures for those with non-university tertiary and university-level education are very close in Finland.

DEFINITIONS

Continuing education and training for adults refers, in principle, to all job-related education and training organised, financed or sponsored by authorities, provided by employers or self-financed.

Job-related continuing education and training as captured by these indicators refers to all organised, systematic education and training activities in which people take part in order to obtain knowledge and/or learn new skills for a current or a future job, to increase earnings, improve job and/or career opportunities in current or other fields, and generally to improve their opportunities for advancement and promotion.

Continuing education and training for adults does not include military training or full-time studies at the tertiary level as defined by ISCED.

P8: Job-related continuing education and training for the adult labour force

Table P8.1:
Participation in job-related continuing education and training as a percentage of the employed population aged 25 to 64

	Year	Gender	Primary education	Lower secondary education	Upper secondary education	Non-university tertiary education	University-level education	All levels of education
During the 12-month period preceding the survey								
Australia	1993	M+W	20	33	35	53	67	38
		Men	18	32	33	50	66	37
		Women	21	34	38	57	69	40
Canada	1993	M+W	6	12	25	35	43	28
		Men	6	13	22	36	40	27
		Women	5	11	28	34	47	30
Finland	1993	M+W	x	27	40	61	61	41
		Men	x	26	37	58	58	38
		Women	x	29	44	63	65	44
France	1994	M+W	8	28	42	72	57	40
		Men	7	26	40	76	46	38
		Women	8	30	46	69	75	43
Germany	1994	M+W	x	15	28	43	50	33
		Men	x	m	29	44	50	35
		Women	x	14	28	40	50	31
Switzerland	1993	M+W	m	16	39	51	53	38
		Men	m	(14)	41	52	52	42
		Women	m	17	37	45	56	34
United States	1995	M+W	7	13	24	36	49	34
		Men	8	11	21	34	45	31
		Women	6	15	27	38	54	36
During the 6-month period preceding the survey								
Sweden	1995	M+W	28	31	41	60	60	44
		Men	27	30	38	58	53	40
		Women	28	32	44	62	68	47
During the 4-week period preceding the survey								
Belgium	1994	M+W	1	1	2	4	6	3
		Men	1	1	3	5	6	3
		Women	0.5	1	2	3	6	2
Denmark	1994	M+W	x	7	14	21	24	15
		Men	x	5	11	19	21	13
		Women	x	8	17	22	29	18
Greece	1994	M+W	m	m	m	m	m	1
		Men	m	m	m	m	m	0.5
		Women	m	m	m	m	m	1
Ireland	1994	M+W	1	2	5	7	8	4
		Men	1	2	4	6	8	3
		Women	1	3	6	8	9	6
Italy	1994	M+W	m	1	2	a	3	1
		Men	0.3	1	2	a	2	1
		Women	m	1	2	a	3	2
Spain	1994	M+W	0.3	1	6	5	8	3
		Men	0.2	1	5	4	7	2
		Women	1	2	8	6	9	4
United Kingdom	1994	M+W	x	3	12	24	24	13
		Men	x	3	11	21	22	12
		Women	x	4	13	26	28	14

Source: OECD Database. See Annex 3 for notes

P8: Job-related continuing education and training for the adult labour force

Table P8.2:
Participation in job-related continuing education and training as a percentage of the unemployed population aged 25 to 64

	Year	Primary education	Lower secondary education	Upper secondary education	Non-university tertiary education	University-level education	All levels of education
During the 12-month period preceding the survey							
Australia	1993	12	25	25	43	53	24
Canada	1993	6	6	15	24	30	16
France	1994	14	22	38	66	75	35
Germany	1994	8	10	19	24	21	16
Switzerland	1993	m	m	m	m	m	33
United States	1995	6	10	11	17	24	14
During the 4-week period preceding the survey							
Belgium	1994	m	m	m	m	m	5
Denmark	1994	m	7	12	10	18	11
Greece	1994	m	m	m	m	m	1
Ireland	1994	0.4	1	4	8	9	2
Italy	1993	m	m	m	m	m	1
Spain	1994	1	5	16	14	35	8
United Kingdom	1994	m	2	7	15	14	6

Source: OECD Database. See Annex 3 for notes

Chapter 4
SCHOOL ENVIRONMENT AND SCHOOL/CLASSROOM PROCESSES

The indicators in preceding chapters have focused on financial and human resources devoted to education as well as on participation in and access to education. Some of these indicators, such as Indicator F3 on expenditure per student or Indicator P32 on student/teaching staff ratios, are sometimes also used as a proxy for the quality of education.

But what can be said directly about the quality of schools? Are schools providing a safe and supportive environment that allows students to devote their energies to learning? Does the way in which instruction is organised and delivered reflect national goals and intentions and live up to best practices? Are schools attracting qualified people with enthusiasm, creativity and commitment into teaching and supporting them with competitive salaries and sustained professional development?

Because of the diverse and complex nature of activities within schools, many of these aspects are not as easily captured as enrolments or expenditure. However, a certain number of national, school and classroom-level characteristics can be assessed, using data reported by those involved in the schooling process or data drawn from policy statements and guidelines. At the national level, such characteristics may include the distribution of decision-making authority across administrative levels or the salaries and working conditions of teachers, including the teaching load and the hours of work. At the school level, aspects such as the time allocated to different parts of the curriculum, the ways in which student progress is monitored and the ways in which students are allocated to classes or groups, can be assessed. This chapter presents ten such indicators.

Indicator P11 compares the amount of intended instruction time for students at the lower secondary level, and the relative emphasis on different fields of study in the curriculum, as measured by the apportionment of instruction time among subject areas. Intended instruction time builds the bridge between the intended curriculum (specified, for example, in national or regional curricular goals and guidelines) and the curriculum that is implemented in classroom instruction. At times, it is also used as a proxy for the achieved curriculum (i.e., the actual educational performance of students in specific curriculum areas).

Indicators P33 and P35 look at teachers' working conditions and, more specifically, at the attractiveness of the teaching profession. Indicator P33 compares the teaching load of teachers across countries and Indicator P35 compares teachers' salaries and payscales. Observed differences in these indicators among countries with comparable standards of economic development provide a rich source for policy reflection.

The chapter concludes with seven process indicators related to primary education [**P22(A) to (G)**]. These were selected in the light of knowledge gained from research on school effectiveness and on what school processes are conducive to student achievement. These seven indicators examine:

- stability in educational staff (as a proxy indicator of consistent education);
- school leadership (with a special focus on the part played by educational versus administrative leadership);
- co-operation between staff, and among headteachers and staff;
- monitoring and evaluation procedures to ascertain the extent to which the goals and intentions have been achieved;
- the ways in which variation in student achievement is addressed by schools and how schools respond to different needs of students;
- the achievement orientation of school policies (relating to the setting and monitoring of standards both at student and at school level); and
- the extent to which parents are informed on various school matters, particularly on the performance of their children, as well as the extent to which parents are involved in instruction or contribute directly to decision-making in schools.

These indicators illustrate differences in educational practices which can be influenced by educational policy. They can act as both "benchmarks" and as examples of "good practices", and are an important element in judging the performance of schools. They should be interpreted in the light of the national context of education.

The data for the system-level indicators on staffing and the intended curriculum time were collected during the school year 1993/94 on the basis of a structured questionnaire, supported by explicit references to formal documents. Differences in results from the 1995 edition of *Education at a Glance* can be largely attributed to a refinement of the methodology. Note that Indicator P11 refers to "intended" rather than "implemented" instruction time. Time devoted to listed subjects may be underestimated in countries where a substantial portion of intended instruction time is flexible (see Annex 3). Teaching time, P33, has been revised to exclude the number of hours per year when schools are closed for national holidays or festivities, and in P35 (compensation of teachers), special care has been taken to treat additional bonuses consistently.

The data for Indicators P22(A) to (G) were collected by means of an international survey of schools, administered during the school year 1995/96 and based upon a probability sample of approximately 400 primary schools per country, which were selected with probabilities proportional to their size. The instruments were administered to primary schools as defined by the national institutional structure of the education system, irrespective of the ages and grades of the students enrolled. The rationale behind this choice was that having information which corresponds to actual school situations would offset any loss of international comparability due to differences in ages and grades. Results are weighted by the number of students enrolled. Technical requirements of sampling and weighting procedures were reviewed and approved by a sampling referee.

P11: Total intended instruction time for students at the lower secondary level

P11: TOTAL INTENDED INSTRUCTION TIME FOR STUDENTS AT THE LOWER SECONDARY LEVEL

This indicator shows the intended instruction time (in hours per year) for the grades in which the majority of students are 12, 13 and 14 years old; as well as how their time is allocated to the different learning areas.

POLICY CONTEXT

The amount of instruction students receive is generally considered a critical factor in determining student outcomes. Time is a limited resource for both students and teachers and its effective use is of paramount importance. The instruction time that can be devoted to each student is closely related to factors such as class size, teaching load (see Indicator P33) and student/teaching staff ratios (see Indicator P32). The optimal balance among these factors may be different for different subject areas and for different levels of education. A related policy issue is the relative importance that should be given to each subject area and, in accordance with this, the allocation of instruction time among the subject areas.

KEY RESULTS

The intended number of instruction hours per year is on average 908 for 12 year-olds, 931 for 13 year-olds and 935 for 14 year-olds. Reading and writing in the mother tongue, together with modern foreign languages, typically accounts for 28 per cent of the intended instruction time for 12-14 year-olds, followed by mathematics and science with about 24 per cent.

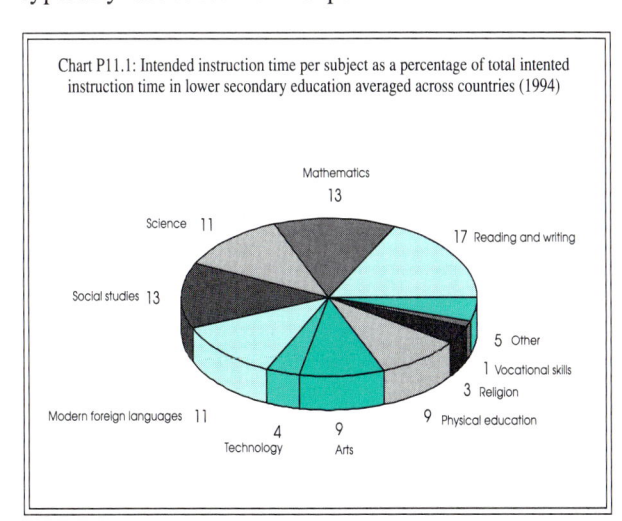

Countries differ both with respect to the overall amount of instruction time that students at different ages receive – for 14 year-olds this ranges from about 700 hours to more than 1 000 hours per year – as well as with respect to its allocation over the different subject areas.

DESCRIPTION AND INTERPRETATION

This indicator shows the intended instruction time (in hours per year) for grades in which the majority of students are 12, 13 and 14 years old. It also gives the percentage of total intended instruction time devoted to major subject areas in the curriculum. Note, however, that the boundaries between different subject areas are sometimes imprecise and may be differently defined across countries. In some countries, a certain portion of time is not pre-allocated in the prescribed curriculum and may not be offered by all schools or taken up by all students. This additional time averages 5 per cent of total instruction time across countries but is as high as 22 per cent in the Netherlands, 16 per cent in Ireland and 10 per cent in Denmark and Portugal. If the additional time is devoted to subjects in the regular curriculum, the percentage of time spent on these subjects in Table P11.2 will be underestimated. Finally, it should be kept in mind that instruction time does not equal learning time. Homework and additional instruction, which are not covered by this indicator, can account for a significant part of the time devoted to studying.

The total intended instruction time for 14 year-olds is highest in Austria (1 073 hours per year) and the Netherlands (1 067 hours) (see Table P11.1). It is lowest in Turkey (696 hours), Sweden (828 hours) and Norway (833 hours). With the exception of Austria, New Zealand and Turkey the amount of instruction time is either stable or increases steadily between 12 and 14 years of age. In a number of countries 12 year-olds are still enrolled at the primary level and will typically continue into the lower secondary level in the following school year. This is usually reflected in a significant increase in intended instruction time between the two grades. Time devoted to mathematics and science for 14 year-olds varies from 167 hours per year in Norway to 390 hours per year in Austria.

On average, about 40 per cent of instruction time is dedicated to the three basic subjects: reading and writing in the mother tongue (17 per cent), mathematics

Chart P11.1: Intended instruction time per subject as a percentage of total intended instruction time in lower secondary education averaged across countries (1994)

- Mathematics 13
- Science 11
- Social studies 13
- Modern foreign languages 11
- Technology 4
- Arts 9
- Physical education 9
- Religion 3
- Vocational skills 1
- Other 5
- Reading and writing 17

137

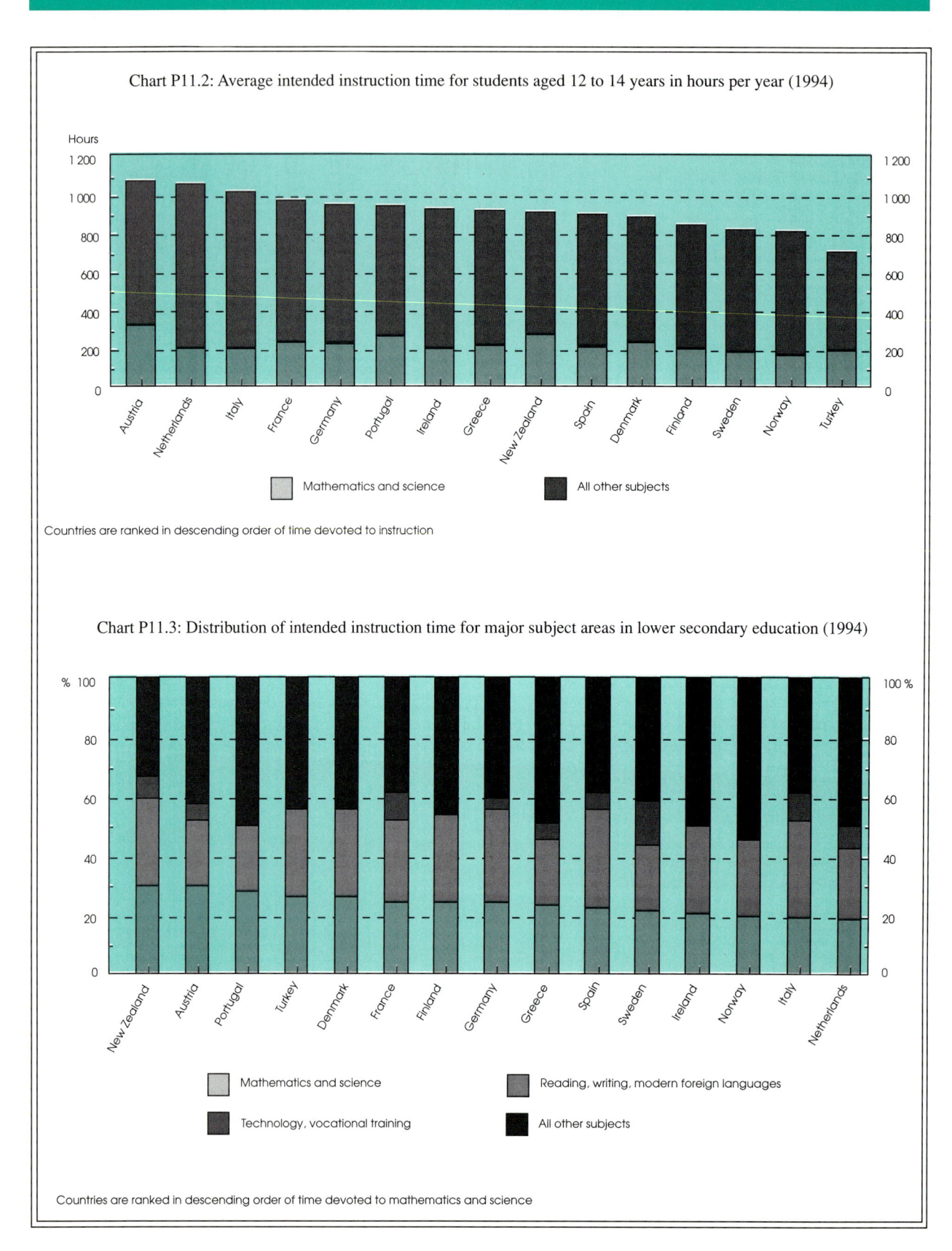

P11: Total intended instruction time for students at the lower secondary level

Chart P11.2: Average intended instruction time for students aged 12 to 14 years in hours per year (1994)

- Mathematics and science
- All other subjects

Countries are ranked in descending order of time devoted to instruction

Chart P11.3: Distribution of intended instruction time for major subject areas in lower secondary education (1994)

- Mathematics and science
- Reading, writing, modern foreign languages
- Technology, vocational training
- All other subjects

Countries are ranked in descending order of time devoted to mathematics and science

P11: Total intended instruction time for students at the lower secondary level

(13 per cent) and science (11 per cent). An average of 13 per cent is devoted to social studies, 11 per cent to modern foreign languages and 9 per cent each to arts and to physical education (see Chart P11.1 and Table P11.2).

DEFINITIONS

Intended instruction time refers to the number of hours per year which students should receive, whether in the compulsory or the flexible part of the curriculum. Compulsory subjects are those that must be taught by each school and taken by each student. Optional subjects form the flexible part of the curriculum. Annex 3 includes more information on country-specific situations with regard to instruction time and curriculum.

The total number of intended instruction hours per year is calculated by multiplying the total number of classroom sessions per year by the duration of one session.

The percentage of the total intended instruction time devoted to a subject is calculated by dividing the total number of sessions per year per subject for 12, 13 and 14 year-old students by the total number of sessions per year for 12, 13 and 14 year-old students.

The intended curriculum is the subject content defined at the national or the education system level. It is embodied in textbooks, curriculum guides, the content of examinations, as well as in policies, regulations, and other official statements produced in connection with the administration of the school system.

If no specific information on the intended curriculum was available, countries reported survey estimates on the implemented curriculum.

The classification of subject areas into the categories used for this indicator is explained in Annex 3.

Data are from the 1995 OECD-INES survey on teachers and curriculum and refer to the school year 1993/94.

P11: Total intended instruction time for students at the lower secondary level

Table P11.1:
Total intended instruction time for students in lower secondary education in hours per year (1994)

	Students 12 years of age	Students 13 years of age	Students 14 years of age	Total students 12 to 14 years of age
Austria	1 105	1 073	1 073	3 251
Belgium	987	987	m	m
Denmark	840	900	930	2 670
Finland	730	912	912	2 554
France	810	1 026	1 026	2 862
Germany	930	960	960	2 850
Greece	918	918	945	2 781
Ireland	935	935	935	2 805
Italy	1 020	1 020	1 020	3 060
Netherlands	1 067	1 067	1 067	3 200
New Zealand	979	875	900	2 755
Norway	805	833	833	2 470
Portugal	949	949	949	2 848
Spain	900	900	900	2 700
Sweden	828	828	828	2 484
Turkey	720	720	696	2 136
United States	m	m	980	m
Country mean	**908**	**931**	**935**	**2 762**

Intended instruction time for mathematics and science in hours per year

	Students 12 years of age	Students 13 years of age	Students 14 years of age	Total students 12 to 14 years of age
Austria	260	325	390	975
Belgium	185	171	m	m
Denmark	210	240	240	690
Finland	182	213	213	608
France	162	270	270	702
Germany	210	225	240	675
Greece	162	243	243	648
Ireland	200	200	200	601
Italy	204	204	204	612
Netherlands	200	200	200	600
New Zealand	275	275	272	822
Norway	171	167	167	504
Portugal	245	338	214	797
Spain	207	207	207	621
Sweden	135	204	204	543
Turkey	192	192	192	576
United States	m	m	295	m
Country mean	**200**	**230**	**234**	**665**

Source: OECD Database. See Annex 3 for notes

P11: Total intended instruction time for students at the lower secondary level

Table P11.2:
Intented instruction time for major subject areas as a percentage of total intended instruction time in lower secondary education (1994)

in %	Reading and writing	Modern foreign languages	Mathematics	Science	Social studies	Technology	Arts	Physical education	Religion	Vocational skills	Other	Total compulsory part	Flexible part
Austria	13	10	16	14	13	6	6	11	6	n	6	100	n
Denmark	20	10	13	12	11	n	9	7	3	x	3	90	10
Finland	13	15	11	13	7	x	14	10	4	n	6	93	7
France	17	11	14	11	13	8	8	11	n	n	n	92	8
Germany	14	17	13	11	11	2	8	9	6	2	n	94	6
Greece	13	11	12	12	12	6	6	9	6	n	16	100	n
Ireland	23	7	12	9	19	n	n	5	6	n	4	84	16
Italy	22	10	10	10	14	10	13	7	3	n	n	100	n
Netherlands	10	14	10	8	11	5	7	9	n	3	1	78	22
New Zealand	21	10	16	13	13	8	9	10	n	n	n	100	n
Norway	17	10	12	8	10	n	13	9	7	n	13	100	n
Portugal	13	10	13	15	17	n	10	10	3	n	n	90	10
Spain	20	13	13	10	10	6	12	10	n	n	6	100	n
Sweden	14	9	11	10	15	3	7	8	x	13	7	97	3
Turkey	20	10	13	13	13	n	9	7	7	n	7	100	n
Country mean	17	11	13	11	13	4	9	9	3	1	5	95	5

Source: OECD Database. See Annex 3 for notes

P33: Teaching time

P33: TEACHING TIME

This indicator shows the statutory number of hours per year a full-time classroom teacher is required to teach.

POLICY CONTEXT

Together with factors such as student/teaching staff ratios and teachers' salaries, teaching time influences the financial resources which governments must devote to education. At the same time, teaching time is an important element of the working conditions of teachers. It also affects the amount of time available for planning and other professional activities. Nonetheless, the time spent actually teaching, which is the portion of human resources in education that is directly involved in the learning process, needs to be given its rightful emphasis as a teacher's primary activity.

KEY RESULTS

At the primary level the annual teaching load is 818 hours on average, but it is over 40 per cent lower for Swedish primary teachers, at one extreme, than for Swiss teachers, at the other. At the lower and upper secondary levels there are fewer teaching hours on average (760 hours at the lower secondary level, 688 and 722 hours at the general and vocational upper secondary levels respectively), but the distribution between the levels of education is similar across countries. It is important to note, however, that these figures do not include non-teaching time.

DESCRIPTION AND INTERPRETATION

This indicator shows the statutory number of hours per year a full-time classroom teacher is required to teach according to formal policy. It is important to bear in mind that these figures include neither non-teaching hours within the school nor work in the community or at home, such as the preparation of lessons or professional development activities and general school tasks, for example staff meetings, or the support of students. The indicator can thus not be interpreted as a measure of the total workload of teachers.

In Greece, Norway and Sweden the teaching load appears to be relatively low at all levels reported, whereas in the Netherlands, Switzerland and the United States it is relatively high. New Zealand and Turkey show relatively high numbers of teaching hours at the upper secondary level. However, the high figures in Turkey partly relate to the fact that the maximum number of hours has been reported in Turkey and that hours to be spent in workshops are included in the figure for vocational education. The teaching load for vocational programmes is higher in most countries than it is for general programmes.

When looking at this indicator jointly with Indicator P35 on teachers' salaries – which is another important determinant of teachers' working conditions – it appears that there is a tendency across countries (although not a general rule) for higher teaching loads to coincide with higher salaries.

DEFINITIONS

Teaching time is defined as the total number of hours per year (1 hour = 60 minutes) during which a full-time classroom teacher is responsible for teaching a group or class of students, according to the formal policy of the country in question.

Teaching hours per year are calculated on the basis of average teaching hours per day multiplied by the number of teaching days per year, or on the basis of teaching hours per week multiplied by the number of weeks per year that the school is open for teaching. This excludes the number of hours per year accounted for by days when the school is closed for festivities and celebrations.

Data are from the 1995 OECD-INES survey on teachers and the curriculum and refer to the school year 1993/94. In New Zealand and the United States, survey data were substituted where no information on statutory teaching hours was available.

P33: Teaching time

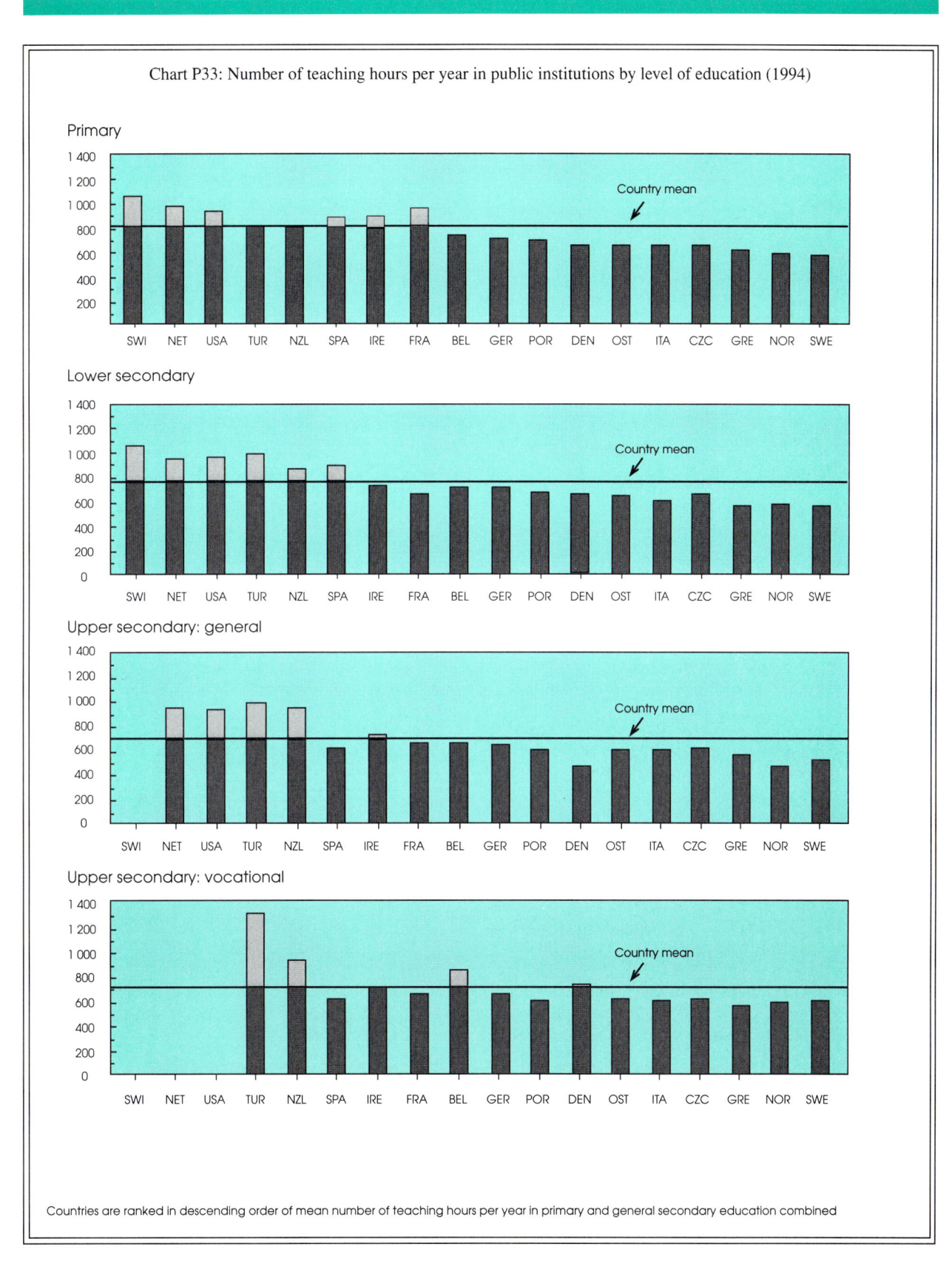

Chart P33: Number of teaching hours per year in public institutions by level of education (1994)

Primary

Lower secondary

Upper secondary: general

Upper secondary: vocational

Countries are ranked in descending order of mean number of teaching hours per year in primary and general secondary education combined

P33: Teaching time

Table P33:
Number of teaching hours per year in public institutions by level of education (1994)

	Primary education	Lower secondary education	Upper secondary education (general)	Upper secondary education (vocational)
Austria	709	651	616	629
Belgium	832	720	660	862
Czech Republic	687	657	627	627
Denmark	750	750	480	750
France	923	660	660	660
Germany	760	712	650	665
Greece	696	569	569	569
Ireland	915	735	735	735
Italy	748	612	612	612
Netherlands	1 000	954	954	m
New Zealand	788	869	950	950
Norway	686	611	476	590
Portugal	828	681	607	607
Spain	900	900	630	630
Sweden	624	576	528	612
Switzerland	1 085	1 056	m	m
Turkey	830	996	996	1 328
United States	958	964	943	m
Country mean	**818**	**760**	**688**	**722**

Source: OECD Database. See Annex 3 for notes

P35: Statutory salaries of teachers in public primary and lower secondary schools

P35: STATUTORY SALARIES OF TEACHERS IN PUBLIC PRIMARY AND LOWER SECONDARY SCHOOLS

This indicator shows the starting, mid-career and maximum statutory salaries of teachers in public primary and lower secondary education. Salaries have been converted into equivalent U.S. dollars using purchasing power parity rates.

POLICY CONTEXT

Good teachers are a key to improved education. Ensuring that there will be enough skilled teachers to educate all children is an important policy concern in all OECD countries. Key determinants of the supply of teachers are the salaries and working conditions of teachers and the costs incurred by individuals in becoming teachers, as compared to salaries and costs for other occupations. Both affect the career decisions of potential teachers and the types of person countries will be able to attract into the teaching profession. Differences between starting and maximum salary levels and the design of payscales can affect career decisions as well.

While salary is one of the malleable rewards of the teaching profession, the pressure to improve the quality of education and to expand access to education is under increasing fiscal constraints – and teachers' salaries represent the most important component of educational spending (see also Indicator F5).

KEY RESULTS

There are considerable differences in annual statutory salaries for teachers among OECD countries, with starting salaries ranging from less than US$ 8 500 to more than US$ 30 000 at the primary level of education; and from less than US$ 7 000 to more than US$ 36 000 at the lower secondary level of education. In most countries statutory salaries are somewhat higher for lower secondary school teachers than for primary school teachers.

Starting salaries of teachers are similar to per capita GDP levels in most countries and after 15 years of experience they are generally above per capita GDP. In most countries teachers are well paid relative to the average earnings of wage and salary workers.

The structure of payscales differs significantly among countries: whereas after 15 years of experience a lower secondary teacher in Turkey can expect less than 1.2 times his or her starting salary, in Portugal the salary level will have almost doubled over the same period. The number of years it takes teachers to progress from their minimum to their maximum salary varies across countries from 9 to 42 years at the primary level of education and from 8 to 42 years at the lower secondary level of education. The average is 25 years for primary and for lower secondary education.

DESCRIPTION AND INTERPRETATION

Annual statutory starting salaries of teachers vary at the primary level from US$ 8 000 to US$ 15 000 in Greece, New Zealand, Sweden and Turkey, up to US$ 26 000 in Germany and US$ 30 600 in Switzerland. The pattern at the lower secondary level is similar although overall levels of salaries are, on average, about US$ 1 000 per year higher than at the primary level.

Comparing teachers' salaries with per capita GDP provides some indication of the economic status of the teaching profession in a country. The indicator shows that the starting salaries of teachers are similar to, or slightly above, per capita GDP in most countries, although there is considerable variation. In Spain and Turkey the starting salary of primary teachers is more than 1.5 times per capita GDP, which suggests that the teaching profession in those countries has a comparatively high standing. At the lower secondary level, starting salary levels are 1.5 times per capita GDP or more in Germany, Ireland, Spain and Switzerland. Starting salaries are lowest relative to per capita GDP in Norway, Sweden and the United States although they are still in the middle range in absolute terms in these countries. After 15 years of experience, statutory salaries are above per capita GDP in most countries.

Chart P35.2 compares the statutory salaries of primary and lower secondary teachers with the 10th, 50th and 90th percentiles of the overall distribution of gross annual earnings of full-time wage and salary workers for selected countries. Although data on average earnings are different in kind from data on statutory salaries and comparisons need therefore be made with caution, they can provide a broad benchmark for teachers' salaries. While primary teachers in Austria, Germany, France and Switzerland fare relatively well when compared against average earnings of full-time wage and salary workers, in Finland, New Zealand and Sweden they obtain

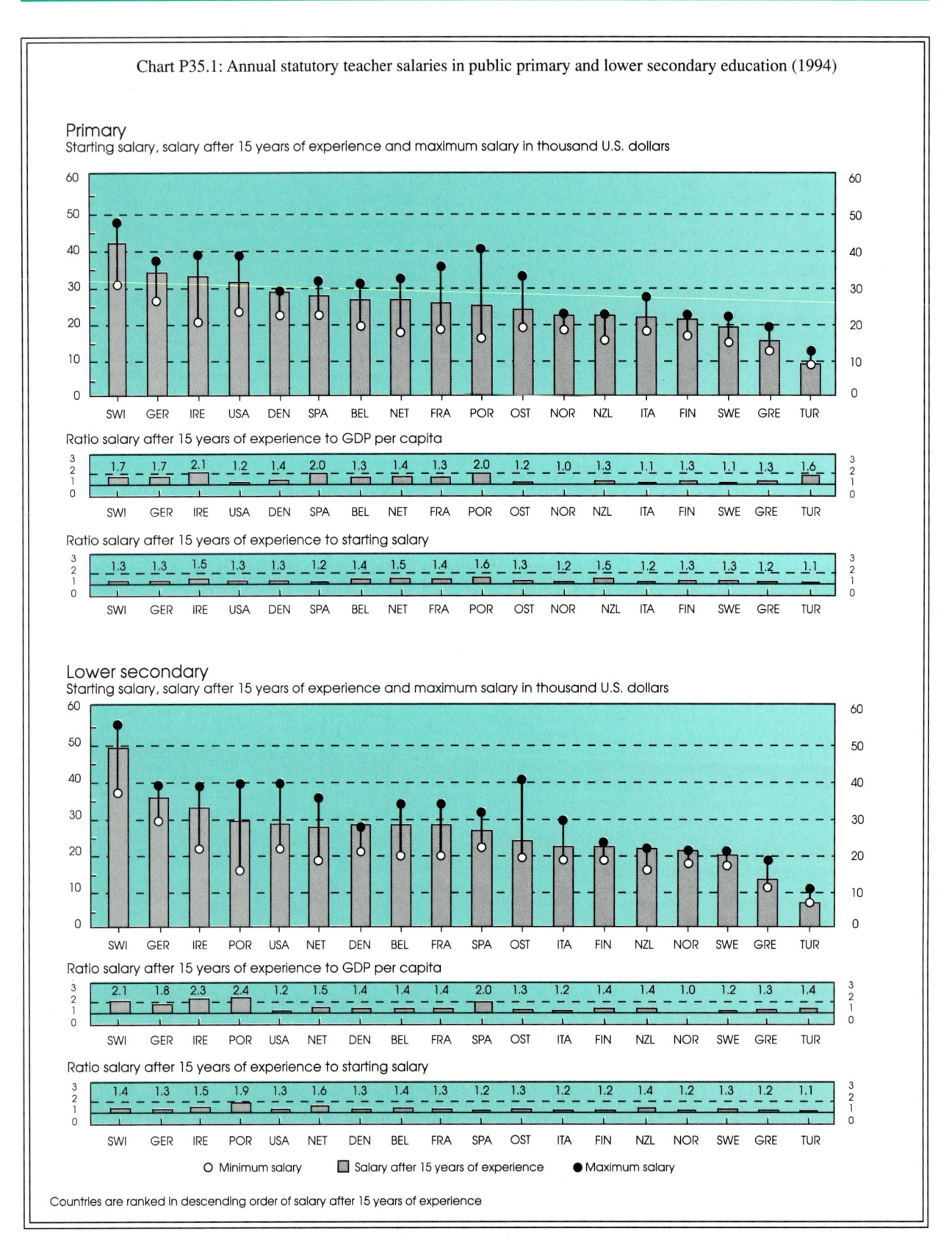

P35: Statutory salaries of teachers in public primary and lower secondary schools

Chart P35.1: Annual statutory teacher salaries in public primary and lower secondary education (1994)

Primary
Starting salary, salary after 15 years of experience and maximum salary in thousand U.S. dollars

	SWI	GER	IRE	USA	DEN	SPA	BEL	NET	FRA	POR	OST	NOR	NZL	ITA	FIN	SWE	GRE	TUR
Ratio salary after 15 years of experience to GDP per capita	1.7	1.7	2.1	1.2	1.4	2.0	1.3	1.4	1.3	2.0	1.2	1.0	1.3	1.1	1.3	1.1	1.3	1.6
Ratio salary after 15 years of experience to starting salary	1.3	1.3	1.5	1.3	1.3	1.2	1.4	1.5	1.4	1.6	1.3	1.2	1.5	1.2	1.3	1.3	1.2	1.1

Lower secondary
Starting salary, salary after 15 years of experience and maximum salary in thousand U.S. dollars

	SWI	GER	IRE	POR	USA	NET	DEN	BEL	FRA	SPA	OST	ITA	FIN	NZL	NOR	SWE	GRE	TUR
Ratio salary after 15 years of experience to GDP per capita	2.1	1.8	2.3	2.4	1.2	1.5	1.4	1.4	1.4	2.0	1.3	1.2	1.4	1.4	1.0	1.2	1.3	1.4
Ratio salary after 15 years of experience to starting salary	1.4	1.3	1.5	1.9	1.3	1.6	1.3	1.4	1.3	1.2	1.3	1.2	1.2	1.4	1.2	1.3	1.2	1.1

○ Minimum salary   ▨ Salary after 15 years of experience   ● Maximum salary

Countries are ranked in descending order of salary after 15 years of experience

P35: Statutory salaries of teachers in public primary and lower secondary schools

comparatively low compensation. The pattern is similar at the secondary level but, overall, teachers at this level appear to have more competitive salaries. Note, however, that in countries with lower average levels of education, teachers are often among the most educated workers and are therefore being compared with persons with, on average, lower formal qualifications. Conversely, in countries with more highly qualified workers, teachers tend to fare worse. In interpreting this indicator, other aspects of the working conditions for teachers need to be taken into account as well, such as the teaching and total working time of teachers compared to that of other professions (see also Indicator P33).

Differences between minimum and maximum salaries are largest in Portugal and smallest in Norway. In Norway most starting teachers have more than the minimum required level of training and are paid accordingly.

In Denmark, Norway and New Zealand teachers have almost reached their maximum salary after 15 years of experience. In Turkey, teachers' salaries at 15 years of experience are scarcely higher than their starting salaries. In Italy and Spain it takes 40 and 42 years respectively for teachers to attain their maximum salary.

In some countries teachers may receive additional bonuses in addition to their gross salaries (see Annex 3). Substantial additional bonuses are found in Finland, France, Greece, New Zealand and the United States. In Turkey, lower secondary teachers are paid additional bonuses for teaching above the compulsory number of hours, which can increase their salaries substantially.

DEFINITIONS

The starting salaries reported refer to the average scheduled gross salary per year for a full-time teacher with the minimum level of training necessary to be fully qualified at the beginning of his or her teaching career. Reported salaries are defined as the sum of wages (total sum of money paid by the employer for the labour supplied minus the employer's contribution to social security and pension funding). Bonuses that constitute a *regular* part of the salary such as a 13th month, or holiday or regional bonuses, are included in the figures. Additional bonuses, for example remuneration for teachers in educational priority areas, for participating in school improvement projects or special activities, or for exceptional performance, are excluded from the reported gross salaries but reported separately in Table P35.

Salaries at 15 years of experience refer to the scheduled salary per year of a full-time classroom teacher with the minimum level of training necessary to be fully qualified and with 15 years of experience. The maximum salaries reported refer to the scheduled maximum salary (top of the salary scale) per year of a full-time classroom teacher with the minimum level of training to be fully qualified for his or her job.

Salary data are reported in accordance with formal policies for public institutions.

Data are from the 1995 OECD-INES survey on teachers and the curriculum and refer to the school year 1993/94. The purchasing power parity (PPP) exchange rates used pertain to GDP and come from the OECD National Accounts Database (see Annex 2). Data on gross average earnings for wage and salary workers are taken from the OECD Earnings Distribution Database. Generally, they refer to overall wages and other remuneration paid in cash in the reference year, before deduction of income tax and social security contributions (for definitions and sources see OECD, *1996 Employment Outlook*).

P35: Statutory salaries of teachers in public primary and lower secondary schools

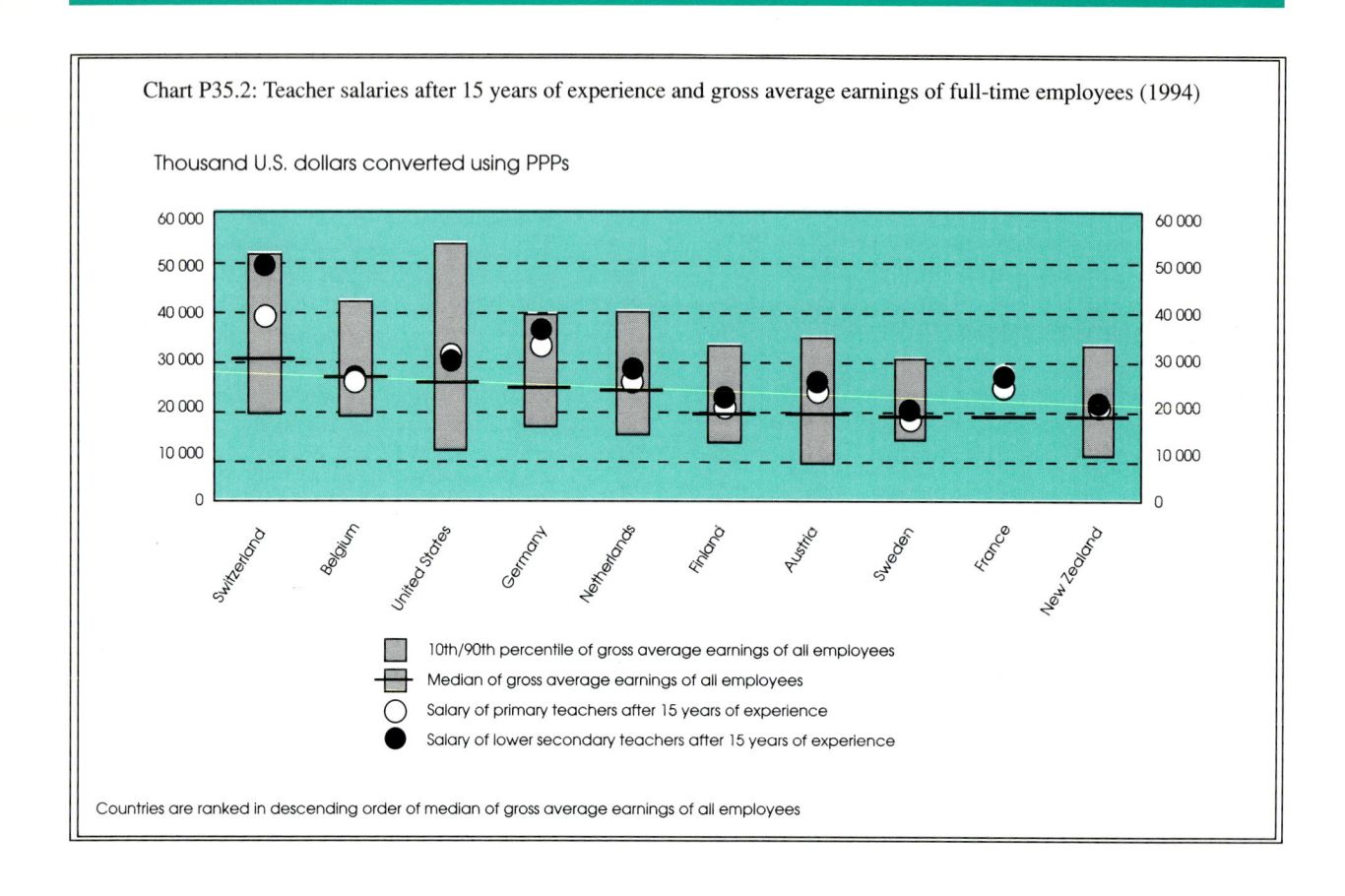

Chart P35.2: Teacher salaries after 15 years of experience and gross average earnings of full-time employees (1994)

Thousand U.S. dollars converted using PPPs

- 10th/90th percentile of gross average earnings of all employees
- Median of gross average earnings of all employees
- ○ Salary of primary teachers after 15 years of experience
- ● Salary of lower secondary teachers after 15 years of experience

Countries are ranked in descending order of median of gross average earnings of all employees

P35: Statutory salaries of teachers in public primary and lower secondary schools

Table P35:
Annual teacher salaries in public institutions at the primary and lower secondary education in equivalent US dollars converted using PPPs (1994)

	Starting salary	Salary at 15 years experience	Salary at top of scale	Ratio of starting salary to per capita GDP	Ratio of salary at 15 years experience to per capita GDP	Ratio of salary at 15 years experience to starting salary	Years from starting to top salary	Percentage additional bonus*
Primary education								
Austria	18 443	23 598	34 136	0.9	1.2	1.3	34	n
Belgium	19 401	26 247	31 269	1.0	1.3	1.4	27	m
Denmark	21 789	28 096	28 096	1.1	1.4	1.3	14	1
Finland	16 558	20 779	22 078	1.0	1.3	1.3	20	14
France	18 496	24 976	34 579	1.0	1.3	1.4	32	12
Germany	26 215	33 321	35 986	1.3	1.7	1.3	22	n
Greece	12 079	14 946	18 726	1.1	1.3	1.2	32	14
Ireland	21 114	32 348	38 188	1.4	2.1	1.5	25	5
Italy	17 605	21 244	27 000	0.9	1.1	1.2	40	m
Netherlands	17 748	26 151	32 680	1.0	1.4	1.5	25	n
New Zealand	14 768	21 581	21 581	0.9	1.3	1.5	9	10
Norway	17 838	21 806	22 036	0.8	1.0	1.2	14	n
Portugal	15 535	24 257	40 277	1.3	2.0	1.6	29	n
Spain	22 850	26 955	32 661	1.7	2.0	1.2	42	n
Sweden	14 617	18 750	21 774	0.8	1.1	1.3	23	n
Switzerland	30 571	40 952	47 000	1.3	1.7	1.3	23	n
Turkey	8 247	8 677	12 827	1.6	1.6	1.1	27	n
United States	22 753	30 716	38 142	0.9	1.2	1.3	16	18
Country mean	**18 702**	**24 745**	**29 946**	**1.1**	**1.4**	**1.3**	**25**	**5**
Lower secondary education								
Austria	19 549	25 533	41 034	1.0	1.3	1.3	34	n
Belgium	19 852	27 997	34 235	1.0	1.4	1.4	27	m
Denmark	21 789	28 096	28 096	1.1	1.4	1.3	14	1
Finland	18 669	22 727	24 351	1.2	1.4	1.2	20	15
France	21 226	27 587	37 351	1.1	1.4	1.3	32	12
Germany	28 760	36 213	39 878	1.5	1.8	1.3	21	n
Greece	12 079	14 946	18 726	1.1	1.3	1.2	32	18
Ireland	22 136	34 248	38 544	1.5	2.3	1.5	24	5
Italy	19 105	23 133	29 980	1.0	1.2	1.2	40	m
Netherlands	17 788	28 191	35 306	1.0	1.5	1.6	25	n
New Zealand	15 769	22 511	22 511	1.0	1.4	1.4	8	17
Norway	17 838	21 806	22 036	0.8	1.0	1.2	14	n
Portugal	15 535	30 079	40 277	1.3	2.4	1.9	29	n
Spain	22 850	26 955	32 661	1.7	2.0	1.2	42	n
Sweden	16 280	20 413	21 774	0.9	1.2	1.3	20	n
Switzerland	36 095	49 095	55 333	1.5	2.1	1.4	21	n
Turkey	6 742	7 172	11 322	1.3	1.4	1.1	27	21
United States	22 265	29 577	39 292	0.9	1.2	1.3	16	23
Country mean	**19 685**	**26 460**	**31 817**	**1.1**	**1.5**	**1.3**	**25**	**7**

* Percentage additional bonus = average of two ratios:
maximum bonus applicable to starting salary and maximum bonus applicable to maximum salary
Source: OECD Database. See Annex 3 for notes

P22(A): Stability in educational staff at the primary level

P22(A): STABILITY IN EDUCATIONAL STAFF AT THE PRIMARY LEVEL

This indicator shows the percentage of teachers at school and of headteachers in charge for at least five years in primary schools, weighted by the number of students enrolled.

POLICY CONTEXT

The stability of the teaching force in a school can have an influence on the consistency and coherence of teaching. Instability may be caused by factors intrinsic to a particular school, such as its working arrangements or social climate, or by extrinsic factors such as the attractiveness of the geographical area where it is situated. The system itself may also cause instability through educational reforms of various kinds, such as the restructuring of school systems, staffing policies, decentralisation and changes in school size.

KEY RESULTS

If stability is considered to exist when at least 75 per cent of the current teaching staff were employed in the same school five years previously, then stability does exist for the majority of students in most countries. However, there are a few countries, notably Greece and Portugal, which have a relatively low percentage of students (24 per cent) attending schools demonstrating such stability. The differences in the stability of teaching staff among the twelve countries for which data are available are generally reflected also in the pattern of stability among headteachers. Reasons for instability cannot be determined from the data. However, major changes in the institutional structure of schools appear not to be the major factor (except in Sweden, where a sizeable proportion of schools had been restructured in the five year period preceding the survey).

DESCRIPTION AND INTERPRETATION

This indicator measures the percentage of students in schools in which *i)* current headteachers, and *ii)* a specified proportion of current teachers were employed five years earlier. Information is also available on whether or not a school existed five years earlier and on whether there have been major changes in the institutional structure of schools (such as a merger or a division into smaller schools). The results are weighted by the number of students enrolled in each school, which means that larger schools will obtain a correspondingly larger weight in the calculation of averages.

Chart P22(A).1 shows the percentage of students attending what are defined as stable schools, i.e., schools in which at least 75 per cent of the teaching staff were employed in the same school five years previously. The

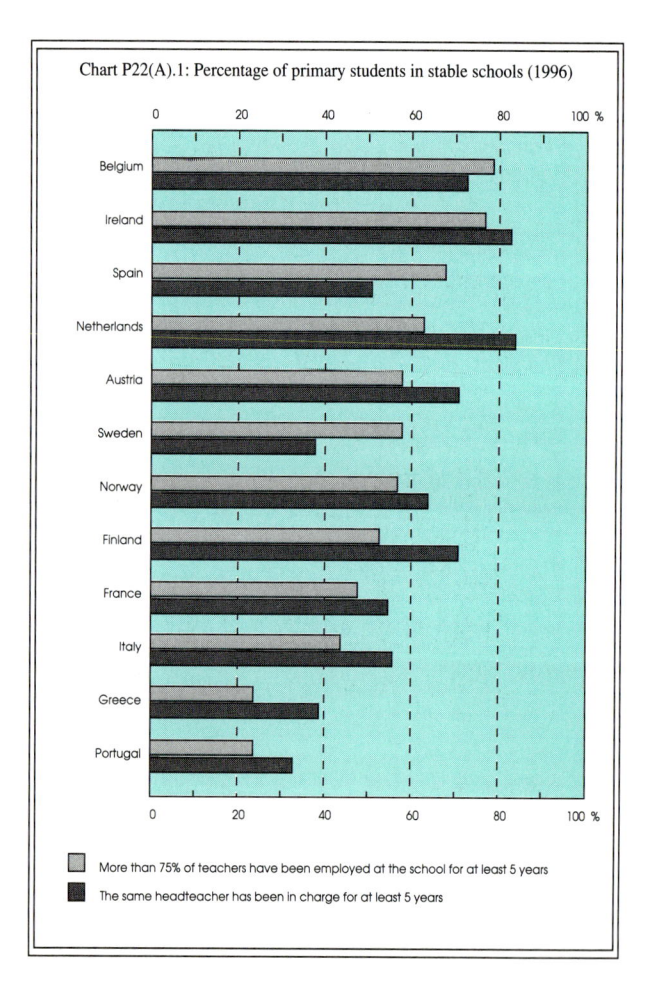

Chart P22(A).1: Percentage of primary students in stable schools (1996)

■ More than 75% of teachers have been employed at the school for at least 5 years
■ The same headteacher has been in charge for at least 5 years

stability rate (taken as the percentage of students in stable schools in a country) ranges from 24 per cent in Portugal and Greece up to 79 per cent in Belgium. The stability rate for headteachers (taken as the percentage of students in schools whose current headteacher has been in place for at least five years) ranges from 33 per cent in Portugal up to 84 per cent in the Netherlands. Both measures account for schools that did not exist five years previously or that have undergone structural change.

P22(A): Stability in educational staff at the primary level

Chart P22(A).2 shows the percentage of students in schools where varying proportions of teachers (0-25 per cent, 26-50 per cent, 51-75 per cent and 76-100 per cent) were already employed five years previously.

As shown in Table P22(A), major changes in the institutional structure of schools during the past five years affect only a small percentage of schools in most countries with the exception of Sweden (55 per cent) and Italy (36 per cent). Moreover, 22 per cent of Swedish primary students attend schools that did not exist five years ago. In nine out of the twelve countries, stability among headteachers is higher than stability in teaching staff.

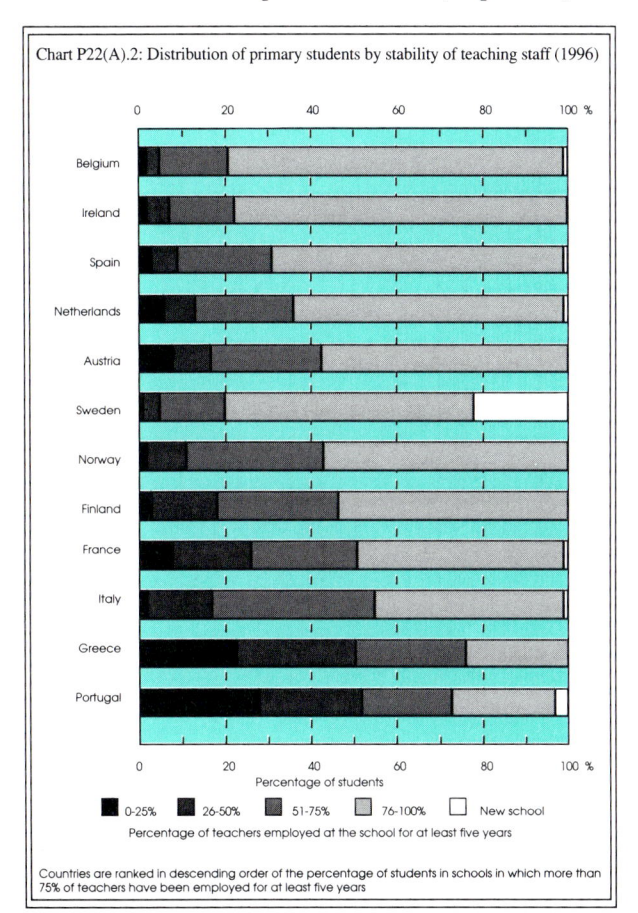

Studies on school effectiveness have shown that the stability of teaching staff and of headteachers adds to the consistency of teaching and to the trust placed in educational institutions. Coherence and consistency in teaching, and a safe and orderly climate, are positively associated with educational achievement. On the other hand, a very low turnover of teachers (in other words a very high stability) could be a sign of rigidity and a lack of dynamism and renewal in schools. It is likely that the optimum lies somewhere in between, but it will depend on local conditions.

Special circumstances may add to the stability or instability in school staff. Examples are a preference for teaching in urban versus rural areas, the geographical or social attractiveness of regions, a halt in recruitment due to policies of retrenchment, the demographic structure of the teaching force, and the supply of and demand for teachers.

DEFINITIONS

Stability in teaching staff is defined in terms of the percentage of currently employed classroom teachers who were already employed at the school five years before the time of the survey (i.e. during the school year 1990/91). Stability among headteachers is defined analogously. Major changes in the institutional structure of schools are defined as mergers, divisions of schools into smaller units, or other major reorganisations. Data are based on the OECD-INES school survey that was conducted during the school year 1995/96. Responses from headteachers are weighted by the number of students enrolled in the school.

Chart P22(A).2: Distribution of primary students by stability of teaching staff (1996)

Countries are ranked in descending order of the percentage of students in schools in which more than 75% of teachers have been employed for at least five years

P22(A): Stability in educational staff at the primary level

Table P22(A): Staff and school stability rates over the past five years (1996)

	Percentage of teachers at school for at least five years					Percentage of headteachers in charge for at least five years			Percentage of schools with changes in institutional structure during past five years	
	0 - 25%	26 - 50%	51 - 75%	76 - 100%	Schools did not exist five years ago	Yes	No	Schools did not exist five years ago	For schools existing five years ago	For schools that were created during past five years
Austria	8	9	26	58	n	71	29	n	12	n
Belgium	2	3	16	79	1	73	26	1	15	1
Finland	3	15	28	53	n	71	28	n	19	n
France	8	18	25	48	1	55	44	1	14	1
Greece	23	28	26	24	n	39	61	n	25	n
Ireland	2	5	15	77	n	83	17	n	6	n
Italy	2	15	38	44	1	56	43	1	36	1
Netherlands	6	7	23	63	1	84	15	1	25	1
Norway	2	9	32	57	n	64	36	n	16	n
Portugal	28	24	21	24	3	33	64	1	25	3
Spain	3	6	22	68	1	51	48	1	17	1
Sweden	1	4	15	58	22	38	40	22	55	22
Country mean	**7**	**12**	**24**	**54**	**3**	**60**	**38**	**2**	**22**	**3**

Data are weighted by the number of primary students enrolled
Source: OECD Database. See Annex 3 for notes

P22(B): School leadership at the primary level

P22(B): SCHOOL LEADERSHIP AT THE PRIMARY LEVEL

This indicator shows the proportion of time which headteachers are assigned to spend in teaching and non-teaching activities in primary schools.

POLICY CONTEXT

In a climate of educational reform, educational leadership and management are of major importance. There are, in particular, increased demands in the areas of financial and human resource management. The literature on school effectiveness indicates that a focus on educational leadership may stimulate performance at the level of schools, teachers and students. However, there is debate on the emphasis that should be given to educational versus administrative leadership, as well as on the amount of working time that headteachers should spend on teaching.

KEY RESULTS

There are large differences in the time headteachers in primary schools are assigned to spend in non-teaching activities. On the one hand in Italy, headteachers have no regular teaching duties at all, and in Belgium and Sweden only a modest amount. On the other hand, in Finland and Spain, headteachers in primary schools spend about half of their working time teaching, and in France and Portugal, they teach for at least 66 per cent of their working hours.

Among non-teaching activities, educational leadership is given roughly comparable weight in all countries. However, it is administrative and organisational duties that take up most of the non-teaching time of headteachers.

DESCRIPTION AND INTERPRETATION

This indicator shows the proportion of time which headteachers are assigned to teaching and non-teaching activities. The results are weighted by the number of students enrolled in each school, which means that headteachers in larger schools will obtain a correspondingly larger weight in the calculation of national averages.

Table P22(B).1 shows the proportion of formal working hours which headteachers are assigned to spend on teaching and non-teaching duties. In the majority of countries, headteachers have teaching obligations, Italy being the only one of the twelve countries for which data are available in which headteachers at primary level have no teaching obligations. At the other end of the scale is Portugal, where headteachers with teaching obligations teach for an average of 25.3 hours per week. Other countries where headteachers have a substantial teaching load are Finland, France, Ireland, Spain and Greece. Note that high values for the standard deviations in Table P22(B).1 indicate that there is considerable variation in the teaching load within countries.

Chart P22(B).1 shows the proportion of time which headteachers estimate they spend on various non-teaching activities, namely educational leadership, administrative and organisational duties, contacts with parents, professional development and other managerial activities. Administrative and organisational duties take up the largest portion of non-teaching time: the average proportion of headteachers' non-teaching working time devoted to administration and organisation ranges from 34 per cent in Greece to 49 per cent in Sweden.

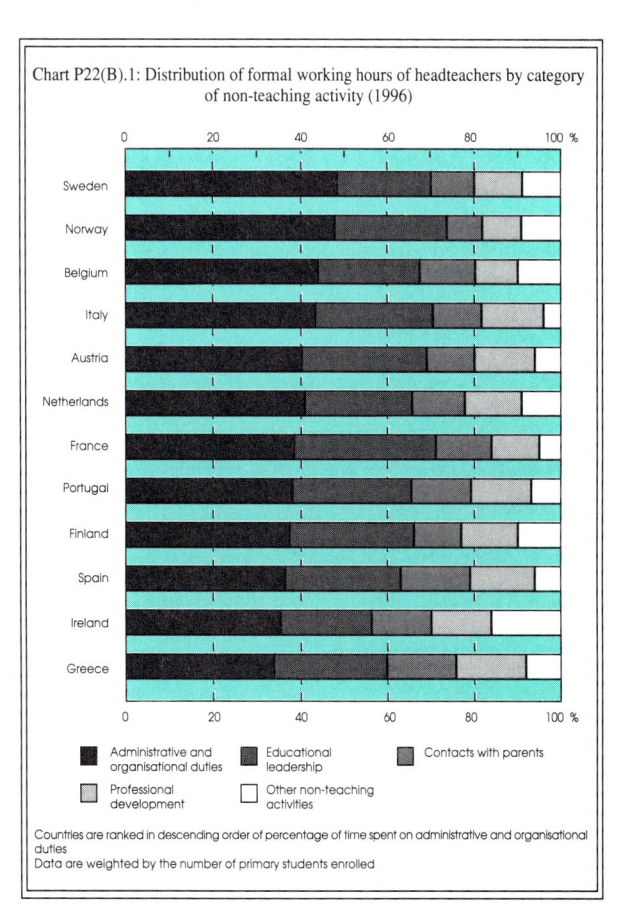

Chart P22(B).1: Distribution of formal working hours of headteachers by category of non-teaching activity (1996)

Countries are ranked in descending order of percentage of time spent on administrative and organisational duties
Data are weighted by the number of primary students enrolled

P22(B): School leadership at the primary level

Chart P22(B).2 reports on the time that headteachers estimate they spend on educational leadership, one of the non-teaching activities. It would appear that headteachers in Italy spend on average significantly more time on educational leadership than those in almost all other countries. The differences in actual time spent on educational leadership, however, are largely explained by the differences in total time headteachers have available for non-teaching activities.

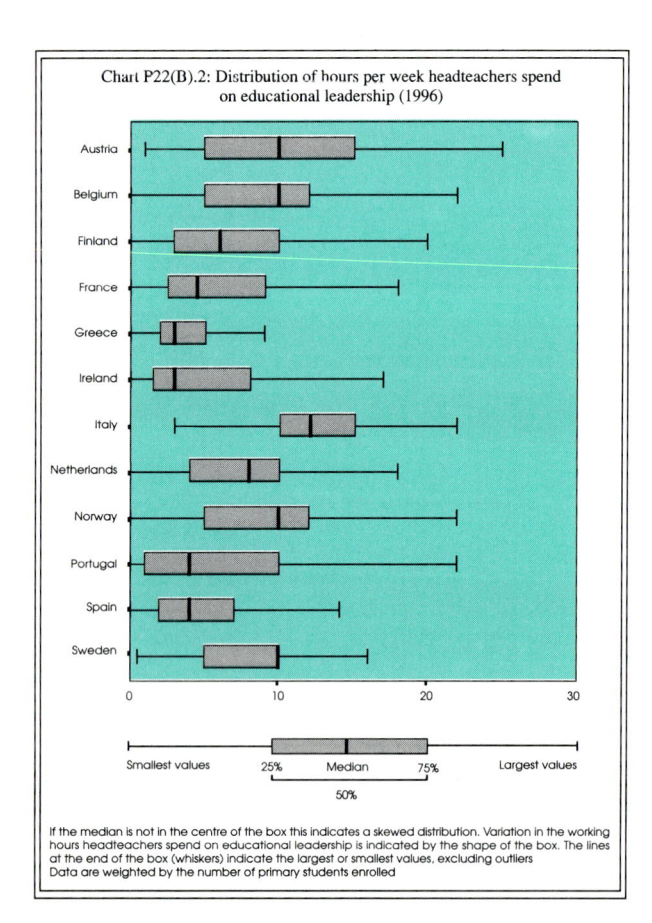

The indicator reflects differences among countries in the roles and functions of headteachers. For example, the relatively heavy teaching load in some countries may reflect the view that headteachers are to be seen as the "first among equals", and should be exemplary teachers rather than managers. Finally, in some countries there is significant variation in this indicator between schools. In Ireland, for example, headteachers of small primary schools teach on a full-time basis whereas headteachers of large primary schools have no teaching duties. The indicator should be interpreted in the context of further information on the amount of administration devolved onto schools, and the level of organisational and professional support provided by local, regional and national authorities.

DEFINITIONS

Data are based on two structured questions in the OECD-INES school survey that was conducted during the school year 1995/96. The first question asked about the number of clock hours per week during which headteachers are formally employed on teaching and non-teaching activities. The second question provided the respondents with five different categories of non-teaching activities: educational leadership, administrative and organisational duties involving internal or external relationships, contacts with parents, professional development and other non-teaching activities. Official statements of various kinds were used as the basis for obtaining information from the responding headteachers about their teaching obligations. The data about non-teaching activities were estimated by the headteachers and thus express the perceived workload. Responses from headteachers are weighted by the number of students enrolled in each school.

Data on working hours per item are based on all cases with valid answers, while percentages of working time per item are based only on cases with valid answer on all items.

Chart P22(B).2: Distribution of hours per week headteachers spend on educational leadership (1996)

If the median is not in the centre of the box this indicates a skewed distribution. Variation in the working hours headteachers spend on educational leadership is indicated by the shape of the box. The lines at the end of the box (whiskers) indicate the largest or smallest values, excluding outliers
Data are weighted by the number of primary students enrolled

P22(B): School leadership at the primary level

Table P22(B).1: Headteacher activities and teaching duties (1996)

	Average percentage of total formal employment of headteachers for: Non-teaching activities	Average percentage of total formal employment of headteachers for: Teaching activities	Characteristics of headteachers with teaching duties: Percentage of headteachers with teaching duties	Characteristics of headteachers with teaching duties: Percentage of statutory working time allocated to teaching	Characteristics of headteachers with teaching duties: Mean number of hours per week employed in teaching (standard deviation in brackets)
Australia	76	24	64	38	14.2 (4.8)
Belgium	92	8	14	58	14.6 (7.7)
Finland	52	48	99	50	15.2 (7.1)
France	34	66	85	78	20.4 (5.6)
Greece	57	43	99	43	13.9 (6.2)
Ireland	47	54	68	79	24.8 (8.5)
Italy	100	a	a	a	a
Netherlands	64	36	77	47	17.9 (8.5)
Norway	77	23	77	30	10.7 (7.8)
Portugal	33	67	92	72	25.3 (13.1)
Spain	52	48	96	50	15.0 (6.9)
Sweden	88	12	25	48	18.9 (15.1)

Data are weighted by the number of primary students enrolled
Source: OECD Database. See Annex 3 for notes

Table P22 (B).2: Non-teaching activities of headteachers (1996)

	Working hours per week on non-teaching activities estimated by headteachers					Percentage of non-teaching time spent on various non-teaching activities				
	Educational leadership	Administrative and organisational duties	Contacts with parents	Professional development	Other non-teaching activities	Educational leadership	Administrative and organisational duties	Contacts with parents	Professional development	Other non-teaching activities
Australia	9.7	13.9	3.5	4.2	2.1	29	41	11	14	6
Belgium	9.4	17.3	4.9	3.8	3.9	24	45	13	10	10
Finland	7.0	9.1	2.2	2.9	2.3	29	38	11	13	10
France	6.3	7.4	2.4	1.8	1.1	33	39	13	11	5
Greece	4.1	5.3	2.5	3.0	1.4	26	34	16	16	8
Ireland	5.2	9.1	3.0	2.9	3.2	21	36	14	14	16
Italy	12.2	19.2	5.0	6.4	2.0	27	43	11	14	4
Netherlands	8.9	14.1	4.0	4.5	3.2	25	41	12	13	9
Norway	9.4	17.7	3.1	3.4	3.2	26	48	8	9	9
Portugal	5.9	7.3	2.1	2.4	1.4	28	39	14	14	7
Spain	5.0	6.8	2.8	2.7	1.4	27	37	16	15	6
Sweden	9.1	21.1	4.0	4.7	4.1	22	49	10	11	9

Data are weighted by the number of primary students enrolled
Source: OECD Database. See Annex 3 for notes

P22(C): STAFF CO-OPERATION

This indicator illustrates the frequency of formal and informal meetings between headteachers and teachers in primary schools.

POLICY CONTEXT

Co-operation between headteachers and teachers and co-operation among teachers are regarded as an important aspect of improved school functioning. The frequency and nature of staff co-operation can be a factor in enhancing school effectiveness.

KEY RESULTS

In most countries there appears to be regular communication and co-operation between headteachers and teachers, particularly at the informal level. There are, however, significant differences among countries with respect to the frequency of meetings of the entire staff convened by the headteacher. Differences in the frequency of informal meetings are less pronounced, although the percentage of students in schools where such informal meetings take place every day ranges from 30 per cent in Belgium to 66 per cent in Finland.

DESCRIPTION AND INTERPRETATION

Co-operation is a complex phenomenon that has various facets. The frequency of formally convened and informal teaching staff meetings, in which the headteacher takes part, is one such facet. Another is co-operation among teachers outside formal meetings. Table P22(C) shows the percentages of schools, weighted by the number of students enrolled, in which informal meetings between the headteacher and some of the staff, and meetings of the entire teaching staff, convened by the headteacher, take place at various frequencies. Chart P22(C) indicates the percentage of schools in which full teaching staff meetings and informal teaching staff meetings are held at least once a week.

There appear to be significant differences among countries with respect to the frequency of meetings involving all staff. In only four countries out of the 12 do more than half of the students attend schools where full staff meetings are held at least once a week. These are Finland, the Netherlands, Norway and Sweden. At the next level of frequency, i.e. full staff meetings that occur at least once a month, it is the same four countries which have the highest values, more than 80 per cent of students being in such schools. In Ireland and Italy, on the other hand, fewer than 25 per cent of students are in schools where full staff meetings take place at least once a month, and the remaining countries demonstrate values of monthly or more frequent full staff meetings ranging from 46 to 73 per cent.

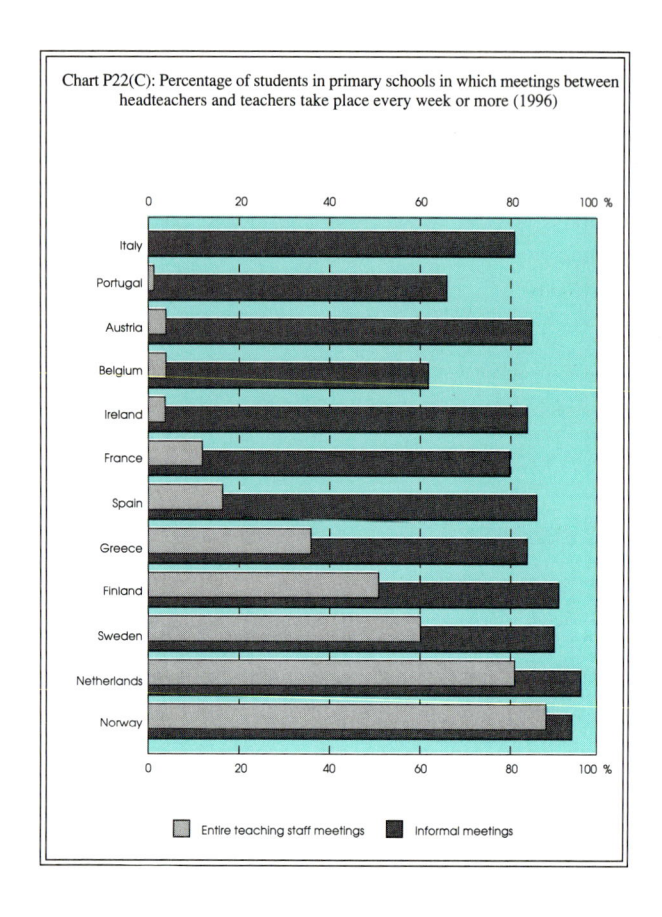

Informal meetings between headteachers and teachers occur more frequently than formal meetings. Countries that show a relatively high frequency of formally convened meetings also show a high frequency of informal meetings. However, countries where full staff meetings are less frequent show high frequencies of informal meetings as well. Thus differences among countries are less pronounced with respect to informal meetings than with respect to meetings of the entire staff convened by the headteacher.

The frequency of meetings and co-operation on certain tasks can only partially capture the complex phenomenon that is formal and informal co-operation.

P22(C): Staff co-operation

Co-operation and communication outside meetings plays an important role as well. Co-operation among staff in schools also depends on less easily measurable factors, such as school culture and climate. It should further be noted that this indicator is based on headteacher perceptions of what is happening in schools.

DEFINITIONS

In an attempt to capture co-operation among staff, this was defined as *i)* meetings of the entire staff convened by the headteacher; and *ii)* informal meetings of the headteacher with one or more members of the teaching staff about educational, administrative or organisational matters. Data are based on the OECD-INES school survey that was conducted during the school year 1995/96. Responses from headteachers are weighted by the number of students enrolled in each school.

Table P22(C):
Frequency of informal meetings between headteacher and teachers and of meetings of entire teaching staff (1996)

	Frequency of informal meetings between headteachers and teachers (as percentages)						Frequency of entire teaching staff meetings (as percentages)				
	Never	1 - 4 times per year	5 - 9 times per year	Every month	Every week	Every day	Never	1 - 4 times per year	5 - 9 times per year	Every month	Every week or more
Austria	n	2	6	7	28	56	n	3	51	42	4
Belgium	n	8	8	22	32	30	n	18	17	61	4
Finland	1	2	2	4	25	66	2	8	9	30	51
France	n	6	7	7	24	57	1	5	21	61	12
Greece	1	2	5	8	22	61	1	5	22	36	36
Ireland	n	6	6	4	26	57	3	52	24	17	4
Italy	n	2	6	11	48	33	n	4	81	16	n
Netherlands	n	1	n	3	38	57	n	1	2	15	81
Norway	n	2	1	2	44	50	n	2	1	9	88
Portugal	n	2	2	31	24	41	4	39	5	51	1
Spain	n	1	3	10	42	43	n	9	31	45	16
Sweden	n	1	2	7	46	44	n	7	10	23	60
Country mean	**n**	**3**	**4**	**10**	**33**	**50**	**1**	**13**	**23**	**34**	**30**

Data are weighted by the number of primary students enrolled
Source: OECD Database. See Annex 3 for notes

P22(D): Monitoring and evaluation at the primary level

P22(D): MONITORING AND EVALUATION AT THE PRIMARY LEVEL

This indicator illustrates the frequency of evaluation and monitoring practices in primary schools, and examines the uses of information from student records.

POLICY CONTEXT

Monitoring students' progress can be an instrument for school improvement as well as a means of accountability towards parents. The methods of monitoring and evaluation used are closely connected to educational aims and intentions, which in turn are embedded in the educational culture. As more sophisticated evaluation techniques become available, national education systems and individual schools are faced with the questions of "how much" student monitoring and evaluation is desirable, and what proportion of this should be structured rather than informal.

KEY RESULTS

There are substantial differences among countries in the frequency with which schools monitor students' progress, and in the purposes to which the information gained from that monitoring is put. In most countries, students' progress at the primary level is recorded at least five times a year in more than half of schools. In Austria this practice takes place every week in the majority of schools.

DESCRIPTION AND INTERPRETATION

The frequency of assessing students' progress during the school year can be indicative of how closely students' progress is monitored. Registering marks and test scores in a way that makes them accessible for inspection by headteachers and other teachers enables this information to be used for the proper guidance of individual students and school self-evaluation. The results in Table P22(D).1 show that recording the progress of individual students is common practice in all countries, although the frequency of such practices differs considerably. In Austria, progress is recorded every week in the majority of schools. Belgium, France, Italy, the Netherlands and Portugal have progress recorded at least five times a year in most schools, while in Sweden 30 per cent of schools do not regularly record student progress in a way that is open for inspection by the principal. The results are weighted by the number of students enrolled in each school, which means larger schools will obtain a correspondingly larger weight in the calculation of national averages.

Many countries use standardised achievement tests in mathematics [not shown in Tables P22(D).1 and P22(D).2], but several countries – Austria, Norway, Spain and Sweden – have specific policies that preclude standardised achievement testing for the purposes of student monitoring or school self-evaluation. The data show that it is common practice to provide a written report on students' progress to parents about three times a year.

The practice whereby schools designate a time for parents to meet their child's teacher to discuss his or her performance is a further indication of the use made of the evaluation of students. The data in Table P22(D).1 show that this practice occurs quite frequently in Austria and Greece (every month of the school year in the majority of schools), and in Spain (every week in most schools).

With respect to the purposes for which information from students' records is used, it appears that "preparing reports for parents" is the most significant in most countries. Preparing individual study plans is also important, as is "providing information about students to teachers in adjacent grade levels" (in most countries these practices occur in the majority of schools). In Greece the most frequently mentioned purposes are "evaluating the functioning of the school" and "preparing study plans for individual students". "Placement of students in classes" is mentioned relatively infrequently as a purpose for using information from students' records [see Table P22(D).2].

It should be noted that the information is based upon data that are aggregated over grade levels in the schools and therefore provides a global picture.

DEFINITIONS

Data are based on the following questions in the OECD-INES school survey that was conducted during the school year 1995/96. Responses from headteachers are weighted by the number of students enrolled in the school. The following questions were asked:

P22(D): Monitoring and evaluation at the primary level

Table P22(D).1:
Percentage of students in schools in which evaluation and monitoring practices that are open for inspection by the principal occur at the following frequencies (average over grades) (1996)

	Never	1-4 times per year	5-9 times per year	Every month	Every week
Recording of progress					
Austria	6	15	7	13	60
Belgium	5	28	40	20	8
Finland	3	68	6	11	12
France	1	42	45	7	5
Greece	5	64	10	12	8
Ireland	15	59	3	10	12
Italy	1	24	23	25	26
Netherlands	4	39	20	10	27
Portugal	3	34	15	34	14
Spain	2	74	8	5	11
Sweden	30	62	1	3	3
Reporting to parents					
Austria	16	71	7	4	3
Belgium	5	26	49	16	4
Finland	4	89	5	1	0
France	1	42	49	5	3
Greece	9	77	7	6	1
Ireland	24	74	0	0	1
Italy	3	79	13	4	2
Netherlands	12	87	1	0	0
Portugal	3	87	4	6	0
Spain	0	93	5	1	0
Sweden	77	15	1	2	5
Discussion with parents					
Austria	5	40	4	4	46
Belgium	4	92	4	0	1
Finland	4	90	3	1	1
France	12	69	10	3	6
Greece	1	25	13	44	17
Ireland	19	79	1	0	1
Italy	1	46	30	21	2
Netherlands	2	92	5	1	0
Portugal	4	56	6	20	13
Spain	1	6	1	6	87
Sweden	3	96	0	0	1

Source: OECD Database. See Annex 3 for notes

P22(D): Monitoring and evaluation at the primary level

- How often in each grade is the progress of individual students registered in records which are open to inspection by the principal? Registering the progress of individual students implies the documentation of students' progress in terms of grades, test scores, and written reports which are open to inspection by the principal.
- Indicate the purposes for which information from students' records is used in the school.
- How often, in each of the following grades, are standardised achievement tests in mathematics/arithmetic administered to students? A standardised achievement test is a test developed or required by the nation, state, district, or other governing organisation and is typically designed for a certain age group/grade.
- How often for each grade does your school provide a written report of student performance or progress to students and their parents?
- How often for each grade does your school designate a time when parents are invited to meet with their children's teachers to discuss their children's performance?

Table P22(D).2:
Percentage of students in primary schools in which information from student records is used for the following purposes (1996)

	For preparing study plans for individual students	For preparing reports for parents	As a basis for the composition of working-groups of students in classes	For providing information about students to teachers in adjacent grade levels	For evaluating the functioning of the school	For placing students in classes	For selecting students for special programmes	For other purposes
Austria	76	97	58	40	31	8	86	14
Belgium	41	90	48	71	35	18	61	6
Finland	45	97	33	66	54	16	19	6
France	75	81	51	61	28	32	36	5
Greece	66	38	30	54	69	5	41	5
Ireland	54	90	48	75	54	24	68	3
Italy	96	91	71	33	34	33	37	6
Netherlands	84	96	32	88	60	18	86	7
Portugal	91	87	56	87	36	33	81	5
Spain	60	96	21	89	64	13	42	7
Sweden	66	72	16	62	45	17	36	9
Country mean	**69**	**85**	**42**	**66**	**46**	**20**	**54**	**7**

Source: OECD Database. See Annex 3 for notes

P22(E): DIFFERENTIATION AT THE PRIMARY LEVEL

This indicator provides information on differentiation practices used across and within classes in primary schools.

POLICY CONTEXT

One of the most important aspects of the educational process is to adapt teaching and instruction to the specific needs of individual students. Since students differ in many ways from one another in aptitudes, social background and motivational and affective characteristics, the task for education is to adapt instruction to match these individual differences. There are various ways of setting about this task: by forming relatively homogeneous classes of students, or by differentiation within more heterogeneous classrooms. Differentiation policies may be related to national views on the issue of equity in education.

KEY RESULTS

With the exception of Greece, a large majority of students are in primary schools where some form of grouping within classes is used. Among the different types of grouping within classes, ability grouping occurs most frequently.

The practice of "team teaching", whereby a teacher collaborates with one or more other teachers to rearrange their students so that students can work at their own level, takes place quite frequently in primary schools in Italy, Norway and Sweden.

Multi-grade primary classes are quite common in France, Ireland, the Netherlands and Portugal.

DESCRIPTION AND INTERPRETATION

Differentiation within schools can be carried out in various ways. One approach consists of allocating students to classes on the basis of ability. In this way either homogeneous classes can be formed or classes can be made intentionally heterogeneous. The practice of allocating students across classes on the basis of their ability occurs relatively infrequently (although within classes it is the most frequent grouping practice); in Austria and Norway it is prohibited through policy directives. In Italy and Portugal it is done expressly for the purpose of ensuring equality between classes. The results for this indicator are weighted by the number of students enrolled in each school, which means larger schools will obtain a correspondingly larger weight in the calculation of national averages.

A phenomenon that is related to differentiation, but can also be used in order to make efficient use of scarce human resources in small schools, is multi-grade classes. These are quite frequent in France, Ireland, the Netherlands and Portugal, where between 60 and 75 per cent of students are in schools in which multi-grade classes exist at the primary level [see Table P22(E)]. In Belgium, Finland and Sweden, between 36 and 53 per cent of students attend schools which have multi-grade classes. On the other hand, in Austria, Italy, Norway and Spain, at most 20 per cent of students attend such primary schools. The use of multi-grade classes can be explained to some degree by the existence of many small schools, largely as an effect of geographic settings.

The practice of team teaching enlarges the possibilities of individualised instruction. This practice occurs when one teacher works with another teacher (or with a class aide or paraprofessional) in the same class at the same time, or when two or more teachers mix and rearrange their classes so that groups of students can work at their own level. Such arrangements occur quite frequently in Italy, Norway and Sweden, where 90, 91 and 92 per cent of students respectively attend schools which apply team teaching in some or all classes at least once a month, and in Austria, Belgium, Finland, France and Spain (where this percentage lies between 62 and 77 per cent); such practices are virtually absent in Greece.

Grouping within classes by age, ability or interest is a common phenomenon in most countries. Ability grouping is the predominant type of grouping within classes in Austria, Belgium, France, Ireland, Italy and the Netherlands.

In interpreting the data on grouping within classes, it should be borne in mind that headteachers were asked to give an overall impression of differentiation practices. It is well known that differentiation within classes is both broadly accepted as a desirable instructional principle, but difficult to implement in practice. Some overstatement of desirable practice cannot be ruled out as a source of upward bias in these figures but there is no evidence that such tendencies in headteachers' responses would endanger the comparability of data across countries.

P22(E): Differentiation at the primary level

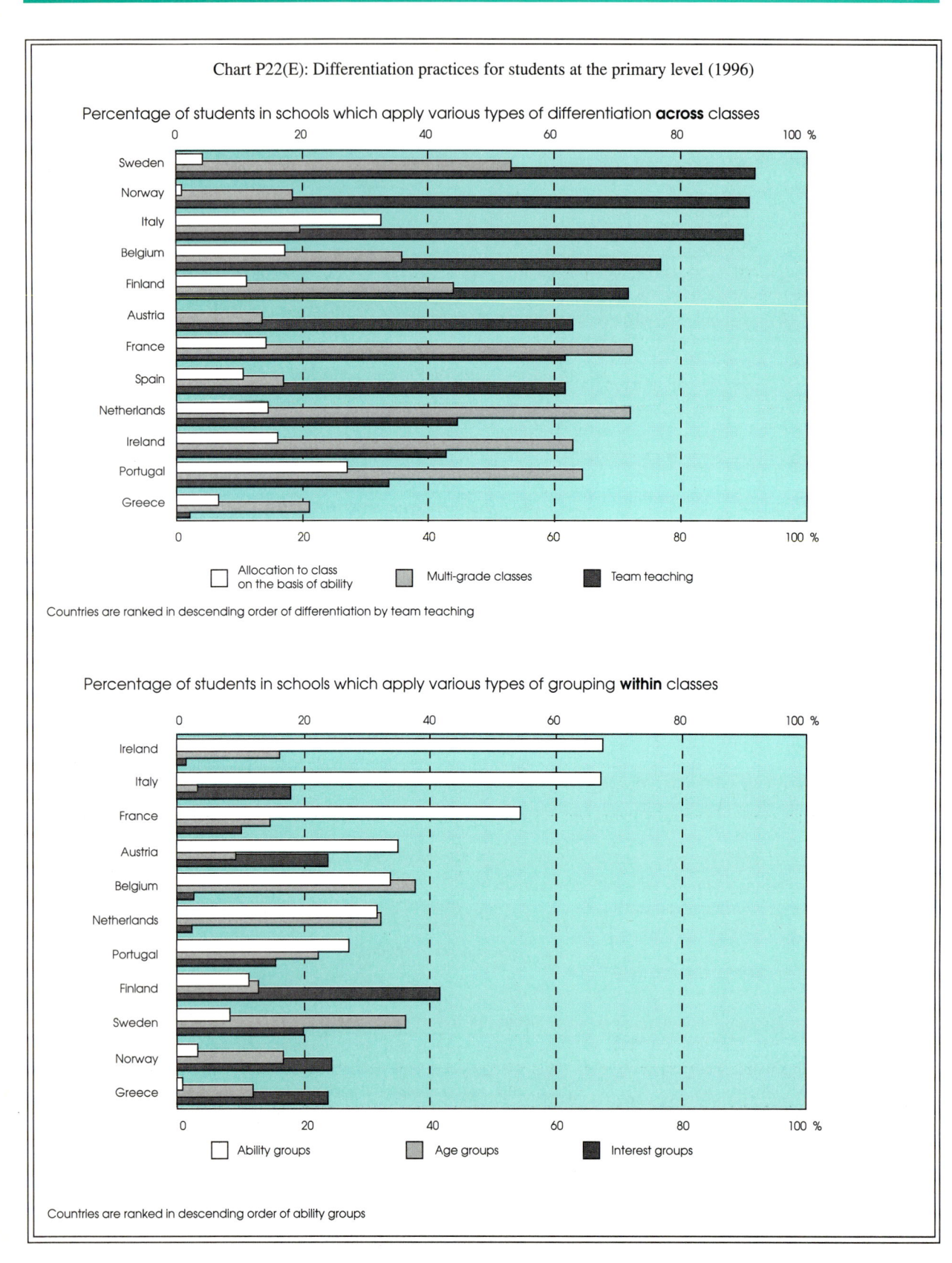

Chart P22(E): Differentiation practices for students at the primary level (1996)

Percentage of students in schools which apply various types of differentiation **across** classes

Countries (top to bottom): Sweden, Norway, Italy, Belgium, Finland, Austria, France, Spain, Netherlands, Ireland, Portugal, Greece

Legend: Allocation to class on the basis of ability | Multi-grade classes | Team teaching

Countries are ranked in descending order of differentiation by team teaching

Percentage of students in schools which apply various types of grouping **within** classes

Countries (top to bottom): Ireland, Italy, France, Austria, Belgium, Netherlands, Portugal, Finland, Sweden, Norway, Greece

Legend: Ability groups | Age groups | Interest groups

Countries are ranked in descending order of ability groups

P22(E): Differentiation at the primary level

DEFINITIONS

Data are based on the following questions in the OECD-INES school survey that was conducted during the school year 1995/96:

- If you have more than one class at a grade level, are students allocated to classes on the basis of ability (i.e., homogeneous grouping)?
- Does your school have multi-grade classes (i.e. children of more than one "grade" combined in one class)?
- What type of student grouping within classes is used most often in your school?
- How frequently does one teacher work with another teacher (or with a class aide or para-professional) in the same classroom, or do two or more teachers mix and rearrange their classes, so that groups of students can work at their own level?

The tables and charts present the percentage of students enrolled in primary schools in which the various differentiation practices are used in one or more classes.

Table P22(E):
Percentage of students in primary schools in which the following differentiation practices are used in one or more classes (1996)

	Differentiation **across** classes			Grouping **within** classes			
	Allocation to class on the basis of ability [1]	Multi-grade classes [2]	Team teaching [3]	No grouping	Ability groups	Age groups	Interest group
Austria	a	14	63	23	36	10	24
Belgium	17	36	77	20	34	38	3
Finland	11	44	72	12	11	13	42
France	14	73	62	14	55	15	10
Greece	7	21	2	55	1	12	24
Ireland	16	63	43	12	68	16	2
Italy	33	20	90	2	68	3	18
Netherlands	15	72	45	23	32	33	2
Norway	1	18	91	6	3	17	25
Portugal	27	65	34	17	28	23	16
Spain	11	17	62	a	a	a	a
Sweden	4	53	92	24	9	37	20
Country mean	**13**	**41**	**61**	**17**	**29**	**18**	**16**

1. Allocation to class on the basis of ability only applies to schools where there is more than one class per grade level
2. For some or all classes
3. At least every month in one or more classes

Source: OECD Database. See Annex 3 for notes

P22(F): Achievement orientation at the primary level

P22(F): ACHIEVEMENT ORIENTATION AT THE PRIMARY LEVEL

This indicator provides information on achievement-oriented practices used in primary schools: comparison of student achievement among schools and over time, setting of achievement standards at student and school level and public recognition of student performance.

POLICY CONTEXT

An active focus on achievement and high expectations of students' performance have been shown to be associated with high student achievement. Common achievement-oriented practices are to set and assess the attainment of explicit achievement standards, and to recognise and reward high levels of performance by students. Comparisons of the standards achieved by different schools, and comparisons of standards over time, can be further important elements of an achievement-oriented strategy. Apart from what schools can do for themselves, governments can enhance achievement orientation directly or indirectly, for example by encouraging intermediate administrative levels to set attainment targets and standards for schools.

KEY RESULTS

Comparing the standards achieved by students in different schools is not a common practice in primary schools in most countries whereas the comparison of student achievement over time is more usual. The setting of achievement standards for individual students is quite common whereas achievement standards for primary schools are not common in many countries. In almost all countries over 50 per cent of the students are in schools that provide public recognition of good progress by students, irrespective of their level of performance.

DESCRIPTION AND INTERPRETATION

Educational standards can be set and assessed in many ways. Comparisons over time give an indication of whether achievement standards within a given school are being maintained, or are rising or falling. Comparisons among schools provide an external reference framework of standards [see Chart P22(F).1]. Finally, achievement standards can be set at the individual or the school level [see Chart P22(F).2]. The results for this indicator are weighted by the number of students enrolled in each school, which means larger schools will obtain a correspondingly larger weight in the calculation of national averages.

Greece and Portugal are the only two countries out of the 12 for which data are available where at least 35 per cent of primary students are in schools which do provide between-school comparisons for all or almost all subject areas. In Austria, Finland, France, Ireland, Italy, Norway and Sweden, fewer than 10 per cent of students

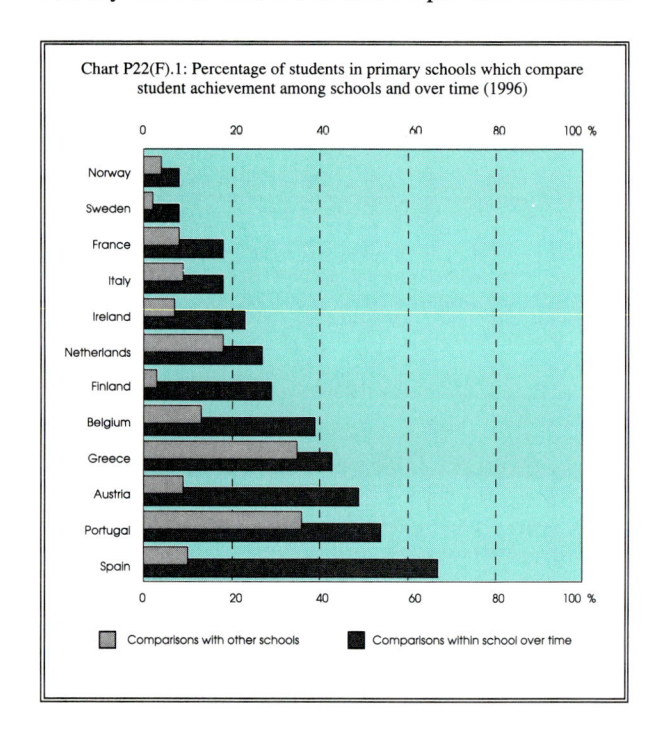

Chart P22(F).1: Percentage of students in primary schools which compare student achievement among schools and over time (1996)

are in such schools. Comparison of students' achievement over time is a more common practice in all countries. In Austria, Portugal and Spain, 49 per cent or more of the students are in schools which compare students' achievement over time, whereas in France, Italy, Norway and Sweden, the figure is below 20 per cent.

On average, about 40 per cent of primary students are in schools that set achievement standards for individual students; Belgium, the Netherlands, Portugal and Spain are the only countries in which more than 50 per cent of students are in schools that set standards for individual students. School-level achievement standards are rarer: only 14 per cent of students attend such schools across all countries. It should be noted,

P22(F): Achievement orientation at the primary level

Chart P22(F).2: Percentage of students in primary schools where achievement standards are set at student and at school levels (1996)

[Bar chart showing countries: Norway, Sweden, Greece, France, Ireland, Italy, Finland, Austria, Belgium, Portugal, Netherlands, Spain — with bars for "Standards for individual students" and "Standards at school level"]

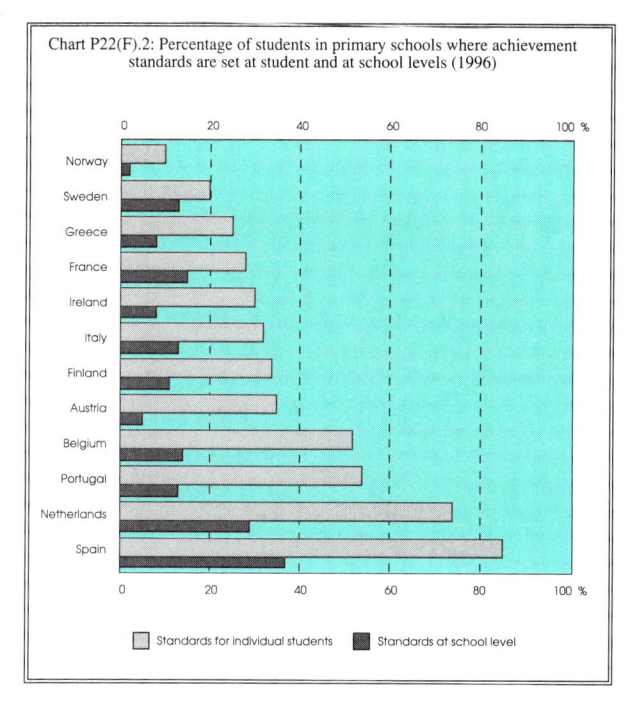

however, that countries have interpreted "setting standards" relatively loosely, and have included a variety of attainment targets.

In almost all countries, over 50 per cent of students are in schools that provide public recognition of good progress by students, irrespective of their level of performance, France being the main exception (29 per cent). With respect to recognition of outstanding student performance, the average proportion of students in schools using this practice across countries amounts to 31 per cent.

While it is reasonable to deduce that some countries favour the assessment of achievement standards more strongly than others, this indicator does not necessarily imply that teachers and schools in the latter aim for or accept lower levels of performance.

DEFINITIONS

Data are based on the following questions in the OECD-INES school survey that was conducted during the school year 1995/96. Responses from headteachers are weighted by the number of students enrolled in the school.

- For how many subject areas do you compare the achievement of students in your school with that of students in other schools?

- For how many subject areas are you able to compare the present average student achievement level in your school with the achievement level five years ago?

- For how many of your former students do you have information on their performance in secondary school?

- Does your school have specific achievement standards for individual student performance?

- Does your school have specific achievement standards at school level?

- Does your school give public recognition to outstanding student performance or student progress (irrespective of level of performance)?

P22(F): Achievement orientation at the primary level

Table P22(F):
Percentage of students in primary schools in which the following achievement-oriented practices are used (1996)

	Achievement focus			Achievement standards		Public recognition	
	Comparison of student achievement among schools in almost all subject areas	Comparison of present student achievement with achievement level 5 years ago in almost all subject areas	Information available on performance in secondary schools by former students	For individual students	At school level	Recognition of outstanding performance	Recognition of progress
Austria	9	49	42	35	5	18	46
Belgium	13	39	46	52	14	23	76
Finland	3	29	18	34	11	85	94
France	8	18	66	28	15	10	29
Greece	35	43	44	25	8	75	85
Ireland	7	23	30	30	8	66	94
Italy	9	18	26	32	13	15	66
Netherlands	18	27	86	74	29	19	72
Norway	4	8	16	10	2	20	74
Portugal	36	54	35	54	13	27	55
Spain	10	67	33	83	37	a	a
Sweden	2	8	23	20	13	19	65
Country mean	**13**	**32**	**39**	**40**	**14**	**31**	**63**

Source: OECD Database. See Annex 3 for notes

P22(G): PARENTAL INVOLVEMENT IN SCHOOLS AT THE PRIMARY LEVEL

This indicator shows the extent to which parents are informed on various educational matters by the school and are involved in the decision-making process and in various school activities in primary schools.

POLICY CONTEXT

Research has shown that a joint effort by the home and the school in the education of students, and the involvement of parents in the school, have a positive impact on student performance. An active policy of informing and involving parents on the part of schools can stimulate good relationships between home and school.

KEY RESULTS

Informing parents on various school matters, particularly on the performance of their children, is general practice in most primary schools in the countries for which data are available. Where structural arrangements exist for parents to participate in school decision-making, these are used more often for matters of organisation and planning than with respect to the curriculum and school staffing. Averaged over countries, about 7 per cent of parents are involved in the actual teaching process at some time during the school year. Although this percentage may appear numerically low, it is by no means educationally insignificant. In other areas (extra-curricular activities and supporting activities such as fund-raising and school maintenance), a somewhat larger percentage of parents are actively involved (generally between 20 and 30 per cent of parents).

DESCRIPTION AND INTERPRETATION

Parental involvement can take various forms, including the provision of regular information to parents by schools on issues such as the progress of their children, the nature of the school's objectives and the pedagogical mission of the school, the involvement of parents in decision-making, and even the direct participation of parents in classroom and other school activities.

It appears from the data summarised in Table P22(G).1 that most primary students in all participating countries are in schools which provide regular information to parents about their children's progress. The table also demonstrates that the majority of students in all countries attend schools which regularly engage parents in supporting their children's school learning at home, the lowest figures being for Austria and the Netherlands (56 per cent). The results for this indicator are weighted by the number of students enrolled in each school, which means larger schools will obtain a correspondingly larger weight in the calculation of national averages.

Table P22(G).1 also shows the percentage of students whose parents are provided with background information by schools about general aims and objectives. Here also, the proportion of such students is consistently above 50 per cent and, taking the two types of information together (school objectives and pedagogical mission), rises to over 75 per cent in all but three cases: Belgium, Ireland and the Netherlands.

The data in Chart P22(G).1 suggest that the involvement of parents in decision-making on organisational matters and school planning issues is more frequent than on matters related to finance and school staffing.

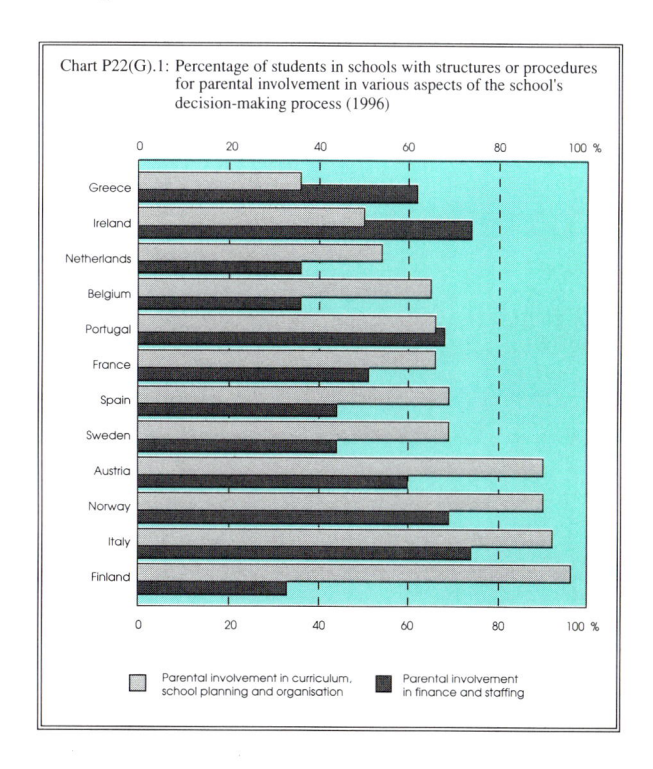

Chart P22(G).1: Percentage of students in schools with structures or procedures for parental involvement in various aspects of the school's decision-making process (1996)

□ Parental involvement in curriculum, school planning and organisation
■ Parental involvement in finance and staffing

P22(G): Parental involvement in schools at the primary level

Table P22(G).1:
Percentage of students in primary schools where parents are informed on various educational matters by the school (1996)

	School informs parents about progress of children		School informs parents on school objectives		School informs parents about pedagogical mission		School engages parents in supporting learning at home	
	Regularly	Occasionally	Regularly	Occasionally	Regularly	Occasionally	Regularly	Occasionally
Austria	75	25	88	8	91	6	56	40
Belgium	89	10	58	25	65	26	83	17
Finland	85	15	82	18	84	16	92	8
France	93	7	84	13	83	11	86	13
Greece	98	2	69	10	90	6	59	36
Ireland	89	11	59	17	53	19	87	11
Italy	99	1	96	2	96	3	71	26
Netherlands	100	n	73	13	70	20	56	43
Norway	100	0	95	5	90	9	90	11
Portugal	98	2	83	9	79	13	78	20
Spain	98	2	90	5	82	11	89	11
Sweden	97	2	95	4	92	5	76	22
Country mean	**93**	**6**	**81**	**11**	**81**	**12**	**77**	**21**

Source: OECD Database. See Annex 3 for notes

Table P22(G).2:
Percentage of students in primary schools with structures or procedures for parental involvement in various aspects of the school's decision-making process (1996)

	Curriculum	School planning	Finance	Staffing	Organisation
Austria	4	61	64	8	83
Belgium	8	55	36	12	49
Finland	92	89	26	20	63
France	4	58	51	11	35
Greece	1	23	61	9	24
Ireland	16	31	81	28	43
Italy	37	73	74	20	85
Netherlands	63	71	42	62	72
Norway	64	67	69	9	78
Portugal	14	55	55	62	50
Spain	33	75	82	27	65
Sweden	34	65	45	14	38
Country mean	**31**	**60**	**57**	**23**	**57**

Source: OECD Database. See Annex 3 for notes

P22(G): Parental involvement in schools at the primary level

Chart P22(G).2: Estimated percentage of parents actually involved in various types of school activities at some time during the school year (1996)

Countries (top to bottom): Belgium, France, Ireland, Spain, Finland, Portugal, Netherlands, Sweden, Greece, Norway, Italy, Austria

Legend: Involvement in teaching process; Involvement in other school and extra-curricular activities; Involvement in other supporting activities

Countries are ranked in ascending order of the percentage of parents involved in other school and extra-curricular activities

When interpreting the results it should be noted that the indicator is based on estimates and judgements by headteachers and on information on national policies.

DEFINITIONS

This indicator focuses on the *active policy* of schools to stimulate parents' involvement. A second aspect is the actual involvement of parents in school affairs. Stimulation of involvement is defined as having policies of informing parents and of engaging them in supporting their children's learning at home, and having structures or procedures for involving parents in decision-making on various issues (curriculum, school planning, finances, staffing and organisation). Actual involvement is measured in terms of parents' participation in various school activities (the teaching and learning process, extra-curricular activities and supporting activities).

Data are based on the OECD-INES school survey that was conducted during the school year 1995/96. Responses from headteachers are weighted by the number of students enrolled in the school.

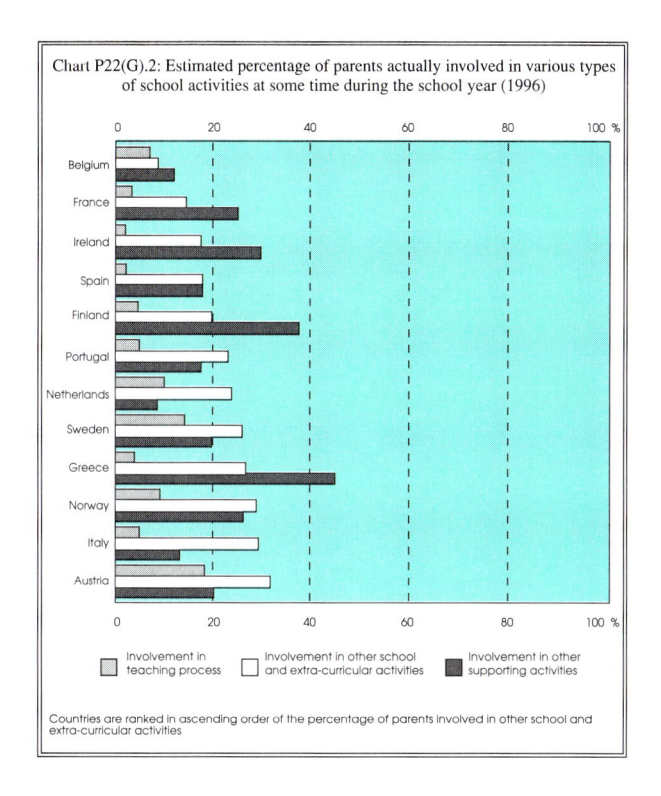

Table P22(G).2 provides further detail. There are marked differences among countries in the degree to which structures exist for joint decision-making over such matters as the curriculum (high percentages of students attending schools offering such structures are found in Finland, the Netherlands and Norway) and staffing (high percentages are found in the Netherlands and Portugal). Such practices are often influenced by national policy.

As shown in Chart P22(G).2, the proportion of parents actually involved in the teaching process is the highest in Austria, the Netherlands and Sweden. A far larger proportion of parents are involved in extra-curricular activities: over 20 per cent of parents in over half the countries under review.

Finally, it should be noted that some of the types of involvement assessed here are different ways of achieving the same effect. To a parent it may be immaterial whether he or she is provided with regular formal information and is invited to comment on school plans, or has the chance to meet staff and to ask questions and exert informal influence by being directly involved in classroom and other school activities.

Table P22(G).3: Estimated percentage of parents actually involved in various types of school activities at some time during the school year (1996)

	Involvement in teaching process	Involvement in other school and extra-curricular activities	Involvement in other supporting activities
Austria	18	32	20
Belgium	7	9	12
Finland	5	20	38
France	3	15	25
Greece	4	27	45
Ireland	2	17	28
Italy	5	29	13
Netherlands	10	24	9
Norway	9	29	26
Portugal	5	23	18
Spain	2	18	18
Sweden	14	26	20
Country mean	**7**	**22**	**23**

Source: OECD Database. See Annex 3 for notes

Chapter 5
GRADUATE OUTPUT OF EDUCATIONAL INSTITUTIONS

This chapter provides a comparison of the graduate output of educational institutions at the upper secondary and tertiary levels of education. Unlike measures of educational attainment, which relate to the stock of knowledge and skills in the population, graduation rates indicate the quantity of output that education systems are currently delivering. They provide an important complement not only to the indicators on attainment but also to the indicators on enrolment and participation that were presented in Chapter 3 and that have provided an overall indication of the size of education systems.

Degrees and other types of certification, which provide formal evidence of involvement and performance over what is often a long period of time, serve as important credentials, indicating to employers and others that students have gained occupationally relevant skills and knowledge.

Cross-country comparisons of qualifications are difficult because educational programmes vary widely – both within and among countries – in duration, academic level and the types of qualifications awarded. However, international comparisons of graduation rates can provide an important insight into the potential flow of persons into the labour force.

Indicator R11 shows graduation rates at the upper secondary level. Although some countries legally allow students to leave the education system at the end of lower secondary education, the completion of upper secondary education has become of utmost importance not only to secure employment and participation in labour markets with rising skill requirements [see also Indicators R21(A) and R21(B)], but also to serve as a basis for subsequent learning later in life. Low upper secondary graduation rates may therefore signal problems for the future.

The remaining indicators in this chapter focus on graduation at the tertiary level of education. Tertiary graduation rates are influenced by the supply of and access to tertiary education programmes and by the demand for higher skills in the labour market. Other factors affecting tertiary graduation rates are the typical duration of programmes, the graduation requirements and the way in which degree and qualification structures are organised within countries, particularly at the university level of education (see **Indicator R12**). Countries which have more exit points from their university (or equivalent) tertiary programmes can offer more transition points into the labour market, thus allowing students to leave the higher education system at different knowledge or skill levels, depending on the current demand for these skills in the labour market, as well as their own aptitudes and interests.

Finally, **Indicators R14 and R15** examine the distribution of tertiary graduates by field of study. Technological innovation affects the industrial, occupational and skill composition of the labour force. New growth industries tend to be those involved in the creation, processing and distribution of information and knowledge. The distribution of university and non-university tertiary graduates by field of study gives an indication of the potential supply of high-level skills in these fields.

R11: Graduates at upper secondary level

R11: GRADUATES AT UPPER SECONDARY LEVEL

This indicator shows the proportion of upper secondary graduates in the population at the typical age of upper secondary completion.

POLICY CONTEXT

The completion of upper secondary education is of utmost importance not only to secure employment and participation in labour markets with rising skill requirements, but also to serve as a basis for subsequent learning later in life. Although some countries legally allow students to leave the education system at the end of lower secondary education, people who do so face poor labour market opportunities [see Indicators R21(A), R21(B) and R24].

One measure of how systems perform in delivering upper secondary education is the graduation rate.

KEY RESULTS

The completion of upper secondary education is increasingly becoming universal. The proportion of students completing a first upper secondary programme is on average 77 per cent across OECD countries and exceeds 80 per cent in more than half of the countries for which data are reported. By contrast, upper secondary attainment in the population aged 25-64 years is around 59 per cent on average across OECD countries (see Indicator C1). Thus, significant progress has been made in almost all countries in increasing the rate of upper secondary completion. Furthermore, gender disparities in upper secondary graduation rates have been successfully eliminated in almost all countries.

In more than half of the countries which distinguish between graduates from general programmes and those from vocational upper secondary programmes, the majority of students complete vocational and technical programmes. In some countries, graduates of upper secondary programmes re-enrol and graduate a second (or subsequent) time, almost always from vocational or apprenticeship programmes.

DESCRIPTION AND INTERPRETATION

In all but two countries the number of upper secondary graduates per 100 persons at the typical graduation age exceeds 63 (see Chart R11). In 14 of the 25 countries for which data are available, the graduation rates are above 80 per cent and in Belgium, Finland, Ireland, Japan, Korea, Norway, Poland and the Russian Federation they exceed 90 per cent. The lowest upper secondary graduation rates are in Mexico (25 per cent) and Turkey (38 per cent).

In over half of countries reporting upper secondary graduation rates for first programmes by gender, graduation rates for women exceed those of men (see Chart R11); in Belgium, Denmark, Finland, Ireland and Spain by over 10 per cent. Only in Austria, the Czech Republic, Norway, Switzerland and Turkey do male graduates outnumber female graduates by more than 5 per cent. The situation is quite different from the attainment levels in the total adult population (see Indicator C2) in which women are often under-represented among persons with upper secondary attainment.

Nine countries – the Czech Republic, Denmark, Finland, France, Germany, Ireland, Italy, the Netherlands, and Spain – reported counts for persons who had re-enrolled in an upper secondary education programme and graduated a second (or subsequent) time. Graduation from a second upper secondary programme was most common in Denmark, Finland, Germany and Ireland, where more than 15 per cent of the population at the typical graduation age completes a second upper secondary programme. However, in other countries, graduates from programmes that may be similar in content to these secondary programmes are counted as tertiary graduates.

The breakdown between general education and vocational/technical education differs widely across countries. Of the 23 countries which make this distinction, ten report that the majority of first programme graduates come from institutions with general programmes and 13 report that they come from vocational institutions or apprenticeship programmes. However, these differences must be interpreted with caution since the classification of programmes as general and vocational is not entirely consistent across countries.

R11: Graduates at upper secondary level

Chart R11: Ratio of upper secondary education graduates to population at typical age of graduation, by type of programme (1994) (first educational programmes)

*   1993 data
** Data by type of programme are not available
Countries are ranked in descending order of ratio of upper secondary graduates to population at typical age of graduation

Distribution of upper secondary graduates and graduation rates by gender

* 1993 data
Countries are ranked in descending order of the proportion of female graduates

R11: Graduates at upper secondary level

DEFINITIONS

Upper secondary graduates are persons who have successfully completed the final year of upper secondary education. In some countries, successful completion requires a final examination; in others it does not. In some countries, students may enrol in and complete additional programmes at the same level of education after initial completion. For this indicator, graduation rates are therefore separated into first and second (or further) upper secondary programmes. Each country has identified a typical age (or average of ages) at which graduation normally occurs (see Annex 1). Graduation rates are obtained by dividing the number of first-time/second-time upper secondary graduates by the population at the typical graduation age. Countries with differentiated upper secondary institutions have, in most cases, reported the numbers of graduates by the type of institution attended. A few countries with upper secondary institutions offering multiple types of programmes have reported the qualifications obtained by graduating students by programme type (general or vocational). Note that in some countries graduation rates may be overestimated due to the fact that some graduates may be counted more than once if they complete multiple programmes at the same level.

R11: Graduates at upper secondary level

Table R11.1:
Ratio of upper secondary graduates to population at typical age of graduation by type of programme (1994)
First educational programmes

	Total M+W	Total Men	Total Women	General M+W	General Men	General Women	Vocational and apprenticeship M+W	Vocational and apprenticeship Men	Vocational and apprenticeship Women
North America									
Canada	70.8	66.4	75.4	m	m	m	m	m	m
Mexico	25.0	m	m	21.5	m	m	3.6	m	m
United States	73.6	71.0	76.3	m	m	m	m	m	m
Pacific Area									
Australia	m	m	m	67.6	62.1	73.4	m	m	m
Japan	92.1	88.9	95.4	67.4	63.8	71.1	24.7	25.1	24.4
New Zealand *	63.9	59.8	68.0	39.0	37.9	40.2	24.8	21.9	27.8
European Union									
Austria *	81.9	84.5	79.2	13.9	11.8	16.1	67.9	72.7	63.0
Belgium *	96.7	89.1	104.7	33.9	30.0	37.9	64.4	60.3	68.6
Denmark *	82.3	75.6	89.3	45.3	37.2	53.8	37.0	38.4	35.4
Finland	93.4	85.5	101.6	43.9	35.6	52.5	48.6	49.0	48.3
France	80.8	78.4	83.4	36.3	30.7	42.1	46.4	49.2	43.5
Germany	88.5	90.5	86.4	22.6	20.4	24.8	65.9	70.1	61.5
Greece *	75.1	72.5	77.8	53.0	45.2	61.1	22.2	27.3	16.7
Ireland	97.5	90.5	104.9	90.0	83.5	96.8	7.6	7.0	8.1
Italy	76.2	72.6	80.0	17.3	15.1	19.6	58.0	56.7	59.3
Luxembourg	m	m	m	m	m	m	m	m	m
Netherlands *	69.4	m	m	33.3	m	m	35.3	m	m
Portugal	m	m	m	38.0	m	m	m	m	m
Spain *	67.9	61.0	75.3	44.6	38.9	50.5	23.1	21.8	24.5
Sweden	74.6	76.5	72.7	25.6	18.0	33.5	50.5	60.2	40.3
United Kingdom	m	m	m	m	m	m	m	m	m
Other OECD countries									
Czech Republic	77.6	81.5	73.6	13.4	10.4	16.5	64.2	71.0	57.1
Hungary *	80.8	m	m	18.4	m	m	60.8	m	m
Iceland	m	m	m	m	m	m	m	m	m
Norway	102.0	117.5	85.9	41.7	35.5	48.2	60.2	82.0	37.7
Switzerland	82.1	86.6	77.3	19.2	17.1	21.4	62.8	69.5	55.9
Turkey	38.4	46.6	29.9	23.6	27.1	20.1	15.1	19.9	10.1
Country mean	**76.9**	**78.7**	**80.9**	**36.8**	**34.5**	**43.3**	**42.2**	**47.2**	**40.1**
Other non-OECD countries									
Korea	91.3	91.3	91.4	54.6	58.9	50.0	36.7	32.4	41.4
Poland	90.3	90.2	90.4	22.3	11.7	33.3	68.0	78.6	57.1
Russian Federation	90.5	m	m	46.8	m	m	43.7	m	m

* 1993 data
Source: OECD Database. See Annex 3 for notes

R11: Graduates at upper secondary level

Table R11.2:
Ratio of upper secondary graduates to population at typical age of graduation by type of programme (1994)
Second or further programmes only

	Total M+W	Total Men	Total Women	General M+W	General Men	General Women	Vocational and apprenticeship M+W	Vocational and apprenticeship Men	Vocational and apprenticeship Women
North America									
Canada	a	a	a	a	a	a	a	a	a
Mexico	a	a	a	a	a	a	a	a	a
United States	a	a	a	a	a	a	a	a	a
Pacific Area									
Australia	a	a	a	a	a	a	a	a	a
Japan	a	a	a	a	a	a	a	a	a
New Zealand *	a	a	a	a	a	a	a	a	a
European Union									
Austria *	m	m	m	m	m	m	m	m	m
Belgium *	x	x	x	x	x	x	x	x	x
Denmark *	16.8	15.1	18.8	3.7	3.1	4.5	13.1	12.1	14.3
Finland	41.3	23.7	59.8	2.3	0.7	3.9	39.1	23.0	56.0
France	11.3	12.3	10.3	a	a	a	11.3	12.3	10.3
Germany	17.8	18.1	17.5	0.6	0.6	0.7	17.0	17.4	16.6
Greece *	a	a	a	a	a	a	a	a	a
Ireland	21.7	13.5	30.2	a	a	a	21.7	13.5	30.2
Italy	9.7	8.1	11.3	a	a	a	9.7	8.1	11.3
Luxembourg	m	m	m	m	m	m	m	m	m
Netherlands *	5.5	m	m	1.7	m	m	3.7	m	m
Portugal	m	m	m	m	m	m	m	m	m
Spain *	13.1	12.3	14.0	a	a	a	13.1	12.3	14.0
Sweden	a	a	a	a	a	a	a	a	a
United Kingdom	a	a	a	a	a	a	a	a	a
Other OECD countries									
Czech Republic	3.8	4.4	3.1	a	a	a	3.8	4.4	3.1
Hungary *	x	x	x	x	x	x	x	x	x
Iceland	m	m	m	m	m	m	m	m	m
Norway	a	a	a	a	a	a	a	a	a
Switzerland	m	m	m	m	m	m	m	m	m
Turkey	a	a	a	a	a	a	a	a	a
Country mean	**6.7**	**5.4**	**8.3**	**0.4**	**0.2**	**0.5**	**6.3**	**5.2**	**7.8**
Other non-OECD countries									
Korea	a	a	a	a	a	a	a	a	a
Poland	m	m	m	m	m	m	m	m	m
Russian Federation	m	m	m	m	m	m	m	m	m

* 1993 data
Source: OECD Database. See Annex 3 for notes

R12: Graduates at the tertiary level

R12: GRADUATES AT THE TERTIARY LEVEL

This indicator shows the number of tertiary graduates as a percentage of the population at the typical age of graduation. For some countries it also shows net graduation rates.

POLICY CONTEXT

Unlike measures of educational attainment, which relate to the stock of knowledge and skills in the population, tertiary graduation rates are an indicator of the current production rate of higher-level knowledge by each country's education system. Countries with high graduation rates at the tertiary level are the most likely to be building or maintaining a highly skilled labour force. The age at which students graduate and become available for the labour market is a factor of importance as well.

KEY RESULTS

For the purpose of this indicator, tertiary qualifications are divided into those equivalent and those not equivalent to a university-level qualification. Tertiary programmes leading to the latter qualifications are typically shorter in duration than the former and are often focused on a specific area of the labour market.

University-level graduation rates across OECD countries are, on average, 16 per cent for short first programmes, 10 per cent for long first programmes, 4 per cent for second programmes and 1 per cent for programmes leading to an advanced research degree.

In addition to the influence that both the supply of tertiary education programmes and the demand for higher skills in the labour market has on tertiary graduation rates, these rates are also affected by the way in which the degree and qualification structures are organised within countries. University-level programmes vary greatly in structure and scope across countries. The duration of programmes leading to the award of a first university-level qualification ranges from three years (e.g. the Bachelor's degree in the United Kingdom in most fields of study) to over five years (e.g. the *Diplom* in Germany and the *Doctorandus* in the Netherlands). It appears that countries whose tertiary education systems offer only long first university-level programmes have, in general, significantly lower overall university-level graduation rates than those that offer also shorter university-level programmes. Longer duration of studies also tends to increase the enrolment stock, and thus the level of required resources, due to a lower turnover rate if entry and drop-out rates are constant. However, when interpreting such differences in university-level graduation rates, the content of the educational programmes, the labour market opportunities they offer and graduation rates for non-university tertiary programmes and upper secondary programmes need to be considered as well.

There is also striking variation among countries in the age at which students graduate and become available for the labour market. Particularly in countries which do not offer short university-level programmes, the transition point is often considerably later.

DESCRIPTION AND INTERPRETATION

Cross-country comparisons of tertiary qualifications are especially difficult because educational programmes vary widely in duration, academic level of content and type of qualification awarded. Nevertheless, international comparisons of graduation rates provide an important insight into the potential flow of persons with high-level qualifications into the labour force.

At the non-university tertiary level, the highest number of graduates per 100 people at the most common graduation age is in Japan, Norway and the Russian Federation (see Table R12.1). In these countries, the number of graduates is equal to or exceeds 26 for every 100 people at the typical graduation age. The lowest non-university tertiary graduation rates are in Mexico, Spain and Turkey, with less than three graduates for every 100 people at the typical graduation age. Non-university graduation rates are affected by the availability of technical and professional education at the tertiary level in a particular country, as well as by the extent to which vocational programmes of similar content are (or are not) offered at the upper secondary level.

First university-level qualifications are classified in this indicator into those with a theoretical duration typically equal to or less than four years (short first university degree programmes) and those with a theoretical duration typically greater than four years (long first university degree programmes).

In countries that offer short first university degrees, such as the Bachelor's in the United States, graduation rates average around 16 per cent across OECD countries (see Chart R12). In Denmark, Ireland,

R12: Graduates at the tertiary level

Japan, Korea, New Zealand, the Russian Federation and the United Kingdom, more than 20 per cent of persons at the typical age group obtain such a degree and in Australia, Canada and the United States, more than 30 per cent. Students tend to graduate around the age of 23 from these programmes.

For long first university degree programmes, such as the German *Diplom* or the Italian *Laurea*, many of which are often regarded as equivalent in academic level to second university degrees in countries such as Australia or the United States, graduation rates average 10 per cent across countries. Graduation rates for long first university-level programmes in Belgium, the Czech Republic, Finland, France, Germany, Portugal and Spain are higher than the graduation rates from second university-level programmes in Australia and the United States, the two countries with the highest second university degree graduation rates.

Graduation rates for second university degrees, such as the Master's in the United States, range from less than 1 to 12 per cent, with an OECD average of nearly 4 per cent. On average, about 1 per cent of the typical age cohort obtain an advanced research degree such as a Ph.D. In Finland and Switzerland it is more than 2.5 per cent and in France more than 5 per cent of a typical age cohort (in France, however, advanced research degrees are defined much more broadly than in most other countries).

Graduation rates from first university-level programmes (short and long) are higher among women than among men in most countries. Only in Germany, Japan, Korea, Switzerland and Turkey are graduation rates among women significantly lower than those among men. For second university degrees, graduation rates for men are slightly higher than those for women in most countries.

Table R12.2 presents net graduation rates for ten countries for which such data are available. These provide a more accurate estimate for first-time graduation rates than the measures presented in Table R12.1, which were obtained by dividing the total graduate output by the typical age of graduation.

The age of university graduation also varies significantly among countries. Table R12.3 indicates, for countries for which this information is available, the 25th, 50th and 75th percentiles of the age distributions of university-level graduates. Of the eleven countries included in this comparison, Finland, Iceland and Sweden show more than 75 per cent of all first-time university-level graduates as 24 years or older. The typical university-level graduation age (see Annex 1) ranges from 21 years in Australia, New Zealand, Portugal, Spain and the United Kingdom (short university-level programmes) to 26 years in Germany and Switzerland (long university-level programmes).

Differences in national university degree structures – examples from seven countries

Annex 3 lists the types of university-level and non-university qualifications awarded in the Czech Republic, France, Germany, Japan, the Netherlands, the United Kingdom and the United States based on data which countries provided through the OECD Taxonomy Survey of Educational Programmes. These countries were selected for presentation because they highlight some of the variability in the national qualification structure at the tertiary level. Several patterns emerge when comparing national qualification structures and the tertiary graduation rates presented in Table R12.1. First, non-university tertiary graduation rates appear to be greatly affected by the availability of occupationally specific education and training at the upper secondary level. Secondly, graduation rates for the first university degree (or equivalent) seem to be influenced by the typical duration of these programmes, as well as by the requirements for earning the qualification.

The level or age group at which vocational and technical education programmes are primarily targeted in a particular country will affect that country's non-university tertiary graduation rate. The seven countries examined can be divided into three broad categories reflecting the level at which they primarily offer technical and vocational education: *i)* those offering technical and vocational qualifications largely at the upper secondary level; *ii)* those offering this level of training mainly at the tertiary level; and *iii)* those offering qualifications at both levels. The Czech Republic and Hungary are examples of countries in the first category. In these countries, students can enrol in specialised trade or vocational schools as early as age 14 and complete their upper secondary education with a specific occupational qualification. The non-university tertiary graduation rates for these countries are low or non-existent. Countries in the second category (e.g. the United States and Canada) offer a rather general programme at the secondary level which allows for relatively minor

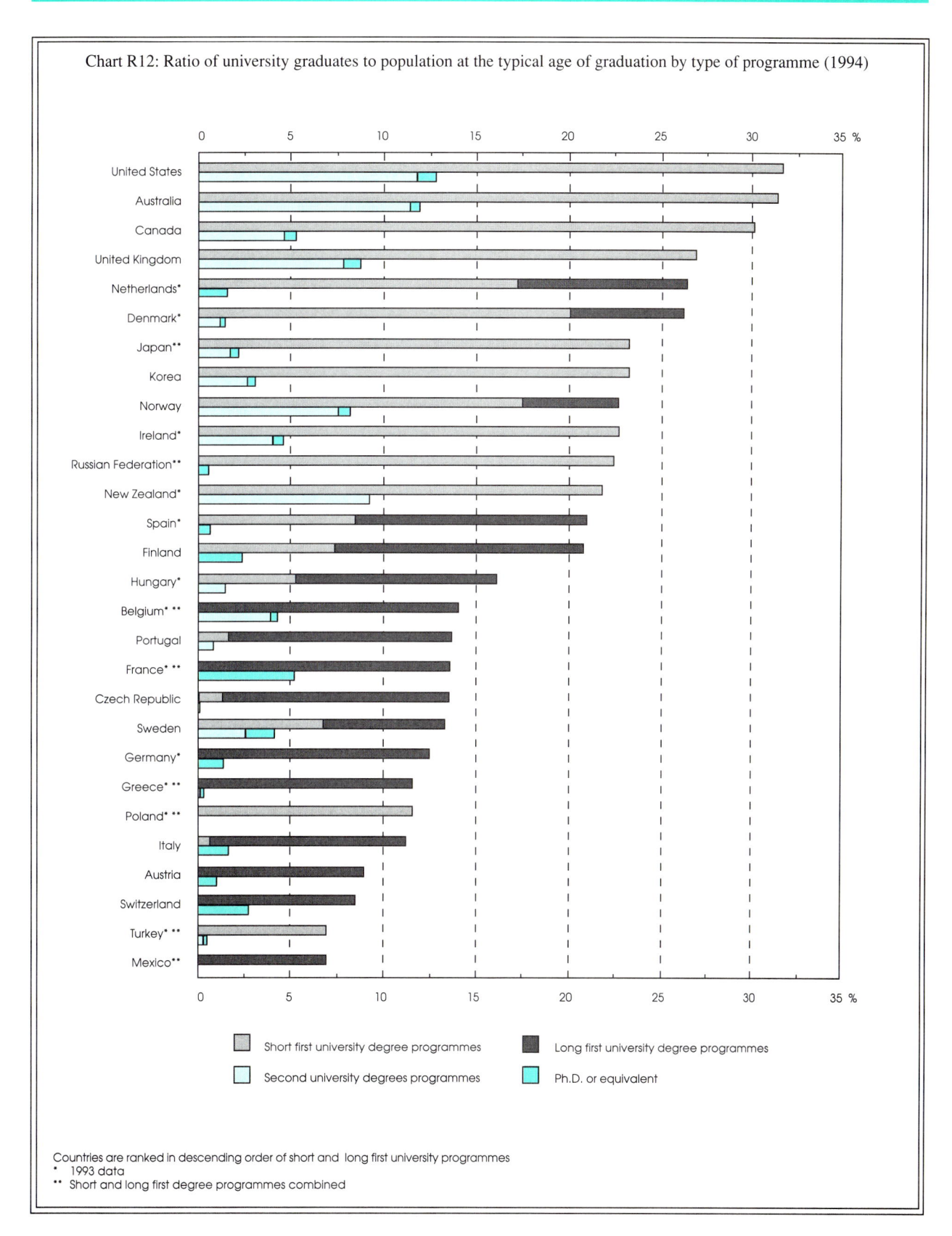

R12: Graduates at the tertiary level

Chart R12: Ratio of university graduates to population at the typical age of graduation by type of programme (1994)

- Short first university degree programmes
- Long first university degree programmes
- Second university degrees programmes
- Ph.D. or equivalent

Countries are ranked in descending order of short and long first university programmes
* 1993 data
** Short and long first degree programmes combined

R12: Graduates at the tertiary level

vocational specialisation. Most occupationally specific education and training in these countries is undertaken after the completion of upper secondary education and, as a result, non-university tertiary graduation rates are relatively high. Countries in the third category offer a variety of vocational and technical programmes which span the upper secondary and tertiary levels of education (e.g. Australia, New Zealand, Germany, the United Kingdom). In these countries, only advanced technical qualifications are awarded at the tertiary level (e.g. the *Meister* qualification in Germany and the Higher National Diploma in the United Kingdom) and the non-university graduation rates are lower than in the second, but higher than in the first, category.

Graduation rates for first university-level qualifications are affected by the typical duration, graduation requirements, and the variety of credentials offered at the tertiary level. In general, countries which do not offer short first university-level programmes have lower first university degree graduation rates than countries which offer short first university degree programmes as well. For example, the first university degree graduation rate in Germany is 12.6, lower than the first university degree graduation rates in the United States (31.8), the United Kingdom (27.0) and Japan (23.4). While the typical duration of a first university degree programme in the latter three countries is four years or less, the typical duration of a first university degree programme in Germany is four to seven years (four to five for a *Fachhochschule Diplom* and five to seven for a university *Diplom*). On the other hand, if the academic level of a first university degree in countries like Germany is regarded as similar to a second university degree in other countries (e.g. a U.S. Master's degree), the gap in high-level qualifications between these countries appears much smaller. Nonetheless, countries which have more exit points from their university (or equivalent) tertiary programmes offer more transition points into the labour market, allowing students to leave the higher education system at different knowledge or skill levels, depending on the current demand for these skills in the labour market, as well their own aptitude and interest.

The graduation rates for advanced research qualifications (Doctorate or equivalent) are affected by both the duration of the programme and the specific graduation requirements. For example France, the country with the highest graduation rate at this level, 5.3 per cent, includes programmes such as the *Diplôme d'études approfondies* (DEA) and the *Diplôme d'études supérieures spécialisées* (DESS). These degrees are lower than the French *Doctorat* and are typically earned within five years of starting tertiary education and do not require a thesis or dissertation. In contrast, the German *Promotion* typically takes between seven and ten years and requires a dissertation of publishable quality. The German graduation rate for the Doctorate or equivalent is 1.5, comparable to other countries which have similar requirements for advanced research qualifications.

DEFINITIONS

Tertiary graduates are people who obtain a university-level or non-university qualification or equivalent in the specified reference year. The indicator distinguishes between five categories of qualifications: those that are equivalent to *i)* a non-university tertiary qualification; *ii)* a first university-level qualification from a programme with a theoretical duration typically equal to or less than four years; *iii)* a first university-level qualification of a theoretical duration typically longer than four years; *iv)* a second university-level qualification at the Master's level; and *v)* an advanced research degree at the doctorate level. For some countries, these distinctions are not always clear and data are not always available for the requested categories. In such cases, graduates have been assigned by the country to the most appropriate category. In many countries the duration of studies also varies significantly between fields of study. For some countries, the non-university tertiary level includes some programmes that in other countries may be classified at the upper secondary level.

For each tertiary category, countries identify the age at which graduation typically occurs. Graduates themselves, however, may be of any age. To obtain graduation rates, the number of graduates is divided by the population at the typical graduation age (see Annex 1). In many countries, defining a typical age at graduation is difficult because graduates are dispersed over a wide range of ages and the duration may differ widely between fields of study. As a result, a more accurate indicator is a net graduation rate. This rate, which represents the sum of age-specific graduation rates, is presented in Table R12.2 for countries which were able to provide information on graduates by single year of age.

Tertiary education graduates generally do not include graduates from programmes offered by private business institutions operating for profit.

R12: Graduates at the tertiary level

Table R12.1:
Ratio of tertiary graduates to population at the typical age of graduation (times 100) by type of programme, men and women (1994)

	Non-university tertiary programmes (A)			Short first university degree programmes (e.g. U.S. Bachelor's) (B)			Long first university degree programmes (e.g. German *Diplom* or Italian *Laurea*) (C)			Second university degree programmes (e.g. U.S. Master's) (D)			Ph.D. or equivalent (E)		
	M+W	Men	Women	M+W	Men	Women	M+W	Men	Women	M+W	Men	Women	M+W	Men	Women
North America															
Canada	m	m	m	30.2	25.5	35.1	x	x	x	4.8	4.9	4.7	0.7	1.0	0.5
Mexico	1.7	m	m	x	m	m	7.1	m	m	x	m	m	x	m	m
United States	21.9	17.9	26.0	31.8	28.4	35.2	x	x	x	11.9	11.2	12.6	1.1	1.4	0.9
Pacific Area															
Australia	m	m	m	31.5	25.4	37.9	x	x	x	11.5	10.4	12.6	0.7	0.9	0.4
Japan	28.3	17.2	40.0	23.4	31.2	15.3	x	x	x	1.9	3.1	0.7	0.5	0.8	0.1
New Zealand *	10.2	6.7	12.9	21.9	19.9	24.0	x	x	x	9.3	9.9	8.7	x	x	x
European Union															
Austria	4.9	2.9	6.9	x	x	x	9.1	10.0	8.2	a	a	a	1.1	1.6	0.7
Belgium *	22.9	19.0	26.9	a	a	a	14.2	15.2	13.1	4.0	4.8	3.1	0.5	0.8	0.3
Denmark *	8.9	11.1	6.6	20.2	16.1	24.6	6.3	7.1	5.4	1.3	1.3	1.3	0.4	0.6	0.2
Finland	25.1	14.0	36.8	7.5	9.3	5.5	13.5	11.8	15.3	x	x	x	2.5	2.9	2.1
France *	25.4	22.1	28.8	x	x	x	13.7	12.9	14.5	a	a	a	5.3	5.6	5.1
Germany *	10.7	9.4	12.1	x	x	x	12.6	14.6	10.4	a	a	a	1.5	2.0	0.9
Greece *	4.6	4.0	5.1	x	x	x	11.7	9.5	13.9	0.2	0.2	0.2	0.3	0.5	0.2
Ireland *	13.9	14.5	13.2	22.8	22.3	23.4	x	x	x	4.1	4.3	3.8	0.7	0.9	0.4
Italy	9.0	6.6	11.5	0.8	0.5	1.0	10.6	9.8	11.5	a	a	a	1.8	2.1	1.6
Luxembourg	m	m	m	m	m	m	m	m	m	m	m	m	m	m	m
Netherlands *	a	a	a	17.4	17.2	17.6	9.3	10.0	8.6	x	x	x	1.7	2.2	1.1
Portugal	6.1	4.0	8.1	1.8	1.2	2.4	12.1	9.2	15.0	0.9	0.8	0.9	a	a	a
Spain *	1.1	1.1	1.1	8.6	6.8	10.4	12.6	11.4	13.9	x	x	x	0.8	0.9	0.6
Sweden	11.6	6.4	17.1	6.9	4.8	9.1	6.6	7.0	6.1	2.7	1.8	3.6	1.6	2.2	0.9
United Kingdom	25.1	21.8	28.5	27.0	26.5	27.5	x	x	x	8.0	8.1	8.0	1.0	1.4	0.6
Other OECD countries															
Czech Republic	5.3	3.2	7.5	1.4	1.2	1.5	12.3	12.5	12.0	x	x	x	0.1	0.1	0.03
Hungary *	a	a	a	5.4	4.6	6.3	11.0	9.9	12.2	1.6	2.0	1.2	a	a	a
Iceland	m	m	m	m	m	m	m	m	m	m	m	m	m	m	m
Norway	47.0	42.0	52.3	17.6	12.5	22.9	5.3	4.8	5.9	7.7	8.7	6.6	0.7	1.1	0.4
Switzerland	24.6	32.1	17.3	x	x	x	8.6	10.9	6.3	a	a	a	2.9	4.0	1.7
Turkey *	2.0	2.2	1.8	7.1	8.8	5.4	x	x	x	0.4	0.5	0.3	0.3	0.4	0.2
Country mean	**13.5**	**11.7**	**16.4**	**15.7**	**14.6**	**16.9**	**10.4**	**10.4**	**10.8**	**3.5**	**3.6**	**3.4**	**1.1**	**1.4**	**0.8**
Other non-OECD countries															
Korea	14.6	12.8	16.5	23.4	26.8	19.7	x	x	x	2.8	4.0	1.6	0.5	0.8	0.1
Poland *	7.5	3.0	12.2	11.7	11.0	12.3	x	x	x	x	x	x	x	x	x
Russian Federation	26.8	m	m	22.6	m	m	x	m	m	a	a	a	0.7	m	m

* 1993 data
Source: OECD Database. See Annex 3 for notes

R12: Graduates at the tertiary level

Table R12.2:
Net graduation rates in university-level education by type of programme (1994)

	Short first university degree programmes (e.g. U.S. Bachelor's)	Long first university degree programmes (e.g. German Diplom or Italian Laurea)	Second university degree programmes (e.g. U.S. Master's)
North America			
Canada	24.8	x	2.6
Pacific Area			
Australia	26.7	x	8.3
New Zealand *	20.1	x	6.0
European Union			
Belgium *	a	13.4	2.9
Denmark *	16.4	5.1	0.8
Finland	5.0	10.0	x
Netherlands *	m	8.2	x
Sweden	5.3	4.8	1.2
Other OECD countries			
Norway	14.2	4.7	6.2
Turkey *	6.4	x	0.5

* 1993 data
Source: OECD Database. See Annex 3 for notes

R12: Graduates at the tertiary level

Table R12.3: Age distribution of university-level graduates (1994)

	Age at 25th percentile[1]	Median age[2]	Age at 75th percentile[3]	Typical age (see Annex 1)
Short first university degrees (e.g. U.S. Bachelor's)				
Australia	20	22	26	21
New Zealand	22	23	25	21
Turkey	22	23	25	25-27
Canada	22	23	26	22
Norway	23	24	28	23
Denmark	21	26	32	25-27
Sweden	24	26	29	22
Finland	24	26	32	22-24
Iceland	24	27	32	m
Netherlands	m	m	m	23
Long first university degrees (e.g. German *Diplom* or Italian *Laurea*)				
Belgium	23	24	25	22-24
Norway	23	25	27	24
Netherlands	23	25	27	25
Iceland	23	26	26	23
Sweden	25	26	30	23-24
Denmark	23	27	29	25-27
Finland	26	27	32	25-26
Second university degrees (e.g. U.S. Master's)				
Turkey	24	26	28	23
Belgium	24	26	32	23-26
Norway	25	26	29	24-28
New Zealand	23	28	37	23
Canada	26	29	37	24
Denmark	27	29	32	26-27
Australia	26	30-34	39	24
Iceland	27	30-34	37	m
Sweden	27	30-34	37	24-27

Countries are ranked in descending order of median age of graduation for each group of university degrees
1. 25 per cent of graduates are below this age
2. 50 per cent of graduates are below this age
3. 75 per cent of graduates are below this age
The vertical bar in the chart indicates the median age of graduation
The horizontal bar in the chart extends from the 25th to the 75th percentile of the age distribution
Source: OECD Database. See Annex 3 for notes

R14: TERTIARY QUALIFICATIONS BY FIELD OF STUDY

This indicator shows the distribution of university graduates over six broad categories of fields of study.

POLICY CONTEXT

Technological innovation affects the industrial, occupational and skill composition of the labour force. New growth industries tend to be those involved in the creation, processing and distribution of information and knowledge. The distribution of university-level and non-university tertiary graduates by field of study provides an important indication of the potential supply of high-level skills in these fields.

KEY RESULTS

When fields of study are classified into six broad categories – namely medical science, natural science, mathematics and computer science, engineering and architecture, humanities, and law and business – one observes that the largest concentration of university-level graduates in all countries is either in the humanities or in law and business. On the other hand, if natural science, mathematics, computer science, engineering and architecture are taken together, more than 40 per cent of the university-level graduates in the Czech Republic, Finland, Germany and the Russian Federation are in these fields.

Although university-level graduation rates do not differ significantly between men and women, female graduates are far less likely to be in scientific fields than are men in all countries. Thus, despite equality of access to tertiary education for men and women (see Indicator R12), the differences between the genders by field of study persist.

DESCRIPTION AND INTERPRETATION

The largest concentration of university-level graduates is in the humanities in all countries except Belgium, France, Italy, Japan, Spain and Switzerland, in which the largest concentration is in law and business. The proportion of university-level graduates in the humanities ranges from 12 per cent in Belgium to 60 per cent in Hungary.

At the non-university tertiary level, the largest concentration of graduates is in law and business in over half of the countries, in the humanities in another six countries, in medical science in Finland, Germany and Sweden and in engineering and architecture in Turkey.

The proportion of women graduating from university programmes in the humanities is higher than that of men in all countries, reaching above 50 per cent of all female graduates in two-thirds of the countries. In medical science programmes, the proportion of women is also in general higher than that of men, except in Greece and Italy. The same pattern holds at the non-university tertiary level, where the proportion of female graduates in medical science programmes reaches above 40 per cent of all female graduates in one-third of the countries.

Less than 25 per cent of the female university-level graduates are in science-related fields (natural science, mathematics, computer science, engineering and architecture) in every country except Korea and Turkey where this is 26 per cent. By contrast, in the Czech Republic, Finland and Germany more than one-half of male university-level graduates are in these science-related fields and in all countries this percentage is higher than 25 per cent. The proportion of women graduating from engineering or architecture programmes is less than 10 per cent of all female graduates in all countries except the Czech Republic and Turkey whereas in 16 countries more than 20 per cent of male university graduates are in engineering and architecture.

As with women graduating from university-level programmes, engineering and architecture are also uncommon for women at the non-university tertiary level. In all countries, except Korea, fewer than 10 per cent of women graduating from non-university tertiary programmes are in engineering or architecture whereas in twelve countries, the percentage for men is over 25.

DEFINITIONS

For this indicator, tertiary graduates who received their qualification in the reference year were divided into categories based on their subject of specialisation. The comparability of the results depends heavily on the extent to which countries are able to apply consistent subject definitions in accordance with ISCED (see Annex 3).

R14: Tertiary qualifications by field of study

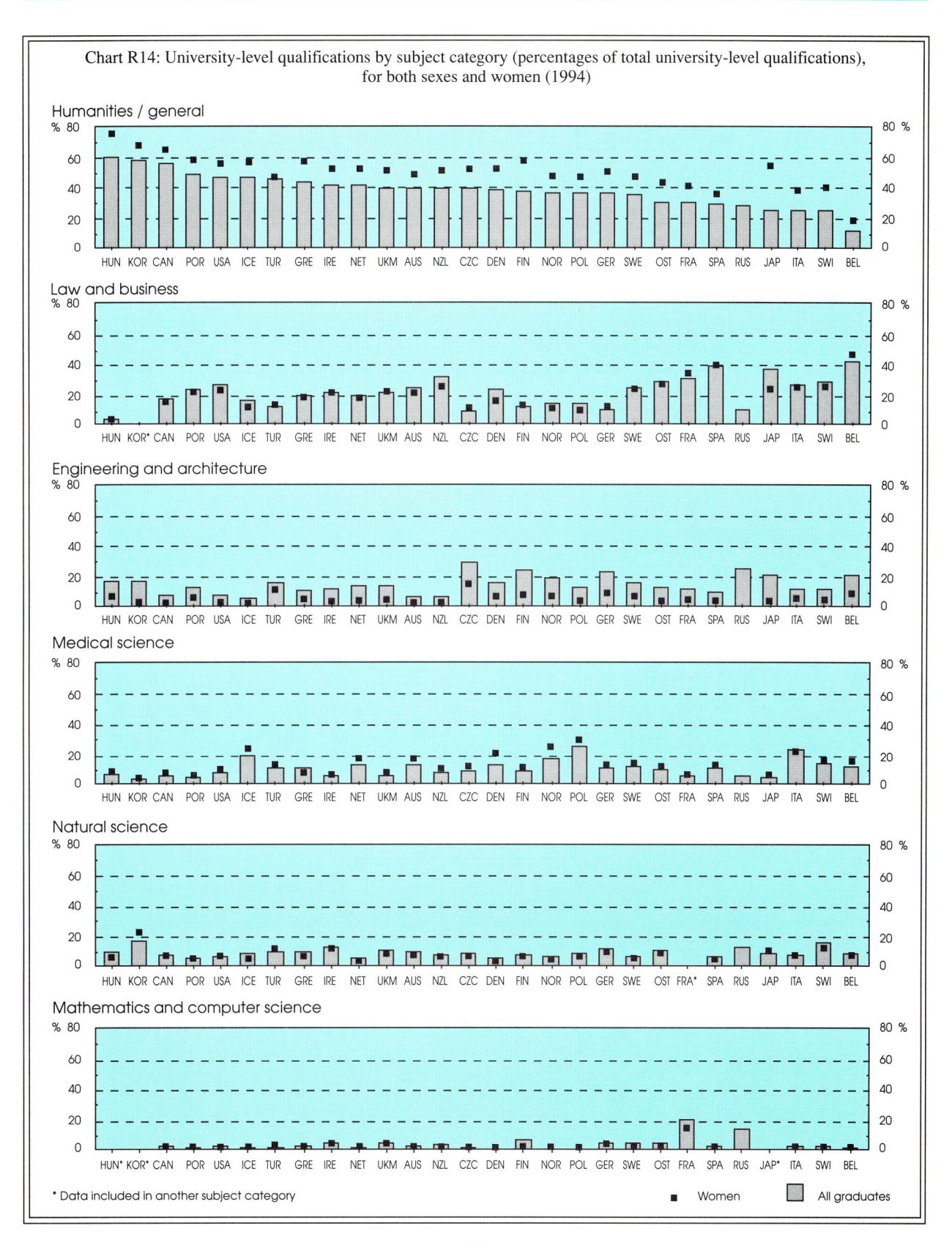

Chart R14: University-level qualifications by subject category (percentages of total university-level qualifications), for both sexes and women (1994)

* Data included in another subject category

■ Women   ▨ All graduates

R14: Tertiary qualifications by field of study

Table R14.1:
Non-university tertiary and university-level qualifications by subject category
(percentages of total non-university and university-level qualifications), **men and women** (1994)

	Medical science Non-university	Medical science University-level	Natural science Non-university	Natural science University-level	Mathematics and computer science Non-university	Mathematics and computer science University-level	Humanities / general Non-university	Humanities / general University-level	Law and business Non-university	Law and business University-level	Engineering and architecture Non-university	Engineering and architecture University-level
North America												
Canada	7.5	6.5	3.6	8.2	1.7	3.7	38.6	56.0	48.1	18.1	n	7.4
Mexico	m	m	m	m	m	m	m	m	m	m	m	m
United States	21.3	8.0	4.3	7.3	2.1	3.3	32.9	46.7	32.4	26.8	6.8	7.6
Pacific Area												
Australia	m	13.6	m	10.6	m	3.8	m	39.5	m	25.4	m	7.1
Japan	10.1	5.2	14.0	9.6	x	x	32.6	25.7	23.1	37.0	18.6	21.5
New Zealand *	15.4	8.4	5.9	8.5	1.2	4.3	58.9	39.4	16.7	32.4	1.6	6.2
European Union												
Austria	8.1	10.2	1.8	11.5	0.8	5.4	63.4	30.7	11.7	28.9	14.2	13.3
Belgium *	13.4	12.5	2.0	9.3	4.3	2.1	28.8	12.3	50.4	42.5	1.1	20.6
Denmark *	5.6	13.6	3.2	6.6	a	1.3	0.9	38.7	90.3	24.2	a	15.5
Finland	57.3	9.7	8.7	8.8	5.3	7.1	5.7	37.3	6.4	12.9	16.6	24.3
France *	0.1	5.9	x	x	15.1	20.9	28.8	30.6	40.4	30.9	15.6	11.7
Germany *	33.0	11.5	6.4	12.6	0.7	5.5	23.9	36.4	11.2	10.8	24.7	23.2
Greece *	29.0	11.6	8.5	10.7	0.8	3.7	4.3	43.5	35.9	19.8	21.5	10.7
Ireland *	0.8	5.9	16.0	13.5	7.7	5.0	8.7	41.7	39.2	22.2	27.6	11.5
Italy	m	23.6	m	8.8	m	2.9	m	25.4	m	27.4	m	11.9
Luxembourg	m	m	m	m	m	m	m	m	m	m	m	m
Netherlands *	a	13.6	a	6.6	a	2.5	a	41.5	a	20.2	a	13.4
Portugal	18.3	5.5	4.3	5.9	2.5	2.5	28.1	49.1	33.7	23.7	13.2	13.3
Spain *	0.6	11.7	0.9	6.8	a	3.7	13.2	29.1	69.6	39.1	a	9.5
Sweden	43.9	12.5	2.0	6.8	2.1	5.2	32.4	35.0	9.3	24.7	10.3	15.9
United Kingdom	24.9	6.5	7.8	11.6	1.3	5.8	12.5	39.5	37.2	22.3	16.3	14.3
Other OECD countries												
Czech Republic	3.5	9.8	21.8	9.7	n	2.5	10.6	39.4	59.0	9.4	5.1	29.2
Hungary *	a	7.4	a	10.8	a	x	a	59.9	a	4.5	a	17.4
Iceland	m	19.9	m	8.9	m	2.8	m	46.4	m	16.6	m	5.5
Norway	0.8	17.7	0.8	7.2	0.7	0.9	63.8	36.7	33.9	14.9	0.1	18.8
Switzerland	m	14.7	m	16.3	m	3.4	m	25.2	m	28.8	m	11.6
Turkey *	29.5	11.5	3.1	10.5	1.7	2.8	2.2	45.9	28.0	13.0	35.5	16.3
Country mean	**15.4**	**11.1**	**5.7**	**9.5**	**2.4**	**4.4**	**23.3**	**38.1**	**32.2**	**23.1**	**10.9**	**14.3**
Other non-OECD countries												
Korea	11.7	4.3	10.4	17.2	n	x	41.5	58.0	x	x	36.3	16.9
Poland *	23.8	25.3	0.8	8.9	a	1.8	23.4	36.5	52.0	14.6	a	13.0
Russian Federation	m	6.6	m	13.9	m	14.9	m	28.6	m	10.5	m	25.5

* 1993 data
Source: OECD Database. See Annex 3 for notes

R14: Tertiary qualifications by field of study

Table R14.2:
Non-university tertiary and university-level qualifications by subject category
(percentages of total non-university and university-level qualifications), **men** (1994)

	Medical science Non-university	Medical science University-level	Natural science Non-university	Natural science University-level	Mathematics and computer science Non-university	Mathematics and computer science University-level	Humanities / general Non-university	Humanities / general University-level	Law and business Non-university	Law and business University-level	Engineering and architecture Non-university	Engineering and architecture University-level
North America												
Canada	2.7	4.4	5.3	9.3	2.1	5.9	28.2	45.0	61.1	21.3	n	14.1
Mexico	m	m	m	m	m	m	m	m	m	m	m	m
United States	9.2	4.8	3.5	8.0	2.5	4.7	34.5	37.6	35.7	31.1	14.3	13.5
Pacific Area												
Australia	m	6.7	m	13.7	m	6.3	m	28.7	m	31.1	m	13.5
Japan	4.7	4.5	1.9	8.8	x	x	14.9	13.2	27.7	43.5	48.9	29.4
New Zealand *	5.2	5.5	9.2	9.5	1.8	6.6	45.8	27.6	33.0	39.9	4.6	9.9
European Union												
Austria	4.1	8.1	3.3	12.7	1.6	7.4	45.6	21.6	12.5	30.0	32.8	20.2
Belgium *	6.6	10.1	2.7	10.0	8.2	2.7	19.5	7.9	61.7	39.0	1.3	29.4
Denmark *	1.0	4.3	3.5	9.1	a	2.1	1.0	23.9	94.5	34.2	a	26.5
Finland	15.4	7.6	14.3	9.3	11.6	11.9	5.9	19.1	3.2	12.2	49.6	39.9
France *	0.1	5.8	x	x	19.6	27.8	20.3	20.5	30.3	27.1	29.6	18.9
Germany *	13.5	10.4	9.6	13.4	1.1	6.0	8.1	27.9	17.5	9.8	50.1	32.5
Greece *	13.7	15.6	9.1	14.9	1.4	5.0	3.9	25.1	35.1	21.2	36.8	18.2
Ireland *	0.1	5.6	12.0	14.3	8.3	6.1	6.3	30.7	27.0	23.1	46.3	20.2
Italy	m	26.1	m	9.5	m	3.1	m	12.3	m	30.0	m	19.0
Luxembourg	m	m	m	m	m	m	m	m	m	m	m	m
Netherlands *	a	8.7	a	8.7	a	4.3	a	32.6	a	21.7	a	21.7
Portugal	7.9	3.7	6.6	6.4	4.8	2.9	14.3	35.7	36.3	26.3	30.1	25.0
Spain *	0.1	8.7	1.0	8.2	a	5.6	5.8	20.9	75.7	39.1	a	17.3
Sweden	19.8	9.3	6.2	7.7	5.6	9.0	15.0	21.4	22.3	25.3	31.1	27.2
United Kingdom	6.0	4.7	11.4	13.4	1.8	7.4	11.9	29.0	41.6	22.1	27.3	23.4
Other OECD countries												
Czech Republic	1.5	6.9	8.1	11.4	n	3.7	11.3	27.5	69.6	7.6	9.5	43.0
Hungary *	a	5.9	a	16.3	a	x	a	42.8	a	4.9	a	30.2
Iceland	m	12.0	m	14.1	m	6.3	m	30.5	m	24.2	m	12.9
Norway	0.3	7.1	1.0	8.9	0.8	1.6	58.5	24.6	39.3	19.5	0.2	34.0
Switzerland	m	13.3	m	18.3	m	4.5	m	17.6	m	30.9	m	15.2
Turkey *	10.2	10.5	4.6	9.9	2.4	2.4	1.5	44.0	24.2	14.1	57.2	19.0
Country mean	5.8	8.4	5.7	11.1	3.7	6.2	16.8	26.7	35.7	25.2	22.4	23.0
Other non-OECD countries												
Korea	6.7	4.3	6.3	13.6	n	x	23.5	51.3	x	x	63.5	25.9
Poland *	11.7	20.0	2.6	10.1	a	1.3	21.8	25.1	64.0	20.1	a	23.4
Russian Federation	m	m	m	m	m	m	m	m	m	m	m	m

* 1993 data
Source: OECD Database. See Annex 3 for notes

R14: Tertiary qualifications by field of study

Table R14.3:
Non-university tertiary and university-level qualifications by subject category
(percentages of total non-university and university-level qualifications), **women** (1994)

	Medical science Non-university	Medical science University-level	Natural science Non-university	Natural science University-level	Mathematics and computer science Non-university	Mathematics and computer science University-level	Humanities / general Non-university	Humanities / general University-level	Law and business Non-university	Law and business University-level	Engineering and architecture Non-university	Engineering and architecture University-level
North America												
Canada	13.0	8.2	1.6	7.4	1.3	1.9	50.4	64.9	33.3	15.5	n	2.1
Mexico	m	m	m	m	m	m	m	m	m	m	m	m
United States	29.9	10.8	4.9	6.8	1.8	2.0	31.8	54.6	30.0	23.0	1.4	2.4
Pacific Area												
Australia	m	18.8	m	8.3	m	2.0	m	47.5	m	21.2	m	2.2
Japan	12.6	6.8	19.4	11.3	x	x	40.6	54.0	21.1	22.4	4.8	3.7
New Zealand *	20.5	11.1	4.2	7.5	0.9	2.1	65.4	50.4	8.6	25.4	0.1	2.8
European Union												
Austria	9.8	12.9	1.2	10.0	0.4	2.6	70.8	43.1	11.3	27.5	6.4	3.9
Belgium *	18.4	15.7	1.5	8.5	1.4	1.4	35.6	18.2	42.1	47.1	1.0	9.1
Denmark *	13.7	21.5	2.7	4.5	a	0.7	0.8	51.3	82.8	15.8	a	6.2
Finland	74.2	12.0	6.5	8.1	2.8	2.0	5.6	56.9	7.7	13.6	3.3	7.3
France *	0.1	6.0	x	x	11.5	14.3	35.5	40.3	48.4	34.6	4.5	4.7
Germany *	48.9	13.2	3.8	11.4	0.4	4.7	36.7	50.1	6.1	12.3	4.1	8.4
Greece *	41.8	8.6	8.1	7.6	0.3	2.7	4.6	57.2	36.4	18.7	8.7	5.1
Ireland *	1.7	6.2	20.8	12.8	7.0	4.0	11.7	52.3	53.8	21.5	5.1	3.2
Italy	m	21.4	m	8.2	m	2.7	m	37.4	m	24.9	m	5.4
Luxembourg	m	m	m	m	m	m	m	m	m	m	m	m
Netherlands *	a	19.0	a	4.3	a	0.6	a	51.4	a	18.4	a	4.1
Portugal	23.5	6.6	3.1	5.6	1.4	2.2	35.0	57.5	32.4	22.1	4.7	6.0
Spain *	1.2	14.0	0.7	5.7	a	2.2	21.1	35.6	63.0	39.2	a	3.2
Sweden	53.2	15.2	0.4	6.0	0.7	2.0	39.2	46.3	4.3	24.2	2.3	6.4
United Kingdom	40.2	8.4	4.9	9.6	0.8	4.1	13.0	50.5	33.6	22.5	7.5	4.8
Other OECD countries												
Czech Republic	4.4	12.9	27.9	7.8	n	1.2	10.3	52.0	54.2	11.4	3.2	14.6
Hungary *	a	8.8	a	6.1	a	x	a	74.8	a	4.1	a	6.2
Iceland	m	24.7	m	5.7	m	0.6	m	56.0	m	12.0	m	1.0
Norway	1.2	26.1	0.6	5.8	0.6	0.3	68.2	46.3	29.4	11.2	0.1	6.7
Switzerland	m	17.3	m	12.4	m	1.3	m	39.2	m	24.9	m	5.0
Turkey *	53.8	13.1	1.1	12.5	0.9	3.4	3.1	46.7	32.9	14.0	8.3	10.3
Country mean	**22.0**	**13.6**	**5.7**	**8.1**	**1.6**	**2.7**	**27.6**	**49.4**	**30.1**	**21.1**	**3.1**	**5.4**
Other non-OECD countries												
Korea	15.9	4.4	13.8	22.7	n	x	56.3	68.5	x	x	14.0	2.9
Poland *	26.9	29.5	0.4	7.7	a	2.2	23.8	46.7	48.9	9.8	a	4.1
Russian Federation	m	m	m	m	m	m	m	m	m	m	m	m

* 1993 data
Source: OECD Database. See Annex 3 for notes

R15: SUPPLY OF HIGH-LEVEL QUALIFICATIONS IN SCIENCE-RELATED FIELDS

This indicator shows the number of tertiary science graduates per 100 000 persons in the labour force.

POLICY CONTEXT

Technological innovation has become an increasingly important component of industries' ability to compete in the global marketplace, and employment is growing in high-technology, science-based sectors ranging from computers to pharmaceuticals. Even beyond their role in science-based sectors, new technologies have an impact throughout economic and social systems.

KEY RESULTS

While in Australia, Ireland, Japan and Korea there are more than 1 200 university-level graduates in science-related fields per 100 000 persons in the labour force aged 25 to 34 years, this number is below 500 in eight OECD countries. It is interesting to note that Japan and Korea also demonstrate very high achievement of students around the age of 13 in mathematics and science (see Indicator R6).

Taking all OECD countries together, the number of tertiary science graduates as a proportion of the labour force aged 25-34 is, on average, twice as high at the university-level (745 graduates per 100 000 persons) as at the non-university tertiary level of education (376 graduates per 100 000 persons). This corresponds roughly to the respective proportions of total enrolments at these levels of education (see Indicator P6).

DESCRIPTION AND INTERPRETATION

The number of persons obtaining tertiary science-related qualifications is an important indicator of the supply of high-level skills and knowledge. However, the indicator does not provide information on the number of graduates actually employed in scientific fields or, more generally, those using their degree skills and knowledge in their employment. It therefore measures a potential supply of skills rather than their utilisation. Furthermore, some countries provide qualifications at the upper secondary level which are equivalent to tertiary qualifications in other countries and which are not taken into account in this indicator.

At the non-university tertiary level, the number of science graduates is comparatively high in Finland, France, Ireland, Japan, Korea and the United Kingdom (more than 600 science graduates per 100 000 persons in the labour force), whereas it is comparatively low in Austria, Denmark and Norway (see Chart R15).

At the university level, the number of science graduates is comparatively high in Australia, Finland, Ireland, Japan, Korea, Norway and the United Kingdom (more than 1 000 science graduates per 100 000 persons in the labour force) while it is low in Austria, Greece, Hungary, Italy, Switzerland and Turkey.

Those countries that tend to award high numbers of university-level science qualifications usually also tend to award higher numbers of science qualifications at the non-university level.

On average across OECD countries, men are almost twice as likely as women to obtain a university-level science qualification, and they are still more than one-and-half times as likely as women to be awarded a science qualification at the non-university tertiary level. Women represent less than 25 per cent of the science graduates at the university-level of education in Finland, Hungary, Japan and the Netherlands.

Gender differences tend to be lower at the non-university tertiary level where programmes are often considerably shorter in duration than at the university level.

At a time when technological innovation is becoming an increasingly important component of industries' ability to compete in the global marketplace, closing the gender gap can be an important policy objective to ensure a sufficient supply of the required skills and knowledge.

DEFINITIONS

This indicator shows the number of persons who obtained a tertiary level qualification in a science-related field per 100 000 persons in the labour force aged 25 to 34

R15: Supply of high-level qualifications in science-related fields

Chart R15: Number of science graduates per 100 000 persons in the labour force 25 to 34 years of age, men and women (1994)

Non-university

[Bar chart showing countries in order: Ireland*, France*, Japan, Korea, Finland, United Kingdom, Germany*, Canada, United States, Sweden, Portugal, Greece*, Belgium*, Turkey*, New Zealand*, Austria, Norway, Denmark*]

University-level

[Bar chart showing countries in order: Japan, Korea, Ireland*, United Kingdom, Finland, Norway, Australia, Denmark*, Netherlands*, United States, Germany*, France*, New Zealand*, Canada, Belgium*, Spain*, Sweden, Switzerland, Poland*, Hungary*, Portugal, Greece*, Italy, Austria, Turkey*]

Legend: Women, Men

* 1993 data

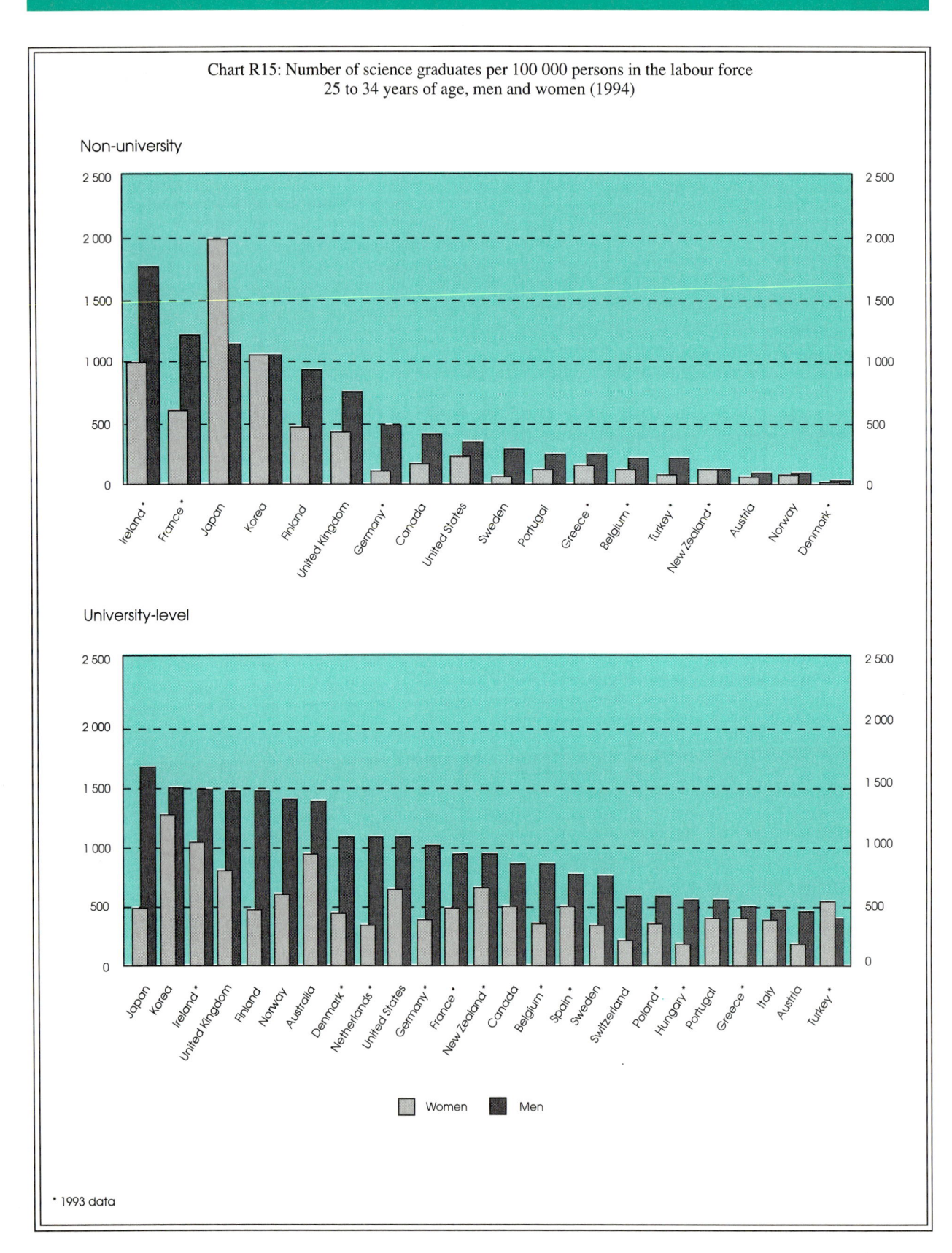

R15: Supply of high-level qualifications in science-related fields

during the reference years. It distinguishes between graduates at the university level of education and the non-university tertiary level.

The indicator takes into account graduates from the following fields of study: "Natural science" (ISCED 42), "Mathematics and computer science" (ISCED 46), "Engineering" (ISCED 54), "Architecture and town planning" (ISCED 58), "Agriculture, forestry and fishery" (ISCED 62) and "Home economics (domestic science)" (ISCED 66). Note that the classification of graduates by field of study has been modified so as to be coherent with the International Standard Classification of Education (ISCED). Thus, the results cannot be compared with those published in earlier editions of *Education at a Glance*.

As with Indicator R14, the results depend heavily on the extent to which subject definitions and classifications are consistent among countries (see also Annex 3).

R15: Supply of high-level qualifications in science-related fields

Table R15:
Number of science graduates per 100 000 persons in the labour force 25 to 34 years of age, men and women (1994)

	Non-university tertiary education			University-level education		
	M+W	Men	Women	M+W	Men	Women
North America						
Canada	299.3	407.2	169.0	698.4	858.9	504.7
Mexico	m	m	m	m	m	m
United States	293.2	343.9	231.5	887.1	1 082.9	649.0
Pacific Area						
Australia	m	m	m	1 205.4	1 393.3	947.4
Japan	1 455.1	1 135.2	1 988.2	1 224.2	1 669.6	481.9
New Zealand *	125.3	130.0	118.9	816.5	938.3	650.7
European Union						
Austria	75.6	89.6	57.7	336.8	462.1	177.1
Belgium *	175.2	220.6	119.7	631.6	853.1	360.0
Denmark *	29.4	38.5	19.3	780.4	1087.0	436.3
Finland	718.1	926.0	465.6	1017.7	1469.7	469.1
France *	935.6	1214.5	599.0	735.0	942.4	484.7
Germany *	320.7	486.8	105.7	739.6	1010.8	388.8
Greece *	208.4	246.0	154.3	458.7	503.9	393.7
Ireland *	1 444.9	1771.7	996.4	1 305.6	1 493.4	1 048.1
Italy	m	m	m	433.4	468.7	382.3
Luxembourg	m	m	m	m	m	m
Netherlands *	a	a	a	775.1	1 085.0	347.6
Portugal	186.2	246.1	120.1	479.4	555.9	395.0
Spain *	1.4	1.4	1.4	658.8	766.4	501.1
Sweden	186.7	292.1	67.4	563.8	762.9	338.3
United Kingdom	612.3	755.1	417.1	1 186.8	1 473.1	795.6
Other OECD countries						
Czech Republic	178.8	m	m	664.0	m	m
Hungary *	a	a	a	374.3	557.5	179.6
Iceland	m	m	m	m	m	m
Norway	85.4	89.5	80.5	1 038.4	1 407.4	603.2
Switzerland	m	m	m	424.0	582.7	209.2
Turkey *	181.2	219.5	76.6	440.7	401.8	542.3
Country mean	**357.8**	**430.7**	**289.4**	**744.8**	**949.0**	**490.7**
Korea	1 053.1	1 055.1	1 048.9	1 427.1	1 500.3	1 276.9
Poland *	m	m	m	483.7	581.0	359.0
Russian Federation	m	m	m	m	m	m

* 1993 data
Source: OECD Database. See Annex 3 for notes

Chapter 6

STUDENT ACHIEVEMENT AND ADULT LITERACY

How well are children performing in mathematics? How good is a particular school? Which university should a student aim for when he or she graduates next year? These are questions many students and parents ask themselves. But how are they to know? At another level, the corollary is: "How good is our education system?" and, "Does it provide young people with the skills and knowledge they will need to enter the labour market and to become effective citizens in a rapidly changing and increasingly complex democratic society?" These are equally legitimate questions, but are similarly difficult to answer straightforwardly.

Answers to these questions all hinge on the availability of valid and reliable information on individual educational outcomes. Without such information, discussion of the quality, equity and effectiveness of education often remains uninformed, anecdotal, and polemic.

This chapter presents two sets of indicators on individual outcomes. The first concerns the achievement of students currently enrolled in the education system in two important areas of the curriculum – mathematics and science. The second set examines the level of functional literacy skills in the adult population. This analysis is taken further in *Education at a Glance – Analysis*.

THE INDICATORS ON STUDENT ACHIEVEMENT

The achievement of students in basic skills such as mathematics, science, reading and cross-curriculum competencies is one of the key criteria for an assessment of the performance of education systems. Students who demonstrate high achievement levels are more likely to be productive workers and members of society when they leave the education system. Student achievement also provides information about the nature and effectiveness of educational processes. In conjunction with information on educational curriculum, staffing, organisation, expenditure, and the home and school environment, it can be used to examine the factors associated with student achievement.

Mathematics and science play a crucial role in equipping young people to meet the responsibilities of adult life in public and private spheres, and they are of particular importance in modern economies, which increasingly depend on scientific discoveries and technological innovation. In most countries, the attention given to mathematics is second only to the emphasis given to instruction in the national language (see Indicator P11), and many countries consider mathematics and science among the most important instructional goals for schools. The emphasis on mathematics and science in national curricula reflects, in part, a widespread interest in identifying and preparing young people to play a leadership role in the research and development activities that underpin modern economies, and a wider need for adults to have the capacity to understand and be able to talk about scientific, technological and environmental issues.

Four indicators review the standards achieved by children at the two grade levels in which most 13 year-olds are enrolled. They draw on the Third International Mathematics and Science Study (TIMSS), an international comparison of performance in mathematics and science tests that was conducted during the school year 1994/95 by the International Association for the Evaluation of Educational Achievement (IEA) and sponsored by the governments of the participating countries. The goal of this study was to measure student performance and, at the same time, to assess some curricular and classroom factors of the social and educational context in which such performance occurs. More than 550 000 students at three grade levels – around the ages of 9 and 13 and in the final year of upper secondary education – as well as some 31 000 teachers and 13 000 schools in 44 countries took part in this study. An extensive analysis of science and mathematics textbooks and curriculum guides used in the participating countries, along with advice from subject specialists, provided data describing what students in the participating countries were expected to learn according to national or regional goals. This information was used to select the topics and assessment items to be included in the achievement tests. A scale was constructed on which tasks of varying difficulty were placed. The ability of students was then measured by a score on this scale.

Indicator R6 provides an indication of the average levels of student achievement in mathematics and science at the higher grade of the two grade levels in which most 13 year-olds are enrolled and which, by convention, is referred to as the "eighth" grade in this publication since in most countries it refers to the eighth year of formal schooling. Differences across countries in average mathematics and science achievement need to be interpreted against the background of curricular emphases, student attitudes and perceptions, and in terms of the social and economic contexts in which students grow up. Achievement is also influenced significantly by school resources and processes and the classroom environment, including the quality of teaching, the resources available for students to use in the classroom (e.g. computers, laboratory equipment), and the nature of the teaching methods used. Finally, test results are clearly affected in important ways by the social context outside school, including the educational and economic resources supporting learning at home, and the availability and content of the mass media (television and the popular press).

Mean achievement may be the primary quality index for classrooms, schools and education systems as a whole. However, overall means can mask significant disparities. It is therefore instructive to compare not only the average performance of countries but also how well the highest and lowest achievers in a country perform in relation to international standards. This is shown by **Indicator R7**, which examines the relative standing of different parts of the achievement distribution. This indicator can also be interpreted as a measure of equity. Teachers, schools and education systems as a whole must cope with the variation in achievement that exists within classes, within schools and within the country. Such variation can result from disparities in resources and in the socio-economic background of students and schools as well as from curricular differences and the way in which instruction is organised and delivered.

Taken together, Indicators R6 and R7 provide a measure of the cumulative yield of formal and informal education in which children participate, from birth to the end of typically the eighth grade.

The third indicator (**R9**) examines the progress in achievement from the seventh to the eighth grade in the sampled population. This indicator, more than the first two, isolates the effects of formal schooling since the effects of family and other social resources are captured at least in part in seventh grade achievement. Thus, the difference in average achievement between the seventh and eighth grades may be viewed largely (although not entirely) as a function of the curriculum and the school. The most important single factor influencing the difference in average achievement between seventh and eighth grades is likely to be the topics covered in the eighth grade, and the extent to which these topics are newly introduced or are a rehearsal of materials introduced in earlier grades.

Finally, **Indicator R10** examines gender differences in mathematics and science achievement. It provides an indication of the extent to which a gender gap is observable before students move on into formal vocational and professional education, which can then affect pathways to further education and training as well as career opportunities later in life (see also Indicators R14 and R15).

THE INDICATORS ON ADULT LITERACY SKILLS

Literacy is a key skill on which the development of other competencies depends. A well-educated and literate workforce gives a country a comparative competitive advantage and helps counteract polarisation and social exclusion. Today, adults need a high level of literacy to function well: societies and economies have become more complex. Even jobs that were once considered "low-skilled" require higher literacy levels than before. Low levels of literacy may relegate certain members of society to the remaining jobs requiring fewer skills and offering lower pay. In addition, at the societal level, with the development of close economic ties among countries, where enterprises locate new plants is increasingly determined by the skill level of the local population. Inadequate levels of literacy and numeracy among a broad section of the population can thus threaten the strength of national economies and social cohesion.

It is against this background that seven countries undertook the first International Adult Literacy Survey (IALS) in 1994. In all, more than 23 000 respondents aged 16 to 65 years were interviewed for about 20 minutes each concerning background characteristics, and then took a 45-minute literacy skill test in their homes in their national languages. Statistics Canada provided overall management and scientific co-ordination for this large-scale operation, supported by international organisations and agencies such as the National Centre for Education Statistics and the Educational Testing Service in the United States.

In IALS, literacy is no longer defined merely in terms of a basic threshold of reading performance, distinguishing the few who completely fail the test (the "illiterates") from nearly all those who reach the minimum threshold (those who are "literate"). Instead, literacy refers to a particular mode of behaviour – namely, the ability to understand and employ printed information in daily activities, at home, at work and in the community – to achieve one's goals, and to develop one's knowledge and potential. By denoting a broad set of information-processing competencies, this conceptual approach points to the multiplicity of skills that constitute literacy in today's advanced industrialised countries. For the purpose of IALS, literacy is operationalised in terms of three scales, each encompassing a common set of skills relevant for diverse tasks: *i) prose literacy* – the knowledge and skills needed to understand and use information from texts, including editorials, news stories, poems and fiction; *ii) document literacy* – the knowledge and skills required to locate and use information contained in various formats, including job applications, payroll forms, public transport timetables, maps, tables and charts; and *iii) quantitative literacy* – the knowledge and skills required to apply arithmetic operations, either alone or sequentially, to numbers embedded in printed materials, such as balancing a cheque book, working out a tip, completing an order form or determining the amount of interest on a loan from an advertisement.

For the indicators in this publication, the ranges of scores achieved were grouped into five proficiency levels. Level 1 indicates persons with very poor skills, where the individual may, for example, be unable to determine the correct amount of medicine to give a child from information printed on the package. At Level 2, respondents can deal only with material that is simple, clearly laid out, and in which the tasks involved are not too complex. By contrast, Levels 3 and 4/5 focus on increasingly higher-order literacy skills, where the ability to integrate several sources of information to solve more complex problems is required. Level 3 is regarded as a suitable minimum by experts in Canada and the United States; it denotes roughly the skill level required for successful high-school graduation and college entry. Levels 4/5 tend to describe respondents who have received some post-secondary education.

Indicator R30 shows the proportion of persons aged 16-65 scoring at each of the four literacy levels on the three different scales. It provides a broad picture of the distribution of literacy skills in a country's population.

Literacy as measured by the International Adult Literacy Survey is not curriculum-based but based on tasks encountered in everyday life, including the work place. It is therefore possible for persons with high levels of formal education to display low literacy and vice versa. The extent of correspondence between education and literacy measured in this way – which is examined by **Indicator R31** – provides some indication of how adequately education systems prepare young people for the world beyond school.

Indicator R32 examines the extent to which the literacy skills of the young differ from those of the older population. This question is of particular interest, because of the light it can shed on the effects of the considerable changes in the enrolment, emphasis and content of educational programmes that have occurred in most countries in recent decades. It points to the need for continuing education and training for those who have left the formal education system.

Indicator R33 examines gender differences in adult literacy skills. The increasing reliance of OECD economies on the participation of women to ensure continued labour force growth, particularly in the face of an ageing population, points to the importance of reducing gender differences.

A NOTE ON STATISTICAL ERROR IN SAMPLE SURVEYS

Like any survey results, the TIMSS and IALS data reported in this chapter are subject to error, which must be taken into account when making comparisons. For this reason, the standard errors of the estimates are reported together with the data. It is important to review the possible sources of the errors that are present, and to reflect on how they constrain the data analysis and the interpretation of observed differences among the countries.

First, the TIMSS and IALS data sets are subject to sampling error because they are based on sample surveys of individuals. The effect of sampling error is to set a lower limit on the size of observed differences which are statistically significant and, thereby, real. Given the high cost of interviewing and testing adults in their homes, the sample sizes used for the IALS study are small. Consequently, many small differences observed among countries are not statistically significant. The sample sizes for students used in the TIMSS survey are larger in most cases. All mean scores and differences are presented together with their standard errors. By adding ± 2 standard errors to the reported means, the reader can obtain a reasonable estimate of the error margins.

Secondly, the TIMSS and IALS results are based on different combinations of test items being administered to each respondent – introducing an additional source of error to the estimates, which should be considered.

Thirdly, subtle differences in design, implementation or patterns of non-coverage or non-response may have introduced non-sampling errors in the TIMSS and IALS studies that can lead to overestimation or underestimation of the true size of population differences. The extent to which non-sampling sources of error are present in the data and bias the results cannot be readily determined. Annex 3 reports non-response rates and the population coverage of the survey results.

R6: Student achievement in mathematics and science

R6: STUDENT ACHIEVEMENT IN MATHEMATICS AND SCIENCE

This indicator compares the average achievement of students in mathematics and science across countries.

POLICY CONTEXT

As enterprises become global in their competitive outlook and dependent upon the wide availability of human talent, international comparisons of student achievement are turning into an essential instrument of evaluation. They contribute to the setting of realistic standards for education systems and are an important instrument for monitoring school quality. Information on student achievement functions also as a measure of accountability for the public trust placed in educational institutions and is of particular interest to the stakeholders in education – taxpayers, students, teachers, parents and employers.

Indicator R6 shows policy-makers whether the relative standing of student achievement in their country is significantly better or worse than that of other countries. Together with Indicator R7 it is an indicator of the comparative yield of education systems in mathematics and science at the upper of the two grade levels in which most 13 year-olds are enrolled. The two domains for which student achievement is compared, mathematics and science, are of particular importance in modern economies that depend on scientific discoveries and technological innovation.

KEY RESULTS

The indicator reveals substantial differences among countries in the average achievement of students in mathematics and science. The difference in mathematics achievement between Japan and Korea, on the one hand, and the OECD average, on the other, exceeds more than twice the typical difference in achievement between students in seventh and eighth grades in OECD countries (see Indicator R9). High achievement levels are not only reached by a small elite in those countries, but more than 75 per cent of the students in Japan and Korea score above the OECD average (see also Indicator R7). This is particularly striking since the financial and human resources which these countries devote to educational institutions are rather modest when compared to the OECD as a whole (see, for example, Indicators F3 and P32). High achievement in mathematics is also shown by students in the Flemish Community of Belgium and in the Czech Republic, whereas students in Portugal lag considerably behind. The average mathematics achievement score for most OECD countries is between 480 and 550 points on a scale that has an overall OECD mean of 516 points and a standard deviation of somewhat less than 100 points. In science, the pattern is similar, with a few notable exceptions and shifts in the rank order of countries. The countries with the highest achievement here are Austria, the Czech Republic, Japan, Korea and the Netherlands. There is slightly less variation across countries in science, especially among the countries with the highest levels of achievement.

DESCRIPTION AND INTERPRETATION

One way to gauge the magnitude of differences in mean achievement among countries is to compare them with the typical difference in achievement between the seventh and eighth grades – an average difference of about 33 points in mathematics and 39 points in science for the OECD countries tested (see Indicator R9). The observed difference in scores between countries with the highest and lowest scores is 153 score points in mathematics and 103 score points in science.

While the relative ranking of most countries is similar in mathematics and science, some countries show substantially higher performance in one discipline than in the other. England, for example, has substantially higher achievement in science than in mathematics, while France performs much better in mathematics than in science (see Charts R6.1 and R6.2). The fact that countries vary in their performance in the two disciplines suggests that variation cannot be explained entirely by the demographic or socio-economic context but may reflect, in part, differences in factors such as curriculum and instruction, which are amenable to policy decisions.

Knowledge about the overall and relative levels of achievement provides useful information for evaluation, particularly when comparisons are made between countries that operate under similar socio-economic conditions. However, there is the fundamental challenge of judging what level of performance is adequate. What does it mean if 10 or 20 per cent of students at a given age fail to provide the correct answers to a set of test items in

R6: Student achievement in mathematics and science

subjects such as mathematics and science? Is this a good result or not? This is where the current debate about achievement standards comes into play. For outcome information to contribute effectively to the evaluation of education systems, it is necessary to identify key points along the performance scale and to define what students should typically know or be able to do at these points.

Information on achievement levels also leads to the more pertinent question of what influences student performance. What factors explain the patterns of performance in different countries, and are they amenable to policy intervention? Knowledge of the determinants of successful student performance enables policy-makers to make informed choices about priorities for the future. Success may be associated, for example, with student attitudes and perceptions, with teachers' instructional practices or with curricular emphases. Future editions of this publication will attempt to explore the factors that can contribute to high standards of performance in school.

The fact that there appears to be neither a strong nor a consistent relationship at the national level between the level of resources (see also Indicators F3 and P32) and student outcomes provides further evidence that country variation cannot be explained alone in terms of financial or staff resource levels and that the search for improvement in school performance must extend to factors that lie beyond material inputs.

Finally, while comparing the relative standing of countries is instructive, different average achievement levels can reflect different aspirations of education systems. Each system has its own values and may go through periods in which certain points of the curriculum are considered more important than others.

DEFINITIONS

The achievement scores are based on tests administered as part of the Third International Mathematics and Science Study (TIMSS), undertaken by the International Association for the Evaluation of Educational Achievement (IEA) during the school year 1994/95. The data are subject to sampling error, which sets a lower limit on the size of observed differences that can be considered statistically significant. Mean scores are therefore reported together with their standard errors. The charts indicate whether differences between pairs of countries are statistically significant or not. The statistical tests used to compare country means were conducted using the Bonferroni adjustment for multiple comparisons at the 95 per cent confidence level. The target population studied in this indicator refers to students at the higher grade of the two grade levels in which most 13 year-olds are enrolled and which, by convention, is referred to as the "eighth" grade since in most countries it refers to the eighth year of formal schooling (see also column 6 in Table R9.1). Countries marked with an asterisk (*) met the IEA/TIMSS sampling standards only partially, countries marked with two asterisks (**) did not meet the IEA/TIMSS sampling standards. The reporting of data on a sub-national level for some countries is based on data availability from the IEA and does not represent a policy decision by the OECD.

Chart R6.1: Multiple comparisons of overall student achievement in **mathematics**, eighth grade (1995)

	Mean	Standard error	Average age	Korea	Japan	Belgium (Fl.)*	Czech Republic	Switzerland*	Netherlands**	Austria**	France	Hungary	Russian Federation	Australia**	Ireland	Canada	Belgium (Fr.)**	Sweden	Germany**	New Zealand	England*	Norway	Denmark**	United States*	Scotland**	Spain	Iceland	Greece**	Portugal
Korea	607	(2.4)	14.2		●	▲	▲	▲	▲	▲	▲	▲	▲	▲	▲	▲	▲	▲	▲	▲	▲	▲	▲	▲	▲	▲	▲	▲	▲
Japan	605	(1.9)	14.4	●		▲	▲	▲	▲	▲	▲	▲	▲	▲	▲	▲	▲	▲	▲	▲	▲	▲	▲	▲	▲	▲	▲	▲	▲
Belgium (Fl.)*	565	(5.7)	14.1	▼	▼		●	▲	●	▲	▲	▲	▲	▲	▲	▲	▲	▲	▲	▲	▲	▲	▲	▲	▲	▲	▲	▲	▲
Czech Republic	564	(4.9)	14.4	▼	▼	●		▲	●	▲	▲	▲	▲	▲	▲	▲	▲	▲	▲	▲	▲	▲	▲	▲	▲	▲	▲	▲	▲
Switzerland*	545	(2.8)	14.2	▼	▼	▼	▼		●	●	●	●	●	▲	▲	▲	▲	▲	▲	▲	▲	▲	▲	▲	▲	▲	▲	▲	▲
Netherlands**	541	(6.7)	14.3	▼	▼	●	●	●		●	●	●	●	●	●	●	●	●	▲	▲	▲	▲	▲	▲	▲	▲	▲	▲	▲
Austria**	539	(3.0)	14.3	▼	▼	▼	▼	●	●		●	●	●	●	●	▲	●	▲	▲	▲	▲	▲	▲	▲	▲	▲	▲	▲	▲
France	538	(2.9)	14.3	▼	▼	▼	▼	●	●	●		●	●	●	●	●	●	▲	▲	▲	▲	▲	▲	▲	▲	▲	▲	▲	▲
Hungary	537	(3.2)	14.3	▼	▼	▼	▼	●	●	●	●		●	●	●	●	●	▲	▲	▲	▲	▲	▲	▲	▲	▲	▲	▲	▲
Russian Federation	536	(5.3)	14.0	▼	▼	▼	▼	●	●	●	●	●		●	●	●	●	●	▲	▲	▲	▲	▲	▲	▲	▲	▲	▲	▲
Australia**	530	(4.0)	14.2	▼	▼	▼	▼	▼	●	●	●	●	●		●	●	●	●	▲	▲	▲	▲	▲	▲	▲	▲	▲	▲	▲
Ireland	527	(5.1)	14.4	▼	▼	▼	▼	▼	●	●	●	●	●	●		●	●	●	●	●	▲	▲	▲	▲	▲	▲	▲	▲	▲
Canada	527	(2.4)	41.1	▼	▼	▼	▼	▼	●	▼	●	●	●	●	●		●	●	▲	▲	▲	▲	▲	▲	▲	▲	▲	▲	▲
Belgium (Fr.)**	526	(3.4)	14.3	▼	▼	▼	▼	▼	●	●	●	●	●	●	●	●		●	●	▲	▲	▲	▲	▲	▲	▲	▲	▲	▲
Sweden	519	(3.0)	13.9	▼	▼	▼	▼	▼	●	▼	▼	▼	●	●	●	●	●		●	●	▲	▲	▲	▲	▲	▲	▲	▲	▲
Germany**	509	(4.5)	14.8	▼	▼	▼	▼	▼	▼	▼	▼	▼	▼	▼	●	▼	●	●		●	●	●	●	●	●	▲	▲	▲	▲
New Zealand	508	(4.5)	14.0	▼	▼	▼	▼	▼	▼	▼	▼	▼	▼	▼	●	▼	▼	●	●		●	●	●	●	●	▲	▲	▲	▲
England*	506	(2.6)	14.0	▼	▼	▼	▼	▼	▼	▼	▼	▼	▼	▼	▼	▼	▼	▼	●	●		●	●	●	●	▲	▲	▲	▲
Norway	503	(2.2)	13.9	▼	▼	▼	▼	▼	▼	▼	▼	▼	▼	▼	▼	▼	▼	▼	●	●	●		●	●	●	▲	▲	▲	▲
Denmark**	502	(2,8)	13.9	▼	▼	▼	▼	▼	▼	▼	▼	▼	▼	▼	▼	▼	▼	▼	●	●	●	●		●	●	▲	●	▲	▲
United States*	500	(4.6)	14.2	▼	▼	▼	▼	▼	▼	▼	▼	▼	▼	▼	▼	▼	▼	▼	●	●	●	●	●		●	●	●	●	▲
Scotland**	499	(5.5)	13.7	▼	▼	▼	▼	▼	▼	▼	▼	▼	▼	▼	▼	▼	▼	▼	●	●	●	●	●	●		●	●	●	▲
Spain	487	(2.0)	14.3	▼	▼	▼	▼	▼	▼	▼	▼	▼	▼	▼	▼	▼	▼	▼	▼	▼	▼	▼	▼	●	●		●	●	▲
Iceland	487	(4.5)	13.6	▼	▼	▼	▼	▼	▼	▼	▼	▼	▼	▼	▼	▼	▼	▼	▼	▼	▼	▼	●	●	●	●		●	▲
Greece**	484	(3.1)	13.6	▼	▼	▼	▼	▼	▼	▼	▼	▼	▼	▼	▼	▼	▼	▼	▼	▼	▼	▼	▼	●	●	●	●		▲
Portugal	454	(2.5)	14.5	▼	▼	▼	▼	▼	▼	▼	▼	▼	▼	▼	▼	▼	▼	▼	▼	▼	▼	▼	▼	▼	▼	▼	▼	▼	

Read across the row to compare a country's mean achievement with the countries listed in the columns of the chart. For example, mean achievement for the United States is significantly lower than for the Czech Republic, not significantly different from Norway, and significantly higher than Portugal

▼ Mean achievement of row country significantly lower than column country

● No statistically significant difference between row and column countries

▲ Mean achievement of row country significantly higher than column country

Countries are ranked by descending order of mean achievement
* Countries met TIMSS sampling requirements only partially
** Countries did not meet TIMSS sampling requirement
Source: International Association for the Evaluation of Educational Achievement (IEA). See Annex 3 for notes

Belgium (Fl.) = Belgium (Flemish Community)
Belgium (Fr.) = Belgium (French Community)

R6: Student achievement in mathematics and science

Chart R6.2: Multiple comparisons of overall student achievement in **science**, eighth grade (1995)

Country	Mean	Standard error	Average age
Czech Republic	574	(4.3)	14.4
Japan	571	(1.6)	14.4
Korea	565	(1.9)	14.2
Netherlands**	560	(5.0)	14.3
Austria**	558	(3.7)	14.3
Hungary	554	(2.8)	14.3
England*	552	(3.3)	14.0
Belgium (Fl.)*	550	(4.2)	14.1
Australia**	545	(3.9)	14.2
Russian Federation	538	(4.0)	14.0
Ireland	538	(4.5)	14.4
Sweden	535	(3.0)	13.9
United States*	534	(4.7)	14.2
Germany**	531	(4.8)	14.8
Canada	531	(2.6)	14.1
Norway	527	(1.9)	13.9
New Zealand	526	(4.4)	14.0
Switzerland*	522	(2.5)	14.2
Scotland**	517	(5.1)	13.7
Spain	517	(1.7)	14.3
France	498	(2.5)	14.3
Greece**	497	(2.2)	13.6
Iceland	494	(4.0)	13.6
Portugal	480	(2.3)	14.5
Denmark**	478	(3.1)	13.9
Belgium (Fr.)**	471	(2.8)	14.3

Read across the row to compare a country's mean achievement with the countries listed in the columns of the chart. For example, mean achievement for the United States is significantly lower than for the Czech Republic, not significantly different from Norway, and significantly higher than Portugal

▼ Mean achievement of row country significantly lower than column country
● No statistically significant difference between row and column countries
▲ Mean achievement of row country significantly higher than column country

Countries are ranked by descending order of mean achievement
* Countries met TIMSS sampling requirements only partially
** Countries did not meet TIMSS sampling requirement
Source: International Association for the Evaluation of Educational Achievement (IEA). See Annex 3 for notes

Belgium (Fl.) = Belgium (Flemish Community)
Belgium (Fr.) = Belgium (French Community)

R7: STUDENT DIFFERENCES IN MATHEMATICS AND SCIENCE ACHIEVEMENT

This indicator compares the distribution of student achievement scores in mathematics and science across countries.

POLICY CONTEXT

The demand for highly-skilled labour in modern economies cannot be satisfied by a small intellectual elite but requires excellence throughout the education system. Both parents and the wider public have become aware of the gravity of the phenomenon of under-achievement and the fact that school-leavers are virtually unemployable if they lack basic skills.

Indicator R7 examines the relative international standing of different parts of the achievement distribution. It shows how well the highest and lowest achievers in a country perform in relation to international benchmarks. The performance of a country's best students in mathematics and science may have implications for the part that country will play in the pool from which tomorrow's mathematicians, engineers and scientists will be drawn. Similarly, a high proportion of students at the lower end of the scale may give rise to concern that a significant proportion of tomorrow's taxpayers and voters will not have the understanding of the basic mathematical and scientific concepts needed for the informed judgements which they will be called upon to make.

An examination of the distribution of achievement scores *within* each country also provides a measure of equity.

Teachers, schools and education systems must address the variation in achievement that exists within classes, within schools and within the country as a whole. Such variation can result from disparities in resources and in the socio-economic background of students and schools as well as from curricular differences and the way in which instruction is organised and delivered. Some education systems deal with this variation explicitly by forming homogeneous student groups through selection either within or between classes and schools, while others leave it as an individual challenge for students and classes.

KEY RESULTS

Less than 5 per cent of students in Portugal reach the average performance standard in mathematics of countries such as Korea, Japan, the Flemish Community of Belgium and the Czech Republic. Only in Switzerland, the Flemish Community of Belgium, Austria and the Czech Republic do more than 25 per cent of students exceed the average performance levels of the two top performing countries.

The difference between the 25th and 75th percentiles of student performance in mathematics exceeds by a factor of two in all countries – and by a factor of four in five countries – the typical progress in achievement that students in OECD countries accomplish between the seventh and eighth grades. In general, countries with great disparities in student achievement in mathematics also show a wide range of achievement in science.

To the extent that achievement gaps at age 13 can be regarded as predictive of achievement disparities at later stages, deficiencies observed at this age can have significant implications both for education systems and for the future highly skilled information society.

DESCRIPTION AND INTERPRETATION

Mean achievement is often used as an outcome measure for classrooms, schools, school types and education systems as a whole. However, overall means can mask significant disparities. In almost all countries disparities in student achievement in mathematics and science present a challenge to the education system. The difference between the 25th and the 75th percentiles of the student achievement distribution in mathematics in Australia, Austria, the Czech Republic, Hungary, Ireland, Japan and Korea is more than four times the average progress in mathematics achievement made by students in OECD countries (33 points) between seventh and eighth grades (see Chart R7.1). In mathematics, two countries (Portugal and Spain) have interquartile ranges of 100 score points or below (that is, about three grade-year equivalents). In science, three countries (Australia, England and the United States) have interquartile ranges of more than 140 score points, while four [Belgium (Flemish Community), France, Portugal and Spain] have ranges of 110 or below. It should be noted that for countries with a higher overall level of achievement, greater disparities would usually be expected. Dividing the interquartile range by the national mean score provides a slightly different picture (see Tables R7.1 and R7.2).

Another way to examine the achievement distributions is to compare the percentage of students in each country who score above the 50th, 75th, and 90th percen-

R7: Student differences in mathematics and science achievement

tiles of the joint OECD distribution of student achievement (see Tables R7.3 and R7.4). As can be seen, more than 58 per cent of the students in Japan and Korea score above the OECD 75th percentile of the mathematics achievement distribution and more than 33 per cent of the students score above the OECD 90th percentile. In Portugal, less than 4 per cent reach the achievement of the OECD 75th percentile.

Questions of interest regarding these results include the following: What are the characteristics of the students in each country who show the best and worst performance? What are the causes for the disparities? And what can education policy do about it? Clearly, the problems that interfere with the success of students and schools are complex and highly inter-related. For example, students who have poor achievement scores may experience the combined impact of growing up poor, living in a poor neighbourhood, having parents with lower levels of education, balancing time for schoolwork with work at home, and lacking the basic skills to escape from a limited track of remedial classes. Young people in these situations have a range of needs, and equipping schools to cope with those needs requires that teachers, administrators and policy-makers understand the causes that put students at risk.

The problem of variation in student achievement is addressed by different countries in different ways, both through the institutional organisation of education systems and through curricular provision. Some countries have implemented selective school systems which restrict access to the more privileged types of school. This is based on the belief that overall achievement can be maximised by arranging relatively homogeneous groups of learners. Other countries seek to equalise educational opportunities by using a mixed system, which may involve more open admission to the academic and intermediate tracks, with some degree of differentiation in core subjects.

DEFINITIONS

Tables R7.1 and R7.2 show the achievement scores of students at the 5th, 25th, 75th and 95th percentiles of the national mathematics and science score distributions. The 5th percentile, for example, refers to the achievement score below which 5 per cent of the population score. Tables R7.3 and R7.4 show the percentage of students who reach the 50th, 75th and 90th percentiles of the joint OECD distribution. For the methodology used for the calculation of the joint OECD distribution see Annex 3.

The achievement scores are based on tests administered as part of the Third International Mathematics and Science Study that was undertaken by the International Association for the Evaluation of Educational Achievement (IEA) during the school year 1994/95. The target population studied in this indicator refers to students at the higher grade of the two grade levels in which most 13 year-olds are enrolled and which, by convention, is referred to as the "eighth" grade (see also column 6 in Table R9.1). Countries marked with one asterisk (*) met the IEA/TIMSS sampling standards only partially, countries marked with two asterisks (**) did not meet the IEA/TIMSS sampling standards. The reporting of data on a sub-national level for some countries is based on data availability from the IEA and does not represent a policy decision by the OECD. Note that the 5th and 95th percentiles of the achievement score distribution need to be interpreted with caution due to relatively small sample sizes.

R7: Student differences in mathematics and science achievement

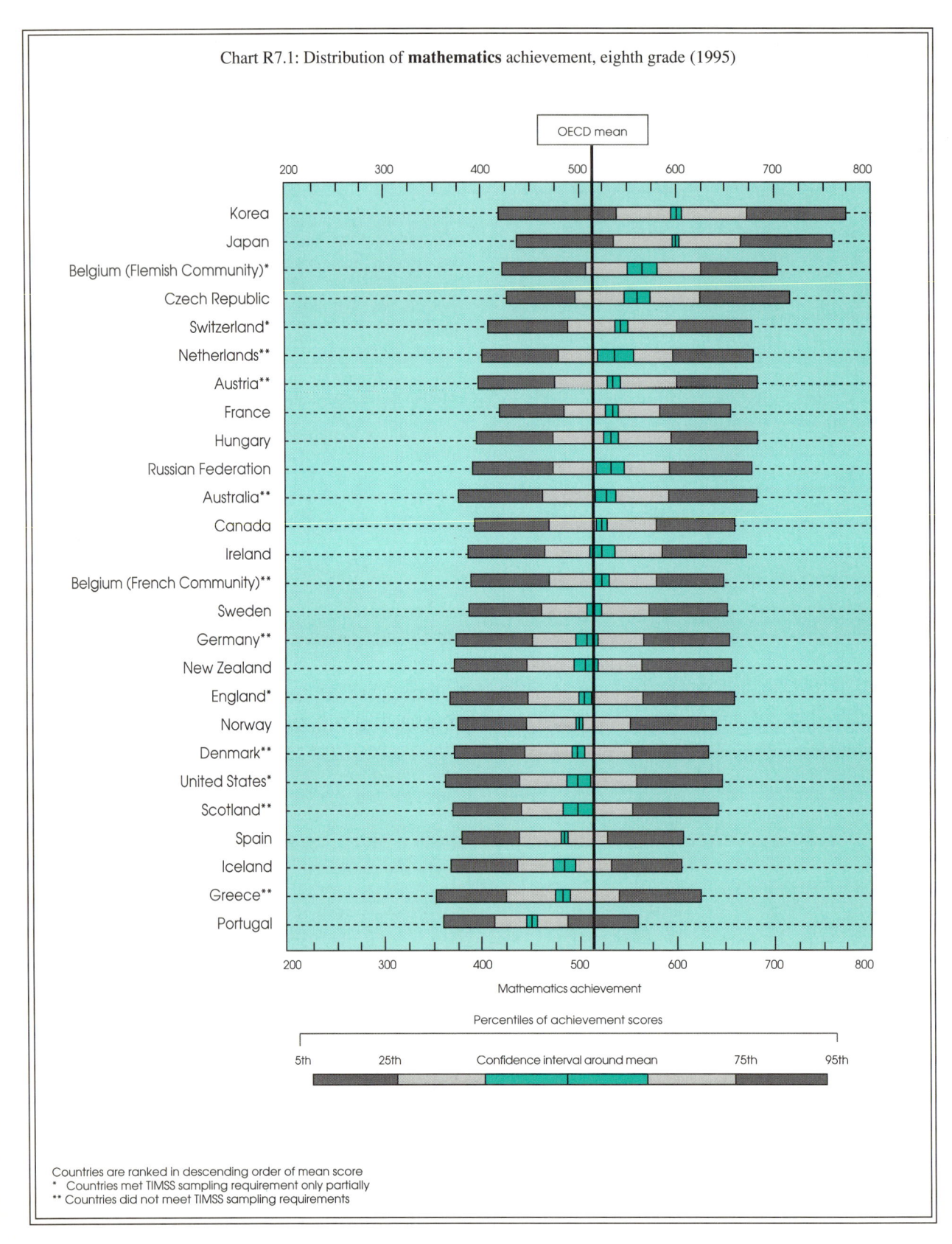

Chart R7.1: Distribution of mathematics achievement, eighth grade (1995)

Countries (in descending order of mean score):
- Korea
- Japan
- Belgium (Flemish Community)*
- Czech Republic
- Switzerland*
- Netherlands**
- Austria**
- France
- Hungary
- Russian Federation
- Australia**
- Canada
- Ireland
- Belgium (French Community)**
- Sweden
- Germany**
- New Zealand
- England*
- Norway
- Denmark**
- United States*
- Scotland**
- Spain
- Iceland
- Greece**
- Portugal

Mathematics achievement

Percentiles of achievement scores: 5th | 25th | Confidence interval around mean | 75th | 95th

Countries are ranked in descending order of mean score
* Countries met TIMSS sampling requirement only partially
** Countries did not meet TIMSS sampling requirements

R7: Student differences in mathematics and science achievement

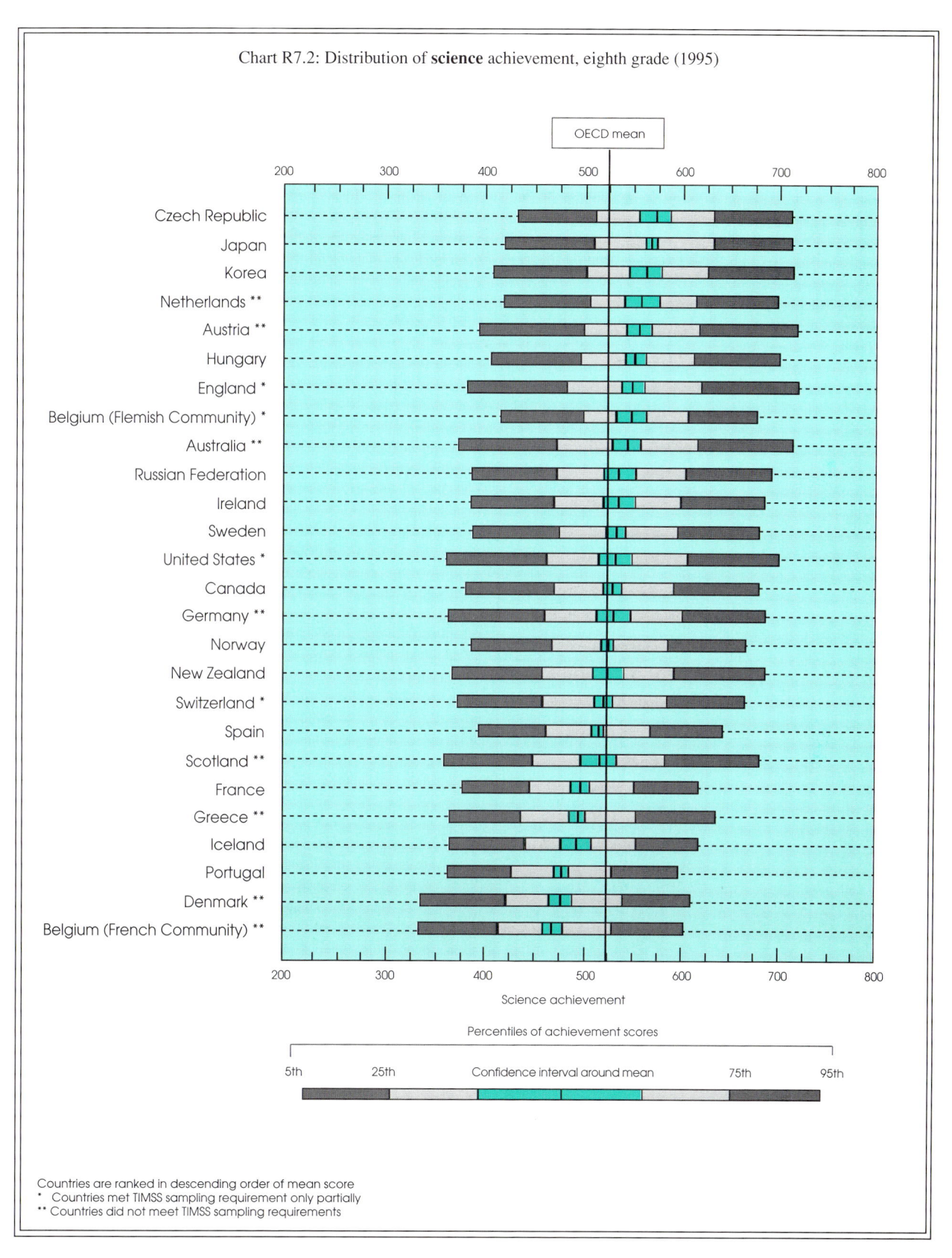

Chart R7.2: Distribution of science achievement, eighth grade (1995)

Countries (ranked in descending order of mean score):
- Czech Republic
- Japan
- Korea
- Netherlands **
- Austria **
- Hungary
- England *
- Belgium (Flemish Community) *
- Australia **
- Russian Federation
- Ireland
- Sweden
- United States *
- Canada
- Germany **
- Norway
- New Zealand
- Switzerland *
- Spain
- Scotland **
- France
- Greece **
- Iceland
- Portugal
- Denmark **
- Belgium (French Community) **

Percentiles of achievement scores: 5th, 25th, Confidence interval around mean, 75th, 95th

Countries are ranked in descending order of mean score
* Countries met TIMSS sampling requirement only partially
** Countries did not meet TIMSS sampling requirements

R7: Student differences in mathematics and science achievement

Table R7.1:
Distribution of **mathematics** achievement scores, eighth grade (1995)

	Mean	5th percentile [1]	25th percentile [1]	75th percentile [1]	95th percentile [1]	Interquartile range [2]	Interquartile range divided by mean
North America							
Canada	527	389	468	587	670	119	0.23
United States *	500	356	435	563	653	128	0.26
Pacific Area							
Australia **	530	372	460	600	690	140	0.26
Japan	605	435	536	676	771	139	0.23
New Zealand	508	366	443	570	663	127	0.25
European Union							
Austria **	539	394	474	608	693	134	0.25
Belgium							
(Flemish Community) *	565	416	502	631	710	129	0.23
(French Community) **	526	385	467	587	658	121	0.23
Denmark **	502	369	443	561	641	118	0.24
France	538	415	484	591	666	107	0.20
Germany **	509	368	448	572	661	124	0.24
Greece **	484	347	422	546	633	124	0.26
Ireland	527	381	462	594	681	132	0.25
Netherlands **	541	397	477	604	688	127	0.23
Portugal	454	357	411	495	569	85	0.19
Spain	487	376	436	536	616	100	0.21
Sweden	519	384	460	579	661	119	0.23
United Kingdom							
England *	506	361	443	570	665	128	0.25
Scotland **	499	364	436	559	649	123	0.25
Other OECD countries							
Czech Republic	564	423	496	633	725	137	0.24
Hungary	537	391	471	602	693	131	0.24
Iceland	487	365	435	540	615	104	0.21
Norway	503	372	445	560	649	115	0.23
Switzerland *	545	401	485	607	685	122	0.22
Country mean	**516**	**380**	**456**	**576**	**660**	**120**	**0.23**
Other non-OECD countries							
Korea	607	418	540	682	786	142	0.23
Russian Federation	536	388	471	600	687	130	0.24

*   Countries met TIMSS sampling requirements only partially
** Countries did not meet TIMSS sampling requirements
1. 5 (or 25 or 75 or 95) per cent of students score below this point
2. Difference between 75th and 25th percentile

Source: International Association for the Evaluation of Educational Achievement (IEA). See Annex 3 for notes

R7: Student differences in mathematics and science achievement

Table R7.2:
Distribution of **science** achievement scores, eighth grade (1995)

	Mean	5th percentile [1]	25th percentile [1]	75th percentile [1]	95th percentile [1]	Interquartile range [2]	Interquartile range divided by mean
North America							
Canada	531	380	472	594	685	121	0.23
United States *	534	359	465	608	705	142	0.27
Pacific Area							
Australia **	545	371	475	619	720	144	0.26
Japan	571	421	514	633	715	118	0.21
New Zealand	526	364	458	594	692	136	0.26
European Union							
Austria **	558	395	499	623	721	125	0.22
Belgium							
(Flemish Community) *	550	416	499	609	681	110	0.20
(French Community) **	471	332	415	532	609	117	0.25
Denmark **	478	334	423	541	615	118	0.25
France	498	375	446	553	623	107	0.21
Germany **	531	362	463	602	691	139	0.26
Greece **	497	363	439	557	643	119	0.24
Ireland	538	383	471	605	694	134	0.25
Netherlands **	560	419	505	619	701	113	0.20
Portugal	480	362	429	531	602	102	0.21
Spain	517	393	465	572	649	106	0.21
Sweden	535	386	476	598	686	122	0.23
United Kingdom							
England *	552	380	485	625	727	141	0.26
Scotland **	517	357	451	584	686	133	0.26
Other OECD countries							
Czech Republic	574	438	513	635	717	121	0.21
Hungary	554	408	497	616	703	119	0.21
Iceland	494	363	442	555	623	112	0.23
Norway	527	385	470	588	671	117	0.22
Switzerland *	522	371	460	587	669	127	0.24
Country mean	**523**	**377**	**464**	**586**	**671**	**122**	**0.23**
Other non-OECD countries							
Korea	565	408	504	629	719	125	0.22
Russian Federation	538	386	475	606	697	131	0.24

* Countries met TIMSS sampling requirements only partially
** Countries did not meet TIMSS sampling requirements
1. 5 (or 25 or 75 or 95) per cent of students score below this point
2. Difference between 75th and 25th percentile

Source: International Association for the Evaluation of Educational Achievement (IEA). See Annex 3 for notes

R7: Student differences in mathematics and science achievement

Table R7.3:
Percentage of students scoring above the 50th, 75th, and 90th percentiles of the joint OECD achievement distribution in **mathematics**, eighth grade (1995)

	Percentage above OECD 50th percentile (507.0)	Standard error	Percentage above OECD 75th percentile (583.3)	Standard error	Percentage above OECD 90th percentile (650.9)	Standard error
North America						
Canada	58.3	(1.1)	26.4	(1.2)	8.3	(0.7)
United States *	45.7	(2.3)	19.5	(1.5)	5.5	(0.6)
Pacific Area						
Australia **	57.7	(1.7)	30.0	(1.6)	11.6	(1.0)
Japan	83.8	(0.6)	58.8	(0.9)	33.5	(0.9)
New Zealand	48.8	(2.2)	20.6	(1.7)	6.5	(0.9)
European Union						
Austria **	61.9	(1.4)	33.3	(1.3)	11.6	(0.8)
Belgium						
(Flemish Community) *	73.6	(2.9)	43.1	(2.4)	18.9	(1.3)
(French Community) **	59.2	(1.7)	26.4	(1.5)	6.1	(0.6)
Denmark **	48.2	(1.6)	18.1	(1.0)	3.9	(0.5)
France	64.1	(1.5)	27.5	(1.5)	7.5	(0.8)
Germany **	49.3	(2.3)	21.5	(1.8)	6.4	(0.8)
Greece **	37.8	(1.5)	13.7	(0.9)	3.8	(0.4)
Ireland	57.3	(2.4)	27.6	(1.9)	9.8	(1.1)
Netherlands **	63.1	(3.3)	32.6	(2.7)	11.6	(1.8)
Portugal	20.0	(1.4)	3.2	(0.5)	0.3	(0.1)
Spain	36.9	(1.2)	10.8	(0.6)	1.8	(0.2)
Sweden	54.4	(1.5)	23.4	(1.2)	6.0	(0.5)
United Kingdom						
England *	48.4	(1.4)	20.6	(1.1)	7.0	(0.6)
Scotland **	44.9	(2.7)	18.1	(2.1)	4.9	(0.9)
Other OECD countries						
Czech Republic	70.7	(1.9)	41.0	(2.4)	19.5	(2.0)
Hungary	60.5	(1.6)	30.8	(1.3)	11.8	(0.8)
Iceland	38.3	(3.0)	11.4	(1.3)	1.5	(0.4)
Norway	46.9	(1.1)	17.9	(0.9)	4.8	(0.4)
Switzerland *	66.0	(1.4)	34.9	(1.2)	11.2	(0.7)
Country mean	**50.9**		**23.8**		**8.3**	
Other non-OECD countries						
Korea	82.9	(0.8)	58.9	(1.0)	35.0	(1.1)
Russian Federation	61.0	(2.6)	30.5	(2.4)	10.6	(0.8)

* Countries met TIMSS sampling requirements only partially
** Countries did not meet TIMSS sampling requirements
Source: International Association for the Evaluation of Educational Achievement (IEA). See Annex 3 for notes

R7: Student differences in mathematics and science achievement

Table R7.4:
Percentage of students scoring above the 50th, 75th, and 90th percentiles of the joint OECD achievement distribution in **science**, eighth grade (1995)

	Percentage above OECD 50th percentile (522.4)	Standard error	Percentage above OECD 75th percentile (593.7)	Standard error	Percentage above OECD 90th percentile (657.0)	Standard error
North America						
Canada	53.2	(1.3)	24.9	(0.9)	8.8	(0.6)
United States *	54.6	(1.9)	29.0	(1.6)	12.2	(0.8)
Pacific Area						
Australia **	58.2	(1.6)	32.7	(1.3)	15.1	(0.9)
Japan	71.0	(0.7)	40.2	(0.8)	17.4	(0.6)
New Zealand	50.5	(1.9)	25.0	(1.5)	10.3	(0.9)
European Union						
Austria **	63.6	(1.6)	34.6	(1.2)	15.8	(0.9)
Belgium						
(Flemish Community) *	63.0	(2.0)	30.3	(1.8)	9.4	(0.8)
(French Community) **	28.1	(1.4)	7.0	(0.6)	1.1	(0.2)
Denmark **	31.8	(1.3)	8.6	(0.7)	2.1	(0.3)
France	37.0	(1.4)	10.8	(0.7)	1.2	(0.2)
Germany **	53.9	(2.1)	27.7	(1.6)	11.1	(1.0)
Greece **	37.4	(1.2)	13.4	(0.7)	3.8	(0.3)
Ireland	56.1	(2.0)	28.5	(1.6)	11.5	(0.9)
Netherlands **	66.6	(2.3)	34.5	(2.3)	11.7	(1.0)
Portugal	27.9	(1.2)	6.4	(0.6)	0.6	(0.1)
Spain	46.5	(1.0)	17.4	(0.7)	4.0	(0.3)
Sweden	55.6	(1.5)	26.1	(1.2)	9.0	(0.7)
United Kingdom						
England *	60.2	(1.4)	33.8	(1.4)	16.6	(0.9)
Scotland **	47.7	(2.2)	22.1	(1.8)	8.1	(1.1)
Other OECD countries						
Czech Republic	72.3	(1.6)	39.5	(2.2)	18.2	(1.5)
Hungary	62.7	(1.4)	33.0	(1.3)	13.1	(0.8)
Iceland	36.0	(2.1)	9.5	(1.3)	2.0	(0.5)
Norway	51.5	(1.1)	23.3	(0.9)	6.9	(0.5)
Switzerland *	50.4	(1.2)	22.2	(0.9)	6.6	(0.6)
Country mean	**48.6**		**22.7**		**8.5**	
Other non-OECD countries						
Korea	67.2	(0.9)	37.9	(0.9)	17.5	(0.8)
Russian Federation	55.6	(1.8)	28.2	(1.2)	10.8	(0.8)

* Countries met TIMSS sampling requirements only partially
** Countries did not meet TIMSS sampling requirements
Source: International Association for the Evaluation of Educational Achievement (IEA). See Annex 3 for notes

R9: DIFFERENCE IN ACHIEVEMENT BETWEEN TWO GRADES IN MATHEMATICS AND SCIENCE

Based on a synthetic cohort, this indicator approximates the gains in mathematics and science achievement over the course of a school year.

POLICY CONTEXT

Education systems need to determine the most appropriate structure of the curriculum and to optimise the nature and quality of instruction so as to maximise achievement gains for all students and at all grade levels. It is of interest to know not just absolute achievement levels, but also how much progress is being made from year to year. A related question is whether the countries with poorer performance at the lower grade are catching up or whether the achievement gap is widening among countries.

This indicator presents an approximation of progress in mathematics and science achievement accomplished between the seventh and eighth grades.

KEY RESULTS

On average, mathematics achievement scores rise 33 points between the seventh and eighth grades, from an average score of 483 in the seventh grade to an average score of 516 in the following grade. Science achievement scores rise an average of 39 points from 484 score points to 523 between these two grades. However, there appears to be no consistent relationship between mean performance and progress between grades seven and eight.

DESCRIPTION AND INTERPRETATION

For most countries, the progress from seventh to eighth grades in the science scale of the Third International Mathematics and Science Study (TIMSS) appears to be somewhat greater than the progress in mathematics (see Charts R9.1 and R9.2). This may reflect a relatively common pattern in the organisation of the curriculum, in which mathematics is given a higher priority in the curriculum in the first years of secondary school, while science is often emphasised at a later stage.

There is no consistent relationship at the country level between mean mathematics achievement in the seventh grade and progress from grade seven to grade eight. The Czech Republic, for example, has both a high seventh grade mean (523) and an above-average gain from seventh to eighth grade (40 points). The Netherlands, however, has a relatively high achievement score in the seventh grade but progress between the seventh and eighth grades is below the OECD average. The situation is similar in science. Whereas Korea, for example, has the highest mean achievement score in science but average progress between the seventh and eighth grades is below the average, Portugal, with a relatively low seventh grade mean, shows an increase in scores which is substantially above the average. These results suggest that the patterns of progress between the two grades are sensitive to specific features of the mathematics and science curriculum. In the case of Portugal, significant grade repetition in the first year of secondary school may also have an impact. In all countries the progress achieved over one grade year is small compared to the differences among students that exist within a grade year.

DEFINITIONS

This indicator presents the mean scores of students in mathematics and science achievement in the lower grade and the upper grade of the target populations as well as the difference between these two means. It should be noted that the indicator is based on a synthetic cohort and does not provide information about the achievement gains of individual students over a school year. The width of the symbols in the charts indicates the confidence interval of the respective means at the 95th per cent level of confidence. The achievement scores are based on tests administered as part of the Third International Mathematics and Science Study that was undertaken by the International Association for the Evaluation of Educational Achievement (IEA) during the school year 1994/95. The target populations studied in this indicator refer to students at the two grade levels in which most 13 year-olds are enrolled and which, by convention, are referred to as the "seventh" and "eighth" grades (see also columns 3 and 6 in Table R9.1). Note that for some countries different grades than the seventh and eighth grade have been sampled (see Tables R9.1 and R9.2). Countries marked with one asterisk (*) met the IEA/TIMSS sampling standards only partially, countries marked with two asterisks (**) did not meet the IEA/TIMSS sampling standards. The reporting of data on a sub-national level for some countries is based on data availability from the IEA and does not represent a policy decision by the OECD.

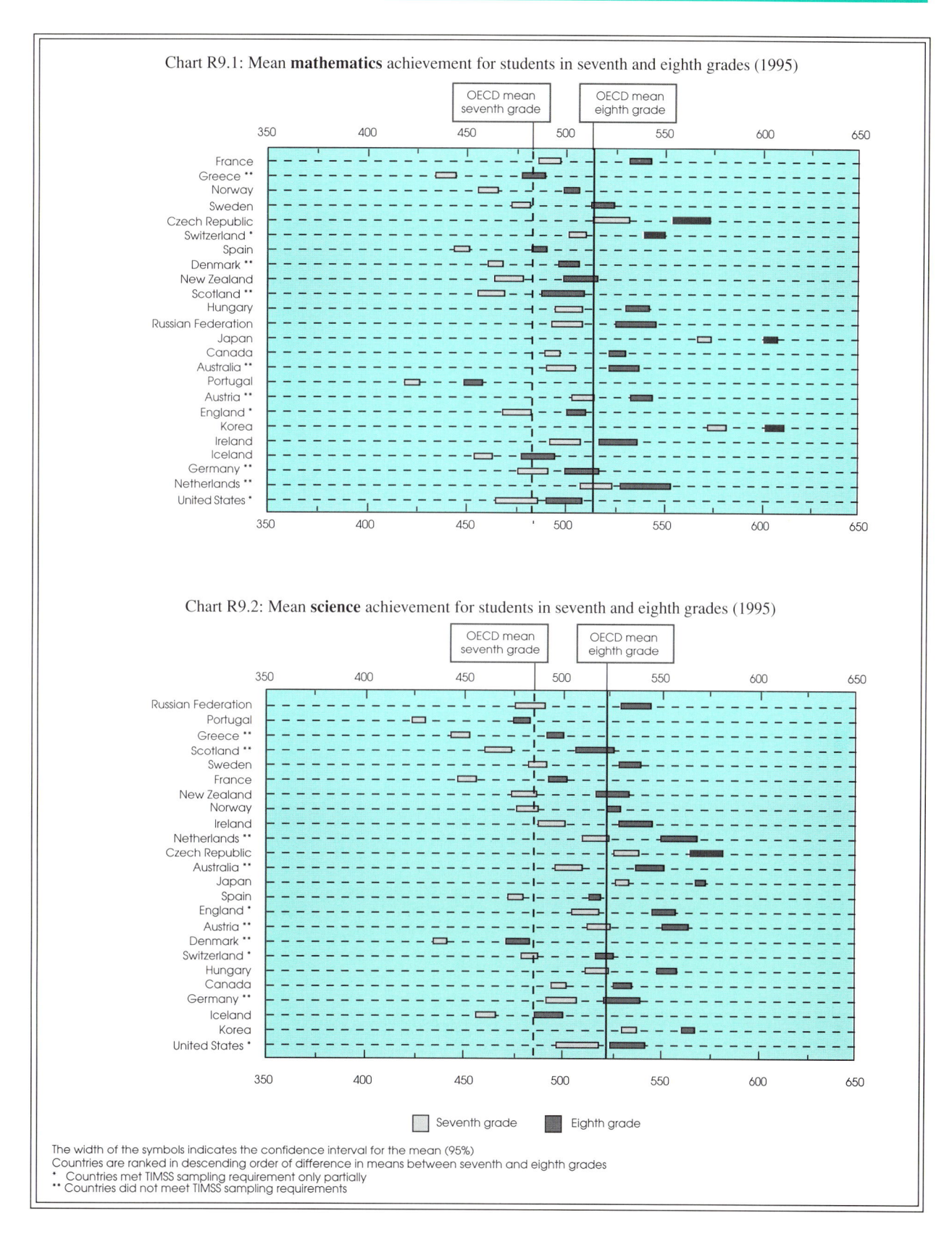

R9: Difference in achievement between two grades in mathematics and science

Chart R9.1: Mean **mathematics** achievement for students in seventh and eighth grades (1995)

Chart R9.2: Mean **science** achievement for students in seventh and eighth grades (1995)

□ Seventh grade   ■ Eighth grade

The width of the symbols indicates the confidence interval for the mean (95%)
Countries are ranked in descending order of difference in means between seventh and eighth grades
* Countries met TIMSS sampling requirement only partially
** Countries did not meet TIMSS sampling requirements

R9: Difference in achievement between two grades in mathematics and science

Table R9.1:
Mean **mathematics** achievement for students in seventh and eighth grades (1995)

	Seventh grade Mean	Standard error	Years of formal schooling	Eighth grade Mean	Standard error	Years of formal schooling	Difference in means	Standard error
North America								
Canada	494	(2.2)	7	527	(2.4)	8	**33**	(3.3)
United States *	476	(5.5)	7	500	(4.6)	8	**24**	(7.2)
Pacific Area								
Australia **	498	(3.8)	7 or 8	530	(4.0)	8 or 9	**32**	(5.5)
Japan	571	(1.9)	7	605	(1.9)	8	**34**	(2.7)
New Zealand	472	(3.8)	7.5 - 8.5	508	(4.5)	8.5 - 9.5	**36**	(5.9)
European Union								
Austria **	509	(3.0)		539	(3.0)		**30**	(4.3)
Belgium								
(Flemish Community) *	m	m	m	m	m	m	m	m
(French Community) **	m	m	m	m	m	m	m	m
Denmark **	465	(2.1)	6	502	(2.8)	7	**37**	(3.5)
France	492	(3.1)	7	538	(2.9)	8	**46**	(4.3)
Germany **	484	(4.1)	7	509	(4.5)	8	**25**	(6.1)
Greece **	440	(2.8)	7	484	(3.1)	8	**44**	(4.2)
Ireland	500	(4.1)	7	527	(5.1)	8	**28**	(6.6)
Netherlands **	516	(4.1)	7	541	(6.7)	8	**25**	(7.8)
Portugal	423	(2.2)	7	454	(2.5)	8	**31**	(3.3)
Spain	448	(2.2)	7	487	(2.0)	8	**39**	(3.0)
Sweden	478	(2.5)	6	519	(3.0)	7	**41**	(3.9)
United Kingdom								
England *	476	(3.7)	8	506	(2.6)	9	**30**	(4.5)
Scotland **	463	(3.7)	8	499	(5.5)	9	**36**	(6.6)
Other OECD countries								
Czech Republic	523	(4.9)	7	564	(4.9)	8	**40**	(7.0)
Hungary	502	(3.7)	7	537	(3.2)	8	**36**	(4.9)
Iceland	459	(2.6)	7	487	(4.5)	8	**27**	(5.2)
Norway	461	(2.8)	6	503	(2.2)	7	**43**	(3.6)
Switzerland *	506	(2.3)	6 or 7	545	(2.8)	7 or 8	**40**	(3.6)
Country mean	**483**			**516**			**33**	
Other non-OECD countries								
Korea	577	(2.5)	7	607	(2.4)	8	**30**	(3.5)
Russian Federation	501	(4.0)	6 or 7	536	(5.3)	7 or 8	**35**	(6.6)

* Countries met TIMSS sampling requirements only partially
** Countries did not meet TIMSS sampling requirements
Source: International Association for the Evaluation of Educational Achievement (IEA). See Annex 3 for notes

R9: Difference in achievement between two grades in mathematics and science

Table R9.2:
Mean **science** achievement for students in seventh and eighth grades (1995)

	Seventh grade Mean	Standard error	Years of formal schooling	Eighth grade Mean	Standard error	Years of formal schooling	Difference in means	Standard error
North America								
Canada	499	(2.3)	7	531	(2.6)	8	**32**	(3.5)
United States *	508	(5.5)	7	534	(4.7)	8	**26**	(7.2)
Pacific Area								
Australia **	504	(3.6)	7 or 8	545	(3.9)	8 or 9	**40**	(5.3)
Japan	531	(1.9)	7	571	(1.6)	8	**40**	(2.5)
New Zealand	481	(3.4)	7.5 - 8.5	526	(4.4)	8.5 - 9.5	**45**	(5.5)
European Union								
Austria **	519	(3.1)		558	(3.7)		**39**	(4.8)
Belgium								
(Flemish Community) *	m	m	m	m	m	m	m	m
(French Community) **	m	m	m	m	m	m	m	m
Denmark **	439	(2.1)	6	478	(3.1)	7	**39**	(3.8)
France	452	(2.6)	7	498	(2.5)	8	**46**	(3.6)
Germany **	500	(4.1)	7	531	(4.8)	8	**32**	(6.3)
Greece **	449	(2.6)	7	497	(2.2)	8	**49**	(3.4)
Ireland	495	(3.5)	7	538	(4.5)	8	**43**	(5.7)
Netherlands **	517	(3.6)	7	560	(5.0)	8	**43**	(6.1)
Portugal	428	(2.1)	7	480	(2.3)	8	**52**	(3.1)
Spain	477	(2.1)	7	517	(1.7)	8	**40**	(2.7)
Sweden	488	(2.6)	6	535	(3.0)	7	**47**	(3.9)
United Kingdom								
England *	512	(3.5)	8	552	(3.3)	9	**40**	(4.8)
Scotland **	468	(3.8)	8	517	(5.1)	9	**49**	(6.4)
Other OECD countries								
Czech Republic	533	(3.3)	7	574	(4.3)	8	**41**	(5.4)
Hungary	518	(3.2)	7	554	(2.8)	8	**36**	(4.2)
Iceland	462	(2.8)	7	494	(4.0)	8	**32**	(4.9)
Norway	483	(2.9)	6	527	(1.9)	7	**44**	(3.5)
Switzerland *	484	(2.5)	6 or 7	522	(2.5)	7 or 8	**38**	(3.5)
Country mean	484			523			**39**	
Other non-OECD countries								
Korea	535	(2.1)	7	565	(1.9)	8	**30**	(2.9)
Russian Federation	484	(4.2)	6 or 7	538	(4.0)	7 or 8	**54**	(5.8)

*   Countries met TIMSS sampling requirements only partially
** Countries did not meet TIMSS sampling requirements
Source: International Association for the Evaluation of Educational Achievement (IEA). See Annex 3 for notes

R10: GENDER DIFFERENCES IN MATHEMATICS AND SCIENCE

This indicator compares the achievement of girls and boys in mathematics and science.

POLICY CONTEXT

All countries place a high level of importance on reducing educational disparities between men and women. Education has a major influence on labour market participation, occupational mobility and quality of life. Gender differences in mathematics and science scores at age 13 can affect pathways in further education and training as well as career opportunities later in life. Gender differences may be related to structural features of the education system as well as to differences in student interests and motivation, which in turn may be affected by culture and the social organisation of work.

KEY RESULTS

Whereas in mathematics the gender gap is moderate – with a slight advantage for boys – the gender difference in science is considerable. It favours boys in all 26 systems, with score differences ranging from around 10 points in Australia, Canada, the Russian Federation and the United States to more than 30 points – almost one grade-year equivalent (in terms of growth) – in Denmark.

DESCRIPTION AND INTERPRETATION

Gender disparities in mathematics tend to be small to moderate (see Chart R10.1). On average, boys score 7 points better than girls on a scale for which a standard deviation is of somewhat less than 100 points. In eight countries the difference in mathematics achievement is statistically significant at the 95 per cent level of confidence.

The situation is different in science. Here, differences in achievement favour boys in all 26 systems and the differences are statistically significant in all systems except Australia, the Flemish Community of Belgium, Ireland, the Russian Federation and the United States (see Chart R10.2). On average, boys in OECD countries score 18 points higher than girls in science, which is almost half the average difference in performance between students in the seventh and eighth grade. This result is very different from student performance in reading. Indicator R4 in the 1993 edition of *Education at a Glance* had shown girls at a similar age level outperforming boys in almost all countries (although many of the differences were not statistically significant). Are these gender differences predictive for later ages and future career choices? While the indicator cannot answer this question directly, it is important to note that, although overall university graduation rates do not differ significantly between men and women, female university graduates are far less likely to be in scientific fields than are men in all countries (see Indicator R14). It needs, however, to be taken into account that between those who took part in the Third International Mathematics and Science Study (TIMSS) and those who obtained a tertiary degree in 1993/94 lies a time difference of around ten years during which the gender gap could have changed.

Countries with relatively large gender differences in science also tend to have large gender differences in mathematics. In both disciplines, for example, the Czech Republic, Denmark and Korea exhibit relatively large gender differences, while Norway, the Russian Federation and the United States exhibit relatively small differences. But there are clear exceptions to this pattern. Hungary, for example, shows no gender differences in mathematics but a large gender difference in science achievement.

In some countries with relatively large gender differences favouring boys, girls nevertheless achieve high scores in comparison with boys and girls in other countries. For example, Japan and Korea both have large differences in mathematics achievement for boys and girls (9 score points in Japan and 17 points in Korea). Nevertheless, the average achievement of girls in both Japan and Korea exceeds the average achievement of both boys and girls in all other countries.

While gender differences in the average performance of boys and girls are an important indicator, gender disparities at the top and bottom ends of the distribution of achievement scores warrant further investigation.

DEFINITIONS

The indicator shows the average difference in mathematics and science achievement scores between boys and girls, together with an indication of whether these differences are statistically significant at the

R10: Gender differences in mathematics and science

95 per cent level of confidence. The achievement scores are based on tests administered as part of the Third International Mathematics and Science Study that was undertaken by the International Association for the Evaluation of Educational Achievement (IEA) during the school year 1994/95. The target population studied in this indicator refers to students at the upper grade of the two grade levels in which most 13 year-olds are enrolled and which, by convention, is referred to as the "eighth" grade (see also column 6 in Table R9.1). Countries marked with one asterisk (*) met the IEA/TIMSS sampling standards only partially, countries marked with two asterisks (**) did not meet the IEA/TIMSS sampling standards. The reporting of data on a sub-national level for some countries is based on data availability from the IEA and does not represent a policy decision by the OECD.

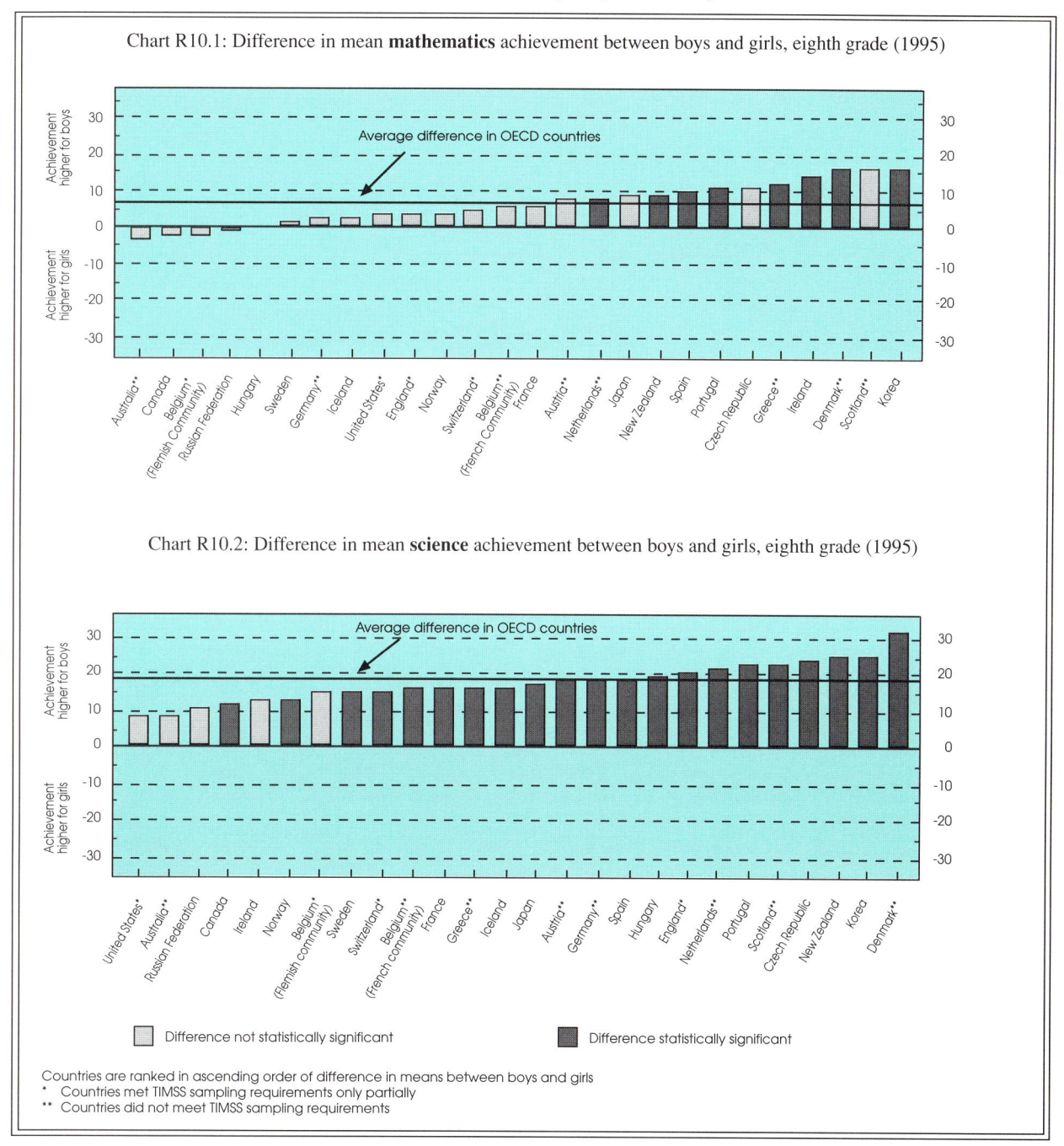

Chart R10.1: Difference in mean **mathematics** achievement between boys and girls, eighth grade (1995)

Chart R10.2: Difference in mean **science** achievement between boys and girls, eighth grade (1995)

Countries are ranked in ascending order of difference in means between boys and girls
* Countries met TIMSS sampling requirements only partially
** Countries did not meet TIMSS sampling requirements

R10: Gender differences in mathematics and science

Table R10.1:
Mean mathematics achievement by gender in eighth grade (1995)

	Boys Mean	Boys Standard error	Girls Mean	Girls Standard error	Difference in means[1]	Standard error
North America						
Canada	527	(3.2)	530	(2.7)	**4g**	(5.6)
United States *	502	(5.3)	498	(4.5)	**4b**	(7.1)
Pacific Area						
Australia **	528	(5.2)	533	(4.5)	**5g**	(6.9)
Japan	609	(2.6)	600	(2.1)	**9b**	(7.9)
New Zealand	513	(5.9)	503	(5.3)	**9b**	(3.9)
European Union						
Austria **	544	(3.2)	536	(4.5)	**8b**	(4.7)
Belgium						
(Flemish Community) *	564	(8.6)	567	(7.4)	**4g**	(11.4)
(French Community) **	530	(4.7)	524	(3.7)	**6b**	(3.3)
Denmark **	512	(3.2)	495	(3.5)	**17b**	(6.2)
France	542	(3.1)	536	(3.8)	**6b**	(9.3)
Germany **	512	(5.1)	509	(5.0)	**3b**	(4.7)
Greece **	490	(3.7)	478	(3.1)	**12b**	(4.7)
Ireland	536	(7.1)	521	(6.0)	**14b**	(4.8)
Netherlands **	545	(7.9)	537	(6.8)	**8b**	(3.1)
Portugal	460	(2.8)	449	(2.7)	**11b**	(3.6)
Spain	492	(2.5)	483	(2.6)	**10b**	(3.9)
Sweden	520	(3.5)	518	(3.2)	**2b**	(7.8)
United Kingdom						
England *	509	(5.2)	505	(3.4)	**4b**	(5.2)
Scotland **	507	(6.9)	490	(5.4)	**17b**	(8.7)
Other OECD countries						
Czech Republic	569	(4.5)	558	(6.3)	**11b**	(8.0)
Hungary	539	(3.7)	538	(3.7)	**0**	(4.2)
Iceland	489	(5.4)	486	(5.6)	**3b**	(4.9)
Norway	505	(2.8)	501	(2.7)	**4b**	(4.8)
Switzerland *	548	(3.6)	544	(3.1)	**5b**	(7.7)
Country mean	**519**		**513**		**7b**	
Other non-OECD countries						
Korea	615	(3.2)	598	(3.4)	**17b**	(6.9)
Russian Federation	535	(6.3)	536	(5.0)	**1g**	(6.0)

*   Countries met TIMSS sampling requirements only partially
** Countries did not meet TIMSS sampling requirements
1. **b** means boys score higher
    g means girls score higher

Source: International Association for the Evaluation of Educational Achievement (IEA). See Annex 3 for notes

R10: Gender differences in mathematics and science

Table R10.2:
Mean **science** achievement by gender in eighth grade (1995)

	Boys Mean	Boys Standard error	Girls Mean	Girls Standard error	Difference in means[1]	Standard error
North America						
Canada	538	(3.0)	526	(3.8)	**12b**	(4.8)
United States *	539	(5.0)	530	(5.3)	**9b**	(7.2)
Pacific Area						
Australia **	551	(5.3)	541	(4.1)	**9b**	(6.7)
Japan	579	(2.4)	562	(2.0)	**17b**	(3.1)
New Zealand	538	(5.4)	513	(5.3)	**25b**	(7.6)
European Union						
Austria **	566	(4.0)	549	(4.6)	**18b**	(6.1)
Belgium						
(Flemish Community) *	558	(6.1)	543	(5.8)	**15b**	(8.5)
(French Community) **	479	(4.8)	463	(2.9)	**16b**	(5.6)
Denmark **	495	(3.5)	464	(3.9)	**31b**	(5.3)
France	506	(2.7)	490	(3.3)	**16b**	(4.3)
Germany **	542	(5.9)	524	(4.9)	**18b**	(7.6)
Greece **	505	(2.6)	489	(3.1)	**16b**	(4.0)
Ireland	545	(6.5)	532	(5.3)	**13b**	(8.4)
Netherlands **	570	(6.5)	550	(5.1)	**21b**	(8.3)
Portugal	491	(2.8)	469	(2.7)	**22b**	(3.9)
Spain	526	(2.1)	508	(2.3)	**18b**	(3.1)
Sweden	543	(3.4)	528	(3.4)	**15b**	(4.8)
United Kingdom						
England *	563	(5.7)	543	(4.3)	**20b**	(7.1)
Scotland **	529	(6.7)	507	(4.8)	**22b**	(8.2)
Other OECD countries						
Czech Republic	586	(4.2)	562	(5.8)	**24b**	(7.2)
Hungary	564	(3.1)	545	(3.6)	**19b**	(4.8)
Iceland	502	(5.0)	485	(4.6)	**16b**	(6.8)
Norway	534	(3.2)	521	(2.0)	**13b**	(3.8)
Switzerland *	529	(3.2)	515	(2.9)	**15b**	(4.4)
Country mean	**532**		**515**		**18b**	
Other non-OECD countries						
Korea	576	(2.7)	552	(2.3)	**25b**	(3.6)
Russian Federation	544	(4.9)	533	(3.7)	**11b**	(6.2)

* Countries met TIMSS sampling requirements only partially
** Countries did not meet TIMSS sampling requirements
1. **b** means boys score higher
Source: International Association for the Evaluation of Educational Achievement (IEA). See Annex 3 for notes

R30: LITERACY AND THE ADULT POPULATION

POLICY CONTEXT

The literacy results presented for this indicator relate to tasks that are performed in everyday life, including the work place. In OECD economies, characterised as they are by the continuous upskilling of jobs, by the greater use of information technology and the information explosion, low levels of literacy may well confine certain members of society to a marginal status and to social dependency, as well as having an adverse impact on the acquisition of new labour force skills required in the work place.

KEY RESULTS

In European countries, literacy levels tend to be more homogeneous than in North America, whether these levels are relatively high (Sweden), relatively low (Poland) or mid-range (Germany, the Netherlands and Switzerland). By contrast, in Canada and the United States there are substantial proportions of persons at all literacy levels and thus a much wider dispersion in literacy and numeracy ability.

The proportion of persons at each level of performance tends to be relatively similar for the three scales in Canada, the Netherlands, Sweden and the United States, and to a somewhat lesser extent in Poland. On the other hand, in Germany and for both linguistic groups tested in Switzerland, there is an increase in performance as one goes from the prose to the document to the quantitative scales.

DESCRIPTION AND INTERPRETATION

Chart R30 shows the proportion of persons aged 16-65 scoring at each of four literacy levels for three different types of materials (prose, document, quantitative). Because sample sizes for the International Adult Literacy Survey (IALS) were relatively small (see Annex 3), caution should be exercised in comparing performance levels across countries, particularly in cases where differences in proportions are small.

For all countries in the survey except Poland and Sweden, the mid-range literacy levels (levels 2 and 3) contain the largest proportion of adults in all scales. In Canada and the United States, persons at these levels account for between 55 and 61 per cent of the population for all three scales. For Germany, the Netherlands and the two linguistic groups in Switzerland, the mid-range levels cover 66 to 75 per cent of the population for the three scales. By contrast, 70 to 75 per cent of the adult population in Sweden is at levels 3 and 4/5, and roughly comparable proportions at the two lowest levels in Poland. Thus in general terms, performance levels tend to be more homogeneous in Europe than in North America.

In Canada and the United States, the relatively lower proportions of adults at mid-range performance levels (levels 2 and 3) are mirrored by generally high proportions at the top level (4/5), but also at the lowest level (1), particularly for the quantitative scale, when compared to most other countries. Germany and the two linguistic groups in Switzerland are noteworthy in a different respect, namely in showing a better performance on quantitative materials than on prose texts. In particular, whereas approximately 45 to 51 per cent of the adult population in these countries is at level 3 or above on the prose scale, the percentage at level 3 or above is about 60 to 67 per cent for the quantitative scale.

Whether these country differences reflect differences in the quality, emphasis, content or structure of national education systems or rather post-schooling effects (continuing education and training, and opportunities to engage in or to pursue literacy-related activities) is difficult to determine. The results presented here are essentially diagnostic in nature. It is the tracing of these results back to differences in national education systems or post-schooling practices that may provide the information required to improve educational output and/or upgrade the functional literacy skills of adults.

DEFINITIONS

The results presented here attempt to measure "functional literacy", that is, respondents are asked to carry out various tasks that might be encountered in everyday life, such as reading instructions on medicine bottles, interpreting train timetables, filling out forms,

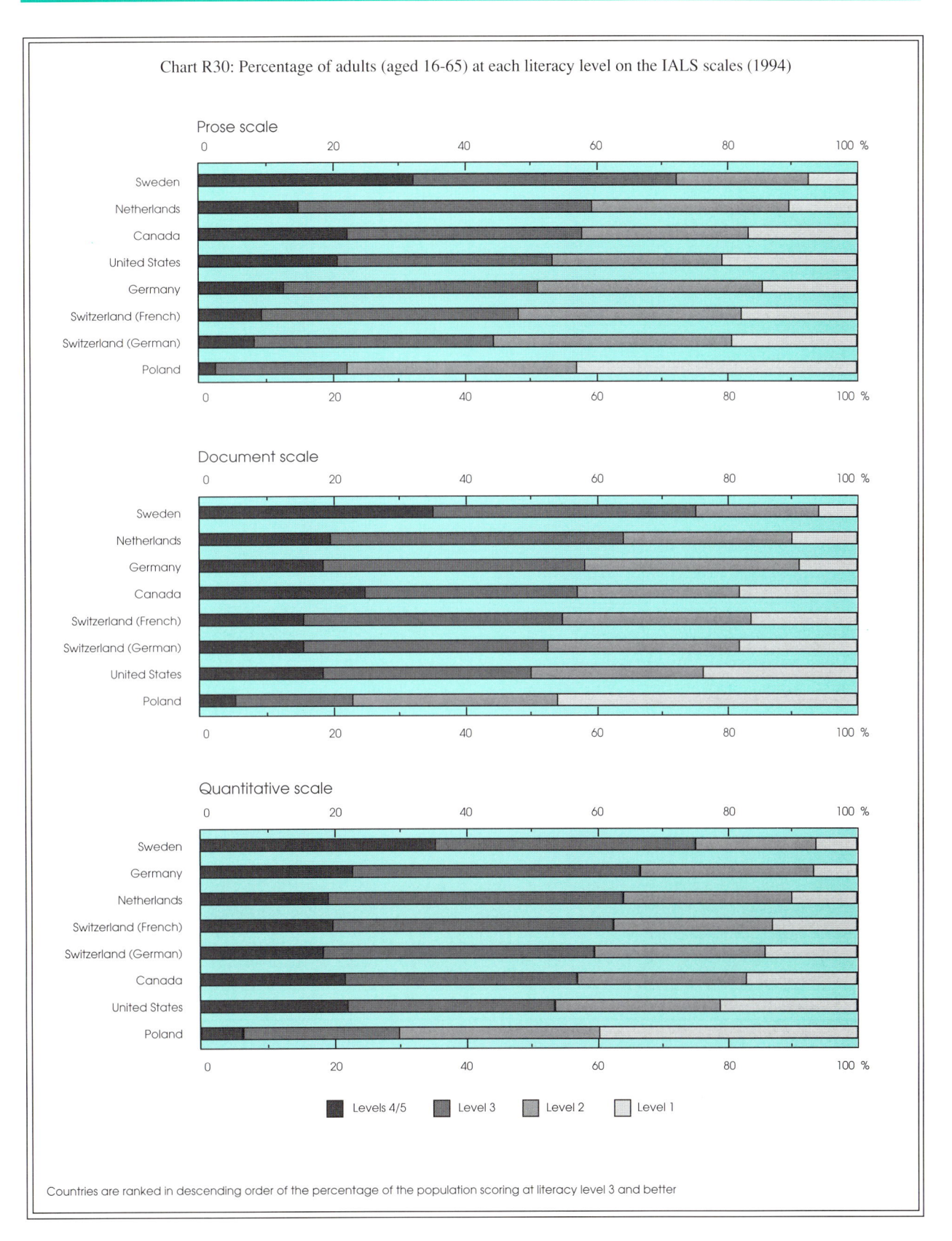

R30: Literacy and the adult population

Chart R30: Percentage of adults (aged 16-65) at each literacy level on the IALS scales (1994)

Prose scale

- Sweden
- Netherlands
- Canada
- United States
- Germany
- Switzerland (French)
- Switzerland (German)
- Poland

Document scale

- Sweden
- Netherlands
- Germany
- Canada
- Switzerland (French)
- Switzerland (German)
- United States
- Poland

Quantitative scale

- Sweden
- Germany
- Netherlands
- Switzerland (French)
- Switzerland (German)
- Canada
- United States
- Poland

Legend: Levels 4/5 | Level 3 | Level 2 | Level 1

Countries are ranked in descending order of the percentage of the population scoring at literacy level 3 and better

R30: Literacy and the adult population

understanding assembly instructions or recipes, etc. They are thus not based on problems taken from an educational curriculum and can be expected to reflect the sort of skills required to function productively in society and the work place.

Because of insufficient sample sizes at the highest literacy level (level 5), this level has been combined with level 4 in the table and chart. The achievement scores are based on tests administered as part of the International Adult Literacy Survey that was undertaken by Statistics Canada during 1994.

Table R30:
Percentage of adults (aged 16-65) at each literacy level on the IALS scales (1994)

	Scale	Level 1 %	Level 1 s.e.	Level 2 %	Level 2 s.e.	Level 3 %	Level 3 s.e.	Levels 4/5 %	Levels 4/5 s.e.
Canada	Prose	16.6	(1.6)	25.6	(1.8)	35.1	(2.4)	22.7	(2.3)
	Document	18.2	(1.9)	24.7	(1.5)	32.1	(1.8)	25.1	(1.3)
	Quantitative	16.9	(1.8)	26.1	(2.5)	34.8	(2.1)	22.2	(1.8)
Germany	Prose	14.4	(0.9)	34.2	(1.0)	38.0	(1.3)	13.4	(1.0)
	Document	9.0	(0.7)	32.7	(1.2)	39.5	(1.0)	18.9	(1.0)
	Quantitative	6.7	(0.4)	26.6	(1.2)	43.2	(0.8)	23.5	(0.9)
Netherlands	Prose	10.5	(0.6)	30.1	(0.9)	44.1	(1.0)	15.3	(0.6)
	Document	10.1	(0.7)	25.7	(0.8)	44.2	(0.9)	20.0	(0.8)
	Quantitative	10.3	(0.7)	25.5	(0.9)	44.3	(1.0)	19.9	(0.8)
Poland	Prose	42.6	(0.9)	34.5	(0.9)	19.8	(0.7)	3.1	(0.3)
	Document	45.4	(1.3)	30.7	(1.0)	18.0	(0.7)	5.8	(0.3)
	Quantitative	39.1	(1.1)	30.1	(1.2)	23.9	(0.6)	6.8	(0.5)
Sweden	Prose	7.5	(0.5)	20.3	(0.6)	39.7	(0.9)	32.4	(0.5)
	Document	6.2	(0.4)	18.9	(0.7)	39.4	(0.8)	35.5	(0.6)
	Quantitative	6.6	(0.4)	18.6	(0.6)	39.0	(0.9)	35.8	(0.7)
Switzerland (French)	Prose	17.6	(1.3)	33.7	(1.6)	38.6	(1.8)	10.0	(0.7)
	Document	16.2	(1.3)	28.8	(1.4)	38.9	(1.3)	16.0	(1.1)
	Quantitative	12.9	(0.9)	24.5	(1.4)	42.2	(1.6)	20.4	(1.0)
Switzerland (German)	Prose	19.3	(1.0)	35.7	(1.6)	36.1	(1.3)	8.9	(1.0)
	Document	18.1	(1.0)	29.1	(1.5)	36.6	(0.8)	16.1	(1.0)
	Quantitative	14.2	(1.0)	26.2	(1.3)	40.7	(1.5)	19.0	(1.3)
United States	Prose	20.7	(0.7)	25.9	(1.1)	32.4	(1.2)	21.1	(1.2)
	Document	23.7	(0.8)	25.9	(1.1)	31.4	(0.9)	19.0	(1.0)
	Quantitative	21.0	(0.7)	25.3	(1.1)	31.3	(0.8)	22.5	(1.0)

s.e.: standard error
Source: Statistics Canada. See Annex 3 for notes

R31: ADULT LITERACY BY LEVEL OF EDUCATIONAL ATTAINMENT

POLICY CONTEXT

One might expect educational attainment and literacy skills to be highly associated. However, literacy as measured by the International Adult Literacy Survey (IALS) is not curriculum-based but instead reflects "functional literacy", that is, the ability to perform literacy-type tasks encountered in everyday life, including the work place. The extent to which education systems adequately prepare young people for the post-school world has traditionally been a question of significant interest to educational policy-makers.

KEY RESULTS

As one might expect, in all countries high prose literacy levels are associated with high levels of educational attainment. However, the correspondence between the two is far from perfect. There are significant proportions of persons with low attainment who achieve relatively high literacy levels and, likewise, not insignificant proportions of persons with high attainment who score lower than one might expect on the basis of their formal qualifications.

In addition, differences across countries in literacy levels do not necessarily reflect differences in levels of educational attainment. For a given level of educational attainment, adults in some countries achieve higher literacy scores on average than persons at the same level in other countries.

DESCRIPTION AND INTERPRETATION

In general, literacy levels increase with the level of educational attainment. In almost all countries that participated in the International Adult Literacy Survey, the proportion of adults with a university education scoring in the two highest prose literacy levels (3 and 4/5) exceeds 80 per cent, attaining 87, 89 and 93 per cent in the Netherlands, Canada and Sweden, respectively (see Table R31). In Poland, on the other hand, it is 58 per cent and in Switzerland (German) 72 per cent.

Although most adults with a university-level education achieve literacy level 3 or above, there is substantial variation among countries in the proportion of university graduates scoring at levels 4 or 5, with 16 per cent in Poland, about 25 in Switzerland (German) 35 per cent in the Netherlands and Switzerland (French), 40 per cent in Germany, 48 per cent in the United States, 59 per cent in Canada and 61 per cent in Sweden.

Among persons with upper secondary education, which is the most common attainment level, there are also significant proportions scoring at level 3 or above in the prose scale, ranging from 31 per cent in Poland to around 50 per cent in Switzerland and the United States to 74 per cent in the Netherlands and Sweden. However, in all countries, persons at this level of attainment tend to score at the mid-range literacy levels.

For the category of persons with lower secondary education, Sweden stands out, with fully 72 per cent of adults at this attainment level scoring at literacy levels 3 and 4/5 and no other country exceeding 45 per cent. Finally, among persons with less than lower secondary education, the percentage reaching level 3 or above ranges from 6 per cent in Poland to roughly 20 per cent in Germany and the Netherlands to 32 per cent in Sweden.

These results suggest that having the "right" formal qualifications is no guarantee of high literacy, and that low educational attainment levels are not necessarily a permanent impediment to achieving it. With the information available, it is difficult to say whether it is the quality or content of basic education in a country such as Sweden which has contributed to the high functional literacy levels observed in that country at all attainment levels, or whether there are institutional or cultural factors that encourage the maintenance and development of literacy skills throughout the life cycle (see Indicator R32 on youth versus adult literacy levels).

DEFINITIONS

For each level of educational attainment, this indicator shows the proportion of adults (aged 16-65) scoring at each literacy level, as measured in the prose scale of the International Adult Literacy Survey. Note that the percentages of persons having attained a specified level of education shown in Table R31 differ from those shown in Indicator C1 due to differences in the classification of the educational attainment.

Because of insufficient sample sizes at the highest literacy level (level 5), this level has been combined with level 4 in the table and chart. The achievement scores are based on tests administered as part of the International Adult Literacy Survey that was undertaken by Statistics Canada during 1994.

R31: Adult literacy by level of educational attainment

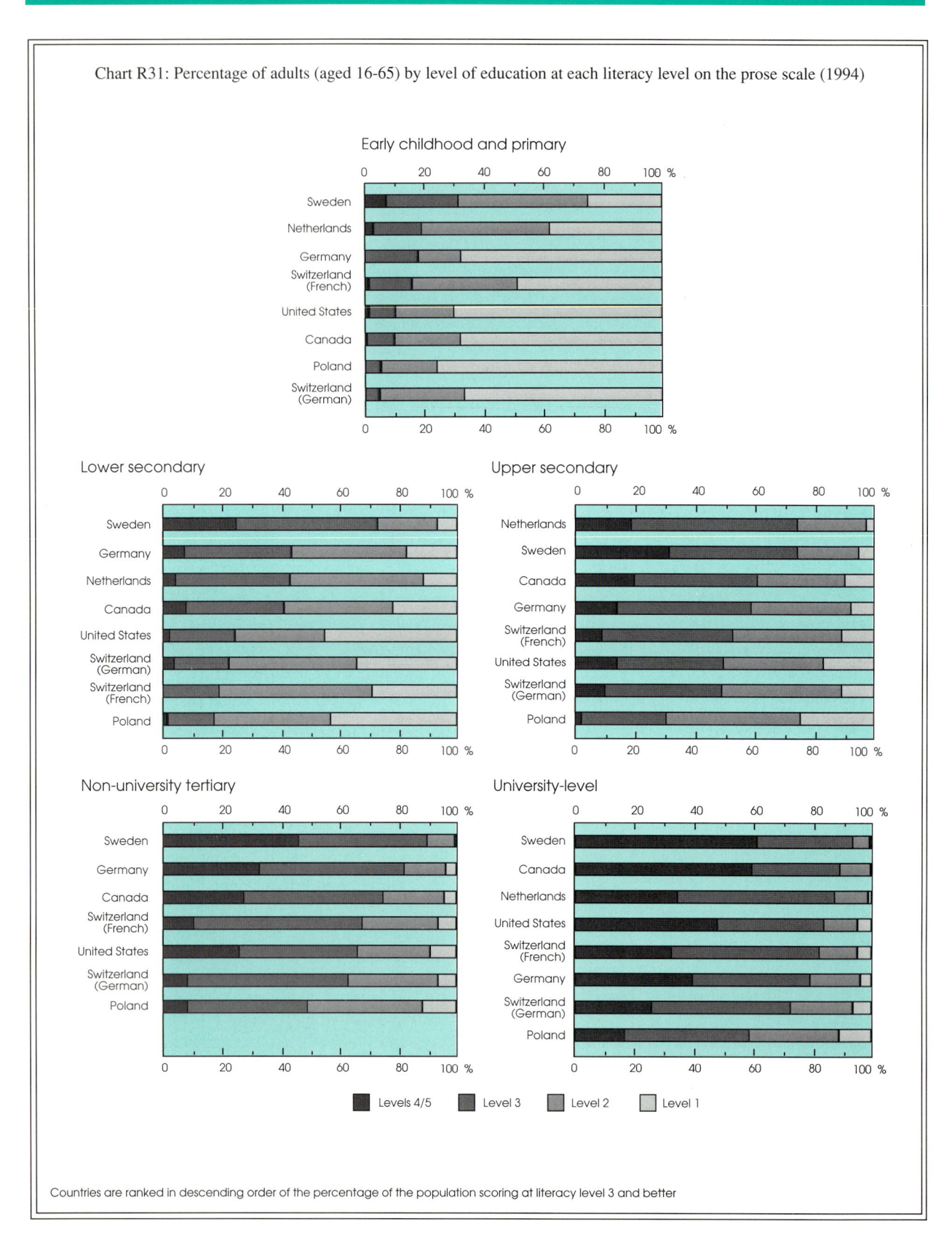

Chart R31: Percentage of adults (aged 16-65) by level of education at each literacy level on the prose scale (1994)

Early childhood and primary
(Countries shown: Sweden, Netherlands, Germany, Switzerland (French), United States, Canada, Poland, Switzerland (German))

Lower secondary
(Countries shown: Sweden, Germany, Netherlands, Canada, United States, Switzerland (German), Switzerland (French), Poland)

Upper secondary
(Countries shown: Netherlands, Sweden, Canada, Germany, Switzerland (French), United States, Switzerland (German), Poland)

Non-university tertiary
(Countries shown: Sweden, Germany, Canada, Switzerland (French), United States, Switzerland (German), Poland)

University-level
(Countries shown: Sweden, Canada, Netherlands, United States, Switzerland (French), Germany, Switzerland (German), Poland)

Legend: Levels 4/5 ■ | Level 3 ■ | Level 2 ■ | Level 1 □

Countries are ranked in descending order of the percentage of the population scoring at literacy level 3 and better

R31: Adult literacy by level of educational attainment

Table R31:
Percentage of adults (aged 16-65) by level of education at each literacy level on the prose scale (1994)

	Level of education	% of population aged 16-65 that has attained each ISCED level	Level 1 %	Level 1 s.e.	Level 2 %	Level 2 s.e.	Level 3 %	Level 3 s.e.	Levels 4/5 %	Levels 4/5 s.e.
Canada	Early childhood, primary	12	67.5	(6.6)	22.1	(3.5)	9.9	(6.8)	0.5	(0.4)
	Lower secondary	20	22.2	(2.2)	36.8	(3.2)	33.0	(4.0)	8.1	(2.5)
	Upper secondary	34	10.0	(3.2)	29.3	(4.5)	41.2	(5.6)	19.5	(0.9)
	Non-university tertiary	17	4.4	(1.8)	20.9	(6.1)	46.9	(7.7)	27.7	(5.0)
	University-level	16	0.2	(0.3)	10.8	(6.0)	29.8	(5.7)	59.1	(9.4)
Germany	Early childhood, primary	1	67.7	(12.7)	14.5	(8.1)	17.8	(8.9)	0.0	(0.0)
	Lower secondary	59	17.5	(1.1)	38.6	(1.4)	36.0	(1.8)	7.9	(1.5)
	Upper secondary	25	7.9	(1.7)	33.6	(3.8)	44.5	(4.4)	14.0	(1.6)
	Non-university tertiary	4	4.1	(1.8)	14.0	(3.1)	49.2	(5.5)	32.6	(3.7)
	University-level	12	4.0	(1.0)	17.0	(3.7)	39.4	(4.2)	39.6	(2.8)
Netherlands	Early childhood, primary	16	37.8	(3.0)	42.1	(3.1)	17.2	(2.4)	3.0	(0.8)
	Lower secondary	28	11.9	(0.9)	44.8	(1.7)	38.3	(1.4)	4.9	(0.7)
	Upper secondary	39	2.7	(0.6)	23.3	(1.4)	55.2	(1.6)	18.8	(1.3)
	Non-university tertiary	a	a	a	a	a	a	a	a	a
	University-level	18	1.3	(0.4)	11.9	(1.4)	52.3	(2.3)	34.5	(2.1)
Poland	Early childhood, primary	26	75.2	(1.3)	19.0	(1.0)	5.7	(0.7)	0.2	(0.2)
	Lower secondary	37	42.5	(1.6)	39.7	(1.8)	15.9	(1.2)	1.8	(0.4)
	Upper secondary	23	24.9	(1.9)	44.4	(2.5)	28.5	(1.8)	2.3	(0.7)
	Non-university tertiary	7	11.8	(2.4)	38.8	(3.7)	40.7	(2.6)	8.6	(1.9)
	University-level	7	11.2	(3.2)	30.4	(2.8)	42.0	(5.1)	16.4	(3.3)
Sweden	Early childhood, primary	13	25.2	(2.6)	42.5	(2.4)	24.7	(2.8)	7.6	(1.1)
	Lower secondary	15	7.0	(1.0)	20.7	(1.4)	47.3	(3.0)	25.0	(2.7)
	Upper secondary	47	5.7	(0.7)	20.5	(1.1)	42.7	(1.6)	31.1	(1.2)
	Non-university tertiary	13	1.4	(0.8)	9.4	(1.4)	43.4	(2.4)	45.8	(2.8)
	University-level	12	0.7	(0.5)	6.3	(1.7)	32.2	(3.8)	60.7	(4.6)
Switzerland (French)	Early childhood, primary	9	48.8	(8.3)	34.7	(7.2)	14.9	(5.6)	1.6	(1.6)
	Lower secondary	14	28.9	(4.6)	51.5	(5.0)	19.6	(5.0)	0.0	(0.0)
	Upper secondary	55	11.1	(1.8)	36.4	(2.3)	43.5	(2.9)	9.1	(0.8)
	Non-university tertiary	9	7.0	(1.9)	25.6	(3.4)	56.8	(4.6)	10.7	(2.8)
	University-level	14	4.8	(2.1)	13.4	(2.7)	49.4	(4.2)	32.4	(3.5)
Switzerland (German)	Early childhood, primary	4	65.8	m	28.8	m	5.4	m	0.0	m
	Lower secondary	15	34.2	(4.9)	42.9	(5.4)	18.7	(4.6)	4.2	(2.1)
	Upper secondary	63	11.0	(1.1)	39.8	(1.9)	39.4	(1.9)	9.8	(1.1)
	Non-university tertiary	11	6.8	(2.9)	30.1	(4.6)	54.1	(4.9)	9.0	(1.7)
	University-level	7	6.7	(2.4)	21.1	(5.6)	46.7	(4.9)	25.5	(5.7)
United States	Early childhood, primary	9	69.3	(4.3)	19.9	(3.5)	8.9	(2.0)	1.8	(0.9)
	Lower secondary	9	44.7	(3.9)	30.1	(3.4)	22.3	(2.4)	2.8	(0.7)
	Upper secondary	44	16.9	(1.6)	33.7	(2.0)	35.4	(2.1)	13.9	(1.8)
	Non-university tertiary	15	9.5	(1.8)	24.8	(2.6)	39.9	(3.5)	25.8	(3.2)
	University-level	22	4.9	(1.2)	11.9	(0.9)	35.7	(2.4)	47.5	(2.7)

s.e.: standard error
Source: Statistics Canada. See Annex 3 for notes

R32: LITERACY SKILLS OF YOUNGER VERSUS OLDER PERSONS

POLICY CONTEXT

To what extent do the literacy skills of the young differ from those of the older population? This question is of particular interest, because of the light it can shed on the effects of the considerable changes in the enrolment, emphasis and content of educational programmes that have occurred in most countries in recent decades. In addition, since the young persons considered here (16-24 year-olds) have in many cases only recently or not yet entered the labour force, comparisons between countries may provide some insight on the extent to which differences in literacy skills are a product of education systems or reflect post-school effects.

KEY RESULTS

Generally, the literacy levels of the young (16-24) are somewhat higher than those of older persons (25-65). In all countries there is a smaller proportion of young persons at the lowest literacy level relative to the older population, and in almost all cases, a larger proportion of young persons at levels 3 and 4/5.

However, the signs of convergence among countries in the literacy skills of the young population are mixed, and depend to a certain extent on the levels already reached by older compatriots.

DESCRIPTION AND INTERPRETATION

Because many young persons in the age group 16-24 have not yet completed their education, it is not immediately obvious that one would expect higher literacy levels for young persons compared to older ones. If literacy skills further develop after the completion of formal schooling, through practice and use in the work place and other settings, then one might expect older persons to be at a relative advantage compared to younger ones, since the literacy test materials are not curriculum-based.

In practice, what one observes is that the prose literacy skills of the young are superior to those of older persons, with between 8 and 16 per cent more persons achieving literacy level 3 or above (Table R32). The only exception to this is the United States, where there is a shift in the distribution of literacy skills towards the middle levels (levels 2 and 3), with relatively fewer young persons in both the highest (4/5) and lowest (1) literacy levels compared to older persons.

For the quantitative scale, young persons in Switzerland in both linguistic groups show an increase of more than 10 percentage points over the two highest levels compared to older persons. Other countries show smaller improvements.

For the document scale, the proportion of young persons achieving at least level 3 exceeds that of older persons by 10 per cent or more in all countries except Germany and Sweden, where the relative increase is some 5 to 7 percentage points.

Generally, the distribution of young persons across literacy levels for all three scales tends to reproduce in a given country that observed for older persons with, however, a shift in the distribution towards higher literacy levels. Young Swedes demonstrate superior performance, in Poland there are relatively fewer young people at high literacy levels than in other countries, and European countries tend to show more homogeneous results than Canada and the United States, although less so than for the entire 16-65 year old population.

Young persons in the age group considered, many of them still in education, are unlikely to manifest significant effects generated by post-school practices. In addition, the general similarity in relative country results for young versus older persons would seem to suggest that both have been subject to the same influences. These could be, for example, persistent characteristics of national school systems that transcend reforms introduced over recent decades, or perhaps wider societal attitudes towards literacy and learning that permeate the school system, the work place and society at large.

DEFINITIONS

The results presented here attempt to measure "functional literacy", that is, respondents are asked to carry out various tasks that might be encountered in everyday life, such as reading instructions on medicine bottles, interpreting train timetables, filling out forms, understanding assembly instructions or recipes, etc. They are thus not based on problems taken from an educational curriculum and can be expected to reflect the

R32: Literacy skills of younger versus older persons

sort of skills required to function productively in society and the work place.

Because of insufficient sample sizes at the highest literacy level (level 5), this level has been combined with level 4 in the table and chart. The achievement scores are based on tests administered as part of the International Adult Literacy Survey that was undertaken by Statistics Canada during 1994.

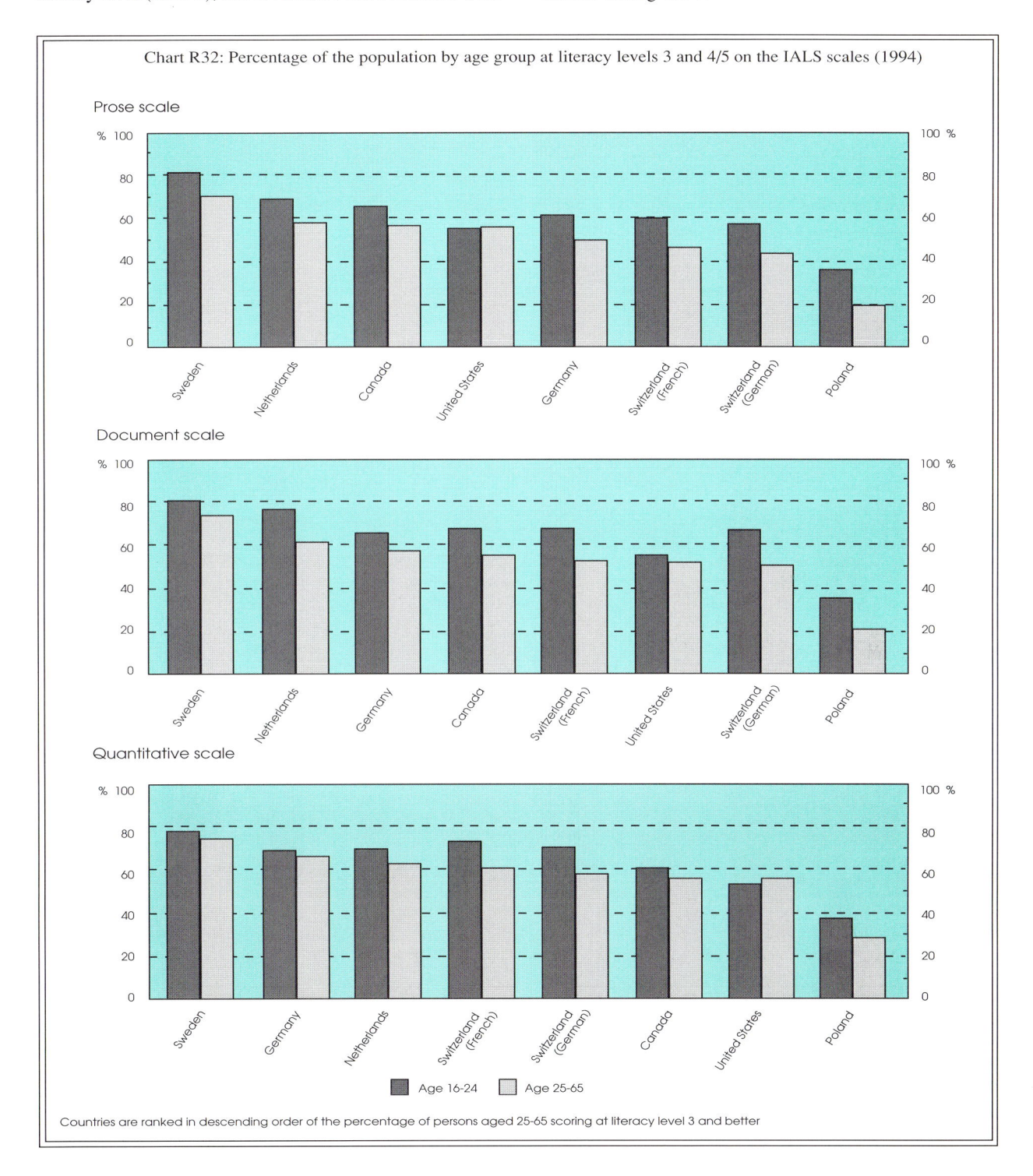

Chart R32: Percentage of the population by age group at literacy levels 3 and 4/5 on the IALS scales (1994)

Prose scale

Document scale

Quantitative scale

■ Age 16-24   □ Age 25-65

Countries are ranked in descending order of the percentage of persons aged 25-65 scoring at literacy level 3 and better

R32: Literacy skills of younger versus older persons

Table R32:
Percentage of the population by age group at each literacy level on the IALS scales (1994)

	Age group	Level 1 %	Level 1 s.e.	Level 2 %	Level 2 s.e.	Level 3 %	Level 3 s.e.	Levels 4/5 %	Levels 4/5 s.e.
Prose scale									
Canada	16-24	11.3	(1.8)	24.0	(2.6)	43.7	(2.4)	21.1	(4.5)
	25-65	17.8	(1.7)	26.0	(1.8)	33.1	(3.1)	23.0	(2.6)
Germany	16-24	8.5	(1.9)	30.3	(3.8)	47.7	(5.1)	13.5	(3.7)
	25-65	15.4	(1.0)	34.9	(0.9)	36.3	(1.4)	13.4	(0.8)
Netherlands	16-24	9.5	(2.1)	21.9	(2.8)	50.6	(3.5)	18.0	(2.3)
	25-65	10.8	(0.6)	31.9	(1.0)	42.6	(0.9)	14.7	(0.6)
Poland	16-24	25.9	(2.1)	38.7	(1.7)	29.9	(1.3)	5.6	(1.0)
	25-65	47.0	(1.0)	33.5	(0.9)	17.1	(0.9)	2.4	(0.3)
Sweden	16-24	3.7	(1.0)	15.9	(1.4)	40.4	(2.0)	40.1	(1.5)
	25-65	8.5	(0.6)	21.5	(0.7)	39.6	(0.8)	30.5	(0.8)
Switzerland (French)	16-24	9.8	(2.7)	30.6	(3.7)	43.4	(4.9)	16.1	(2.4)
	25-65	19.3	(1.3)	34.4	(1.6)	37.6	(1.8)	8.7	(0.8)
Switzerland (German)	16-24	7.1	(1.8)	36.0	(3.5)	43.2	(4.9)	13.7	(3.0)
	25-65	21.4	(1.1)	35.6	(1.8)	34.8	(1.3)	8.1	(0.8)
United States	16-24	15.0	(0.9)	31.0	(1.4)	37.0	(1.4)	18.0	(1.1/0.3)
	25-65	20.0	(0.7)	24.8	(1.3)	32.3	(1.3)	23.0	(1.3)
Document scale									
Canada	16-24	10.6	(1.4)	22.1	(3.9)	35.2	(2.1)	32.1	(4.9)
	25-65	19.8	(2.3)	25.3	(2.1)	31.3	(2.3)	23.5	(1.2)
Germany	16-24	4.9	(1.2)	29.7	(3.4)	44.3	(4.9)	21.1	(3.8)
	25-65	9.7	(0.8)	33.3	(1.2)	38.6	(0.8)	18.5	(1.2)
Netherlands	16-24	6.6	(1.9)	17.1	(2.1)	50.9	(3.2)	25.4	(2.7)
	25-65	10.9	(0.6)	27.7	(0.9)	42.6	(1.0)	18.7	(0.7)
Poland	16-24	31.7	(2.4)	33.5	(2.0)	26.3	(1.8)	8.6	(0.9)
	25-65	48.9	(1.4)	30.0	(1.1)	15.9	(1.0)	5.1	(0.3)
Sweden	16-24	3.0	(0.7)	16.7	(1.9)	39.3	(1.8)	40.9	(1.8)
	25-65	7.0	(0.5)	19.4	(0.9)	39.5	(0.8)	34.1	(0.8)
Switzerland (French)	16-24	7.7	(2.1)	25.2	(2.6)	40.2	(4.4)	26.8	(4.4)
	25-65	18.0	(1.4)	29.6	(1.7)	38.6	(1.9)	13.8	(0.9)
Switzerland (German)	16-24	6.8	(2.0)	27.0	(4.5)	39.0	(4.4)	27.2	(3.5)
	25-65	20.1	(1.1)	29.4	(1.5)	36.2	(1.0)	14.3	(1.0)
United States	16-24	14.0	(0.7)	30.0	(1.2)	37.0	(1.5)	18.0	(1.1/0.3)
	25-65	23.5	(0.8)	25.1	(1.2)	31.8	(1.1)	19.5	(0.9)
Quantitative scale									
Canada	16-24	10.6	(1.0)	28.9	(5.0)	43.6	(2.6)	16.9	(3.0)
	25-65	18.3	(2.2)	25.5	(2.7)	32.9	(2.3)	23.3	(1.8)
Germany	16-24	4.6	(0.9)	26.5	(3.6)	48.3	(2.7)	20.6	(3.3)
	25-65	7.0	(0.4)	26.6	(1.3)	42.3	(1.1)	24.1	(0.8)
Netherlands	16-24	8.3	(2.1)	21.8	(2.7)	49.7	(3.3)	20.2	(2.8)
	25-65	10.7	(0.7)	26.4	(1.0)	43.1	(1.1)	19.8	(0.8)
Poland	16-24	29.3	(2.8)	32.8	(2.7)	31.4	(1.9)	6.5	(0.9)
	25-65	41.7	(1.1)	29.5	(1.1)	21.9	(0.7)	6.9	(0.4)
Sweden	16-24	4.8	(0.6)	17.7	(2.0)	39.0	(2.4)	38.5	(1.9)
	25-65	7.1	(0.6)	18.8	(0.9)	39.0	(0.9)	35.2	(0.9)
Switzerland (French)	16-24	5.9	(2.1)	21.1	(2.6)	45.5	(5.2)	27.4	(4.3)
	25-65	14.3	(1.0)	25.1	(1.6)	41.5	(1.4)	19.0	(0.8)
Switzerland (German)	16-24	6.7	(2.5)	23.2	(4.3)	46.2	(3.6)	23.9	(3.1)
	25-65	15.4	(1.0)	26.7	(1.5)	39.8	(1.5)	18.1	(1.4)
United States	16-24	17.0	(0.9)	30.0	(1.1)	36.0	(1.0)	17.0	(0.9/0.4)
	25-65	19.7	(0.7)	24.4	(1.1)	31.6	(0.9)	24.3	(1.0)

s.e.: standard error
Source: Statistics Canada. See Annex 3 for notes

R33: ADULT LITERACY BY GENDER

POLICY CONTEXT

In recent decades the labour force participation of women in OECD countries has been continuously increasing, while that of prime-age men has been falling. The increasing reliance of OECD economies on the participation of women to ensure continued labour force growth, particularly in the face of an ageing population, will require the enhancement of women's work-place skills, particularly in quantitative areas, where performance differences persist.

KEY RESULTS

The relative prose literacy performances of men and women are mixed across countries. However, for document literacy, a somewhat higher proportion of men than women are at the higher literacy levels in Europe. Quantitative literacy results show almost uniformly better scores for men than women.

DESCRIPTION AND INTERPRETATION

In Canada and the United States, women tend to show higher levels of prose literacy than men. In both linguistic groups in Switzerland, the reverse is true, whereas in the rest of the countries covered in Table R33, the distribution of prose literacy for women is comparable to that of men.

On the document scale, with the exception of Canada and the United States, there are relatively more men than women attaining at least level 3 (some 6 to 7 percentage points more on average). On the quantitative scale, the proportion of men attaining at least level 3 exceeds that of women by about 9 percentage points on average, with Canada again being an exception.

The educational attainment levels of women do tend to be somewhat lower than those of men in almost all countries (see Indicator C2), which may account for some of the differences observed. However, results fairly similar to those described here have been observed in reading and mathematics achievement tests for students, with girls generally performing better in reading and boys in mathematics. Whether these results reflect the effect of gender stereotyping, unequal opportunities or other factors is difficult to say.

In addition, there is clearly substantial overlap in the distribution of literacy skills of men and women within a country as well as substantial variation in the relative scores of men and women among countries. For example, proportionally more women in Sweden score at levels 4 or 5 than do men in every other country, and this holds for all scales. Literacy levels are thus substantially malleable, and it is likely that educational and societal factors contribute significantly to the performances that are observed.

DEFINITIONS

The results presented here attempt to measure "functional literacy", that is, respondents are asked to carry out various tasks that might be encountered in everyday life, such as reading instructions on medicine bottles, interpreting train timetables, filling out forms, understanding assembly instructions or recipes, etc. They are thus not based on problems taken from an educational curriculum and can be expected to reflect the sort of skills required to function productively in society and the work place.

Because of insufficient sample sizes at the highest literacy level (level 5), this level has been combined with level 4 in the table and chart. The achievement scores are based on tests administered as part of the International Adult Literacy Survey that was undertaken by Statistics Canada during 1994.

R33: Adult literacy by gender

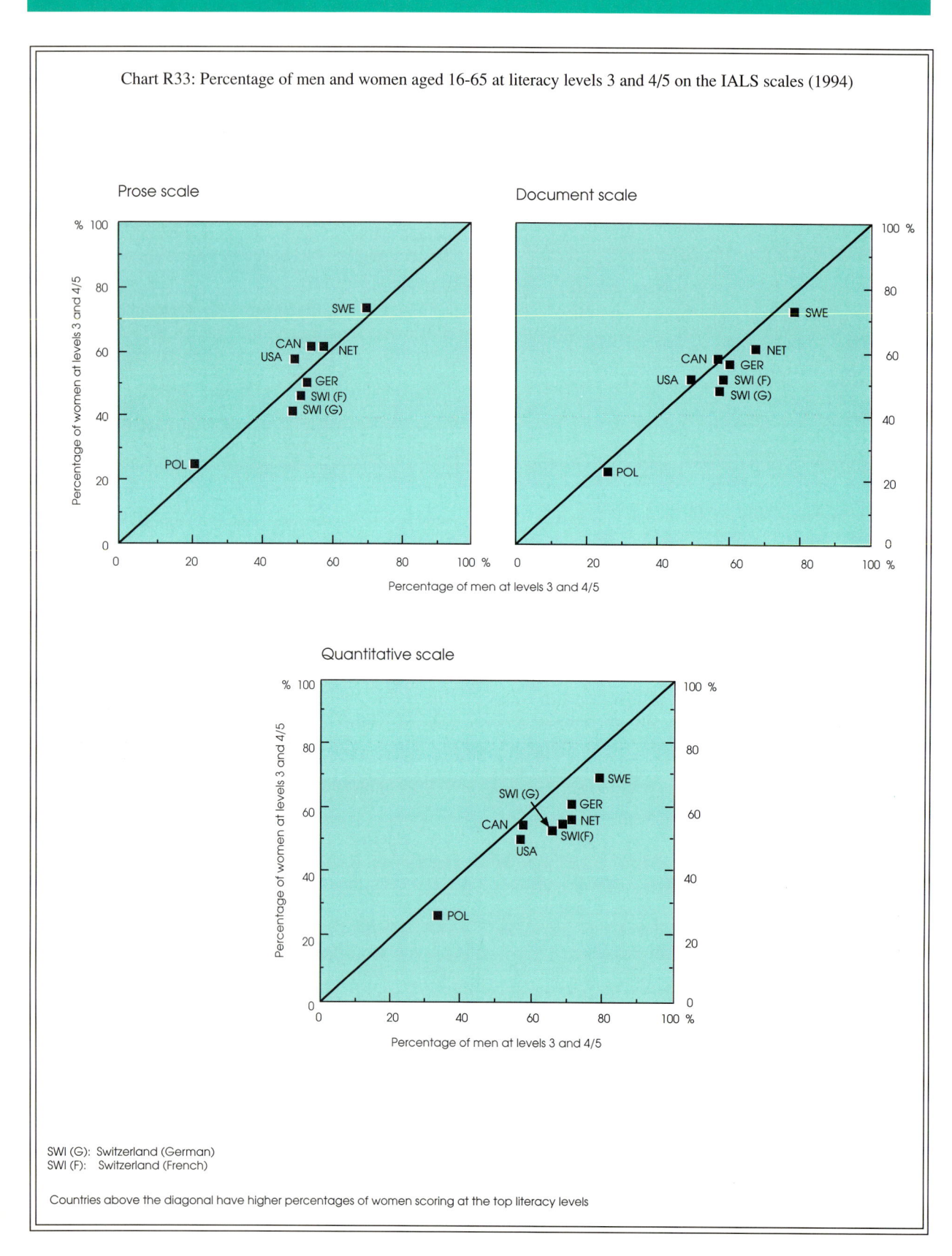

Chart R33: Percentage of men and women aged 16-65 at literacy levels 3 and 4/5 on the IALS scales (1994)

Prose scale

Document scale

Quantitative scale

SWI (G): Switzerland (German)
SWI (F): Switzerland (French)

Countries above the diagonal have higher percentages of women scoring at the top literacy levels

R33: Adult literacy by gender

Table R33:
Percentage of men and women (aged 16-65) at each literacy level on the IALS scales (1994)

	Scale	Level 1 Men %	s.e.	Level 1 Women %	s.e.	Level 2 Men %	s.e.	Level 2 Women %	s.e.	Level 3 Men %	s.e.	Level 3 Women %	s.e.	Levels 4/5 Men %	s.e.	Levels 4/5 Women %	s.e.
Canada	Prose	19.0	(2.0)	14.3	(1.9)	26.6	(3.5)	24.7	(3.5)	37.0	(3.3)	33.2	(2.4)	17.4	(2.3)	27.8	(4.7)
	Document	17.0	(1.8)	19.3	(2.9)	25.7	(2.6)	23.8	(1.9)	31.8	(2.8)	32.3	(1.9)	25.4	(1.7)	24.7	(1.6)
	Quantitative	17.2	(2.4)	16.6	(3.0)	24.9	(4.5)	27.2	(2.7)	33.8	(3.7)	35.9	(1.5)	24.1	(1.9)	20.2	(3.8)
Germany	Prose	15.4	(1.4)	13.3	(1.6)	31.8	(2.0)	36.7	(2.0)	37.9	(1.7)	38.0	(1.9)	14.9	(1.6)	12.0	(1.4)
	Document	7.8	(1.0)	10.1	(0.9)	31.0	(1.7)	34.4	(2.3)	38.7	(1.2)	40.2	(1.3)	22.4	(1.9)	15.3	(1.4)
	Quantitative	5.7	(0.8)	7.6	(0.7)	22.7	(1.6)	30.5	(2.3)	42.9	(1.3)	43.5	(1.4)	28.7	(1.8)	18.4	(1.1)
Netherlands	Prose	10.5	(1.0)	10.5	(0.9)	31.3	(0.9)	28.8	(1.3)	43.6	(1.0)	44.6	(1.6)	14.6	(1.1)	16.0	(0.8)
	Document	8.5	(1.0)	11.9	(1.0)	23.9	(1.2)	27.7	(1.1)	45.0	(1.4)	43.3	(1.2)	22.7	(1.2)	17.1	(0.9)
	Quantitative	8.2	(1.0)	12.4	(1.0)	20.8	(1.2)	30.4	(1.3)	46.4	(1.5)	42.1	(1.2)	24.6	(1.3)	15.1	(1.0)
Poland	Prose	43.3	(0.6)	42.0	(1.7)	35.4	(1.1)	33.7	(1.4)	18.7	(0.8)	20.8	(0.7)	2.6	(0.5)	3.5	(0.5)
	Document	43.7	(1.5)	47.0	(1.7)	31.1	(1.5)	30.4	(0.9)	18.7	(0.8)	17.4	(1.3)	6.4	(0.5)	5.2	(0.4)
	Quantitative	36.2	(1.2)	42.0	(1.4)	29.7	(1.6)	30.6	(1.4)	26.1	(1.2)	21.7	(1.2)	8.0	(0.7)	5.7	(0.5)
Sweden	Prose	7.9	(0.7)	7.1	(1.0)	20.9	(1.3)	19.8	(1.0)	39.9	(1.0)	39.5	(1.6)	31.3	(1.1)	33.6	(1.5)
	Document	5.0	(0.3)	7.3	(0.7)	16.8	(0.9)	21.0	(1.4)	39.6	(1.2)	39.3	(1.7)	38.6	(1.3)	32.4	(1.2)
	Quantitative	5.2	(0.5)	8.0	(0.7)	15.3	(1.0)	21.8	(1.6)	37.6	(1.2)	40.4	(1.7)	41.9	(1.2)	29.8	(1.1)
Switzerland (French)	Prose	17.1	(1.9)	18.2	(1.5)	31.2	(2.1)	36.2	(1.8)	40.9	(2.5)	36.4	(1.8)	10.8	(1.4)	9.2	(0.9)
	Document	14.0	(1.5)	18.5	(1.8)	27.0	(1.9)	30.6	(1.8)	40.3	(2.0)	37.5	(1.6)	18.7	(2.1)	13.4	(1.4)
	Quantitative	11.0	(1.4)	14.8	(1.1)	19.8	(1.9)	29.1	(1.8)	43.8	(2.0)	40.7	(2.0)	25.4	(1.9)	15.5	(1.4)
Switzerland (German)	Prose	17.9	(1.5)	20.7	(1.7)	32.9	(2.3)	38.4	(1.8)	40.0	(2.2)	32.1	(1.6)	9.2	(1.4)	8.7	(1.2)
	Document	15.2	(1.6)	21.1	(1.7)	26.7	(2.7)	31.4	(1.6)	39.7	(1.4)	33.6	(1.8)	18.4	(1.4)	13.9	(1.8)
	Quantitative	12.2	(1.6)	16.1	(1.8)	22.2	(2.5)	30.2	(2.0)	41.9	(2.6)	39.6	(1.6)	23.7	(2.1)	14.2	(1.6)
United States	Prose	22.2	(1.2)	19.3	(1.1)	28.0	(1.3)	23.9	(1.5)	29.8	(1.4)	34.7	(1.5)	20.0	(1.6)	22.1	(1.5)
	Document	25.2	(1.4)	22.4	(1.0)	24.9	(1.5)	26.7	(1.5)	30.4	(1.4)	32.3	(1.2)	19.5	(1.3)	18.5	(1.1)
	Quantitative	20.9	(1.2)	21.0	(1.2)	22.2	(1.6)	28.1	(1.1)	29.9	(1.6)	32.5	(0.9)	27.1	(1.2)	18.4	(1.5)

s.e.: standard error
Source: Statistics Canada. See Annex 3 for notes

Chapter 7

LABOUR MARKET OUTCOMES OF EDUCATION

Education is a means by which the values, traditions and culture of a society are transmitted from generation to generation while at the same time being the source of social and scientific progress. It has two obvious effects on productivity. On the one hand, education can help in the development of scientific knowledge, which translates into technological improvements and productivity gains. On the other hand, education helps to increase the skills and qualifications of workers and thus makes them more able to accomplish particular tasks as well as to adapt to new job requirements. The contribution of education to economic performance and to the achievement of goals which societies consider important thus manifests itself for the individual in the ability to find and to hold a job in the labour market and in the wages which enterprises, governments and individuals are willing to pay for the work or services performed.

This chapter examines labour force outcomes of education for the working-age population as a whole and for various demographic sub-groups. The two indicators chosen to provide information on labour force outcomes are the unemployment rate and mean annual earnings. Although the actual level of these is influenced by many factors not directly related to educational attainment (for example fiscal and monetary policies, the state of the business cycle, employment policies and labour market rigidities), the relative values of these indicators for different levels of educational attainment provide valuable information on the importance which societies and economies attribute to increased levels of attainment.

Indicator R21(A) provides the general background for this chapter, presenting data on the unemployment rates of the adult labour force by educational attainment. Young people are the principal source of new skills in our societies, and **Indicator R21(B)** shows how they perform in the labour market at various ages according to their educational attainment level. The transition from school to work is a difficult period for many young people, and societies have an interest in seeing that this transition occurs as smoothly as possible. **Indicator R24** shows that despite the reductions in the size of the youth cohort observed in many countries over the past decade, the transition period remains difficult, even for the university-educated in some countries.

Finally, no examination of the outcomes of education would be complete without a look at earnings, which represent both the return on the investment in education and the incentive that ensures economies a steady supply of highly educated workers. **Indicator R22** shows the earnings of workers (both men and women) at various attainment levels, relative to those of persons with upper secondary attainment.

R21(A): Unemployment and education

R21(A): UNEMPLOYMENT AND EDUCATION

This indicator shows the unemployment rates of the adult labour force by level of educational attainment.

POLICY CONTEXT

To the extent that educational attainment is an indicator of skill, it acts as a signal to employers of the likely knowledge, capacities and work place performance of candidates for employment. Unemployment rates by educational attainment measure the extent of labour market demand for different levels of skill. The adequacy of workers' skills and the ability of an economy to supply jobs that match available skills are issues of significant policy interest in most countries.

KEY RESULTS

Unemployment rates in OECD countries generally decrease as the level of educational attainment of workers increases. This is a result that appears to hold generally across countries with widely different distributions of educational attainment in their populations (see Table C1.1 for background) and with labour markets subject to varying degrees of governmental regulation and rates of job creation.

A second result is that, if one outlier country is excluded from the data, the range of unemployment rates across OECD countries for persons with university-level attainment is relatively narrow. Indeed, what distinguishes countries from one another is the ability of their economies to provide employment opportunities for persons at the other end of the spectrum, namely those with relatively low educational attainment.

Finally, in most OECD countries, the labour market position of persons aged 25-64 with less than upper secondary education has deteriorated relative to that of the overall labour force in recent years.

DESCRIPTION AND INTERPRETATION

Unemployment rates for persons aged 25-64 in 1994 among OECD countries listed in Table R21(A) range from a low rate of 3 to 4.5 per cent in Austria, Norway and Switzerland to a high rate of about 20 per cent in Spain. Even under these very different labour market conditions, however, it is generally the case in most countries that persons with higher levels of educational attainment are subject to lower rates of unemployment. With few exceptions, this holds regardless of the overall rate of unemployment in a country or of its overall distribution of educational attainment and regardless of whether the range of unemployment rates across educational levels is large (Denmark, Finland, Ireland and the United States) or small (Italy, Switzerland, Turkey). This is a telling illustration of a generalised demand for more highly skilled workers in all OECD countries.

The notable exceptions to this result concern countries where the share of the labour force engaged in self-employment is still relatively large (over 30 per cent or more), such as Greece, Portugal and Turkey. Most of the self-employed persons in these countries consist of traditional farmers, craftsmen and shopkeepers of limited education who are effectively not subject to unemployment unless they lose their means of subsistence entirely. In these countries there has also been significant emigration of persons with low attainment levels in recent decades and the proportion of the labour force in agriculture remains high.

Over all reporting countries, the average rate of unemployment among persons aged 25-64 in the labour force in 1994 with below upper secondary education was approximately 12 per cent, among those with university-level education about 5 per cent, and over all levels about 8 per cent. These averages, however, mask varying dispersions in unemployment rates across countries for different levels of attainment.

If one excludes Spain, the dispersion in adult unemployment rates across countries for persons with university-level attainment covers a relatively narrow range, from a low of 1.5 per cent in Norway to a high of 6.6 per cent in Finland. By contrast, rates for persons with less than upper secondary education range from 4.9 per cent in Austria to 22.7 per cent in Finland, with countries present over the entire spectrum [see Chart R21(A)].

Since persons with less than upper secondary education in many countries still comprise a substantial proportion of the working-age population and of the labour

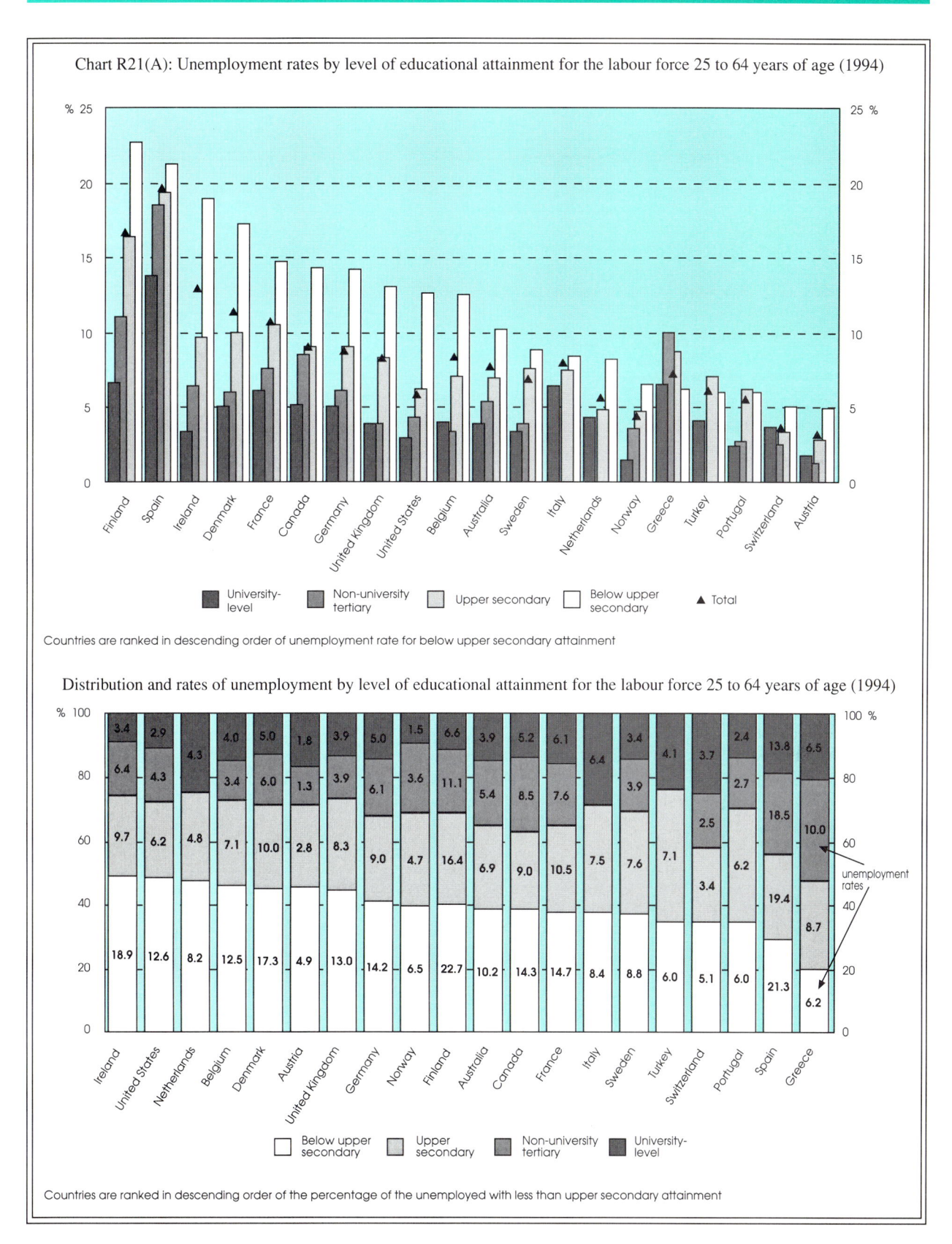

R21(A): Unemployment and education

Chart R21(A): Unemployment rates by level of educational attainment for the labour force 25 to 64 years of age (1994)

Legend: University-level | Non-university tertiary | Upper secondary | Below upper secondary | ▲ Total

Countries (in descending order of unemployment rate for below upper secondary attainment): Finland, Spain, Ireland, Denmark, France, Canada, Germany, United Kingdom, United States, Belgium, Australia, Sweden, Italy, Netherlands, Norway, Greece, Turkey, Portugal, Switzerland, Austria

Countries are ranked in descending order of unemployment rate for below upper secondary attainment

Distribution and rates of unemployment by level of educational attainment for the labour force 25 to 64 years of age (1994)

Country	Below upper secondary	Upper secondary	Non-university tertiary	University-level
Ireland	18.9	9.7	6.4	3.4
United States	12.6	6.2	4.3	2.9
Netherlands	8.2	4.8	4.3	—
Belgium	12.5	7.1	3.4	4.0
Denmark	17.3	10.0	6.0	5.0
Austria	4.9	2.8	1.3	1.8
United Kingdom	13.0	8.3	3.9	3.9
Germany	14.2	9.0	6.1	5.0
Norway	6.5	4.7	3.6	1.5
Finland	22.7	16.4	11.1	6.6
Australia	10.2	6.9	5.4	3.9
Canada	14.3	9.0	8.5	5.2
France	14.7	10.5	7.6	6.1
Italy	8.4	7.5	—	—
Sweden	8.8	7.6	3.9	3.4
Turkey	6.0	7.1	4.1	—
Switzerland	5.1	3.4	2.5	3.7
Portugal	6.0	6.2	2.7	2.4
Spain	21.3	19.4	18.5	13.8
Greece	6.2	8.7	10.0	6.5

Countries are ranked in descending order of the percentage of the unemployed with less than upper secondary attainment

R21(A): Unemployment and education

force in most countries (see Indicator C1), an economy's ability to provide jobs for adult persons at this level has a significant effect on the overall unemployment rate. Over the 1989 to 1994 period, in a climate of generally increasing unemployment and continuing upskilling of jobs, the position of this group relative to that of the rest of the labour force has, with some exceptions (Germany, Ireland, the Netherlands and Norway), deteriorated in many reporting countries, and most notably in Canada, Denmark, Finland, Spain, Sweden, the United Kingdom, and the United States.

DEFINITIONS

The unemployed are defined, in accordance with the ILO guidelines on unemployment statistics, as persons who are without work, actively seeking employment and currently available to start work. The unemployment rate is defined as the number of unemployed persons as a percentage of the labour force. Persons less than 25 years of age have been excluded from the statistics, in order to base the analysis as much as possible on persons who have completed their education.

Table R21(A):
Unemployment rates by level of educational attainment for the labour force 25 to 64 years of age (1994)

	Below upper secondary education	Upper secondary education	Non-university tertiary education	University-level education	All levels of education
North America					
Canada	14.3	9.0	8.5	5.2	9.2
United States	12.6	6.2	4.3	2.9	5.8
Pacific Area					
Australia	10.2	6.9	5.4	3.9	7.7
European Union					
Austria	4.9	2.8	1.3	1.8	3.3
Belgium	12.5	7.1	3.4	4.0	8.3
Denmark	17.3	10.0	6.0	5.0	11.5
Finland	22.7	16.4	11.1	6.6	16.7
France	14.7	10.5	7.6	6.1	10.8
Germany	14.2	9.0	6.1	5.0	8.7
Greece	6.2	8.7	10.0	6.5	7.2
Ireland	18.9	9.7	6.4	3.4	12.9
Italy	8.4	7.5	a	6.4	7.9
Netherlands	8.2	4.8	a	4.3	5.7
Portugal	6.0	6.2	2.7	2.4	5.5
Spain	21.3	19.4	18.5	13.8	19.8
Sweden	8.8	7.6	3.9	3.4	6.8
United Kingdom	13.0	8.3	3.9	3.9	8.2
Other OECD countries					
Norway	6.5	4.7	3.6	1.5	4.3
Switzerland	5.1	3.4	2.5	3.7	3.6
Turkey	6.0	7.1	a	4.1	6.0
Country mean	**11.6**	**8.3**	**5.3**	**4.7**	**8.5**

Source: OECD Database. See Annex 3 for notes

R21(B): Youth unemployment and education

R21(B): YOUTH UNEMPLOYMENT AND EDUCATION

This indicator shows unemployment rates for young persons by level of educational attainment.

POLICY CONTEXT

Youth represent the most important source of new skills in our societies. In most OECD countries educational policy has aimed at encouraging young people to complete upper secondary education. With the continuing upskilling of jobs, persons with low attainment are at a distinct disadvantage in the labour market. Even with increasing educational attainment, unemployment among young people in many countries is high. This is a waste of human resources and can be a risk factor socially for both the individual and society at large.

KEY RESULTS

In the OECD countries, the unemployment rates of young people are consistently higher than those of older age groups, often twice as high, and sometimes three or more times.

Nowhere is the handicap of low educational attainment more evident in the labour market than among the young, who cannot compensate for this through work experience and skills learned on the job. With some exceptions, each increment in the formal qualifications of young people results in a lower unemployment rate in the early stages of working life.

Finally, in a number of countries young workers with even tertiary-level attainment have high unemployment rates.

DESCRIPTION AND INTERPRETATION

In 1994 the average rate of unemployment in the OECD countries was 19 per cent among those aged 20-24 and 13 per cent for 25-29 year-olds.

There are, however, a number of reasons why these rates need to be nuanced. First of all, the younger of these age groups contains considerable numbers of persons still in school. Those not in school consist in part of

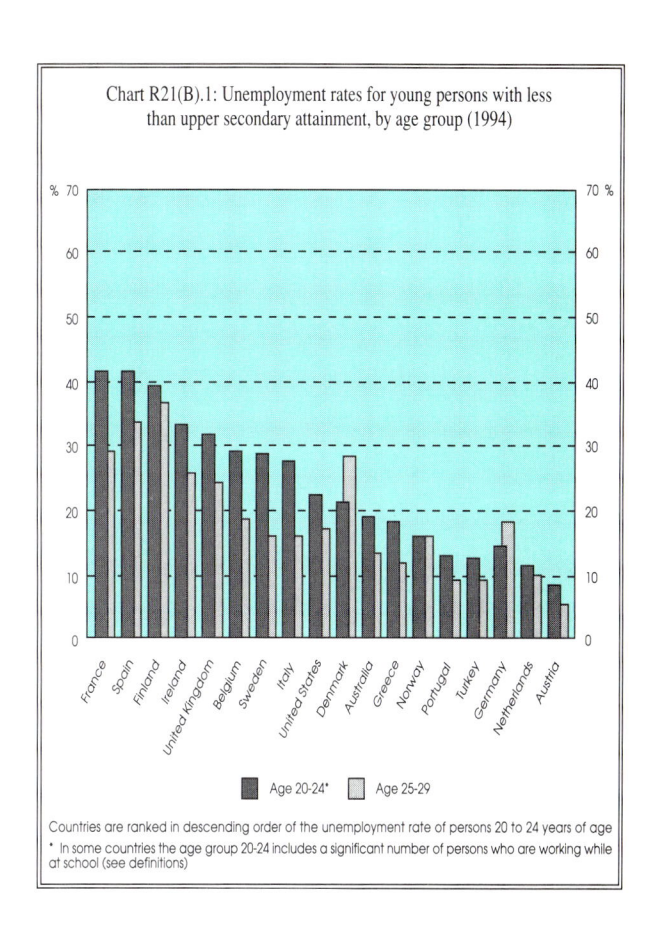

Chart R21(B).1: Unemployment rates for young persons with less than upper secondary attainment, by age group (1994)

Countries are ranked in descending order of the unemployment rate of persons 20 to 24 years of age
* In some countries the age group 20-24 includes a significant number of persons who are working while at school (see definitions)

"drop-outs" and of persons who have completed their education at a certain level but are not pursuing their studies. They do not thus constitute a representative sample of the 20-24 population, but rather a sub-group that is biased towards lower levels of attainment.

In addition, because of seniority provisions in collective bargaining agreements, young workers are generally the first to be laid off by firms that are in difficulty. Finally, in some countries, many new jobs which are created are temporary, or of limited duration, and young workers may pass through a period of unstable employment before the transition to a more permanent job is made. Notwithstanding these qualifications, the problematic nature of youth unemployment remains, and is particularly evident for young persons of low educational attainment.

Unemployment rates for persons aged 20-24 with less than upper secondary education are exceedingly high in many countries [see Chart R21(B).1], particularly in Finland, France and Spain (about 40 per cent) but also in

R21(B): Youth unemployment and education

Belgium, Ireland, Italy, Sweden and the United Kingdom (between 27 and 33 per cent). In the older age group (25-29), persons with less than upper secondary education generally fare somewhat better than the younger group. However, the labour market situation of persons aged 25-29 in this attainment group is still highly unfavourable, with unemployment rates exceeding 20 per cent in Denmark, France, Ireland and the United Kingdom and over 30 per cent in Finland and Spain.

With the completion of upper secondary education, the unemployment picture of persons aged 20-24 improves significantly relative to persons at lower levels of attainment, except in Finland and Southern Europe [see Chart R21(B).2]. In the latter region, there may be a buffering effect for youth with low attainment levels, due to the continuing prevalence of traditional occupations such as farming, shopkeeping and crafts, which are often associated with family businesses. In addition, in the economies of these countries the supply of young persons at higher attainment levels greatly exceeds the demand for their skills. Indeed, even at tertiary levels, unemployment rates for young people aged 25-29 remain high in most of Southern Europe, particularly in Greece, Italy and Spain (some 15 to 30 per cent).

In other countries in Chart R21(B).2, with the exception of Denmark, Finland and France where unemployment rates for university-educated 25-29 year-olds still exceed 10 per cent, persons of that age with university education are only slightly more subject to unemployment than corresponding older workers.

DEFINITIONS

The unemployed are defined, in accordance with the ILO guidelines on unemployment statistics, as persons who are without work, actively seeking employment and currently available to start work. The unemployment rate is defined as the number of unemployed persons as a percentage of the labour force.

R21(B): Youth unemployment and education

Chart R21(B).2: Unemployment rates by level of educational attainment for persons 25 to 29 years of age (1994)

Countries are ranked in descending order of unemployment rate for below upper secondary attainment

Distribution and rates of unemployment by level of educational attainment for persons 25 to 29 years of age (1994)

Legend: Below upper secondary | Upper secondary | Non-university tertiary | University-level

Countries are ranked in descending order of the percentage of the unemployed with less than upper secondary attainment

R21(B): Youth unemployment and education

Table R21(B):
Youth unemployment rates by age group and level of educational attainment (1994)

	Below upper secondary education		Upper secondary education		Non-university tertiary education	University-level education	All levels of education	
	20-24	25-29	20-24	25-29	25-29	25-29	20-24	25-29
North America								
Canada	m	m	14.1	12.5	10.0	6.4	15.0	11.5
United States	22.3	17.2	10.6	7.8	4.7	3.1	10.8	7.4
Pacific Area								
Australia	18.8	13.2	11.1	8.2	m	5.4	13.9	9.6
European Union								
Austria	8.3	5.4	3.4	2.9	0.7	4.6	4.5	3.4
Belgium	29.1	18.5	16.9	11.1	4.6	8.7	20.4	11.7
Denmark	21.1	28.2	12.5	11.8	9.0	10.3	15.7	15.8
Finland	39.0	36.4	30.7	19.1	19.3	12.0	32.4	21.4
France	41.5	28.9	27.7	16.0	10.6	11.0	28.6	16.1
Germany	14.4	18.1	8.7	8.6	5.6	5.8	9.1	8.7
Greece	18.0	11.9	31.7	15.1	17.5	19.9	27.8	15.3
Ireland	33.3	25.7	15.3	10.6	7.3	5.1	20.3	14.2
Italy	27.4	15.9	34.5	16.3	m	28.4	30.8	17.0
Netherlands	11.4	10.0	7.5	5.4	m	7.4	m	7.1
Portugal	12.8	9.1	18.7	9.9	5.2	6.3	14.2	8.8
Spain	41.3	33.4	42.0	28.3	26.7	32.5	42.3	31.4
Sweden	28.6	15.8	16.4	10.6	5.8	5.6	16.7	9.9
United Kingdom	31.8	24.2	13.8	10.7	3.2	4.3	15.0	10.3
Other OECD countries								
Norway	16.0	16.0	11.5	6.7	6.2	4.5	11.1	7.1
Switzerland	x	x	(5.9)	(3.4)	m	m	(7.1)	(4.6)
Turkey	12.6	9.0	28.3	13.4	m	11.1	17.3	10.0
Country mean	**23.8**	**18.7**	**18.7**	**11.8**	**9.1**	**10.1**	**19.2**	**12.5**

Source: OECD Database. See Annex 3 for notes

R22: EDUCATION AND EARNINGS FROM EMPLOYMENT

This indicator shows the mean income from work of persons at a given level of educational attainment divided by the mean income from work of persons with upper secondary attainment.

POLICY CONTEXT

One (but not the only) way in which markets ensure the availability of sufficient numbers of persons needed to fulfil the skill requirements of modern economies and societies, is through monetary incentives, in particular through enhanced earnings from attaining higher levels of education. The pursuit of higher levels of attainment can also be viewed as an investment in human capital. The higher earnings that result represent the return on that investment and the premium paid to enhanced skills and/or to higher productivity. Finally, earnings differentials by educational attainment may be a reflection of differences in supply or in access to education.

KEY RESULTS

With a few minor exceptions, average earnings increase with educational attainment in all reporting OECD countries, for both men and women 25-64 years of age. However, there is considerable variation between countries in the earnings rewards for increased attainment, with certain countries showing a much broader range in earnings dispersion by educational attainment than others.

In all countries and at all attainment levels, the earnings of women are on average approximately one-half to three-quarters of the earnings of men, a result that is partly due to differences in the incidence of part-time work. In addition, there is only a relatively weak tendency for earnings differences between men and women to decrease with educational attainment.

DESCRIPTION AND INTERPRETATION

The earnings data in Tables R22.1 and R22.2 differ among countries in a number of ways that may render some country-to-country comparisons of relative earnings problematical. Caution should therefore be exercised in interpreting the results. In particular, for countries reporting annual earnings, differences in the incidence of part-year work among persons with different levels of educational attainment will have an effect on relative earnings that is not reflected in the data for countries reporting weekly or monthly earnings (see Definitions below).

University education offers a substantial earnings advantage compared to secondary education (see Table R22.1). Among countries reporting annual gross earnings, the earnings premium for university-level education ranges from about 40 per cent for men aged 25-64 in Denmark, Italy, the Netherlands and Switzerland to around 90 per cent in Finland and France. For women in the same age range, the premium is high in Ireland (87 per cent), Portugal (88 per cent) and exceptionally so in the United Kingdom, where university-level educated women show over twice the earnings of women with upper secondary education. On the other hand, the earnings premium is lower (about 40 per cent or less) for women in Austria, Denmark, Italy, the Netherlands and Spain.

Such variations in earnings premiums (before taxes) between countries reflect the effect of a number of factors, among them minimum wage legislation, the strength of unions, the coverage of collective bargaining agreements, the supply of workers at the various educational attainment levels, the relative work experience of the workers with high and low attainment, the distribution of employment by occupation and the relative incidence of part-time and part-year work among workers with varying levels of educational attainment.

University education appears to enhance earnings relative to secondary-level education more for women than for men in Australia, Belgium, Canada, Ireland, the Netherlands, Portugal, Switzerland, the United Kingdom and the United States, whereas the reverse is true in Austria, Denmark, Finland, France, Germany, Italy, New Zealand, Norway, Spain and Sweden.

Non-university tertiary education in all countries yields a considerably smaller earnings advantage than university education. The advantage of non-university tertiary education is typically 10 to 30 per cent among both men and women aged 25-64. In the United Kingdom the earnings advantage is 50 per cent for women, whereas in New Zealand and Spain men and women with non-university tertiary education actually show somewhat lower earnings than men and women with upper secondary attainment.

R22: Education and earnings from employment

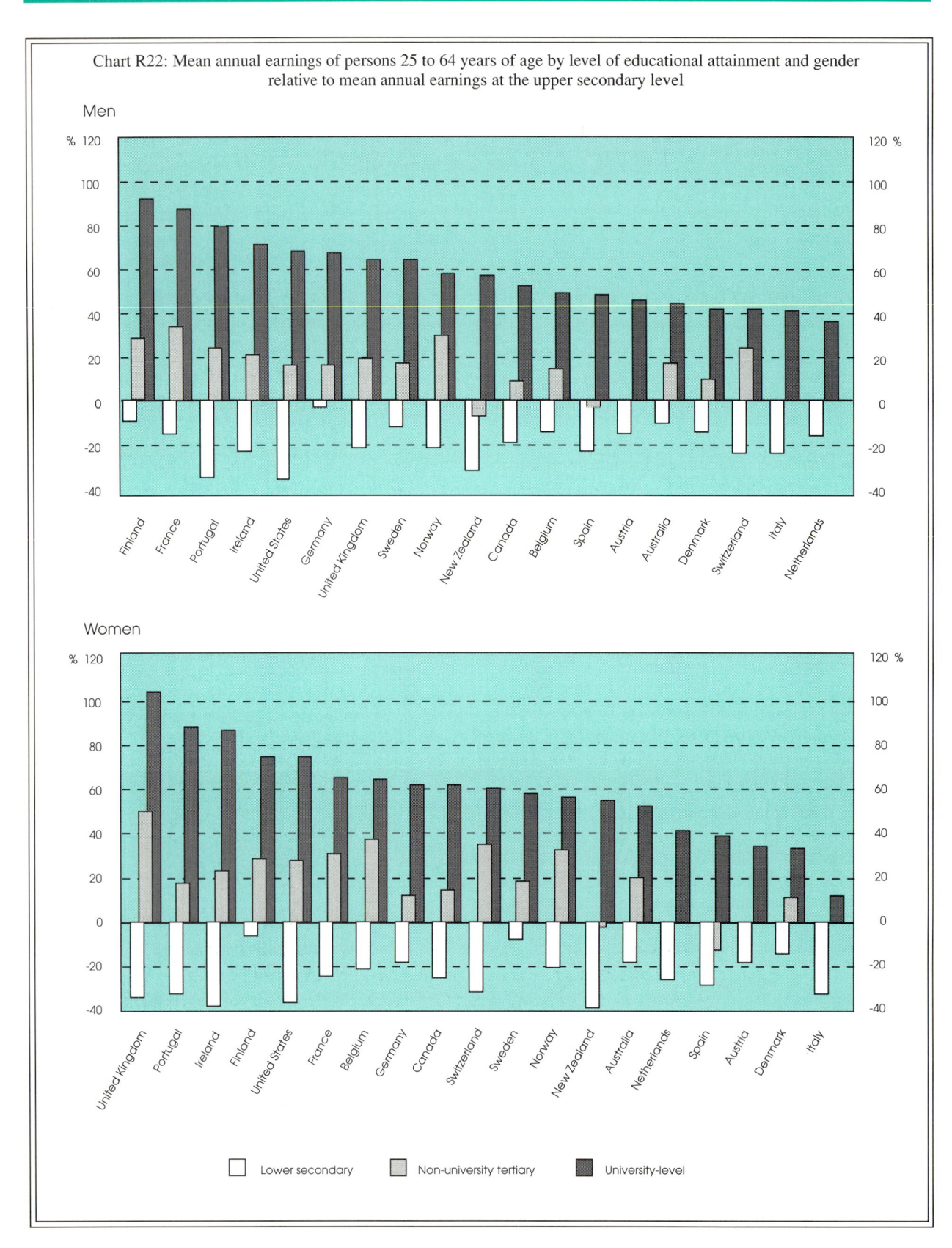

Chart R22: Mean annual earnings of persons 25 to 64 years of age by level of educational attainment and gender relative to mean annual earnings at the upper secondary level

Men

Women

Lower secondary — Non-university tertiary — University-level

R22: Education and earnings from employment

Earnings of men and women with less than upper secondary attainment are approximately 60 to 90 per cent of those of persons who have completed upper secondary education. In general, men with lower levels of education fare slightly better than women relative to upper secondary completers of the same gender.

Women's earnings range from about one-half (the Netherlands, New Zealand, Switzerland and the United Kingdom) to about three-quarters (Austria, Denmark, Finland, France, Italy, Portugal and Spain) of those of men (see Table R22.2). In countries in the first group, women show a much higher incidence of part-time work than men. In the second group, the picture is mixed, with Finland and Southern European countries showing low rates of part-time work in general but Austria, Denmark and France higher incidences for women than for men.

In a number of countries (Australia, Canada, Germany, the Netherlands, New Zealand, but especially in Ireland, Switzerland and the United Kingdom) earnings differentials between men and women tend to decrease with educational attainment. However, with the exception of the latter three countries, most of the reduction in earnings differentials has already occurred for persons at the upper secondary level. Moreover, in a number of other countries, namely Austria, Denmark, Finland, France, Italy and Sweden, the reverse relationship tends to be true, that is, earnings differences between men and women tend to increase with educational attainment, albeit weakly. Thus, although higher attainment levels do generally result in higher earnings for both men and women, they do not seem to contribute substantially to reductions in earnings inequality between the genders.

DEFINITIONS

Relative earnings from employment are defined as the mean income from work (before tax and excluding social transfers) of persons at a given level of educational attainment divided by the mean income from work of persons with upper secondary school attainment. This quotient is then multiplied by 100. The estimates are restricted to persons with income from employment during the reference period.

Earnings data in Tables R22.1 and R22.2 and Chart R22 for most countries are annual earnings. However, for France, Spain and Switzerland earnings data are monthly and for Australia they are weekly. Earnings for Italy are after taxes. Data cover only employees in Australia and France, and only earnings from the main employer in Australia. In Spain, persons who work less than fifteen hours per week are excluded.

The observed differences in relative earnings across countries therefore reflect not only differences in wage rates, but also differences in coverage, in the number of weeks worked per year and in hours worked per week. To the extent that lower levels of educational attainment are associated with fewer hours of work (in particular with part-time work) and with less stable employment (a greater likelihood of temporary employment or more susceptibility to unemployment over the course of a year), the relative earnings figures shown for the higher education levels in the tables and chart will be magnified over and above what would be observed from an examination of relative rates of pay.

R22: Education and earnings from employment

Table R22.1:
Relative earnings of persons 25 to 64 years of age with income from employment (upper secondary education = 100) by level of educational attainment and gender

	Year	Men Lower secondary education	Men Upper secondary education	Men Non-university tertiary education	Men University-level education	Women Lower secondary education	Women Upper secondary education	Women Non-university tertiary education	Women University-level education
North America									
Canada	1994	81	100	109	152	74	100	114	162
United States	1994	64	100	116	168	63	100	127	175
Pacific Area									
Australia	1993	90	100	117	144	81	100	120	152
New Zealand	1994	68	100	93	157	61	100	97	155
European Union									
Austria	1991	85	100	a	146	81	100	a	134
Belgium	1992	86	100	115	149	78	100	137	164
Denmark	1993	86	100	110	142	86	100	111	133
Finland	1993	91	100	128	192	94	100	129	175
France	1994	85	100	134	187	75	100	131	165
Germany	1994	97	100	116	167	81	100	111	162
Ireland	1993	77	100	121	171	62	100	123	187
Italy	1993	76	100	a	141	67	100	a	112
Netherlands	1993	84	100	a	136	73	100	a	141
Portugal	1993	65	100	124	179	67	100	117	188
Spain	1993	77	100	97	148	71	100	87	139
Sweden	1993	88	100	117	164	92	100	118	158
United Kingdom	1994	79	100	119	164	66	100	150	204
Other OECD countries									
Norway	1993	79	100	130	158	79	100	132	156
Switzerland	1994	76	100	124	142	68	100	135	160

Source: OECD Database. See Annex 3 for notes

R22: Education and earnings from employment

Table R22.2:
Mean annual earnings of women as a percentage of mean annual earnings of men 25 to 64 years of age, by level of educational attainment

	Year	Lower secondary education	Upper secondary education	Non-university tertiary education	University-level education	Total
North America						
Canada	1994	54	60	62	63	61
United States	1994	60	61	67	64	62
Pacific Area						
Australia	1993	59	65	67	68	62
New Zealand	1994	46	51	54	51	47
European Union						
Austria	1991	80	83	a	76	77
Denmark	1993	73	73	74	68	72
Finland	1993	82	81	81	73	78
France	1994	66	75	73	66	71
Germany	1994	53	64	62	62	59
Ireland	1993	45	56	57	61	59
Italy	1993	67	75	a	60	72
Netherlands	1993	44	51	a	53	49
Portugal	1993	72	69	66	73	72
Spain	1993	70	77	69	72	79
Sweden	1993	69	67	68	64	68
United Kingdom	1994	41	49	62	61	49
Other OECD countries						
Norway	1993	63	63	64	62	63
Switzerland	1994	47	53	57	60	49

Source: OECD Database. See Annex 3 for notes

R24: UNEMPLOYMENT RATES OF PERSONS LEAVING EDUCATION

This indicator shows the unemployment rates of persons who, at the beginning of a given year, were not enrolled in full-time education or training and who in the course of the preceding year had completed education at a particular level of the education system.

POLICY CONTEXT

The transition from school to work is a critical period for young people. This is the point at which the knowledge and skills imparted to them by modern education systems come up against the actual skill requirements of labour markets and enterprises. The extent to which school learning translates into work place skills and performance, and the work habits acquired at this stage, have a significant effect on social integration and future labour force activity and earnings. Since young workers represent the future production potential of economies, societies have an interest in ensuring that the transition occurs reasonably smoothly.

KEY RESULTS

The transition from school to work is a gradual one, with the unemployment rates of young persons one year after leaving school slowly decreasing as more and more of them find suitable jobs. Five years after leaving school, rates have nearly reached the levels characteristic of adult workers.

The handicap of low educational attainment makes itself felt very quickly in the labour market, with exceedingly high unemployment rates one year after leaving school, and persistent unemployment even five years later. This situation improves as one moves up the attainment ladder. Indeed, highly-educated young people are in general more fully integrated into the labour force in the first year after leaving school than their less-educated counterparts after five years.

DESCRIPTION AND INTERPRETATION

With about 90 per cent of an age cohort entering upper secondary education in many OECD countries (see Indicator R11), leavers from lower secondary education constitute a highly vulnerable group. They have lower rates of participation in the labour force and significantly higher rates of unemployment than leavers from upper secondary education. Labour markets in OECD countries discriminate strongly on the basis of educational attainment at entry into the labour force (see Chart R24). As a result, there are few opportunities for those with lower levels of education to overcome deficiencies in formal qualifications through on-the-job training or the accumulation of work experience. Even after five years, leavers from the lower secondary level of education have higher unemployment rates than the average for the total labour force after one year.

Leavers from upper secondary education also have relatively high rates of unemployment upon leaving school in some countries. In Finland, France and Spain the unemployment rates for this group are above 35 per cent after one year and remain at nearly 20 per cent (in Spain over 30 per cent) after five years. In Italy and Spain, almost one-half of university graduates in the labour force have still not found work one year after graduating. Labour demand in these countries is simply not able quickly to absorb the number of university graduates leaving the education system each year. In other countries, in particular Australia, Canada, Denmark, Finland, Ireland, Switzerland and the United States, university graduates rapidly move into jobs and show relatively low unemployment rates in the first year after completion of education.

To a certain extent, the difficult transition from school to work may be viewed in part as a "frictional" phenomenon that reflects inefficiencies in the matching of youth qualifications and job requirements and a lack of correspondence between the knowledge and skills imparted by education systems and the needs of labour markets. However, education systems are not designed purely to generate a steady supply of productive workers, but have larger societal aims, which include, for example, the formation of an informed citizenry capable of participating intelligently in public and social life. For many persons who leave school with low attainment, both of these aims may be threatened. Indeed, the inability to find gainful employment may result in social marginalisation that persists throughout life.

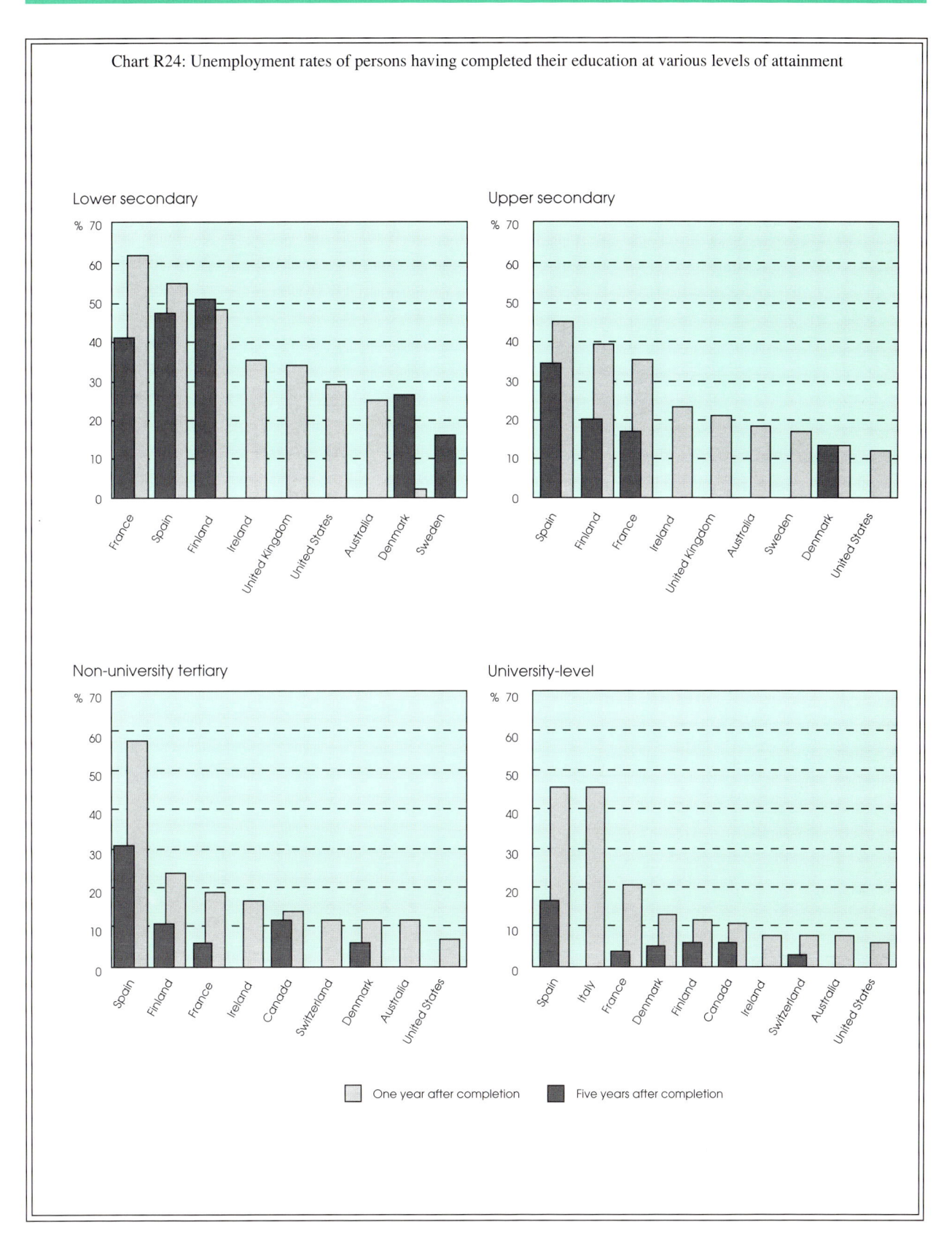

R24: Unemployment rates of persons leaving education

Chart R24: Unemployment rates of persons having completed their education at various levels of attainment

Lower secondary

Upper secondary

Non-university tertiary

University-level

☐ One year after completion   ■ Five years after completion

R24: Unemployment rates of persons leaving education

DEFINITIONS

"Leavers" from a particular level of the education system are defined here as persons who:
- at the beginning of a given year (whether the school year or the calendar year) were not enrolled in full-time education or training; and
- in the course of the preceding year had completed education at a particular level of the education system.

For some countries (Denmark, Ireland, the United States), the data include persons who may not have actually completed their education in the preceding year ("drop-outs"). Sources for the data may be administrative (Denmark, Finland, Switzerland) or sample surveys (all other countries). Sample surveys include Labour Force Surveys (France, the United States), special graduate or school leavers' surveys (Australia, Canada, Ireland, Sweden and the United Kingdom) or general purpose panel surveys (Spain).

R24: Unemployment rates of persons leaving education

Table R24: Unemployment rates of persons having completed their education at various levels of attainment

	Year	Gender	Lower secondary education	Upper secondary education	Non-university tertiary education	University-level education
One year after completion						
Australia	1994	M+W	25	18	12	8
		Men	28	14	16	m
		Women	21	25	m	m
Canada	1992	M+W	m	m	14	11
		Men	m	m	16	10
		Women	m	m	12	11
Denmark	1993	M+W	2	13	12	13
		Men	1	11	13	15
		Women	4	15	12	11
Finland	1994	M+W	48	39	24	12
		Men	49	46	25	12
		Women	48	34	23	13
France	1994	M+W	62	35	19	21
		Men	57	26	11	17
		Women	70	47	28	27
Ireland	1994	M+W	35	23	m	m
		Men	34	22	m	m
		Women	37	24	m	m
Ireland	1995	M+W	m	m	17	8
		Men	m	m	19	10
		Women	m	m	15	7
Italy	1994	M+W	m	m	m	46
		Men	m	m	m	43
		Women	m	m	m	48
Spain	1994	M+W	55	45	58	46
Sweden	1994	M+W	m	17	m	m
		Men	m	21	m	m
		Women	m	14	m	m
Switzerland	1993	M+W	m	m	12	8
United Kingdom	1994	M+W	34	21	m	m
United States	1994	M+W	29	12	7	6
		Men	24	11	9	7
		Women	36	13	6	6
Five years after completion						
Canada	1991	M+W	m	m	12	6
		Men	m	m	15	7
		Women	m	m	8	6
Denmark	1993	M+W	26	13	6	5
		Men	23	11	6	5
		Women	29	15	6	5
Finland	1994	M+W	51	20	11	6
		Men	54	22	13	6
		Women	46	19	10	7
France	1994	M+W	41	17	6	4
		Men	40	15	5	5
		Women	41	19	7	3
Spain	1994	M+W	47	34	31	17
		Men	39	21	13	29
		Women	56	49	56	10
Sweden	1992	M+W	16	m	m	m
		Men	19	m	m	m
		Women	13	m	m	m
Switzerland	1993	M+W	m	m	m	3

Source: OECD Database. See Annex 3 for notes

ANNOTATED ORGANISATION CHARTS OF EDUCATION SYSTEMS

The organisation charts represent the institutional structure of education systems. They provide information on:

- the ISCED levels of education to which major types of educational programmes and institutions have been assigned for the purpose of the OECD education indicators;
- typical student flows and recognised exit points in the education system;
- the degrees and qualifications awarded after the successful completion of major educational programmes;
- the theoretical duration of studies in the programme types as well as typical starting and ending ages.

Except where otherwise indicated, the size of the graphical elements provides no indication of the size of the enrolment in the corresponding educational institutions.

Institutional structures are colour-coded by ISCED level of education (colour codes are explained at the left hand side of each diagram). In addition, programmes specifically designed for part-time attendance are indicated in *pink*. Vocational education and training programmes are indicated in *mauve*. Arrows in *blue* indicate common student flows. For some countries numbers on these blue arrows indicate the proportion of completers who take this route. Blue triangles indicate recognised exit points of the education system. Names on *grey* background indicate types of educational institutions or programmes. Names on *red* background indicate degrees and qualifications awarded after successful completion of the corresponding programme. Arabic numbers indicate typical starting and ending ages. Roman numbers indicate theoretical years of study in the corresponding programme.

The organisation charts as well as the accompanying descriptions have been prepared and approved by the national education authorities. The terminology used may vary from country to country and may differ from the terminology that has been used in the description of the indicators.

Australia / Australie

Education System Diagram

Typical age / **ISCED levels** / **Years of study**

ISCED 7 (age 23+)
- DOCTORATES (IX)
- MASTER'S DEGREES AND POST-GRADUATE DIPLOMAS (VI, VII, VIII)

ISCED 6
- BACHELOR'S DEGREE (IV, V)
- ADVANCED DIPLOMA, DIPLOMA (I, II, III)

UNIVERSITY

ISCED 5 (age 18)
- CERTIFICATE IV
- DIPLOMA
- ADVANCED DIPLOMAS

ISCED 3
- CERTIFICATE III (includes most trades)
- CERTIFICATE II
- CERTIFICATE I

VOCATIONAL EDUCATION & TRAINING

VOCATIONAL EDUCATION AND TRAINING SECTOR

ISCED 3 (typical age 16–17)
- SENIOR SECONDARY CERTIFICATES OF EDUCATION (XI, XII)

UPPER SECONDARY EDUCATION

ISCED 2 (age 12–15)
- VII, VIII, IX, X

LOWER SECONDARY EDUCATION

ISCED 1 (typical age 5–12)
- Kindergarten / Preparatory year
- I, II, III, IV, V, VI, VII

PRIMARY EDUCATION

ISCED 0 (typical age 3–5)
PRE-SCHOOL EDUCATION

SPECIAL EDUCATION

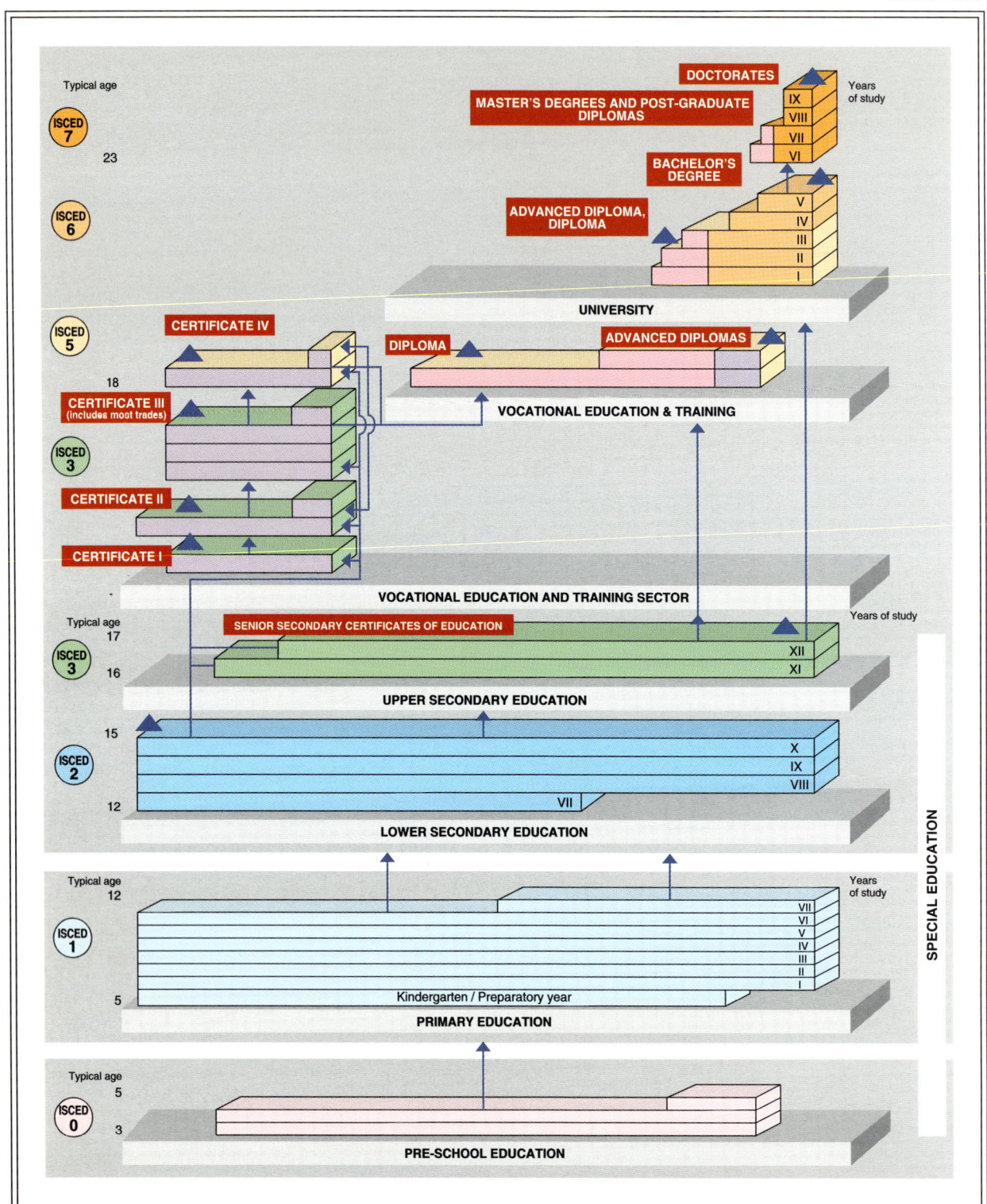

Colour codes (for details see page 249): **Pink** - Programme designed for part-time attendance. **Mauve** - Vocational education and training. **Blue triangle** - Recognised exit point of the education system. **Blue arrow** - Typical student flow. The size of the graphical elements provides no indication of the enrolment in the corresponding educational institutions.

Codes couleur (voir la page 249) : *Rose - Programmes expressément à temps partiel. Mauve - Enseignement et formation professionnels. Triangle bleu - Point de sortie officiel du système éducatif. Flèche bleue - Progression typique des élèves ou étudiants. La taille des différents blocs ne représente pas la proportion des effectifs dans les établissements d'enseignement correspondants.*

Australia

1. GENERAL CONTEXT

Australia is an island continent occupying almost 8 million square kilometres and has a population of about 18 million. Largely due to immigration, the population has a younger age structure than most other developed countries. It is also highly urbanised with 71.5 per cent of people living in state/territory capital cities (including Canberra, the national capital) and is concentrated in two distinct and widely separated coastal regions. The largest lies in the south-east and east, while there is a smaller concentration in the south-west corner. The centre and north of Australia are sparsely populated.

Australia has a federal political structure comprising six state and two territory governments as well as a federal (Commonwealth) government. The Australian Constitution does not grant the Commonwealth responsibility for education. The Commonwealth, however, has played an increasingly important role in funding education, particularly at university level, and also in co-ordination. The states and territories administer their own school and Technical and Further Education (TAFE) systems. While there is no national education system as such, there are few significant differences among the state systems and, over the last decade in particular, state Education Ministers in association with the Commonwealth have worked to minimise problems associated with differences in year levels and nomenclature.

Australia has a diversified economy, which in recent years has been subject to increased international competition due to a general reduction in protection for domestic industries and some deregulation of the financial sector. In general, the goods-producing industries such as agriculture, manufacturing, mining and utilities have been experiencing declining shares of output and employment, while service-providing industries have been growing.

Education in Australia is dominated by public institutions (though non-government schools are important). Government schools enrol about 71 per cent of the school population and operate under the direct responsibility of the state Education Minister. The scattered rural population has necessitated a large number of very small primary schools, although their number is declining. Non-government schools operate under conditions determined by government registration authorities and are required to meet specified education standards and use satisfactory premises. Almost all non-government schools have some religious affiliation, mostly with the Catholic Church. Almost all tertiary students attend a public university or TAFE college.

There has been an emphasis in education policy on ensuring basic equality of resource provision in the public systems and on assisting low-income private schools (most of which are in the Catholic sector). Distance education continues to play an important role, not only in rural areas, but increasingly for tertiary study in urban centres as well.

2. EDUCATIONAL STRUCTURE AND ENROLMENTS

Early childhood education is available, normally on a part-time basis, before commencing primary school. Most children start primary school at the age of 5, and primary education covers 7 or 8 years depending on the state concerned. Secondary education commences at around age 12 and continues for 6 or 5 years (depending on the length of primary education). There are around 1.8 million primary and 1.3 million secondary students.

Education is compulsory between the ages of 6 and 15 (16 in Tasmania) and about three-quarters of students now complete Year 12, the final year of secondary education, twice the proportion as compared to 1980. The growing diversity of the senior secondary school population has stimulated major reviews of the secondary curriculum, pedagogy and assessment.

The tertiary sector comprises colleges of Technical and Further Education (TAFE), private vocational education providers and universities. Vocational education and training is mainly delivered through the TAFE college system, although private providers, senior secondary schools and universities also play a role. About 300 TAFE colleges provide a wide variety of courses, including pre-employment programmes, apprenticeships, off-the-job training, retraining programmes and adult education. TAFE enrols more than a million students, although most of these are enrolled part-time and in relatively short courses. Vocational education and training in Australia is being reorganised through the Modern Australian Apprenticeship and Traineeship system (MAATS), which aims to extend entry-level training to a wider range of enterprises. Australian governments are committed to quality in vocational education and training and this has found expression in client surveys, pilot projects on quality assurance and a best practice demonstration programme.

The higher education sector went through substantial change during the late 1980s. The former "binary system" consisting of universities and colleges of advanced education was replaced by a Unified National System (UNS) consisting of only universities. Under the binary system, universities were seen as centres of scholarship and research, while colleges were seen as possessing more vocational objectives. Associated with the establishment of the UNS was the amalgamation of many former colleges of advanced education with universities to achieve sizes where economies of scale could be realised both in terms of cost-efficiency and educational effectiveness. This resulted in a decrease in the number of higher education institutions which are now part of the UNS, from 78 in 1982 to 36 in 1995, and an increase in the average size of each institution, from 4 000 in 1982 to 17 000 in 1995. The university sector as a whole provides a full range of undergraduate and post-graduate programmes, although not all institutions offer programmes in every discipline.

Changes to the structure of the higher education sector occurred in a climate of rapid growth in student enrolments. Over the decade to 1995, the number of students enrolled in higher education increased by 63 per cent to 604 000. Within this environment of strong growth, there was a significant shift to post-graduate studies with the number of post-graduate degree students growing by 178 per cent to 74 000 in 1995. The number of female students grew more quickly than males, with women currently accounting for 54 per cent of all students compared to 49 per cent in 1985. A feature of student attendance at higher education institutions in Australia is the high proportion of students who attend on other than a full-time basis. In 1995 some 41 per cent of students attended higher education either part-time or externally.

About 50 per cent of Year 12 graduates enter university within a year or two of completing secondary school. Entry to higher education is normally based on academic results in either school or external examinations and is restricted by the number of places funded by the government. About one in seven commencing

Australia

undergraduate students is now admitted on the basis of special entry provisions, rather than on the basis of school performance.

Education assistance and income support is provided through Commonwealth programmes aiming to promote equality in educational opportunities. Particular areas of focus are persons on low incomes, Aboriginal and Torres Strait Islander people and those living in geographically isolated areas. Expenditure on AUSTUDY, the major student income support scheme, amounted to A$ 1 573 million in 1995/96 or an average A$ 3 266 per recipient. Expenditure on ABSTUDY, providing income support for Aboriginal and Torres Strait Islander students, amounted to a further A$ 128 million in 1995/96. In addition, expenditure under the Assistance for Isolated Children scheme was A$ 28 million in 1995/96. Most allowances under the schemes of assistance are subject to a means-test, which includes an income and an assets test.

3. EDUCATIONAL FINANCE AND COSTS

The Commonwealth and state governments provide about 92 per cent of the funds spent on education. The contribution drops by about 10 percentage points if income support and other grants to students/households are excluded. The states provide about 60 per cent of all public expenditure on education, and the Commonwealth 40 per cent.

State and territory governments provide about 90 per cent of the funding for government schools and the Commonwealth about 10 per cent. The Commonwealth is the major source of public funding for non-government schools, providing 65 per cent compared with 35 per cent by state governments. The Commonwealth also provides supplementary resources to the states for TAFE.

Owing to an environment of fiscal restraint in recent years, there have been greater calls for educational institutions to be more accountable for the funds they receive. In the school system, emphasis is now placed on assessing and reporting student performance and on evaluating teachers.

Government schools do not charge fees, while the private school sector levies tuition fees, which can vary substantially among different types of schools. University students pay about one-fifth of the average cost of a higher education place (about A$ 2 400 for an equivalent full-time student load in 1994). Students can decide between paying the annual sum on enrolment each semester or deferring payment until their earnings exceed a certain level. Under the latter arrangement, repayments are collected through the income tax system. TAFE colleges generally charge only low fees. Universities and TAFE colleges are now encouraged to raise more of their funds independently through enrolling overseas students (many of whom pay full fees), tailoring fee-paying courses for industry and attracting commissioned research.

Cost estimates per student are highly sensitive to the definitions applied. In 1994 expenditure per student (excluding private transportation costs and household incidental expenditure but including university research costs) was about A$ 4 100 per annum for primary school students, A$ 6 300 for secondary school students, A$ 3 000 for TAFE students (A$ 8 400 per full-time equivalent) and A$ 11 750 for university students (A$ 15 200 per full-time equivalent).

4. CURRICULUM AND ASSESSMENT

There is no common school curriculum across the country, although the differences among states are not substantial in most curriculum areas. In 1989 the states and the Commonwealth agreed on broad goals for schooling, and there have been a number of co-operative curriculum developments since that time. Within each state, a central authority specifies broad guidelines and, increasingly, some of the fine details of curriculum as well. The curriculum is most precisely specified at the upper secondary level, at which most states issue school certificates. These normally combine external and school-based assessment. At these levels, students generally have more scope to specialise. A recent survey indicated that around 25 per cent of Year 12 students specialise in mathematics and science courses, 25 per cent in humanities and arts and 10 per cent in commerce, while the remainder study subjects from a diverse range of fields.

In most schools, students are automatically promoted between year levels according to age. There is considerable interest in developing profile statements that provide detailed accounts of student achievement in a wide range of academic, personal and social areas.

Curriculum development in the TAFE sector is usually a collaborative activity between educators and representatives of industry and government. Universities have responsibility for their own curricula and assessment, although in some disciplines industry bodies play a significant role.

5. TEACHERS

Schools employ about 200 000 teachers (in full-time equivalent terms) and a further 50 000 persons in non-teaching positions. The majority of school teachers are female, especially among early childhood and primary teachers. The states are responsible for determining acceptable teacher qualifications. Teacher training occurs in universities with Bachelor of Education being a common qualification. The normal length of initial training for secondary teachers is currently four years, and three years for primary teachers. Many teachers subsequently upgrade their qualifications. As part of the general movement towards greater accountability, most school systems have moved to give more emphasis to merit, as opposed to seniority, in promotion decisions.

The combination of an ageing teaching force, relatively stable student enrolments and restrictions in government expenditure has meant that there is currently an oversupply of primary and secondary teachers, and teacher education faculties in universities have been reduced in size over the past decade.

In full-time equivalent terms, there are about 81 000 people employed by universities, of which about 36 000 are academic staff. A significant trend in recent years has been a move away from tenured employment of academic staff in favour of greater emphasis on contract employment.

Austria

1. GENERAL CONTEXT

Austria is a landlocked country in the centre of Europe. It covers an area of 83 858 square kilometres and has a population of 8 million. About 97 per cent of the population speak German, but there are small ethnic minorities of Slovenians, Croatians, Hungarians and Czechs. About 78 per cent of the population are Roman Catholic. Although there is some international migration, the population is ageing and it is expected that the school population will decrease after the year 2000.

In 1995 about 7 per cent of the labour force were employed in agriculture/forestry, 32 per cent in industry and 61 per cent in the service sector. GDP per capita was US$ 20 210 in 1994 (in purchasing power parity). Unemployment was 3.7 per cent in 1995.

Austria has a federal political structure comprising 9 provinces (*Länder*) and a federal government. General legislation for all educational matters rests with the federal parliament. Provincial parliaments can pass minor bylaws concerning compulsory schools. The organisation of schools and the curriculum and arrangements of school life are much the same throughout the country. School inspection and administration are carried out by the Ministry of Educational and Cultural Affairs as well as by lower-level bodies at the regional level (*Land*) and district level (*Bezirk*).

Thirty two per cent of the 25-64 year-old population have not completed more than compulsory school, 62 per cent have a qualification at the upper secondary level, and 7 per cent have some kind of post-secondary qualification. In recent years, educational attainments have risen significantly. Among the 20-24 year-old population, 80 per cent have a qualification above compulsory school.

2. EDUCATIONAL STRUCTURE AND ENROLMENTS

Pre-primary education is not compulsory but the majority of 3 to 6 year-olds attend some type of pre-primary education, and demand exceeds supply. Education is compulsory between the ages of 6 and 15 years. All schools are co-educational, and about 6 per cent of the pupils attend private schools which are mostly run by the Roman Catholic Church or affiliated institutions. Most private schools conform to State laws and can issue certificates equivalent to those of State schools.

Primary school (*Volksschule*) has four grades. If the school authorities consider that a child is not mature enough to attend the first grade of primary school, the child is placed in a pre-school class in primary school. This is the case for about 10 per cent of the children.

Lower secondary school also has four grades. Children have an option to enter either the general secondary school (*Hauptschule*) or the lower cycle of the academic secondary school (formally known as *allgemeinbildende höhere Schule* but commonly known as the *Gymnasium*). To enter the *Hauptschule* they must have completed the last grade or primary school, whereas to enter the *Gymnasium* they must have high attainments in primary school. On average about 30 per cent of an age cohort enter the *Gymnasium*, a fraction that varies widely, however, between urban and rural areas. The curriculum is similar in both types of school. There is little transfer between school types. Over the last 30 years this level of school has been subject to controversy between proponents and opponents of comprehensive schooling.

There are special schools for children with mental or physical disabilities (*Sonderschulen*). In 1995 enrolment was 2 per cent (primary level) and 2.6 per cent (lower secondary level). Numbers are decreasing as "mainstreaming" has become the norm, but the parents decide whether their child should enter a regular or a special school.

Students who do not continue full-time schooling at the upper secondary level usually enrol in the *Polytechnischen Lehrgang* which lasts for one year. Most of them proceed with vocational training afterwards. The special feature of the dual vocational programme is that apprentices get a practical training in firms where they are employed and attend school (*Berufsschule*), typically for one day a week. Successful completion results in a vocational licence. About one-quarter of all firms (50 000 of 200 000) train apprentices for 227 different trades and occupations. Between 40 and 45 per cent of an age cohort receives this type of education.

For students who continue full-time schooling at the upper secondary level, there is a choice between three types:

- The intermediate vocational and technical school (*berufsbildende mittlere Schule*) is basically a full-time school equivalent to the dual system programme. In 1994 enrolment was 13 per cent of the relevant age group.
- The higher vocational and technical school (*berufsbildende höhere Schule*) lasts for 5 years. Students graduate with a *Reifeprüfung*, a final examination which qualifies for admission at universities. At the same time they have a vocational qualification equivalent to that gained in the dual system. In 1994 enrolment was 24 per cent of the relevant age group.
- The upper cycle of the *Gymnasium* lasts for 4 years. At the end, students take the *Reifeprüfung*. In 1994 enrolment was 18 per cent of the relevant age group.

In 1994, 30 000 students (32 per cent of the relevant age group) graduated with a *Reifeprüfung*. In the same year, 28 000 students continued with some sort of post-secondary education. Post-secondary education can be divided into courses which are regarded as higher education (*Universitäten, Kunsthochschulen, Fachhochschulen*) and other courses (e.g. teacher training for compulsory schools). About 90 per cent of all students at the post-secondary level are enrolled in universities. There is "open access" which means that all students who have passed the *Reifeprüfung* are entitled to enrol in any Austrian university. The first degree is the *Diplom*, a degree often considered equivalent to a Master's degree. The minimum duration of programmes leading to this degree is 4-5 years. The actual study duration, however, is 7.5 years on average. This is partly due to the fact that all students are considered full-time students even though many of them may actually study part-time. After the *Diplom* students can continue with a doctoral course (*Doktoratsstudium*).

Kunsthochschulen and *Fachhochschulen* do not have open access. Enrolment in *Kunsthochschulen* requires an entrance examination to prove artistic talent. Entrance in *Fachhochschulen* (which exist since 1994) is restricted by the number of places available.

Austria

3. EDUCATIONAL FINANCE AND COSTS

Attendance at State schools and universities is free. Additionally, the State provides family allowances and free transportation up to the age of 27, direct study grants, talent scholarships, subsidies for studies abroad and subsidised health insurance for students.

Ownership of public educational institutions is shared by different levels of government. Compulsory schools are run by the municipalities (*Gemeinden*), their teachers are employed by the *Länder*, but their salaries are refunded by the federal government. *Berufsschulen* are run by the *Länder*; for these schools the federal government refunds only half of the teachers' salaries. All other schools and all public institutions of higher education are run and funded by the federal government.

In 1993, public expenditure for pre-school and school education was Sch 87.1 billion. Public expenditure for post-secondary education was Sch 22.3 billion. The total educational expenditure represented 5.3 per cent of GDP.

4. CURRICULUM AND ASSESSMENT

Syllabuses, which can be considered as "frame curricula", are uniform throughout the country for all schools. They are prepared by expert commissions within the Ministry of Educational and Cultural Affairs after having been shaped by a complex consultation process involving all influential social interest groups (e.g. employers' and employees' organisations, churches, teacher associations and so on), the provinces and subject matter specialists. These syllabuses specify the general aims of each subject at each grade level as well as the didactic principles; they also contain a table of subjects listing the number of lessons per grade per week. The selection and further specification of the objectives in the syllabus, as well as the way in which they are taught, are left to the individual teachers. In practice, however, it is the textbooks which define the content and methods to a large extent. All textbooks and other instructional materials must be approved by expert commissions of the Ministry.

Promotion from one grade to the next is on the basis of continuous assessment carried out by the class teacher and leading annually to a "school report" with marks between 1 (excellent) and 5 (poor). Students who fail in two subjects (or in one subject if they are considered not mature enough) have to repeat the class. Repetition in compulsory school is rare, but in the more selective schools, especially in higher vocational and technical schools, more than 10 per cent of the students are not eligible for promotion. There are policy efforts to reform the system of promotion. Upper secondary school ends with an examination.

Study courses at universities are regulated by federal law and "fine-tuned" by universities' study commissions. These regulations provide an even wider framework than at the school level and leave individual teachers broad discretion to shape their course. Failure at universities is significantly higher than in schools. Fewer than 50 per cent of the first time entrants complete their studies with a *Diplom*.

There is no external evaluation of schools or universities and no external assessment of student achievement. The system of educational statistics is well developed but only for input variables.

5. TEACHERS

About 119 000 teachers are employed in the school system, representing 3 per cent of the labour force. About 65 per cent are women and 8 per cent work in private institutions; 78 000 are *Landeslehrer* who teach in compulsory schools and 41 000 are employed by the federal State (*Bundeslehrer*).

There are two major types of teacher qualifications. *Landeslehrer* undergo three-year courses at teacher training academies and perform their training at training schools attached to the academies. *Bundeslehrer* who teach at academic secondary, intermediate and upper vocational schools are trained in two academic subjects at universities. About 20 per cent of training time is devoted to education. After graduating from this course they undertake a one-year school-based induction phase organised by the school authorities.

Attendance at teacher in-service training courses is voluntary except for new curricula introduction courses. These courses are provided by pedagogical institutes that exist in every province.

In 1995 the total academic staff of *Universitäten* and *Kunsthochschulen* was 10 700 in full-time equivalents, 2 300 of whom were professors. About one-quarter of all teaching is done by free-lance lecturers. Employed academic staff usually start with a temporary 4-year contract, during which time they are supposed to finish their doctoral degree. After a further 6 years of temporary contract, they are supposed to finish their *Habilitation* which gives them full teaching authorisation in their field. *Habilitation* is also a prerequisite for appointment as a professor.

Austria

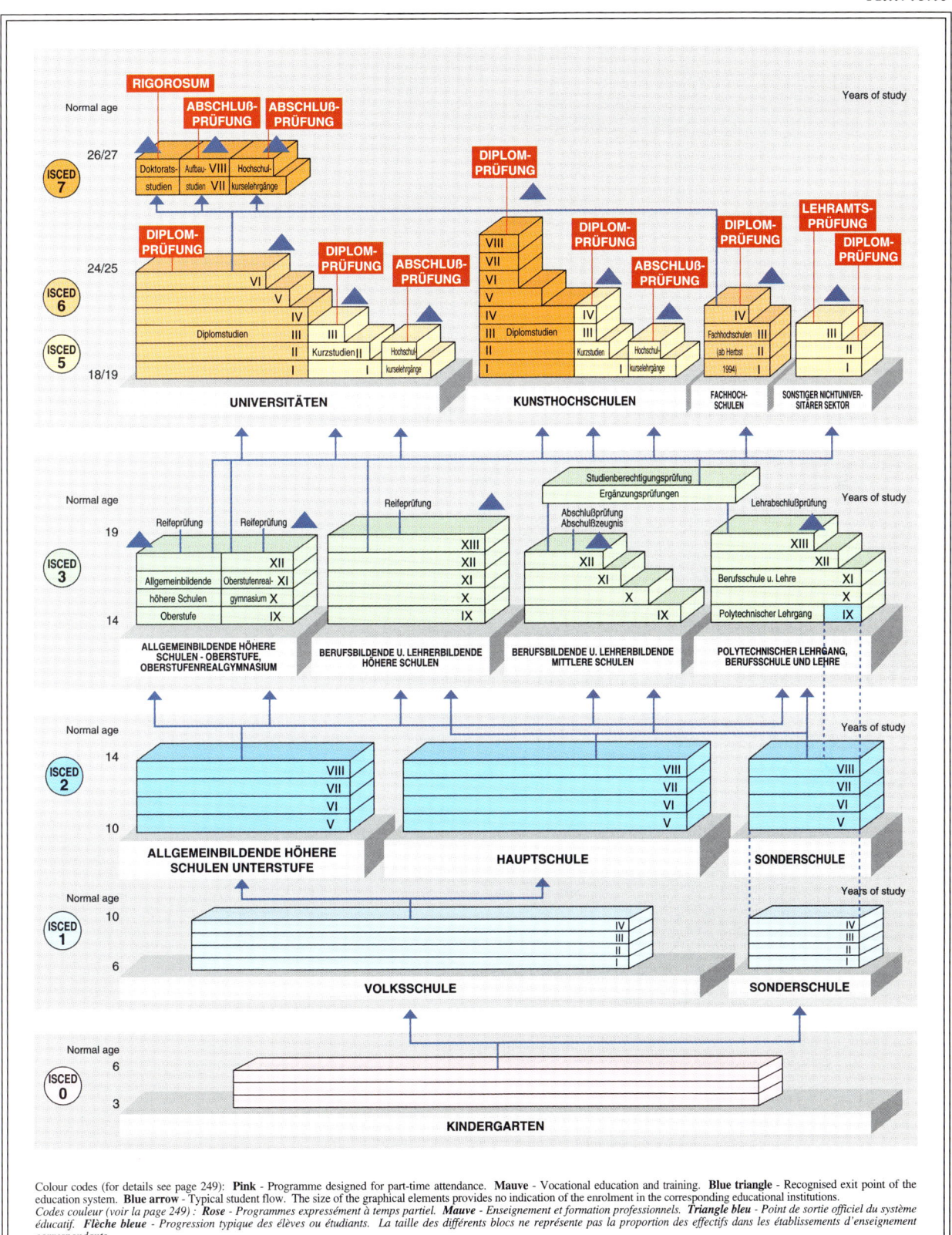

Autriche

Belgium (Flemish Community)

Belgique (Communauté flamande)

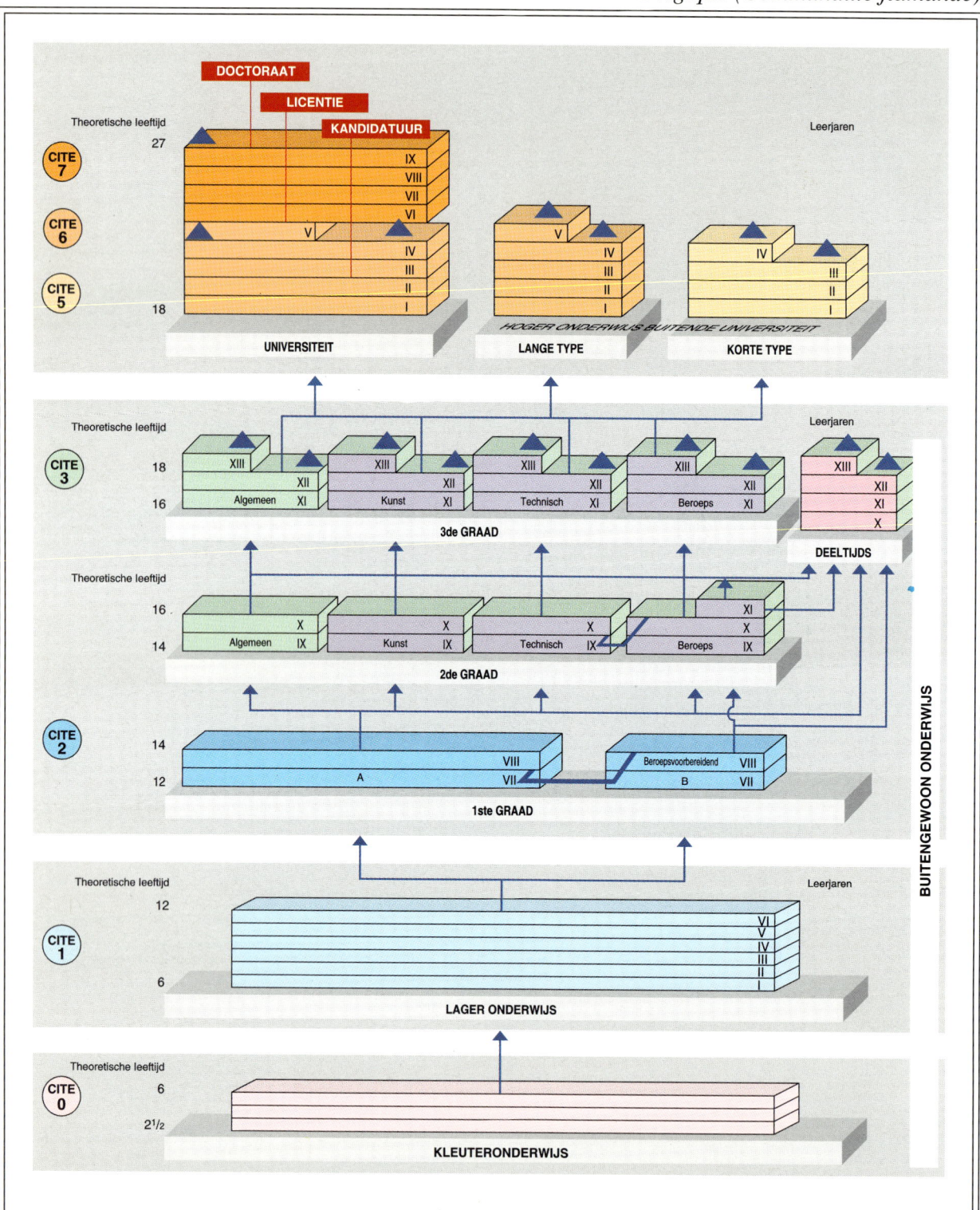

Colour codes (for details see page 249): **Pink** - Programme designed for part-time attendance. **Mauve** - Vocational education and training. **Blue triangle** - Recognised exit point of the education system. **Blue arrow** - Typical student flow. The size of the graphical elements provides no indication of the enrolment in the corresponding educational institutions.
*Codes couleur (voir la page 249) : **Rose** - Programmes expressément à temps partiel. **Mauve** - Enseignement et formation professionnels. **Triangle bleu** - Point de sortie officiel du système éducatif. **Flèche bleue** - Progression typique des élèves ou étudiants. La taille des différents blocs ne représente pas la proportion des effectifs dans les établissements d'enseignement correspondants.*

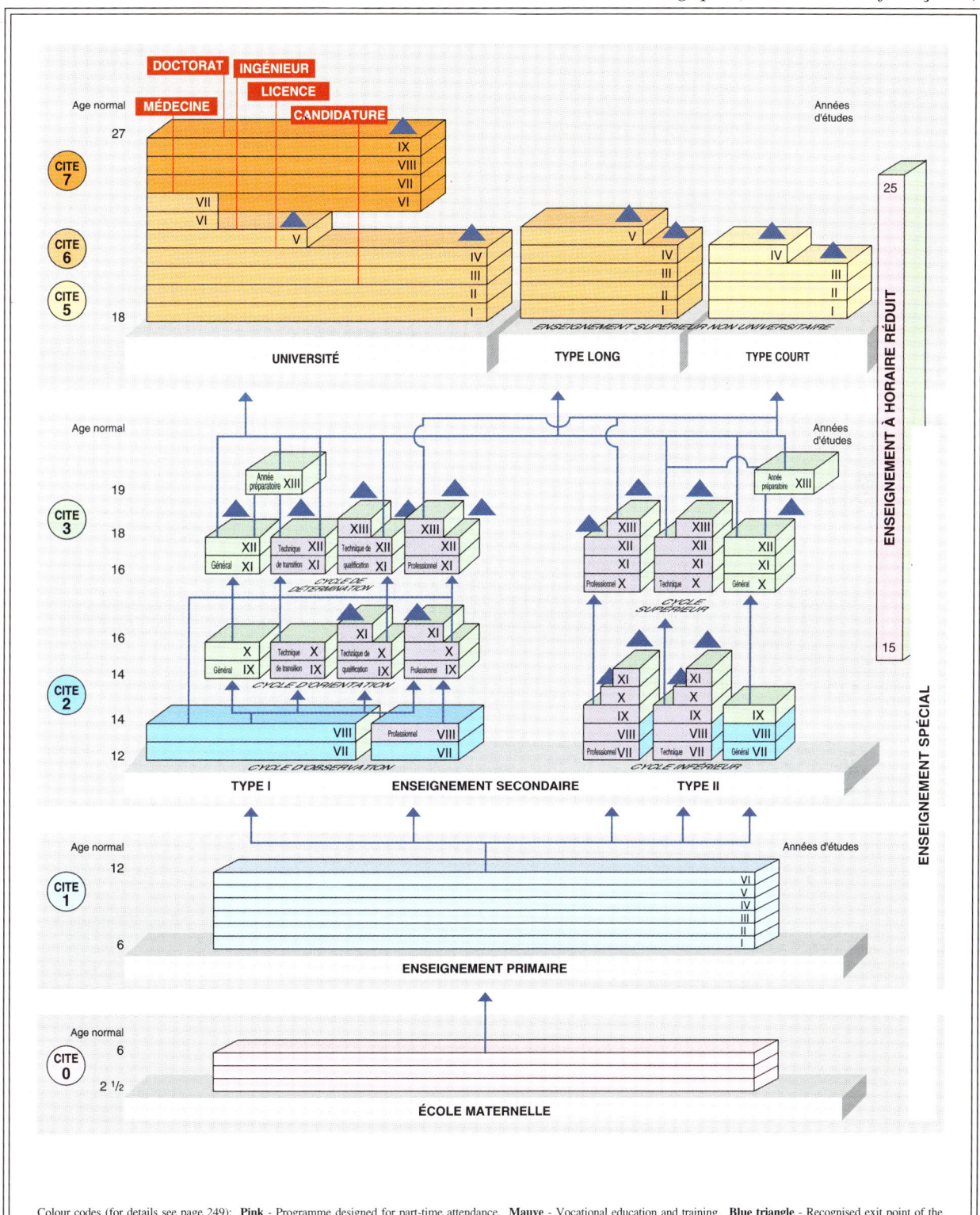

Belgium (French Community)

Belgique (Communauté française)

Colour codes (for details see page 249): **Pink** - Programme designed for part-time attendance. **Mauve** - Vocational education and training. **Blue triangle** - Recognised exit point of the education system. **Blue arrow** - Typical student flow. The size of the graphical elements provides no indication of the enrolment in the corresponding educational institutions.

*Codes couleur (voir la page 249) : **Rose** - Programmes expressément à temps partiel. **Mauve** - Enseignement et formation professionnels. **Triangle bleu** - Point de sortie officiel du système éducatif. **Flèche bleue** - Progression typique des élèves ou étudiants. La taille des différents blocs ne représente pas la proportion des effectifs dans les établissements d'enseignement correspondants.*

Belgium (Flemish and French Communities)

1. GENERAL CONTEXT

Belgium has an area of 30 518 square kilometres and a population of 10 million with a density of 331 inhabitants per square kilometre. Since 1970 the rate of demographic growth has been well below 1 per cent per year. Foreigners represent 9 per cent of the population but 11 per cent of the school population. Despite continuing immigration of young foreigners, the average age of the population is increasing. More than 60 per cent of all immigrants are from the European Union, Italy in particular.

The State of Belgium was created in 1830 and is a constitutional and parliamentary monarchy. A progressive federalisation movement, in existence since 1970, resulted in the adoption of a constitutional amendment in 1988, under the terms of which the country became a federation of three regions: Flanders in the north, Wallonie in the south and Brussels, the capital, in Flemish territory. However, in respect of private and cultural matters, including education, there is a second federal subdivision into three linguistic communities: the Flemish Community, consisting of the region of Flanders and the Flemish-speakers in the region of Brussels; the French Community, consisting of the major part of the region of Wallonie and the French-speakers in the Brussels region; and the German-speaking Community at the eastern end of Wallonie. Each community has its own parliament, government and ministries. The Flemish, French and German Ministries of Education are responsible for their own education systems, with 57.5, 42 and 0.5 per cent of the school population respectively.

There has been a decrease in the number of children enrolled in pre-school, primary and secondary education, but an increase, especially since 1990, of students in higher education. It should also be noted that in 1995 the unemployment rate was 10 per cent of the workforce but 24 per cent among young people under the age of 25.

The following describes the education systems in the Flemish- and French-speaking communities.

2. EDUCATIONAL STRUCTURE AND ENROLMENTS

The 1983 compulsory school attendance act obliges parents to see that their children attend school for 12 years – from the month of September in the year of the student's 6th birthday until the end of June of the year in which the student turns 18. Compulsory school attendance applies for Belgians as well as for foreigners. Under special conditions children may also be educated at home. As from the age of 15-16, compulsory attendance can be part-time in the framework of the "dual" system of education and training.

Before compulsory education, early childhood education is provided for children from the age of two-and-a-half to six, and nearly all children are enrolled. For example, 97 per cent of three year-olds and 100 per cent of four and five year-olds are enrolled in this stage of education.

Primary education normally covers six years, from the age of 6 to 12.

It is at the secondary education stage that the Flemish and French Communities begin to differ. The Flemish system has three cycles of two years each. This structure may be modified by the addition of an optional third year in the third cycle of general, technical, artistic and vocational secondary education and by a third year in the second cycle of vocational secondary education.

The French system has three cycles of two years each, called *observation* (12-13 years), *orientation* (14-15 years) and *détermination* (16-17 years). After the three cycles, a seventh optional year of general, technical, artistic and vocational programmes may follow, the successful completion of which, in the case of vocational education, opens entry to higher education.

When students graduate at the end the seventh year in the vocational streams, they have the right to enter higher education, except in engineering where they must sit an entrance exam. As of 1997, the Flemish Community will also organise an entrance exam for medical studies.

Special education for children with disabilities runs parallel to early childhood, primary and secondary education. These children may also follow regular education while benefiting from special aid programmes.

At the secondary level there are also adult education programmes and vocational courses organised by bodies other than the Ministry of Education for those, both young people and adults, who have dropped out of school but wish to acquire new qualifications.

There are three types of higher education institutions: universities and non-university higher education institutions which organise both short (one cycle) and long (two cycles) programmes. At university there are three cycles: the first covers two or three years. The second cycle, also covering two or three years, leads to a *licence* or the equivalent. The third cycle leads to a doctorate or an equivalent degree.

Non-university education programmes with two cycles are similar in structure to the first two cycles of university-level education. Short programmes last for three years. At the secondary level there are adult education and various vocational programmes.

3. EDUCATIONAL FINANCE AND COSTS

The general principle of financing education was fixed in January 1989 by a law according to which each Community finances educational institutions in the form of a block grant to the schools within its jurisdiction and for which it receives block grants from the federal State. This block grant is to cover teachers' salaries and the running, maintenance and replacement costs of equipment and buildings. The subsidy received by a school is based on its enrolment and the type of education it provides.

Compulsory schooling is free and parents cannot be asked to contribute. In higher education, however, enrolment in any course of studies is subject to payment of a registration fee.

About 85 per cent (in the Flemish Community) and 88 per cent (in the French Community) of educational expenditure is on teachers' salaries. In the Flemish and French Communities, 42.5 per cent and nearly 43 per cent of the total annual budget are allocated to secondary education respectively.

Belgium (Flemish and French Communities)

4. CURRICULUM AND ASSESSMENT

The authorities have the task of making the minimum expectations of the community clearly known with regards to education. This is necessary to ensure the quality of education.

In the Flemish Community, the "attainment target" concept has been introduced for this purpose. Attainment targets are minimum aims that must be reached by the majority of students in their respective disciplines. The targets relate to knowledge, insight, educational attitudes and skills.

As far as early childhood, special education and the first year of the *B*-programme of secondary schooling (a special year with an adapted curriculum for children who experience learning difficulties in their primary schooling) are concerned, the term "developmental objectives" is used to refer to the skills a school must strive for but need not actually achieve.

The aim is not to replace the curricula with the attainment targets or development objectives. Curricula will remain the responsibilities of the organising powers. They will, however, have to include the attainment targets or developmental objectives.

As from 1 September 1997, developmental objectives for nursery schools and attainment targets for primary education will come into effect. Attainment targets will be developed for secondary education as well.

The inspectorate examines whether the attainment targets or developmental objectives are effectively realised and whether the other obligations (among other things the minimum schedule) are correctly observed. The inspectorate is not subject-oriented or meant to assess individual teachers; it aims to assess the school as a whole.

In the French Community, committees presided over by members of the inspectorate develop the curriculum which must then be approved by the Minister of Education. If a network of schools produces its own curriculum, it must also be approved by the Minister.

It should be noted that in order to give the whole education system maximum coherence, three objectives for schools were adopted in 1992: to promote students' personal development, to train them in how to build their knowledge and to enable them to play an active role in economic life and become responsible citizens in a free society.

The "attainment target" consists of basic skills defined by all schools. These basic skills are used as a measure for evaluation, a process for which each school is responsible.

Materials for study (textbooks and exercises) are produced by inspectors or teachers and marketed by private companies.

Within schools, assessment is carried out by teachers. Standardised diagnostic tests for the different subjects are produced in order to help teachers in their work in the French Community.

In Belgium, mastery of languages is of crucial importance. Not only is the Belgian federation based on the existing linguistic communities, but having bilingual Brussels as the political centre of Europe implies the need for effective communication. In Flemish primary schools children already learn French and in the secondary education system students study two foreign languages (French and English) for six years.

5. TEACHERS

There are over 200 000 teachers at all levels of education. Women teachers are in the majority. In early childhood education, almost 100 per cent of teachers are women. For early childhood, primary and lower secondary education, teachers are trained for three years in non-university higher institutions. Upper secondary teachers are trained in their specific subject matter and must, in addition, attend post-graduate courses in order to prepare them to teach at that level.

Teaching at university level requires a doctorate or an equivalent degree.

Canada

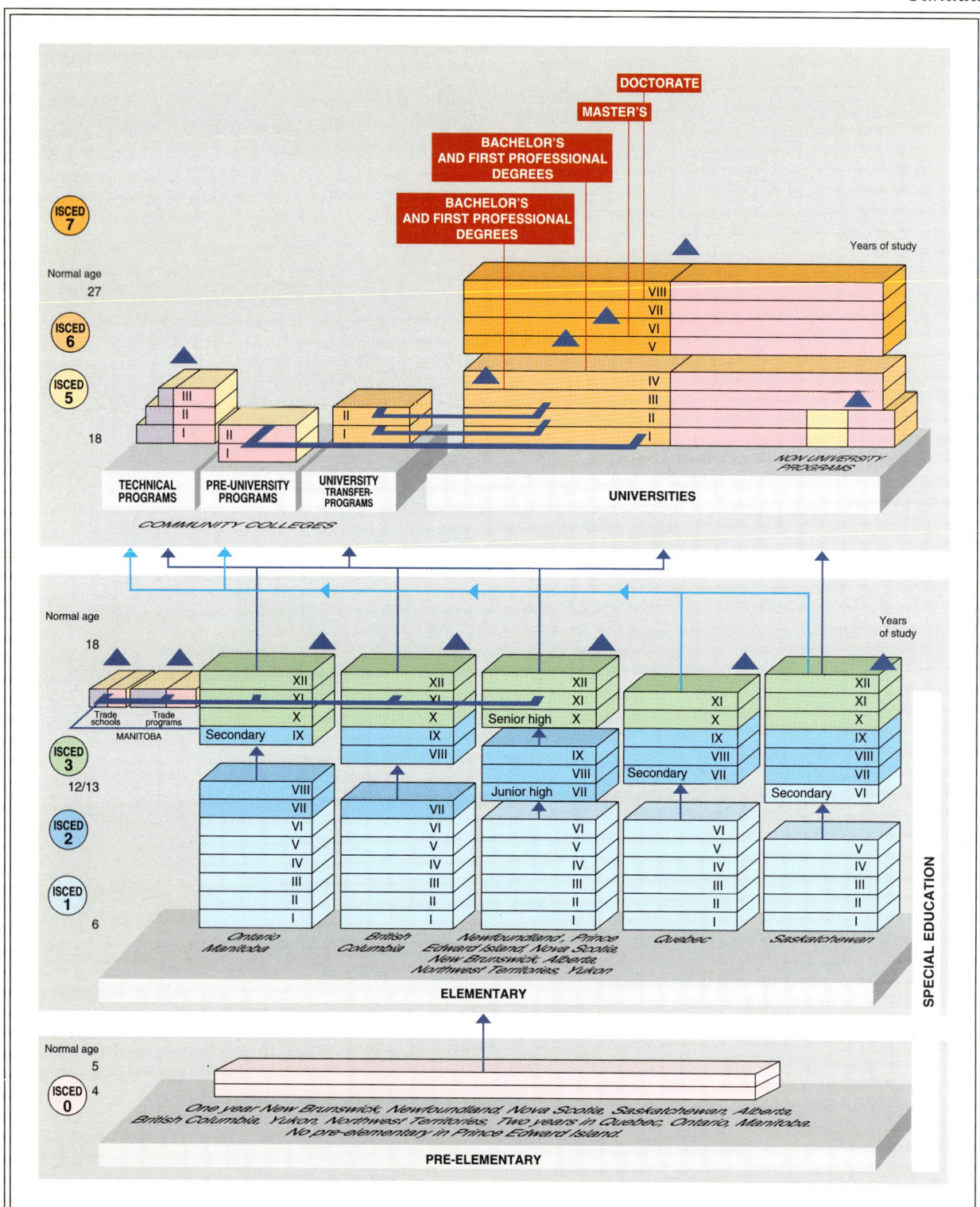

Colour codes (for details see page 249): **Pink** - Programme designed for part-time attendance. **Mauve** - Vocational education and training. **Blue triangle** - Recognised exit point of the education system. **Blue arrow** - Typical student flow. The size of the graphical elements provides no indication of the enrolment in the corresponding educational institutions.

Codes couleur (voir la page 249): *Rose* - Programmes expressément à temps partiel. *Mauve* - Enseignement et formation professionnels. *Triangle bleu* - Point de sortie officiel du système éducatif. *Flèche bleue* - Progression typique des élèves ou étudiants. La taille des différents blocs ne représente pas la proportion des effectifs dans les établissements d'enseignement correspondants.

Canada

1. GENERAL CONTEXT

Canada spans six time zones from east coast to west and stretches over 9 970 000 square kilometres, an area almost as large as Europe. Yet it has only approximately 30 million inhabitants, the majority of whom live along the southern border and in the large industrial centres. Canada has two official languages: English, the mother tongue of approximately 61 per cent of the population, and French, the mother tongue of approximately 26 per cent. Most French speakers live in Quebec, but there are also many French speakers in New Brunswick, Ontario and Manitoba. In Canada, education is available in both official languages, but to a greater or lesser degree, depending on the region.

Education is the responsibility of each of the ten provinces and two territories. Therefore, while the educational structures and institutions across the country are similar in many ways, they have been developed by each jurisdiction to respond to the particular circumstances and historical and cultural heritage of the population it serves. The Government of Canada is directly responsible for education in the Canadian Armed Forces, education of Canada's Aboriginal peoples (status Indian, registered Métis and Inuit) and education and training in the Correctional (penitentiary) Service.

There is no federal or central ministry or department of education. For this reason, in 1967, the ministers responsible for education established the Council of Ministers of Education, Canada (CMEC) to be the national voice for education in Canada and the ministers' mechanism for consultation, action on matters of mutual interest and co-operation with national education organisations and various federal departments. It is also the body that represents Canadian education internationally.

Several trends are evident in education in Canada today, many of which are directly or indirectly related to the need for more accountability to the public. Most notable is the increase in co-operation and sharing of services at the regional and national levels in areas such as curriculum and learning outcomes development, assessment of student achievement, programme evaluation, information technology and distance education and the transferability of credits between post-secondary institutions. Initiatives are also under way in most jurisdictions to help students make the transition from school to the work place, many of which involve changes to vocational and technical education, apprenticeship programmes, guidance and career counselling and co-operative programmes.

2. EDUCATIONAL STRUCTURE AND ENROLMENTS

It is estimated that the school-age population will continue to shrink as a percentage of the total population, but the demand for non-compulsory early childhood education could increase if there are further increases in women's labour force participation rates. As well, increases in the demand for post-secondary education could come from increased participation rates resulting from the demands of the labour market.

There was a total of 16 233 public and private educational institutions in Canada in 1993/94. Of these, 12 441 offered elementary instruction; 3 509 secondary education; 206 college-level education; and 77 university-level instruction. In the past few years, for the whole of the country, the number of elementary and secondary institutions has increased, while the number of colleges and universities has remained fairly stable. Approximately 5.5 million students are enrolled in public and private elementary and secondary institutions in Canada. Nearly one million students are enrolled full-time in post-secondary institutions.

Early childhood education programmes are operated by the local education authorities and provide one or two years of pre-grade 1 education for 4 and 5 year-olds in all provinces and territories except Prince Edward Island.

Public education is provided free to all Canadian citizens and permanent residents until the end of secondary school – normally age 18. The ages for compulsory schooling vary from one jurisdiction to another, but are normally from age 6 or 7 to age 16.

In each province or territory, a ministry or department of education is responsible for elementary and secondary education. Elementary education covers the first six to eight years of compulsory schooling. Afterwards, children proceed to secondary education. A great variety of programmes – vocational (job training) as well as academic – are offered at the secondary level. The first years of secondary schooling are devoted to compulsory subjects, with some optional subjects included. In the latter years, the number of compulsory subjects is reduced, permitting students to spend more time on specialised programmes that prepare them for the job market or on specific courses needed to meet the entrance requirements of the college or university of their choice. Secondary school diplomas are granted to students who pass the compulsory and optional courses of their programmes.

Special-needs students, such as the physically or mentally disabled, the gifted, etc., are accommodated in the public schools in various ways. In some cases, separate programmes are available to meet their needs; in others, these students are integrated into the regular classroom and, to the extent possible, follow the regular programme of instruction.

Private or independent schools, which provide an alternative to publicly funded schools, may operate in any province or territory if they meet the general standards prescribed by that jurisdiction for elementary and secondary schools. Although in most cases they closely follow the curriculum and diploma requirements of the department or ministry of education, they function independently of the public system and charge fees. Five provinces – Alberta, British Columbia, Manitoba, Quebec and Saskatchewan – provide some form of financial assistance to these schools.

The point of transition from elementary to secondary school varies. The elementary-secondary continuum is sometimes broken into schools that group together, for example, kindergarten to grade 6, grades 7 to 9 (junior high), and 10 to 12 (senior level). In Quebec, secondary education ends after the eleventh year of schooling (*secondaire V*). Approximately two-thirds of secondary students go on to post-secondary institutions. Of these, nearly 60 per cent go to college-level institutions and the other 40 per cent to university-level institutions.

Once secondary school has been successfully completed, a student may apply to a college or a university, depending on the region and on whether he or she qualifies. Quebec students must first obtain a college diploma in order to be admitted into a

Canada

university programme. The colleges, called *cégeps* (*collèges d'enseignement général et professionnel*), offer both a general programme that leads to university admission and a professional programme that prepares students for the labour force. In Ontario, students presently must complete six additional courses to be admitted to a university programme, although this requirement is gradually being phased out.

Post-secondary education is available in both government-supported and private institutions, some of which award degrees. Colleges such as technical and vocational institutions, community colleges, *cégeps* and other institutes of technology offer six-month to three-year programmes for continuing education and for developing skills for careers in business, the applied arts, technology, social services and some health sciences. In general, colleges award diplomas or certificates only.

Programmes leading to degrees are offered in universities. It is possible to study at three different levels, that lead to a Bachelor's (3-4 years), Master's (further 1-2 years) or doctoral (3-5 years after Master's) degree. Not all universities offer graduate studies (Master's and doctorates). In addition to degree programmes, most universities offer diploma and certificate programmes. These can be either at the under-graduate or graduate level and can range from one to three years in duration.

3. EDUCATIONAL FINANCE AND COSTS

The amount of funding available for education and the method of funding varies from jurisdiction to jurisdiction. Among the factors that contribute to the wide variety of relative education expenditures are the size of the population, participation rates, taxation resources and levels and local priorities for education.

Various levels of government (local, provincial/territorial and federal) spent a total of about C$ 56 billion on education and training in 1993/94, up from approximately C$ 45 billion in 1989/90. The amounts provided for elementary and secondary education that come from local and provincial or territorial revenues vary significantly due to the variations in school finance systems and fiscal policy — in some provinces there is no direct local taxation on property for education while, in one jurisdiction, school boards receive more than half of their revenue from local taxation directly related to education. At the post-secondary level, the majority of operating funds is provided to post-secondary institutions by the provinces. The balance of the funding comes from tuition fees, contract research, endowments and sale of services. The federal government also provides some funding for post-secondary education, mainly through the *Canadian Health and Social Transfer* programme as well as in the form of student aid and sponsored research.

While the share of funds spent by trade/vocational institutes, colleges and universities remained fairly stable between 1989/90 and 1993/94, the share spent on elementary and secondary education increased over the same five-year period, accounting for much of the overall growth. Nearly two-thirds of the amount spent on elementary and secondary education covers instructional costs, which comprise mostly salaries for teaching and administrative staff, but also include instructional supplies and services, desks and equipment used in instruction and computer services.

4. CURRICULUM AND ASSESSMENT

There is no common curriculum across the country but the differences among the provincial and territorial programmes are not substantial in most curriculum areas.

There is regional collaboration on curriculum development for the core subjects of mathematics, science and language, with the western provinces and territories (British Columbia, Alberta, Saskatchewan, Manitoba, Yukon and the Northwest Territories) working together as one group and the Atlantic provinces (Newfoundland, Prince Edward Island, Nova Scotia and New Brunswick) as another. Most provinces and territories are collaborating through CMEC in a pan-Canadian project to develop a framework of common general and specific learning outcomes for science, from kindergarten to end of secondary. Jurisdictions will then use this framework as a basis to develop their own regional or provincial curriculum.

There is also considerable diversity in Canadian assessment and examination practices. Jurisdictions base their assessment programmes on their own curriculum. No common instrument is used by all provinces and territories. However, all jurisdictions participate in the School Achievement Indicators Program, a national assessment of 13 and 16 year-olds in mathematics content and problem-solving, reading and writing (first language only) and science.

All but two jurisdictions have some type of provincial assessment programme. The focus tends to be on the basics – mostly English or French as a first language and mathematics – with some provinces including other subjects such as science and social sciences. Jurisdictions usually assess students at two or more levels, and subjects are usually assessed on a rotating cycle. As well, nine jurisdictions have high school exit examinations for graduating students. The stakes for students range from 30 to 50 per cent of the final mark in exam courses, with the remainder contributed by teachers for class work. At the post-secondary level, there is no common test for all students.

5. TEACHERS

In the period between 1984/85 and 1992/93, the elementary-secondary educator workforce increased by nearly 13 per cent, even though total enrolment increased by only 5 per cent. While the number of male elementary and secondary educators has remained fairly constant over time, the number of female educators increased consistently between 1984/85 and 1992/93. Women now make up nearly two-thirds of the elementary-secondary educator workforce, but only hold one-third of administrative positions. The average age of educators increased from 34 years in 1972/73 to 42 years in 1992/93, with only 23 per cent below the age of 35. In the decade from 2001 to 2010, more than 45 per cent of the 1992/93 educator workforce will be retiring or nearing retirement.

In 1993/94, there were 27 114 full-time college teachers and 36 957 full-time university teachers. Like the elementary-secondary educator workforce, the full-time post-secondary teacher workforce is also ageing.

Czech Republic

1. GENERAL CONTEXT

The Czech Republic covers an area of 78 864 square kilometres and has just over 10 million inhabitants. It is located in Central Europe and borders Germany, Austria, Slovakia and Poland. Most of the population is Czech and the remaining part consists of Slovaks (3.1 per cent) and small numbers of Poles, Germans and Romanys. There is a relatively high population density and a continuing process of urbanisation.

From 1948 until 1989 the Czech and Slovak Republics (Czechoslovakia) were part of the Soviet bloc. After the "Velvet Revolution" in 1989, Czechoslovakia became again a democratic country. In 1993 it was divided into two independent countries – the Czech Republic and the Slovak Republic. The transition from a centrally regulated economy to a market economy began in 1990. The changes in 1989 also had repercussions for the education system. After 1990 the monolithic uniform State education system was abandoned and it became possible to establish private and church schools. The compulsory teaching of Russian was also discontinued. The new postulates of education were the needs of the individual and the principles of humanism and democracy. Many of the central responsibilities devolved to the regions and the schools. The State undertook to ensure that all schools – state, private, and ecclesiastic – were able to develop under comparable conditions. At the same time there was a strive to reduce the curriculum in basic schools and the upper secondary level in order to permit diversity according to local needs within a framework of established educational standards.

2. EDUCATIONAL STRUCTURE AND ENROLMENTS

The language of instruction is Czech although minority groups are provided with an education in their native languages. Compulsory education, now covering nine grades, has a long tradition. Six-year compulsory school attendance was introduced in 1774, and in 1869 a compulsory eight-year school attendance for all children aged six to fourteen was enacted.

Pre-school education (kindergarten) caters for children from the age of 3 until they enter primary school. The primary objective of pre-school education is the development of the skills and knowledge of children, their speech and thinking, mostly through playing. Entry to primary school follows normally at age 6, provided that the child is judged sufficiently mature.

Primary and lower secondary school together form 9 years of basic education. Basic education has two stages: the first (grades 1-5) corresponds to primary education and the second (grades 6-9) to lower secondary education. In primary school, the child receives the core knowledge through general, polytechnical, physical and aesthetic education. Lower secondary school provides obligatory instruction in the mother tongue, mathematics, natural science, civics, history, geography, physics, chemistry and other subjects including a foreign language. Each subject at this stage is taught by a different teacher. Talented students can attend a school with an extended curriculum in language, mathematics, sport, etc. Students are tested through oral and written examinations where they are graded on a 1 to 5 scale. At the middle and at the end of a school year, students receive a school report. Parents are informed about the progress of their child at regular meetings.

Upper secondary schools prepare students for further studies at the university level or at one of the newly established institutions at the non-university tertiary level of education, or they prepare students for direct entry into the labour market. Since 1990, many private schools have been established following a long-standing national tradition. Upper secondary education has traditionally been very diversified. In 1996 there were four types of upper secondary schools with a total enrolment of 588 875 students: *i) gymnasia* (16 per cent); *ii) secondary technical schools and conservatoires* (32 per cent); *iii) secondary vocational schools* (34 per cent) and *iv) integrated schools* which provide education that can be found at both specialised and vocational schools (18 per cent).

Students enter this stage typically at the age of 15 on the basis of entrance examinations and their basic school results. After completing four grades of upper secondary school, students take a matriculation exam (*maturita*) with both written and oral components.

Gymnasia (grammar schools) provide students with a broad and thorough general education and prepare them for university-level or non-university tertiary education. Studies conclude with the matriculation examination (*maturita*). Each student must take two compulsory subjects (Czech language and literature and a foreign language of his/her choice) as well as two optional subjects.

Secondary specialised schools and *conservatoires* exist since the 18th century. They are classified as vocational/technical schools at ISCED 3 although their curricula are comparable to many non-university tertiary programmes in other countries. They provide a broad general education as well as specialised education in particular fields. They prepare students to become nurses, technicians, designers, secretaries, bank clerks, people working in tourism, lower-level managers, librarians, accountants, receptionists, hotel managers, etc. After four years, there is a matriculation exam in two compulsory and three optional subjects. A shorter 3-year track was recently introduced. These programmes are practically oriented and end with an exam but not a *maturita*. Secondary specialised schools are divided into technical schools (which are further specialised in engineering, construction, civil building, electrotechnical, geodesy, etc.), schools for economists, commercial academies, agricultural or forestry schools, pedagogical schools, art schools and others. They also include nursing schools administered by the Ministry of Health. The conservatory is a specialised secondary school with 5 to 8 years of study in music, drama and dance.

Secondary vocational schools, in which most of the instruction is school-based, prepare their students directly for specific classes of occupations but they also provide 4- to 5-year courses ending with a matriculation exam (similar to that in the specialised technical schools) which provides access to university. Secondary vocational schools specialise mostly in engineering and technical areas and more recently also in management. They also provide general education, including mother tongue, history, mathematics and the sciences. Study at these secondary vocational schools ends with an apprenticeship exam. Graduates of four-year programmes take both the apprenticeship exam and the *maturita*.

Czech Republic

Integrated schools are new in the Czech education system. They offer vocational courses as in vocational schools and specialised vocational schools.

Special education is intended for handicapped children who cannot be integrated within the regular school system. It is available at the pre-primary, primary, lower secondary and upper secondary levels. Special schools have smaller class sizes, require more individualised teaching methods, have a modified curriculum and sometimes longer school attendance. There is an attempt to integrate children as far as possible into mainstream schools.

Tertiary education consists of non-university schools and universities. Because of very diversified upper secondary programmes, there was no immediate need for institutions at the non-university tertiary level. However, since 1990 several non-university tertiary institutions have been created and their number is expected to grow. Universities represent the highest educational level. They are granted full autonomy by law. There are 23 universities, and in recent years a number of new faculties have been established. Normally students must sit an entrance examination to enter a university although, occasionally, a student with good results at the upper secondary level may be admitted directly. Women represent 45 per cent of all students. Technical universities attract a relatively high number of students. Seventy per cent of the students are enrolled in long first university degree programmes with a typical duration of 5 years. Since 1990 a shorter Bachelor's programme has been introduced which is either practically oriented or the first stage of a five-year university programme. Some programmes (like medicine, architecture and veterinary medicine) take six years and primary school teacher training takes four years. University study ends with the defence of a thesis as well as State exams. A post-graduate doctoral course takes three years.

Adult education is an inseparable part of the education system. It is carried out by upper secondary schools and the tertiary education sector within the framework of the education system. Students study the same curricula as their young colleagues, take the same examinations and receive the same degrees.

An inseparable part of the Czech system of education is the training of children and young people outside formal school hours. This training is organised by the school as well as by other institutions and organisations such as leisure centres, basic art schools and language schools. There are also young technician clubs run by experts. School groups or clubs ensure the care for the children of working mothers.

3. EDUCATIONAL FINANCE AND COSTS

The major part of the education budget is borne by the State although education also receives funding from the private sector. Salaries account for more than 30 per cent of the education budget. Education is free in all state and church schools as well as in universities. Some fees are paid in private schools but the State pays a per capita subsidy of some 70 to 100 per cent of what a student in a state school costs. Scholarships are awarded to students from low-income families.

4. CURRICULUM AND ASSESSMENT

Syllabuses and curricula are developed by teams of educationalists and academics in co-operation with teachers and representatives of professional groups. They must be approved by the Ministry. Since 1990, each school can adapt up to 10 per cent of the curriculum according to local needs. In the fourth year of the *gymnasium* up to 40 per cent of the curriculum can be established at the school level.

Textbooks and other teaching materials are developed by private publishers. However, they must be approved by the Ministry. School principals can (with State funding) purchase any approved textbook on the market. The distribution of textbooks is the responsibility of the publishing companies. The main problem with curriculum development is the determination of the core subjects for the different types and levels of education as well as the co-ordination among subjects.

Continuous oral and written tests are held throughout primary and secondary education. There is an entrance examination to secondary school, the content of which is established under the responsibility of the school principal. Twice a year, secondary students receive a school report and parents are informed about their children's progress. School monitoring and evaluation services are currently being implemented.

5. TEACHERS

In the school year 1993/94 there were 24 148 teachers in kindergarten, 27 420 at the primary level, 45 460 at the lower secondary level, 9 344 in upper secondary grammar schools, 60 291 in upper secondary vocational and technical schools and 21 056 at the tertiary level.

Primary, secondary and special school teachers receive their training either in university faculties of education or in special teacher-training programmes within subject-matter faculties at universities. Kindergarten teachers receive their training at the secondary school level.

Teachers typically study two subjects at the university. However, since there is a shortage of foreign language teachers, some faculties are organising single-subject Bachelor's degree courses. Secondary vocational school teachers must have studied in technical, economic, art or agricultural faculties. During training all teachers practice teaching at schools under the supervision of a senior teacher. Supplementary courses for future teachers are also organised for university graduates in other than their teaching subjects. In upper secondary schools there are also many external part-time teachers such as doctors and nurses from hospitals for the courses for future nurses.

The number of compulsory teaching hours per week is: 31 in kindergartens, 23 at the primary level of basic school, 22 at the lower secondary school level and 21 in secondary schools.

Czech Republic

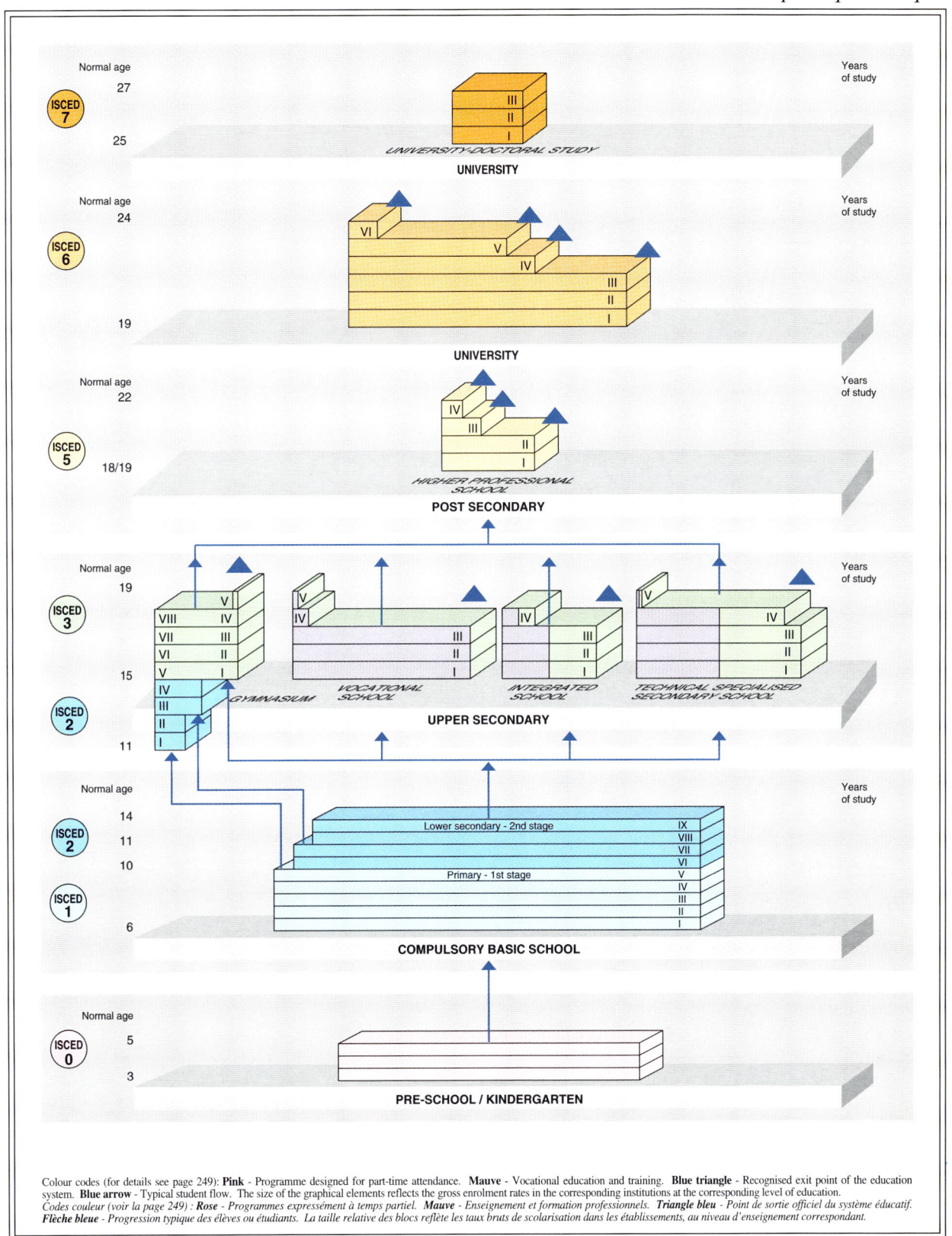

République tchèque

Denmark

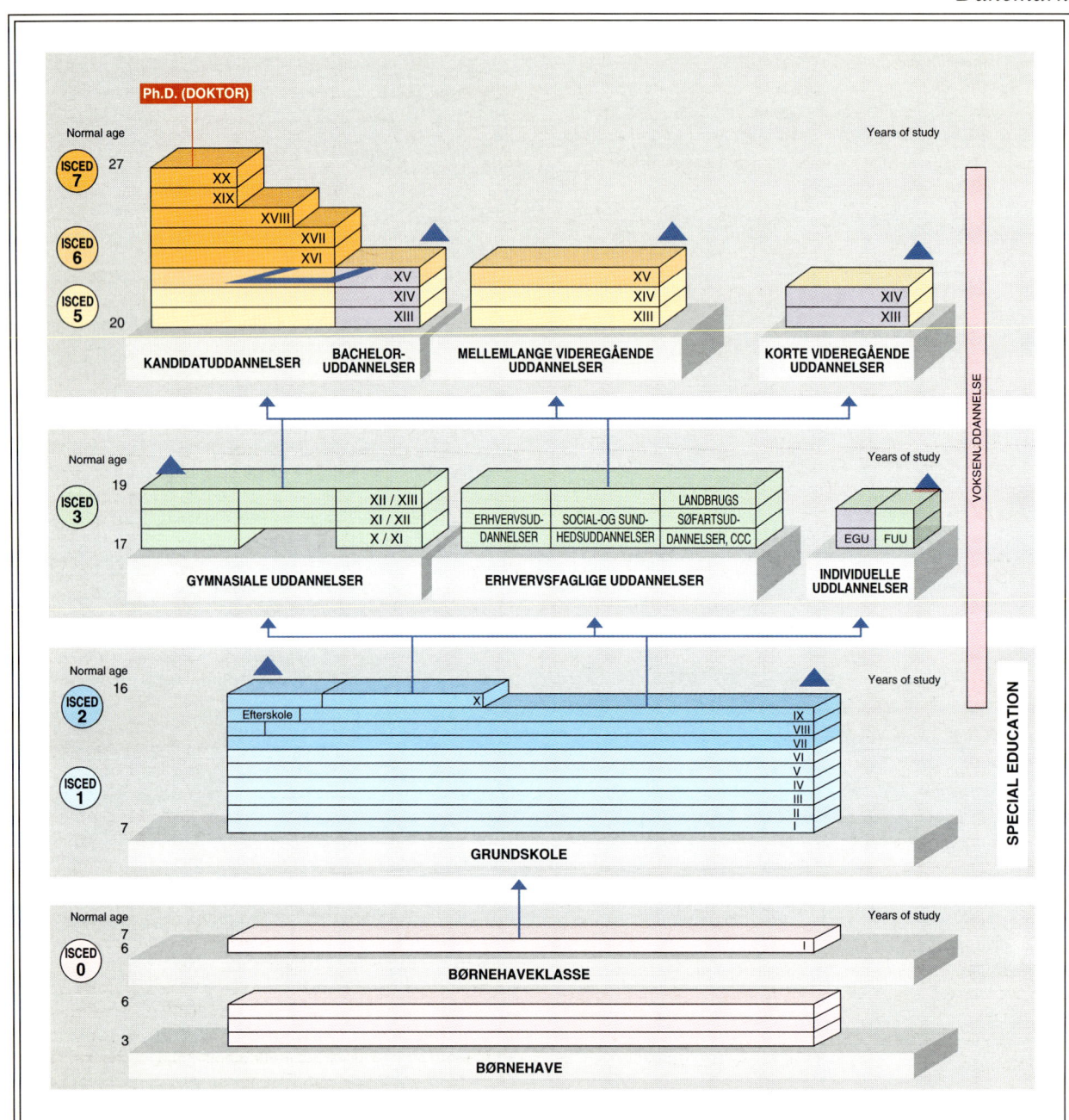

Danemark

Colour codes (for details see page 249): **Pink** - Programme designed for part-time attendance. **Mauve** - Vocational education and training. **Blue triangle** - Recognised exit point of the education system. **Blue arrow** - Typical student flow. The size of the graphical elements provides no indication of the enrolment in the corresponding educational institutions.
*Codes couleur (voir la page 249) : **Rose** - Programmes expressément à temps partiel. **Mauve** - Enseignement et formation professionnels. **Triangle bleu** - Point de sortie officiel du système éducatif. **Flèche bleue** - Progression typique des élèves ou étudiants. La taille des différents blocs ne représente pas la proportion des effectifs dans les établissements d'enseignement correspondants.*

Denmark

1. GENERAL CONTEXT

Denmark, in north-western Europe, covers an area of 43 080 square kilometres and has a population of 5.3 million people. The population is highly urbanised with about 60 per cent of people living in cities with more than 10 000 inhabitants and a population density as high as 120 inhabitants per square kilometre. The proportion of elderly citizens is relatively large and increasing. However, since the mid-1980s, the birth rate has been increasing significantly.

Denmark has a constitutional monarchy and is governed by a democratically-elected government and a parliament, the *Folketing*, in a multi-party system. Constitutionally, education is a central government responsibility although the regional and local authorities play an important role in lower levels of education and in upper secondary education.

The public sector predominates in Danish education. Private schools are mostly at the primary and lower secondary education levels (including pre-primary classes in primary schools and kindergartens), but there are also a few private general upper secondary schools (private *Gymnasia*). Instruction in private schools is comparable to that in public schools but the framework for the organisation of teaching is more flexible. Private schools are heavily subsidised with the State covering more than 80 per cent of expenditure.

The main issues in the educational debate have been the supply of and demand for graduates of vocational upper secondary education and tertiary education, lifelong learning and differentiated teaching within classes. In the middle of the 1990s, the central topics in the policy debate were education and training for all and the quality of education.

Since the mid-1980s, an increasing number of decisions have been decentralised to regional and local governments as well as to the schools and institutions themselves.

Over half of the labour force holds an upper secondary education qualification. Opening up the economy to greater international competition, especially in the European Union, has been associated with extensive initiatives to increase skill levels through education and training and to secure a better balance between the supply and demand for specific skills and qualifications. The government is committed to achieving an upper secondary completion rate of at least 90 per cent by the year 2000.

2. EDUCATIONAL STRUCTURE AND ENROLMENTS

Pre-primary education is optional. About 60 per cent of 3 to 4 year-olds attend kindergarten or age-integrated institutions. Nearly 99 per cent of 6 year-olds are enrolled in pre-primary programmes in kindergartens, age-integrated institutions or, most frequently, in pre-school classes in primary schools. Most children start primary school at the age of 7. Education is compulsory for nine years and commences on 1 August in the calendar year of the child's 7th birthday. The municipal *Folkeskole* (primary and lower secondary school) is comprehensive up to grade 10. Grade 10 is optional, but in 1994 some 60 per cent of an age cohort were enrolled at this grade level. Schools must provide children with subject-related qualifications and prepare them broadly for their role as citizens in a democratic society. Schools co-operate closely with the parents. The point of departure is taken in the individual student's abilities and intentions. Students are normally taught in classes where they remain together throughout the whole period of basic schooling. Teaching is differentiated within the framework of the class. There are 200 school days per year, and children attend school for five days a week with anywhere between 20 and 36 lessons per week depending on the grade level. A total of 606 000 children are enrolled in primary and lower secondary education.

In total 220 000 students are enrolled in upper secondary education. At this level education is either preparatory for further education [*Gymnasium*, higher preparatory exam (HF), higher commercial exam (HHX) and higher technical exam (HTX)] or vocationally oriented [vocational education and training programmes (EUD), basic social and health training programmes (SOSU), agricultural, forestry, home economics and maritime programmes]. Additional opportunities for young people were recently established through two individually organised programmes: vocational basic training (EGU) and open youth education (FUU). Irrespective of the type of youth education, great emphasis is placed on developing students' personal qualifications. To enter vocational upper secondary education, the completion of compulsory education is normally the only admission requirement. For the general programmes, the applicant qualifies to enter by passing the leaving examination of the *Folkeskole* in a number of specific subjects and by being recommended for further education by the lower secondary school. The duration of an upper secondary programme is typically 3 years but varies between 2 and 5 years. Students are usually 16-19 years of age. In 1994, 95 per cent entered upper secondary education and 78 per cent of the age cohort completed this level.

The tertiary sector provides short programmes, medium-term programmes (including Bachelor's degree programmes) and long university programmes (including Ph.D. programmes). Institutions range from vocational schools, teacher training colleges and business schools to universities. In 1996, about 47 per cent of the age cohort entered tertiary education with 34 per cent completing their programmes. The proportion of students entering and graduating from tertiary programmes is rising. In total, about 170 000 students are enrolled in tertiary education. Entry requirements to short-term higher education programmes are either vocational education and training or a general upper secondary qualification. Entry requirements for medium-term and long tertiary programmes are normally a general upper secondary qualification or, for some long-term programmes (*kandidat* programmes), a Bachelor's degree. There is open admission to most higher education programmes. It is, however, up to the individual school, college or university to establish admission requirements based on examination results which are, in some cases, supplemented with credits obtained for vocational experience.

Denmark

3. EDUCATIONAL FINANCE AND COSTS

Most education is publicly financed. The local authorities fund the *Folkeskole* and pre-primary education including kindergartens and age-integrated institutions. The county authorities fund special schools such as the *Gymnasium* and general upper secondary schools, and the State funds all other types of regular education including vocational schools, teacher training colleges and universities. Financial support for students is also funded by the State, through the State education grant and loan scheme. The State provides about 40 per cent of all expenditure for education, county authorities about 10 per cent and local authorities about 50 per cent.

Only private schools (independent primary and lower secondary schools, continuation schools and private *Gymnasium*) charge tuition fees. For vocational schools, business colleges, colleges of education and universities, the allocation of public grants is regulated according to fixed national rates per full-time student.

The regulation of the expenditures for primary and lower secondary education has been difficult to anticipate and control due to demographic changes in recent years. This has been a topic in the debate. Other issues in the educational debate have been and still are admission to tertiary education and the relationship between the level of expenditure and quality in education.

4. CURRICULUM AND ASSESSMENT

There is a common curriculum intended as a guideline for primary and lower secondary schools. While the national parliament (the *Folketing*) sets the general aims of the school (*Folkeskole*) and the Ministry of Education the objectives for the individual subjects, it is up to the local education authorities and the individual schools to decide how these aims and objectives are to be accomplished. In order to help local authorities and individual teachers, the Ministry of Education issues curriculum and teaching guidelines for the individual subjects.

The curriculum is specified in most detail at the upper secondary level. In general upper secondary school, the Ministry of Education sets the objectives for the individual subjects and issues detailed regulations on the content of the subjects, their scope and their inclusion in other subject areas. The actual planning and organisation of the individual subjects are, to the extent possible, jointly carried out by the teacher and the students. All programmes comprise compulsory and optional subjects. To a certain extent, it is therefore possible for each student to compose his or her own programme of study. In vocational upper secondary education, which normally comprises both school-based and work-based components, students generally have more scope to specialise. The framework of the curriculum at this level is developed in collaboration with the social partners. Just over half of the young persons entering upper secondary education choose general programmes. There is now much emphasis on encouraging young people to enter vocational education and training, especially the technical programmes.

At universities and other tertiary education institutions, the Ministry of Education lays down broad regulations for educational programmes. However, it is up to the single institution to define the content of the programmes in detail.

In primary and lower secondary schools, children are normally automatically promoted from one grade to the next. At the end of compulsory education there are optional leaving examinations in single subjects but there is no overall examination. In upper secondary education, students are normally automatically promoted to the next grade. Although the school can advise on promotion, the final decision is up to the students. In tertiary education, promotion is dependent on results from tests and examinations.

5. TEACHERS

Teachers are trained at different types of institutions. Pre-school teachers are trained at colleges for pre-school teachers and kindergarten training colleges. The duration of these programmes is 3 and a half years. The training of teachers for primary and lower secondary school (*Folkeskole*) takes place at colleges of education and lasts for 4 years. Teachers for general and vocational upper secondary education normally have a university degree corresponding to a Master's degree and/or a vocational level of education and some professional experience from the labour market. Teachers at universities and other tertiary institutions are normally graduates with a Master's degree or a Ph.D.

In total, about 90 000 persons are employed as teachers, corresponding to about 80 000 full-time equivalent teachers. The number of people employed in the education sector in non-teaching positions is about 60 000. Student/teacher ratios are relatively low and the overall spending on education is high by OECD standards, especially for primary and lower secondary schools.

Many teachers subsequently up-grade their qualifications. The criteria for promotion of teachers is normally seniority. The combination of an ageing teaching force, decreasing student enrolments in primary and lower secondary education and public expenditure restrictions has meant that there have been few jobs for new teachers in the past 15 years and the number of colleges of education has declined. However, with the increase in the number of children in the year groups now entering school, a growing demand for new teachers is expected.

Finland

1. GENERAL CONTEXT

The Republic of Finland has an area of 358 000 square kilometres and a population of 5.1 million inhabitants with an average density of 16 inhabitants per square kilometre. The majority (64 per cent) of the population lives in urban or suburban areas including one-fifth of the population in the capital region.

There are two national languages: Finnish and Swedish. Approximately 93 per cent of Finns speak Finnish and 6 per cent speak Swedish. Sami is the mother tongue of roughly 2 000 people. Citizens have the right to use their own language in all official business (i.e. Finnish or Swedish) and when specifically stipulated the Sami language as well. The same applies to education.

There were major financial problems in the early 1990s forcing retrenchments in the annual budgets. From 1990 to 1993 public expenditure rose from 41 to 62 per cent of GNP. The unemployment rate rocketed from 3.5 per cent in 1990 to roughly 17 per cent in 1995. Finding a job has become most difficult for young people: the unemployment rate for the under 25 year-olds in 1995 was about 31 per cent.

As retrenchment occurred, there were budget cuts in education. Differences among regions with regards to financial investment in education increased. At the same time, a national study commissioned by the Ministry of Education suggested that there seemed to be no evidence of any systematic decline in student achievement.

The main criteria used in the development of the education system are assuring quality and equality in education and the principle of lifelong learning. Special attention is paid to basic educational rights and services, wherein everyone is entitled to an education that corresponds to his or her developmental level, and an emphasis is placed on the central role of education for reforming working life and production structures.

2. EDUCATIONAL STRUCTURE AND ENROLMENTS

Early childhood education for the 3 to 6 year-olds is mainly the responsibility of the social welfare authorities and is organised in children's day-care centres (kindergartens). In certain cases, the pre-school education of 6 year-olds can also take place in conjunction with a comprehensive school. This is particularly the case in sparsely-populated areas. Nearly 60 per cent of all 6 year-olds are enrolled in pre-school education.

Primary and lower secondary education, which is compulsory for all school-age children, takes place in nine-year comprehensive schools. It is divided into a lower stage of six grades and an upper stage of three grades. An optional tenth grade is also possible. At the lower stage, there were 384 000 pupils in 1995 while the number of students at the upper stage was 197 000. At the optional tenth grade level there were about 3 200 students. Comprehensive schools, with very few exceptions, are maintained by the municipalities.

School education begins in the year when a child turns 7 and normally lasts for ten years. However, compulsory education is usually completed in nine years. For certain groups of disabled children, compulsory school begins at age 6 and can continue for a period of eleven years.

Special education within the comprehensive school system takes place either in special comprehensive schools, in special classes of regular comprehensive schools, or in the form of integrated teaching in normal education. The general trend is to decrease segregation and increase integration. In 1995, approximately 94 000 students (i.e. 16 per cent of comprehensive school students) were enrolled in special education of some type. In most of these cases (79 per cent of students) this special education comprised part-time remedial teaching mainly for students with speech or reading/writing disabilities. For some special groups, there are state-owned special schools (e.g. schools for pupils with impaired hearing or vision).

Upper secondary education is provided for all comprehensive school-leavers, both in senior secondary schools and in vocational schools. Approximately 90 per cent of compulsory school-leavers continue their studies completing some form of education at the upper secondary level. Nearly 50 per cent of the age group take the national matriculation examination and slightly more than 50 per cent complete vocational education.

The completion of *senior secondary education* is scheduled to take about three years. Since these schools are now ungraded, studies may be accomplished in a shorter or longer time than this, with an allowed maximum of four years. The enrolment figure for senior secondary day schools in 1995 was 109 000. The senior secondary schools are run mainly by the municipalities.

Vocational education at the upper secondary level takes two to three years. A development programme was begun in 1996 with the purpose of extending the minimum length of vocational education to three years while broadening the scope of diplomas and incorporating longer periods of work practice into all programmes. Initial vocational education and training is provided mainly in educational institutions run and owned by the municipalities. The number of students in this sector was about 130 000 in 1994. There are special vocational institutions for certain groups of the disabled, but most of special education in vocational education takes place in conjunction with regular education.

Tertiary education consists of advanced vocational education and education at the university or the non-university tertiary level. Polytechnics (*ammattikorkeakoulut, AMK-institutions*) are included in the non-university sector. The university and the non-university sectors form higher education.

Advanced vocational education (following upper secondary education) is provided in college programmes of two to four years' duration. The entry requirement is either the national matriculation examination (at the end of senior secondary school) or initial vocational education at the upper secondary level. For the most part, advanced vocational training has been, or is currently being, transferred to higher education in the non-university sector (see below).

The *university sector* consists of 20 universities, of which ten are multi-faculty institutions and ten specialist institutions. All universities are engaged in both education and research and have the right to award doctorates. The national matriculation

Finland
Finlande

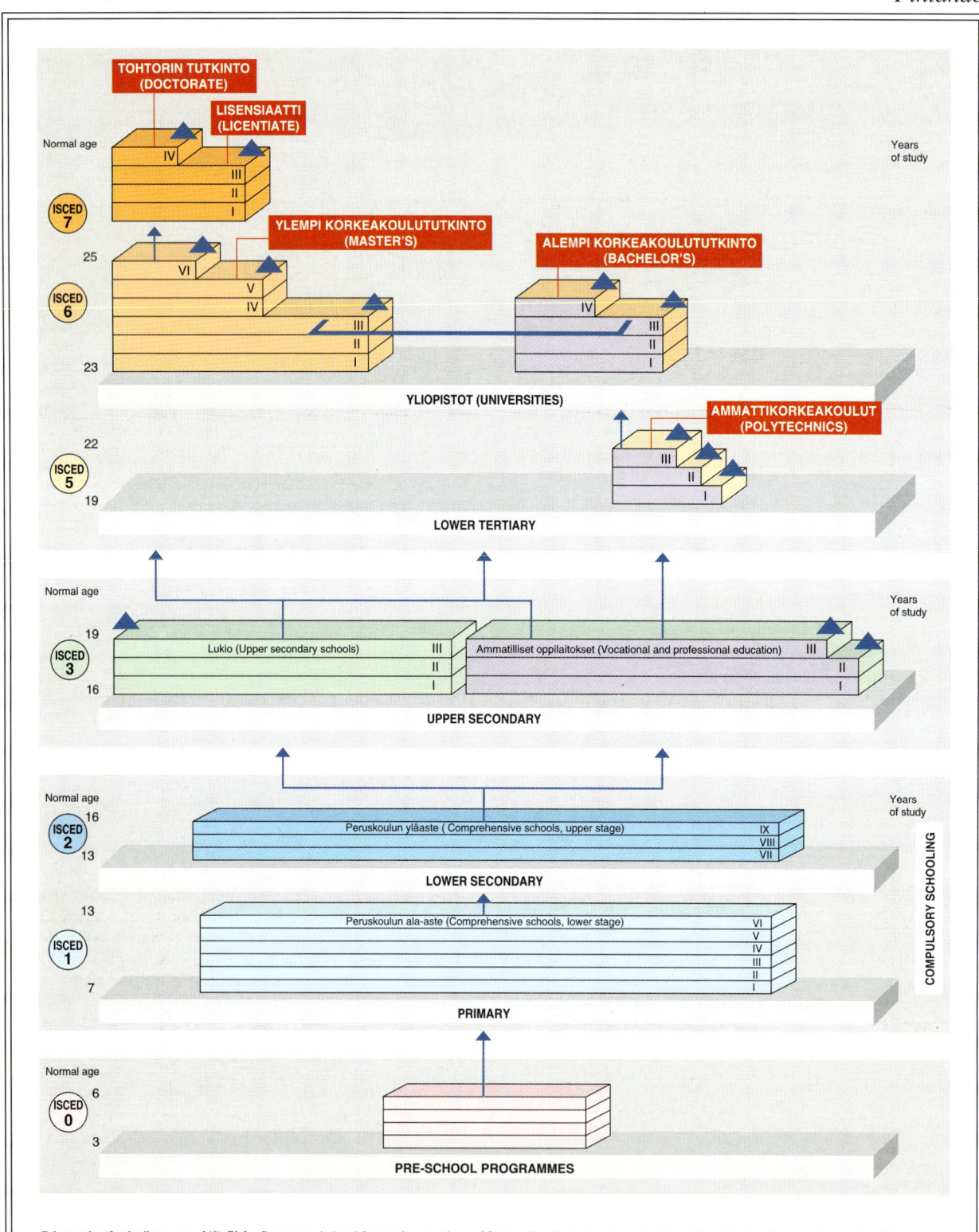

Normal age

- ISCED 7
- ISCED 6 — 25, 23
- ISCED 5 — 22, 19

TOHTORIN TUTKINTO (DOCTORATE) — IV
LISENSIAATTI (LICENTIATE) — III, II, I
YLEMPI KORKEAKOULUTUTKINTO (MASTER'S) — VI, V, IV, III, II, I
ALEMPI KORKEAKOULUTUTKINTO (BACHELOR'S) — IV, III, II, I

YLIOPISTOT (UNIVERSITIES)

AMMATTIKORKEAKOULUT (POLYTECHNICS) — III, II, I

LOWER TERTIARY

Normal age — ISCED 3 — 19, 16

Lukio (Upper secondary schools) — III, II, I
Ammatilliset oppilaitokset (Vocational and professional education) — III, II, I

UPPER SECONDARY

Normal age — ISCED 2 — 16, 13

Peruskoulun yläaste (Comprehensive schools, upper stage) — IX, VIII, VII

LOWER SECONDARY

ISCED 1 — 13, 7

Peruskoulun ala-aste (Comprehensive schools, lower stage) — VI, V, IV, III, II, I

PRIMARY

COMPULSORY SCHOOLING

Normal age — ISCED 0 — 6, 3

PRE-SCHOOL PROGRAMMES

Colour codes (for details see page 249): **Pink** - Programme designed for part-time attendance. **Mauve** - Vocational education and training. **Blue triangle** - Recognised exit point of the education system. **Blue arrow** - Typical student flow. The size of the graphical elements reflects the gross enrolment rates in the corresponding institutions at the corresponding level of education.

Codes couleur (voir la page 249) : *Rose* - Programmes expressément à temps partiel. *Mauve* - Enseignement et formation professionnels. *Triangle bleu* - Point de sortie officiel du système éducatif. *Flèche bleue* - Progression typique des élèves ou étudiants. La taille relative des blocs reflète les taux bruts de scolarisation dans les établissements, au niveau d'enseignement correspondant.

Finland

examination provides general access to university education. Access to the university sector can also be gained through a vocational diploma at the advanced level. In 1995 there were approximately 133 000 students in universities (ISCED levels 6 and 7).

The *non-university sector* of higher education consists of 28 *AMK-institutions*, nine of which have a permanent licence while the others (19) are still operating under a temporary licence in the autumn of 1996. The *AMK-institutions* comprise more than 150 educational institutes and colleges providing advanced and higher vocational education. Experimentation with this system started in 1991 with the aim of improving the standard and quality of vocational education and simplifying the complex structure of the education system. In 1994, the number of students in the non-university sector of higher education was about 75 000 and in 1995 about 81 000. Of all non-university students in higher education in the autumn of 1995, some 32 000 were enrolled in *AMK-institutions*. In the autumn of 1996 this sector was providing entry for 15 000 new students; according to the government plans, this number will be raised to 24 000 by the millennium. General eligibility for *AMK-institutions* is gained through upper secondary education.

3. EDUCATIONAL FINANCE AND COSTS

The state subsidy system has been developed in a direction that gives the municipalities more latitude in their decision-making. As state subsidies are no longer earmarked, the municipalities can freely decide how they use these funds as long as they meet their educational obligations.

Expenditure for comprehensive and senior secondary schools and vocational institutes is divided between their maintainers (municipalities) and the State. Since 1993, the state subsidy system has been based on a calculated unit cost confirmed annually by the Ministry of Education. The state subsidy is granted on the basis of these unit costs and number of students.

The amount of state subsidies varies according to the capacity of the students' home municipality to finance educational services. In 1993, the state subsidy covered, on average, 59 per cent of the running costs of comprehensive schools, whereas for senior secondary schools and vocational institutes the percentages were ç68 and 56 per cent respectively.

All universities are owned by the State and financed directly from the state budget. Universities currently obtain approximately 16 per cent of their total funding from external sources, and this share appears to be increasing. The financing of universities has been geared towards providing more incentive for results. In the academic year 1993/94, about 3 per cent of the total funding was awarded as incentives on the basis of results. The *AMK-institutions*, on the other hand, though receiving state subsidies, are municipal or privately-owned educational institutions.

4. CURRICULUM AND ASSESSMENT

There are legal stipulations concerning the length of the school year and school week and the subjects that are compulsory and optional. Optional courses may include other subjects than those mentioned in the stipulations. The Council of State (i.e. the Government) decides on the distribution of lesson hours among the various school subjects. The National Board of Education issues the curriculum framework for the comprehensive schools; this contains guidelines concerning the national goals and contents of school education as well as the legal stipulations about student assessment. Standardised forms for school reports are also provided. The Framework Curriculum for the Comprehensive School was reformed in 1994. A school's curriculum has to be approved by the municipality. In practice, school-based curricula have been approved almost without exception. This approach supports teachers' commitment to the implementation and development of the curriculum.

Furthermore, at the end of each school year (except for grades 1 to 4 where verbal descriptions can be used), students' performance must be assessed in the form of written school reports with numerical grading. When completing comprehensive school, the student receives a school-leaving certificate which provides general eligibility for studies at the upper secondary level. There is no school-leaving examination in the comprehensive school.

After comprehensive school all students are eligible for senior secondary schools. Due to limited places, the students are selected on the basis of their comprehensive school certificates. The curricula of senior secondary schools are regulated in the same way as in the comprehensive school. The curricula are school-based and designed in the form of courses. Each course (38 hours) includes student assessment, usually with numerical grades. At the end of the senior secondary school there is the national matriculation examination, the compulsory and optional subjects of which are legally stipulated. In addition to the certificate of matriculation, students receive a separate school-leaving certificate. Passing the matriculation examination gives general eligibility for university education.

The provision of student places in vocational education at the upper secondary level is designed to offer all comprehensive and senior secondary school-leavers an opportunity to continue their studies. Studies in a vocational institute comprise general studies, which are common to all institutes, as well as more occupationally-oriented studies. The National Board of Education also issues the framework curriculum for vocational schools. These curriculum guidelines were reformed in 1995/96. Vocational education is now divided into education sectors (7) which in turn are subdivided into educational fields (30) and further into various diplomas (77). The length of the diploma studies is defined in terms of study weeks; a study year comprises 40 study weeks. The length of basic diploma studies is 80 to 120 study weeks. Students' performance is assessed in terms of integrated study sections. Upon completion of this education, students are granted a vocational diploma. Vocational education is still undergoing further changes.

The duration of studies for a diploma in vocational colleges ranges from 80 to 120 study weeks and in *AMK-institutions* from 140 to 180 study weeks. All vocational diploma studies include either graduate work or a thesis as well as work practice.

In higher education, the national degree regulations define the objectives, extent and overall structure of degrees. Within the framework of these regulations, the universities decide on the

Finland

content and structure of their degrees in more detail. They also decide on their annual curricula and forms of instruction. Finnish university degrees correspond to Bachelor's, Master's and Doctor's degrees. In most fields, students can also take a voluntary Licentiate's degree before proceeding to a Doctorate. The Bachelor's degree takes a minimum of three years. The minimum duration for a Master's degree is five years.

5. TEACHERS

All teacher training takes place at universities. The training of kindergarten teachers, which was transferred to the universities in full in 1995/96, is a three-year programme which leads to the equivalent of a Bachelor's degree. The training of classroom teachers for the lower comprehensive school comprises a programme with extensive studies in education, basic study in several subjects and specialised studies in one or two subjects; it corresponds to a Master's degree.

Subject teachers teach one or two subjects at the lower or upper stage of the comprehensive school or in the senior secondary school. They have a Master's degree which consists of subject-specific studies in relevant university departments and pedagogical studies.

Vocational subject teachers are required to have a relevant university degree or post-secondary national diploma, 1 to 3 years of work experience and teacher training. The teacher's diploma is awarded by universities or other institutions at the higher education level. Teachers of general studies are required to have a Master's degree and teacher training.

In the *AMK-institutions*, for a Senior Lecturer a doctoral or Licentiate degree is required, while lecturers need a Master's degree or equivalent. Exceptions may be made to this rule in special cases. Teachers must have at least 3 years' work experience in their respective fields.

France

1. GENERAL CONTEXT

France is a Republic under whose constitution, adopted in 1958, the President of the Republic, who has been directly elected by universal suffrage since 1962, enjoys substantial and wide-ranging powers. The President appoints the Prime Minister, who is responsible both to the President and the Parliament.

France is divided into 22 regions, each of which contains from 2 to 8 *départements*. In all, there are 96 metropolitan *départements*, 4 overseas *départements*, 2 *collectivités territoriales* (Mayotte, Saint-Pierre-and-Miquelon) and 3 overseas territories (French Polynesia, New Caledonia and Wallis and Futuna).

France has a population of 58 million which is growing at an annual rate of slightly over 0.3 per cent. The population density is 105 inhabitants per square kilometre and 73.4 per cent of the population live in urban areas.

France has a labour force of 25 million people of whom 3 million are currently unemployed, resulting in an unemployment rate of 12 per cent. Some 1.5 million people (or 5.9 per cent of the labour force) are employed in the education of young people. Two-thirds of this staff, or approximately 1 million people, are civil servants (out of a total of 2.3 million). Thus, nearly half of all civil servants work in the education sector.

In 1993/94, France's school and university population amounted to over 14 million, i.e. a quarter of the total population. These children and students mainly attended public and private establishments supervised by the Ministry of National Education although some attended establishments supervised by the Ministry of Health (some 100 000 students) and Agriculture (some 200 000 students).

Despite far-reaching changes introduced in the 1980s, the French education system continues to be largely controlled by the State which still retains a number of basic powers such as the recruitment and remuneration of teachers, the framing and implementation of education policy and national curricula and the sole right to confer university diplomas, of which the *baccalauréat* is considered to be the first level.

However, over the past ten years there has been a trend towards both devolution (with the transfer of some decision-making powers to regional administrations) and decentralisation in response to the conferring of new responsibilities to elected regional and local authorities under legislation enacted between 1982 and 1985.

Each level of government (communes, *départements* and regions) has been made responsible for a given level of education. Communes have responsibility for the provision and financial management of nursery schools and primary schools. The *départements* are responsible for the maintenance and construction of *collèges* (lower secondary schools). The regions have the same responsibilities for *lycées* (upper secondary schools) and are also responsible for educational planning (regional education plans, forward investment plans).

At the same time, secondary schools have been made more independent and their legal status adjusted accordingly. Universities, which have been largely autonomous since 1968, have been given even greater autonomy in the administrative, financial, educational and scientific spheres since the Act of 1984.

Over the past ten years, the education system has been substantially expanded as part of the effort to ensure that 80 per cent of each age cohort would stay on at school to the *baccalauréat* level. There has been a substantial increase in access to upper secondary education, and today approximately 70 per cent of young people, twice as many as in 1980, try to obtain the *baccalauréat*.

This trend has led to a massive increase in enrolment in higher education, especially in the first cycle. Today there are some 2.1 million students enrolled in universities compared with just over a million in 1980.

2. EDUCATIONAL STRUCTURE AND ENROLMENTS

Since 1967 education has been compulsory from the age of 6 to 16.

The school year normally comprises 36 weeks of lessons from September to June, and the average amount of classroom instruction per week ranges from approximately 26 hours in primary education to as much as 30 hours or more in secondary education.

i) Education is divided into three main levels:

- *primary education* (or first level): pre-primary education (before the age of six) and primary education (from the age of 6 to 11) are provided in nursery schools and primary schools respectively. The initial stage of early learning is followed by a stage of learning basic skills and then by more in-depth learning. Nursery school attendance gradually became widespread during the 1960s and 1970s. Today some 2.5 million children attend nursery schools, as do all children between the ages of 3 and 5.

   In primary education, the number of children repeating classes has steadily declined. Fewer than a quarter of all children repeat a grade during primary school compared with over half of all children 30 years ago.

- *secondary education* (or second level): the first cycle (from the age of 11 to 15) is provided in *collèges*, and the second cycle (from the age of 15 to 18 or 19) is provided in vocational, general or technical lycées. It leads to the award of the *baccalauréat*, divided into general (56 per cent of successful candidates in 1996), technical (29 per cent) and vocational (15 per cent) and which still boasts of considerable status. The introduction of the vocational option in 1985 led to a sharp increase in access to the *baccalauréat* by making it possible for holders of an initial vocational certificate (CAP, Certificate of Vocational Aptitude and BEP, Diploma of Vocational Studies) to continue their studies.

- *higher education* is open to all holders of the *baccalauréat*. It comprises the following:
   - selective streams (*numerus clausus*, generally with more applicants than places). These include University Institutes of Technology (IUT) and

France

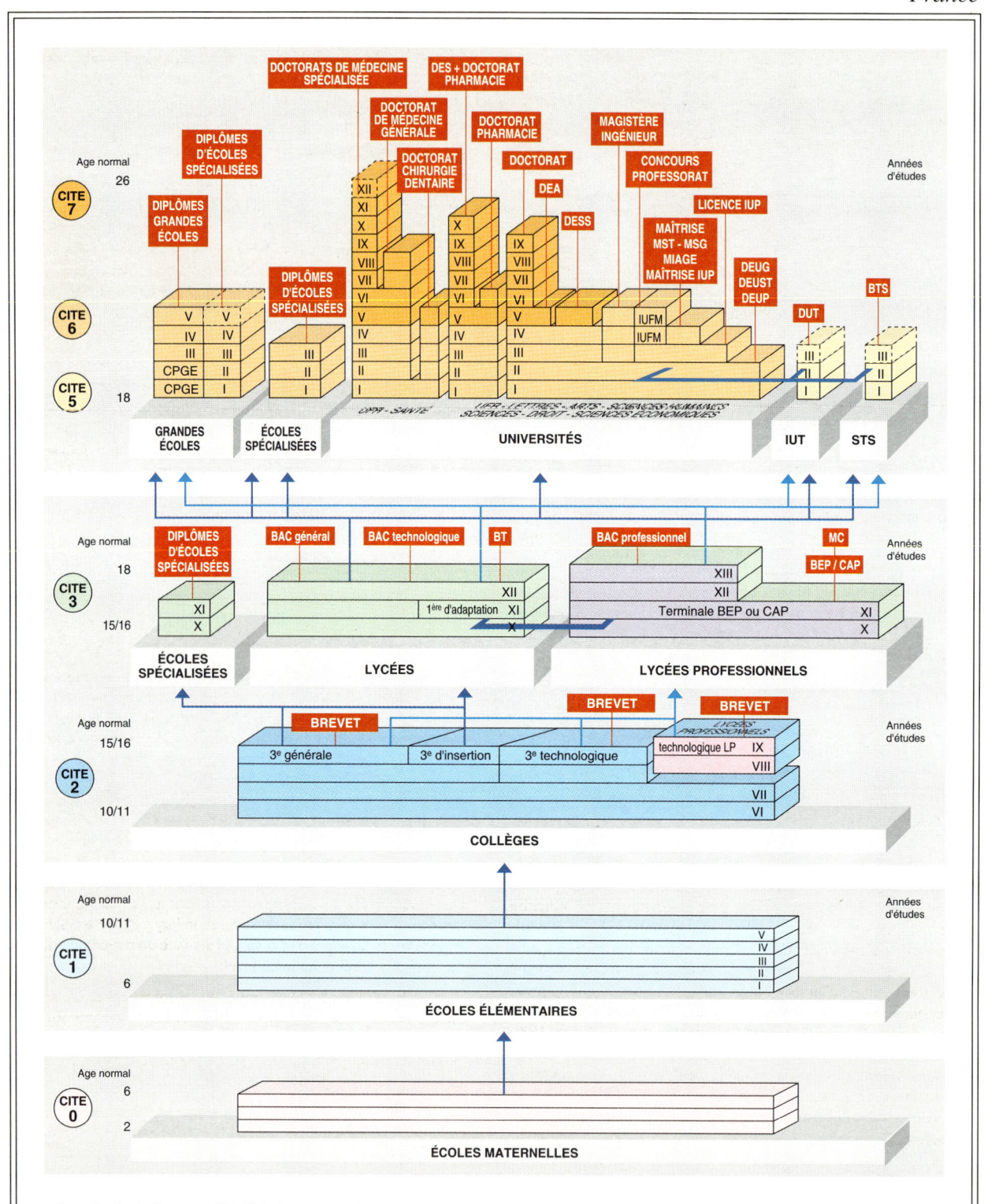

CITE 7 (Age normal 26)
- DIPLÔMES GRANDES ÉCOLES
- DIPLÔMES D'ÉCOLES SPÉCIALISÉES
- DOCTORATS DE MÉDECINE SPÉCIALISÉE
- DES + DOCTORAT PHARMACIE
- DOCTORAT DE MÉDECINE GÉNÉRALE
- DOCTORAT CHIRURGIE DENTAIRE
- DOCTORAT PHARMACIE
- DOCTORAT
- DEA
- DESS
- MAGISTÈRE INGÉNIEUR
- CONCOURS PROFESSORAT
- MAÎTRISE MST - MSG MIAGE MAÎTRISE IUP
- LICENCE IUP
- DEUG DEUST DEUP
- DUT
- BTS

CITE 6 / CITE 5 (Age 18)
Grades: CPGE I–V (Grandes Écoles); I–V (Écoles Spécialisées); I–XII (Universités – médecine/santé); IUFM; DUT I–III; BTS I–III

Institutions: GRANDES ÉCOLES · ÉCOLES SPÉCIALISÉES · UNIVERSITÉS (UFR – LETTRES – ARTS – SCIENCES HUMAINES – SCIENCES – DROIT – SCIENCES ÉCONOMIQUES) · IUT · STS

CITE 3 (Age 18 → 15/16)
- DIPLÔMES D'ÉCOLES SPÉCIALISÉES (X, XI)
- BAC général / BAC technologique (X, XI 1ère d'adaptation, XII)
- BT
- BAC professionnel (X, XI Terminale BEP ou CAP, XII, XIII)
- MC
- BEP / CAP

Institutions: ÉCOLES SPÉCIALISÉES · LYCÉES · LYCÉES PROFESSIONNELS

CITE 2 (Age 15/16 → 10/11)
- BREVET
- 3e générale · 3e d'insertion · 3e technologique (VI–IX)
- BREVET technologique LP (VIII, IX) – LYCÉES PROFESSIONNELS

Institution: COLLÈGES

CITE 1 (Age 10/11 → 6)
Grades I–V
Institution: ÉCOLES ÉLÉMENTAIRES

CITE 0 (Age 6 → 2)
Institution: ÉCOLES MATERNELLES

Colour codes (for details see page 249): **Pink** - Programme designed for part-time attendance. **Mauve** - Vocational education and training. **Blue triangle** - Recognised exit point of the education system. **Blue arrow** - Typical student flow. The size of the graphical elements provides no indication of the enrolment in the corresponding educational institutions.

Codes couleur (voir la page 249) : **Rose** - Programmes expressément à temps partiel. **Mauve** - Enseignement et formation professionnels. **Triangle bleu** - Point de sortie officiel du système éducatif. **Flèche bleue** - Progression typique des élèves ou étudiants. La taille des différents blocs ne représente pas la proportion des effectifs dans les établissements d'enseignement correspondants.

France

preparatory classes for the entrance examination to the *grandes écoles* (CPGE) and the higher technician sections (STS), with the vast majority of these preparatory classes taught in *lycées*. Admission to engineering and business *grandes écoles* is by competitive examination following completion of one to three years of special preparatory classes or several years of university education.

– by contrast, all holders of the baccalauréat are entitled to enrol in a university. In addition to the lengthy training for the health care professions (medicine, dentistry, pharmacy), universities provide three cycles of education leading successively to the Diploma of General University Studies (DEUG, at the end of the first cycle), the licence and Master's degree in the second cycle and the Diploma of Advanced Studies (DEA), the Diploma of Specialised Higher Studies (DESS) and the doctorate in the third cycle.

ii) The share of *private education* varies depending on the levels concerned: 13.8 per cent of children in the first level, 20.6 per cent in lower secondary education, 22.2 per cent in the upper secondary vocational cycle, 21.3 per cent in general and technical upper secondary education and 29.3 per cent in the final years of the *lycée*. At the primary and secondary levels, the vast majority of private schools (mainly Catholic) are under contract with the State being responsible, in particular, for teachers' salaries. In non-university higher education, the share of independent private institutions is much larger. There are very few private universities, all of which are government-dependent.

iii) *Special education* is mostly provided in primary and secondary schools but also in special institutions under the control of the Ministry of National Education or the Ministry of Health. It caters for nearly 5 per cent of students with various types of physical or mental disabilities.

iv) In addition to school-based education, *apprenticeship* training is another means of providing training for young people above the age of 16. Students who participate in this form of training learn a trade partly in employment under an apprenticeship trainer and partly in educational institutions referred to as *Centres de formation d'apprentis* (CFA). Apprentices are bound by a special type of work contract. Over three-quarters of them are enrolled at CFAs run by trade chambers, chambers of commerce and industry, professional associations or joint bodies. The other CFAs are run by vocational *lycées* or regional authorities. Since 1987, apprenticeship training can lead to all secondary or higher education diplomas (CAP, BEP, the vocational *baccalauréat*, the Advanced Technician's Diploma, the University Diploma of Technology, the *licence* and even engineering degrees). It concerns nearly 15 per cent of an age cohort.

v) Each year one out of five wage-earners participates in *adult education*, with management in the lead. It is an important activity of the public education sector. It has long been established through social promotion action in particular. Since the 1989 orientation act, it forms an integral part of the schools' functions.

Over the past twenty years secondary educational institutions have been grouped into GRÉTAs (*Groupement d'établissements*).

3. EDUCATIONAL FINANCE AND COSTS

Out of a total education expenditure of some FF 500 billion in 1993, the budget of the Ministry of National Education amounted to 281.7 billion, of which 90.9 per cent was for staff expenditure (including pensions). This budget represents 4 per cent of GDP. Excluding pensions, it can be broken down as follows: 25 per cent for primary education, 54 per cent for secondary education, 16 per cent for higher education and 5 per cent for the general administration of education.

The State funds two-thirds of total expenditure on education, which is far more than the share of the regional and local authorities (20 per cent) and those of enterprises and households. The educational expenditure of households tends to increase with the level of education. In 1992, household expenditure ranged from FF 1 000 per year at the beginning of secondary education to FF 1 600 per year in *lycées*. To these schooling costs must be added the enrolment fees charged in higher education which can be high in selective streams.

Students from the age of 6 to 18 may receive allowances at the commencement of the school year. Lower secondary students may be given financial aid, and *lycée* and university students may be awarded study grants. One *lycée* student out of four and one university student out of six received such grants.

There are three main sources of funding for adult training: the State, regional and local authorities and enterprises (which must devote 1.5 per cent of their wage bill to training). Total expenditure in 1993 amounted to some FF 50 billion. Initiatives in favour of the unemployed are mainly funded by the State.

4. CURRICULUM AND ASSESSMENT

The curriculum is defined in terms of subject matter and specifies the number of hours to be devoted to each subject. The curriculum is established by commissions made up of inspectors general, university, primary and secondary school teachers and experts from outside the Ministry. There are no regional variants to the curriculum set at national level.

In addition to the common, mandatory curriculum, students choose among optional courses. Over 20 languages are offered in secondary education. The vast majority of students choose English as their first foreign language and approximately half take Spanish as a second language.

Furthermore, over the past 4 or 5 years, reinforcement and remedial classes for small groups of students have become more widespread.

In lower and upper secondary education, students are differentiated (repeating, moving up to the next class, changing streams) according to a procedure involving the teachers, management and parents of students within each school. While

France

teachers' opinions come first, parents may appeal and insist that their children move up to the next class instead of repeating, or repeat instead of changing to another stream against their wishes, depending on their educational level. At each school a specialised team of advisors helps students, parents and teachers to solve any problems.

The Ministry of Education organises surveys on a regular basis to observe the level of achievement of all children after two years of primary education. These take place at the beginning and end of the *collège* and at the beginning of the *lycée* and are supplemented by the monitoring of children's progression through the system and studies on students' learning skills and social behaviour in school. Increasing attention is being paid to serious under-achievement which often ultimately leads students to leave school without a qualification. Given the growing difficulties young people face in finding a job, it is increasingly necessary to ensure that each student has a minimum qualification (at least the level of the CAP – Certificate of Vocational Competence – or the BEP – Diploma of Vocational Studies). In 1994, 8 per cent of young people left school without reaching the minimum level, compared with 15 per cent in 1980. Apprenticeship training is partly responsible for this decline as there has been a renewed interest in this form of training over the past two years. At the same time, there has been an increase in the number of placement schemes offered by schools under which *lycée* students (in particular those preparing the CAP, BEP, vocational *baccalauréat* and BTS) can gain work experience or follow training courses in enterprises.

5. TEACHERS

In 1993, there were some 900 000 classroom teachers of whom 90 per cent were employed by the Ministry of National Education. The other categories of staff in the education sector include inspectors and managers, educational advisors and guidance counsellors, documentalists and clerical and service staff. A substantial majority of educational staff are women (66 per cent). They account for 95 per cent of teachers in pre-primary schools, 75 per cent at the primary level, 55 per cent in secondary schools and 30 per cent in higher education.

Since 1991, all teachers receive training in teacher training university institutes (IUFM). The entrance requirement for these institutes is the *licence*. At the end of the first year, students must pass one of the two competitive examinations (*Professeur des écoles* or *Professeur d'enseignement secondaire*) in order to be admitted to the second year as teacher-trainees, for which they will receive a salary. At the end of the second year, they obtain the status of a normal civil servant and their qualification (*Professeur des écoles* or *Professeur d'enseignement secondaire*). Their training includes both theoretical training in how to teach different subjects and teaching practice.

The rise in enrolments and the number of teachers retiring has required an active recruitment policy whereby it has sometimes proved difficult to recruit staff to teach certain subjects. However, the large numbers of students entering the IUFMs is estimated as sufficient to meet future demand for teachers.

Throughout their careers, teachers are able to participate in continuing training programmes managed at the *département* or regional level. Primary school teachers are legally entitled to 36 weeks of training during their teaching career. For secondary teachers no set amount of training is specified in their contracts.

All teachers are subject to inspection visits after which they are rated. This rating is taken into account in their career development (transfers, advancement).

Germany

1. GENERAL CONTEXT

Since reunification in 1990, the Federal Republic of Germany now has an area of 357 000 square kilometres and a population of 81 million. Nearly 7 million are non-nationals (i.e. 8.5 per cent). The population density is 227 persons per square kilometre. One in three citizens lives in one of the 84 cities (each populated by more than 100 000 inhabitants) while the majority of the population live in villages and small towns.

The country consists of 16 states (*Länder*) (among them 3 city states), 29 *Regierungsbezirke* (the largest administrative division of a *Land*), 517 *Kreise* (administrative districts) with 115 of them being *kreisfreie Städte* (towns not belonging to a *Kreis*) and 402 *Landkreise* (rural districts), as well as 15 770 municipalities (*Gemeinden*).

Responsibility for the education system is determined by the federate state structure. Important decisions concerning structure and content of education are taken by the federal government together with the states as well as by the employers and employees, the latter with respect to the dual vocational training system.

The states are responsible for the major part of the education system, covering the school, higher education, adult education, continuing education and also cultural affairs sector. Schools are, as a rule, institutions maintained by municipalities and the states while higher education institutions are state-level institutions. There are also schools as well as higher education institutions maintained by the churches or private sponsors.

The fact that each state is responsible for education implies that the curricula and leaving certificates of the various schools differ from one state to another. The Standing Conference of *Länder* Ministers of Education (*Kultusministerkonferenz*) carries out important co-ordination activities. The federal government and the states co-operate in the planning and funding of higher education buildings and also jointly support pilot experiments in all sectors of the education system. The latter is carried out by the *Bund-Länder* Commission for Educational Planning and Research Promotion (BLK).

2. EDUCATIONAL STRUCTURE AND ENROLMENTS

The education system covers pre-primary, primary, secondary and higher education as well as continuing education.

Pre-primary education, typically for 3 to 6 year-olds, is optional. It does not form part of the state school system and is administered by the Youth Services (*Jugendhilfe*). The institutions responsible for kindergartens are in most cases churches, voluntary welfare organisations or municipalities and sometimes enterprises or associations.

Compulsory schooling lasts for 12 years, from age 6 to age 18. There are nine or ten years (depending on the state) of full-time compulsory education and the rest is compulsory part-time or full-time education. Part-time education takes place in part-time vocational schools within the framework of the dual vocational training system.

Primary schools comprise four years except in Berlin and Brandenburg where it is six years. After primary school children transfer to the first level of secondary education of which there are four general school types: *Hauptschule*, *Realschule*, *Gymnasium* and *Gesamtschule*. There are some variations in the different states.

About 30 per cent of the children enter the *Hauptschule* which provides a basic general education from grades 5 to 9 or 10 before entry to vocational education. The *Realschule* is located somewhere between the *Hauptschule* and the *Gymnasium* and provides its pupils with an enhanced general education from grades 5 to 10. It ends with a school-leaving certificate entitling holders to continue their education, in full-time vocational or advanced vocational schools. In 1993 about 40 per cent obtained this certificate.

The *Gymnasium* (usually grades 5 to 13) takes in about 30 per cent of the relevant age group. Grades 11-13 comprise the second level of secondary education wherein the traditional classes are abandoned in favour of a course system. The *Abitur* (secondary school-leaving certificate) is obtained at the end of grade 13 entitling the student to enter university-level tertiary education.

The *Gesamtschule* (comprehensive school) also provides a general education in a setting where children of all abilities are mixed. The grade levels are the same as in the *Gymnasium*. However, given the existence of the *Gymnasium* and *Realschule*, the *Gesamtschule* often has to compete for pupils.

After completing general compulsory education – typically at age 15 – students transfer to the second level of secondary education according to the leaving certificates obtained at the end of the first level. This second level provides education and training in general education and full-time vocational schools as well as vocational training under the dual system.

There is a great variety of vocational training opportunities: in part-time vocational schools, full-time vocational schools, advanced vocational schools, vocational grammar schools and trade and technical schools.

Most school-leavers are trained in the so-called "dual system" which combines practical enterprise-based training with academic education in a part-time vocational school; studies are thus shared by the private and public sectors. The federal government is responsible for non-school vocational education while the individual states are in charge of vocational schools. In 1994, about 1.6 million young people underwent training for one of some 450 recognised training occupations of highly differing popularity.

Apart from apprenticeship and vocational school, there are other routes to vocational training for young people. Two examples are the full-time vocational school (*Berufsfachschule*), which prepares students for entry into an occupation, and the advanced vocational school (*Fachoberschule*), which admits students from the *Realschule*. The students can obtain a *Fachhochschulreife* (entrance qualification for technical and vocational higher education).

The *Zweiter Bildungsweg* (second educational route) provides young people with the opportunity to catch up with what they missed during regular schooling. *Abendgymnasien* (evening grammar schools) enable gainfully employed people to prepare for the *Abitur* examination while continuing to work.

Germany

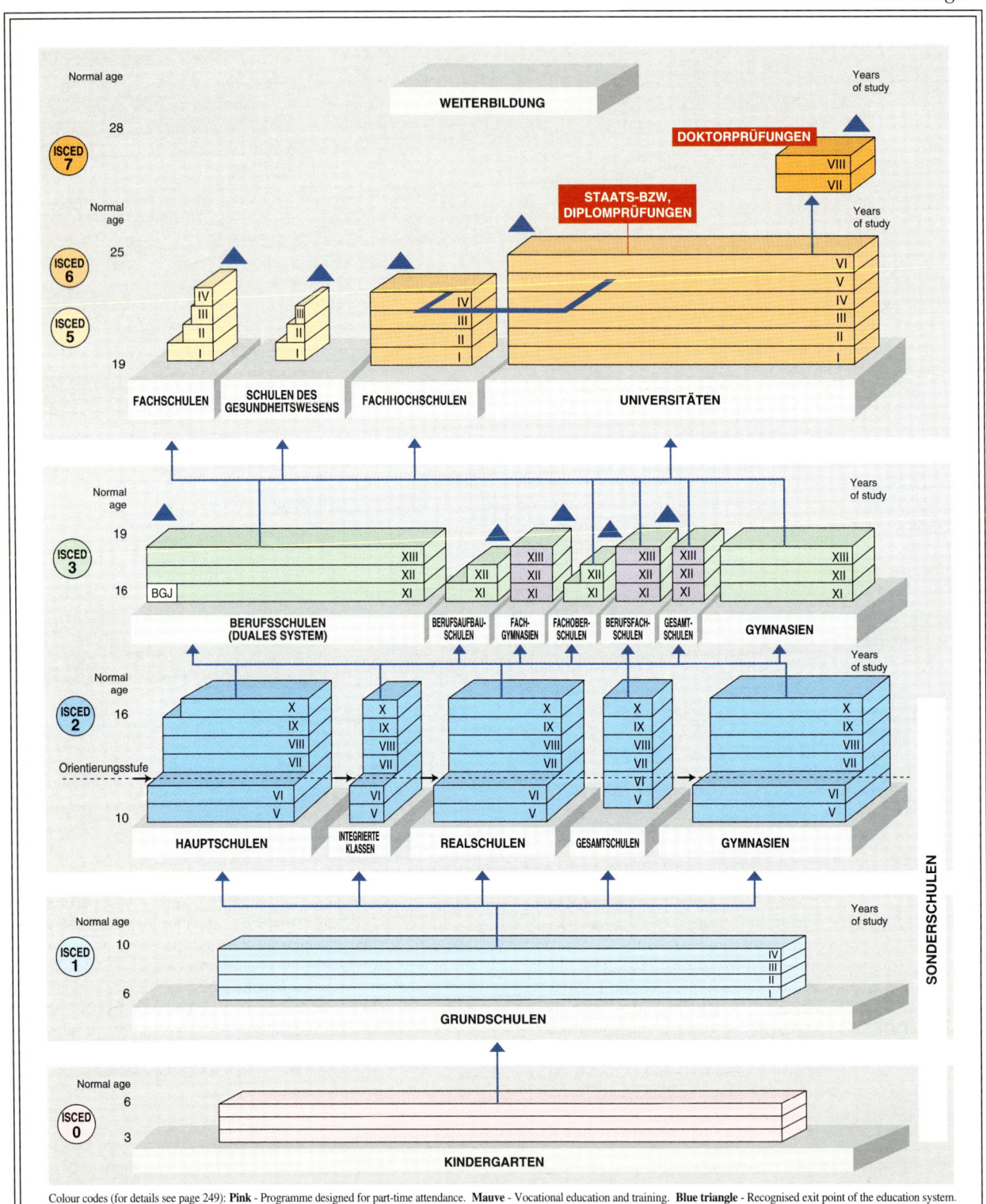

Allemagne

Normal age	ISCED	Institution	Years of study
28	ISCED 7	WEITERBILDUNG	
		DOKTORPRÜFUNGEN	VIII, VII
25	ISCED 6	STAATS-BZW, DIPLOMPRÜFUNGEN	VI, V, IV, III, II, I
	ISCED 5	FACHSCHULEN / SCHULEN DES GESUNDHEITSWESENS / FACHHOCHSCHULEN / UNIVERSITÄTEN	IV, III, II, I
19			

Normal age	ISCED	Institution	Years of study
19	ISCED 3	BERUFSSCHULEN (DUALES SYSTEM) / BERUFSAUFBAU-SCHULEN / FACH-GYMNASIEN / FACHOBER-SCHULEN / BERUFSFACH-SCHULEN / GESAMT-SCHULEN / GYMNASIEN	XIII, XII, XI
16		BGJ	

Normal age	ISCED	Institution	Years of study
16	ISCED 2	HAUPTSCHULEN / INTEGRIERTE KLASSEN / REALSCHULEN / GESAMTSCHULEN / GYMNASIEN	X, IX, VIII, VII, VI, V
10		Orientierungsstufe	

Normal age	ISCED	Institution	Years of study
10	ISCED 1	GRUNDSCHULEN	IV, III, II, I
6			

Normal age	ISCED	Institution
6	ISCED 0	KINDERGARTEN
3		

SONDERSCHULEN

Colour codes (for details see page 249): **Pink** - Programme designed for part-time attendance. **Mauve** - Vocational education and training. **Blue triangle** - Recognised exit point of the education system. **Blue arrow** - Typical student flow. The size of the graphical elements reflects the gross enrolment rates in the corresponding institutions at the corresponding level of education / At ISCED 3, after completing a first programme, many students follow a second or further programme at the same level.

Codes couleur (voir la page 249) : *Rose* - Programmes expressément à temps partiel. *Mauve* - Enseignement et formation professionnels. *Flèche bleue* - Progression typique des élèves ou étudiants. *Triangle bleu* - Point de sortie officiel du système éducatif. La taille relative des blocs reflète les taux bruts de scolarisation dans les établissements, au niveau d'enseignement correspondant. Au niveau CITE 3, de nombreux jeunes après avoir terminé leur premier cursus secondaire de deuxième cycle, en suivent un autre, ou plusieurs.

Germany

In 1994, there were a total of 325 state and state-recognised higher education institutions which included 112 universities and higher education institutions of equal status (such as technical universities, comprehensive universities and colleges of education), 46 colleges of art and music, 167 technical colleges (*Fachhochschulen*) and colleges of public administration. There exist also special types of higher education institutions such as those with restricted access for the armed services.

In 1994/95 there were nearly 1.9 million students in higher education. In 1994, some 267 000 new students entered higher education. Enrolment in higher education has expanded rapidly since the 1960s, and the government has attempted to cope with the situation by extending or constructing universities, hiring more teachers and considerably increasing funding. New study courses have been introduced, and studies have been more strongly oriented to subsequent practical occupational work. However, average study time is considered to be too long. A reform of study structures to improve the efficiency of higher education is under discussion.

Studies at the universities and other higher education institutions of equal rank are concluded with a *Diplom*, *Magister* or state examination. Following these degrees, it is possible to proceed to doctoral or post-graduate studies. The *Fachhochschulen* provide more practical-oriented training which is concluded with the *Diplom* examination, most often in the fields of engineering, economics, social work/social studies, design and agriculture. Almost one in three first-year students chooses this type of institution which has a shorter standard period of study than the universities. Hesse and North Rhine-Westphalia established the so-called *Gesamthochschulen* (comprehensive universities) in the 1970s. They combine various types of higher education institutions under one roof and offer a correspondingly greater number of possible study courses and degrees. The University for Distance Education at Hagen, with an enrolment of almost 42 500 students in 1995, was established in 1976.

In 1994 just under 40 per cent of students in the former territory of the Federal Republic and more than 46 per cent in the new states were women.

Continuing education is becoming increasingly important and comprises, with equal importance, the areas of general and vocational education. More than 10 million citizens avail themselves of the numerous offers of continuing education annually. It is offered by municipal institutions, particularly *Volkshochschulen* (adult education centres), private providers, institutions of the churches, trade unions, chambers of commerce, political parties and associations, enterprises and public administration, schools for parents and *Familienbildungsstätten* (church-sponsored family-oriented adult education centres), academies, *Fachschulen* (trade and technical schools) and higher education institutions as well as distance education providers. Continuing education programmes are also offered by radio and television.

3. EDUCATIONAL FINANCE AND COSTS

The majority of educational institutions are public. Attendance at all public schools is free. Instructional materials (mainly textbooks) are provided either free or on a lending basis. In some cases parents must contribute according to their income. Specific groups of learners receive government training assistance. Government funding of the education system is based on decision-making processes within the political/administrative system within which various forms of government expenditure on education are co-ordinated depending on the responsibilities of the federal government, the states and the municipalities as well as in accordance with educational policy and other requirements.

Decisions concerning educational funding are taken at three levels: federal government, state, and municipalities, but the states and the municipalities shoulder more than 90 per cent of the educational expenditure.

In 1993 the joint educational budget of the federal government, the states and the municipalities amounted to DM 159.8 billion. This accounted for 5.06 per cent of GDP and 13.82 per cent of the overall public budget, with 1.17 per cent of the overall public budget going to the pre-primary sector and non-school youth education, 7.13 per cent to schools, 3.74 per cent to higher education institutions, 0.39 per cent to continuing education, 0.72 per cent to support and assistance measures and 0.67 per cent to joint federal government and state research funding.

In addition, the private sector made available DM 115.6 billion for education and research in the fields of vocational education and training, continuing vocational education, research and development in 1993. Of this total DM 28.8 billion was accounted for by in-company training under the dual system provided by industry and other training institutions. Part-time vocational schools, which together with industrial companies fulfil the educational mission of the dual system, are financed by public funds.

The expenditure of the states and the municipalities on education (excluding research funding) increased from DM 69.4 billion in 1980 to DM 146.1 billion in 1993 (old and new *Länder*). Federal government expenditure increased from DM 4.2 billion to DM 6.4 billion over the same period (excluding research funding).

4. CURRICULUM AND ASSESSMENT

The state ministries of education (with a few exceptions in vocational and technical education) determine their curricula in accordance with existing legislation, and they do so in three ways: *i)* tables prescribing the number of periods per week and subject by school type and grade level; *ii)* curriculum guidelines; and *iii)* the authorisation of textbooks. Whereas the general aims of education are laid down in school legislation (often as preambles to Acts of Parliament), specific objectives are given in the context of curriculum guidelines. These include syllabuses, recommendations on teaching methods and, sometimes, model lesson plans. Only the syllabus is considered to be obligatory.

For promotion from grade to grade, it is the teachers who decide on the basis of teacher-made tests, class work and homework. The results are reported in the form of written reports or marks on a six-point scale. Informal tests (in the higher grades of up to five hours' duration) are given with a prescribed minimum frequency. Because of the variety of assessment procedures, students' marks or scores are not comparable across states or even classrooms because

Germany

they depend on individual judgement and potentially quite different achievement tasks. Grade repeating is not extensive. The second level of secondary education is somewhat different in that credits are awarded on a 16-point scale and are weighted and accumulated over a four-semester period.

Study and examination regulations in higher education institutions are under evaluation to improve the quality of the higher education system and its outcomes. In schools as well as in higher education institutions, European topics have increasingly entered the curriculum.

There is no national assessment although the states now co-operate in some international surveys of educational achievement.

5. TEACHERS

Teachers are specially trained for each type of school. While all teachers attend higher education, study courses vary in accordance with state legislation. The prospective primary and secondary school teacher usually studies for six semesters. A longer study period is required for teachers at *Realschulen*, *Gymnasien* and vocational schools. At the end of their studies, all trainee teachers must pass the first state examination. This is followed by an additional two-year programme of combined practical and theoretical training culminating with a second state examination. Teachers, as a rule, become civil servants with life tenure.

Pre-primary school teachers do not have the training or status of teachers. They are mostly state-recognised educators trained at the *Fachschulen für Sozialpädagogik* (schools for social work/social studies).

In higher education there are a variety of full-time staff who work in domains other than that of academics. No special training is required. Candidates for a teaching post must have the necessary qualifications, a doctorate for example, and, where appropriate, suitable experience.

Greece

1. GENERAL CONTEXT

Greece (*Hellas*) consists of a mainland (81 per cent of which is mountainous) in south-eastern Europe and numerous islands in the Aegean and Ionian Seas. The area covers 131 957 square kilometres and the population is 10.4 million inhabitants (estimated figures from the National Statistical Service – 1/1/1995). There is a declining birth rate.

The new Greek State was established in 1828 and has witnessed many socio-political changes. Since 1975 the country has been a republic with a President, a Prime Minister, 300 Deputies, 13 Regions and 54 Administrative Departments (*Nomos*). The language of the country is Greek (*Hellenika*) which descends from ancient Greek through 3 000 years of continuous use and modification.

Major urban centres are inhabited by 58 per cent of the population (1981). Greater Athens alone accounts for about 30 per cent of the country's population, 60 per cent of private investments, 47 per cent of the industrial manpower and almost all the administrative and cultural activities. After the destructive effects of World War II and the devastating civil war (1944-49) and their difficult aftermath, the country achieved a rapid entry into the group of developed countries.

In 1994, the per capita income was US$ 11 315, and in 1993, 11 per cent of the population were employed in agriculture, 25 per cent in industry and 64 per cent in services while the unemployment rate was 10.1 per cent in 1995.

Constitutionally, education is a government responsibility and is provided free at all levels from pre-school to university. The education system remains predominantly centralised and the funding is basically provided from the centre. Since 1981, there has been a gradual process towards decentralisation of education and many decisions and the management of funds are administered at the *Nomos* or municipality levels.

Education is predominantly public – totally at the tertiary level and almost entirely at the primary and secondary levels. However, outside the formal education system there are a considerable number of private schools for foreign languages, liberal studies, coaching candidates for entrance into higher education, etc.

Education policy has many goals which range from the provision of compulsory education for all to the reduction of unemployment, from the modernisation of the curricula to the conservation of the cultural tradition and from catering for the high demand for higher education to achieving all of these goals despite insufficient resources. Not all of these goals are easy to achieve, and the output of the education system does not always respond to the changing needs of the economy and the labour market.

2. EDUCATIONAL STRUCTURE AND ENROLMENTS

Formal education

Kindergarten education is not compulsory. It lasts for one or two years and enrols children between 4 and 5 years of age. In 1992/93 there were 5 409 schools in the public sector with 7 743 teachers and 128 940 children. In the private sector there were 141 schools with 256 teachers and 6 017 children. Higher enrolments would be expected if more schools had been provided. In 1992, the enrolment rate was 48.9 per cent for 4 year-olds and 61.5 per cent for 5 year-olds.

Primary school education is compulsory, lasts for six years and caters for children aged 6 to 12 years. In 1992/93 there were 7 116 State schools with 36 363 teachers and 725 278 children, while there were 404 private schools with 2 487 teachers and 55 494 children. There has been a sizeable reduction in enrolments due to a declining birth rate. One of the problems has been the existence of many small schools with one or two teachers in mountainous or isolated areas. An effort is under way to reduce their number by merging school-units and providing school transport. Although only 3 per cent of the Greek population belongs to linguistic and cultural minorities, special schools have been set up to offer instruction in their native languages and cultures.

Lower secondary education is compulsory, lasts for three years and caters for children aged 12 to 15 years. In 1993/94 there were 1 857 schools, 29 459 teachers and 443 641 students. For 14 year-olds, the enrolment rate was 97.6 per cent and for 15 year-olds 94.3 per cent.

Upper secondary education is not compulsory, lasts for three years and caters for students aged 15 to 18 years. In 1993/94 there were the following types of upper secondary schools:
- *General Lyceums*: 1 170 schools, 17 729 teachers, 255 584 students.
- *Technical-Vocational Lyceums*: 353 schools, 8 636 teachers, 114 667 students.
- *Integrated Lyceums*: 25 schools (which have since increased to 39), 1 878 teachers, 22 084 students. This type was first introduced in 1984 and differs from the other categories in that it offers a greater variety of courses that link technical and general education.

Tertiary education takes place in universities and technological education institutes (*TEI*). University education lasts for between four and six years. In 1993/94, there were 18 institutions, with 9 354 teachers and 109 335 students. In 1992, the enrolment rate for 18 to 21 year-olds was 15.6 per cent.

Technological education lasts for three to four years for students aged 18 or over. In 1993/94 there were 13 institutions, with 5 427 teachers and 77 928 students. In 1992, the enrolment rate for the age group 18-21 was 8.2 per cent.

Efforts are underway to create and develop a high standard of graduate studies, which should result in fewer students pursuing graduate studies abroad. For the whole university sector an effort is being made to modernise the structure as well as the content and teaching methods in order to achieve a higher quality of studies.

Non-formal education

Non-formal education comprises programmes for adults organised by the Secretariat for Adult Education and training

Greece

programmes under various ministries (e.g. Employment, Agriculture, etc.) as well as various special programmes such as reception classes for immigrant children, in-service training for public servants, vocational training and the like.

There are also the Institutes for Vocational Training (*IEK*). In the public sector in 1994/95, there were 59 institutes with 4 000 teachers and 13 000 students which provided 62 different types of courses, while in the private sector there were 73 institutes with 13 592 students providing 37 different types of courses. This type of education started in 1992 in order to cater for students who had completed secondary education but needed vocational training to improve their opportunities in the labour market.

3. EDUCATIONAL FINANCE AND COSTS

In 1995 the national government supplied more than 95 per cent of the funds for education. The remaining part came from support from the European Union. Subsidies from the European Union are expected to rise over the coming years.

State expenditure (current and capital) for all education under the Ministry of Education has, in constant prices, increased gradually.

The proportion of government expenditure allocated to education was, in the period 1970-1994, an average of 10 per cent. However, during the 1990s, this proportion decreased to an average of around 7 per cent. On the other hand, public education expenditure as a proportion of GDP has increased gradually from 2 per cent in 1970 to 4 per cent in 1994. This is explained partly by the increase in overall public education expenditure and, partly, by the low rate of growth in GDP.

Irrespective of State expenditure on education, a very large number of parents devote a considerable amount of private expenditure to the coaching of their children; either to support them during secondary school or to prepare them for the Higher Education entrance examinations. This expenditure, together with the expenditure of families for their children to pursue higher education degrees or post-graduate degrees abroad, foreign language courses or other private lessons, would raise Greek educational expenditure to about 6.5 per cent of GDP if they were added to public expenditure.

4. CURRICULUM AND ASSESSMENT

For all primary and secondary schools, there is a nation-wide uniform curriculum, the scope and content of which is established by the Ministry of National Education. A single formal syllabus is prepared by the Pedagogic Institute and ratified by the Ministry. Textbooks are prepared by individuals or teams following specific guidelines, selected by the Pedagogic Institute and again ratified by the Ministry. There is a single textbook for every subject at each grade level. There is also a Teacher's Guide for each grade level providing suggestions about teaching methodology for selected content. Significant reforms are planned, including new curricula and textbooks, expansion of information technology, professional orientation, development of school libraries, etc.

Any curriculum development faces challenges such as familiarising the students with the complete evolution of the Greek language and its textual development (Ancient Greek, Medieval Greek, 19th Century Greek and so on).

The quality, implementation and outcomes of the curriculum are the subject of considerable debate and are also influenced by such factors as the financing of education and the provision of sufficient classroom stock to afford the flexibility needed for the implementation of new curricula.

The forms of assessment used include descriptive evaluation in primary education and quantitative evaluation in secondary education. Work has begun on establishing national tests for upper secondary education.

In primary education pupils are automatically promoted, but this practice is currently being reconsidered.

5. TEACHERS

Teachers for all school levels have to be tertiary graduates, either from pedagogical departments (for primary school teachers) or from the faculties of the respective disciplines (for secondary education teachers). The career development of teachers depends to a great extent on their obtaining post-graduate degrees.

In 1993/94 there were 7 859 teachers (16 students per teacher) employed in pre-school education, 37 214 teachers (19:1) in primary education, 28 139 teachers (15:1) in lower secondary education, 29 733 teachers (13:1) in upper secondary education, 5 800 teachers (16:1) in *TEI*s and 9 100 teachers (13:1) in the *AEI*s.

The modern and efficient training of primary and secondary school teachers is a priority area and various new policies are being applied in both pre- and in-service training. In the second Community Support Framework of the European Union there is provision for Dr 35 billion for innovation in teacher training (compulsory or voluntary training, intensive seminars, distance training, special training days, etc.).

There are serious problems with regards to the teaching force. One is the seniority system whereby teachers are on a waiting list for career development. Some believe that eliminating the seniority principle would encourage clientelism, while others claim that it inhibits the emergence of a "younger" and more effective teaching force. Other problems include low salaries, lack of incentives and excessive administrative duties which distract teachers from their main commitment to teaching as such.

Greece

Grèce

Post-Graduate Studies (ISCED 7)
- DOCTORATE
- MASTER'S (VI, VII, VIII, IX, X)

ISCED 6 / ISCED 5 — Higher Education (Normal age 18–23)

Universities (18 institutions):
- DIPLOMAS OF TECHNICAL UNIVERSITIES
- DIPLOMAS OF MEDICINE SCHOOLS
- DIPLOMAS OF DENTISTRY SCHOOLS
- DIPLOMAS OF AGRICULTURE SCHOOLS
- DIPLOMAS OF OTHER UNIVERSITY SCHOOLS

Technological Education Establishments (14 institutions)

ISCED 3 — Post-secondary Vocational
- EPL — VOCATIONAL TRAINING (1 YEAR)
- IEK — INSTITUTE OF VOCATIONAL TRAINING (1 YEAR)

Upper Secondary (Normal age 14½–17½)
- GEL — GENERAL LYKEION (X, XI, XII)
- EPL — INTEGRATED LYKEION (X, XI, XII)
- TEL — TECHNICAL AND VOCATIONAL LYKEION (X, XI, XII)
- TES — TECHNICAL AND VOCATIONAL SCHOOL (XI, XII)

ISCED 2 — GYMNASION (Normal age 11½–14½)
Years VII, VIII, IX

ISCED 1 — DIMOTIKO (PRIMARY SCHOOL) (Normal age 5½–11½)
Years I, II, III, IV, V, VI

ISCED 0 — NURSERY SCHOOL (Normal age 3½–5½)

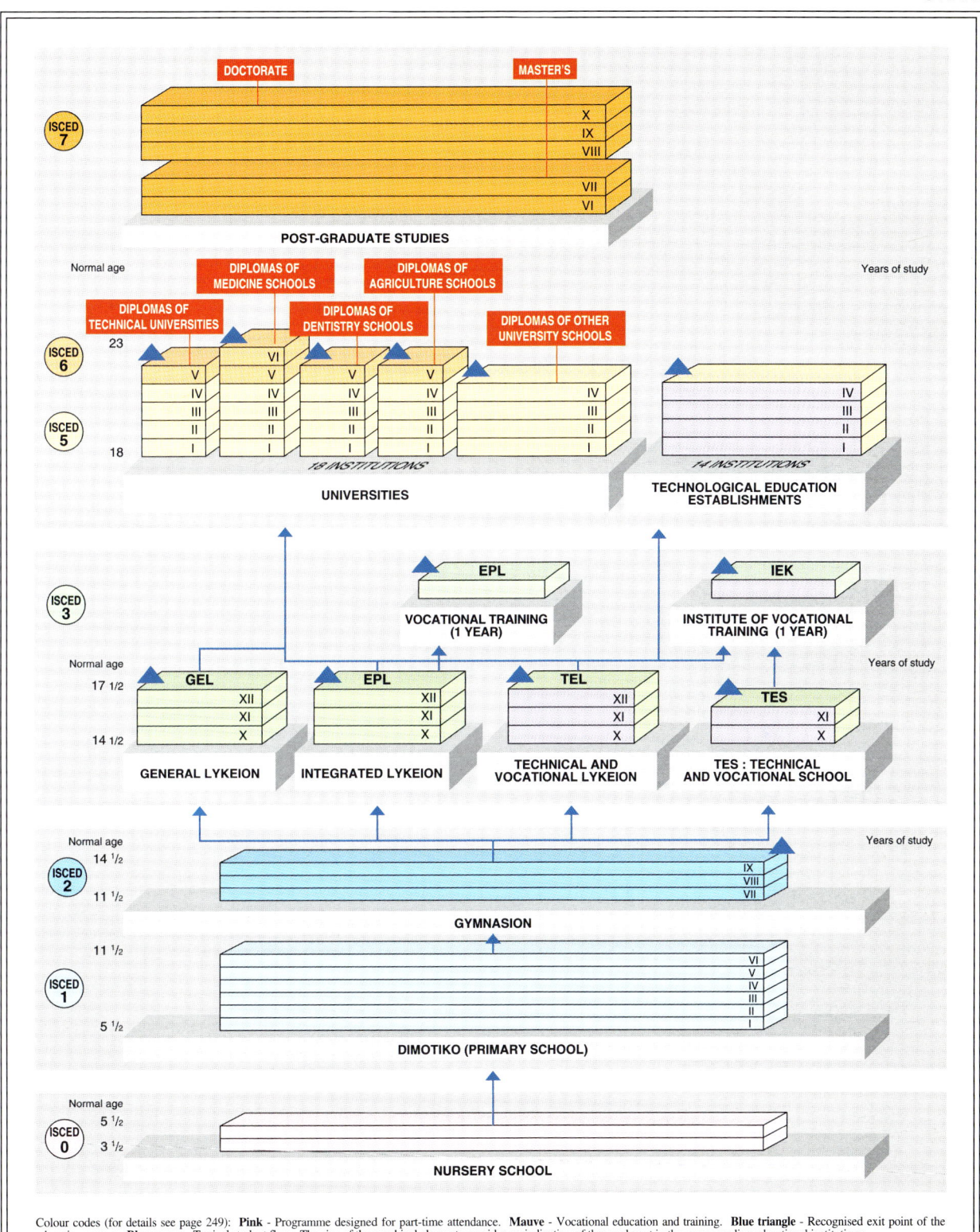

Colour codes (for details see page 249): **Pink** - Programme designed for part-time attendance. **Mauve** - Vocational education and training. **Blue triangle** - Recognised exit point of the education system. **Blue arrow** - Typical student flow. The size of the graphical elements provides no indication of the enrolment in the corresponding educational institutions.

*Codes couleur (voir la page 249) : **Rose** - Programmes expressément à temps partiel. **Mauve** - Enseignement et formation professionnels. **Triangle bleu** - Point de sortie officiel du système éducatif. **Flèche bleue** - Progression typique des élèves ou étudiants. La taille des différents blocs ne représente pas la proportion des effectifs dans les établissements d'enseignement correspondants.*

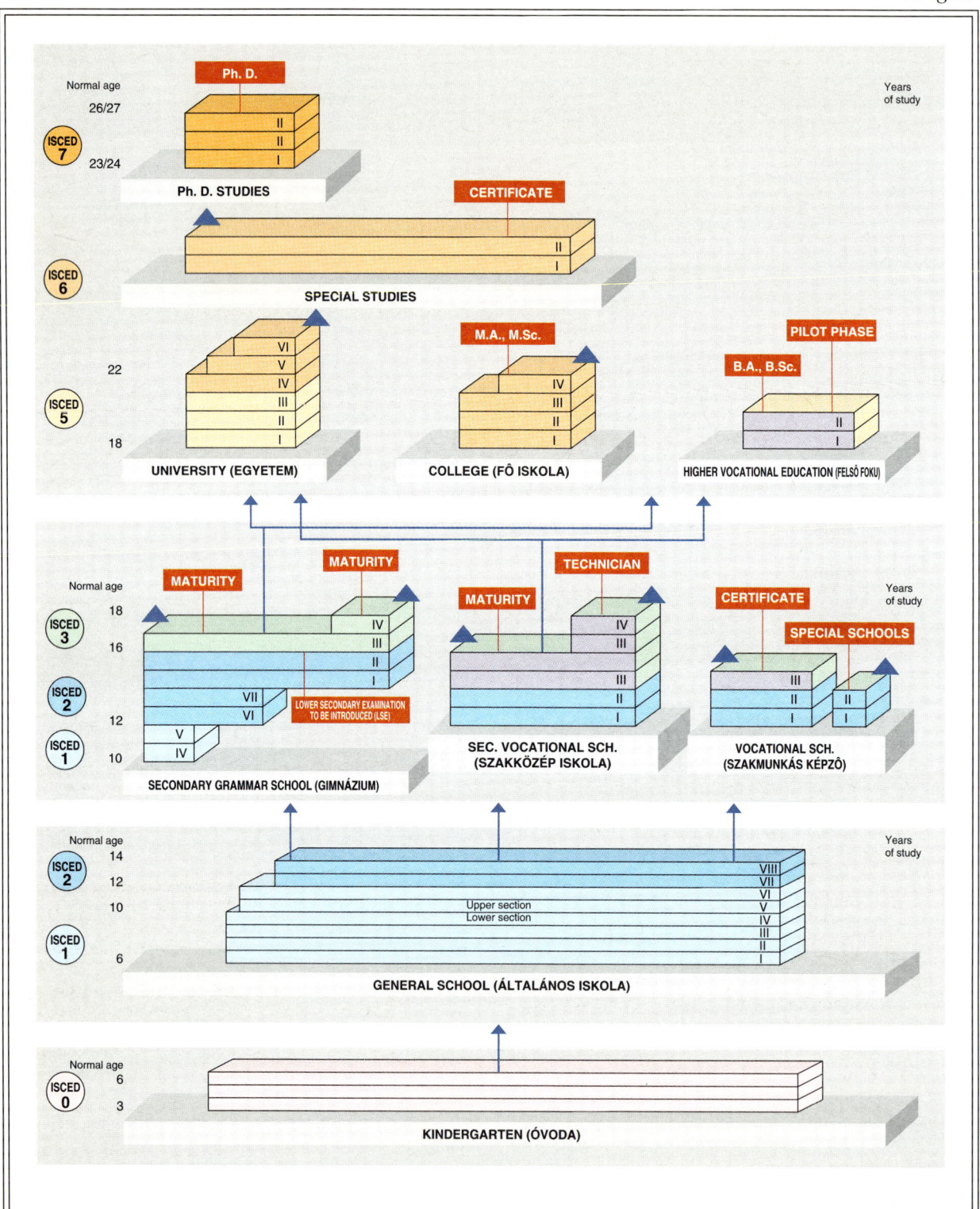

Hungary

Hongrie

ISCED 7 — Normal age 26/27, 23/24 — Ph. D. STUDIES (Ph. D.)

ISCED 6 — SPECIAL STUDIES (CERTIFICATE)

ISCED 5 — Normal age 18–22 — UNIVERSITY (EGYETEM) (M.A., M.Sc.) — COLLEGE (FÔ ISKOLA) (M.A., M.Sc.) — HIGHER VOCATIONAL EDUCATION (FELSÔ FOKU) (B.A., B.Sc. — PILOT PHASE)

ISCED 3 — Normal age 16–18 — SECONDARY GRAMMAR SCHOOL (GIMNÁZIUM) (MATURITY) — SEC. VOCATIONAL SCH. (SZAKKÖZÉP ISKOLA) (MATURITY / TECHNICIAN) — VOCATIONAL SCH. (SZAKMUNKÁS KÉPZÔ) (CERTIFICATE) — SPECIAL SCHOOLS

ISCED 2 / ISCED 1 — Normal age 10–14 — LOWER SECONDARY EXAMINATION TO BE INTRODUCED (LSE)

ISCED 2 / ISCED 1 — Normal age 6–14 — GENERAL SCHOOL (ÁLTALÁNOS ISKOLA) — Upper section / Lower section

ISCED 0 — Normal age 3–6 — KINDERGARTEN (ÓVODA)

Colour codes (for details see page 249): **Pink** - Programme designed for part-time attendance. **Mauve** - Vocational education and training. **Blue triangle** - Recognised exit point of the education system. **Blue arrow** - Typical student flow. The size of the graphical elements reflects the gross enrolment rates in the corresponding institutions at the corresponding level of education.

Codes couleur (voir la page 249) : Rose - Programmes expressément à temps partiel. Mauve - Enseignement et formation professionnels. Triangle bleu - Point de sortie officiel du système éducatif. Flèche bleue - Progression typique des élèves ou étudiants. La taille relative des blocs reflète les taux bruts de scolarisation dans les établissements, au niveau d'enseignement correspondant.

Hungary

1. GENERAL CONTEXT

The Republic of Hungary in eastern-central Europe covers an area of 93 000 square kilometres and has a population of 10.3 million inhabitants (1994) with a density of 111 inhabitants per square kilometre. In spite of trends towards urbanisation, there are still many small villages with their own elementary school, and a considerable part of the variation in student achievement is explained by the urban or rural location of schools.

The population is fairly homogeneous with 98 per cent Hungarians. Ethnic minorities include Germans, Slovaks, Serbs, Croats, Romanians and Slovenes and a sizeable Gypsy population.

In 1994 GDP per capita was US$ 4 019. Despite its low economic standing compared, for example, to its neighbour Austria where per-capita GDP is nearly seven times that in Hungary, education has a high standing. In 1994 the active workforce accounted for 40 per cent of the total population with just over 58 per cent in the service sector, 33 per cent in industry and 9 per cent in agriculture. Unemployment is a recent phenomenon. In 1994 some 10 per cent of the workforce were unemployed.

A move towards decentralising the school system has had implications for curriculum development, the examination system and the different levels at which decisions are taken. Responsibility for education is shared among three levels: the central government as represented by the Ministry of Culture and Education and the Ministry of Labour for vocational education; the municipalities, churches and foundations which maintain schools and the schools themselves (including school boards consisting of representatives of teachers, parents and maintainers). The government provides basic funding, the ministries guide education (through the core curriculum and the examinations system) and the Ministry of Culture and Education exercises legal supervision on the whole system. The municipalities are expected to complement the funds allocated by the State, sometimes by collecting money from the parents for textbooks. School boards carry out advisory tasks for the school.

2. EDUCATIONAL STRUCTURE AND ENROLMENTS

Early childhood education takes place in kindergartens for the 3-6 year-olds. In 1993 there were 4 712 kindergartens and they enrolled about 90 per cent of an age cohort. Before 1990 they were run either by the State or by major factories. At the beginning of the 1990s, most kindergartens were maintained by municipalities, but some were also provided for by churches and the private sector.

Young children attend kindergarten for an average of 3.2 years. In practice, every 5 year-old attends kindergarten as mandatorily prescribed by the 1993 Education Act (with possible exemptions). The last year in a kindergarten is thus a year of preparation for school, at the end of which kindergarten teachers examine whether the child is mature enough for school. Those who are not may stay on for another year. More than 80 per cent of kindergarten teachers have tertiary-level qualifications.

The most important institution of *basic education* is the 8-grade general school. Admission occurs flexibly between the ages 6 and 7. This type of school includes the primary level (four years in the lower grades) and the lower secondary level (the next four years, or upper grades). As basic education takes eight years to complete while compulsory schooling lasts for 10 years, children who do not enter secondary schools may continue for the remaining two years in a general school or in special vocational schools.

In rural areas many small and mostly ungraded schools were closed prior to 1985 for the sake of improving the standard of teaching. In 1970 there were 5 450 general schools including 3 103 entirely or partly ungraded schools. By 1993 only 586 out of 3 771 general schools had remained partly or entirely ungraded and 1 127 provided only elementary grades. Since then, many municipalities have reopened some of the small rural schools. The enrolment in general schools was just over one million children in 1993.

Basic education for the disabled is organised partly in specialised institutions, partly in special classes in regular schools.

After the 8-grade general school, there are three main types of upper secondary education. In 1993, about 24 per cent entered the academic *secondary grammar school*, 32 per cent the secondary vocational school, 36 per cent the *three-year vocational school*, 6 per cent the *special vocational school* and about 2 per cent dropped out of school.

The school type providing general education preparing for the Mature Examination for the Certificate of Secondary Education (MCSE) is the *secondary grammar school*. It covers different durations depending on the institution: mainly 4 grades following the 8-grade basic education but, for special or supplementary courses, it can be 5-grades long; besides, 6- or 8-grade grammar schools following the 6- or 4-grade basic education have been instituted and expanded since the early 1990s. By this time, there were 4-grade secondary grammar schools that extended downwards for either two or four years. (The notion of the German *gymnasium* has always had high prestige.) These types of grammar schools are also different with respect to the content and level of education. Although the main objective of grammar schools is to prepare for higher education, a number of them also regard preparing for the labour market as an important objective.

The school type which prepares for the MCSE while at the same time providing vocational training is the *secondary vocational school*, with traditionally 4-year programmes. But it now also covers three types of provision with different objectives: *i)* The five-year secondary technical school training medium-level technical experts (technicians), *ii)* the formerly four-year, now increasingly five-year, secondary schools preparing mainly for vocations in the service sector and *iii)* the four-year secondary vocational schools which prepare for the Certificate of Secondary Education and grant qualifications at skilled worker level.

The three-year vocational school, which does not prepare for the MCSE, is still the largest component of the vocational sector. Yet despite decreasing enrolments over the past few years, it still attracts the largest number of young people after their eight-year basic education. Enrolment in the two-year typist and stenographer training school and the three-year health care vocational school is also decreasing. The special vocational school deserves particular attention: since 1990 it admits non-handicapped children alongside

Hungary

the disabled. Here, students unable to gain admittance to any of the other secondary-level institutions are offered a two-year programme.

In 1993, there were 270 secondary grammar schools, 446 secondary vocational schools and 150 comprehensive secondary schools enrolling 138 198 grammar school students and 192 388 vocational school students in full-time courses. In addition there were 332 three-year vocational schools enrolling 174 187 students. The 23 three-year health-care vocational schools enrolled 4 224 full-time students and the 49 two-year typist training schools 3 494 students. There were also 125 special vocational schools enrolling 17 298 students.

Higher education consists of general courses and professional training outside the school system, through which higher-level qualifications acknowledged by the State can also be obtained. The so-called post-secondary education is still in an experimental phase and waiting to be integrated into the formal education system. This is why ISCED 5 data are not reported for the school year 1993/94.

There are both universities and colleges (the latter are organised following the model of the German *Fachhochschule*). Universities generally impart high-standard theoretical knowledge, while colleges offer more practically oriented and shorter courses. Part of the university and college structure is specialised: the former classic European university structure was broken up into faculties (medical, agricultural, economic and technical) early in the 1950s, and colleges were also organised around these specialisations to meet the demands of the economy. Early in the 1990s, a number of church-run higher education institutions were established. At present there are 89 independent institutions, of which 30 are universities (25 State and 5 church-maintained universities) and 59 are colleges (32 State, 23 church-run and 4 run by foundations). Universities may offer both university and college-level education. Church-run higher education institutions increasingly offer courses other than theology (e.g. teacher training). In 1993, 103 713 full-time and 30 243 part-time (evening and correspondence) students were enrolled altogether.

The minimum duration of university graduate education is four years (eight semesters), but the typical duration is usually five years and can range up to six years. In specialised post-graduate education, the minimum period is one year, generally two and exceptionally three. Doctoral studies take three years. University post-graduate education now also includes doctoral studies formerly carried out in the separate research sector. This is why ISCED 7 data are reported for enrolments but not for graduates.

According to the 1993 Higher Education Act, admission to university or college graduate education requires the MCSE or an equivalent. The entrance requirement for post-graduate education is a university or college degree or diploma and, for doctoral studies, a university degree or equivalent.

Adult education mainly takes the form of evening and/or correspondence courses. Distance learning is beginning to spread, primarily in higher education.

3. EDUCATIONAL FINANCE AND COSTS

According to national statistics for 1993, the education budget amounted to 231 527 million Hungarian Forint (HUF) for current expenditure and HUF 13 838 million for capital expenditure. In addition to direct expenditure for educational institutions, this expenditure includes school-meals, day care, student hostels and student grants.

4. CURRICULUM AND ASSESSMENT

Although there is a common core curriculum, provisions are also made for local components. Each school is encouraged to add further components to the core curriculum and many schools do so. Curricula that are considered valuable are made known throughout the country. Before the "change", Russian was a compulsory subject for all students. Now English and German are in high demand but, despite a retraining programme, there is a shortage of teachers.

There are two major transition points in the system. The first is the transition from general school into secondary school. Access to the different types of secondary programmes is regulated by student marks in general school. If compulsory education is extended by two years as is currently intended, then a national examination at the end of grade 10 will need to be introduced. The second transition point is at the end of grade 12, when students must decide whether or not to take the final school-based examination. Besides the secondary school-leaving examination, universities have their own entrance examinations.

5. TEACHERS

Teachers are trained at colleges and universities. Pre-primary and primary teachers undergo a three- or four-year training programme, lower secondary teachers a four-year programme and secondary school teachers a five-year programme. In 1992 there were 35 colleges and universities training 40 000 undergraduate future teachers. The present system has been criticised as being too subject-matter oriented, with insufficient educational theory and practice. It is anticipated that there will be several reforms in teacher training. After many years of teacher shortage, there is now some unemployment among teachers.

In 1993 there were about 90 000 basic school teachers, 12 000 secondary grammar school teachers, 15 000 vocational secondary school teachers, 11 000 vocational school teachers, 1 200 typist, health and special vocational teachers and 6 500 special basic education teachers. In-service training courses are encouraged but not compulsory. Such courses are held in county pedagogical institutions or are school-based.

In higher education 16 761 full-time and 1 926 part-time lecturers were employed in 1993. Since 1995 a reduction of higher education staff is on the agenda.

Ireland

1. GENERAL CONTEXT

Ireland is a peripheral island in north-western Europe, occupying 69 000 square kilometres and with a population of almost 3.6 million people of whom nearly 50 per cent are aged under 29 years. Dublin, the capital city, and its suburbs account for almost one-third of the population. In 1986/87 well over a quarter of the population was undergoing full-time education or training (27 per cent in 1994/95).

The Irish economy grew by over 7 per cent in 1995 and continued strong economic growth is forecast. Gross National Product (which excludes all profits earned in the multinational sector) grew by 7.3 per cent. Gross Domestic Product grew by 10.1 per cent. Although 52 000 new jobs were created in 1995, unemployment is high and most serious among the unqualified, the unskilled and the young. Unemployment also affects many who are qualified, such as teachers. A number of key initiatives in education and training have been largely financed from sources of the European Union. Some critics allege that the teaching of foreign languages is inadequate, but many schools have established flourishing exchange programmes.

The State has constitutional responsibility for the national education system. Many of the proposals for comprehensive change and development of the education system, contained in the White Paper on Education "Charting our Education Future", are being implemented. These include the establishment of ten Education Boards (EBs) functioning in an effective partnership with the Department of Education, the providers of education, parents and local community interests, including the business sector and locally elected representatives. The Department of Education will concentrate primarily on strategic planning, quality assurance and budgetary responsibilities.

There has been a strong emphasis in recent years on the links between education and the economy. Ireland has had no choice but to develop its industrial capacity at speed, and this has necessitated a drive to expand vocational and technical education and enhance its quality. This expansion has been accompanied by a parallel drive to widen access to post-compulsory general education in the cause of equality and opportunity. It is a major official objective to increase the percentage of the 16 to 18 year-old age group completing senior cycle to at least 90 per cent by the year 2000 (in 1995 it was 77 per cent, but only 33 per cent in 1970). The expansion of education at second level into a mass participation system is also emerging in tertiary education.

The structure of the system of education in Ireland owes much to history. Irish schools are owned, not by the State, but by community groups, traditionally religious groups. It is in general an aided system: the State does not itself operate the schools (with a few minor exceptions) but assists other bodies, usually religious, to do so. Almost 92 per cent of the population of Ireland are Roman Catholics and religious authorities play a pre-eminent role in the realm of education.

Until the 1960s the education system was both static and gravely under-resourced. In the compulsory sector many of the classes were much too large, and almost a quarter of teachers were untrained. The upper secondary sector was small and fee paying. Higher education was elitist. In 1967 free education became available at the second level and this, coupled with the beginning of economic expansion, led the State to assume an increasingly interventionist role. Money was allocated to build new schools and post-secondary institutions, and thousands of new teachers were appointed. School enrolments doubled between 1960 and 1970, and almost trebled between 1963 and 1986. The system expanded up to the mid-1980s.

2. EDUCATIONAL STRUCTURE AND ENROLMENTS

Education is compulsory from the age of 6 to 15 years and is divided into a six-year primary and a three-year lower secondary cycle. Parents may have their children educated at home provided that certain standards can be assured; however, this is an unusual practice. Parents may send their children to any State-funded school of their choice no matter where it is located, provided that accommodation is available. In addition, groups of parents and others are free, in principle, to set up their own schools and to receive the statutory subventions of the State, subject to conforming to the general regulations applying to all school authorities.

The primary sector comprises primary schools (3 200), special schools (116) and non-aided private primary schools (68). Aided primary schools account for 98 per cent of children in the primary sector.

Primary schools are mostly denominational in their intake and management, and located in parishes; however, no child may be refused enrolment on the ground of religion in any school where a place is available. The ultimate responsibility for each primary school (with the exception of the multi-denominational schools), lies with the "patron" who is, as a rule, the Bishop of the relevant denomination. He delegates managerial authority to a school board. Although compulsory primary schooling does not start until the age of 6, virtually all young children attend school from the age of 5 and approximately 53 per cent do so from the age of 4. The Irish education system has had a long-standing commitment to early schooling. The "infant school" (a two-year programme catering for 4-7 year-olds) is treated as a part of the national compulsory school provision and curriculum, although it is differentiated for the purposes of the UOE (UNESCO, OECD, EUROSTAT) data collection. In effect, all children spend eight years being educated continuously up to the end of primary school. Some young people will complete no fewer than 14 years of schooling from 4 to 18 years of age. There are around 114 000 pre-primary students, 381 000 primary students and 4 000 students over 13 years of age who are being educated in special schools. Enrolments are falling in this sector.

There is a limited number of compensatory programmes provided by the State for 3 year-olds, including programmes for children of travellers, children living in areas of particular disadvantage and children with special educational needs.

Virtually all primary school pupils proceed directly to secondary education, commonly referred to as "second-level" or post-primary education.

Second-level education commences at about age 12 and continues for five or six years. It consists of a three-year junior

Ireland

Irlande

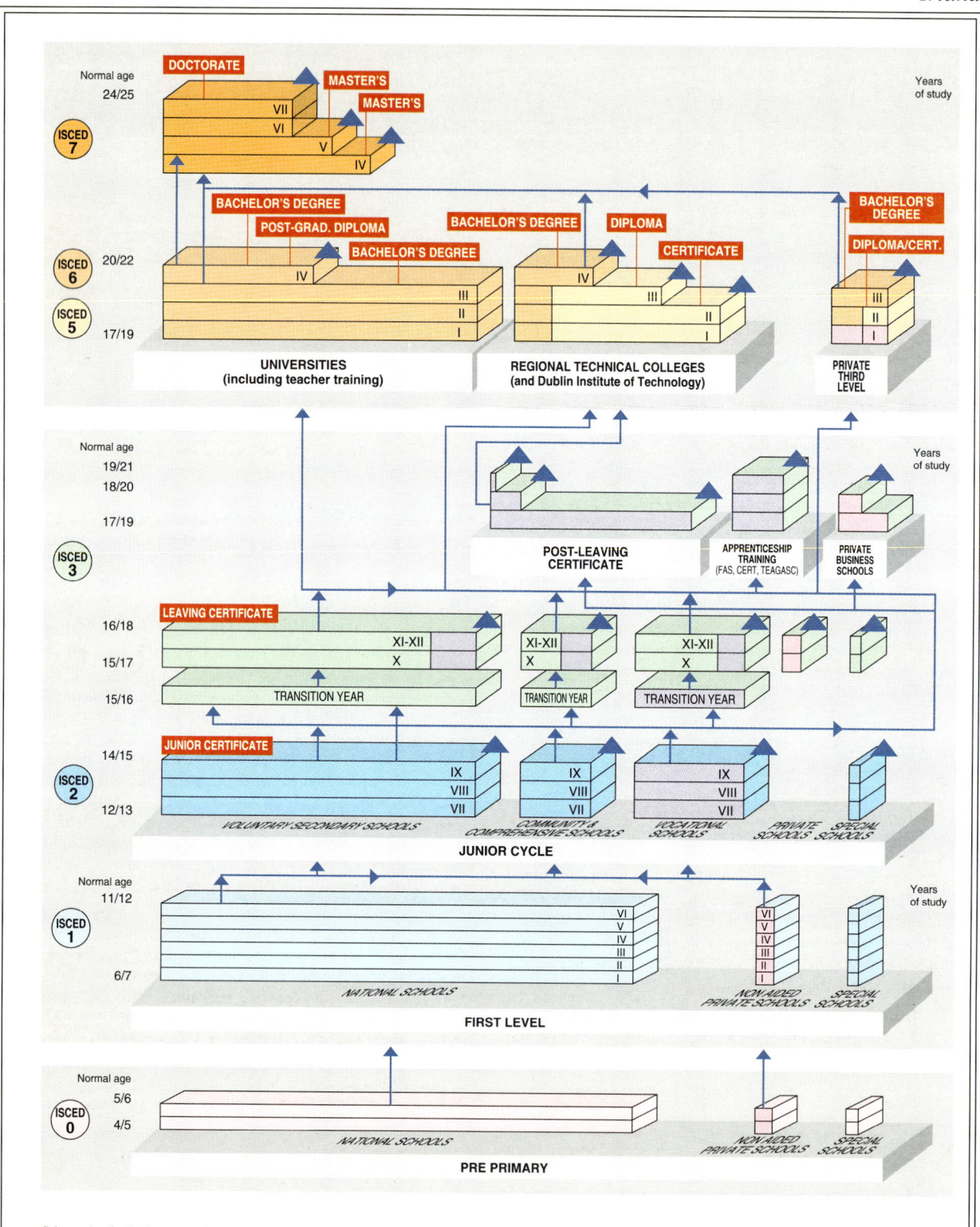

Ireland

cycle followed by a two- or three-year senior cycle. Participation in post-compulsory education continues to rise with over 91 per cent of 16 year-olds, 82 per cent of 17 year-olds and 64 per cent of 18 year-olds in full-time education. The Junior Certificate examination is taken after three years. In the senior cycle there is an optional one-year Transition Year Programme followed by a choice of three two-year Leaving Certificate programmes. The Leaving Certificate examination is held at the end of the Senior Cycle in post-primary schools. Students normally sit for the examination at the age of 17 or 18. The second-level sector comprises secondary, vocational, community and comprehensive schools. However, there is little provision of vocational education in second-level schools in the sense of programmes that are geared towards direct labour market entry. There are almost 370 000 students in this sector, attending a total of 768 publicly-aided schools. In addition there are 19 other State-aided educational institutions outside the main second-level system and a further 15 non-aided schools. Twelve per cent of schools have under 200 students and fewer than 10 per cent have over 800 students. Secondary schools, educating 60 per cent of second-level students, are privately owned and managed. The majority are conducted by religious communities and the remainder by Boards of Governors or by individuals. Vocational schools, educating 26 per cent of all second-level students, are administered by Vocational Education Committees, which are sub-committees of local authorities. Community and comprehensive schools, educating 14 per cent of second-level students, are administered by Boards of Management and are allocated individual budgets by the State.

As well as the courses provided in third-level institutions, a wide range of vocational education and training courses are offered within the second-level education sector for students who have completed second level. The principal programmes are Post-Leaving-Certificate courses which have grown rapidly in recent years (18 000 enrolled in 1995/96). This area is evolving within an emerging national certification framework which will provide alternative routes of progression for students through the education system and will meet the needs of the economy for high-quality vocational competencies, formally validated and certified to national and international standards. In addition, off-the-job training for designated craft apprentices is provided in colleges and training centres. While traditionally a young person was apprenticed on completion of compulsory schooling, in practice an increasing percentage of apprentices have now already achieved Leaving Certificate standard. (Statistics for these courses are included in the overall figures for second level.)

There are also programmes on offer for young people who leave school without any formal qualification, for adult and continuing education and training and second-chance education.

Enrolments in tertiary education have increased steadily, from 20 700 in 1965/66 to 41 500 in 1980/81, to 67 400 in 1984/85 and to 96 700 in 1994/95 (full-time figures only). In 1995 almost 50 per cent of students who completed their Leaving Certificate entered an aided tertiary institution in the Republic of Ireland. Entry to higher education is normally based on academic results in the Leaving Certificate examination and is restricted by the number of places available and sometimes by quotas. Just under 4 per cent of commencing undergraduate students are now admitted on the basis of prior informal study or work experience, but it is planned to increase this proportion. About 7 per cent of tertiary students are engaged in graduate study.

The higher education sector comprises the universities, the technological colleges (both of which are self-governing institutions which receive an annual state grant and grants for capital purposes), the teacher training colleges (which are privately managed but largely financed by the State), as well as some non-state aided private higher education colleges. There are about 122 000 students (almost 97 000 of whom are full-time) enrolled in 32 publicly aided higher education institutions. In addition there are 23 other non-aided colleges and institutions in this sector.

3. EDUCATIONAL FINANCE AND COSTS

The major portion of public expenditure on education is borne by central government funds. The State supplies more than 90 per cent of the funds for education. In the private school sector tuition fees vary substantially among different types of schools. Public expenditure per primary school student is about Ir£ 1 400 per annum, Ir£ 2 200 per secondary student and Ir£ 3 700 per tertiary student.

The current and capital costs of primary schools, including the full cost of teachers' salaries, are predominantly funded by the State and supplemented by local contributions. In addition, special funding arrangements are in place for some schools which, for example, are in disadvantaged areas and/or cater for children with special needs. While parents are required to pay for textbooks and necessary equipment, there are grants available for needy pupils.

At second level over 95 per cent of the cost of teachers' salaries are met by the State. In addition, allowances and capitation grants are paid to the 95 per cent of secondary schools which participate in the free education scheme. These schools do not charge fees but may ask for a voluntary subscription from parents. The estimated State support for secondary schools amounted to Ir£ 397 million in 1994. Vocational schools are funded, through Vocational Education Committees, to the extent of about 93 per cent of the total cost of provision. The balance is provided by receipts generated by the committees. Community and comprehensive schools are allocated individual budgets by the State.

Higher education institutions receive income from a State Grant, tuition fees paid by students (post-graduate and non-European Union nationals) and income earned from research and development and other activities. The government abolished undergraduate tuition fees for first-time, full-time students in publicly-funded tertiary institutions as of 1996/97. University students are required to pay about Ir£ 150 per year towards the cost of registration, examinations and student services. Government-funded Student Support Schemes help to promote access to tertiary education through the payment of maintenance grants which are means-tested.

4. CURRICULUM AND ASSESSMENT

There are different levels of responsibility for the development and implementation of the curriculum. At the national level, the curriculum is formulated by the Minister for Education,

Ireland

on the advice of the National Council for Curriculum and Assessment, and the Department of Education oversees its implementation through its inspectorate. At the school level, the particular character of the school makes a vital contribution. Adaptation of the curriculum to suit the individual school is achieved through the preparation and continuous updating of a school plan. There is no formal assessment at the end of primary school but school principals may transfer a cumulative record card of pupils' profiles to the school to which they transfer. Within primary schools promotion from one grade to the next is automatic. Standardised testing for the 7 and 11 year-old age groups will be introduced for diagnostic purposes.

All five types of secondary school at second level offer a broad curriculum but with different emphases. The second-level curriculum is a derivation of the "classical humanist" tradition with an overlay of scientific/technological/technical/commercial subjects. With increasing diversity of the student population, consequent upon increased retention rates, curriculum planners have made substantial changes to the curriculum in recent years. There is no real specialisation at upper secondary level with most students taking seven subjects. The examinations that are held for the different secondary school pupils have been mentioned in Section 2 above.

Tertiary institutions have responsibility for their own curricula and assessment, although in some discipline areas professional/industrial bodies play a significant role.

5. TEACHERS

Over 4 per cent of the total labour force in Ireland are employed as teachers. There have been few openings for new teachers since the mid-1980s. Teacher training occurs in higher education institutions. The normal length of initial training for primary teachers is three years. Teachers at the second level first complete an undergraduate degree of their choice (3-4 years) and then proceed to do a one-year post-graduate teaching qualification course (Higher Diploma in Education). Teacher training colleges for particular curricular specialisms are an exception to this pathway.

The primary schools are staffed by almost 21 000 teachers, and second level schools employ approximately 23 000 teachers (in full-time-equivalent terms). Teachers are employed by the management authorities of the schools in which they teach, but their salaries are paid directly by the Department of Education. Approximately 55 per cent of primary schools have four or fewer teachers. The pupil/teacher ratios in 1995/96 were comparatively high at 22.8:1 at the primary level.

Italy

1. GENERAL CONTEXT

Italy has an area of 301 000 square kilometres and a population of about 57 million inhabitants. Italian is spoken by almost the entire population but there are also several ethnic-linguistic minorities. Italy is a parliamentary republic since 1946 and, administratively, composed of 20 regions, five of which have an autonomous special status. Since the 1950s there has been a gradual process of decentralisation, and in the 1970s many responsibilities, including some concerned with education, were transferred from State to local authorities (regions, provinces, councils).

The Ministry of Education has general responsibility for the supervision and co-ordination of all educational activities carried out in the country by State and private institutions, the planning, study and promotion of education and the supervision of all educational institutions. It promotes curriculum and syllabus changes and the in-service training of the teaching staff. It authorises experimentation affecting curriculum and teaching hours and directly administers activities concerning the budget and the recruitment and transfer of staff. Finally, it controls and administers the automation of services.

Regional responsibilities include: school building and maintenance, educational assistance (i.e. medical and psychological services for students, including handicapped students), management of vocational and handicraft education, provision of training, specialisation and requalification of teachers and provision of counselling and guidance services. Provinces provide equipment, services and non-teaching staff to the schools. Councils, at the local level, manage the services necessary for running the schools in their own areas; these include welfare services, grants and the supervision of school attendance.

State schools predominate with an enrolment of more than 90 per cent of all students. The exception is early childhood education where the private sector serves almost half of the whole population of 3 to 6 year-old children.

About 34 per cent of the population aged 26 to 64 have an upper secondary or tertiary education degree (university degree, university diploma, upper secondary school diploma, vocational qualification). At present, several initiatives are underway in order to increase the participation in upper secondary and post-secondary courses, particularly in the vocational sector.

2. EDUCATIONAL STRUCTURE AND ENROLMENTS

Education is compulsory for all children from 6 to 14 years of age (eight years of school attendance) but a bill is currently with Parliament to increase the length of compulsory education.

Early childhood education is not compulsory. The *scuola materna* (3-6 years) is, however, attended by 93 per cent of children.

Compulsory education includes the *scuola elementare* (elementary school), which lasts five years (6-11) and the *scuola media* (lower secondary school, comprehensive), which lasts three years (11-14).

More than 80 per cent of pupils continue their studies in a variety of secondary school types: *ginnasi e licei* (general education) with a duration of five years; *istituti magistrali* (elementary teachers' training schools) four years plus one additional year to enter university; *istituti tecnici* (technical education with different specialisations) five years; *istituti professionali* (vocational education for various working activities fields) five years with a first diploma after three years' attendance; *istituti d'arte* and *licei artistici* (Fine Arts institutes and schools 3+2 and 4+1 years, respectively). Vocational training is organised by the regions under the responsibility of the Ministry of Work and Social Security.

Important reforms were undertaken in technical and vocational education in the past decade. In the technical institutes there has been a curriculum reform in order to prepare young people adequately for future jobs. Post-diploma courses have been introduced for higher professional qualifications. Vocational institutes have also undergone a curriculum reform. A diploma in all languages of the European Union has been created for pupils who have successfully completed a three-year course after compulsory schooling in order to increase their job mobility. In the last two years of the five-year course some teaching hours are devoted to job-training activities under the responsibility of the regions. This reform should result in a broader basic education for students that is then followed by vocational training.

Each school is requested to inform the public about its own educational programme formulated according to educational, methodological and organisational choices.

About 76 per cent of all upper secondary graduates (54 per cent of the age group) enrol in tertiary programmes, which include the so-called "schools with special goals" (*scuole dirette a fini speciali*), offering 2/3-year full-time courses, almost all vocationally-oriented; the university diploma courses (*corsi di diploma universitario*), usually lasting three years; the medium-long university programmes (*corsi di laurea*); and the academies. In all, there are 75 universities or higher education institutions, many of which have separate branches located in different towns. Most of them are State universities, but there are also a few "free", non-state, universities, faculties and institutes. Together they serve a population of more than 1.6 million students. A number of institutions, both public and private and the so-called "third age universities" serve a large number of adults in the area of adult education and lifelong learning.

3. EDUCATIONAL FINANCE AND COSTS

Educational expenditure was 5.2 per cent of GDP in 1993. The central government covers a little less than 80 per cent of public institutions' expenditure. The remaining 20 per cent is covered by regions, provinces and municipalities. The share of central government financing is slightly higher (84 per cent) in the case of early childhood, primary and secondary education. These numbers reflect the different responsibilities of different administrative levels.

Compulsory education in primary school and the *scuola media* is free of charge. Households contribute financially towards enrolment and tuition fees, examination and graduation fees in secondary school according to a means-test. There are also grants

Italy

for excellent students. Private schools usually receive a contribution from the government.

Since the early 1980s there has been a slight decrease in public expenditure for education as a percentage of total public expenditure. In 1993 the expenditure per pupil was US$ 4 107 in primary schools and US$ 5 313 in secondary schools.

4. CURRICULUM AND ASSESSMENT

The Minister of Education enacts national programmes that are approved by Parliament and gives his approval for experimental curricula in selected schools.

In elementary schools a new curriculum was implemented in 1990. This included innovations such as: team teaching, modular units, content organised in disciplinary areas and the introduction of a foreign language from grade 3 onwards. New syllabuses were issued by the Ministry for each subject in the *scuola media* in 1979. So far, there is no new set of curricula for the secondary school although there are some experimental curricula being tested. Of the 80 per cent of pupils who graduate from the *scuola media* and enter secondary education, 17 per cent fail at the end of the first year. Despite this, general schools are still considered to have high standards. There is also much curriculum reform in the vocational and technical schools.

In elementary school, assessment is carried out by teachers in the form of a short report about each child's achievement in various subjects. At the end of grade 5, the pupils have to pass an exam, *licenza elementare*, to be able to enter the lower secondary school (*scuola media*).

In the *scuola media,* the council of teachers of each class not only has the task of setting the objectives to be reached by each pupil in each subject, but also has to undertake an analytical evaluation at the end of each term and at the end of the school year using a descriptive form (*scheda di valutazione*) about each pupil's achievement. The final exam at the end of the third year, *esame di licenza*, consists of three written tests and an oral interview. It is a State exam. The final diploma awarded to pupils who have successfully passed the exam is an indispensable document for entry to further education or vocational training or, indeed, to obtain a job.

In upper secondary education, marks (on a scale from 1 to 10) are awarded for each subject at the end of each year and pupils who do not reach the minimum (6/10) have to repeat the school year. According to law, the final exam (*maturità*) gives access to all university faculties. Reports from teachers of the school and the pupil's school career documents are taken into consideration by an external committee (headed by a president, a university professor or a secondary school headmaster) when deciding on a final mark for a student in the *maturità*. The written exams are set by the Ministry of Education and are the same all over the country for any one subject. There is no central institution for monitoring the system of education although discussions are underway about establishing one.

5. TEACHERS

Since 1990 all teachers must receive their initial training at a university. Prior to 1990 this was the case for secondary school teachers only and other teachers attended teacher training institutions.

Initial teacher training stresses the importance of a sound, subject-centred preparation for secondary school teachers. The professional psycho-pedagogical training takes place in in-service training. Teachers who successfully pass the qualification exam (*abilitazione*) are officially listed as qualified teachers. They then have to be successful in an open competition in order to obtain a post as a fully qualified teacher in a State school. In certain cases a teacher may obtain such a post on the basis of the qualification exam and previous teaching experience which can take the place of the national competition. Initial training also includes theoretical and practical training during the first year of service in the school as a state teacher under the supervision of a tutor.

Italy

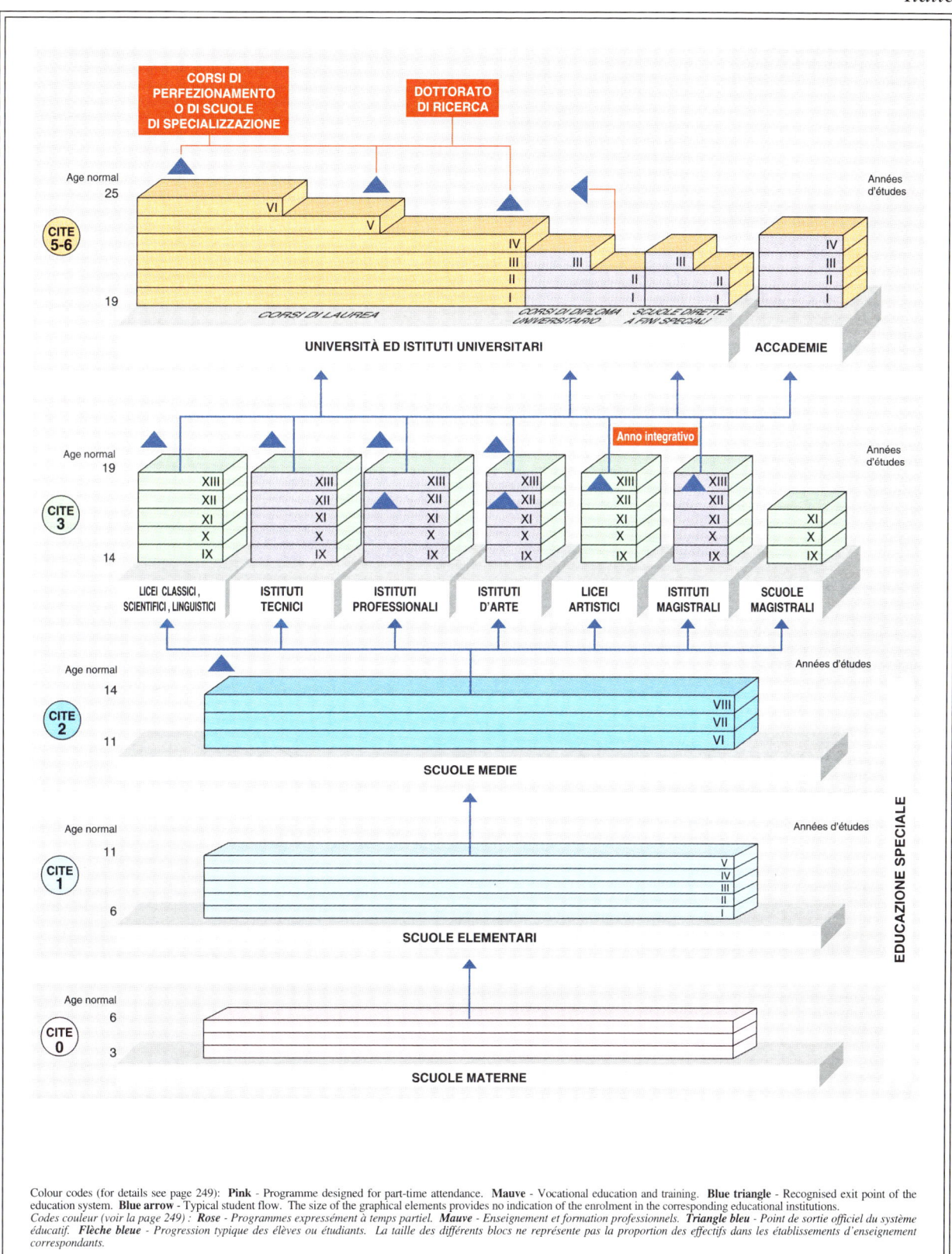

Italie

Japan

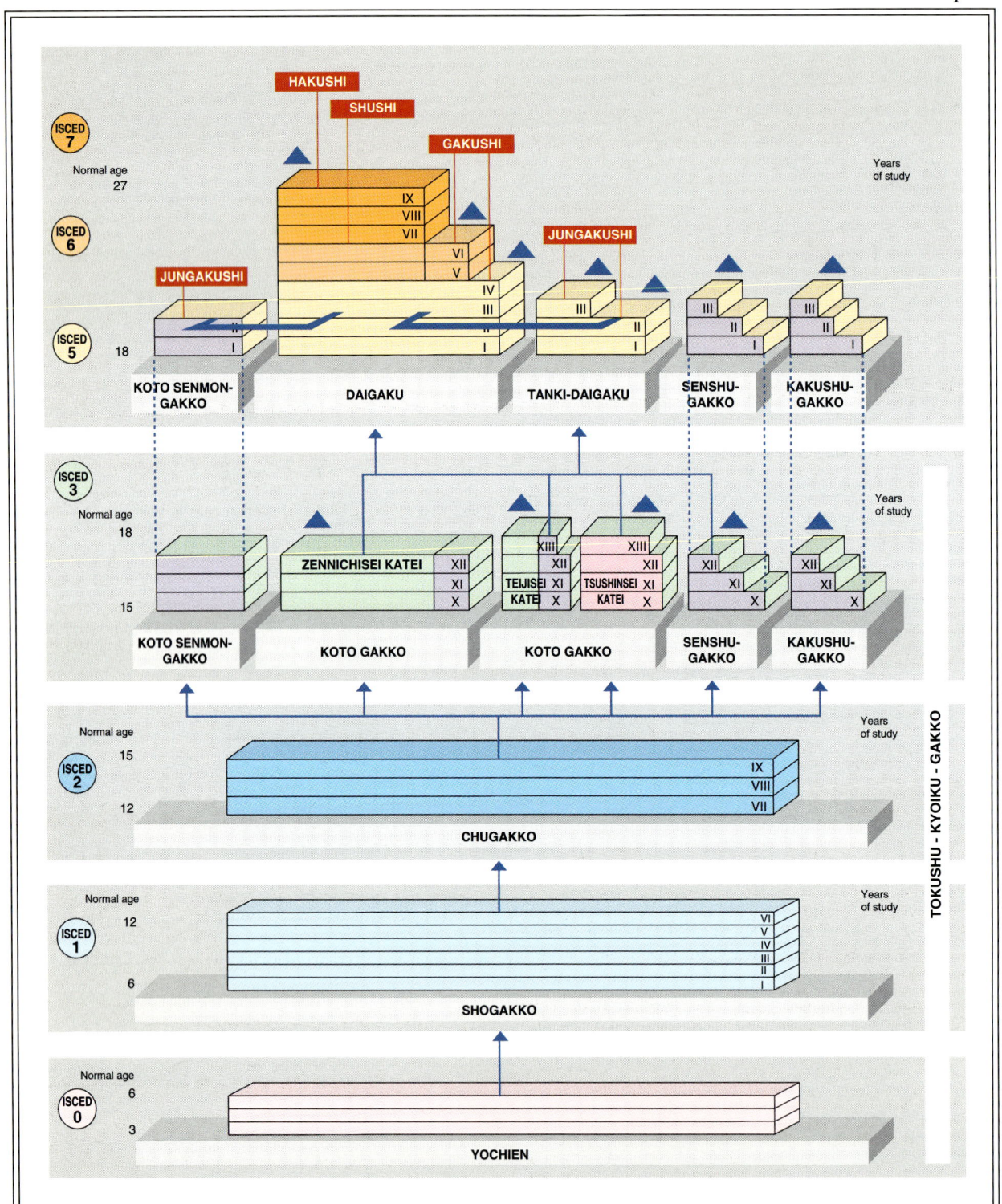

Japon

Japan

1. GENERAL CONTEXT

Japan is a country with an area of about 380 000 square kilometres and a population of about 125 million people. The proportion of the population aged under 14 years is 16 per cent, between 15 and 64 years it is 70 per cent and over 65 years it is 14 per cent (1994). In the last few years there has been a decrease in the number of children born. In 1994, about 6 per cent of the employed population was working in the primary sector, 34 per cent in the secondary sector and 60 per cent in the tertiary sector.

There are 47 prefectures in Japan and about 3 200 municipalities within these prefectures. Prefectures and municipalities are local self-governing bodies.

Educational administration at the national level is conducted by the Ministry of Education, Science, Sports and Culture. Some universities and junior colleges and almost all colleges of technology are directly maintained and supervised by the Ministry.

The Ministry of Education, Science, Sports and Culture provides guidance, advice and assistance to prefectural boards and municipal boards of education. Prefectural boards of education administer schools (mainly upper secondary and special education) established by the prefectures, whereas municipal boards of education administer mainly elementary and lower secondary schools established by the municipalities.

Until the end of World War II a "multi-track" education system was in force. After the war, under the Fundamental Law of Education and the School Education Law enacted in 1947, a "single-track 6-3-3-4" system was established.

2. EDUCATIONAL STRUCTURE AND ENROLMENTS

Kindergartens cater for children aged 3, 4 and 5 and provides them with one- to three-year courses. It is compulsory to attend both elementary school (ages 6 to 12) and lower secondary school (ages 12 to 15) or to attend a special education school for a period of nine years, from the age of 6 to 15. Upper secondary schools (catering to children aged 15 to 18 or over) offer, in addition to full day courses, day/evening and correspondence courses. Full-day courses last for three years, while day/evening and correspondence courses can last longer. Out of those graduating from lower secondary schools, about 95 per cent advance to upper secondary schools.

Institutions of higher education include universities, junior colleges and colleges of technology. In addition, special training colleges offering post-secondary courses provide a further type of higher education. Advancement rate to universities (new entrants as a percentage of the 18 year-old age cohort) is about 25 per cent and to non-universities (including post-secondary courses of special training colleges) about 30 per cent.

Universities offer courses of at least four years' duration leading to a Bachelor's degree. Graduate courses normally last for five years, consisting of initial two-year courses leading to a Master's degree and followed by three-year courses leading to a doctoral degree. Junior colleges offer two- or three-year programmes in different fields of study. Colleges of technology accept those who have completed lower secondary schooling and offer five-year programmes.

In addition to the above-mentioned institutions, there are educational institutions known as «special training colleges» and «miscellaneous schools» which offer a variety of practical vocational and technical educational programmes. The great majority of these schools are privately controlled.

There are national, local public and private institutions at all levels of education. The percentage of enrolments in private educational institutions at each level of education is less than 1 per cent for compulsory education schools (elementary and lower secondary schools), about 30 per cent for upper secondary schools, about 70 per cent for universities, about 90 per cent for junior colleges and about 5 per cent for colleges of technology.

3. EDUCATIONAL FINANCE AND COSTS

Educational expenditures for the national government are classified into three categories: *i)* direct expenditures for national educational activities, such as expenditures for operating national universities and schools, *ii)* specific subsidies for the educational activities of other institutions such as those of prefectures, municipalities, private schools and research organisations, and *iii)* the local allocation of a tax grant, a part of which is expended for education.

The educational expenditures of the prefectures include direct expenditures for educational activities operated by the prefectures, the payment of salaries of personnel employed in elementary, lower secondary, day/evening upper secondary and special education schools established by municipalities, subsidies to private kindergartens, elementary, lower and upper secondary schools and special education schools and subsidies for designated educational activities operated by the municipalities. The educational expenditures of municipalities are for educational activities operated by the municipalities such as elementary and lower secondary schools.

National and local public schools imparting compulsory education (elementary and lower secondary schools) do not charge tuition fees. National and local public educational institutions other than these (upper secondary schools, institutions of higher education) and all private educational institutions charge tuition fees.

4. CURRICULUM AND ASSESSMENT

Curriculum standards for elementary, lower secondary and upper secondary schools are prescribed in the "Courses of Study" issued by the Minister of Education, Science, Sports and Culture.

The "Courses of Study" provide the basic framework for curricula including the aims of each subject and the aims and content of teaching at each grade. Revised "Courses of Study" were issued in March 1989 and came into effect in elementary schools in April 1992, in lower secondary schools in April 1993 and in upper secondary schools for the first year classes beginning in April 1994. Each school organises its own curriculum on the basis of the

Japan

"Courses of Study" taking into consideration the actual conditions of the community and of the school itself as well as the development level and characteristics of its pupils.

In most of these schools students are automatically promoted from one grade to the next. A certificate of graduation is conferred according to a school-based assessment.

The upper secondary school admits entrants based on a selection process that takes into consideration such materials as student credentials obtained from the lower secondary schools, scholastic test records and other factors. Each university and junior college, either national, local public or private, selects its entrants according to its own admission procedures, using the applicant's upper secondary school credentials, scholastic tests, interviews, short papers, practical skill tests and other means. One of the scholastic tests, a standard nation-wide test, is conducted by the NCUEE (National Centre for University Entrance Examination). Except for junior colleges, all national and local public universities as well as some private universities use this examination. In addition to this, each university administers its own tests.

5. TEACHERS

Teachers of elementary and secondary schools are required to have relevant teacher certificates, which are awarded by prefectural boards of education. To obtain the certificates students are required, in addition to the basic qualifications such as the completion of a Bachelor's degree course, to acquire the prescribed number of credits for teaching specialised subjects in courses approved by the Minister of Education, Science, Sports and Culture.

There are three classes of regular teacher certificates: advanced, first class and second class. Teachers holding an advanced class certificate have earned a Master's degree. Those holding a first class certificate have earned a Bachelor's degree, and those holding a second class certificate have earned a title of associate, obtained upon the completion of junior college.

Various systematic programmes are conducted in in-service training at national, prefectural and municipal levels, at schools and at other levels. A system of induction training for beginning teachers was created in 1989. It is conducted for all beginning teachers in national and local public elementary and secondary schools and takes place during the year after their appointment.

Korea

1. GENERAL CONTEXT

The Republic of Korea (South Korea) covers an area of 90 000 square kilometres and has a population of 44.5 million people (1994) of whom one-quarter live in the capital city, Seoul. The population density is 449 inhabitants per square kilometre and the annual population growth rate is 0.90 per cent. GNP per capita is US$ 8 483 with a growth rate of 8.2 per cent. The percentages of the workforce in the different sectors are: 7 in the primary sector, 27 in the secondary sector and 66 in the tertiary sector.

The Ministry of Education is the central authority responsible for discharging the constitutional mandates for education. The Ministry develops national education plans, implements them, publishes and approves textbooks for elementary and secondary education, enacts laws related to education, executes the educational budget, directs and co-ordinates subordinate agencies for educational policy planning and implementation and supervises the municipal and provincial boards of education, the institutes of higher education and other national schools.

The municipal and provincial offices of education are responsible for the administration of elementary and secondary education in their areas. There are 15 such offices of which six are municipal and six are provincial. All operate under the authority of their Board of Education and the Ministry of Education. Each board consists of between 7 and 26 members (depending on the size of the area) elected by the municipal and provincial assemblies. Half of the members must have had at least 15 years of teaching experience. Each board elects a superintendent for four years.

The lowest unit of administration is the district office. There are 179 district offices of education. These offices carry out the administration of the schools under their supervision, maintain educational facilities, enact educational regulations and supervise all kindergartens, elementary and middle schools.

2. EDUCATIONAL STRUCTURE AND ENROLMENTS

The present structure of education was introduced in 1949. It consists of six years of elementary or primary school, three years of middle school, three years of high school and four years of college or university.

The Education Law of 1949 established the minimum number of school days for the completion of one academic year. Elementary, middle and high schools should have more than 220 school days. Universities, colleges, teacher colleges, colleges of education and junior colleges should hold classes for at least 30 weeks per year. The same law stipulated that there should be the following types of schools: *i)* elementary, middle and high schools as well as colleges and universities (which constitute the backbone of the education system); *ii)* junior colleges, air, correspondence and open universities; *iii)* teacher colleges and colleges of education; *iv)* trade schools and trade high schools; *v)* civic schools and civic universities; *vi)* special schools; *vii)* kindergartens and *viii)* miscellaneous schools.

Pre-primary education is carried out in kindergartens for 3 to 5 year-olds. Just over 20 per cent of 3 and 4 year-olds and about 60 per cent of 5 year old children are enrolled. A national curriculum for kindergarten as well as teaching materials are provided by the Ministry of Education. Most of the kindergartens are private although the Ministry is making efforts to increase the number of public kindergartens and improve the quality of education at that level.

Education is compulsory and free from 6 to 14 years of age and takes place in elementary schools and middle schools (lower secondary education). All primary schools are co-educational and provide four to six hours of instruction per day. Over 99 per cent of the children progress from the elementary to the middle school, which lasts for three years. Students are allocated at random from the district where they live to a middle school in the district. In 1995, there were a total of 2 481 848 middle school students. Admission to high school is on the basis of examination results and, where appropriate, a "school-life document" completed over the middle school years.

Parents must pay fees for high school. There are basically two types of high schools: general (academic) high schools and vocational high schools. In the general high school, students choose between one of the following tracks at the beginning of the second year: humanities and social sciences, natural sciences and vocational. Within vocational education, there are 29 agricultural high schools, 175 technical high schools, 248 commercial high schools and 9 fishery and marine high schools. These prepare students for entering the workforce. It is worth noting that in 1994 technical high schools began to apply the "dual" system on an experimental basis whereby, after two years of attendance, students were trained in the work place. There are also 239 comprehensive high schools offering a mixture of academic and vocational education. There are 29 comprehensive vocational high schools that offer more than one vocational subject. Finally, there are 15 science high schools for scientifically talented youngsters. After two years of study in a science high school, a student may enter the Korea Advanced Institute for Science and Technology. In 1995 there were 911 453 students in all of the vocational high schools and 1 246 427 in the general high schools. Together, they represented about 88 per cent of an age group. About 40 per cent of an age group goes on to higher education.

Institutions of higher education can be divided into four types: colleges and universities, teacher colleges and colleges of education, junior colleges and others such as theological colleges and seminaries. All are under the authority of the Ministry of Education. The presidents of private universities are elected by the Board of the institution but subject to the approval of the Minister of Education. The period of study is from four to six years. Entrance depends on high school achievement marks, the scores on the government-administered scholastic achievement test or the universities' own entrance examination. In 1995 there were 1 187 735 students in colleges and universities, 19 650 in teacher colleges, 569 820 in junior colleges and 112 728 in graduate schools.

3. EDUCATIONAL FINANCE AND COSTS

There are three sources of educational finance: the central government, local governments and private entities. Grants from the central government and tuition fees are the major sources of finance. The major source of government funding is tax revenue,

Korea

which covers the expenditure of the Ministry of Education and those of national universities and institutes as well as the expenditure of local governments for elementary and secondary education. The 1995 budget of the Ministry of Education provides funds for general accounts, education transfers to local governments, national property management, fiscal investment and financing, rural development tax management and national university hospitals.

The total budget for education in 1995 (including general accounts and special accounts and excluding national university hospital budgets) was 12 496 billion won, which accounts for 22.7 per cent of the total public sector budget. Securing financial resources is of vital importance to funding local education and compensating local administrative authorities for their services. Furthermore, the funding of local education should provide for the upgrading of educational quality and a balanced development of various aspects of education. The total revenue of the 15 provincial and metropolitan education authorities in 1995 was 12 696 billion won. The major source of funding for private education are entrance fees and tuition fees. The government enacted a law exempting private schools from taxation in the acquisition and sale of properties and is providing subsidies to compensate for shortages in remuneration and operational costs. Loans are provided to help private schools with the expansion and renovation of facilities. The government's coverage of research grants, students' activities, scholarships and annuities is increasing.

4. CURRICULUM AND ASSESSMENT

The curriculum for each level of schooling and the criteria to be used for the development of textbooks and instructional materials are prescribed in educational laws. Curricula are revised periodically, and the last revision took place in 1992. Implementation of the new curriculum began in 1995 and is still underway. The Ministry of Education convenes committees for developing the curricula. The committees are composed of school teachers, subject-matter specialists, curriculum specialists, professors and educational administrators. A final version is promulgated by the Ministry. At the elementary school level, all textbooks are written by educational research institutes authorised by the Ministry. At the secondary level, this is also true for the Korean language, Korean history and moral education. The Ministry reviews, revises and finally approves these textbooks known as Type 1 textbooks. Other (Type 2) textbooks are developed by private publishers and are then reviewed and approved by a special committee at the Ministry. Type 1 textbooks are the only textbooks allowed for those particular subjects, whereas schools can select from several of the approved Type 2 textbooks. Local input to the curriculum is very limited.

Promotion from one grade to another is generally automatic. Certificates are awarded at the end of each level of schooling and are based on internal assessment. Applicants for vocational education sit an entrance examination. Applicants for the academic high school take a city or provincial examination. Colleges and universities select their students on the basis of the composite score of the Scholastic Achievement Examination for College Entrance (SAECE) and on high school academic records. There is also a National Learning Ability Test for College (NLATC) that can be given by colleges and universities and that they can use in the selection process.

Teachers keep detailed records of student achievement which are based on objective achievement tests, essay tests, and affective assessments. Regional assessment is undertaken at the elementary and middle levels. Participation by schools is mandatory. National assessments are undertaken in thirteen subjects areas at grade 7 and twelve subjects at grade 10. The tests are constructed by the National Institute of Educational Evaluation. In addition to the above, the Korean Educational Development Institute (KEDI) undertakes about 50 major projects in different aspects of education each year.

5. TEACHERS

Institutions responsible for teacher education vary in type and level, but all courses are of four years' duration. They include teacher colleges, colleges of education, teacher education courses or departments of education in colleges and universities, junior colleges, air and correspondence colleges and graduate schools of education. These institutions recruit nearly 40 000 teachers per year. Kindergarten teachers are trained at four-year colleges, junior colleges and air and correspondence colleges. Elementary teachers are trained in teacher colleges. Students are exempt from entrance fees and tuition fees and are entitled to scholarships but, in return, they must serve in state schools as teachers for an agreed number of years. Secondary school teachers must be graduates of colleges of education, departments of education or teacher education courses in colleges or universities or graduate schools of education. Students must pay some tuition. The entrance examination is very strict.

In 1995, there were 25 576 kindergarten teachers, 138 369 elementary school teachers, 99 931 middle school teachers, 56 441 general high school teachers, 42 656 vocational high school teachers and 45 087 college and university teachers.

Korea

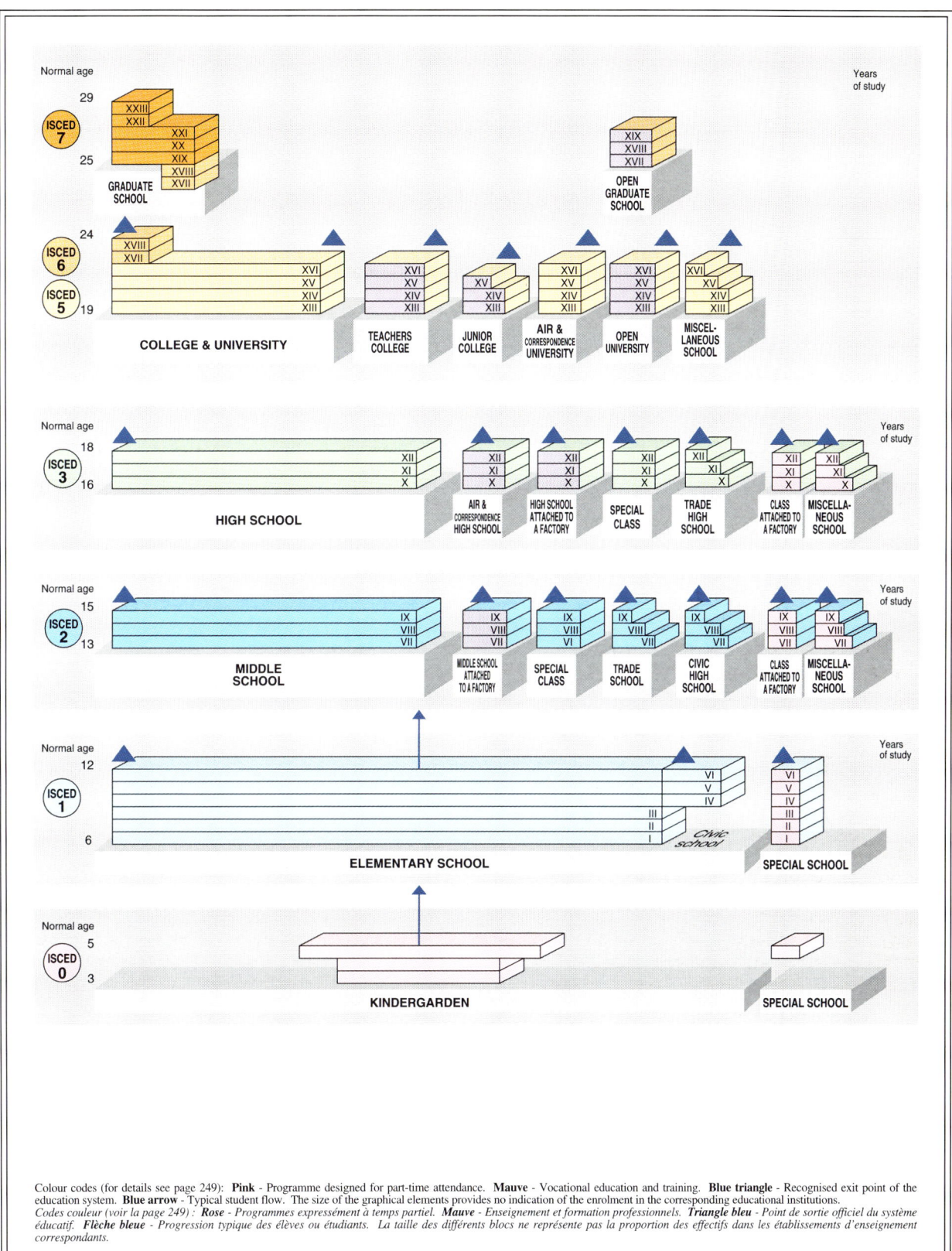

Corée

Colour codes (for details see page 249): **Pink** - Programme designed for part-time attendance. **Mauve** - Vocational education and training. **Blue triangle** - Recognised exit point of the education system. **Blue arrow** - Typical student flow. The size of the graphical elements provides no indication of the enrolment in the corresponding educational institutions.
*Codes couleur (voir la page 249) : **Rose** - Programmes expressément à temps partiel. **Mauve** - Enseignement et formation professionnels. **Triangle bleu** - Point de sortie officiel du système éducatif. **Flèche bleue** - Progression typique des élèves ou étudiants. La taille des différents blocs ne représente pas la proportion des effectifs dans les établissements d'enseignement correspondants.*

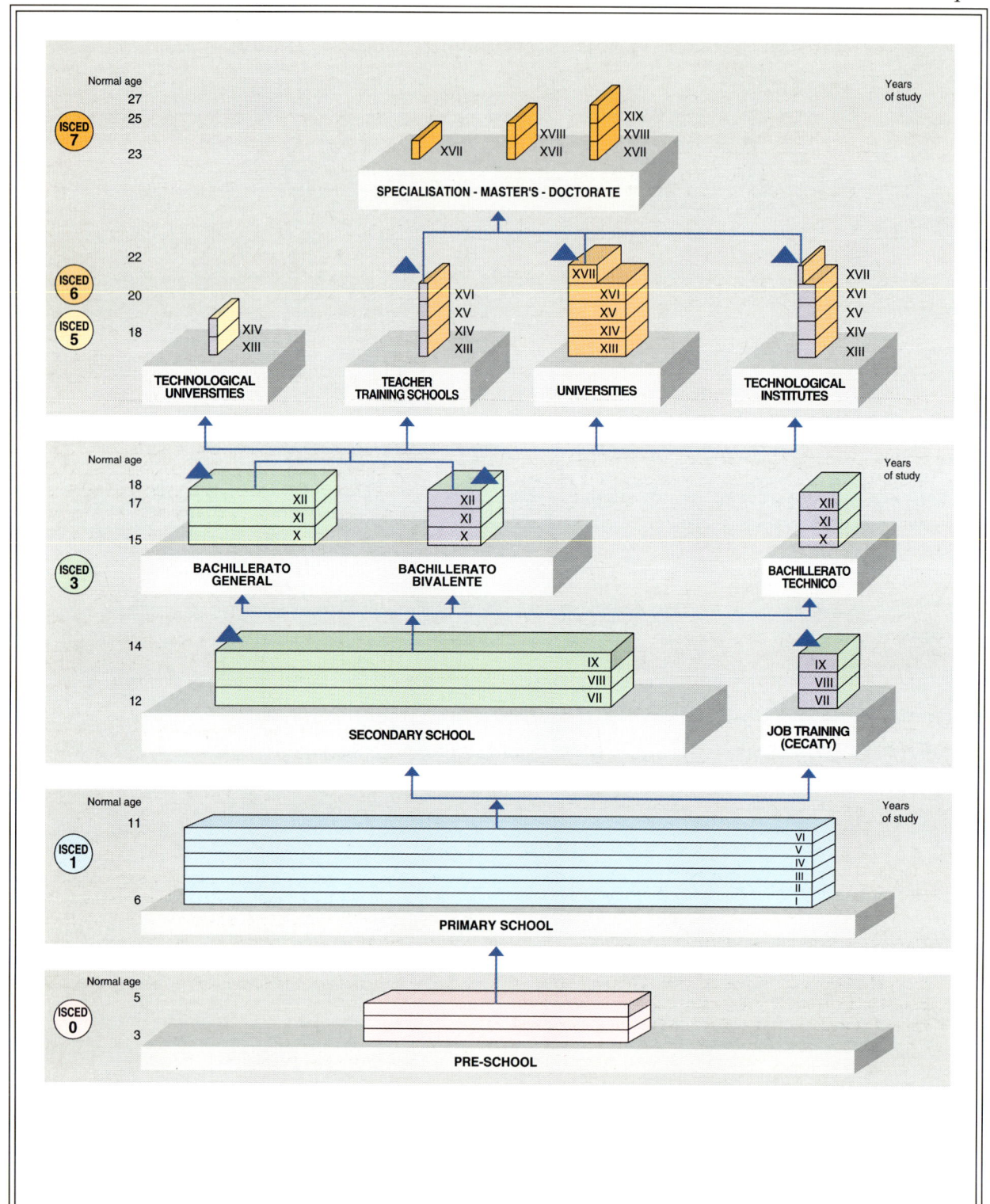

Mexico

Mexique

Mexico

1. GENERAL CONTEXT

The United States of Mexico is a federal country with an area of nearly 2 million square kilometres and a population of over 80 million people (1990). It has a high population growth rate and although between 1970 and 1990 there was a decrease in the growth rate, 60 per cent of the population is below the age of 24 years. An enormous effort was required to provide educational services to such an expanding population, and this explains why enrolment in the formal school system is only 31 per cent of the total population. The population is unevenly distributed and its density ranges from 43 to 5 500 inhabitants per square kilometre. Just over 70 per cent of the inhabitants live in urban areas, and from 1970 to 1990 the percentage of the population living in cities of more than 100 000 inhabitants increased from 23 to 44 per cent. The country is divided into 38 states.

In 1990 there were 24 million persons in the labour force, and of these 20 per cent were female. Nearly 23 per cent worked in agriculture, 28 per cent in the secondary sector and 46 per cent in the tertiary sector. The public sector deficit representing 16 per cent of GDP in 1987 turned into a financial surplus in 1993. According to the 1990 census, schooling levels for the total population were still low but 83 per cent of 15 to 19 year-olds had completed primary school. More than 10 per cent of the population, but only 4 per cent of the 15 to 19 year-olds, were considered illiterate.

Until 1992 there were parallel systems of administration, supervision and certification of basic education by both the federal and state governments. An exception was and is the Federal District where education is fully under the responsibility of the Ministry of Education. In 1993 state governments became responsible for all public schools. Until the end of the century there is a transition period from a centralised to a decentralised administration of education. The Ministry of Education, with a reduced size, remains the body in charge of normative and policy-making functions in education. Specifically, it is responsible for formulating national plans and curricula; authorising teaching material for basic education and teacher training, implementing the textbook programme for primary education; establishing evaluation procedures for the system as a whole and maintaining programmes such as in-service teacher training, literacy programmes and programmes aimed at reducing inequalities among regions.

2. EDUCATIONAL STRUCTURE AND ENROLMENTS

Early childhood education is optional. Children may enter at the age of 4 and it is strongly advocated that 5 year-olds attend. 45 per cent of 4 year-olds and over 72 per cent of 5 year-olds attend early childhood education establishments. About 8.5 per cent of these children are in private institutions. Schools work from 9 a.m. till noon and many of the schools have two classes of 20 pupils each.

The official age of entry to primary school is 6 years but children can enter primary school between the ages of six and fourteen years. Although late-comers have been reduced nearly to zero, re-entrance has resulted in 30 per cent over-age students in every grade. The total number of students in the formal system rose from 3.2 million students in 1950 to 24.6 million in 1990. Despite the fact that this growth required the creation of more than 550 000 places per year, the enrolment of all children in the basic education age group is still far from being achieved. Enrolment rates vary between areas in the north of the country and around the Metropolitan Area of Mexico City which have high rates, and those areas in the south-east of the country which have low rates.

Basic education comprises early childhood education, primary school (six years) and lower secondary school (three years). The total enrolment in primary school was more than 14 million in 1994 and over four million in lower secondary school. Lower secondary education comprises two tracks — the general track and the vocational and technical track. In remote areas, public schools provide education by transmitting recorded lessons to students by means of a television network and the assistance of a tutor. The survival rate of those entering the first grade of primary school up to the end of nine years of education was fewer than 42 per cent in the early 1990s. Just over 6 per cent of all children are enrolled in private primary schools and over 8 per cent in lower secondary schools.

Following basic education there is middle level education with two tracks; students can either follow technical studies for three or four years or the upper secondary school called *bachillerato* for an average period of three years, the latter enabling them to enter higher education. Fewer than 50 per cent of an age group are enrolled in these two forms of education. Before 1980, 90 per cent of all students at this level were in the upper secondary school and the remainder in technical studies, but after 1980 there was a large increase in the number of technical schools, and by 1992, 20 per cent of students were in technical education. While 30 per cent of students are enrolled in private institutions of technical education, 22 per cent are enrolled in upper secondary schools.

Higher education comprises three categories of institutions: a system of federal technology institutes (including the National Polytechnic Institute); state and autonomous universities together with the National Autonomous University of Mexico and teacher-training institutes. There is at least one university in each state and the larger universities have campuses in different cities. The faculties of management and social sciences enrol the largest proportion of students (47.7 per cent) followed by technology (34.1 per cent) and medicine (8 per cent). Fewer than 2 per cent of students are enrolled in natural sciences and mathematics. Most of the institutions offer courses lasting from 4 to 7 years which include teacher training for basic education. Graduate courses include specialisation, Master's and doctoral courses although most avenues for pursuing graduate studies are still to be found outside the country.

3. EDUCATIONAL FINANCE AND COSTS

In 1992 total expenditure on education was US$ 16.7 billion representing 4.7 per cent of GDP. Government expenditure as a percentage of total expenditure on education was 91 per cent, of which 77 per cent came from federal funding. The percentage of the federal budget allocated to education rose from 11.6 per cent in 1983 to 20.3 per cent in 1992 and to 23.7 per cent in 1993. It is worth noting that since 1978 there have been 42 classrooms built each day. In 1994 the percentage distribution of the education

Mexico

budget to the different levels of education were: pre-school 8.7 per cent; primary 37.3 per cent; secondary 20.8 per cent; *bachillerato* 13.5 per cent; teacher training 1.4 per cent; universities, technological institutions and graduate level 18.2 per cent.

4. CURRICULUM AND ASSESSMENT

The federal government, through the Ministry of Education, is responsible for designing the curricula for basic education and teacher training. Curricular modifications and revisions are made by means of a participatory process through the National Technical Council of Education and involve the existing network of state and technical councils in each school. The resulting syllabuses are to be approved by the Ministry of Education and are compulsory for all basic education. Some local variation is allowed. Since 1993 the same principle of arriving at a core syllabus has been used for the upper secondary education cycle. For new textbooks the Ministry calls for proposals that are evaluated by a jury composed of different groups of specialists, academic experts and representatives of social groups. At the higher education level, there are many different curricula depending on the faculty. In the National Autonomous University of Mexico there is a body known as the University Council, composed of faculty members, student representatives, directors of schools, departments and institutes, that can authorise changes or modifications to the curriculum.

In basic education, promotion from one grade to the next is the responsibility of the teachers in the school who must comply with certain Ministry norms. In 1993 a national standard examination was introduced. At the end of each cycle of education a certificate is awarded upon successful completion of the studies. For transfer from one cycle of education to the next there are examinations. The educational statistics division in Mexico was established in the early 1970s and collects data on a series of education indicators each year.

5. TEACHERS

Teacher training became part of higher education in 1984. Early childhood education and basic school teachers undergo a 4-year course. Teacher training syllabuses are currently being revised for the three cycles of basic education i.e. early childhood, primary and lower secondary. A shortage of early childhood teachers and a surplus of primary teachers led to a retraining programme for primary teachers to become early childhood teachers. Despite this, total enrolment in teacher training institutions is less for early childhood than for primary education. A career in teaching has become less attractive given comparatively low salaries, and many teachers have left education for better paid jobs.

Netherlands

1. GENERAL CONTEXT

The Netherlands is one of the smaller Member countries of the OECD. It has a population of more than 15 million, a surface area of 41 500 square kilometres and is one of the most densely-populated countries in the world. Several major economic centres are clustered in its highly fertile delta area, and it has an advanced, open economy. The export of products and services accounts for over 50 per cent of GNP. Since the 1960s the Netherlands has also exported natural gas but it has hardly any other raw materials.

The Netherlands is a constitutional monarchy since 1848 and has a two-chamber parliamentary system since 1815. The twelve provinces and approximately 630 municipalities have a relatively independent role. The provincial authorities mainly play a supralocal role in physical planning, environmental protection and socio-cultural affairs. The municipality is responsible for preserving local autonomy. In the field of education this is reflected in the fact that it is the municipal authorities that are in charge of public schools, whereas education policy is generally made at national level.

Freedom of education, which is laid down in the Constitution, finds expression in virtually all facets of the Dutch education system. The threefold freedom — to found schools, to organise them and to determine the principles on which they are based — is the reason for the wide variety of schools in the Netherlands. Under the terms of the Constitution, the government funds public and private schools on an equal basis. Almost 65 per cent of all pupils attend privately-run schools. Freedom of education is subject to restrictions laid down in the Compulsory Education Act which stipulates that children, until they reach the age of 16, must attend, on a full-time basis, an educational establishment which complies with statutory requirements. In addition, all 16 and 17 year-olds are required to attend school at least part-time until they turn 18.

More than half of the labour force holds at least a qualification at the upper secondary level.

2. EDUCATIONAL STRUCTURE AND ENROLMENTS

Primary education (basisonderwijs) caters for children from the ages of 4 to about 12 (in principle eight consecutive years of schooling). Nearly all children attend school from the age of four, although de jure compulsory education starts at the age of five. There are around 1.4 million children enrolled in primary education, which lays the foundation for secondary education.

Secondary education follows ordinary and special primary education. Secondary education comprises: pre-university education (VWO; 6 years; age 12-18), senior general secondary education (HAVO; 5 years; age 12-17), junior general secondary education (MAVO; 4 years; age 12-16), pre-vocational education (VBO; 4 years; age 12-16), senior secondary vocational education (MBO; maximum 4 years; age 16-20) and adult general secondary education (VAVO). Most secondary teaching takes place within schools offering a variety of the types of secondary education mentioned above. Around 1.2 million pupils are enrolled in secondary education.

Since the start of the school year 1993/94, VBO, MAVO, HAVO and VWO all begin with a period of basic secondary education which lasts three years. The aim is to provide pupils between the ages of 12 and 15 with a broad general education with no strict dividing line between general and technical subjects. Basic secondary education is not a separate type of school but is a revised curriculum that is taught in all types of secondary schools that follow on directly from primary school.

Senior secondary vocational education (MBO) currently falls under the Secondary Education Act. MBO is vocationally oriented, leading to middle management positions in industry, service industry and government. MBO lasts a maximum of four years. Longer courses (three or four years) lead to middle management jobs and are associated to higher vocational education (HBO). Interim courses (maximum three years) lead to an independent profession and short training courses (maximum two years) lead to a starting profession and possibly moving on to the long MBO.

The apprenticeship system (LLW) is general vocational training under the joint responsibility of education, government and the social partners. Following one or two days at school, the other days comprise practical training in industry or trainee workshop. This apprenticeship system is for young people from 16 years of age, with or without VBO or MBO certificates. It lasts for one to three years.

Special education is provided in separate schools catering for either the primary or secondary age group or both. Special education for pre-school children with developmental difficulties is provided in units attached to special primary schools. Each special school is geared to the particular learning difficulties that children may encounter in the course of their schooling. Special primary schools cater for children aged from 3 or 4 to 12 years, while special secondary schools are for children aged 12 and over. The maximum age is 20. In 1994 there were around 113 000 pupils in special education.

Tertiary education, for students aged 18 and over, comprises higher professional education (HBO) and university education (WO) (universities). There are 73 higher professional education institutions (*hogescholen*) and 13 universities, including three universities which focus predominantly on engineering and technology, and one agricultural university. Over 400 000 students are enrolled in tertiary education.

There is also one establishment providing open higher distance education, the Open University, with more than 50 000 students. HBO and WO have a two-tier system. The first phase, or undergraduate level, may last up to four years, while the propaedeutic stage lasts no longer than one year.

Higher education institutions have the power to set up and close courses, provided that they take into account the need for an efficient distribution of courses around the country.

3. EDUCATIONAL FINANCE AND COSTS

The Ministry of Education, Culture and Science administers almost all central government expenditure on education, while the

Netherlands

Ministry of Agriculture, Nature Management and Fisheries funds agricultural education.

Under the terms of the Constitution, all schools – public and private – are funded on an equal basis. This means that government expenditure on public schools must be matched by expenditure on private schools. The relationship between educational institutions and the government is characterised by a large measure of institutional autonomy; the role of the government is merely to create the right conditions.

Education is free of charge up to the age of 16. Some schools ask for a parental contribution, but such contributions are voluntary and may not constitute an obstacle to the admission of pupils. Secondary school pupils have to pay for their books and learning materials, travel costs and – where applicable – the cost of living away from home.

Pupils aged 16 and over who are attending a government-funded secondary or special school also have to pay annual school fees, the level of which is set each year by the government (in 1996 Gld 1 576). The same applies to the tuition fees for students in tertiary education (in 1996 Gld 2 400).

Pupils under the age of 18 who are in full-time education at regular or special secondary schools or studying full-time in higher education can apply for a study cost allowance. The level of the allowance depends on parental income. All students between the ages of 18 and 27 enrolled in full-time secondary or higher education are entitled to a non-repayable basic grant, the size of which depends on the type of education and on whether or not the student is living away from home. Depending on their parents' income, students may be able to claim a supplementary grant which, like the basic grant, does not have to be repaid. Students can also claim an interest-bearing loan which must be repaid after the completion of their studies.

4. CURRICULUM AND ASSESSMENT

In the Primary Education Act, school subjects that must appear in the curriculum of primary education are defined, in an integrated form when possible. Although these subjects are compulsory, schools are free to decide how much time they devote to each subject. The government does not prescribe methods for assessing the progress of primary school pupils. Rather, the methods of assessment and reporting are recorded by each individual primary school in its school work plan.

For basic secondary education, national attainment targets have been set for the subjects in the core curriculum. These attainment targets are compulsory minimum standards which schools are expected to achieve by the end of the period of basic secondary education. Under the aegis of the Minister of Education, Culture and Science, tests are set for each subject in the core curriculum, with the exception of physical education. These tests are based on the attainment targets and are administered for each subject or group of subjects. The method of testing is recorded in the school work plan. The school-leaving examinations in VBO, MAVO, HAVO and VWO comprise two parts: internal school examinations and national examinations. Pupils who pass the examination receive a national certificate.

MBO courses are taught in accordance with a school work plan describing the organisation and content of teaching. The competent authority of a school submits the school work plan to the Inspectorate for approval. Examinations are generally set by the institutions themselves. The diplomas awarded at the end of the courses are identical throughout the country.

For the institutions at tertiary level the government lays down no more than a framework, within which these institutions have to operate. Those students passing the final examination of a HBO course have the right to use the title *ingenieur* or *baccalaureus*. The students passing a final examination at a university have the right to use one of the following titles: *ingenieur* (technical universities and agricultural university), *doctorandus* or *meester* (law graduates).

To obtain a doctorate and be entitled to use the title "Dr.", students have to complete a thesis with the support of one or more supervisors. Alternatively, university graduates may take up a four-year appointment as trainee research assistants, during which time they are expected to produce a thesis.

5. TEACHERS

Teacher training courses for the various sectors of education form part of higher education and can be subdivided into:

- Teacher training for full competence in primary education in all subjects and for all age groups (HBO).
- General teacher training for a second-degree and a first-degree qualification in secondary education. Second-degree teachers may give lessons in the first three years of HAVO and VWO and in all years of VBO, MAVO or MBO and first-degree teachers in the complete secondary system. Full-time training for the second-degree qualification lasts for four years with special training in a single subject. A first degree can then be attained after three years of part-time training (HBO).
- Teacher training in technical subjects for a second-degree qualification at the Netherlands Pedagogic Technical College. The course lasts five (full-time) or seven (part-time) years (HBO).
- Teacher training at five colleges for physical education for a first-degree qualification. The course lasts four years (HBO).
- University teacher training for a first-degree qualification in secondary education in the subject completed at the university. It is a one-year course. Passing an undergraduate exam, in which a two-month orientation towards the teaching profession is part of the study programme, is a requirement for admission (WO).

Netherlands

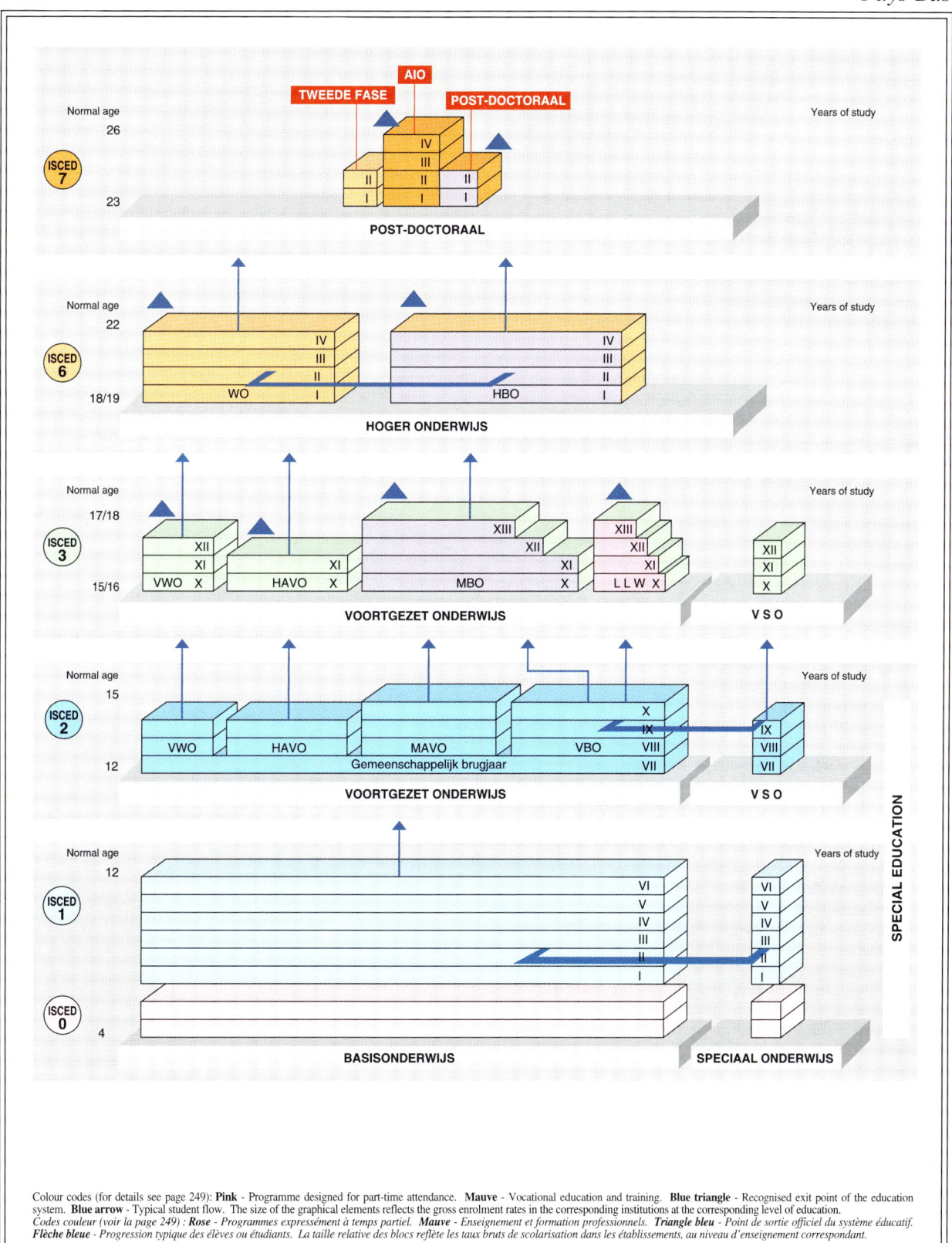

Pays-Bas

Normal age

- ISCED 7: 23–26 — POST-DOCTORAAL (TWEEDE FASE, AIO, POST-DOCTORAAL)
- ISCED 6: 18/19–22 — HOGER ONDERWIJS (WO, HBO)
- ISCED 3: 15/16–17/18 — VOORTGEZET ONDERWIJS (VWO, HAVO, MBO, LLW) / VSO
- ISCED 2: 12–15 — VOORTGEZET ONDERWIJS (VWO, HAVO, MAVO, VBO, Gemeenschappelijk brugjaar) / VSO
- ISCED 1: 4–12 — BASISONDERWIJS / SPECIAAL ONDERWIJS
- ISCED 0

SPECIAL EDUCATION

Colour codes (for details see page 249): **Pink** - Programme designed for part-time attendance. **Mauve** - Vocational education and training. **Blue triangle** - Recognised exit point of the education system. **Blue arrow** - Typical student flow. The size of the graphical elements reflects the gross enrolment rates in the corresponding institutions at the corresponding level of education.

Codes couleur (voir la page 249) : Rose - Programmes expressément à temps partiel. Mauve - Enseignement et formation professionnels. Triangle bleu - Point de sortie officiel du système éducatif. Flèche bleue - Progression typique des élèves ou étudiants. La taille relative des blocs reflète les taux bruts de scolarisation dans les établissements, au niveau d'enseignement correspondant.

New Zealand

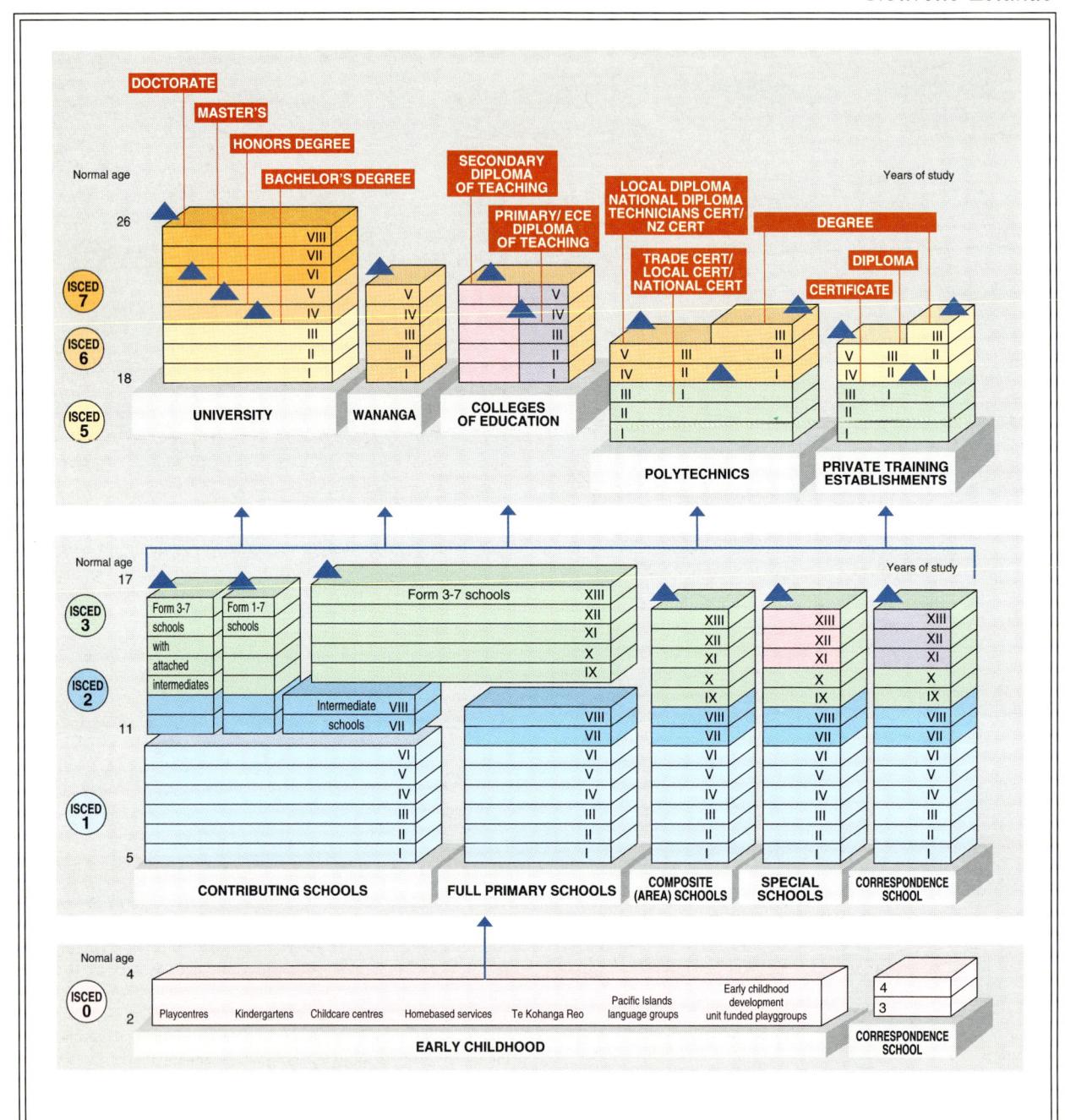

Nouvelle-Zélande

Colour codes (for details see page 249): **Pink** - Programme designed for part-time attendance. **Mauve** - Vocational education and training. **Blue triangle** - Recognised exit point of the education system. **Blue arrow** - Typical student flow. The size of the graphical elements provides no indication of the enrolment in the corresponding educational institutions.

*Codes couleur (voir la page 249) : **Rose** - Programmes expressément à temps partiel. **Mauve** - Enseignement et formation professionnels. **Triangle bleu** - Point de sortie officiel du système éducatif. **Flèche bleue** - Progression typique des élèves ou étudiants. La taille des différents blocs ne représente pas la proportion des effectifs dans les établissements d'enseignement correspondants.*

New Zealand

1. GENERAL CONTEXT

New Zealand is an island nation in the South West Pacific, comprising two main islands (the North and South Islands) and a number of smaller islands, with a total land area of about 270 000 square kilometres. The population of 3.6 million is multicultural in character, highly urbanised and becoming increasingly diverse through immigration. The majority of the population, about 79 per cent, is of European, mainly British, descent. The indigenous Maori population constitutes about 13 per cent of the population, while about 5 per cent are of Pacific Islands Polynesian descent, and 3 per cent Asian. In comparison with other OECD countries, New Zealand has a relatively young population with about 40 per cent aged between 5 and 29. This is particularly true for the Pacific Islands and Maori populations, a fact reflected in the school population in which over 20 per cent are Maori and about 7 per cent Pacific Islanders. The main language of the country is English, but the Maori language (*te Reo Maori*) is an official language and it is currently undergoing a strong revival.

New Zealand has a democratic system of government based on the Westminster parliamentary system. There is a unicameral House of Representatives with members of parliament elected on a first-past-the-post system. This year a major change in the system of government is taking place with the introduction of a new electoral system based on proportional representation.

The economy is heavily dependent on overseas trade, and over the past 20 years it has moved away from its traditional dependence on dairy, meat and wool exports. Forestry, horticulture, fishing, manufacturing and tourism have become increasingly important, and new niche markets have been developed. In the second half of the 1980s, major economic and social reforms were carried out. The reforms, which led to the reorganisation of social services, including education, were concerned about using resources more efficiently and a delivering higher-quality social services with devolution of responsibility. Improvements in the efficiency and responsiveness of the education system were key objectives of the education reforms. Considerable emphasis has been placed on raising the skill levels of school-leavers to enable them to participate in the workforce and to undertake further education and training. At present, about 25 per cent of the adult population (25 to 64 years of age) have an educational attainment at the tertiary level, and participation rates are improving. In 1992, 56 per cent of New Zealanders aged 5 to 29 years were in full-time education and a 5 year-old could expect to have 14.6 full-time-equivalent years of education.

The reform in the economic sector has resulted in major structural changes that have created one of the most open and deregulated economies in the world. As a result of these reforms the economy has achieved one of the highest growth rates (around 4 per cent) among OECD countries, while maintaining one of the lowest rates of inflation, between 1 and 2 per cent over recent years, and overseas debt has been substantially reduced. However, the unemployment rate is still relatively high at around 8 per cent, and it is double this rate for the 15-19 year-old age group. Furthermore, it is disproportionately high for Maori and Pacific Islanders populations at over 20 per cent. Maori and Pacific Island populations, lower socio-economic groups, the unskilled and the unemployed have not benefited as much from the economic reforms as have the rest of the population, and there are greater disparities between rich and poor. These factors are having negative consequences for the educational opportunities available to these groups.

2. EDUCATIONAL STRUCTURE AND ENROLMENTS

New Zealand has an integrated national education system. The Ministry of Education provides policy advice for the government to help implement education policy and to see that resources are used efficiently and fairly. The Education Review Office evaluates the performance and effectiveness of educational institutions, and the New Zealand Qualifications Authority has responsibility for examinations and qualifications. The Education Act (1989) provides for free education in the 2 667 State primary and secondary schools administered by locally-elected boards of trustees. These schools provide education for around 450 000 primary students and over 230 000 secondary students. Attendance is compulsory from the age of 6 until 16, although most children start formal schooling at the age of 5. The majority of students begin secondary school at age 13 and spend four or five years at school, with about 50 per cent completing five years of secondary education. Student/teacher ratios are around the OECD mean. State secondary schools are "comprehensive" in that they offer programmes leading to both academic and vocational careers. Maori medium education is supported through the provision of bilingual and immersion programmes in mainstream schools or through a small number of schools (currently 34) which are specifically designated Maori medium schools (*kura kaupapa Maori*). There are 127 private schools partly funded by the government, catering for around 4 per cent of the school population.

Beyond secondary school level, students may undertake further education and training in one of the 25 polytechnics offering a diverse range of largely vocational programmes from certificate to degree level for around 90 000 students, in one of seven universities offering undergraduate and post-graduate diploma and degree qualifications for around 105 000 students, in one of five colleges of education offering teacher training for around 12 600 students, in a wide range of private training establishments or with an employer in industry. A relatively new development is the provision of *wananga*, i.e. polytechnic and university level programmes specifically for Maori and with an emphasis on Maori language and culture. Two have been set up to date by Maori tribal authorities, and they are recognised by the government for funding purposes.

Early childhood care and education are available to children under 6 years of age (almost all 5 year-olds are in the formal school system) through home-based services and through a wide range of centre-based services, such as kindergarten, play centres and private child-care centres, which provide part-day and full-day programmes. To provide a Maori language and cultural environment, Maori communities have established *kohanga reo* in which Maori preschool children can learn Maori language and culture. Pacific Islands communities are also establishing early childhood centres where their own languages are used. All early childhood education services must meet minimum government requirements, and to be eligible for a government funding grant, services must also have a

New Zealand

negotiated charter. Enrolments in early childhood education have increased by nearly 35 per cent over the last five years, and nearly 100 per cent of 4 year-olds attend early childhood education.

3. EDUCATIONAL FINANCE AND COSTS

Educational expenditure is about 16 per cent of total government expenditure and around 6 per cent of GDP. Compulsory schooling is funded by the government. Each State school receives a grant for operating costs and the board of trustees is responsible for ensuring that the school is properly maintained and controlling the school's expenditure. The funding of capital works is the responsibility of the Ministry of Education. The costs of teachers' salaries (excluding senior management salaries), school transport, major capital works and long-term maintenance are paid directly by the Ministry of Education. Since 1996, however, schools have the choice of directly resourced salaries or the continuation of central delivery of their staffing salary entitlement. Supplementary funding is available to schools for the delivery of programmes to students with special needs, for innovative curriculum delivery in rural schools, for senior programmes in secondary schools, for Maori language immersion programmes and to compensate schools in disadvantaged socio-economic areas.

For tertiary institutions, a new funding mechanism based on an Equivalent Full-Time Student (EFTS) system was introduced in 1991. Universities, polytechnics, colleges of education and *wananga* receive state subsidies for the number of EFTS in each of the course-cost categories at their institution. The funded places are provided by the government in advance of the funding year, and funding is inclusive of capital works.

4. CURRICULUM AND ASSESSMENT

New Zealand has had a national curriculum for many decades, but in late 1990 a major programme of reform of the curriculum was begun. In 1993 *The New Zealand Curriculum Framework* (NZCF) was released and, together with new national curriculum statements, it provides the basis for programmes in schools. The NZCF states a range of broad principles which underpin and give direction to all teaching and learning in schools, specifies seven essential learning areas which describe in broad terms the knowledge and understandings which all students will learn, sets out the eight essential skills to be developed by students through the context of the essential learning areas and outlines the desirable attitudes and values. The NZCF provides direction to the development of more specific national curriculum statements, and new statements have been finalised in English, mathematics, science, senior sciences (biology, chemistry and physics) and technology, with developmental work under way in other learning areas. Parallel statements are also being developed in the Maori language. The main assessment information will come from ongoing school-based assessment as part of the normal teaching and learning process. In addition, information will be obtained at key points in the education system, such as school entry, the start of year 7 (form 1) and the start of year 9 (form 3, when most students begin secondary school). Commencing in 1995, national education standards are being monitored on a four-year rolling cycle by assessing nationally representative samples of students at ages 8 and 12. The four-year cycle will enable all essential learning areas and essential skills in the NZCF to be assessed. Complementing the NZCF is the development of a new *National Qualifications Framework* (NQF). The NQF, which follows a standards-based model, is being phased in over the next few years, and it will bring together senior secondary education, industry training and tertiary education and training into one co-ordinated qualifications system.

5. TEACHERS

Early childhood teachers undertake a three-year programme offered at each of the five colleges of education; they may also gain their teaching qualifications through provider-developed programmes of study while concurrently employed in an early childhood centre. The normal course of training for primary teachers is three years at a college of education. Approximately 80 per cent of primary teacher trainees undertake university degree study, and conjoint programmes are offered at all institutions. Two options are available to secondary teacher trainees. For graduates there is a one-year post-graduate course, and there is also a four-year course of consecutive or concurrent study for suitably qualified school-leavers. A wide range of professional education in-service courses is available, most of which provide credits towards diploma qualifications and service increments. When compared internationally, New Zealand has a relatively small range between starting and maximum salaries. Relative to other professional occupations, the New Zealand teaching body has an older age profile with a mean age of 43 years. This fact, coupled with rising student enrolments, will have a significant impact on the number of teachers required into the 21st century.

Norway

1. GENERAL CONTEXT

The legislative and financial command as well as the overall responsibility for education lies with parliament – the "*Storting*". The *Storting* sets the principal objectives for education and decides on the general administrative structure. The government exercises its authority in matters of education through the Ministry of Education, Research and Church Affairs. This ministry has the overall responsibility for all levels of education from primary and secondary to higher education, including adult education.

Norway is divided into 19 counties, or regional administrative units, and 435 municipalities. The municipalities are responsible for running the primary and lower secondary schools. This includes the responsibility for the building and maintenance of schools, for appointing teachers and for most of the financing. At the upper secondary level these responsibilities are assumed by the 19 counties. The Ministry of Education, Research and Church Affairs is responsible for the individual institutions at both the university and the non-university sectors.

A characteristic feature of the education system has always been the dominating position of the State. Compared with other countries, Norway has few private schools and no specific private school tradition. Private schools are primarily considered as supplementary and not supposed to compete with public instruction. Private higher education institutions may receive state funding only for recognised study programmes, but they are not automatically entitled to such support. In 1996 there were 19 private higher education institutions which received state funding for part of their activities.

Norway has a scattered population, and there are many small school units in remote and sparsely-populated areas. In 1994 only 3 per cent of primary and lower secondary schools had more than 400 pupils. In the municipalities there are about 1 000 schools (about one-third of all primary and lower secondary schools) that do not have separate classes for all age groups because the number of pupils is too small. About 25 per cent of these schools are ungraded, i.e. all the pupils are brought together in one and the same classroom. The number of pupils in each class tends to be quite small in many remote areas compared with class sizes in urban schools. At the lower secondary stage most of the schools are larger, with 2 or 3 parallel classes at each level.

2. EDUCATIONAL STRUCTURE AND ENROLMENTS

Provision of child-care services is the responsibility of the municipalities. A large part of the overall service is provided by private organisations under municipal supervision. Fifty-five per cent of all children between 0 and 6 years of age attend child-care institutions. The coverage is low for the youngest children, increases with age and is about 80 per cent for 6 year-olds.

In 1996, full-time compulsory education covered nine years, from age 7 to age 16. As from the academic year 1997/98, in accordance with new legislation passed by the *Storting*, children will start their compulsory education during the year they reach the age of 6. This will extend the period of compulsory education to ten years instead of nine.

Compulsory education in Norway is co-educational, and classes are organised by age. Neither subject nor level of achievement is a determining factor. An exception is made in the case of optional courses, which are organised around subject matter.

Students normally start upper secondary education at the age of 16. All upper secondary courses lead after 3 years (or, in the case of vocational courses, normally 4 years) to higher education (or a recognised vocational qualification). Regional authorities that are responsible for upper secondary education are required by law to offer places substantially in excess of the needs of the 16-19 age group, 37.5 per cent of the average 16-19 age cohort, in order to provide mature students with the opportunity of receiving an upper secondary education.

A large-scale reform of upper secondary education was implemented as from August 1994. The reform implied the introduction of a statutory right (but no obligation) to three years of upper secondary education for all between the ages of 16 and 19. Foundation courses have been co-ordinated and their number has been reduced from 109 to 13. They now provide a broad knowledge base for specialisation and lifelong learning. For trades recognised under the Act Concerning Vocational Training, the model proposed will combine two years in school with subsequent training in industry. Regional authorities are under legal obligation to establish follow-up services linked to an existing authority. Such services have as their main purpose the following-up of young people who are not in employment, have not applied for or accepted a training place or who have dropped out of their training. The aim of the service is to ensure that all young people, as far as possible, have the opportunity to obtain a recognised qualification.

Ninety-eight per cent of the 16-19 age group are in education or employment but most (over 90 per cent) are in education. The remaining 2 per cent of the age group that, at any one time, are both outside the education system and without employment are contacted by the follow-up service. Only 0.3 per cent prove to be uninterested in the help provided by the follow-up service in finding work or training. Eighty-two per cent of students with a statutory right to upper secondary education progress from a foundation course to an advanced course.

The structural reforms of higher education in Norway in the mid-1960s and the considerable expansion in this sector in the following decade, aimed at creating equal access to higher education for all, irrespective of economic status, social or geographical background.

The structure of higher education was, until the early 1990s, characterised by a high degree of decentralisation. The non-university sector was reorganised as of 1 August 1994, a process through which 98 (regional) colleges were merged into 26 new ones. The reorganisation took place during a period of increased interest in and demand for higher education – thus creating challenges, both quantitatively and qualitatively. The student population increased by about 60 per cent, from around 100 000 to more than 160 000 students, from the end of the 1980s to the mid-1990s – due to increased unemployment as well as to a change in the general attitude towards pursuing higher education. As demand for higher education seems to be flattening out, the present challenges for the

Norway

sector are less concerned with growth and more with consolidation of the new structures, further development of "Network Norway" as well as with measures to ensure quality education.

3. EDUCATIONAL FINANCE AND COSTS

Total public expenditure on education is about NKr 60 million. This constitutes 7.6 per cent of the GNP. Relative to per-capita GDP, per-student expenditure (all levels combined) is 31.5 per cent. Over 50 per cent of the total public expenditure is on primary and secondary education.

Decentralisation of decision-making has been a general trend in Norwegian education since the late 1980s. A major step in the direction of decentralisation was made by the introduction of a new sector grant system in 1986. The former earmarking of grants for primary and secondary education from central to local/county authorities was then replaced by a system in which local and regional authorities receive a lump sum covering all central government subsidies for school education, culture and health services. As a consequence, the municipalities and counties now enjoy greater autonomy in educational provision.

The institutions of higher education are awarded a framework budget within which they have a considerable amount of freedom concerning the detailed internal allocations and expenditures, so long as the set goals (the expected level of activity) are achieved.

4. CURRICULUM AND ASSESSMENT

The Core Curriculum states the goals and principles for primary, secondary general and vocational and adult education while providing a common basis for curriculum development within all these educational sectors. The common Core Curriculum for all of these stages (and for adult education) underlines how the different stages of education are linked by common goals.

The legal basis for the content of teaching in compulsory school is found in the Curriculum Guidelines drawn up by the Ministry of Education. The present guidelines were adopted in 1987. The Curriculum Guidelines indicate how much time should be devoted to the different subjects in terms of weekly periods per subject for each of the three-year blocks of compulsory education. The guidelines give local authorities and individual schools some freedom to develop local curricula and to adapt the guidelines to local needs and conditions. A new curriculum for primary and lower secondary education has been developed, defining the principles, guidelines and subject syllabuses for the new ten-year compulsory education. This curriculum will be introduced in 1997, when the reform is to be put into effect.

In upper secondary education a single set of syllabuses is used by all groups. The choice and adaptation of methods are the responsibility of the professional teacher who is assisted by the teaching guides that accompany the syllabuses.

The main objectives of assessment in primary and lower secondary education are to define and assess to what extent the objectives are being achieved, judge whether or not progress is being made and also suggest what steps might be taken to achieve better progress. Marks are not used in primary education. What is to be assessed is the pupil's overall competence in relation to the objectives described in the Core Curriculum and the syllabuses for the different subjects. Thus, the assessment must be comprehensive and related to both process and result.

Upon leaving compulsory school, all pupils receive a certificate indicating which subjects have been studied, the most recent marks for the year's work and final examination results. These marks form an important criterion that is used for deciding on a student's continuing in upper secondary school.

In the upper secondary school, marks are given in all subjects. These marks, which reflect the individual general level of competence in each subject, appear on the student's certificate alongside examination marks and have the same status as examination marks. An upper secondary school certificate is awarded on the successful completion of a three-year course of studies and this gives the student the "right" to enter higher education. Craft certificates and journeyman's certificates are awarded for successful completion of vocational training.

5. TEACHERS

In Norway all teacher education for primary and secondary schools is regulated by the Act concerning the Training of Teachers. Teachers are usually recruited from colleges of education and universities. Most of the colleges of higher education provide training for teachers of general subjects. Candidates with a traditional university background have to take a one-year programme in practical teacher training.

The municipality is mainly responsible for the in-service education of teachers employed in primary and lower secondary education. One of the responsibilities of the universities and regional colleges will be to provide or organise "in-service" courses and formal post-graduate education in their own subjects for primary and lower secondary school staff.

The rate of unemployment is low among teachers. Teacher training has been expanded in recent years to meet the demographic challenges in the years to come, including an ageing teacher force and a growing number of pupils.

Student/teacher ratios in Norwegian schools are among the lowest in Europe, reflecting the high overall spending and the decentralised school structure.

Norway

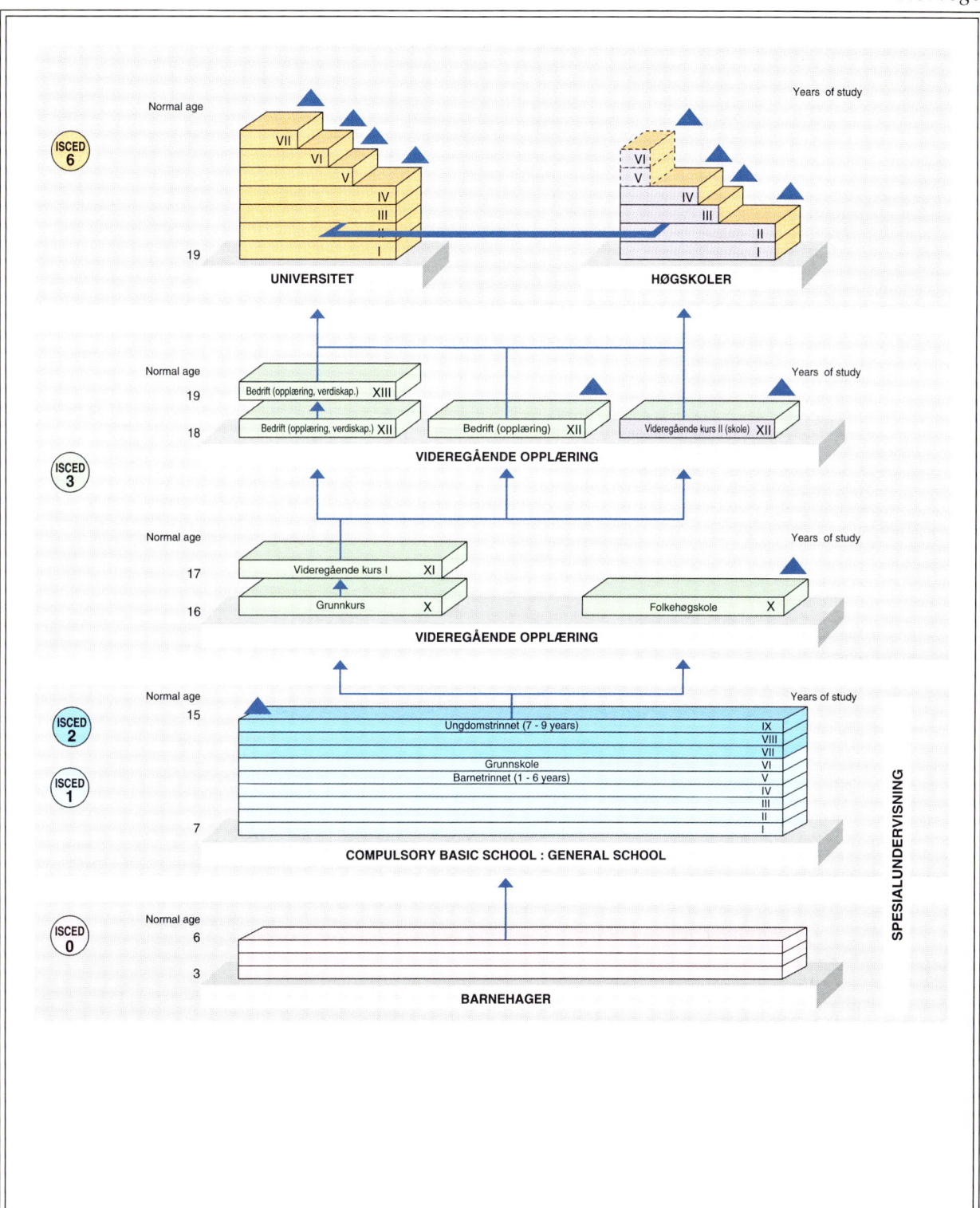

Norvège

ISCED	Level	Age	Programme
ISCED 6	Tertiary	19+	UNIVERSITET / HØGSKOLER (I–VII)
ISCED 3	Upper secondary	18–19	VIDEREGÅENDE OPPLÆRING — Bedrift (opplæring, verdiskap.) XII–XIII; Bedrift (opplæring) XII; Videregående kurs II (skole) XII
		16–17	VIDEREGÅENDE OPPLÆRING — Grunnkurs X, Videregående kurs I XI, Folkehøgskole X
ISCED 2	Lower secondary	13–15	Ungdomstrinnet (7–9 years) — Grunnskole (VII–IX)
ISCED 1	Primary	7–12	Barnetrinnet (1–6 years) — Grunnskole (I–VI) — COMPULSORY BASIC SCHOOL: GENERAL SCHOOL
ISCED 0	Pre-primary	3–6	BARNEHAGER

SPESIALUNDERVISNING

Colour codes (for details see page 249): **Pink** - Programme designed for part-time attendance. **Mauve** - Vocational education and training. **Blue triangle** - Recognised exit point of the education system. **Blue arrow** - Typical student flow. The size of the graphical elements provides no indication of the enrolment in the corresponding educational institutions.

Codes couleur (voir la page 249) : Rose - Programmes expressément à temps partiel. Mauve - Enseignement et formation professionnels. Triangle bleu - Point de sortie officiel du système éducatif. Flèche bleue - Progression typique des élèves ou étudiants. La taille des différents blocs ne représente pas la proportion des effectifs dans les établissements d'enseignement correspondants.

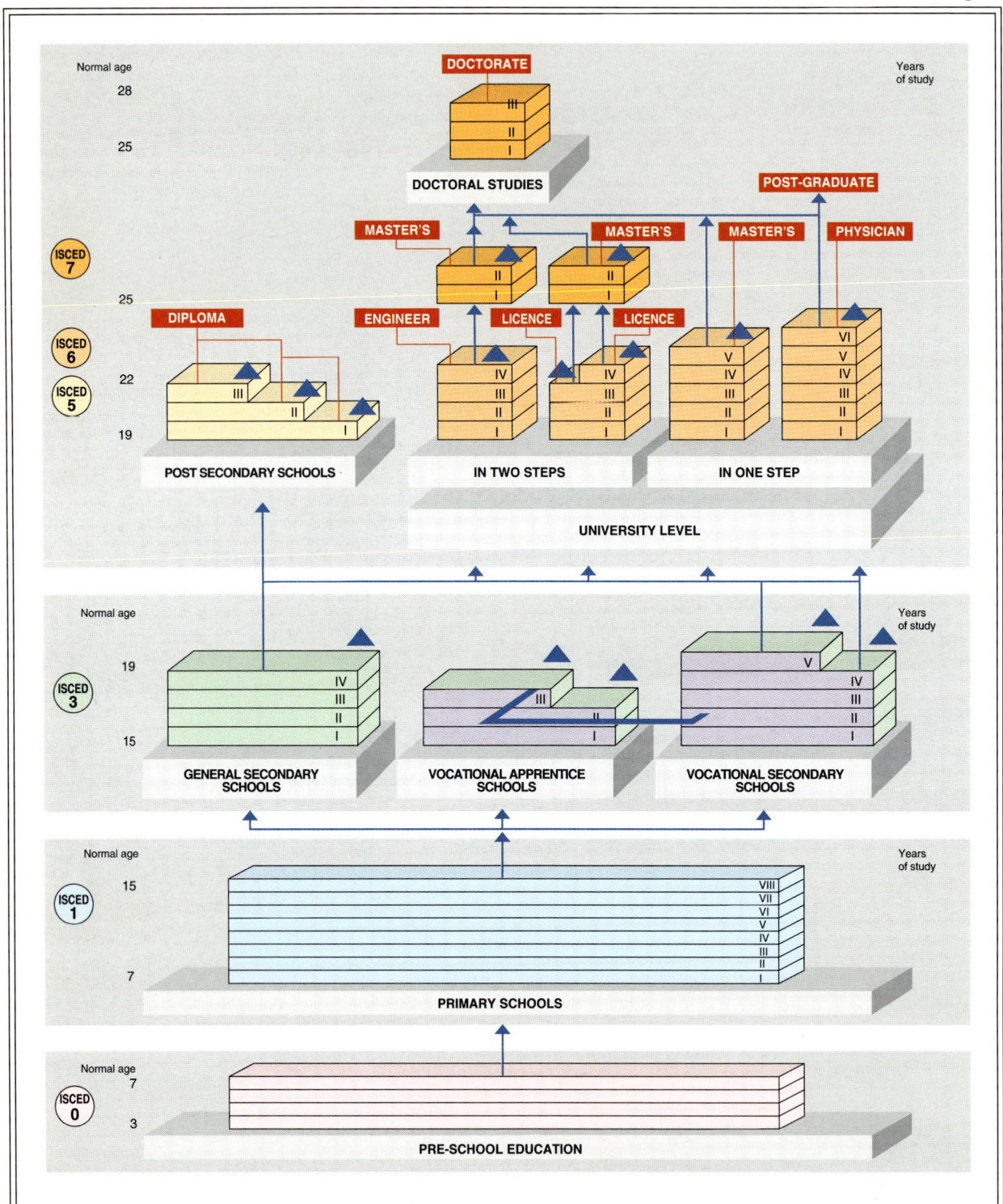

Poland

Pologne

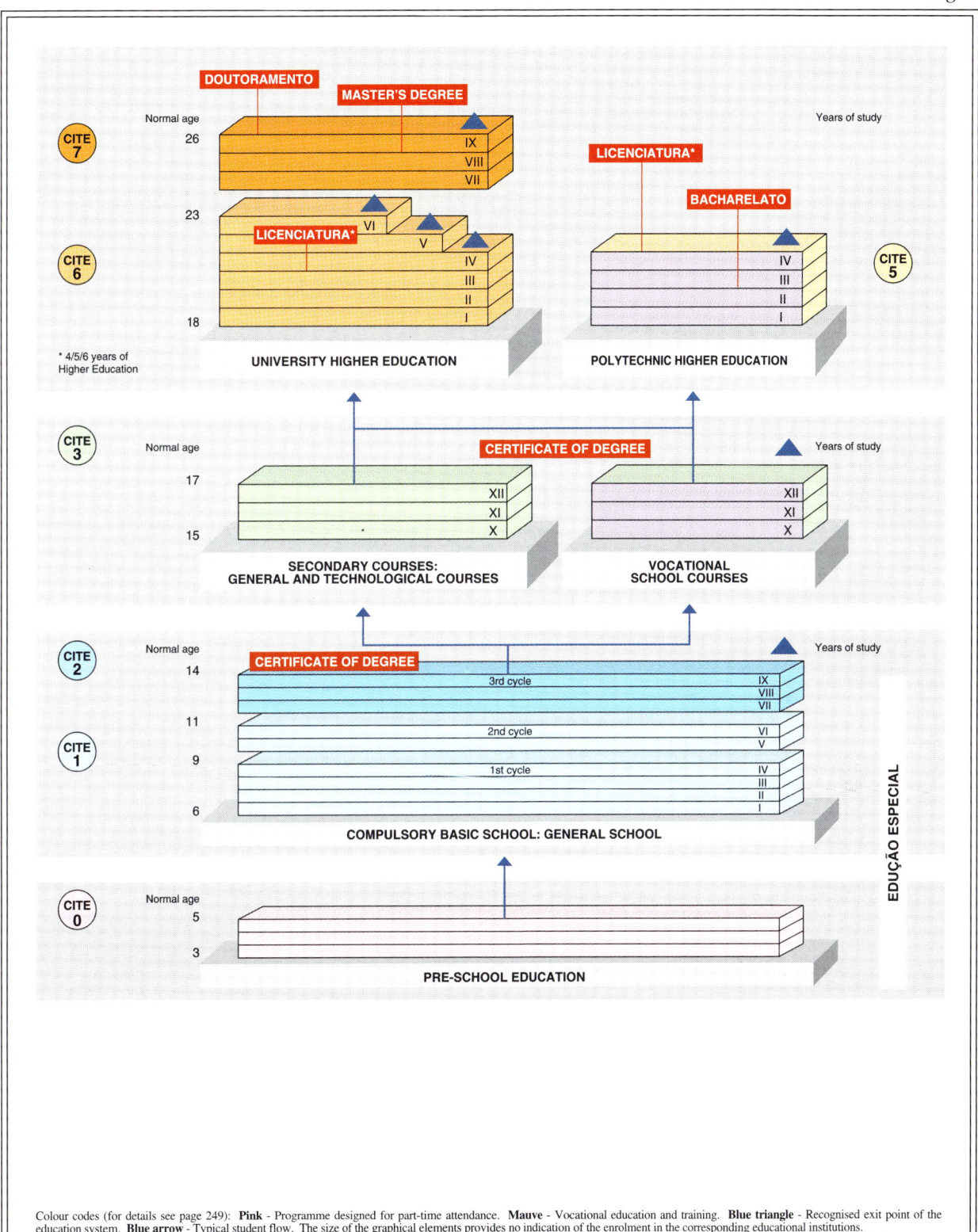

Portugal

CITE 7
- DOUTORAMENTO
- MASTER'S DEGREE
- Normal age: 26
- IX, VIII, VII

CITE 6
- LICENCIATURA*
- Normal age: 23 – 18
- I, II, III, IV, V, VI

UNIVERSITY HIGHER EDUCATION

*4/5/6 years of Higher Education

CITE 5
- LICENCIATURA*
- BACHARELATO
- I, II, III, IV

POLYTECHNIC HIGHER EDUCATION

CITE 3
- Normal age: 15 – 17
- CERTIFICATE OF DEGREE
- X, XI, XII

SECONDARY COURSES: GENERAL AND TECHNOLOGICAL COURSES

VOCATIONAL SCHOOL COURSES

CITE 2 / CITE 1
- Normal age: 6, 9, 11, 14
- CERTIFICATE OF DEGREE
- 1st cycle (I, II, III, IV)
- 2nd cycle (V, VI)
- 3rd cycle (VII, VIII, IX)

COMPULSORY BASIC SCHOOL: GENERAL SCHOOL

EDUCAÇÃO ESPECIAL

CITE 0
- Normal age: 3 – 5

PRE-SCHOOL EDUCATION

Years of study ▲

Colour codes (for details see page 249): **Pink** - Programme designed for part-time attendance. **Mauve** - Vocational education and training. **Blue triangle** - Recognised exit point of the education system. **Blue arrow** - Typical student flow. The size of the graphical elements provides no indication of the enrolment in the corresponding educational institutions.
Codes couleur (voir la page 249) : *Rose* - Programmes expressément à temps partiel. *Mauve* - Enseignement et formation professionnels. *Triangle bleu* - Point de sortie officiel du système éducatif. *Flèche bleue* - Progression typique des élèves ou étudiants. La taille des différents blocs ne représente pas la proportion des effectifs dans les établissements d'enseignement correspondants.

Portugal

1. GENERAL CONTEXT

Portugal comprises a mainland area (88 944 square kilometres) and the two autonomous regions of the Azores and Madeira (together 3 041 square kilometres). It has a population of 9.8 million inhabitants (1991). Between 1981 and 1991, the population grew by 0.28 per cent. The majority of the population inhabits the north of the country, the coastal areas and the urban centres where most schools are to be found.

Nearly 57 per cent of the workforce is in the tertiary sector, just over 32 per cent in the secondary sector and the rest in the primary sector. Unemployment is just above 7 per cent. Nearly 70 per cent of the workforce have six or fewer years of schooling, just over 3 per cent have a higher education qualification and the rest have between seven and twelve years of schooling.

The Ministry of Education defines the policy for formal and non-formal schooling as well as for physical education. Initial vocational education, provided by vocational schools, is the joint responsibility of the Ministry of Education and the Ministry of Employment and Social Security. Apprenticeship training as well as continuing training for those already in employment is the responsibility of the Ministry of Employment and Social Security.

The organisational framework of the Ministry of Education involves central, regional and local bodies. There are five Regional Departments in the mainland and an Educational Secretary in each of the two autonomous regions responsible for operating and managing education in their areas. The central structure of the Ministry comprises a number of advisory, technical assistance, planning and research units responsible for the orientation, co-ordination, control and evaluation of the education system. These units are the General-Directorate for Higher Education, the General-Directorate for Basic and Secondary Education, the General-Directorate for Adult Education, the Educational Resources Management Department, the Technological, Artistic and Vocational Education Bureau, the Educational Innovation Institute and the Programming and Financial Management Department.

Each school is run by three bodies: the school committee, the pedagogical committee and the administrative committee. In some schools an executive director is designated.

2. EDUCATIONAL STRUCTURE AND ENROLMENTS

Pre-school education is optional and provided for children between the ages of 3 and 5. There are State and private networks of institutions (generally nursery schools) run by the Ministry of Education and the Ministry of Solidarity. In 1994 the enrolment was about 57 per cent of an age group. The government's objective is to attain an enrolment rate of 90 per cent by the year 2000.

Basic education is universal, free and compulsory and lasts for nine years. Eight per cent of pupils are in private schools. Basic education comprises three cycles:
- The first cycle lasts four years, covers general education and is taught by generalist teachers.
- The second cycle lasts two years and is organised as a basic introduction to interdisciplinary subject areas. Usually there is one teacher per subject area.
- The third cycle lasts three years and is taught according to a standard curriculum by one teacher per subject or group of subjects. Upon successful completion of basic education, the student receives a certificate.

Secondary education is not compulsory, lasts three years and enrols about 60 per cent of an age group. It is provided in secondary and vocational schools. About 12 per cent of children attend private schools. General courses (CSPOPE) and technological courses (CSPOVA) are provided in secondary schools. Transfer between the two types of courses is automatic. In secondary education each teacher is responsible for one subject area.

Vocational schools, set up on a decentralised and partnership basis, aim primarily at meeting local and regional needs.

Higher education is provided in universities and polytechnical institutes, and about 20 per cent of an age group are enrolled in higher education courses. Of these 20 per cent, 37 per cent are enrolled in private institutions.

Special education is provided for about 10 per cent of children and takes place either in special schools or in regular schools (mainstreaming).

In 1991 about 13 per cent of adults were deemed to be illiterate. Most of these persons are from rural areas and include more women than men. Both state and private institutions provide recurrent education courses as a complement to, or as a substitute for, school education.

3. EDUCATIONAL FINANCE AND COSTS

Education expenditure is estimated to be about 5.6 per cent of GDP and about 21 per cent of the state budget. The allocation to the different levels of education is approximately 2.4 per cent to early childhood education, 59.2 per cent to basic education, 18.4 per cent to secondary schooling and 17.3 per cent to higher education. Special education and adult education are allocated 2.7 per cent.

4. CURRICULUM AND ASSESSMENT

There is a national curriculum for basic education although some optional subjects are also allowed.

In the first cycle, optional subjects focus on personal/social development and religious subjects. The same applies to the second cycle with additional foreign language options, and in the third cycle, the same options exist plus other foreign languages, music and technological options. Some vocational schools deliver courses corresponding to the third cycle predominantly oriented to working life.

There is also a national curriculum for secondary education, or rather two sets of overlapping curricula because there are two different secondary tracks: general courses predominantly leading to further pursuit of studies at the tertiary level of education and technological courses predominantly oriented to the working life.

Vocational schools constitute an alternative to the normal education system. They aim primarily at meeting local and regional needs through diversified courses and curricula within each area of training.

Portugal

Textbooks are typically written by teachers and published commercially. The Ministry of Education establishes criteria that schools must follow when selecting textbooks.

Assessment takes various forms. In basic education, school committees decide on a student's promotion from one grade to the next based on the teacher's continuous assessment in the first cycle. In the second and third cycles as well as in secondary education, teachers award marks in each subject and the school committees use these for their assessment. There is little grade repetition. At the end of basic education and again at the end of secondary education, national achievement tests are administered and their results are used whenever decisions are taken about the award of a certificate. At the end of secondary education, the results from national achievement tests are used for decisions about entry to higher education.

5. TEACHERS

In 1994, out of the total of 170 000 teachers, 3 per cent were working in early childhood education, 25 per cent in the first cycle of basic education, 20 per cent in the second cycle, 42 per cent in the third cycle and in secondary education, about 9 per cent in higher education and 1 per cent in other schools.

Teachers in pre-school and the first cycle of basic education receive a three-year initial training course in polytechnic institutions. For teachers in the two other cycles of basic education and in secondary education, there are two forms of training: *i)* a 4 to 5-year course (subject matter plus education) at a university for those without any qualifications; and *ii)* a two-year in-service course involving theoretical and practical training for those with a first degree having already been selected to teach in a school.

Russian Federation

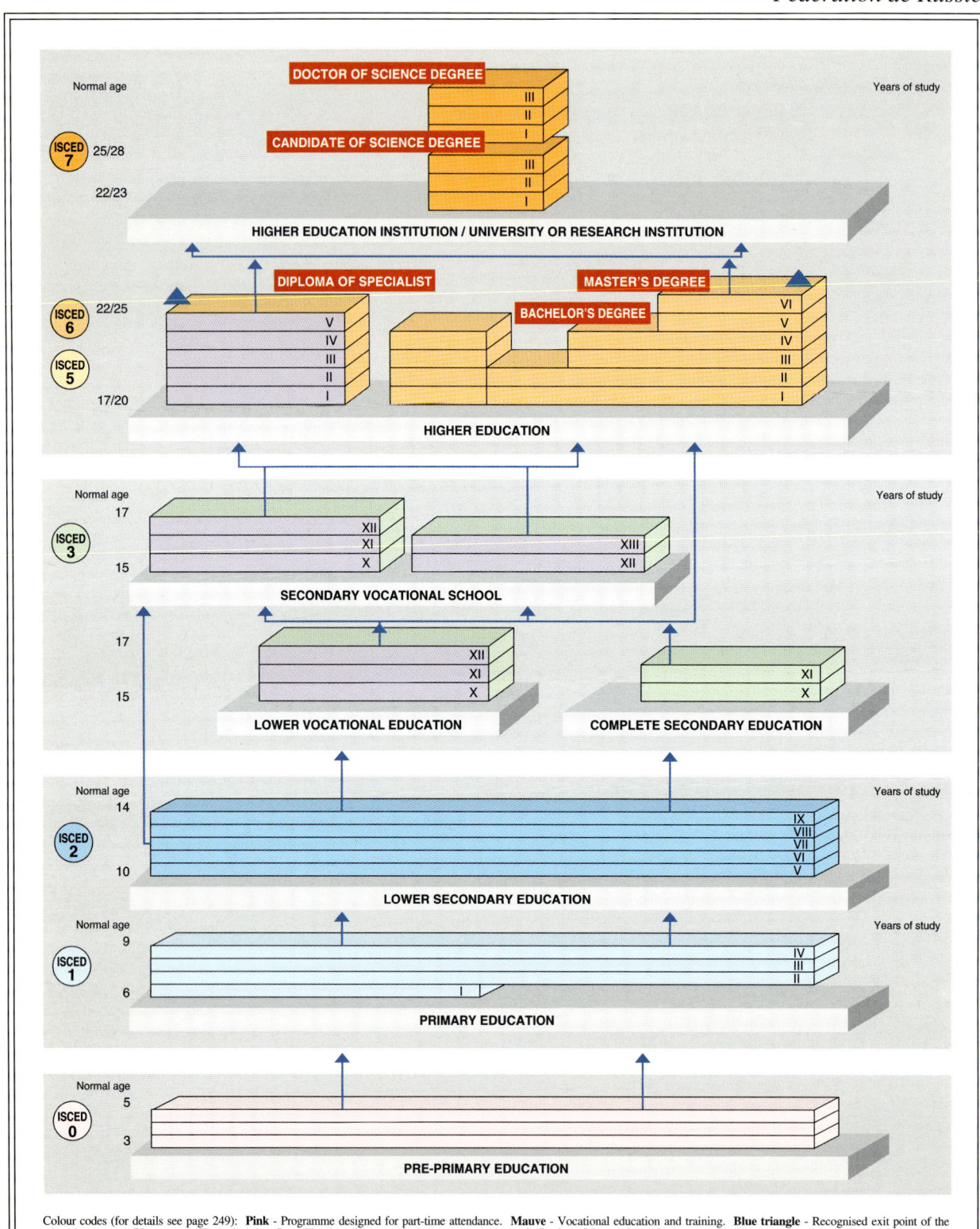

Fédération de Russie

Russian Federation

1. GENERAL CONTEXT

Russia lies across Eastern Europe and North Asia, occupies 17 075 400 square kilometres and has a population of nearly 148 million of which 73 per cent live in urban areas. There are twelve cities with over one million inhabitants each. Together with a decreasing population growth rate, there has been a reduction in the size of the population under working age. About 35 per cent of the total population are potential consumers of initial educational services.

The population contains over 130 nationalities, with students from 80 language backgrounds enrolled in school. Upper secondary education is provided in three of these languages. With the exception of teacher training, all higher education is taught in Russian.

Out of 1 000 persons aged 15 years or over, 151 have completed or partly completed higher education, 219 vocational secondary, 285 upper secondary, 202 lower secondary, 100 primary education and 43 have no primary education (mainly people over 60). Among the employed, 12 per cent have not completed their secondary education.

Access to education is one of the primary constitutional rights of all citizens. Primary, lower secondary and general upper secondary education are all generally available and free. Secondary and higher vocational education at state and municipal educational institutions are also free but on a competitive basis.

The Russian Federation has a complex administrative structure with 89 territorial areas (*oblasts*, *krays*, *obrugs* and republics). The State plays a leading role at all education levels. At the federal level, responsibility is shared between the federal, regional and local authorities. Federal laws apply throughout the whole country. Local and regional authorities can promulgate laws and issue regulations provided that they do not contravene federal laws.

The three principal goals of educational development are formulated in light of the demands of social and economic development: self-realisation of the individual, development of everyone's learning potential and strengthening of the civic society.

2. EDUCATIONAL STRUCTURE AND ENROLMENTS

Early childhood education is not compulsory. Children may, as a rule, attend kindergartens for one to three years at ages 3-5(6). There were 72 800 early childhood public (state) institutions at the end of 1993, attended by 6.8 million children. By the beginning of 1995, there were 400 000 children still in need of early childhood education. In many regions parents must now pay for part of the services provided, and the remaining part is reimbursed by local authorities and enterprises. This new situation has led to a dramatic decrease in enrolments.

Primary education is compulsory. There were 17 141 schools in 1996, but this number is decreasing continuously. Depending on the curriculum offered, primary schooling covers 3 or 4 years. Children enter primary school at the age of 7 (or 6).

Lower secondary education is also compulsory. There were 13 943 schools in 1996, but their number is also decreasing. This cycle lasts 5 years. At the end of this cycle students are awarded a certificate of basic secondary education. Schooling is compulsory up to the age of 15.

Upper secondary education is provided in two-stage secondary schools and *gymnasia*. The number of state day-time upper secondary schools was 35 219 in 1996 and is increasing. Final-year students, typically 16 or 17 years old, receive a school-leaving certificate. These schools sometimes provide lower vocational education and award a corresponding certificate.

About 64 per cent of day-time schools' lessons are conducted in a single shift, but 25 per cent of the school children study in a second or third shift. In recent years, this situation has changed slightly in that more pupils are now enrolled in second and third shifts.

Lower vocational education and, as a rule, the upper secondary cycle are provided by vocational schools frequently referred to as *lyceums*. At the end of this course students are awarded a certificate of lower vocational education. There are 4 203 vocational schools enrolling 1 699 000 students.

In order to be admitted to a secondary vocational institution, a person must have completed basic lower secondary education, the upper secondary cycle or lower vocational education. Depending on the student's initial level of education, a 3 to 5-year training programme is carried out by means of programmes with different curricula. The main types of secondary vocational institution are *technicums* (1 895) and colleges (679) altogether enrolling 1 870 800 students. Colleges may be either independent or departments within higher education institutions. Graduates are awarded a diploma of secondary vocational education in their field of study.

To enter a higher vocational institution a student must have completed secondary education. In 1995/96 the number of higher vocational institutions was 759 with a total enrolment of 2 777 500. There were 402 300 graduates, a total that reflects a decline owing to reduced admissions over the previous period.

Higher education in Russia is complex, there being programmes at different levels and of different durations and purposes. It is carried out in colleges, institutes, universities and academies.

The sector is structured in three stages. The first corresponds to initial higher education. The second, for which the entry requirement is the Bachelor's degree, provides basic higher education. The courses consist of two components: education and research. Successful candidates are awarded a Master's degree. The third stage, which is traditional in Russia and lasts for 5 to 6 years, is increasingly in popular. Graduates are awarded a specialist diploma.

Students may continue their studies at the post-graduate level where the training of research and teaching staff is provided. The system is organised in two stages: *i)* post-graduate (3-4 years); and *ii)* doctoral (3 years). At the end of each stage, students must successfully defend a thesis leading to the degree of candidate or doctor of science, respectively. Post-graduate courses are available

Russian Federation

in 506 higher education and 828 research institutions. In 1995 there were 62 300 post-graduate students of whom 11 400 had completed their courses, including 2 600 who had defended their theses. The doctoral course is available in 217 higher education and 167 research institutions. In 1995 there were 2 200 students enrolled of whom 464 completed their courses, including 137 who defended their theses.

Apart from the state institutions, at all levels except for the post-graduate level, there are private educational institutions, some of which charge tuition fees.

3. EDUCATIONAL FINANCE AND COSTS

Economic instability had implications on educational finance. Having declared education a priority area, the State is not in a position to provide the financial resources required for its development. The funding available to educational institutions is often only sufficient to pay for salaries and municipal services. Premises and library stocks are in a poor condition in most institutions. There is a shortage of textbooks, other manuals and teaching and learning aids.

Under the new legislation, the State guarantees an allocation of 10 per cent of the national income to meet educational needs. The Ministry of Finance is increasingly transferring responsibility for educational finance to regional and local authorities, thus delegating to them the strategic development and implementation of education within their areas. At the same time, this leads to regional disparities in the provision of educational services due to the unequal financial capacity of the regions.

The share of educational expenditure in GDP has increased slightly. In 1994 it was about 4.5 per cent, still below the level reached at the beginning of the 1970s. However, according to preliminary data, the share decreased again in 1995 to 3.4 per cent. At the same time, the real expenditure per pupil, particularly in early childhood and compulsory school education, fell dramatically.

Institutions are authorised to acquire additional financial resources by charging for educational services. In 1996 a private sector began to take shape at all levels of education. Currently 4.9 per cent of the total student population is enrolled in 193 private higher education institutions, a number which is rapidly increasing and becoming a mass phenomenon in the two largest cities, Moscow and St. Petersburg. Tuition fees range from US$ 300 to 6 000 per year (about 1.5 to 30 million rubles). By comparison, the average salary in April 1996 was 770 000 rubles and the minimum salary was 76 000 rubles.

The new educational law has established a system of educational credits but the exact nature of its implementation has not yet been determined.

According to preliminary data, the average monthly salary of the educational workforce in 1995 was 308 000 rubles. The average monthly salary in higher education institutions was 75 per cent of the average salary in the economy and 118 per cent of the average salary in the education sector (excluding social bonuses). A new law envisages a salary not lower than that of civil servants.

4. CURRICULUM AND ASSESSMENT

Standards are being set in state education. Incorporating federal and regional components, they define the minimum level of achievement for basic education, the maximum number of hours of study and the basic knowledge required of students.

Educational programmes can be subdivided into general (early childhood, primary, lower secondary, upper secondary) and vocational (primary, secondary, undergraduate, post-graduate). While state bodies define the core curriculum, the content is designed and delivered by each institution. The innovative contribution of individual teachers to the learning process is encouraged.

The implementation of additional general and vocational programmes, not only for personal development but also for the professional training and retraining of both young people and adults, is of great importance. The content of additional programmes is varied and frequently designed to match new labour market demands. The duration of programmes ranges from several months to several years.

5. TEACHERS

Teaching is an important sphere of employment. At the beginning of the 1994/95 school year, 1 508 900 teachers were employed in schools under the jurisdiction of the Ministry of Education (including school managers who also usually teach). Seventy-four per cent have a degree, 3 per cent have not completed a degree, 20 per cent have completed secondary vocational teacher training and 3 per cent have completed secondary vocational or general secondary education without teacher training. Among primary school teachers the education level is lower, with 45 per cent having a degree. Teaching is essentially a female profession, with 84 per cent of secondary school teachers and 99 per cent of primary school teachers being women.

The training of teachers is carried out at primary and secondary institutions (vocational schools, *technicums*, colleges) and in higher education institutions. The duration of programmes is 2 to 3 years in the former and 3 to 5 years in the latter. Further professional training may be acquired, but there are few educational institutions or teachers that can afford it. Some support for talented young teachers is provided by the Soros Foundation.

Only a proportion of the graduates from teacher training institutions actually take up teaching, mainly because salaries are so low. For the same reason, practising teachers, especially young ones, are leaving the profession. At the beginning of the 1994/95 school year, the number of vacancies in state schools for teachers in Russian language and literature was 3 400, history 2 100, mathematics 1 900, physics 1 300 and other subjects about 1 000. However, the greatest number of vacancies was for foreign language teachers, where there were 8 300 positions to fill. By contrast, the situation is more or less stable in higher vocational institutions although the teaching force is ageing.

Spain

1. GENERAL CONTEXT

With an area of 504 759 square kilometres, Spain is the second largest country in Western Europe. In 1991 it had a total population of 38 872 268 inhabitants. While the population density, 77 inhabitants per square kilometre, is relatively low compared to that of other Western European countries, the distribution of this population is very uneven, with a higher concentration in and around the country's capital and a very low population density in the central areas. The age structure corresponds to that of a mature population, with about 25 per cent of young people under 16.

The current population is the result of the historical inter-relationships among groups of very different origins, with different traditions and different languages (in addition to Castilian Spanish, which is the official language for the State as a whole), such as Galician, Basque and Catalan. The form of government, according to the Constitution of 1978, is that of a constitutional monarchy. The Spanish nation comprises 17 Autonomous Communities (which are divided into a total of 50 provinces) and two special municipalities (Ceuta and Melilla).

Spain's recent history has seen far-reaching upheavals of huge significance for the country's current situation. With the passing of the 1978 Constitution, the former centralised territorial organisation was replaced by a new decentralised model, with one of the many changes being the sharing of responsibilities for education matters among the State, the Autonomous Communities and the municipalities.

2. EDUCATIONAL STRUCTURE AND ENROLMENTS

The structure of the Spanish education system was reformed by the Constitutional Law on the General Ruling of the Education System (LOGSE). While this law was passed in October 1990, its full implementation will take ten years. At most educational levels, therefore, the structure set up by the previous law, the General Law on Education (LGE) of 1970, is still in force and will remain so until it is gradually supplanted by the new levels and cycles.

The education structure of the LGE has four levels: early childhood education, Basic General Education (EGB), General Unified Baccalaureate (BUP) and university education. Vocational training, although not included in the 1970 law as an "educational level" in the strict sense of the term, is, together with the BUP, part of what in Spain is known as *enseñanzas medias* (equivalent to the second cycle of secondary education in other countries).

Early childhood education was the first level to be reformed by the LOGSE, with the change taking effect for the 1991/92 school year.

The EGB covers basic and compulsory education for all Spaniards between the ages of 6 and 14. By the 1993/94 school year, the new law had been applied to the first four years of primary education, with the last four still regulated by the EGB. The Baccalaureate consists of three school years. Students who wish to move on to higher education after the Baccalaureate have to complete the Pre-university Guidance Course (COU), after which they can take university entrance examinations. Vocational training (VTI) is divided into two levels: first grade (2 years) and second grade (2 or 3 years).

The new education system established by the LOGSE defines a structure more akin to that of other Western European countries. Early childhood education under the system extends up to the age of six and is optional. Primary education, comprising six academic years (from 6 to 12 years of age) is compulsory and free of charge. The term "secondary education" covers compulsory secondary education (ESO), which spans the four academic years between ages 12 and 16; the Baccalaureate, which covers two academic years and is a non-compulsory stage; and vocational training at the intermediate level, which is organised into modules of variable length. The LOGSE also covers vocational training at the advanced level, as post-secondary education.

University education is also undergoing a process of reform (Law on University Reform of 1983). University courses can be followed at *Escuelas Universitarias*, *Escuelas Técnicas Superiores* or university faculties. In the first of these, the courses have single (3-year) cycles whereas in the second and third, courses last for at least two cycles (5-6 years), after which access can be gained to the third cycle to obtain a doctorate.

Enrolments for the 1993/94 academic year can be broken down as follows: 1 083 330 children in infant education; 2 444 613 in primary education (1st to 4th) and the 5th year of EGB; 1 836 325 students in the upper cycle; 1 370 239 in BUP, the second cycle of the ESO and the 1st year of LOGSE Baccalaureate; 395 521 in COU and the 2nd year of the LOGSE Baccalaureate, 422 951 in VTI and level II modules; 16 412 in VTII, level III modules and advanced vocational training and, finally, 1 420 021 at university.

3. EDUCATIONAL FINANCE AND COSTS

Education in Spain is funded both publicly and privately. Public financing is provided by the central educational administration and by regional governments and local authorities, although there are also contributions from other ministries. Private financing is provided by private institutions and citizens.

Schools in the general state system are free up to the university level. Private schools which meet certain conditions may receive funding from the public authorities (direct grant schools). The non-direct grant schools do not receive financing of any type and can act with complete autonomy on matters concerning their internal organisation, the selection of teaching staff, admission of students and financial management. At public universities, students must pay part of the cost of their education through enrolment fees. The remaining part of the universities' income is received through contributions from the public administration and private institutions. In private universities, students must meet the full cost of their courses.

In order to compensate for inequalities in education, the education system offers a series of grants and study awards (for travel, accommodation, materials, exemption from fees), which are

Spain

of particular importance at non-compulsory levels of education, as well as for services which complement compulsory education, such as school transport, meals and boarding.

In 1994 Spain spent 5.8 per cent of its GDP on education. A breakdown of these resources according to their origin shows that about 80 per cent of the money spent on education was of public origin, whilst the remaining 20 per cent came from private sources.

4. CURRICULUM AND ASSESSMENT

In the upper cycle of EGB (ages 11 to 14), the curriculum is divided into courses. There are Pedagogical Guidelines, created in 1971, which are flexible and orientational. These guidelines point to greater specialisation in subject areas when compared to the more general guidelines in lower cycles. Assessment is designed to be continuous, although there is a test at the end of each year to permit those students who have not received a positive overall assessment to move up to the following year and to give them the opportunity of passing the subjects in which they were not successful. In the second cycle of secondary education, there is no set syllabus in the strict sense, since there is only an outline Baccalaureate curriculum which divides subjects into a common core (those which all students are obliged to take), optional subjects and technical-vocational education. The COU aims at broadening students' basic instruction, guiding them towards choosing a career and preparing them intellectually for higher education. In the BUP and COU, assessment is continuous, and a grade is awarded for each subject.

The LOGSE is introducing a new, more open approach to the design and development of the curriculum. The components which make up the curriculum provide aims for abilities, contents, teaching methods and the assessment criteria used at each of the different levels, stages, cycles, grades and subject matters into which education is divided. In order to guarantee an education common to all students and to ensure validity for the qualifications awarded, the basic aspects of the curriculum have been set for the whole country. Taking this as a basis, there are three levels at which the curriculum is then defined in greater detail: the Autonomous Region which establishes its curriculum according to the characteristics of its particular territory; the school, which establishes the curriculum according to the characteristics of its students and environment; and the school's teaching staff, who work out the programmes, adapting them to each specific group of students.

Assessment of early childhood education must be global, continuous and formative; in primary education it must be continuous and global; and in compulsory secondary education it must be continuous and integrating according to the different subjects on the curriculum. At earlier stages, when the student fails to reach the specified targets, the teachers will take the necessary steps to provide for extra educational assistance and, if need be, adapt the curriculum. For those students who fail to reach the standards set by the ESO, specific social guarantee programmes are set up with a view to offering basic, vocational training. Assessment at the Baccalaureate level is continuous and is dependent on subject, according to the educational objectives and evaluation criteria set in the curriculum of each education authority. In vocational training, as in the other types of education provided for in the LOGSE, assessment is continuous, and is carried out by vocational modules.

5. TEACHERS

The total number of teachers has steadily increased since 1975, from just over 300 000 to more than 500 000 at present.

The initial teacher training required to give classes at the different levels of education is as follows. For early childhood and primary stages, the qualification of *Maestro* (3-year teacher training course) is required. A secondary school teacher has to be a tertiary graduate, architect or engineer (with a 5/6-year course) and to have followed a teacher training course. In certain areas of vocational training, it is possible to become a teacher with the qualification of *diplomado*, "technical architect" or "technical engineer" (3-year courses). In general, to gain access to a teaching post at university level, a doctorate is required, although there are some teaching categories which only require the qualification of Graduate, Architect or Engineer.

Substantial changes have been introduced in in-service teacher training since the LOGSE was passed. Training is being actively promoted by education authorities, who are increasing the supply and using incentive schemes (recognition of courses for promotion purposes, transfer competitions, financial rewards, etc.). In-service teacher training programmes seek to align the curricula more closely to the needs resulting from new educational practices. The institutions involved in this process in recent years have included universities (through their educational departments, ICEs) and teachers' centres.

Spain

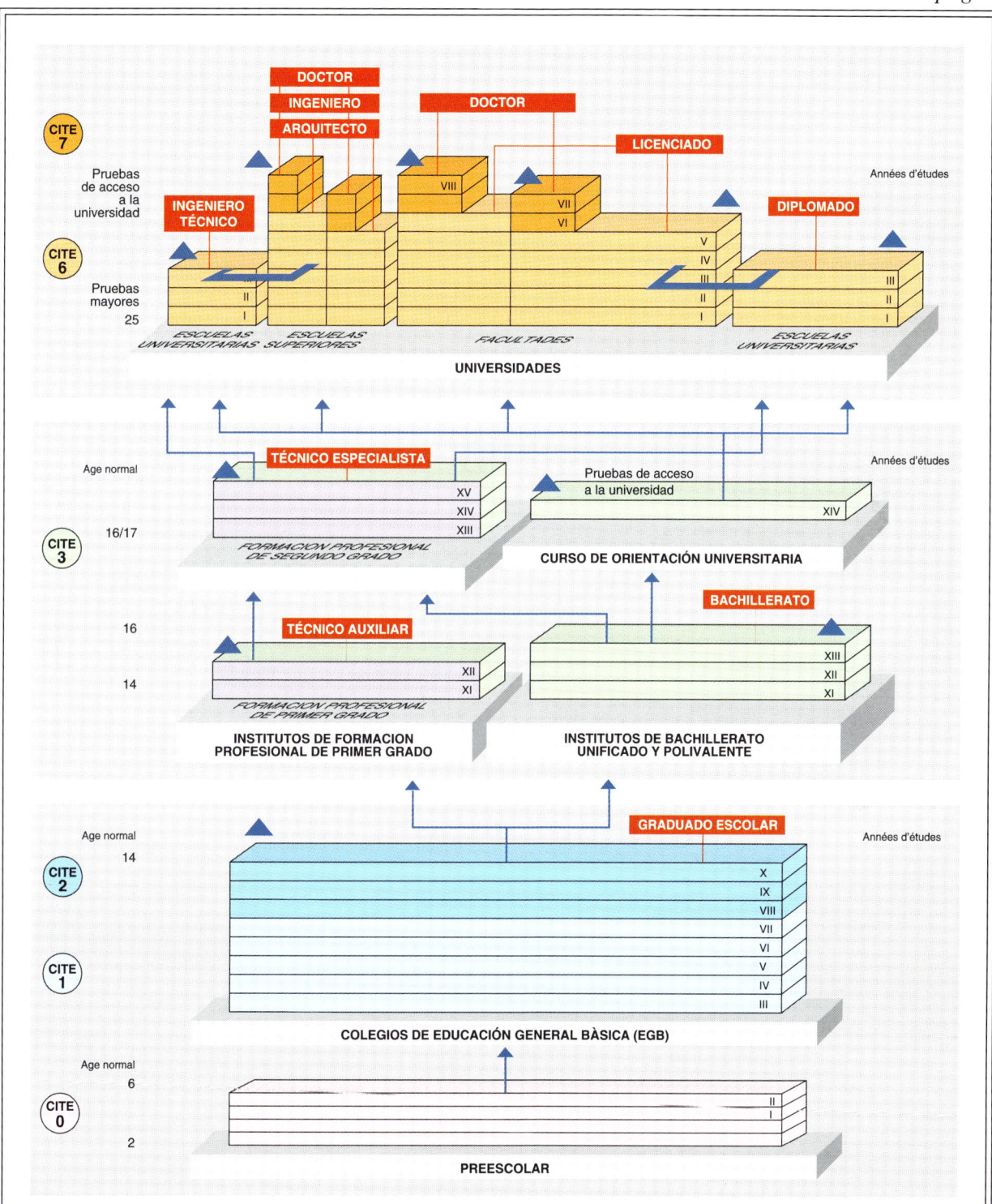

Espagne

Diagram: Structure of the Spanish Education System (1993/94)

CITE 7 / CITE 6 — UNIVERSIDADES
- ESCUELAS UNIVERSITARIAS SUPERIORES: INGENIERO TÉCNICO (I–II), DOCTOR / INGENIERO / ARQUITECTO (up to VIII)
- FACULTADES: DOCTOR, LICENCIADO (I–VII)
- ESCUELAS UNIVERSITARIAS: DIPLOMADO (I–III)
- Pruebas de acceso a la universidad
- Pruebas mayores 25

CITE 3 (Age normal 16/17)
- FORMACION PROFESIONAL DE SEGUNDO GRADO — TÉCNICO ESPECIALISTA (XIII–XV) — INSTITUTOS DE FORMACION PROFESIONAL DE PRIMER GRADO
- CURSO DE ORIENTACIÓN UNIVERSITARIA (XIV) — Pruebas de acceso a la universidad

(Age 14–16)
- FORMACION PROFESIONAL DE PRIMER GRADO — TÉCNICO AUXILIAR (XI–XII)
- BACHILLERATO (XI–XIII) — INSTITUTOS DE BACHILLERATO UNIFICADO Y POLIVALENTE

CITE 2 / CITE 1 (Age normal 14)
- COLEGIOS DE EDUCACIÓN GENERAL BÀSICA (EGB) — GRADUADO ESCOLAR (III–X)

CITE 0 (Age normal 2–6)
- PREESCOLAR (I–II)

Colour codes (for details see page 249): **Pink** - Programme designed for part-time attendance. **Mauve** - Vocational education and training. **Blue triangle** - Recognised exit point of the education system. **Blue arrow** - Typical student flow. The size of the graphical elements provides no indication of the enrolment in the corresponding educational institutions. The diagram presents the structure of the Spanish education system during the school year 1993/94 on which the indicators are based. The current education system differs from the one represented here due to changes implemented following the Education Act of October 1990. *Codes couleur (voir la page 249) : Rose - Programmes expressément à temps partiel. Mauve - Enseignement et formation professionnels. Triangle bleu - Point de sortie officiel du système éducatif. Flèche bleue - Progression typique des élèves ou étudiants. La taille des différents blocs ne représente pas la proportion des effectifs dans les établissements d'enseignement correspondants. L'organigramme représente la structure du système éducatif tel qu'il était en 1993/94, année scolaire de référence pour les indicateurs. Le système éducatif actuel est différent de celui-ci à la suite de réformes apportées par la loi d'octobre 1990 sur la direction générale du système d'enseignement.*

Sweden

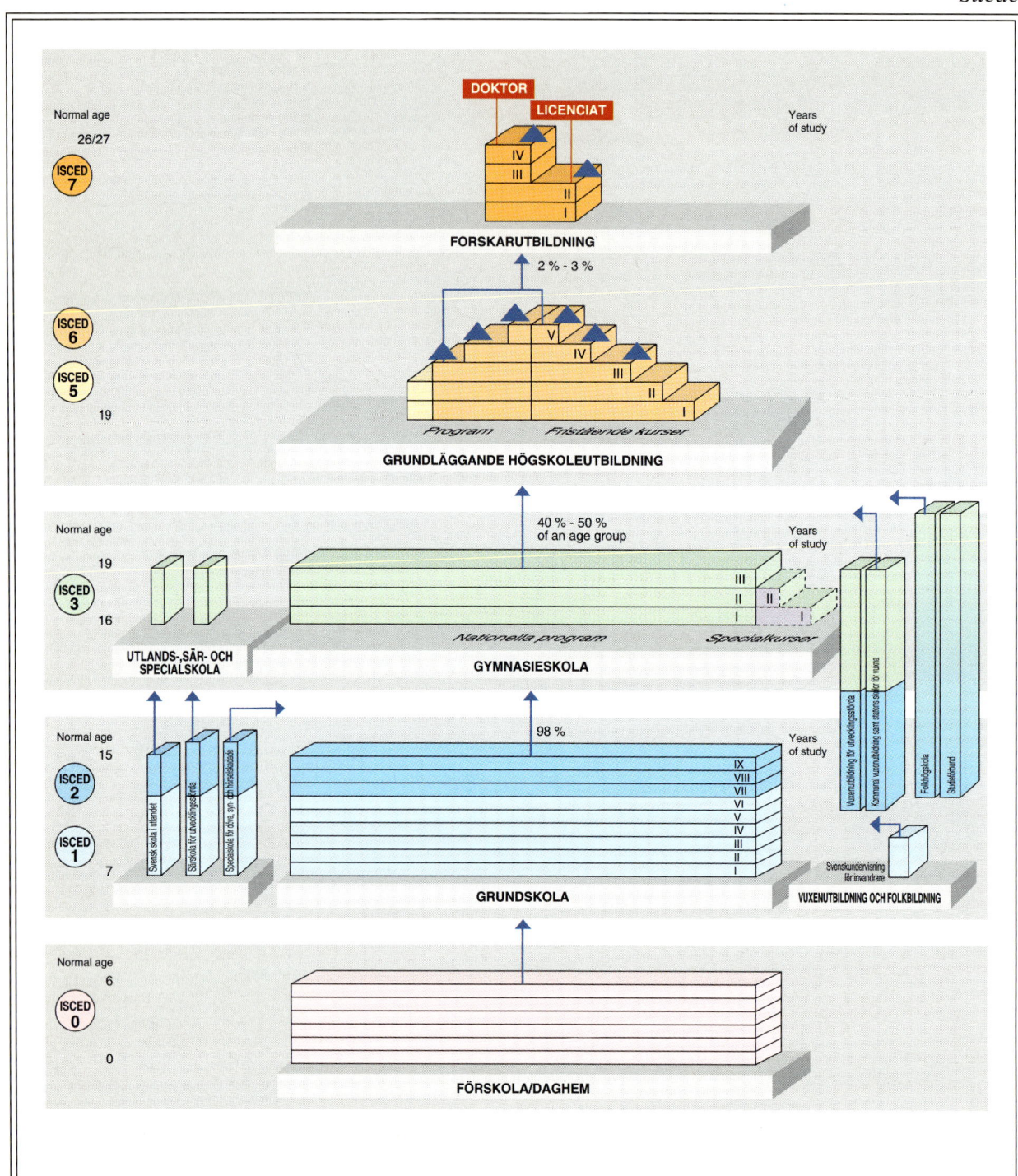

Suède

Colour codes (for details see page 249): **Pink** - Programme designed for part-time attendance. **Mauve** - Vocational education and training. **Blue triangle** - Recognised exit point of the education system. **Blue arrow** - Typical student flow. The size of the graphical elements provides no indication of the enrolment in the corresponding educational institutions.
*Codes couleur (voir la page 249) : **Rose** - Programmes expressément à temps partiel. **Mauve** - Enseignement et formation professionnels. **Triangle bleu** - Point de sortie officiel du système éducatif. **Flèche bleue** - Progression typique des élèves ou étudiants. La taille des différents blocs ne représente pas la proportion des effectifs dans les établissements d'enseignement correspondants.*

Sweden

1. GENERAL CONTEXT

Sweden has an area of 450 000 square kilometres and a population of 8.8 million inhabitants (1994). The population density is low, with only 21 inhabitants per square kilometre. There has been a low population growth rate for decades, but this has been balanced by an increased average life expectancy and increased immigration. Immigrants and their children number over 2 million, resulting in Swedish now being taught as a foreign language for immigrants in school. Nearly all immigrant children study their mother tongue as a language in school, and all immigrant adults are offered education in Swedish.

The economically active population was about 3.9 million in 1994. Nearly 39 per cent work in public service sectors, about 28 per cent in mining, manufacturing and construction, 15 per cent in wholesale and retail trades, 8 per cent in finance and insurance, 7 per cent in transport, storage and communications and about 3 per cent in agriculture (including forestry, fishing and hunting).

Sweden has a constitutional monarchy with a parliamentary representative democracy written into the Constitution. Sweden is administratively divided into 24 counties (*län*) and 288 municipalities (*kommuner*). There has been political stability for many years, and this has been accompanied by a comparatively conflict-free labour market. Through social welfare legislation, there are high standards for all in such areas as unemployment insurance, basic old-age and supplementary income-related pensions and health and medical care as well as child and housing allowances. The reforms in the education system, including, for instance, free schooling and higher education, are part of this welfare programme.

Compulsory schools and upper secondary schools are comprehensive, designed to accommodate all those in the relevant age group. Education for adults equivalent to the education offered by the compulsory and upper secondary schools is part of the public school system. Swedish education is a structurally uniform system, from pre-school and its integration with the elementary level of compulsory school to upper secondary schooling, adult education and higher education.

Compulsory schooling and upper secondary education are subordinate to the local school board in each municipality. At the central level they are subordinate to the government, including the Ministry of Education. There has been a gradual decentralisation of responsibilities. Since 1991 municipalities and county councils have had the joint responsibility for organising and implementing school activities. A central inspectorate for upper secondary schools was abolished in 1980, and the regional inspectorate for compulsory schooling was abolished in 1991, whereby their responsibilities were taken over by local boards and school heads. Since 1993 the role of the State has been further limited by a radical reform of the higher education system.

2. EDUCATIONAL STRUCTURE, ENROLMENTS AND COSTS

The establishment of day nurseries, nursery schools and corresponding pre-school care institutions (*förskola och barnomsorg*) had been seen predominantly as a social welfare enterprise. These institutions are managed by municipal administrations and by a central board of health and social affairs. There has been a gradual integration between the activities of the pre-school and compulsory school. In 1996 the Swedish government decided to move the responsibility for this sector from the Ministry of Health and Social Affairs to the Ministry of Education and Science. Early childhood institutions have sometimes after-school facilities for children in compulsory school.

In 1994 there were about 650 000 children in day nurseries, pre-schools and other child-care institutions. This corresponds to 350 000 full-time-equivalents in the age group 0-6 years. There are about 15 000 institutions and slightly more than 110 000 pre-school teachers and other personnel employed. The total public cost was about SKr 38 billion.

Compulsory education (*Grundskolan*) normally starts at the age of 7 and lasts until 16 years of age (grades 1-9), but in 1994 about 7 per cent began compulsory school at the age of 6. There has been much discussion about a general reform aimed at extending compulsory school until the age of 16 (grades 1-10). This has not been implemented, but there is the provision of a one-year general pre-school class in each school. Education at grades 1-6 is usually classified as primary education and at grades 7-9 as lower secondary education. There are compulsory national tests for grades 8 and 9.

A central principle of the Swedish education system is the provision of equal opportunity for all, irrespective of ethnic background or area of residence. Compulsory schooling in Sweden thus has a broad orientation adapted to all students.

In 1994 about 930 000 students in grades 1 to 9 attended 5 800 compulsory schools, where they were taught by slightly more than 90 000 teachers. This figure includes Swedish schools abroad (*Svensk skola i utlandet*), schools for children with impaired hearing/vision and physical disabilities (*specialskola*), compulsory schools for the mentally handicapped (*särskola*) and Sami schools for Sami-speaking children in the north of the country. The total public cost was about SKr 44 billion.

All young people who have completed nine years of compulsory school are qualified to enter upper secondary schools (*Gimnasieskolan*). About 98 per cent do so. The three-year general track, the two-year general track and two-year vocational tracks were replaced in 1994 by 16 study programmes (*nationella program*) of three years' duration. Of these, 14 are primarily vocationally oriented, with the remaining two preparing primarily for higher studies. Students have some flexibility in composing their own programme. Four evaluatory marks are awarded with the criteria for each specified in the different syllabi. The completion of a three-year programme in upper secondary school provides general eligibility for tertiary education.

In 1994 there were 310 000 students enrolled in upper secondary education, which included 630 schools and 29 000 teachers. The total public cost was about SKr 21 billion, including student loans and grants of about SKr 2.5 billion.

To be admitted to tertiary education, a student must first fulfil the general eligibility requirements, which are common to all programmes or courses, and then meet the specific eligibility requirements, which are usually imposed on applicants by the

Sweden

individual university or university college. In selecting students, one or more of the following criteria are applied: school marks, results in the university aptitude test (a national non-compulsory test) which is common for all institutions of higher education, a special test (e.g. interviews), previous education or work experience.

Roughly 30-35 per cent of an age group participate in higher education (*Högskolan*) before the age of 25 and a further 10-15 per cent after the age of 25. From 1977 to 1993 undergraduate (first degree) programmes were grouped into five labour-market related sectors: technical, administrative-economical-social, medical-paramedical-health, teaching, and cultural-informational.

In addition, separate courses were offered (*fristående kurser*) that usually varied in length from five weeks to one and a half years. In 1991 a major reform was initiated aiming at a deregulation of the unitary system of higher education and greater autonomy for the institutions.

In 1993 a new Higher Education Act came into effect. The dimensioning of different programmes and the allocation of grants to institutions became more dependent on the requirements of the individual students and the achievements of the individual institutions. The organisation of studies and range of courses offered were to be determined locally and students were given greater freedom in choosing their study routes.

Under the new regulations there are two kinds of first degrees: general and professional. Three different general degrees are awarded: diploma (*högskoleexamen*) after completion of at least 80 points (one year is normally 40 points), Bachelor's degree (*kandidatexamen*) after completion of 120-140 points and Master's degree (*magisterexamen*) after completion of 160 points or more. Professional degrees (*yrkesexamen*) are awarded upon completion of programmes leading to specific profession, e.g. medicine, dentistry, teacher training, engineering, nursing, design, etc.

The post-graduate degrees are Licentiate and doctoral degrees. In many fields it is possible to obtain a Licentiate degree approximately two years after the completion of the first degree. Studies for a doctorate take a minimum of four years

Adult and non-formal education at all ISCED levels plays a major role in the Swedish education system. Universities and university-colleges have accepted adults since the beginning of the 1970s. In 1994 roughly one-third of all new entrants to separate courses were older than 25 and enrolled part-time frequently in evening classes; they can be classified as students in continuing or further education for adults.

In the academic year 1994/95, there were about 270 000 students participating in first degree programmes or separate courses. In full-time-equivalents, this corresponds to 220 000 and to 230 000 in the beginning of the autumn term 1994.

There were also nearly 20 000 post-degree students registered in 1994/95, including non-active students. This corresponds to about 15 000 active students (roughly 11 000 full-time-equivalents). There are about 70 institutions, including seven state universities and 22 000 teachers and scientists. The total public cost for higher education including research in universities was about SKr 31 billion, including student loans and grants of about SKr 6.5 billion.

At ISCED levels 2-5 there is popular adult education (*folkbildning*), municipal adult education (*kommunal vuxenutbildning*) and adult labour market educational arrangements. Popular adult education is of two types: folk high schools (*folkhögskola*) and evening study circles (*studieförbund*). The folk high schools are run by county councils, organisations and associations. In 1994 there were slightly more than 130 folk high schools with 30 000 students (full-time-equivalents). In the same year, more than two million persons (150 000 full-time-equivalents) were involved in study circles.

Municipal adult education, which is offered to about 200 000 people (100 000 full-time-equivalents) a year in 280 municipalities, consists mostly of courses equivalent in content to compulsory school, upper secondary courses and special vocationally oriented courses.

Public labour market training (*arbetsmarknadsutbildning*) provides vocational education for those who are unemployed or in danger of losing their jobs. In 1994 there were about 50 000 persons (full-time-equivalents) in such training.

A large part of all job-related training is financed by the enterprises (*personalutbildning*). Employers themselves organise most of this training, but there are certain occupational groups for whom the higher education system is frequently enlisted as a natural educational arranger. For example, the higher education system organises, by commissioned education, a large share of supplementary education for teachers and for medical employees. In 1994 roughly 3 000 000 employees (about 200 000 full-time-equivalents) participated in job-related training courses financed by the enterprise.

In 1994 the total number of teachers in adult education was roughly 20 000 (full-time-equivalents). The total public cost for adult education, excluding higher adult education and job-related training financed by the enterprises, was about SKr 9.5 billion, including student loans and grants of about SKr 3.5 billion.

In 1994 the total cost for the State, the municipalities and the county councils, in the sector of education and research, (excluding the costs for the Police college and the Academy of Military Sciences) was about SKr 146 billion.

Switzerland

1. GENERAL CONTEXT

Switzerland is an inland country of 41 300 square kilometres (about one-fourth of which is unproductive) and a population of 7 million people. Seventeen per cent of the population is under 15 years of age, while 15 per cent is over 64 years old. The average life expectancy continues to rise, and in 1996 it was 80.8 years for women and 74.1 years for men. The country has a federal structure comprising 26 cantons (with 3 029 communes). The cantons range in size from 15 000 to 1 162 000 inhabitants.

Constitutionally, education is a cantonal responsibility, although the federal government plays a role in funding universities and in planning, implementing and funding vocational education. Since the cantons have constitutional responsibility for education, there is no national education system as such, although all cantonal systems have the same basic structure. Variations occur mainly in the offer of programmes at the post-compulsory level and in the configuration of compulsory schooling. The communes also play a role in funding and administering compulsory education, although the definition of this role and its importance vary among cantons. In short, there is considerable diversity in the education system.

There is the further diversity of cultures and languages. The four official languages are: German, French, Italian and Romansch or Rhaeto-Romanic, with each used as the language of instruction in a well defined territory. Twenty-two of the 26 cantons have unilingual education systems, three are split between German and French and one, Grisons, has three instructional languages – German, Italian and Romansch. Seventy-three per cent of children attend German-speaking compulsory schools, 22 per cent French, 5 per cent are taught in Italian and 0.5 per cent in Romansch. Children coming from homes where another language is spoken are expected to use the language of instruction of their school.

Some 70 per cent of the population live in urban areas. Labour force participation has traditionally been very high among men (around 80 per cent of the population aged 15 and over). Women attained a participation rate of 57 per cent in 1994, with slightly more than 50 per cent working part-time. Since 1991 the unemployment rate has risen from 1.8 to 5.2 per cent. Six per cent of the workforce is in agriculture, 34 per cent in industry and 61 per cent in the tertiary sector. Switzerland was an early industrial country, and the tertiarisation of its economy has been relatively recent.

Switzerland enjoyed economic growth with very low unemployment from the 1950s to the beginning of the 1990s. Economic growth led to heavy immigration; in 1994 about 19 per cent of the population consisted of foreign nationals. About one-fifth of these were born in Switzerland, and the 1990 census revealed that 6 per cent of Swiss nationals were born in another country. The integration of immigrants' children is a major challenge for the education system.

The public sector predominates in Swiss education, with privately-funded schools enrolling only 5 per cent of all students. All university students attend public institutions while one-fifth of non-university higher vocational education students attend private schools. This picture grossly misrepresents the role of the private sector in Swiss education. The country has a "two-ladder" post-compulsory system and dual-system apprentices, who constitute the majority at the upper secondary level, receive the school part of their full-time education in a government school while the enterprise part takes place in the private sector.

The education system has been described as highly selective, streaming students into programmes with either a basic curriculum or a broader based one as early as after 5 or 6 years of primary school. The selection into different programmes in upper secondary education is also rather rigid. All upper secondary and tertiary education is optional – young people are under no obligation to continue their education and public authorities are not required to assure educational opportunities for all.

2. EDUCATIONAL STRUCTURE AND ENROLMENTS

Almost all children (98 per cent) attend kindergarten for an average of 1.8 years before commencing primary school. Primary school starts at 6 or 7 years of age and lasts for four, five or six years depending on the canton. There are about 440 000 primary school students. Lower secondary education commences at 11 or 12 years of age and lasts for three to five years depending on the canton. This makes a total of nine years of compulsory education in all cantons. There are about 280 000 lower secondary students. Some cantons have organised their lower secondary level in a comprehensive form; in others, the different types of programmes can be classified into two groups: those schools with a basic required curriculum and those with an extended required curriculum. In 1994, 31 per cent of students attended the first type and 69 per cent either the second type or a comprehensive form.

Even though upper secondary education is not compulsory, an estimated 93 per cent (1994) of the cohort entered education at this level, and 85 per cent graduated from a programme of more than two years' duration. Nearly 20 per cent of the cohort (1995) attempted more than one programme in upper secondary education, with the most frequent case being attendance at a short (one or two years' duration) general programme followed by entering vocational education. Three-quarters of the cohort enter vocational education and two thirds finish a programme of two or more years' duration. Seventeen per cent of the cohort graduate from a programme giving access to university education.

The tertiary sector is composed of ten universities, several different types of colleges of higher vocational education and many part-time vocational education courses. The latter usually lead to an examination approved by a public or professional body. All universities are public, while many of the programmes in the higher vocational education sector are private. Thirteen per cent of young adults enter one of the universities and 27 per cent a higher vocational education course/programme. Some of the higher vocational colleges will be promoted to *Fachhochschulen* from 1997 on, thus diversifying the tertiary sector.

In 1992/93 almost two million adults (40 per cent) attended at least one continuing education course. Only 19 per cent of these courses were offered by the public sector. Thirty-one per cent were organised by the employer and 50 per cent by another private entity,

Switzerland

with most of the private organisations being market-oriented providers of continuing education. Educational policy in the fields of higher vocational and continuing education supports this pattern as there is a strong reliance on market forces to arrive at a pattern of efficient qualification of the workforce.

3. EDUCATIONAL FINANCE AND COSTS

Public expenditure for education amounts to 5.4 per cent of the country's GDP, a figure comparable to that of other European countries. The federal government provides about 12 per cent of the public funds for education, while the cantons provide 53 per cent and the communes the remaining 35 per cent. Roughly speaking, the federal government finances a portion of the universities and vocational education, while the communes finance kindergarten and a part of compulsory school. The rest is paid by the cantons.

Compulsory and upper secondary public schools do not charge tuition. At the tertiary level, tuition fees vary significantly between different institutions and cantons.

The three year average for 1990, 1991 and 1992 of public expenditure per lower secondary student was US$ 6 400, well above the OECD mean of US$ 4 760 for all secondary education, and close to the country with the highest per-student expenditure, namely the United States with US$ 6 470. (Both figures quoted are adjusted for the purchasing power parity when transforming them into US dollars).[1]

4. CURRICULUM AND ASSESSMENT

With the exception of vocational education, there is no nation-wide common school curriculum. However, for compulsory education, the conference of cantonal education ministers has established a series of targets defining the expected competencies in several key subject areas such as mathematics, the mother tongue and the first foreign language. For upper secondary general education, the targets have been set for the university entrance exam and the intermediate diploma. All of these inter-cantonal agreements pertaining to the expected level of competence allow for cantonal variation in the curricula leading up to the goals.

In contrast, the national curricula for vocational education in the form of apprenticeships are very detailed. They are compulsory for both the school-part and the enterprise-part and are established after intensive consultation with representatives of industry and trade unions.

There is an entrance requirement or exam for all post-compulsory programmes and for streams with a broader based curriculum in lower secondary education (with the notable exception of the universities which have up to now admitted all persons with a *maturité*). Assessment within a programme is usually school-based, with promotion between year levels not being automatic. In compulsory education, for example, one in six students repeats at least one grade. Diplomas at the end of post-compulsory programmes are usually granted after passing a government board approved school-based exam. Again, relatively high failure rates are not uncommon.

5. TEACHERS

The education of kindergarten, primary and lower secondary (basic demands) teachers is the responsibility of the cantons. Teachers educated in one canton were not necessarily qualified to teach in other cantons. While the cantonal teachers' education used to be a strong basis for the development of cantonal school cultures, this is now rapidly changing. The education of teachers, however, is still far from uniform across the country. Nevertheless, some broad common features can be identified. All upper secondary teachers are educated in university-level institutions. The teachers of lower secondary programmes which provide the broader based curriculum are also educated at the university. In some cantons, the teachers in programmes providing the basic curriculum are taught in specialised teacher education colleges, usually at the tertiary level. Some primary teachers still attend 5-year colleges beginning after compulsory school. The others are educated at the tertiary level in teacher colleges. The policy established in 1995 plans to split all teacher education into an upper secondary part equivalent to the *maturité* and a tertiary part of at least three years' duration devoted to the acquisition of professional knowledge and skills.

Statistics on Swiss teachers are as yet incomplete, but will be completed by the year 2001. In compulsory schools some 62 200 teachers occupied 51 000 full-time posts, with 46 per cent of all teachers having part-time status. The proportion of women teachers in primary and lower secondary is 68 and 36 per cent, respectively, one of the lowest proportions among OECD countries.

Swiss teachers work longer hours than teachers in other OECD countries and enjoy salaries well above the GDP per capita. Salaries are higher at higher levels of education, and there is considerable variation among cantons for the same category of teachers.

References

Gretler A. (1995) "Switzerland". In: Postlethwaite T. Neville (Ed.). *International Encyclopaedia of National Systems of Education*. Second Edition. Pergamon. Oxford.

OECD (1995). *Education at a Glance - OECD Indicators*. Paris.

OFS (1995). *Les indicateurs de l'enseignement en Suisse – l'enseignement en mutation dans notre pays*, Berne.

---

1. Country currency translated into US dollars by using the purchasing power parity (PPP) exchange rate. Sources: OECD, *Education at a Glance – OECD Indicators*, Paris 1995; OFS, *Les indicateurs de l'enseignement en Suisse – l'enseignement en mutation dans notre pays*, Berne 1995. **The figure cited for Switzerland does not correspond to the one published by the OECD, but to the one published by OFS.**

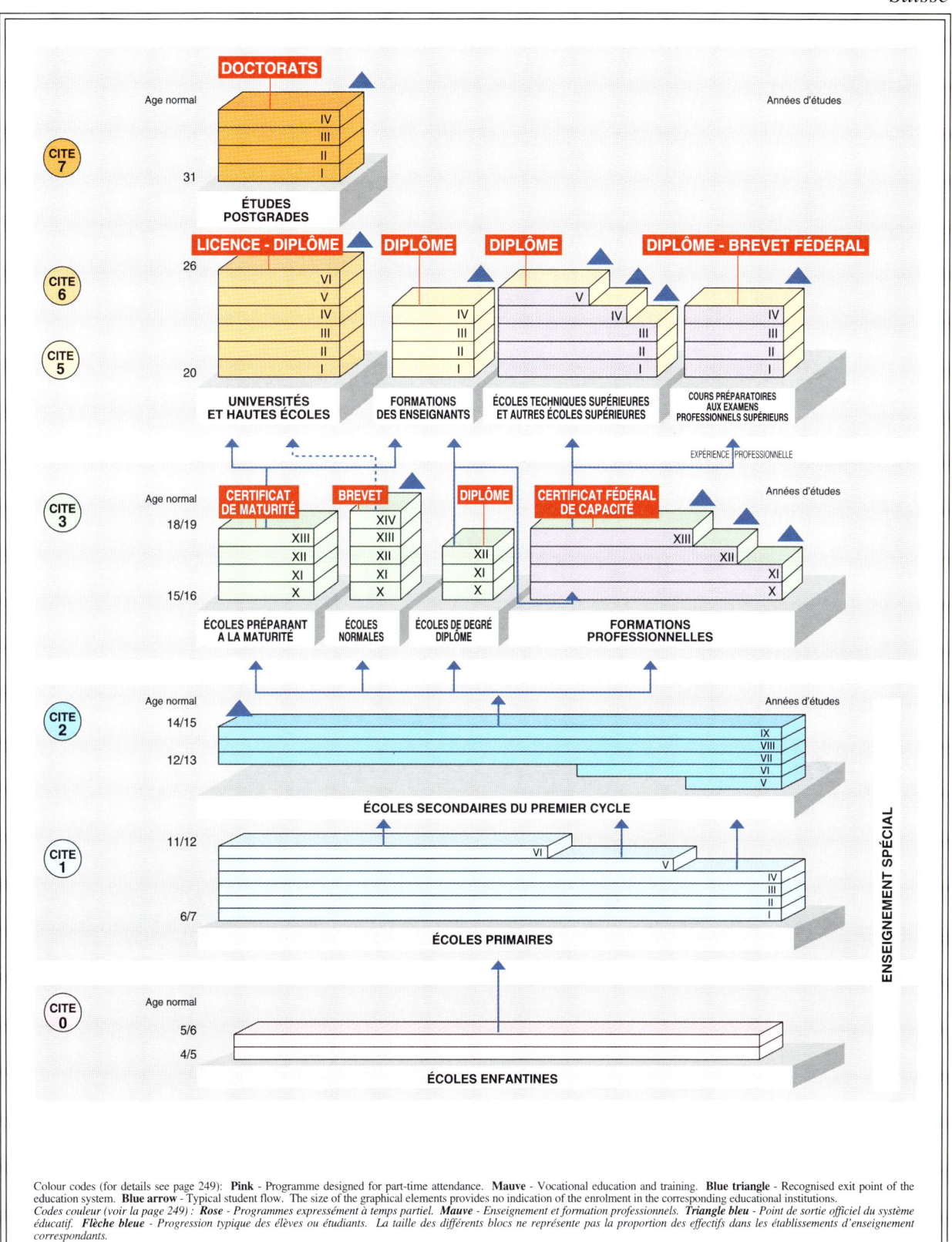

Switzerland

Suisse

Turkey

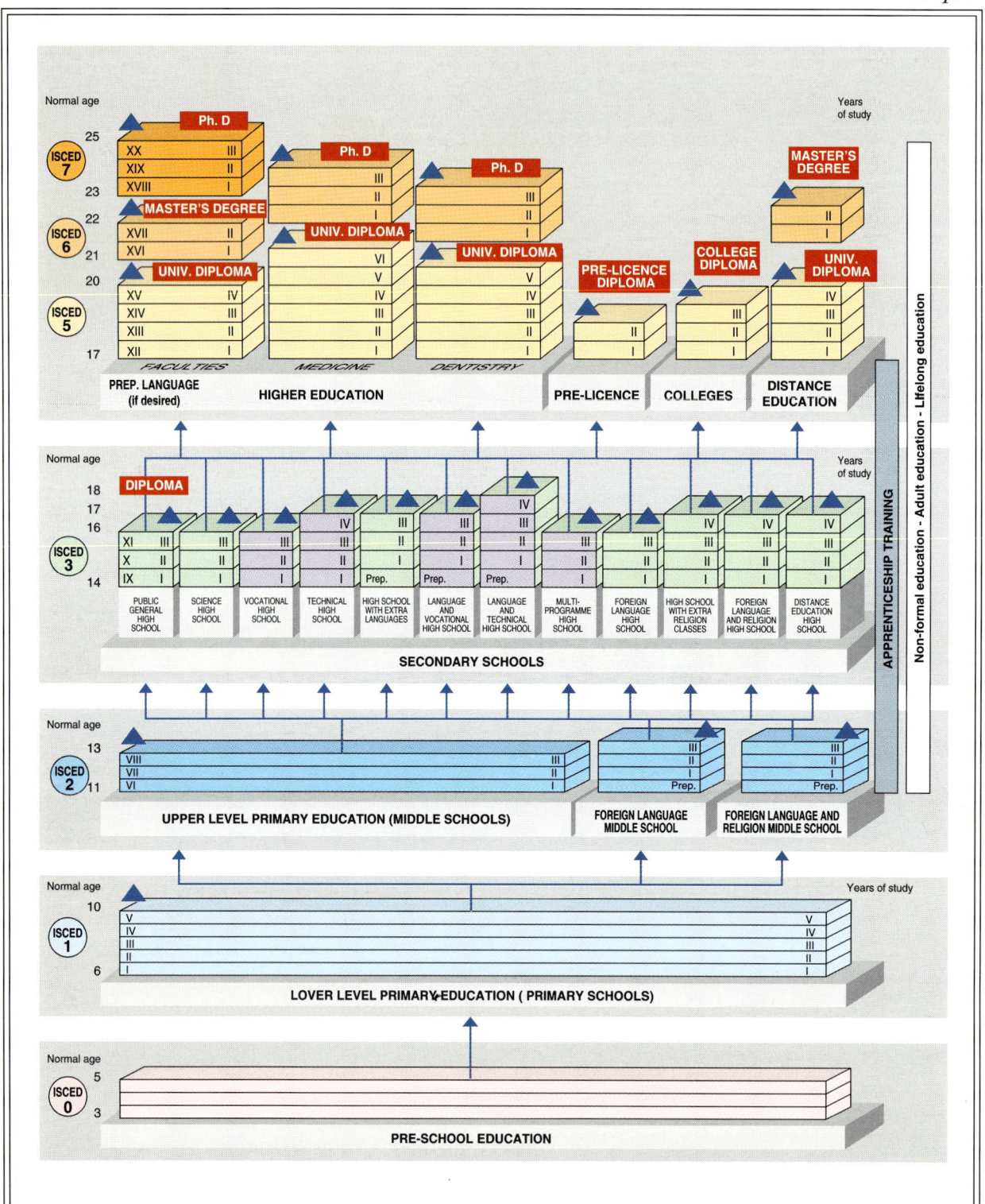

Turquie

Turkey

1. GENERAL CONTEXT

Turkey lies at the junction of Europe and Asia and is situated at the north-east of the Mediterranean. It has an area of 814 578 square kilometres and a population of about 60 million, of whom about 60 per cent live in urban areas. The annual population growth is about 1.7 per cent. There has been a continuing urbanisation of the population, primarily from eastern and south-eastern Anatolia to the large cities of western Anatolia. The centres receiving these migrants are being challenged to provide sufficient infrastructure, education and health services. Cities with high urbanisation rates are facing educational problems such as large class sizes and double-shift schools. In urban areas, about one-third of the population is under the age of 5, whereas in rural areas the figure is two-fifths of the population. In 1990 the literacy rates were 96 per cent for men and 84 per cent for women.

In 1990 about 50 per cent of the labour force was employed in agriculture, 15 per cent in industry and 35 per cent in the service sector. There is an increasing demand for technical and vocational education. The unemployment rate is just over 8 per cent of the workforce, and it is particularly high among secondary school graduates.

2. EDUCATIONAL STRUCTURE AND ENROLMENTS

Early childhood education, for children under the age of six who have thus not yet reached the age of entry to primary school, is optional. It is provided by the Ministry of National Education, the General Directorate of Social Welfare and the Child Protection Agency. There are kindergartens where children can go at age 3 and pre-school classes for 4 and 5 year-olds. The Ministry of National Education supervises private or institutional (work place) kindergartens, sets up educational and health requirements and establishes teachers' educational requirements. Pre-school teachers must have completed a four-year university course in early childhood education. There are approximately 200 000 children attending pre-school.

Primary education is designed for 6 to 12 year-olds. In 1995 there were 6 896 762 primary students, with 5 per cent being enrolled in private schools. The net enrolment rate was 95 per cent. There are still fewer girls than boys who enter and graduate from primary school. The reasons for this include early marriages, limited means of transportation and family attitudes giving higher priority to the education of boys. All primary schools are co-educational and all state schools are free. In rural areas where the population is sparse, there is one school for a group of villages. These are known as "regional primary schools" and have boarding facilities. There are 180 school days a year and five hours of instruction per day.

For those aged between 12 and 13 years, there are three main types of junior high schools: academic, clerical and technical. The duration of junior high school programmes is generally three years. The enrolment in 1995 was 2 651 076, meaning that only some 40 per cent of children proceed to junior high school. Of these some 10 per cent are enrolled in private schools.

Children may then continue with a three-year programme at the upper secondary level in either the general high school (enrolment: 1 277 115) or in the vocational and technical high school (enrolment: 946 121). Nation-wide, there are 175 days of instruction yearly and five hours of instruction per day. Upper secondary education prepares students for entry either into higher education or the work place.

Higher education refers to all educational institutions providing at least two years of education beyond upper secondary education. It includes universities, institutes, higher schools, conservatories and higher vocational schools. The total enrolment at this level is 1 407 039 students.

Non-formal education courses are run by the Ministry of National Education for nearly one million people who either never entered formal education or later dropped out.

Special education services are provided by the Directorate of Special Education and Counselling. Nearly 20 000 pupils are in such schools or special classes, with nearly half of them being at the primary level.

3. EDUCATIONAL FINANCE AND COSTS

The percentage of the national budget allocated to education is nearly 22 per cent, which amounts to 2.24 per cent of GNP. The government is trying to increase the share of private sector funding as well as the share for local administrations. The Ministry also funds a number of scholarships – for 81 448 secondary school students in 1995/96.

There is a deficit from the past regarding school buildings, facilities and teachers, and more resources will be required to compensate for this deficit.

4. CURRICULUM AND ASSESSMENT

There is a national curriculum. National programmes are prepared by special expert committees appointed by the Ministry of National Education. The programmes are for all subject areas and all levels of education. The committees comprise subject matter experts and teachers from both universities and schools. The draft curricula are reviewed by the Ministry and when approved, textbooks are written and introduced to the schools on an experimental basis to begin with. The textbooks used at all levels are either produced or approved by the Ministry.

Assessment is carried out by teachers across all levels of education. In grades 1 to 3, this is carried out informally, but in grades 4 to 8 teacher-created written and oral examinations are also used. To move from one level of education to another, the graduation certificate of the previous level of education is important. The graduation certificate is awarded by the school administration on the basis of teacher evaluation of achievement over the years in the school. Some schools work on a credit system, requiring a specified minimum number of credits to obtain a graduation certificate. There are no external examinations.

Turkey

5. TEACHERS

In 1995 there were 532 093 teachers at all levels of education, of which 9 622 teachers at the pre-primary level, 22 979 in primary schools, 69 533 in general high schools, 70 158 in vocational and technical education, 36 778 in non-formal education and 47 267 in higher education. Efforts are being made to increase the number of teachers. Teacher education is undertaken by three types of institutions: *i)* higher schools of education which prepare primary school teachers; *ii)* faculties of education preparing secondary school teachers; and *iii)* faculties of science and literature offering programmes in basic social sciences. All training courses last four years. Teacher training programmes consist of: 62.5 per cent subject matter knowledge, 12.5 per cent general culture and 25 per cent pedagogical matters. The practice training takes place in schools near the training establishments. Upon completing their courses, new teachers are assigned to schools by the Ministry of National Education. They are on probation for one or two years depending on the results they obtained at the end of their training. In-service training courses are offered by the In-service Training Department of the Ministry of National Education.

United Kingdom (England and Wales)

1. GENERAL CONTEXT

The United Kingdom comprises Great Britain (England, Scotland, and Wales) together with Northern Ireland. The territory, occupying just over 244 000 square kilometres, lies just west of the European mainland. The total population is about 56.8 million (47.3m in England, 5.1m in Scotland, 2.8m in Wales and 1.6m in Northern Ireland).

The UK economy is growing: GDP rose by 4.0 per cent in 1994 and 2.5 per cent in 1995 as a whole. Inflation is low. Labour market reforms have created a flexible labour market and unemployment is falling, and is below the average in the European Union.

The Government Minister with overall responsibility for education and training in England and Wales is the Secretary of State for Education and Employment who heads the Department for Education and Employment. The Department's main role in respect of education is to set and administer the statutory framework of the education system and to establish national education policy, working with other central and local government bodies, the churches (who part-fund some schools) and its Non-Departmental Public Bodies (NDPBs). The Secretaries of State for Scotland, Wales and Northern Ireland are responsible for the education system in their jurisdictions.

The public sector predominates in British education, although there is a growing diversity of providers. In England, 8 million children attend school, over 90 per cent going to the publicly-financed State schools, of which there were 24 000 in 1994/95. The government has funded significant growth in the Further Education and Higher Education sectors in recent years. Just over 67 per cent of young people attain a good standard at the end of compulsory schooling and 44 per cent achieve qualifications suitable for entry into higher education. About 24 per cent of the workforce have advanced professional, management, academic or vocational qualifications.

Government policies are directed at enhancing choice and diversity in education and training, advancing knowledge through supporting high-quality research, increasing transparency and accountability, improving quality in the education and training system and the standards achieved by pupils, students and trainees.

In order to improve national competitiveness and individual success, the Department has endorsed a challenging set of National Targets for Education and Training for the year 2000 as the focus for its education and training effort. Employers, schools and colleges, Training and Enterprise Councils, and individuals all have a role in working towards these targets.

2. EDUCATIONAL STRUCTURE AND ENROLMENTS

Over 90 per cent of 3 and 4 year-olds receive some form of pre-compulsory education provision. Twenty-seven per cent are admitted to maintained nursery schools and classes; 26 per cent are admitted to infant classes in maintained primary schools (mainly 4 year-olds in reception classes), 4 per cent are admitted to special or independent schools, and a substantial proportion attend private nursery schools or playgroups. The government is introducing a voucher scheme to provide, over time, a nursery education place for all 4 year-olds whose parents want one.

Education is compulsory from age 5 to 16. In England in 1994/95, there were 3.5 million children aged 5 and over in primary schools and 2.7 million children under school-leaving age in secondary schools.

In most areas a two-tier system of primary (ages 5-11) and secondary schools (ages 11-16) operates, but some areas have a three-tier system of first, middle and upper or high schools. Although the majority of schools are comprehensive, some areas also have grammar and secondary modern schools which cater specifically for children in the higher and lower ability ranges, respectively. The development of secondary schools specialising in particular subject areas, such as technology or languages, is encouraged.

In some areas choice is enhanced by the existence of Grant-Maintained Schools (directly funded by government) and City Technology Colleges. The proportions of these different categories of schools vary between the primary and secondary sectors and in different parts of the country.

Provision for most children with special educational needs is made in mainstream primary and secondary schools and further education colleges. Some children with special educational needs attend, for all or part of their schooling, special schools. Young people who have attended special schools may go on to colleges of further education and to higher education.

At the end of compulsory schooling, 16-19 year-olds may study in either the sixth form of a school, or at one of over 450 colleges in the Further Education (FE) sector. They are offered qualifications within a framework of General Certificate of Education (GCE) A/AS Level Qualifications, broad-based General National Vocational Qualifications (GNVQs), and job-specific National Vocational Qualifications (NVQs). Students may study for one of these qualifications or a combination of them within the same programme. Typical full-time courses last one or two years.

Following a review of 16-19 year-olds' qualifications the government is developing a new framework of qualifications based on existing qualifications and on common national certificates. A new national diploma will be introduced to recognise achievement in studies both in depth and in breadth. Action will be taken to strengthen A levels, GNVQs and NVQs. There will also be a new-style AS level. It is anticipated that the framework will be substantially in place by September 1998.

It is the government's intention that all 16 and 17 year-olds not in full-time education should be in training or in a job – preferably with training. All 16 and 17 year-old school-leavers are entitled to a Youth Credit. Youth Credits provide the mechanism to access Modern Apprenticeships and Youth Training. Eighty-eight per cent of 16 year-olds, 79 per cent of 17 year-olds and 59 per cent of 18 year-olds participated in education and training in 1994/95.

Separate provision is made to allow young people in schools, FE-sector colleges and elsewhere to receive careers education and guidance. As well as provision by institutions

United Kingdom (England and Wales)

Royaume-Uni (Angleterre et Pays de Galles)

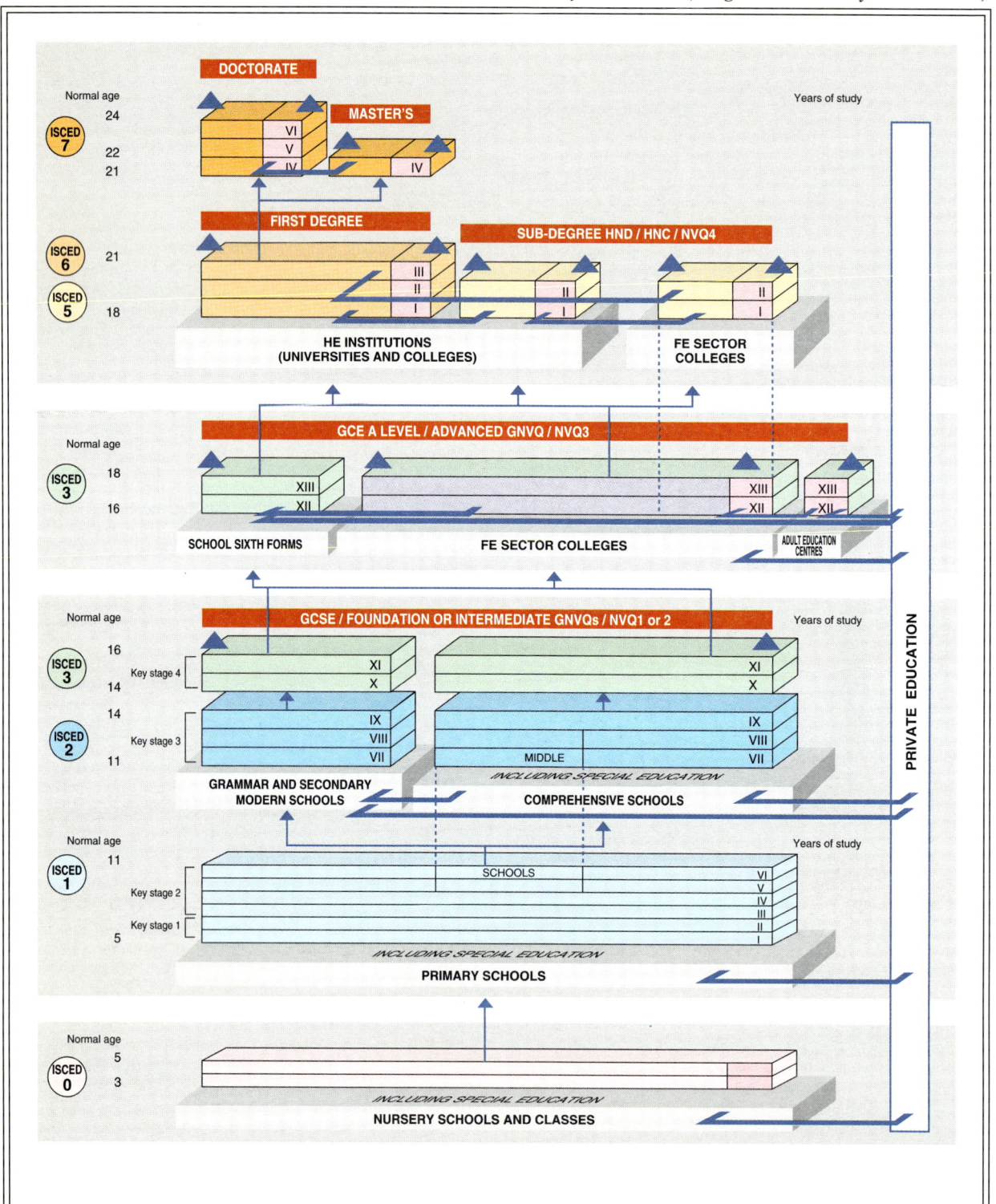

ISCED 7 — Normal age 24, 22, 21 — DOCTORATE / MASTER'S

ISCED 6 — Normal age 21 — FIRST DEGREE / SUB-DEGREE HND / HNC / NVQ4

ISCED 5 — Normal age 18 — HE INSTITUTIONS (UNIVERSITIES AND COLLEGES) / FE SECTOR COLLEGES

ISCED 3 — Normal age 18, 16 — GCE A LEVEL / ADVANCED GNVQ / NVQ3 — SCHOOL SIXTH FORMS / FE SECTOR COLLEGES / ADULT EDUCATION CENTRES

ISCED 3 — Normal age 16, 14 — Key stage 4 — GCSE / FOUNDATION OR INTERMEDIATE GNVQs / NVQ1 or 2

ISCED 2 — Normal age 14, 11 — Key stage 3 — GRAMMAR AND SECONDARY MODERN SCHOOLS / COMPREHENSIVE SCHOOLS (MIDDLE) — INCLUDING SPECIAL EDUCATION

ISCED 1 — Normal age 11, 5 — Key stage 2, Key stage 1 — PRIMARY SCHOOLS — INCLUDING SPECIAL EDUCATION

ISCED 0 — Normal age 5, 3 — NURSERY SCHOOLS AND CLASSES — INCLUDING SPECIAL EDUCATION

PRIVATE EDUCATION

Colour codes (for details see page 249): **Pink** - Programme designed for part-time attendance. **Mauve** - Vocational education and training. **Blue triangle** - Recognised exit point of the education system. **Blue arrow** - Typical student flow. The size of the graphical elements provides no indication of the enrolment in the corresponding educational institutions.

*Codes couleur (voir la page 249) : **Rose** - Programmes expressément à temps partiel. **Mauve** - Enseignement et formation professionnels. **Triangle bleu** - Point de sortie officiel du système éducatif. **Flèche bleue** - Progression typique des élèves ou étudiants. La taille des différents blocs ne représente pas la proportion des effectifs dans les établissements d'enseignement correspondants.*

United Kingdom (England and Wales)

themselves, there are local careers services which work under contract to the Secretaries of State. There are separate arrangements for young people at HE institutions.

Nearly one in three young people entered higher education in 1994/95 – double the rate of participation in 1988. In England, 150 universities and colleges of higher education receive public funds to provide higher education – that is study above Advanced level (GCE A level, the Scottish equivalent, or advanced level GNVQ/NVQ level 3).

Universities and colleges are autonomous bodies, responsible for managing their own financial, administrative and academic affairs, including curricula, admissions and examinations. Universities award their own degrees; most colleges award degrees validated by another institution with degree-awarding powers.

Many undergraduate courses are Bachelor degree courses requiring three or so years' full-time study. Also offered are shorter undergraduate courses leading to diplomas; post-first-degree qualifications such as the post-graduate certificate of education; post-graduate taught courses leading to Master's degrees; and post-graduate research courses leading to qualifications such as Doctorates. Part-time courses, taking longer to complete, are also offered at all levels.

In addition to traditional universities and higher education colleges, the Open University offers, through the medium of distance learning, a range of higher education courses to those over 18 who might otherwise be unable to take advantage of the higher education system.

The education of adults is a crucial part of the government's policy to increase participation and attainment at all ages and all levels. Adults may resume their education at any age, and have access to a wide range of further and higher education courses, including appropriate short courses. Some lead to formal qualifications and some are less formal courses, often undertaken as leisure activities. There were over 3 million students at FE-sector colleges in 1994/95: the majority were aged over 21 mainly studying part-time. Mature entrants to higher education also now outnumber young people. Access courses facilitate the admission to undergraduate courses for mature students or those with non-traditional or non-formal qualifications.

3. EDUCATIONAL FINANCE AND COSTS

In 1994/95, State funding for education in the UK was £35 000 million or 5.2 per cent of GDP. In addition in England, £1 500 million was spent on training such as Modern Apprenticeship and Youth Training Schemes.

Although the bulk of resources are provided by the government, these are largely spent by Local Education Authorities (with 85 per cent mandatorily delegated by them to schools) or by the relevant agencies — the Funding Agency for Schools (direct funding of Grant-Maintained Schools) or the Further Education Funding Agency (funding colleges in the FE-sector). The higher education councils are responsible for distributing public funding to higher education institutions.

Government schools do not charge tuition fees but about 7 per cent of school pupils attend fee-charging independent schools. Independent schools range from small kindergartens to large day and boarding schools and from new experimental schools to ancient foundations. A Government-funded Assisted Places Scheme enables around 35 000 secondary pupils in England and Wales from low-income families to attend selected independent schools. From September 1996 the Scheme is being doubled over time to 70 000 places and extended to cover the whole range of compulsory education.

While universities and higher education colleges receive public funding, they are private, rather than public sector bodies. Most home full-time undergraduates have their university tuition fees paid for them by the Local Education Authorities. They also have access to a publicly-funded means-tested maintenance grant and to student loans. A National Committee of Inquiry has been established (February 1996) to make recommendations on how the purposes, shape, structure, size and funding of higher education (including student support) should develop to meet the needs of the UK over the next 20 years.

The government has launched a Private Finance Initiative designed to promote partnership between the public and private sectors, encouraging the private sector to invest in public sector projects. For the education sector, this principally means improvements in the capital stock (mainly buildings) by the application of the private sector's capital resources and management skills.

4. CURRICULUM AND ASSESSMENT

All pupils of compulsory school age in State schools must follow the National Curriculum. It is divided into four key stages which correspond to different school year groups. Key Stages 1 and 2 constitute the primary phase, and Key Stages 3 and 4 the secondary phase.

The National Curriculum is at the heart of the drive to improve standards and to provide a minimum entitlement for pupils in State schools. Established by the Education Reform Act of 1988 and revised in January 1995, it sets out what subjects pupils should study, what they should be taught, and what standards they should achieve.

The subjects to be studied vary at each Key Stage (KS). At KS1 and 2 the subjects are English, mathematics, science, technology, history, geography, art, music and physical education. A modern foreign language is added at KS3. At KS4, schools have been given flexibility to develop courses appropriate to pupils' aptitudes and needs. The minimum requirement is English, mathematics, science, physical education, information technology, design and technology and a modern foreign language. In addition, all schools are required to provide religious education and, in secondary schools only, sex education.

Regular assessment of pupils in schools, and the publication of the results, acts as a check on their progress. All 7 year-olds (end of KS1) are tested and assessed by their teachers in English and

United Kingdom (England and Wales)

mathematics; 11 year-olds and 14 year-olds (KS2 and 3) are tested and teacher-assessed in English, mathematics and science. At 16 (KS4) public examinations (usually GCSE) are the main means of assessing attainment. The government has pledged that all 5 year-olds will be tested. It is planned that a nation-wide baseline assessment and testing policy will be introduced from September 1997.

The Office for Standards in Education (OFSTED) works closely with the Department for Education and Employment and is responsible for running a system whereby schools are inspected every 4 years to monitor the quality of education and identify areas where schools can and should improve. This is part of a range of government strategies for improving schools.

Colleges in the FE-sector offer a wide range of courses and qualifications, both academic and vocational. The Further Education Funding Council operate their own inspection of colleges.

Universities have responsibility for their own curricula and assessment. External scrutinies of the quality of teaching and learning are carried out by the higher education funding councils. External scrutinies of the quality assurance systems are carried out by the Higher Education Quality Council. There are plans for a single quality agency in higher education from 1997.

5. TEACHERS

Over 500 000 full-time equivalent staff are employed in State-funded education institutions of whom 390 000 are school teachers and assistants, 70 000 are lecturers in FE and 55 000 are lecturers in HE. Teacher training mostly takes place in higher education institutions through either a 3- or 4-year Bachelor of Education degree or a 9-month post-graduate Certificate in Education. Both include a substantial period spent by trainee teachers in schools. There are also a small number of school partnerships which offer school-based initial teacher training.

The Teacher Training Agency (TTA) is responsible for the funding and quality control of Initial Teacher Training and for work in the continuing professional development of serving teachers. The TTA is currently developing a national framework of standards for teaching at various key stages, from newly-qualified teacher to headteacher. In addition, the TTA supports professional development for school managers, including a scheme to train newly-promoted headteachers (HEADLAMP). The development of a professional qualification for those who aspire to become headteachers is proposed. The TTA is also responsible for commissioning and disseminating research on effective classroom and training practice.

United States

1. GENERAL CONTEXT

The United States is a large and diverse country occupying about 9 628 000 square kilometres, with a population of 260 million people. The country has a federal system of government comprising 50 states, the District of Columbia, and associated territories. Constitutionally, education is a state responsibility, although most states have delegated authority to operate and finance schools to about 15 000 local education authorities, or school districts. The federal government plays a limited role in the governance of education, but provides funding to states and school districts, mostly to support programmes for students with special educational needs. It also provides financial aid to students in the form of scholarships and loans to support their participation in post-secondary education.

The public sector tends to predominate at the elementary and secondary education levels, with public schools enrolling about 90 per cent of the nation's 48 million school children. Private schools generally receive only small amounts of public funding, although private school children who qualify for federal programmes are guaranteed service under these programmes. A large majority of students in higher education are enrolled in public institutions, although private institutions enrol nearly 22 per cent of the nation's 14 million students.

After a period of enrolment decline during the 1970s and early 1980s, elementary and secondary school enrolments have grown by almost 12 per cent during the last decade. Although a few states have continued to lose students, many have seen large increases in their student population. It is anticipated that by 1997 public school enrolments will surpass the previous high reached in 1971 and will continue to increase into the next century. The demand for qualified teachers will therefore continue to influence education policy in future years.

Immigration and other demographic factors have also contributed to changes in the school population over this period. In 1993, about one-third of children in public elementary and secondary schools were from minority backgrounds – a slight increase over the 30 per cent in the mid-1980s. An increasing number of children also come from families where English is not the home language. As a result, many school districts have established programmes, some with federal and state support, to provide special programmes for teaching English as a second language.

2. EDUCATIONAL STRUCTURE AND ENROLMENTS

Compulsory education begins at age 6 or 7 in the majority of states, but most children enter kindergarten in an elementary school at the age of 5. Elementary school typically lasts for 7 years (including kindergarten through grade 6), although the duration, including kindergarten, may be as short as 5 years or as long as 9 years in some states and school districts. Secondary education typically commences around age 12 and continues for about 6 years. There are about 24 million children in public elementary schools (grades K-6) and almost 19 million children in public secondary schools (grades 7-12). Private elementary and secondary schools enrol another 5 million children.

Compulsory schooling ends at age 16 in over half the states, but a large majority of young adults continue their education and receive regular high-school diplomas. In the period 1990 to 1996, high-school graduates as a proportion of the 17 year-old population have been between 71 and 73 per cent. However, since many students complete their high-school education through alternative programmes, such as night schools and the General Educational Development (GED) programme, the proportion of young adults having completed high school is considerably higher.

The structure of higher education is quite diverse, with nearly 1 600 public institutions and almost 2 000 private institutions offering a wide range of programmes. Community colleges generally offer vocational education and/or the first two years of training at the college level. Universities typically offer a full undergraduate course of study leading to a Bachelor's degree, as well as first-professional and graduate programmes leading to advanced degrees. Vocational and technical institutions offer training programmes which are designed to prepare students for specific careers.

Institutions of higher education enrol about 14 million students, with about 5.5 million in two-year institutions and just under 9 million in four-year institutions. Most two-year college students attend public institutions (almost 96 per cent), while enrolments in four-year institutions are about two-thirds public and one-third private. An additional 1 million students are enrolled in non-collegiate post-secondary institutions.

3. EDUCATIONAL FINANCE AND COSTS

States and local school districts provide the vast majority of funds for public elementary and secondary education. In 1993, school revenues totalled around US$ 248 billion, with states providing just under 46 per cent, and local school districts about 45 per cent of the total. The federal share was just under 7 per cent and private fees comprised the other 3 per cent. After a long period of growth, state revenues peaked at just under 50 per cent of the total in the mid-1980s, but have since declined to current levels.

Since the mid-1960s, the federal government has funded school programmes to assist students with special educational needs and to improve overall school quality. The federal share of funding for elementary and secondary education peaked during the late 1970s, but with the growth in budget deficits since that time, the share of funding declined, reaching a low of about 6 per cent in the late 1980s.

Current expenditures per enrolled student in public elementary-secondary schools are about US$ 5 500 per student. In the period 1990 to 1996, expenditures per student were relatively stable, as states and the federal government were under great pressure to reduce taxes or shift funding to other domestic programmes.

Both public and private institutions of higher education charge tuition fees, but fees vary substantially between the two sectors and between two-year and four-year institutions. In 1994/95, average undergraduate tuition and fees paid by students in all institutions of higher education were about US$ 4 000 per

United States

student. However, tuition and fees for undergraduate students in private institutions averaged about US$ 11 100 per student, compared to about US$ 2 150 in public institutions. The average cost of tuition in public four-year institutions was over twice as great as those in two-year institutions — US$ 2 700, compared with US$ 1 200 per student.

Funding for public and private institutions tends to come from different sources. Private institutions receive over half their revenues from tuition and fees, gifts, and income from endowments, and one-sixth of their revenues from government funding. Public institutions receive less than one-fourth of their funding from private sources and about half their revenues from federal, state, and local governments. Federal funds mainly support student financial aid, but some institutions also receive substantial funding for research and development.

4. CURRICULUM AND ASSESSMENT

Curriculum and assessment are state and local responsibilities. The United States does not have a national curriculum or curriculum framework. Most states have developed curriculum frameworks and performance standards. The specification of the curriculum and selection of textbooks are usually delegated by the states to local school districts. Currently, the federal government is sponsoring the development of curriculum standards in numerous subject areas and encouraging states to implement voluntary standards that promote improved student performance. Efforts to establish curriculum standards are also underway by teacher associations such as the National Council of Teachers of Mathematics and the American Federation of Teachers.

Most states and the District of Columbia have some form of mandated state-wide testing programme to assess individual student performance against state-established performance standards. Twenty states also have mandatory promotion/graduation tests. Most of these tests are geared to ensuring minimum standards.

The most widely represented subject areas for testing are reading, mathematics, and language arts. Language arts typically include, in addition to reading, other elements of language development such as spelling, vocabulary, grammar, and composition. The tests are administered at a variety of grade levels, and are used by a majority of states as a means of monitoring student progress, as a criterion for grade promotion, for curriculum improvement, to influence policy, as a means of holding schools accountable, or any combination of the above.

The schools use either norm-referenced tests, criterion-referenced tests, or a combination of both. The most frequent type of testing in the United States is conducted using teacher-developed examinations. These tests monitor individual student progress.

At the national level, the United States Department of Education administers the National Assessment of Educational Progress (NAEP). NAEP provides information on selected basic skills for a sample of students at three grade levels. NAEP results are reported for the nation as a whole, by region, gender, racial/ethnic group, parental education, community type and, on a voluntary basis, by state. Results have not traditionally been reported for individual school systems, schools, or students; therefore, there have been no consequences for students based on their test scores. In the future, however, school districts will be able to obtain NAEP results for the whole district, but not for individual students.

5. TEACHERS

Public elementary and secondary schools employ about 2.5 million teachers and 250 000 principals, assistant principals, counsellors, and librarians; total school and district staff is about 4.8 million. Student/teacher ratios are about 17:1 and overall pupil/staff ratios around 9:1. Student/teacher ratios are a little above the OECD average, although overall spending is relatively high by OECD standards.

Each state has its own standards for teacher education, which occurs in a wide variety of higher education institutions. The typical teacher education programme consists of four years of training, with emphasis on the pedagogy, i.e., the methodology of instruction. Student teachers also participate in brief practicums. Teacher education reforms encourage a fifth year of study to integrate theory and practice better, as well as to provide student teachers with additional time to develop subject-area content expertise.

States grant teaching licenses in over 50 fields. To become fully licensed, new teachers are typically provisionally licensed for up to three years. During this period, most states require that new teachers pass a competency test and demonstrate their ability to teach.

Teachers, especially those certified to teach in mathematics, the sciences, special and bilingual education, are in short supply. This shortage is a continuation of the type of spot shortages that have characterised the teacher labour market at different times. However, there have also been changes in the overall labour market that affect the teaching profession. Teaching was traditionally viewed as a "women's profession" with high turnover and low salaries. As opportunities for women expanded and salaries continued to lag behind those of jobs requiring similar preparation, the supply and qualifications of teachers declined. Since the late 1980s both the supply and qualifications of teachers have improved. For much of the 1980s teacher salaries improved relative to other jobs. The education reforms currently being introduced emphasise the need for professional development for existing teachers, improved induction programmes for new teachers, and greater participation by all teachers in education decision-making.

Reference

U.S. Department of Education, Office of Educational Research and Improvement, National Center for Education Statistics. 1995. *Digest of Education Statistics 1995*. Washington DC.

United States

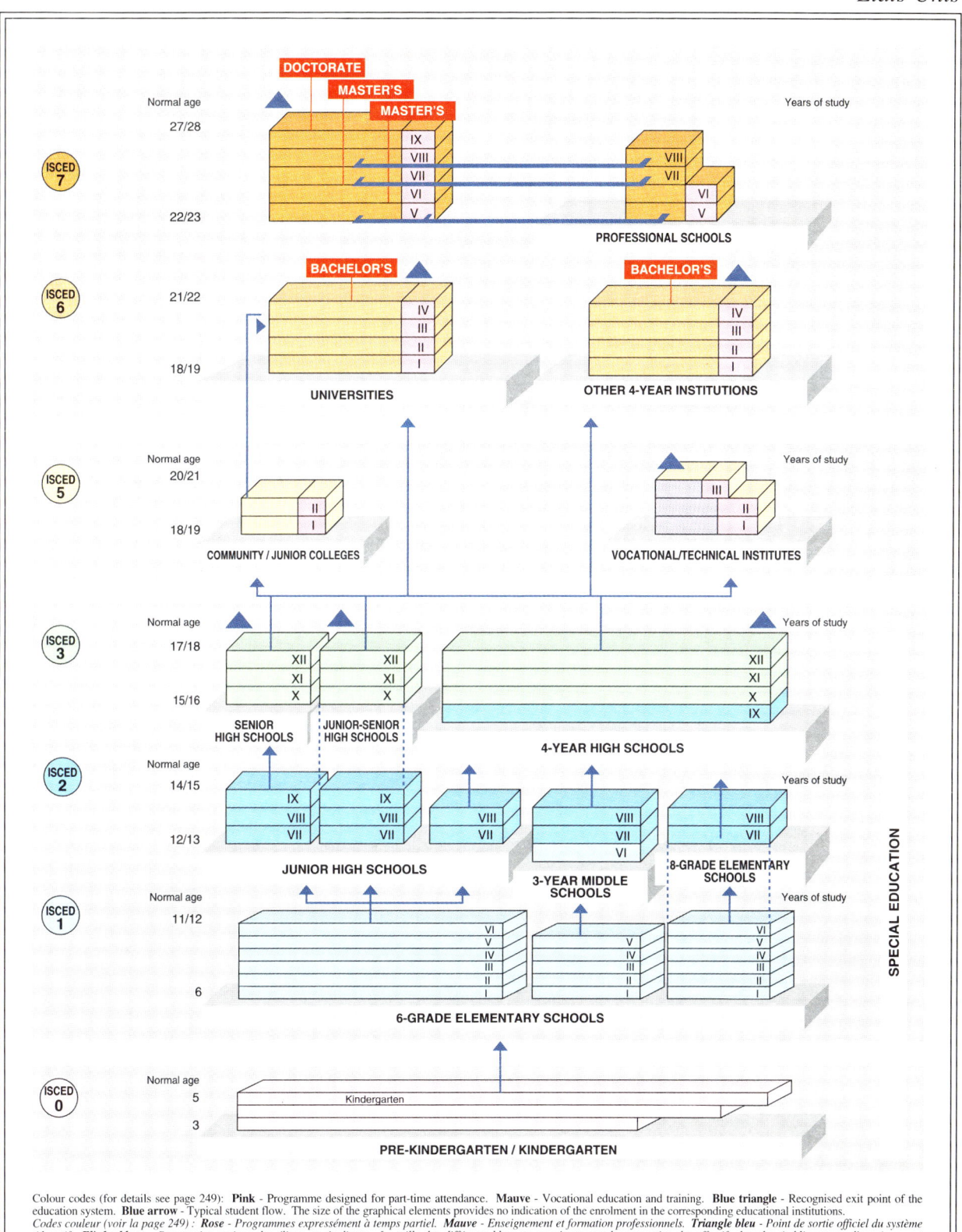

États-Unis

ISCED 7
- Normal age 27/28 – 22/23
- **DOCTORATE**, **MASTER'S**, **MASTER'S**
- Levels V–IX
- PROFESSIONAL SCHOOLS (V–VIII)

ISCED 6
- Normal age 21/22 – 18/19
- **BACHELOR'S**
- UNIVERSITIES (I–IV)
- OTHER 4-YEAR INSTITUTIONS (I–IV)

ISCED 5
- Normal age 20/21 – 18/19
- COMMUNITY / JUNIOR COLLEGES (I–II)
- VOCATIONAL/TECHNICAL INSTITUTES (I–III)

ISCED 3
- Normal age 17/18 – 15/16
- SENIOR HIGH SCHOOLS (X–XII)
- JUNIOR-SENIOR HIGH SCHOOLS (X–XII)
- 4-YEAR HIGH SCHOOLS (IX–XII)

ISCED 2
- Normal age 14/15 – 12/13
- JUNIOR HIGH SCHOOLS (VII–IX)
- 3-YEAR MIDDLE SCHOOLS (VII–VIII)
- (VI–VIII)
- 8-GRADE ELEMENTARY SCHOOLS (VII–VIII)

ISCED 1
- Normal age 11/12 – 6
- 6-GRADE ELEMENTARY SCHOOLS (I–VI)
- (I–V)
- (I–VI)

ISCED 0
- Normal age 5 – 3
- Kindergarten
- PRE-KINDERGARTEN / KINDERGARTEN

SPECIAL EDUCATION

Colour codes (for details see page 249): **Pink** - Programme designed for part-time attendance. **Mauve** - Vocational education and training. **Blue triangle** - Recognised exit point of the education system. **Blue arrow** - Typical student flow. The size of the graphical elements provides no indication of the enrolment in the corresponding educational institutions.

*Codes couleur (voir la page 249) : **Rose** - Programmes expressément à temps partiel. **Mauve** - Enseignement et formation professionnels. **Triangle bleu** - Point de sortie officiel du système éducatif. **Flèche bleue** - Progression typique des élèves ou étudiants. La taille des différents blocs ne représente pas la proportion des effectifs dans les établissements d'enseignement correspondants.*

ANNEXES

Annex 1 – Typical ages and reference years

TABLE A1.1: TYPICAL CUMULATIVE YEARS OF SCHOOLING BY LEVEL OF EDUCATION

Table A1.1 shows the typical number of years of schooling that a person with a specified highest completed level of education has obtained. Note that in some cases the numbers are higher than the cumulative number of years that would normally lead to the completion of a specific level of education, reflecting the incidence of partial completion of the next higher level of education. For example, for the United States the number of years shown in Table A1.1 for lower secondary education is ten years, whereas the theoretical cumulative duration of this level would be 9 years. The increase by one years reflects participants who have only completed lower secondary education but who have also participated in programmes at the upper secondary level without completing this level.

	Primary education	Lower secondary education	Upper secondary education	Non-university tertiary education	University-level education
Australia	8	11	13	15	16
Austria	4	9	13	15	19
Belgium	6	9	12	14	16
Canada	6	9	12	15	16
Denmark	6	9	13	14	18
Finland	5	9	12	14	16
France	5	9	12	14	16
Germany	4	10	13	15	19
Greece	6	9	12	15	23
Ireland	7	10	13	15	16
Italy	5	8	13	13	20
Netherlands	6	10	12	a	17
New Zealand	6	11	13	15	16
Norway	6	9	12	14	16
Portugal	6	8	12	14	16
Spain	6	10	12	14	17
Sweden	7	9	12	14	16
Switzerland	6	9	13	16	19
Turkey	6	8	11	14	16
United Kingdom	6	9	13	15	16
United States	7	10	12	14	16

Annex 1 – Typical ages and reference years

TABLE A1.2: TYPICAL AGES

TYPICAL STARTING AGES

The typical starting age is the typical age at the beginning of the first school/academic year of the corresponding level and programme.

Table A1.2.1:
Typical starting age, tertiary levels of education

	Type of programme		
	Non-university tertiary education (ISCED 5)	University-level education, first stage (ISCED 6)	University-level education, second stage (ISCED 7)
Australia	18	18	22
Austria	18 - 19	18 - 19	22 - 25
Belgium	18 - 19	18 - 19	22 - 24
Canada	18	18	22
Czech Republic	18 - 20	18 - 20	18 - 25
Denmark	21 - 22	19 - 23	19 - 26
Finland	19 - 20	19 - 20	21 - 23
France	18 - 19	18	21
Germany	19	19	26
Greece	17 - 19	17 - 19	21 - 25
Hungary	a	18 - 19	23 - 25
Iceland	20	20	24
Ireland	17 - 18	17 - 18	20 - 24
Italy	19	19	23
Japan	18	18	22
Korea	18	18	22
Luxembourg	m	m	m
Mexico	18	18	24
Netherlands	a	18	19
New Zealand	18	18	21
Norway	19	19	m
Poland	19	19 - 20	22 - 26
Portugal	18	18	22
Russian Federation	15 - 18	17 - 19	22 - 25
Spain	18	18	23
Sweden	19	19	22 - 24
Switzerland	19 - 25	20	26
Turkey	17	17	21
United Kingdom	18	18	21
United States	18	18	22

Annex 1 – Typical ages and reference years

TYPICAL GRADUATION AGES

The typical graduation age is the age at the end of the last school/academic year of the corresponding level and programme when the degree is obtained. The typical age is based on the assumption of full-time attendance in the regular education system without grade repetition.

Table A1.2.2: Typical graduation age, upper secondary level, first educational programmes

	Type of programme				
	All	General programmes	Vocational and technical programmes	School-based vocational and technical programmes	Combined school and work-based vocational and technical programmes
Australia	19	18	20	20	20
Austria	17 - 19	18	17 - 19	17 - 19	18 - 19
Belgium	18 - 20	18	18 - 20	18 - 19	18 - 20
Canada	18	m	m	m	m
Czech Republic	18 - 20	18 - 20	18 - 20	18 - 20	18 - 20
Denmark	19 - 20	19 - 20	19 - 20	19 - 20	19 - 20
Finland	19	19	18 - 19	18 - 19	18 - 19
France	18 - 20	18	18 - 20	18 - 20	18 - 20
Germany	19	19	19	19	19
Greece	17 - 19	17 - 19	17 - 19	17 - 19	a
Hungary	16 - 18	18	17 - 18	18	17
Iceland	20	20	20	20	20
Ireland	17 - 18	17 - 18	17 - 18	17 - 18	17 - 18
Italy	17 - 19	19	17 - 19	17 - 19	a
Japan	18	18	18	18	a
Korea	18	18	18	18	18
Luxembourg	m	m	m	m	m
Mexico	18	18	18	18	a
Netherlands	18 - 19	18 - 19	19 - 20	19	18 - 21
New Zealand	18	18	18	18	a
Norway	19	19	19	19	19
Poland	18 - 20	19	18 - 20	18 - 20	18 - 20
Portugal	18	17	18	18	18
Russian Federation	18	17	18	18	a
Spain	16 - 18	17 - 18	16 - 18	16 - 18	18
Sweden	18 - 19	19	18 - 19	18 - 19	a
Switzerland	18 - 20	18 - 20	18 - 20	18 - 20	18 - 20
Turkey	17	17	17 - 19	17 - 19	17 - 18
United Kingdom	16 - 18	16	18	18	18
United States	18	m	m	m	m

Annex 1 – Typical ages and reference years

Table A1.2.3: Typical graduation age, upper secondary level, second educational programmes

	Type of programme				
	All	General programmes	Vocational and technical programmes	School-based vocational and technical programmes	Combined school and work-based vocational and technical programmes
Austria	18 - 20	a	18 - 20	18 - 20	a
Czech Republic	21 - 23	a	21 - 23	21 - 23	21 - 23
Denmark	22 - 23	22 - 23	22 - 23	22 - 23	22 - 23
Finland	20 - 21	21	20 - 21	20 - 21	20 - 21
France	19 - 20	a	19 - 20	19 - 20	19 - 20
Germany	22	25	22	22	22
Iceland	20	20	20	20	20
Ireland	18 - 19	a	18 - 19	18 - 19	18 - 19
Italy	19	a	19	19	a
Netherlands	19 - 20	19	20	20	20
Portugal	18	18	18	18	18
Spain	19	a	19	19	a

Note: Only countries which report second or further educational programmes at the upper secondary level are listed

Annex 1 – Typical ages and reference years

Table A1.2.4: Typical graduation age, tertiary levels of education

	Type of programme					
	Non-university tertiary education (ISCED 5)	University-level education, first stage (ISCED 6)		University-level education, second stage (ISCED 7)		
	All programmes	Short programmes	Long programmes	All second programmes	Second programmes (e.g. U.S. Master's)	Ph.D. or equivalent
Australia	20	21	x	25	24	25
Austria	20 - 22	x	22 - 25	24 - 27	a	24 - 27
Belgium	21 - 23	a	22 - 24	23 - 30	23 - 26	26 - 30
Canada	21	22	x	27	24	27
Czech Republic	21 - 24	21 - 23	23 - 25	26 - 28	x	26 - 28
Denmark	23 - 24	25 - 27	25 - 27	26 - 35	26 - 27	29 - 35
Finland	21 - 22	22 - 24	25 - 26	29 - 30	25 - 26	29 - 30
France	20 - 21	x	22	26	a	26
Germany	21	x	26	29 - 31	a	29 - 31
Greece	20 - 22	x	21 - 25	23 - 30	23 - 27	26 - 30
Hungary	a	21 - 22	23 - 24	26 - 28	26 - 28	a
Iceland	23	23	m	m	m	m
Ireland	18 - 21	20 - 22	23 - 24	21 - 27	21 - 24	24 - 27
Italy	21	22	23	25	a	25
Japan	20	22	x	27	24	27
Korea	20	22	x	29	24	29
Luxembourg	m	m	m	m	m	m
Mexico	23	x	23	28	26	28
Netherlands	a	23	25	28	x	28
New Zealand	21	21	x	25	23	25
Norway	20 - 21	23	24	24 - 29	24 - 28	25 - 29
Poland	20 - 22	22 - 23	23 - 26	24 - 29	24 - 26	27 - 29
Portugal	21 - 22	21 - 22	22 - 24	26 - 27	26 - 27	a
Russian Federation	19 - 20	20 - 23	22 - 25	26	a	26
Spain	20	21	23	26 - 28	x	26 - 28
Sweden	20 - 22	22	23 - 24	24 - 29	24 - 27	26 - 29
Switzerland	23 - 29	x	26	31	a	31
Turkey	19	25 - 27	x	25 - 27	25 - 27	25 - 27
United Kingdom	20	21	x	26	22	26
United States	20	22	x	27	24	27

Annex 1 – Typical ages and reference years

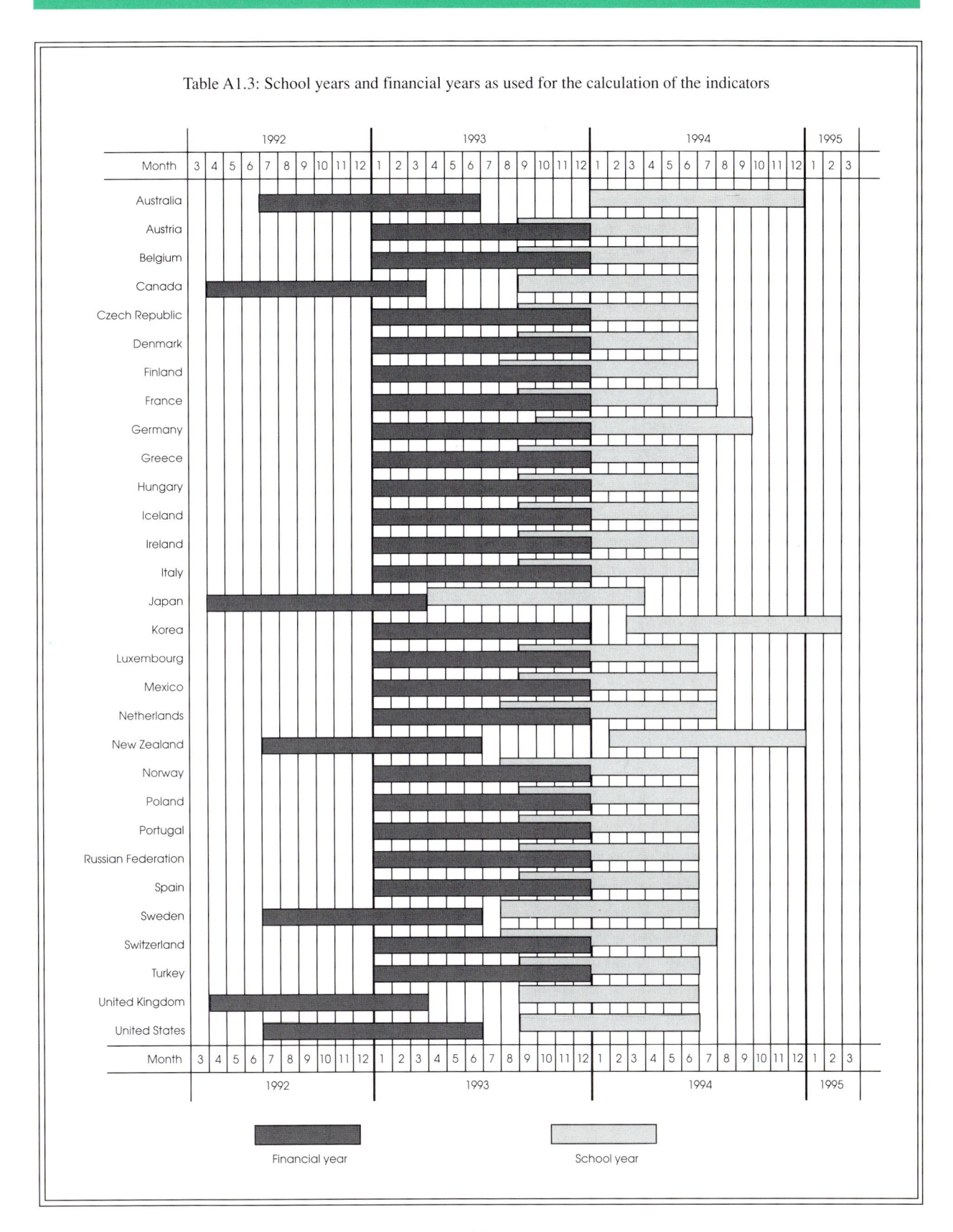

Table A1.3: School years and financial years as used for the calculation of the indicators

Annex 2 – Basic reference statistics

TABLE A2: BASIC REFERENCE STATISTICS

| | Basic reference statistics (reference period: calendar year 1993) |||||||
	Gross Domestic Product*	Purchasing Power Parity exchange rate*	Unadjusted market exchange rate*	Comparative price levels of GDP (United States=100)*	Total public expenditure*	Adjustment factor*	Population size
Australia	414 680	1.3592	1.4706	92	164 345	1.006166	17 573 000
Austria	2 124 072	13.865	11.632	119	1 130 797	1	7 993 000
Belgium	7 268 607	37.303	34.597	108	4 153 072	1	10 084 000
Canada	705 987	1.2630	1.2901	98	363 654	1.007880	28 941 000
Czech Republic	910 600	10.4	29.153	36	420 085	1	10 325 700
Denmark	873 237	8.7859	6.4839	136	557 124	1	5 189 000
Finland	482 397	6.0862	5.7123	107	298 566	1	5 066 000
France	7 082 790	6.5728	5.6632	116	3 896 899	1	57 655 000
Germany	3 154 900	2.1029	1.6533	127	1 593 350	1	81 179 000
Greece	16 760 352	184.34	229.25	80	6 735 323	1	10 368 000
Hungary	3 537 800	57.1	m	m	1 240 800	1	10 310 200
Iceland	410 860	82.926	67.603	123	168 566	1	265 000
Ireland	32 173	0.65477	0.67725	97	13 876	1	3 563 000
Italy	1 550 150 000	1 533.8	1 573.7	97	885 711 000	1	57 070 000
Japan	465 972 000	184.31	111.2	166	162 742 000	1.004823	124 670 000
Korea	267 145 900	620.9	802.67	77	56 084 600	1	43 663 405
Luxembourg	m	39.620	34.597	115	m	1	393 000
Mexico	1 127 584	1.8200	3.1156	58	206 989	1	91 210 000
Netherlands	579 040	2.1344	1.8573	115	339 020	1	15 290 000
New Zealand	78 804	1.5158	1.8505	82	31 501	1.013804	3 470 750
Norway	733 665	8.9309	7.0941	126	436 546	1	4 312 000
Poland	1 557 800 000	8 533	m	m	50 200	1	38 418 100
Portugal	13 625 623	116.96	160.8	73	m	1	9 876 000
Russian Federation	158 000 000	205.4	m	m	m	1	148 295 000
Spain	60 905 100	116.96	127.26	92	24 424 000	1	39 086 000
Sweden	1 442 181	9.8332	7.7834	126	1 069 134	1.013233	8 718 000
Switzerland	342 850	2.1316	1.4776	144	123 445	1	6 938 000
Turkey	1 981 866 000	5 989.8	10 984.6	55	m	1	59 489 000
United Kingdom	628 384	0.63735	0.66676	96	286 333	1.024528	58 191 000
United States	6 259 900	1	1	100	2 335 600	1.010901	258 120 000

* See explanations below

Annex 2 – Basic reference statistics

Explanations:

Gross Domestic Product (GDP) refers to the producers' value of the gross outputs of resident producers, including distributive trades and transport, less the value of purchasers' intermediate consumption plus import duties. GDP is expressed in local money (in millions). For countries which provide this information for a reference year different from the calendar year (such as Australia and New Zealand) adjustments are made by linearly weighting their GDP between two adjacent national reference years to match the calendar year. The following formula is used: $GDP = w_{t-1}(GDP_{t-1}) + w_t(GDP_t)$, where GDP_{t-1} and GDP_t are the GDP estimates for the two years and w_{t-1} and w_t are the weights applicable, based on the starting and ending months of the national reference year for the reporting of national GDP data.

Purchasing Power Parity exchange rates (PPP) are the currency exchange rates that equalise the purchasing power of different currencies. This means that a given sum of money when converted into different currencies at the PPP rates, will buy the same basket of goods and services in all countries. In other words, PPPs are the rates of currency conversion which eliminate the differences in price levels among countries. Thus, when expenditure on GDP for different countries is converted into a common currency by means of PPPs, it is, in effect, expressed at the same set of international prices so that comparisons among countries reflect only differences in the volume of goods and services purchased.

The **unadjusted exchange rates** are par or market exchange rates that have been averaged over the calendar year 1993. They have been calculated by the International Monetary Fund, and are published in *International Financial Statistics*.

The **comparative price level of GDP** is obtained by dividing the purchasing power parity exchange rate by the corresponding unadjusted exchange rate and multiplying the result by 100. This provides an indication of the relative price level in a country compared with the United States. For example, for Portugal the exchange rate to the U.S. dollar equals 117 while the market exchange rate is equal to 161. The comparative price level of GDP for Portugal is therefore 73 per cent. This means that in Portugal the same basket of goods costs only 73 per cent of what it would cost in the United States.

Total public expenditure as used for the calculation of the education indicators corresponds to the sum of the following items (for details refer to "Accounts for General Government": Table 6 in *National Accounts - Detailed Tables, Volume II*, OECD, Paris, 1995): Total public expenditure = Total current disbursements and net saving + (Capital: gross accumulation) Increase in stocks + (Capital: gross accumulation) Gross fixed capital formation + (Capital: gross accumulation) Purchases of land net + (Capital: gross accumulation) Purchases of intangible assets net + (Capital: gross accumulation) Capital transfers – (Capital: finance of gross accumulation) Net saving – (Capital: finance of gross accumulation) Capital transfers. Total public expenditure is expressed in local money (in millions).

The **adjustment factor** is used to shift the reference period for expenditure data from the national financial year to the calendar year 1993.

Sources:

OECD countries (unless otherwise specified below)
- OECD *National Accounts*, 1995
- OECD *Economic Outlook*, 1995

Czech Republic
- GDP: *Short-term Economic Indicators, Central and Eastern Europe*, OECD/CCET, July 1995
- PPP: Estimated figures provided by OECD/STD (Unit for PPP)
- Population and total public expenditure: Department of Demography, Prague University of Economics

Hungary
- GDP: *Short-term Economic Indicators, Central and Eastern Europe*, OECD/CCET, July 1995
- PPP: Estimated figures provided by OECD/STD (Unit for PPP)
- Population and total public expenditure: Ministry of Finance, Budapest

Korea
- GDP: *International Financial Statistics,* International Monetary Fund, June 1995
- PPP: Estimated figures provided by the World Bank
- Population: Korean Educational Development Institute
- Total public expenditure: *International Financial Statistics*, International Monetary Fund, June 1995

Mexico
- Total public expenditure: National Institute of Geographical and Computerised Statistics, Mexico

New Zealand
- Total public expenditure: Ministry of Education, Wellington

Norway
- Total public expenditure: The Royal Norwegian Ministry of Education, Research and Church Affairs, Oslo

Poland
- GDP: *Short-term Economic Indicators, Central and Eastern Europe*, OECD/CCET, July 1995
- PPP and total public expenditure: Estimated figures provided by OECD/STD (Unit for PPP)
- Population: Central Statistical Office of the Republic of Poland, Warsaw

Russian Federation
- GDP: World Bank (caution: it is GNP rather than GDP)
- PPP: Estimated figures provided by the World Bank
- Population: Centre for Education Research and Science, Moscow

Annex 3 – Sources, methods and technical notes

This annex provides notes on the coverage of the indicators as well as on the interpretation of the indicators and on methods and sources. It is organised by indicator.

**INDICATORS C1: EDUCATIONAL ATTAINMENT OF THE ADULT POPULATION;
C2: GENDER DIFFERENCES IN EDUCATIONAL ATTAINMENT OF THE ADULT POPULATION; AND
C11: RATES OF LABOUR FORCE PARTICIPATION BY LEVEL OF EDUCATIONAL ATTAINMENT**

Notes on specific countries

Coverage

Czech Republic: Data refer to 1991 and cover both the Czech Republic and the Slovak Federal Republic. Non-university tertiary education is included in university-level education.

Denmark: Category 24 to 64 years of age includes all ages.

Spain: Persons aged 16 years and over are included. The population aged 15 years or less has been allocated to ISCED 2.

Norway: Persons for whom the level of educational attainment is unknown are allocated to ISCED level 0/1.

New Zealand: Persons not in private households (i.e. those living in boarding houses, hotels, army camps, hospitals, etc.) are excluded.

Turkey: Illiterate persons and persons with no school-leaving diploma are excluded (not included in ISCED 0/1).

United Kingdom: Only people aged 16 and over are included in the survey.

Notes on interpretation

Austria: The definitions of the labour force and unemployment have changed since the last data collection in order to follow Labour Force Survey (LFS) definitions. Data are therefore not comparable with data in the 1995 edition of *Education at a Glance*.

France: The definitions of ISCED levels have changed, so that they are more similar to EUROSTAT definitions and more easily compared with other countries. Data for 1994 are therefore not directly comparable with data for other years. The main change consists in taking into account the programmes followed, and not only the diplomas awarded. Some categories have therefore been shifted from ISCED level 1 to ISCED level 2.

Notes on methodology

Austria, **Italy**: Annual averages are based on surveys conducted at the end of each quarter.

Belgium: The data are based on an original sample of about 35 000 households (33 075 households interviewed, a total of 81 000 persons, of whom 67 000 were aged 15 or over).

Definitions of the International Labour Organisation (ILO) have been used. The allocation to ISCED levels is based on the highest certificate or diploma obtained in initial or further education. Training which is not formally certified is not included.

Canada: The Labour Force Survey is conducted on a monthly basis, and then annual averages are produced from the data. Data have been rounded to the nearest 1 000 and all values less than 4 000 have been suppressed to adhere to LFS release criteria.

Finland: Annual estimates are calculated as the average of monthly estimates.

Sweden: For Indicators C1 and C2: Data are based on the total register of the population. Both self-reported data from the 1990 census and administrative data from examination registers are used. For Indicators C11 and R21: Annual averages are based on monthly Labour Force Surveys.

Sources

Australia: Australian Bureau of Statistics, "Transition from Education to Work", May 1994 (unpublished data).

Austria: Austrian Central Statistical Office, Microcensus, 1994.

Belgium: Labour Force Survey, Spring 1994.

Canada: Statistics Canada, Labour Force Survey, 1994.

Denmark: Statistical register of education, "The labour force and unemployment", November 1993.

Finland: Labour Force Survey, 1994.

France: *Enquête Emploi* (Labour Force Survey), March 1994.

Germany: Labour Force Survey, April 1994.

Greece: National Statistical Service, Labour Force Survey, 1994.

Ireland: Irish Labour Force Survey, 1994.

Italy: Labour Force Survey, 1994.

Netherlands: Labour Force Survey, 1994.

Norway: Labour Force Survey, 1994.

New Zealand: Household Labour Force Survey, Sept. 1994 Quarter.

Portugal: National Institute of Statistics, Permanent Employment Inquiry.

Spain: *Encuesta de Población Activa* (Labour Force Survey), 1994.

Annex 3 – Sources, methods and technical notes

Sweden: For Indicators C1 and C2: Register on educational attainment of the population, December 1994. For Indicators C11 and R21: Labour Force Survey, 1994.

Switzerland: *ESPA: Enquête suisse sur la population active* (Swiss Labour Force Survey), April/June 1994.

Turkey: Household Labour Force Survey, SIS, average April and October 1994.

United Kingdom: Labour Force Survey, Spring 1994.

United States: U.S. Department of Commerce, Bureau of the Census, Current Population Survey, March 1994.

INDICATOR C3: THE RELATIVE SIZE OF THE YOUNG POPULATION

Sources

OECD Demographic Database, 1995 release.

INDICATOR F1: EDUCATIONAL EXPENDITURE RELATIVE TO GROSS DOMESTIC PRODUCT

General notes

Notes on methodology

- Reference period

Statistics on educational expenditure relate to the calendar year 1993. GDP consumer price deflators from the OECD National Accounts database are used to adjust the data on expenditure where the national financial year does not coincide with the calendar year. In order to make this adjustment, the data on educational finance are multiplied by the ratio of GDP price levels between the calendar year for which data are published and those of the preceding calendar year, in proportion to the fraction of the national financial year that overlaps with the previous calendar year. The following two limitations of the use of such deflators should be recognised: *i)* The adjustments relate to changes in general (GDP) price levels but not to the price levels for educational services. The assumption is made that educational costs are measured in terms of national income foregone so that a GDP price index is justified. *ii)* No allowance has been made for real growth in educational expenditure (increases in excess of inflation or smaller increases) that might have taken place during the corresponding period of adjustment. It would only be possible to take real growth into account retrospectively. Nevertheless, the adjustment for inflation does eliminate one significant source of non-comparability of expenditure figures.

For countries for which GDP is not reported for the calendar year, GDP is estimated as: $w_{t-1} (GDP_{t-1}) + w_t (GDP_t)$ with w_t and w_{t-1} being the weights for the respective portions of the two calendar years.

- Assumptions concerning the allocation of financial aid to students

Indicator F1 distinguishes between public financial aid to students and/or households that is attributable to household payments to educational institutions for educational services (e.g. tuition fees) and other public aid to students/households (such as subsidies for student living costs). The following coefficients are used to estimate the proportion of public financial aid to households that is destined for educational institutions.

	Primary (ISCED 1)	Secondary (ISCED 2/3)	Tertiary (ISCED 5/6/7)	All levels of education combined
Australia	0	0	0.46	0.24
Canada	0	0	0.329	0.329
Ireland	0	0	0.42	0.27
Mexico	0	0	0.0074	0.0128
Netherlands	0	0.3	0.3	0.3
New Zealand	0.5	0.5	0.5	0.5
United Kingdom	0.5	0.5	0.5	0.5
United States	0.50725	0.50725	0.50725	0.50725

- Calculation of estimates in Charts F1.2(B) and (C)

The estimates in Charts F1.2(B) and (C) were calculated as follows: Let $B(i)$ be the percentage of persons 5 to 29 years of age in the total population of country i, divided by the average percentage of 5 to 29 year-olds in all OECD countries for which data are available. Let $A(i)$ be the expenditure for educational institutions as a percentage of GDP in country i. The expected difference for country i shown in Chart F1.2(B) was then calculated as $A(i)/B(i) - A(i)$. Similarly, let $C(i)$ be the percentage of students 5 to 29 years of age enrolled in the population 5 to 29 years of age in country i, divided by the average percentage of 5 to 29 year-olds enrolled in all OECD countries for which data are available. The expected difference for country i shown in Chart F1.2(C) was then calculated as $A(i)/C(i) - A(i)$.

Notes on specific countries

Coverage

Australia: Educational expenditure *excludes* private expenditure on early childhood education; household expenditure on educational items and services other than fees and payments made to educational institutions; payments to private vocational education and training institutions; and payments to two private universities.

Annex 3 – Sources, methods and technical notes

Austria: Expenditure classified as "not allocated by level" *includes* the main non-tertiary level scholarships, schoolbooks and free travel arrangements for students, and expenditure on adult and special education.

Belgium, **Czech Republic**, **Greece**, **Mexico**, **New Zealand**, **Norway**, **Switzerland**, **United Kingdom**: Expenditure from private sources is *not included*.

Belgium: Research expenditure is *included* only if covered by funds provided by the Community education authorities. Research funds from other public and private sources are *excluded*.

Czech Republic: Public expenditure on upper secondary and tertiary education *includes* estimates of child allowances, meals, accommodation, and transport subsidies. In some cases, the allocation of expenditure by level of education is estimated on the basis of enrolments.

Denmark: Expenditure on adult education programmes that are similar in content to programmes in the normal school system has been allocated to the corresponding level of education. Expenditure on other adult education programmes has been allocated to the upper secondary and tertiary levels of education. The allocation of expenditure on early childhood, primary and lower secondary education is estimated on the basis of the corresponding enrolments.

Finland: Expenditure on adult education is *excluded*. Research expenditure *includes* general university and business enterprise funds but not other separately identifiable R&D funds. Government transfers and payments to private entities, except financial aid to students, are *excluded*. Expenditure by households, except school meal charges, and expenditure by other private entities are also *excluded*. Ancillary services are *included* as current expenditure other than compensation of staff.

France: Expenditure "not allocated by level" *includes* expenditure on special education in primary and lower secondary education and expenditure on arts education. All separately identifiable R&D expenditure is *excluded*; however, compensation of university teaching staff (and other regular university staff) is *included*, a portion of which is attributable to research.

Germany: Expenditure on the following types of programmes/institutions are *not included* in total expenditure: colleges of nursing; agricultural training and research centres; training of trainee civil servants in public service; support payments for dependent children made to persons undergoing education/training; allowances paid to teachers enjoying the status of civil servants for medical treatment and health insurance; scholarships granted by private institutions; purchases of commodities and educational services by households. Payments by private households and other private entities to government-dependent institutions are *excluded*. Almost all expenditure on research performed by the higher education sector is *included*.

For the period 1970-90 the data refer to the former territories of the Federal Republic of Germany. From 1975 onwards, coverage of financial statistics has increased. Since 1985, university research is *included*.

Hungary: Expenditure "not allocated by level" *includes* educational services provided by independent institutions in the fields of educational and psychological counselling, methodology and administration. Financial data for non-tertiary level education *only include* expenditure reported under educational headings, whereas data for tertiary level education *include* all expenditure by tertiary institutions, whatever the heading, *except* in the case of medical institutions of higher education. In addition, expenditure on early childhood education *includes* meals, expenditure on primary and lower secondary education *includes* student hostels, day-care in schools and meals, and expenditure on upper secondary education *includes* meals, hostels, and expenditure on work places for apprentices.

Iceland: Expenditure by private entities other than households and all capital expenditure by or on private institutions are *excluded*. Funds from foreign sources are also *excluded*.

Ireland: Educational expenditure *includes* mainstream higher education research. Only household expenditure on the running costs of schools is *included*. Household expenditure on school transport, schoolbooks and other educational materials is *excluded*. Expenditure by private entities other than households is *only included* for tertiary education. Child benefits for students in tertiary education (who would not qualify for benefit if they were not enrolled in full-time education) are *not included*. Such benefits apply to less than 20 per cent of such students.

Italy: Expenditure from international sources has not been taken into account for upper secondary education and for vocational training at the regional government level. Expenditure on private institutions at all levels of education except university *only includes* expenditure by public sources. Private expenditure on vocational training in higher education is not negligible.

Japan: Expenditure "not allocated by level" *includes* expenditure on special training colleges, miscellaneous schools and educational administration. No separately identifiable research expenditure has been taken into account but compensation of teaching staff (and other regular staff) in universities is *included*.

Korea: Expenditure "not allocated by level" *includes* expenditure by research institutes, non-educational organisations supporting educational activities, teacher training institutions and libraries, *but not* expenditure by central government or household expenditure on independent private institutions. For primary and lower secondary education, expenditure by the central government is *excluded*. Central government expenditure on primary and secondary schools affiliated to universities is included in tertiary level

Annex 3 – Sources, methods and technical notes

expenditure. Compensation of "other educational, administrative, and professional staff" in public institutions of early childhood education is *not included*.

New Zealand: Expenditure "not allocated by level" *includes* policy advice, management of contracts/administration of payments, provision and support of the curriculum, ministerial servicing, payment of salaries and allowances, provision of information, provision of teaching/learning accommodation, provision of housing for teachers and caretakers, losses on sales of fixed assets, restructuring expenses, provision for retirement and long-service leave, and capital investment.

Norway: Expenditure on early childhood education in government-dependent institutions is *included* in expenditure on primary education.

Spain: Public expenditure on education is *underestimated* because contributions paid by employees are only partially included. Expenditure on research has been *partially included*. Some tertiary institutions have all R&D expenditure in their budgets; others have only general university funds and certain types of contracts.

Payments to independent private institutions for tertiary education are *underestimated* because only payments by private entities to universities for R&D are included. Expenditure by private entities other than households on private institutions and scholarships are *underestimated*. Funds from foreign sources received by central government are *not included*.

Sweden: Early childhood education at pre-schools and day-care centres from the age of three is *included*. Expenditure on the educational element is *estimated*. Expenditure on municipal adult education is *included* and reported under primary, lower and upper secondary education. Expenditure on all research performed in higher education institutions is *included*.

Switzerland: Funds from foreign sources for public institutions are *not included*.

United Kingdom: Only general university funds and grants from the Department for Education and Employment are *included*. All other separate R&D funds are *excluded*. Funds originating in the public sector spent by households on tuition fees are *included*, *but not* amounts spent by households from their own resources. Expenditure relating to nursing and paramedical non-university tertiary programmes is *not included*.

United States: All research expenditure is *included* except funds for major federal R&D centres administered by universities.

Notes on interpretation

Denmark: Expenditure on early childhood education is slightly *overestimated*.

Finland: Capital expenditure cannot be compared with figures shown in the 1995 edition of *Education at a Glance*.

Hungary: Expenditure on tertiary education cannot be compared with figures shown in the 1995 edition of *Education at a Glance*, because expenditure on non-tertiary level education by tertiary-level institutions has now been *excluded*. Furthermore, figures now *exclude* non-scholarship grants, and expenditure associated with loans to students and securities.

Sweden: In comparison with the 1995 edition of *Education at a Glance*, two main changes have been made in the reporting of data, in accordance with the new definitions: *i)* Expenditure on the educational element in day-care institutions has been *estimated*, taking expenditure per student to be the same as in pre-schools for 6 year-olds. In the 1995 edition of *Education at a Glance*, all expenditure on children above 3 years of age in day-care institutions was reported. *ii)* Expenditure on research, regardless of funding source, has now been *included* in tertiary education. Since research in the government sector is to a great extent performed in higher education institutions, expenditure on tertiary education increases by more than one-third when research is included. Private payments other than to educational institutions only cover public financial assistance (grants and loans) for private payments, i.e. for students' living costs and, in tertiary education, for books.

Switzerland: Expenditure figures cannot be compared with figures shown in the 1995 edition of *Education at a Glance*.

Notes on methodology

Australia and **New Zealand** report educational expenditure and national account data for the period July to June. For these countries, the "calculated" ratio of national GDP price levels adjusts the expenditure data to the calendar year. GDP figures are adjusted by creating a weighted average for the two adjacent reference years.

Austria, **Belgium**, **Czech Republic**, **Denmark**, **Finland**, **France**, **Germany**, **Hungary**, **Ireland**, **Italy**, **Korea**, **Mexico**, the **Netherlands**, **Norway**, **Poland**, **Russian Federation**, **Spain**, **Switzerland** and **Turkey** report both educational expenditure and national account data by calendar year. No adjustment is therefore needed.

Canada, **Japan** and **United Kingdom** report educational expenditure for the period April to March. **Sweden** and **United States** report educational expenditure for the period July to June. Enrolment and financial data are adjusted as appropriate to accord with the calendar year.

Australia: Figures on expenditure by source are based on 1992/93 financial year data provided by the Australian Bureau of Statistics. These data are supplemented with averaged 1992 and 1993 calendar year data (provided by major educational organisations) to apportion total expenditure across ISCED levels and expenditure categories. The ISCED level data for the Technical and Further Education (TAFE) institutions were apportioned by expenditure item based on data supplied by the New South Wales TAFE and then apportioned across ISCED levels according to student hours.

Annex 3 – Sources, methods and technical notes

Finland: Scholarships and other grants to students/households broken down by level of education are estimates.

Hungary: Government expenditure on public institutions is estimated by subtracting the income from the expenditure of public institutions. Private payments to public institutions are taken as income of public institutions. Private payments to government-dependent institutions are estimates. Funds from foreign sources that are directly paid to service providers are not included.

Mexico: The proportion of public financial aid to students that is attributable to household payments to educational institutions is estimated and applies for federal public expenditure. Private expenditure on independent private institutions is estimated. Expenditure by local government on public institutions and the distribution of regional and local government expenditure across ISCED levels are also estimated.

Sources

1995 UNESCO/OECD/EUROSTAT (UOE) data collection on education statistics. National sources are:

Australia: Department of Employment, Education and Training, Higher Education Division, Canberra; Australian Bureau of Statistics, "Expenditure on Education Finance" collection; in the case of regional government expenditure, state government data (for public institutions) and school data (for private institutions) were used; "Collection of National Financial Data on Vocational Education and Training", 1992/93; New South Wales Technical and Further Education, unpublished data.

Austria: Austrian Central Statistical Office, Vienna.

Belgium: French Community: Ministry of Education, Research and Training, Brussels; Flemish Community: Education Department, Brussels; German Community: Ministry of the German-speaking Community, Eupen.

Canada: Statistics Canada, Ottawa.

Czech Republic: Institute for Information on Education, Prague.

Denmark: Ministry of Education, Department of Economic Affairs, Copenhagen.

Finland: Statistics Finland, Helsinki; Ministry of Education, Helsinki.

France: Ministry of National Education and Culture, Directorate of Evaluation and Planning, Paris.

Germany: Federal Office of Statistics, Wiesbaden.

Greece: Ministry of National Education and Religious Affairs, Directorate of Investment Planning and Operational Research, Athens.

Hungary: Ministry of Finance, Budapest.

Iceland: Ministry of Culture and Education, Reykjavik.

Ireland: Department of Education, Statistics Section, Dublin.

Italy: ISTAT, Rome; Ministry of Public Education, Statistical Service, Rome.

Japan: Ministry of Education, Science, Sports and Culture, Research and Statistics Planning Division, Tokyo.

Korea: Korean Educational Development Institute, Educational Information Research Center, Seoul.

Mexico: Secretariat of Public Education.

Netherlands: Central Bureau for Statistics, Department for Statistics of Education, Voorburg; Ministry of Education and Science, Zoetermeer.

New Zealand: Ministry of Education, Wellington.

Norway: Statistical Central Office, Division for Population, Education and Regional Conditions, Kongsvinger; The Royal Norwegian Ministry of Education, Research and Church Affairs, Oslo.

Poland: Central Statistical Office, Republic of Poland, Warsaw.

Portugal: Ministry of Education, Office of Research and Planning, Department of Programming, Lisbon.

Russian Federation: Centre for Science Research and Statistics, Moscow.

Spain: National Institute of Statistics, Sub-directorate General of Social Research and Statistics, Madrid; Ministry of Education, Planning Office, Madrid; Ministry of Labour, Madrid.

Sweden: Swedish National Agency for Education (*Skolverket*), Stockholm; Swedish National Agency for Higher Education (*Hogskoleverket*); Statistics Sweden, Örebro.

Switzerland: Federal Statistical Office, Berne.

Turkey: State Institute of Statistics, Ankara.

United Kingdom: Department for Education and Employment, Darlington.

United States: Department of Education, Office of Educational Research and Improvement, National Center for Education Statistics, Washington, D.C.

Annex 3 – Sources, methods and technical notes

INDICATOR F3: EXPENDITURE ON EDUCATIONAL SERVICES PER STUDENT

See also notes on Indicator F1.

General notes

Notes on methodology

- Reference period

Indicator F3 refers to the calendar year 1993. For countries for which the financial year and/or the school year does not match the calendar year, corresponding adjustments are made. For countries in which the financial year closely matches the calendar year but for which the school year is different from the calendar year, the enrolment data are weighted to match the calendar year. For countries in which the school year closely matches the calendar year but in which the financial year is different from the calendar year, the enrolment data remain unchanged but the GDP price deflators mentioned under F1 are used to match the financial data to the calendar year. For countries in which neither the school year nor the financial year matches the calendar year, the enrolment data are weighted to match the financial year and afterwards the above-mentioned GDP price deflators are used to adjust the financial year data to accord with the calendar year.

- Influence of R&D expenditure on tertiary education expenditure

Comparisons of expenditure on tertiary education, and especially per tertiary student, can be misleading because the figures for universities and other tertiary institutions include substantial expenditure on research. The research share of total tertiary spending varies among countries, partly because of differences in the proportion of total national research and development (R&D) performed by the higher education sector.

Another reason why research spending distorts comparisons of expenditure per tertiary student is that research outlays have not been included to the same extent in the tertiary expenditure figures of all countries. For example, while some countries have excluded separately funded or separately budgeted research, others, such as Hungary and Sweden, have essentially included all research outlays by institutions of higher education in their tertiary expenditure statistics.

A comparison of expenditure per student including and excluding R&D for selected countries is shown in Annex 3 in the 1995 edition of *Education at a Glance*. The results shown there indicate that research spending constitutes a significant portion of total expenditure on tertiary education. They also show that there is wide variation in the estimated research share of total tertiary expenditure. For the handful of countries that were covered by this comparison, the subtraction of R&D expenditure from tertiary education expenditure reduced the estimated expenditure per student by amounts ranging from 14 to 37 per cent.

It follows that international differences in spending per tertiary student shown in this indicator, and in spending on tertiary education as a percentage of GDP shown in Indicator F1, partly reflect differences among countries in the research roles of institutions of higher education. The spending differences do not necessarily reflect differences in the amounts spent per student to support the teaching functions of tertiary institutions.

Recognising these problems, policy-makers in several countries have asked for an indicator that distinguishes between expenditure on research and expenditure on teaching, and that compares countries with respect to expenditure per tertiary student net of the cost of research. Unfortunately, this request is difficult to satisfy. One obstacle is that some countries do not have complete data on the research outlays of their tertiary institutions. Another obstacle is conceptual: an important activity of universities, the "training by doing" of students to be researchers (especially post-graduates) can be described with equal validity as either teaching or research. It is therefore very difficult to measure these two components consistently.

The OECD-INES Technical Group is currently undertaking a study to obtain insight into the ways in which countries estimate the R&D share of total tertiary expenditure.

- Estimation of typical duration of tertiary studies

The estimates of the cumulative expenditure on education over the average duration of tertiary studies were obtained by multiplying Indicator F3 by an estimate of the average duration of tertiary studies. The latter estimate was approximated by the rate of turnover of the existing stock of enrolments, obtained through the ratio of flow data (entrants and leavers) to the corresponding numbers of students enrolled. The formula $D = (S_{t-1} + S_t)/(Z_t + A_t)$ was used for this calculation, where S_t is the number of students enrolled at the end of year t, S_{t-1} is the number of students at the beginning of year t (approximated by the number of students enrolled at the end of the preceding school year), Z_t is the number of students who are in their first year of study in year t, and A_t is the number of leavers in the school year t (approximated by $S_{t-1} + Z_t - S_t$). Full-time equivalents have been used to estimate enrolments. The number of entrants to full-time programmes has been used to estimate the inflow. All participants are included, even those who will eventually not obtain a degree.

The estimate is based on a number of simplifying assumptions: First, it is assumed that transition ratios are constant over time. Secondly, expenditure for the current reference year is assumed to be representative for the total duration of studies. OECD trend data indicate that real expenditure per student is fairly constant.

Annex 3 – Sources, methods and technical notes

Notes on specific countries

Coverage

Finland: Figures *include* day care and pre-school education as well as meals provided for 3-6 year-olds in day-care centres, generally 8 to 10 hours a day, five days a week.

Spain: For financial data, students in open universities have been considered part-time students. Financial data for private institutions at ISCED level 6 *only include* university institutions.

Notes on interpretation

Denmark: Expenditure on early childhood education is slightly overestimated. Data differ from those published in the 1995 edition of *Education at a Glance* due to an improved alignment between the expenditure and enrolment data.

Netherlands: Expenditure per student is higher than in the 1995 edition of *Education at a Glance*, because expenditure previously classified as "not allocated by level" is now attributed to the various levels of education and because participants in apprenticeship programmes have been converted to full-time equivalents.

United Kingdom: In the 1995 edition of *Education at a Glance*, high expenditure per student figures for public tertiary education were due to the classification of Further Education colleges as public institutions. Now all universities and Further Education colleges are considered government-dependent private institutions.

Notes on methodology

Denmark: Kindergartens are classified as public institutions. There are changes from the 1995 edition of *Education at a Glance* in the adjustment of full-time students enrolled on 1 October to figures corresponding to accounts and expenditure data for the total school year. The average duration of tertiary studies in Denmark (see Chart F3.4) is based on ISCED levels 6 and 7 only.

Hungary: The separation of financial figures for primary and lower secondary education is estimated on the basis of the numbers of students enrolled.

Sweden: Only children 3 years and older in early childhood education institutions are included. Expenditure on the educational element and total expenditure on the age group, are estimated. Expenditure on primary and lower secondary education (*grundskola*) is not available separately. The breakdown between these levels is estimated from teachers' salaries and the numbers of teaching periods. Expenditure on special education at primary, lower and upper secondary levels, and on municipal adult education, is also estimated. Students in municipal adult education have been converted to full-time equivalents at primary, lower and upper secondary education according to the type of course they attend. Full-time equivalents for students in tertiary education have been calculated according to the registered course load (as a percentage of a full-time course load). In the last edition of *Education at a Glance*, data for this calculation were not available and all students were counted as full-time.

Switzerland: Expenditure per student is very high at university level. This is mainly due to the structure of the university system: a high number of university students in relation to the size of the country, the small size of some universities, the wide range of provision at each university, and therefore the relatively low student/teaching staff ratios. Furthermore, teachers' salaries at university level are comparatively high, and university expenditure also includes expenditure on research and development.

Sources

1995 UNESCO/OECD/EUROSTAT (UOE) data collection on education statistics. For details see sources for *Indicator F1*.

INDICATOR F3-R: INTER-REGIONAL DISPARITIES IN EXPENDITURE ON EDUCATIONAL SERVICES PER STUDENT

See also notes on Indicator F3.

General notes

Sources

The indicators of regional disparities in expenditure per student and student/teaching staff ratios were produced from a variety of different sources. These sources included regular statistical reports on education, special reports on regional education indicators, and unpublished tables containing data on education. Most of this material was produced by Ministries of Education or National Statistical Offices, but some reports were prepared by other government agencies. The citations that follow are examples of the statistical publications that were used to produce the regional indicators: *Estadistica de la Enseñanza en España, 1992/93,* published by the Ministerio de Educación y Ciencia in Spain; *Estadistica Basica del Sistema Educativo Nacional*, published by the Secretaria de Educación Publica in Mexico; and *Schüler, Klassen, Lehrer und Absolventen der Schulen, 1984 bis 1993*, published by the Sekretariat der Kultusministerkonferenz in Germany. Special reports on education that highlight national and/or regional education data include: *National Report on Schooling in Australia*, published by the Ministerial Council on Education, Employment, Training and Youth Affairs in Australia; *Géographie de l'École*, published by the Ministère de l'Éducation nationale de l'Enseignement supérieur et de la Recherche in France; and *The Swiss Educational Mosaic — A Study in Diversity*, published by the Federal Statistical Office in Switzerland.

Annex 3 – Sources, methods and technical notes

INDICATOR F5: EDUCATIONAL EXPENDITURE BY RESOURCE CATEGORY

See also notes on Indicator F1.

General notes

Notes on methodology

Initial public spending includes both direct public expenditure on educational institutions and transfers to the private sector. Initial private spending includes tuition fees and other student or household payments to educational institutions, less the portion of such payments offset by public subsidies. The final public and private portions are the percentages of education funds spent directly by public and private purchasers of educational services. Final public spending includes direct public purchases of educational resources and payments to educational institutions, but excludes transfers to households and other private entities. Final private spending includes tuition fees and other private payments to educational institutions (whether or not offset by public subsidies). Direct household purchases of educational goods and services are excluded from the main calculations of initial and final portions of expenditure.

Notes on specific countries

Coverage

Canada, **Norway**: Figures provided for secondary education *also include* expenditure on primary education.

Czech Republic, **Germany**, **Norway**: Figures cover expenditure on *public* institutions *only*.

Ireland, Hungary, Korea, Sweden: Data on expenditure by resource category refer to expenditure on public institutions only, but the figures on average staff and teacher compensation per student have been *estimated* on the basis of expenditure per student in both public and private institutions.

Switzerland: Compensation of teachers and other staff does *not include* expenditure on social security and other non-salary compensation. These items are, however, included in total expenditure, which is therefore greater than the sum of compensation of teachers and other staff.

Notes on methodology

Denmark: The breakdown of expenditure by category is estimated.

Sources

1995 UNESCO/OECD/EUROSTAT (UOE) data collection on education statistics. For details, see sources for *Indicator F1*.

INDICATOR F12: PUBLIC FUNDS BY LEVEL OF GOVERNMENT

See also notes on Indicator F1.

General notes

Notes on methodology

See also notes on *Indicator F5*.

Notes on specific countries

Notes on interpretation

Czech Republic: In comparison with the 1995 edition of *Education at a Glance*, a significant increase in central government expenditure can be observed, due to an increase of over 50 per cent in central government expenditure during 1993 while local government expenditure has remained practically unchanged.

Finland: The initial sources of funds for central and local government in 1993 are not comparable with those reported in the 1995 edition of *Education at a Glance* because the system of educational finance has been reformed.

Notes on methodology

Hungary: Regional governments (counties) and municipalities have been regarded as local government agencies because regional governments have no significant redistributive role: they provide services which are not provided by municipalities in the region.

Japan: Expenditure by prefectures and municipalities (regional and local funds) cannot be reported separately.

Sources

1995 UNESCO/OECD/EUROSTAT (UOE) data collection on education statistics. For details, see sources for *Indicator F1*.

INDICATOR F13: PROPORTION OF PUBLIC EXPENDITURE SPENT ON EDUCATION

See also notes on Indicator F1.

General notes

Notes on methodology

- Trend data

The data include public subsidies which are not attributable to household payments for educational institutions. For 1992 and

Annex 3 – Sources, methods and technical notes

1993, possible inconsistencies with the 1995 edition of *Education at a Glance* may arise because reporting practices changed in 1992.

- Calculation of estimates in Chart F13.1(B)

The estimates in Chart F13.1(B) were calculated as follows: Let $B(i)$ be the percentage of persons 5 to 29 years of age in the total population of country i, divided by the average percentage of 5 to 29 year-olds in all OECD countries for which data are available. Let $A(i)$ be the expenditure on educational institutions as a percentage of total public expenditure in country i. The expected difference for country i shown in Chart F13.1(B) was then calculated as $A(i)/B(i) - A(i)$.

Notes on specific countries

Coverage

Australia: Trend data: The 1993 figure *includes* estimates for research carried out in universities.

Belgium: Public subsidies to the private sector *include* scholarships only.

Germany: Trend data: For the period 1985-92 data refer to the former territories of the Federal Republic of Germany.

Mexico: Trend data: *Only includes* federal (central) public education expenditure.

Portugal, **Turkey**: Figures on total public expenditure from OECD National Accounts are *not available* for 1993.

Sweden: Trend data: The 1985-91 figures do *not include* expenditure on adult education and include only the (estimated) educational element of early childhood education for 6 year-olds. The 1992 figures *include* municipal adult education and all expenditure on early childhood education (for children aged 3 and over). The 1993 figures include adult education but only the (estimated) educational element of expenditure on early childhood education (3 and over).

Sources

1995 UNESCO/OECD/EUROSTAT (UOE) data collection on education statistics. For details, see sources for *Indicator F1*.

INDICATOR P1: PARTICIPATION IN FORMAL EDUCATION

General notes

Notes on methodology

Statistics which relate participation data to population data are published for the reference date that was used by national authorities for these statistics. The assumption is made that age references in the enrolment data refer to 1 January of the reference year. Population data are, where necessary, linearly interpolated to 1 January as the reference date (which for most countries is a good proxy for the mid-point of the school year) except for **Australia**, **Korea** and **New Zealand** where 1 July is used as the reference date for both enrolments and population data.

The dates or periods at which students, educational staff and educational institutions were counted have not been provided to the Secretariat by all countries. Nevertheless, it is known that some countries collect these statistics through surveys or administrative records at the beginning of the school year while others collect them during the school year, and yet others at the end of the school year or at multiple points during the school year. It should be noted that differences in the reference dates between, for example, enrolment data and population data can lead to errors in the calculation (e.g. net enrolment rates exceeding 100 per cent) in cases where there is a significant decrease or increase over time in any of the variables involved. If the reference date for students' ages used in the enrolment data differs from the reference date for the population data (usually 1 January of the reference year), this can be a further source of error in enrolment rates.

Participation rates are based on head counts of enrolments and do not differentiate between full-time and part-time enrolments.

Calculations of school expectancy for a 5 year-old child are based on head counts instead of full-time equivalents, which were used in the 1995 edition of *Education at a Glance*.

Trend data: Because of the revision of the OECD-INES data-collection instruments in 1985, there are differences in coverage prior to that date.

Notes on specific countries

Coverage

Australia: Private vocational education and training institutions are *not included*.

Austria, **Germany**, **Norway**, **Portugal**, **Spain**: Figures for government-dependent private institutions *also include* some independent private institutions.

Belgium: Data for independent private institutions are *not available*. Since institutions of this type are not very numerous, data for all types of institution are only slightly underestimated.

Germany: Students pursuing doctoral studies are not obliged to register at university and it is not possible to estimate their number. Trend data: for the period 1985-92, data refer to the former territories of the Federal Republic of Germany.

Hungary: Disabled students have been *included* in the figures for the primary and lower secondary level of education.

Annex 3 – Sources, methods and technical notes

Netherlands: Only educational programmes with a theoretical duration of more than 12 months are *included*.

United Kingdom: Data on vocational programmes at upper secondary level in independent private institutions are *not available*. Their number is quite small but not negligible.

Notes on interpretation

Australia: Figures for 1994 are not fully comparable with those published in the 1995 edition of *Education at a Glance*, since the classification of vocational education and training (VET) has changed. Some student streams classified in previous years as non-university tertiary education have been allocated to lower levels of education, especially to the upper secondary level. Full-time equivalent enrolments are low compared with total head-count enrolments, because students in VET are mostly part-time. Also, apprentices are considered part-time instead of full-time students, since the new VET sector recording system does not separately identify apprentices.

Germany: Most private institutions are government-dependent.

Iceland: Data for early childhood education are not available. The results for all levels of education combined may therefore be slightly underestimated.

Ireland: Net enrolment rates exceed 100 for some ages. The reason lies partly in the nature of the provisional population estimates supplied by the Central Statistics Office, partly in a possible over-reporting of enrolments by schools, and partly in the fact that enrolment data are collected by a "year of birth" definition, so that the reference years for enrolment (collected on 30 September) and population data do not match.

Japan: Net enrolment rates exceed 100 for some ages because there are different reference dates for school enrolment and demographic data.

Mexico: Net enrolment rates exceed 100 in some years because there are different reference dates for the school enrolment and the demographic data.

New Zealand: The 5-14 year-old participation rate is over 100 because of a census undercount. Education in New Zealand is compulsory from 6 to 16 years of age, and all 5 year-olds attend school or pre-school.

Notes on methodology

Czech Republic: All data on enrolments by age are estimates (with the exception of children in early childhood education). The so-called "extraordinary students" (studying only some courses) are classified as part-time students. Adult students are classified as full-time students, since they follow the same curriculum and take the same examinations as other students.

Denmark: All ordinary formal education is classified as full-time education. The number of students refers to the number of persons enrolled on 1 October.

Hungary: Age distribution data (by single age) are not available for tertiary education.

Japan: Figures broken down by age are estimates for primary, lower secondary and upper secondary education.

Mexico: Teacher training programmes are classified as programmes at the non-university tertiary level. Job-related training is classified as lower secondary education.

Norway: Figures broken down by age are estimates for primary and lower secondary education.

United States: No distinction is made between full-time and part-time students in upper secondary education.

Sources

1995 UNESCO/OECD/EUROSTAT (UOE) data collection on education statistics. For details, see sources for *Indicator F1*.

INDICATOR P2: PARTICIPATION BY YOUNG CHILDREN

See also notes on Indicator P1.

Notes on specific countries

Coverage

Australia, Iceland: Data on early childhood education are *not available*.

Austria: Figures refer only to kindergartens and pre-primary classes in primary schools. Day-care centres are generally *excluded*.

Denmark: Early childhood education *includes* children above 3 years of age in kindergartens, "age-integrated institutions" and pre-primary classes in primary schools. Children in crèches (normally below 2 years of age) are *excluded*. Children in private day-care/child-minding institutions are also *excluded*. Children in private kindergartens (receiving substantial public subsidies) are *included* in public institutions.

United Kingdom: At ages 2 to 4, early childhood education refers to public nursery schools and to nursery classes in public primary schools. Children in educational programmes such as play groups and day-care facilities are *excluded*: data are therefore underestimated.

Notes on interpretation

Czech Republic: There are no private kindergartens.

Denmark: In contrast to the 1995 edition of *Education at a Glance*, "age-integrated institutions" (similar to kindergartens) have now been *included*.

Annex 3 – Sources, methods and technical notes

Hungary: Deviations from figures published in the 1995 edition of *Education at a Glance* can be attributed, in part, to the fact that age groups are defined differently.

Ireland, Japan, Mexico, New Zealand: See also notes on *Indicator P1*. In contrast to the 1995 edition of *Education at a Glance*, day nurseries are now *included*.

United Kingdom: Ages are calculated at 31 August, but children are counted in the following mid-January, so some children are actually older than their measured age.

Notes on methodology

Denmark: Age groups for children in pre-primary classes in primary schools are estimated. A small number of children enrolled in both kindergartens and pre-primary classes in primary schools are classified as enrolled in primary school.

Japan, Norway: See notes on Indicator P1.

Poland: Figures on enrolments in early childhood programmes and enrolments by single year of age are estimates.

Sources

1995 UNESCO/OECD/EUROSTAT (UOE) data collection on education statistics. For details, see sources for *Indicator F1*.

INDICATOR P3: PARTICIPATION IN EDUCATION TOWARDS THE END OF COMPULSORY SCHOOLING AND BEYOND

See also notes on Indicator P1.

General notes

Notes on methodology

In contrast to the 1995 edition of *Education at a Glance*, calculations are now based on head counts instead of full-time enrolments.

Notes on specific countries

Coverage

Austria: The age distribution for non-university tertiary education is *not available*. But non-university tertiary education enrolments are negligible, in comparison with all tertiary education combined.

Belgium: Some students in full-time vocational programmes are *included* in general programmes of lower secondary education.

Czech Republic, Denmark, Hungary, Norway: See notes on *Indicator P1*.

Ireland: In upper secondary education, age 20 refers to ages 20-24. In part-time upper secondary education, age 24 refers to ages 24 and over. Persons aged 13 and over enrolled in special schools are classified as "not allocated by level".

Japan: For tertiary-level enrolments, data broken down by single age are *not available*.

Mexico: For first-degree university-level enrolments, data broken down by single age are *not available*.

Poland: In upper secondary education, data broken down by single age are *not available* for the age group 20-24.

Portugal: Distribution by age does *not include* enrolments for Madeira and Açores.

Sweden: Adult students in primary and secondary education are *not classified* by age.

United Kingdom: Vocational education figures are normally *only available* for students in their last two years of upper secondary education. Enrolments in private institutions for vocational programmes in upper secondary education are *excluded*. Students in private tertiary education aged 19 and over are *excluded*, in order to avoid possible double counting with public sector provision.

Notes on interpretation

Australia: In comparison with the 1995 edition of *Education at a Glance*, there is a significant change in the proportion of upper secondary students enrolled in general programmes relative to those enrolled in vocational programmes. This can be attributed to the review of non-university tertiary education: the majority of vocational programmes previously allocated to non-university tertiary education (ISCED 5) are now considered upper secondary education (ISCED 3). There are a large number of people enrolled in Technical and Further Education (TAFE) courses in upper secondary education outside the typical age group, and a large proportion of these attend part-time.

Belgium: In comparison with the 1995 edition of *Education at a Glance*, there are some changes in the proportion of students enrolled at age 15, 16 and 17: these are due to the fact that compulsory schooling now ends at 17 years of age, and that there are a great number of foreign students – mostly from France and Luxembourg – in the schools of the French Community (especially in vocational and technical programmes) who are now included. The increase in enrolment rates in this age group is also due to improvement in data collection (particularly for combined school and work-based programmes). Data shown in the 1995 edition of *Education at a Glance* were underestimated. The classification of general and vocational programmes has changed: various programmes which were considered general programmes in the 1995 edition of *Education at a Glance* are now included as vocational and technical programmes.

Annex 3 – Sources, methods and technical notes

Czech Republic: The classification of general and vocational programmes has changed by comparison with figures shown in the 1995 edition of *Education at a Glance*: various programmes which were considered general programmes in the 1995 edition are now included as vocational and technical programmes. These programmes combine both general and technical education, but prepare students for particular groups of occupations.

Italy: The classification of general and vocational programmes has changed by comparison with figures shown in the 1995 edition of *Education at a Glance*: Istituti Magistrali (teacher training institutions), which were considered general programmes in the 1995 edition, have now been reclassified as vocational programmes.

Japan: *See notes on Indicator P1.*

New Zealand: There are considerable deviations from figures shown in the 1995 edition of *Education at a Glance* due to the inclusion of "Training Opportunity Programmes" at the upper secondary level.

Spain: *See also notes on Indicator P1.* In the typical age group for all upper secondary first programmes, ages 14 to 17, the enrolment rate is greater than 100 because of repeaters and partial matriculations.

United Kingdom: Enrolment in vocational courses is inflated by large numbers of adults taking one or two courses at the upper secondary level who are much older than the typical age. Participation rates are slightly under-reported due to the lack of reliable estimates of the number of enrolments in independent private institutions at upper secondary level (vocational and technical programmes).

Notes on methodology

Czech Republic, **Finland**, **Greece**, **Ireland**: Figures broken down by single age are estimates.

Greece: For the distribution of enrolments by single age, no distinction is made between lower and upper secondary education.

Japan, **Mexico**, **United Kingdom**: *See notes on Indicator P1.*

Sources

1995 UNESCO/OECD/EUROSTAT (UOE) data collection on education statistics. For details, see sources for *Indicator F1*.

INDICATOR P6: PARTICIPATION IN TERTIARY EDUCATION

See also notes on Indicator P1.

Notes on specific countries

Coverage

Austria: *See notes on Indicator P3.*

Germany: Trend data: For the period 1985-92, data refer to the former territories of the Federal Republic of Germany.

Notes on interpretation

Australia: *See notes on Indicator P1.* By comparison with the 1995 edition of *Education at a Glance*, the number of non-university tertiary enrolments has decreased significantly. This is because a substantial number of vocational programmes previously allocated to non-university tertiary education are now included in lower and upper secondary education.

Canada: The number of students enrolled in non-university tertiary education has significantly increased by comparison with figures provided in the 1995 edition of *Education at a Glance*. This can be attributed to the fact that prior to 1992/93, enrolment data only included provincially registered schools, required to meet certain provincial standards. A survey conducted in 1992/93 for the first time provided information on enrolments for non-registered private schools, which are now included.

Hungary: The higher education system consists of universities (4 to 6 years of study) and colleges (3 to 4 years of study). In 1991, colleges were reported as non-university tertiary education. In 1992, colleges with 3 years of study were reported as non-university tertiary education, while colleges with 4 years of study were reported as university-level education, first stage. Now all colleges are considered university-level education, first stage. Post-graduate education in colleges is considered university-level education, first stage, while post-graduate education in universities is considered university-level education, second stage.

Italy: Figures have considerably increased in comparison with the 1995 edition of *Education at a Glance* because vocational programmes at non-university level have now been included.

Japan: *See notes on Indicator P1.*

Notes on methodology

Czech Republic, **Hungary**, **Finland**: *See notes on Indicator P1.*

Ireland, **Mexico**, **Poland**: Ages 22-25 include ages 26-29.

Sources

1995 UNESCO/OECD/EUROSTAT (UOE) data collection on education statistics. For details, see sources for *Indicator F1*.

INDICATOR P8: JOB-RELATED CONTINUING EDUCATION AND TRAINING FOR THE ADULT LABOUR FORCE

Notes on specific countries

Coverage

Australia: Estimates of continuing education and training *include* persons studying part-time, enrolled for the whole or

Annex 3 – Sources, methods and technical notes

part of the year in external courses; training courses organised and run internally at the work place; and training courses run outside the work place (including some government training programmes). Persons enrolled only in full-time programmes at any time during the twelve months preceding the survey, and people pursuing only on-the-job training, are *excluded*.

Belgium: Data refer to every form of continuing education and training, and not only to job-related training. The 0.2 per cent of employees who attend full-time formal education are *included*.

Denmark: Persons in formal education are *included*.

Finland: Only the training of employees which is sponsored by employers is *included*.

France: In contrast to data shown in the 1995 edition of *Education at a Glance*, employees of small enterprises who have received training are now also *included*.

Germany: Initial training of students over 25 years of age in vocational schools and in the dual system is *not included*. Forms of continuing vocational training other than formal courses are also excluded: e.g. participation in short events such as lectures or half-day seminars, familiarisation at the work place, computer-aided learning at the work place, workshop circles and learning workshops. Data on training for the unemployed *include* formal training as well as on-the-job training if it is subsidised by the Federal Labour Agency.

Italy: Persons enrolled in ordinary school courses are *not included*.

Sweden: Data refer to a period of 6 months. Only training supplied or sponsored by employers is *included*.

United States: Data do *not include* full-time students. Persons who completed upper secondary education but did not obtain a diploma are *included* in lower secondary education. Employed persons who were on vacation during the survey week were *included* in the total number of persons employed.

Notes on methodology

Australia: These data are taken from a special household survey using a smaller sample than the one used to generate data for Indicators C1, C2, C11 and R21. The survey only asked questions about training courses attended over the last twelve months.

Belgium: *See also notes on Indicator C1.* The training rate for the unemployed is based on very few cases.

Denmark: Sample size: 15 600 with 11 741 respondents, of whom 6 633 were employed and 961 unemployed. Results are weighted.

France: The Labour Force Survey in France does not include questions on participation in continuing education and training during the 12-month or 4-week period preceding the survey. An estimate has been made taking from the Labour Force Survey the structural distribution of persons in continuing training at the time of the survey, and taking from an administrative source the total number of persons (employed and unemployed) who have participated in continuing training during the year.

Greece, **United Kingdom**: *See notes on Indicator C1.*

Switzerland: The training rate for the unemployed is based on very few cases.

United States: Data are from a telephone survey conducted on a nationally representative sample of all civilian, non-institutionalised persons in the 50 states and the District of Columbia.

Sources

Australia: Australian Bureau of Statistics, Survey of Education and Training, March to May 1993. Extracted from the published Unit Record File.

Belgium: Labour Force Survey, Spring 1994.

Canada: Supplement to the monthly Labour Force Survey, January 1994.

Denmark: Labour Force Survey, April 1994.

Finland: Supplementary Survey of Labour Force Survey, 1993.

France: Administrative data source (Ministry of Labour); Labour Force Survey, March 1994.

Germany: Training for employed persons: *Berichtsystem Weiterbildung* (Continuing education reporting system), 1994; training for the unemployed: Statistics of the Federal Labour Agency.

Greece: Labour Force Survey, 1994.

Ireland: Labour Force Survey, 1994.

Italy: Labour Force Survey, April 1994.

Spain: Labour Force Survey, second quarter 1994.

Sweden: Labour Force Survey, June 1995.

Switzerland: Supplement to Labour Force Survey, April-June 1993.

United Kingdom: Labour Force Survey, Spring 1994.

United States: U.S. Department of Education, National Household Education Survey (NHES), January - April 1995.

INDICATOR P11: TOTAL INTENDED INSTRUCTION TIME FOR STUDENTS AT THE LOWER SECONDARY LEVEL

General notes

Notes on methodology

List of possible subjects that are taught under the headings used in Indicator P11 (non-exhaustive enumeration, derived from notes provided by Member countries):

Annex 3 – Sources, methods and technical notes

Reading and writing in the mother tongue:
    reading and writing in the mother tongue
    reading and writing in a second "mother tongue"
    reading and writing in the national language as a second language (for non-natives)
    language studies
    public speaking
    literature

Modern foreign languages:
    foreign languages

Mathematics:
    mathematics
    mathematics with statistics
    geometry

Science:
    science
    physics, physical science
    chemistry
    biology, human biology
    environmental science
    agriculture/horticulture/forestry

Social studies:
    social studies
    community studies
    contemporary studies
    economics
    environmental studies
    geography
    history
    humanities
    legal studies
    liberal studies
    studies of one's own country
    social sciences
    ethical thinking
    philosophy

Technology:
    introduction to technology, including information technology
    computer studies
    construction/surveying
    electronics
    graphics and design
    home economics
    keyboard skills
    word processing
    workshop technology/design technology

Arts:
    arts
    music
    visual arts
    practical art
    drama
    performance music
    photography
    drawing
    creative handicraft
    creative needlework

Physical education:
    physical education
    gymnastics
    dance
    health

Religion:
    religion
    history of religions
    religious culture

Vocational skills:
    vocational skills (preparation for specific occupations)
    technical skills
    domestic science
    accountancy
    business studies
    career education
    clothing and textiles
    polytechnic programmes
    secretarial studies
    tourism
    handicraft

Other:
    Subjects that cannot be classified under one of the above headings are labelled "other".

Sources

The data for Indicator P11 were collected by means of an administrative questionnaire administered during the school year 1995/96 through National Delegates of the OECD-INES Network C. Responses were supported by references to formal guidelines and regulations.

Notes on specific countries

Coverage

Belgium: For the Flemish Community, data refer to general programmes only, school year 1992/93. For the French Community, data refer to the school year 1993/94.

Denmark: Vocational skills is not a subject as such, but an obligatory topic to be included in other subjects. "Other" subjects *include* "class time", which is one extra lesson a week for the class teacher. Technology is *included* in mathematics.

Finland: Technology is *included* in arts. Geography is *included* in science. "Other" subjects *include* home economics (114 lessons a year at age 13) and student guidance (76 lessons a year at ages 13 and 14).

Annex 3 – Sources, methods and technical notes

France: At ages 13 and 14, data *refer to* general programmes only.

Germany: Timetables of special schools (*Sonderschulen*) are *not included*. "Modern foreign languages" also *includes* classical languages such as Latin.

Greece: "Other" subjects *include* Ancient Greek literature (four lessons a week), home economics (one lesson a week), and, at age 14 only, civic education (one lesson a week).

New Zealand: The compulsory portion of the curriculum *excludes* languages other than English and religion. Data on the flexible part were not collected as part of the survey. Vocational skills are not distinguished apart from the list of essential skills in the New Zealand school curriculum.

Norway: "Other" subjects *include* home economics, student class councils and optional subjects (e.g. a second foreign language).

Spain: "Other" subjects *include* religion and its alternative, ethical thinking (54 hours a year).

Sweden: Technology is *included* in science for the 12 year-old age group. Religion is *included* in social studies. "Other" subjects *include* French/German and/or mother tongue for immigrants, and/or optional subjects.

Turkey: "Other" subjects *include* handicraft, accountancy, typewriting, road safety, computer studies, tourism and environmental science, public speaking and writing, nutrition, co-operation, family relations, etc.

Notes on interpretation

Austria: The flexible portion consists of optional subjects. Every student may choose a maximum of three. Not all optional subjects listed in the curriculum are offered at every school and no student is obliged to choose one.

Belgium: Education at the secondary level comprises three 2-year cycles. ISCED 2 is defined as following a non-specific curriculum, which corresponds for Belgium to the first cycle of secondary education.

Finland: According to comprehensive school legislation, the time of one lesson is 60 minutes, which includes at least 45 minutes' teaching or other classwork and at least 10 minutes' break.

Germany: The curriculum not only differs from *Land* to *Land*, but also among different types of school within each *Land*. In addition, some curricula allow the school to decide, in some subjects, whether to have one lesson more or one lesson less per week in that particular year or the following one. Not all students (about 50 per cent) study a second foreign language. Some students take other subjects instead, which may be vocational or technical. There may be up to 160 alternative lessons per year.

Greece: Private independent schools are under the same legislation as public schools concerning the minimum number of hours for each subject, but they may increase the teaching hours of subjects if they wish.

Ireland: Figures refer to the junior cycle in post-primary schools, which caters for the 12-14 year-olds.

The obligatory subjects are Irish, English, mathematics, history and geography, civics and physical education, plus at least two subjects from an approved list. Religion is regarded as an essential part of the curriculum in all schools. The vast majority of students in this age group take a science subject, usually for a minimum of 4 periods of 40 minutes each per week. In vocational schools it is not obligatory to teach history and geography. These schools can opt instead for more practical or vocational subjects.

There are no regulations regarding the amount of time to be spent on the different subjects of the curriculum. In general, approximately 21 hours and 20 minutes per week are spent on the compulsory portion of the curriculum and about 6 hours and 40 minutes per week on the flexible portion.

Italy: In 25 per cent of lower secondary schools, 340 additional hours are provided, which may be devoted to different subjects (curricular or extra-curricular activities).

New Zealand: The National Education Guidelines make it mandatory for all state and state-integrated schools to meet the requirements of the New Zealand Curriculum, which sets out seven essential learning areas (language and languages, mathematics, science, social sciences, technology, arts, and health and physical education) and seven essential skills (communication, numeracy, information, problem-solving, self-management, social and co-operative, physical work and study), but no apportionment of time is laid down.

In 1994, languages other than English was not compulsory except in a small number of schools where the *reo Maori* was compulsory. The most common language other than English was Maori, followed by French and Japanese. The learning area of technology consisted primarily of home economics and woodwork. A growing number of schools also included computer studies.

Religion is not taught in New Zealand's state secular education system, which comprises 90 per cent of schools. However, most state-integrated schools and independent schools include up to one hour per week of religious instruction in their compulsory curriculum.

Portugal: Figures refer to the third cycle of basic education (ISCED 2), which caters for the 12-14 year-olds. The "school-focused area" is one of the compulsory components of the curriculum. This is a cross-curricular component aiming at applying the knowledge acquired in individual subjects to multi-disciplinary activities and projects. It covers 95-110 hours per year taken from the curricular time assigned to the various subjects.

Annex 3 – Sources, methods and technical notes

Within the flexible portion of the curriculum, students must choose one of three optional subjects: second foreign language (105 lessons per year), music (105-175 lessons per year) or technology (105-175 lessons per year). For music, technology and physical education, the number of lessons per week may be increased from 3 to 5 if the necessary premises are available.

Spain: The curriculum specifies for what subjects 65 per cent of the school timetable must be used (55 per cent in the case of Autonomous Communities with their own language). The rest is laid down by the government of each Autonomous Community.

Sweden: The curriculum is defined in stages: one covers ages 10-12 and another ages 13-15, with an element of choice in how subjects are distributed over the years. Data reported are an average of the two stages.

Notes on methodology

France: The school year was taken to be 36 weeks long.

Germany: The curriculum differs among *Länder* and types of school. A typical pattern was extracted from the individual curricula and from a framework which was set by an agreement of the Committee of Ministers of Education (*Kultusministerkonferenz*). It was not possible to calculate a weighted average of all possible curricula. Normally the curriculum is expressed in lessons per week, sometimes also in lessons per year. In order to calculate the total number of lessons per year, the common practice in Germany is to multiply the number of lessons per week by 40, although there are fewer than 40 weeks of school if religious and public holidays are taken into account.

New Zealand: 100 schools representing a broad cross-section of New Zealand state, state-integrated, and private independent primary, secondary and composite schools were sent a questionnaire on the number of hours and lessons per week in form 2 (age 12), form 3 (age 13) and form 4 (age 14) for the subjects listed in the survey.

The curriculum is based on the average number of lessons per week times the required minimum number of weeks per year. The sums do not take account of occasional interruptions to the weekly programme, such as sports events, special assemblies, etc.

Portugal: The total number of lessons per year was computed on the basis of 184 teaching days (38.6 teaching weeks per year minus 9 public holidays = 36.8 weeks of 5 days).

United States: A stratified cluster sample (unweighted N = 16 883) was drawn from the population of students who were enrolled in 8th grade in 1987/88, for whom 9th grade transcripts were collected a year later (14 year-olds). Less than 5 per cent were excluded: these were students who could not participate in the study in 8th grade because of limited English proficiency or severe physical disability, and who were not enrolled in 12th grade in spring 1992. Data refer to average lessons actually taken: not all of them are compulsory.

Sources

Austria: Curriculum of the *Realgymnasium*.

Belgium: Curriculum of the three educational networks; Ministerial Circular, 13 May 1993.

Finland: Framework Curriculum for the Comprehensive School, 1985.

France: Regulations governing curricula.

Germany: Timetables of the different schools and *Länder*.

Greece: Ministry of Education, National Government Bulletin 185/A (Decree 447/93), 1993.

New Zealand: National Survey, New Zealand Ministry of Education, Data Management and Analysis, Policy Division, Nov.-Dec. 1995; National Education Guidelines, The New Zealand Curriculum Framework Education Act 1989, Section 65.

Norway: Curriculum Guidelines for Compulsory Education.

Netherlands: *Wet v.o.; Inrichtingsbesluit dagscholen VWO-HAVO, MAVO-VBO; Besluit kerndoelen en adviestabel basisvorming* 1993-1998.

Portugal: Guidebook for the school year.

Spain: Primary Education Academic Planning Service, Ministry of Education and Science.

Sweden: National Curriculum (*Läroplan för grundskolar*).

United States: National Education Longitudinal Survey (NELS 88), second Follow-up Transcript Component Aug. 1992 - Mar. 1993.

INDICATOR P22(A): STABILITY IN EDUCATIONAL STAFF AT THE PRIMARY LEVEL

General notes

Notes on methodology

The data for Indicator P22 were collected by means of an international survey of schools administered during the school year 1995/96 through National Delegates of the OECD-INES Network C. The target population of this survey were all schools at the primary level of education as defined by the national institutional structure of the education system, irrespective of the ages and grades of the students enrolled. The survey instruments were administered to school principals.

Sampling procedures were based upon an implicitly stratified probability sample of approximately 400 schools per country

Annex 3 – Sources, methods and technical notes

selected with probabilities proportional to their sizes. Samples were stratified by the size of schools and, in most countries, by geographical region. Additional implicit stratification variables were used as appropriate in the participating countries.

For 9 of the 12 participating countries the sample was selected at the international level on the basis of national sampling frames provided by the countries. In France, the sample was selected nationally in accordance with international guidelines. Italy and Spain used variants of the internationally proposed sample design that were approved by the Sampling Referee. Greece selected an equal probability sample of schools.

The response rates for the survey varied among countries from 56 to 83 per cent. The distributions of national relevant marker variables, such as geographical location, urbanisation and school denomination, were analysed to check the "representativeness" of the samples, particularly in cases where response rates were below 80 per cent (Belgium, France, Greece, Ireland and Portugal). The results of this analysis showed that the distribution of these variables in the samples were comparable to the corresponding population statistics.

Sources

1995/96 OECD-INES Network C School Survey.

Notes on specific countries

Notes on interpretation

Italy: Between 1985 and 1990, primary education underwent a process of renewal: new programmes were approved in 1985 and the new system was set out in a 1990 law. Primary school attendance is compulsory for children between 6 and 11 years of age.

The five years of primary school are divided into two cycles according to the developmental levels of the children: in the first cycle (two years) basic skills predominate, while the second cycle gradually introduces students to advanced concepts. The law provides for the presence of three teachers for every two classes or four for every three classes. Classes are made up of no more than 25 students, with a limit of 20 for classes containing a handicapped child, for whom a support teacher is provided in order to speed up integration and learning.

Schools are grouped into organisational units called *circoli didattici* (from one to ten schools, four on average). Schools belonging to a *circolo didattico* may be situated in different towns and are co-ordinated by a headteacher, who has an office in one of the schools but no teaching function. Data refer to such organisational units.

The low stability rating is due to both transfer and retirement of many teachers, as well as to the redistribution of schools within *circoli didattici*, which over the last few years was an attempt to make these units more efficient.

Portugal: Children at ISCED level 1 attend first cycle schools (primary schools) for the first four grades and second cycle schools or comprehensive schools for the following two grades. There are about 9 300 first cycle public schools, many of which are small and isolated: 50 per cent of them merge grades 1 to 4 in the same class. Although classes should have children from one age group, a class may include children from different age groups and schooling levels.

Second cycle schools (grades 5 and 6) and comprehensive basic schools (grades 5 to 9) both deliver the second cycle of basic education (grades 5 and 6) which is organised as a basic introduction to interdisciplinary subject areas, usually with one teacher per subject area or subject.

Figures on stability among headteachers are to be interpreted in the light of a formal policy allowing for the election of the headteacher every year in first cycle schools, and every two years in second cycle schools and comprehensive schools. However, about 50 per cent of the schools keep their headteachers for longer periods.

Spain: Spain appears in this survey as one of the OECD countries with the highest percentage of schools with more than 75 per cent of teachers remaining at the same school for more than five years, although it has been involved in a major educational reform in the last few years. Educational policy promotes the stability of teachers.

Headteachers do not have the same percentage of stability over 5 years in this survey. The Education Act establishes that the School Board must elect a new headmaster every three years (and from now on every four years) although the former headteacher may also be re-elected.

Notes on methodology

Greece: Schools were sampled with equal probability of selection. The sample in Greece does not meet the OECD-INES Network C sampling requirements.

INDICATOR P22(B): SCHOOL LEADERSHIP AT THE PRIMARY LEVEL

See general notes on Indicator P22(A).

Notes on specific countries

Notes on interpretation

Ireland: Headteachers of small primary schools teach on a full-time basis, while headteachers of large primary schools have no teaching duties at all.

Portugal: Notwithstanding the existence of formal and explicit job specifications for headteachers, figures for the time spent by headteachers on various tasks (averaged over schools) cover two quite different situations:

Annex 3 – Sources, methods and technical notes

a) First cycle schools (ISCED 1), where headteachers, although expected to invest some time in managerial activities, are formally employed only on teaching (35 hours per week like any classroom teacher).

b) Second cycle and comprehensive schools (ISCED 2), where headteachers are formally employed on both teaching and managerial activities. Depending on the size of the school, second cycle headteachers are to spend between half and none of their total working time (35 hours per week) on teaching.

The mean number of hours computed for headteachers' teaching activities includes the preparation and marking times formally allowed.

Spain: It is not only the headteacher who runs the school. The main decisions are taken by a school council (made up of the headteacher, the deputy head, students, teachers, parents, non-teaching staff and a member of the municipal council). The day-to-day running of the school is undertaken by a team composed of the headteacher, the deputy head and the secretary. Furthermore, there are heads of departments who co-ordinate and are responsible for groups of teachers.

INDICATOR P22(C): STAFF CO-OPERATION

See general notes on Indicator P22(A).

Notes on specific countries

Notes on interpretation

Finland: In the 1970s and early 1980s Finland had a national curriculum. During the second half of the 1980s and early 1990s Finland had a municipal (local) curriculum, which was prepared by the municipalities on the basis of the national core curriculum. During the last two or three years, each school has prepared its own (school-based) curriculum on the basis of the national core curriculum. Curriculum planning in schools is one reason why in recent years there have been many meetings in Finnish schools.

Italy: To become a headteacher it is necessary to have a degree, to have passed a national selection examination, and to have taught for at least 5 years.

Formal meetings of the entire staff convened by the headteacher refer to meetings of all the teachers within a *circolo didattico*, the organisational unit of a group of schools.

Portugal: The distribution of values on the frequency of staff meetings is to be directly related to the different organisational categories of the schools involved: first cycle, second cycle, and comprehensive schools. Data are therefore meaningful when analysed by stratum.

INDICATOR P22(D): MONITORING AND EVALUATION AT THE PRIMARY LEVEL

See general notes on Indicator P22(A).

Notes on specific countries

Notes on interpretation

Austria: According to an ordinance based upon the School Instruction Act (*Schulunterrichtsgesetz*), performance of students is partly determined by assessing active participation in classroom work. In the first three grades, this form of assessment is the only accepted way of evaluating students' progress. In practice it comprises short questions which are to be answered during lessons and brief written tests (about 10-15 minutes) in mathematics and German (dictations and writing down short texts from memory). It lies within the discretion of the teacher how often this is done. The method of assessing active participation in classroom work may be an explanation for the relatively high frequency of evaluation activities in Austria. There is no standardised achievement testing.

Italy: Classes normally remain stable, made up of the same students from the first to the fifth year. Data concerning use of student evaluation for placing students in classes refer to those coming from other schools, redistribution from oversized classes, etc.

Portugal: There are two main types of student assessment: formative and summative evaluation. The former takes place throughout the school year and is intended to provide students, their parents or guardians and their teachers with information on their learning progress and on the attainment of curriculum objectives. Summative evaluation takes place at the end of each school term and at the end of each cycle, but not before the second grade.

In the first cycle (grades 1 to 4) summative assessment takes the form of a descriptive report, while in the second cycle (grades 5 and 6) it consists in giving marks between 1 and 5, together with a summary of the reports given during the formative assessment. For the purposes of transition, the summative assessment which takes place at the end of each cycle is expressed as a "Pass" or "Fail".

Spain: Standardised tests for the evaluation of students are not used. The approach to educational evaluation is qualitative rather than quantitative. Evaluation must be a continuous process at every level and its main purpose is to monitor students' progress with a formative intention, helping them and informing their parents about the learning process.

Annex 3 – Sources, methods and technical notes

INDICATOR P22(E): DIFFERENTIATION AT THE PRIMARY LEVEL

See general notes on Indicator P22(A).

Notes on specific countries

Notes on interpretation

Italy: Since the 1990 reform, every primary school teacher works with 2 or 3 classes, and each class has 2 or more teachers. Two teachers may be present in class at the same time, for limited periods, to carry out specific activities such as group work. Classes can be formed on the basis of ability groups, so that they contain the same proportions of groups at different levels.

Portugal: Heterogeneous grouping of students in classes is recommended. The policy of "streaming" students within classes is only used as a means of temporarily supporting students with learning difficulties. There are different types of support: individual tutoring, aptitude grouping for a period of time, specific timetabling arrangements, or alternative curricula. However, a number of schools use streaming on a permanent basis.

Figures on multi-grade classes apply only to first cycle schools (grades 1 to 4). Because of their small size, 50 per cent of these schools merge grades 1 to 4 in the same class. First cycle classes never exceed 25 children.

INDICATOR P22(F): ACHIEVEMENT ORIENTATION AT THE PRIMARY LEVEL

See general notes on Indicator P22(A).

INDICATOR P22(G): PARENTAL INVOLVEMENT IN SCHOOLS AT THE PRIMARY LEVEL

See general notes on Indicator P22(A).

Notes on specific countries

Notes on interpretation

Austria: As schools have little financial autonomy, the explanation for the relatively high percentage of schools where parents are involved in financial decision-making may lie in the law that gives parents the right to advise the school on the use of money which is directly given to the school. Most of a school's budget is, however, not administered by the school itself but by the education authorities.

With regard to staffing, Austrian schools do not act as employers: teachers are allocated to schools and employed by the federal or *Land* government. The result of the survey (8.3 per cent of schools reported that they had parental involvement in staffing matters) is hence somewhat surprising. However, the responses may have been influenced by the fact that the Austrian questionnaire also covered the allocation to classes of teachers already appointed to the school.

According to the School Instruction Act, each school must inform parents about the progress of their children by written report twice a year. The 75 per cent of cases in which schools regularly inform parents about children's progress refer to information given in addition to these compulsory reports.

Finland: In recent years, schools have prepared their own curriculum. Parents have therefore occasionally had more opportunities to become involved in curriculum and school planning.

Italy: Since 1974, some decisions concerning school life (e.g. school budget, choice of textbooks) have been taken by an elected committee of parents and teachers.

Parents do not take any part in the dismissal or recruitment of staff. But there may be cases in which staff organisation is discussed with parents (19.9 per cent).

Portugal: Figures on parental involvement are to be interpreted as the percentage of students who attend schools which have structures for participation and decision-making, and not as the percentage of students whose parents are actually involved in school decision-making.

Although the reliability of the values relating to involvement in decision-making about staffing is doubtful, the figures may be explained by the weight of first cycle schools (grades 1 to 4) in the sample. Non-teaching staff are not allocated to these schools, and very often parents are involved in their appointment.

INDICATOR P31: STAFF EMPLOYED IN EDUCATION

General notes

Coverage

The coverage of support staff is still uneven across countries. In some countries, such as the United States, "other support staff" includes bus drivers, custodians, clerical staff, district administrators and other non-professional staff which in many other countries, especially in Europe, are under the auspices of non-educational authorities and not included. For the definition of a teacher for the purpose of this indicator, see the *Glossary*.

Notes on methodology

To ensure comparability of the data with the 1995 edition of *Education at a Glance*, data on the number of teachers are

Annex 3 – Sources, methods and technical notes

divided by the number of persons in the total labour force, not by the number of persons employed. Between-country differences in this indicator are thus affected by differences among countries in unemployment rates.

In contrast to the 1995 edition of *Education at a Glance*, calculations are based on head counts instead of full-time equivalents.

Notes on specific countries

Coverage

Australia: Teachers *include* some principals, deputy principals and senior teachers who are mainly involved in administration.

Belgium: Primary and lower secondary education *includes* only primary education; upper secondary education *includes* all secondary education.

Finland: The total does *not include* teaching staff in kindergartens.

France: Primary and lower secondary education also *includes* upper secondary education.

Germany: Data on teachers of the work-based component of combined school and work-based programmes are *not available*.

Greece: Figures are underestimated because part-time teachers in early childhood and primary institutions are *not included*. Secondary part-time teachers in private institutions are also *excluded*.

Iceland: Data are *not available* for the following institutions: two out of the six government-dependent private institutions at primary and lower secondary level, the one independent private institution at primary and lower secondary level, the two private institutions at upper secondary level, three out of the 14 public institutions which offer vocational programmes at upper secondary level, and the two private institutions at non-university tertiary level.

Japan: Principals and deputy principals are *included* in "teachers".

Mexico: Data on "educational, administrative and professional staff" are *not available* for university-level education.

Netherlands: In contrast to the 1995 edition of *Education at a Glance*, teaching staff now *includes* principals and deputy principals. Teaching staff relates only to programmes designated for full-time attendance by students.

Sweden: For primary, lower and upper secondary education, not only teachers in ordinary comprehensive schools are *included* (*grundskola* and *gymnasieskola*), but also teachers in municipal adult education and in special education for severely handicapped and mentally retarded students. Figures for teachers broken down by level of education are estimates.

"Support staff" *only includes* support staff in public tertiary institutions.

Switzerland: For university-level education, only teachers paid from the regular budget are *included*, while those paid from external sources are *excluded* (200-300 persons, 100-150 in full-time equivalents).

United Kingdom: Figures on teachers in upper secondary education are *not included*. Educational personnel in nursing and paramedical non-university tertiary programmes are *not included*.

Notes on interpretation

Switzerland: Teachers at university level are not only involved in teaching, but also in research activities and services, in the following estimated proportions: teaching: 40-45 per cent; research and development: 35-40 per cent; services and other activities: 15-25 per cent.

Notes on methodology

Czech Republic: Separate figures for full-time and part-time personnel are not available. In the following cases, the distribution of staff by level of education is estimated from the number of students: basic schools (covering primary and lower secondary education), some *gymnasiums* (some of which cover both lower and upper secondary education), and some schools at upper secondary level which also offer post-secondary education.

Denmark: Most figures are estimates.

Finland: For central government institutions, figures on educational, administrative, professional and support staff are estimated on the basis of local government institutions. For government-dependent private institutions, the distribution between teaching and non-teaching staff and between the genders has been estimated.

France: The numbers of teachers in private institutions of tertiary education and in independent private institutions of secondary education are estimates. A significant proportion of educational and support staff has been estimated.

New Zealand: In primary and secondary education, most schools cover more than one level of education, so that exact numbers of teachers at each level are not known. These have been estimated according to the number of students.

Spain: The distribution of teachers by educational level is estimated, especially between early childhood, primary and lower secondary education, and between upper secondary and non-university tertiary education.

Sources

1995 UNESCO/OECD/EUROSTAT (UOE) data collection on education statistics. For details, see sources for *Indicator F1*.

Annex 3 – Sources, methods and technical notes

INDICATOR P32: RATIO OF STUDENTS TO TEACHING STAFF

See general notes on Indicator P31.

Notes on specific countries

Coverage

Germany: Trend data: For the period 1985-92, data refer to the former territories of the Federal Republic of Germany.

Sweden: Trend data: In the figure referring to 1994, students and teachers in municipal adult education are *included*.

Notes on interpretation

New Zealand: The decrease in the student/teaching staff ratio for early childhood education is largely explained by the improved coverage of data on staff in Maori pre-schools.

Sources

1995 UNESCO/OECD/EUROSTAT (UOE) data collection on education statistics. For details see sources for *Indicator F1*.

For sources on regional disparities in student/teaching staff ratios, see sources for *Indicator F3-R*.

INDICATOR P33: TEACHING TIME

General notes

Sources

The data for Indicator P33 were collected by means of an administrative questionnaire administered during the school year 1995/96 through National Delegates of the OECD-INES Network C. Responses were supported by references to formal guidelines and regulations.

Notes on specific countries

Coverage

Denmark: Teaching, preparation, and correction of papers are *included*.

Germany: For upper secondary vocational programmes, only teachers for the school-based portion of combined school- and work-based programmes are *included*.

Greece: For upper secondary vocational programmes, some laboratory hours are *included*.

Netherlands: Data for primary education *relate to* grades 5 to 8 (ages 9 to 12). For grades 3 and 4, data are the same as for early childhood education.

Portugal: For primary education, figures *refer only* to first cycle teachers (grades 1 to 4), who make up 50 per cent of all teachers in primary education. For secondary education, figures refer both to second and third cycle teachers (grades 5 to 9).

Sweden: For general programmes in upper secondary education, figures *refer to* teachers of general subjects in both general and vocational programmes. For vocational programmes in upper secondary education, figures *refer to* teachers of vocational subjects in vocational programmes.

Turkey: Figures for vocational programmes *include* practice hours spent in workshops at school.

United States: Figures *refer to* teachers at "regular", military-operated, "non-regular" (e.g. special education, vocational), and Bureau of Indian Affairs operated public institutions as well as teachers at private institutions (including religious and non-religious schools).

Notes on methodology

Austria: The staff law for teachers stipulates only the teaching time and not the average working time. Teaching time varies between 20 and 24/25 hours a week, depending on the type of school. A lesson lasts 50 minutes. All provisions concerning teaching time are based on the assumption that, together with other tasks a teacher has to fulfil, this amounts to a total of 40 hours a week.

Belgium: The maximum number of lessons a week in primary education is 28 (of 50 minutes). The school year consists of 36 weeks (37 weeks less 5/6 days public holidays). A teacher with a full-time appointment spends 23.33 hours per week teaching, 839.88 hours per year. Figures for vocational programmes at upper secondary level are estimated.

Denmark: In primary and secondary education, one lesson lasts 45 minutes, and the school year consists of 40 weeks. The maximum teaching time is 750 hours per year (3.75 hours per day). The hours of teaching for vocational programmes at upper secondary level vary from school to school. Figures for hours per day and per week are therefore estimated.

France: In early childhood and primary education, figures refer to official compulsory teaching time (26 hours times 35.5 weeks). At secondary level, figures refer to actual teaching hours per week, in relation to FTEs, including extra hours (18.6 hours times 35.5 weeks). In the data collection relative to 1991/92, hours per week did not include extra hours. An equivalent figure for 1993/94 would be 17.2 hours per week. Figures for lower secondary education are based on data for upper secondary education.

Germany: Decrees establish how many lessons (of 45 minutes) a specific type of teacher in a specific type of school is supposed to teach per week. It is assumed that the total working time (teaching plus other duties) will be the same

Annex 3 – Sources, methods and technical notes

as for all civil servants. Working days per year amount to 238 (365 – 52 Sundays – 75 days' holiday); teaching weeks per year are hence 39.7 (238:6, there being a 6-day week); and teaching days per year 190.5 (39.7 times 5.1 less the weighted average number of closed days, 11.8).

Greece: At primary level, there are 25 teaching hours per week. At secondary level, there are 21 teaching hours per week. The teaching year excludes Christmas and Easter holidays (about 4 weeks). For secondary education, the examination period is excluded (3 weeks).

Ireland: The school day for a primary teacher lasts 4 hours 40 minutes at ISCED 0 and an hour longer at ISCED 1. This time includes school assembly and recreational breaks. In secondary education, the length of the school day allows for a minimum of 6 hours of instruction. A teacher teaches on average 4.40 hours per day, i.e. 22 hours per week.

Italy: The number of teaching hours per year has been calculated as an average. The law establishes that the minimum number of actual school days (excluding public holidays and Sundays) must be 200. The minimum number of weeks is therefore 34 (6 working days a week). Italian norms also establish the number of teaching hours per week (25 for early childhood education, 22 for primary education, 18 for secondary education).

Netherlands: The law establishes the minimum number of teaching hours per year for early childhood education (880 hours) and primary education (1 000 hours). Given 40 school weeks, the minimum number of teaching hours per week is 22 in early childhood education and 25 at primary level. There are no survey results available about daily practice in schools.

New Zealand: 100 schools representing a broad cross-section of state, state-integrated, and private independent primary and secondary schools were asked for an assessment of the teaching and working hours per week. At primary level, figures represent the minimum number of teaching hours according to government regulations: 394 half-days, where a half-day constitutes a minimum of 2 hours' instruction, i.e. 197 days or 39.4 weeks. In practice, all primary schools provide more than 4 hours per day, averaging 4.8 hours or 23.8 hours per week.

At lower secondary level, figures represent the mean between those for primary and upper secondary education. Formal regulations require secondary students to be taught for 380 half-days a year (38 weeks), where a half-day constitutes 2.5 hours.

Norway: For primary education, the school year consists of 188 working days (five days per week, 38 weeks per year, two public holidays). The hours of teaching for a full-time teacher consist of 925 lessons of 45 minutes per year, i.e. 686 hours per year (3.7 hours per day, 18.5 hours per week).

Portugal: In early childhood, primary and secondary education, the working week for full-time teachers is 35 hours; the school year is 42 working weeks, of which 38.6 are devoted to teaching.

In early childhood and primary education, a full-time teacher spends 22.5 hours per week (25 hours less five breaks of 30 minutes) teaching. At lower secondary level, a full-time teacher spends 18.3 hours per week teaching (22 lessons of 50 minutes). At the top of the career ladder, a minimum of 38 per cent of the appointment is to be devoted to teaching. At the upper secondary level, a full-time teacher spends 16.7 hours per week teaching. At the top of the career ladder, a minimum of 33 per cent of the appointment is to be devoted to teaching.

Sweden: The number of teaching hours per week during the 178 days (36 weeks) of the school year is regulated for different types of teacher through national agreements between teachers' organisations, and the Swedish Association of Municipalities. For example, in upper secondary education, there are different agreements for teachers in general subjects, vocational subjects, artistic and practical subjects. Figures are roughly estimated according to the number of teachers in each group at the different levels.

Switzerland: Teaching time varies considerably by category of teacher and canton. The data represent a mean weighted by the number of teachers in each category and canton.

Turkey: Figures refer to the maximum number of teaching hours per week. Teachers must teach for a minimum compulsory amount of time, but may teach extra hours up to the figures provided for teaching time. For example, a teacher working in lower secondary education must teach 18 hours a week, but may teach 12 hours more if needed. In upper secondary education, the compulsory number of teaching hours per week is 15.

United States: Hours per year are calculated from hours per week and weeks per year. Hours per day at secondary level include time when students are moving from one class to another. Teachers do not have a formal break during this time.

Sources

Austria: School Period Act, "Staff Hours for Teachers", Austrian School Statistics.

Belgium: Flemish Community: *Onderwijszakboekje 1993-1994, Jaarkalender basisonderwijs, secund. onderwijs 1993-1994.*

French Community: Ministerial Circular, 13 May 1993.

Czech Republic: Ministry of Education, Youth and Sport of the Czech Republic, Act No. 503/1992 (official regulations and circulars of the Ministry of Education).

Denmark: Collective agreements.

France: For early childhood and primary education: service regulations; for secondary education: survey on conditions of service for teachers in public secondary national education.

Germany: Official regulations; school calendar; documents of the *Kultusministerkonferenz* (Committee of Ministers of Education, KMK).

Annex 3 – Sources, methods and technical notes

Greece: National legislation.

Ireland: Department of Education, official Regulations and Circulars.

Italy: National legislation: DPR 399/88; L 476/86; DPR 417/74.

Netherlands: For early childhood and primary education: *Wet Basisonderwijs* and *Rechtspositiebesluit Basisonderwijs*; for secondary education: *Rechtspositiebesluit Onderwijspersoneel*.

New Zealand: Education Act 1989 sections 20, 25, 65; State collective contracts for primary teachers (section 2.9) and secondary teachers (sections 4.1 to 4.6), 1994; key staff from Ministry of Education, Catholic Schools' Council, Independent Schools' Association, and New Zealand Education Institute; National survey (data on samples), Nov./Dec. 1995.

Norway: Agreements between the Ministry of Education and the teachers' unions on working hours and working conditions.

Portugal: Teaching Career Statute; School Calendar Bill (Desp. 123/ME/93).

Spain: For public institutions: Primary Education Planning Service, Ministry of Education and Science; for private institutions: National Institute of Quality and Evaluation, Ministry of Education and Science.

Sweden: National agreements.

Switzerland: Salary statistics, Swiss Teachers' Umbrella Organisation (*Association faîtière des enseignantes et des enseignants suisses, ECH*); Statistics on teachers 1993/94, Federal Statistical Office.

United States: National survey (stratified cluster sample, N = 55 447): Schools and Staffing 1993/94 (SASS).

INDICATOR P35: STATUTORY SALARIES OF TEACHERS IN PUBLIC PRIMARY AND LOWER SECONDARY SCHOOLS

General notes

Sources

The data for Indicator P35 were collected by means of an administrative questionnaire administered during the school year 1995/96 through National Delegates of the OECD-INES Network C. Responses were supported by references to formal guidelines and regulations.

Data on gross average salaries for persons employed full-time are taken from the OECD Earnings Distribution Database. For definitions, see Annex 3 in the *OECD Employment Outlook, 1996*.

Notes on specific countries

Coverage

Austria: There are only very few additional bonuses. Additional work is in most cases *included* in teaching time. This reduces the teaching obligation stipulated by law and may result in better paid overtime teaching.

France: Teachers in public institutions: data refer to school teachers for primary education and certified teachers for secondary education.

Germany: All data on salaries refer only to the former territories of the Federal Republic of Germany. Data on independent private institutions are *not available*. Salaries in private government-dependent institutions are the same as in public institutions.

Greece: Only overtime compensation is included as additional bonuses. This is 390 120 drachmas per year for early childhood and primary education and Dr 526 662 per year for secondary education. However, there are further possible occasional benefits such as marriage (Dr 8 000 per month), first child (Dr 4 000 per month), second child (Dr 4 000 per month), three children (Dr 16 000 per month), four children (Dr 26 400 per month), etc.

Italy: Only teachers in public institutions are *included*. Additional remuneration, though it exists, is *not included*.

New Zealand: No data are available for salaries of full-time classroom teachers with 15 years' experience. In 1994, virtually every teacher with 15 years' experience had reached the top of the appropriate salary scale consistent with their level of qualifications.

Portugal: Data *refer to* teachers having attended a three-year higher education course and professional training (Teaching Career Statute, public schools).

Sweden: *See notes on Indicator P33.*

Switzerland: Only teachers in public institutions are *included*. Figures for salaries of teachers with 15 years' experience refer to salaries of teachers with 11 years' experience.

Turkey: The salary of primary teachers *includes* 10 regular bonuses for extra teaching hours. The salary of lower secondary teachers covers 18 teaching hours. Additional bonuses cover 30 teaching hours.

United States: *See also notes on Indicator P33.* The figures for starting salaries and salaries of teachers with maximum qualifications at the top of the scale refer to teachers subject to salary schedules only (98.6 per cent of public school teachers). Salaries of teachers with 15 years' experience and salaries of teachers with minimum training at the top of the salary scale refer to all teachers, regardless of whether their salary is set by a formal schedule.

Annex 3 – Sources, methods and technical notes

Additional bonuses include extra compensation earned for extra-curricular or additional activities (such as coaching, student activity sponsorship, or teaching evening classes) and other earned income from teaching such as merit pay bonuses or state supplements.

Notes on interpretation

Denmark: In continuation schools at lower secondary level, there is an extra DKr 5 000 on the starting salary in boarding schools and an extra DKr 2 300 in additional bonuses.

Finland: Qualified teachers starting their career in 1993 all have a university degree. Teachers with 15 years' experience have qualifications which are not at university level.

Germany: Teachers with special tasks or functions can be promoted to the next salary group in some cases so that their gross salary is higher, although this is not counted as bonus. In early childhood education, there is a bonus system for whole salary groups. After four years of work, everybody in the salary group receives this bonus as part of the ordinary salary.

With regard to teachers at the top of the salary scale, each teaching category demands a different level of qualification and offers a different salary scale. The category which requires the longest or the highest level of training or education receives the largest salary throughout the scale. The starting salary is related to the actual age of the teacher at the time, so that the number of years taken to reach the top of the scale varies.

Greece: 90-95 per cent of teachers have a gross starting salary of 169 624 drachmas per month. There is also a small percentage of starting teachers who have a salary bonus because of higher qualifications: a teacher with a Master's degree receives a bonus of Dr 3 000 per month, and Dr 6 000 per month for a doctorate. After 32-35 years of teaching, there is a special bonus to the maximum salary of Dr 5 200 per month.

Ireland: In early childhood and primary education, salaries include an allowance of Ir£ 716 for a teacher with a basic degree. In secondary education, salaries include an allowance of Ir£ 716 for a teacher with a basic degree and Ir£ 228 for a teacher with the Higher Diploma in Education.

For salaries of teachers with maximum qualifications at the top of the salary scale, the amount of Ir£ 26 589 includes the maximum allowances of Ir£ 2 385 for a doctorate and Ir£ 480 for the Higher Diploma in Education (Hons). It does not contain any Post of Responsibility Allowance.

In early childhood and primary education, a full-time classroom teacher with 15 years' experience could receive one of the following additional bonuses: *i)* Vice-Principal: Ir£ 1 144 to Ir£ 4 818; *ii)* Post of Responsibility A Level: Ir£ 2 587; *iii)* Post of Responsibility B Level: Ir£ 1 144. At secondary level, a full-time classroom teacher with 15 years' experience could receive one of the following allowances: *i)* Post of Responsibility A Level: Ir£ 2 587; *ii)* Post of Responsibility B Level: Ir£ 1 144.

New Zealand: The only additional bonuses in 1994 were an isolation allowance, which varied from NZ$ 293 to NZ$ 3 000 depending on the degree of isolation, and a staffing incentive allowance of NZ$ 947 for starting teachers who took up full-time teaching positions in identified schools with a record of staffing shortage. A full-time classroom teacher with several years' experience can apply for a senior teacher's allowance (for primary teachers, NZ$ 2 306), or positions of responsibility (up to a maximum additional NZ$ 12 202, for secondary teachers). Primary teachers with maximum qualifications also qualify for increments of NZ$ 1 562.

Years from starting to top salary vary according to the starting qualifications of secondary teachers: eight years with a Bachelor's degree on average, seven years with an honours Bachelor's or Master's degree, and six years for a few teachers with the highest qualifications (Ph.D. or honours Master's).

Spain: Salaries of teachers in early childhood, primary and secondary education are the same. After 15 years' experience, salaries rise by five *trienios*. A *trienio* is a small supplement which is added for every three years of service (in both public and private institutions). For teachers in public institutions, another supplement is added: two *sexenios*. A *sexenio* is a new supplement added after every six years provided that the teacher has completed 100 hours of in-service training in that period of six years. The *trienios* have a different value at different ISCED levels (and vary between public and private institutions), while *sexenios* have the same value at all educational levels.

The retirement age is 65. In early childhood, primary and lower secondary education, it is assumed that teachers can begin their professional career at age 21 and can accumulate a maximum of 14 *trienios* (42 years). At upper secondary level, the initial training requirement is higher. It is assumed that teachers can begin their professional career at age 24, accumulating a maximum of 13 *trienios* (39 years). But until 1994 only a maximum of three *sexenios* was granted to public school teachers. No bonuses are given in addition to salary.

United States: The minimum training is a Bachelor's degree, and the maximum qualification is one year of training beyond a Master's degree. The top of the scale is 20 or more years of experience. Among teachers who receive additional bonuses, 95 per cent receive a smaller bonus than the maximum.

Notes on methodology

Finland: The basic salary is constructed from the Teachers' Wage & Salary Agreement. Data from National Statistics are used to compute average regional compensations including average compensation of teaching hours and other tasks which exceed hours covered by the basic salary. The percentage of the population covered is 98 per cent of primary and lower secondary education, 95 per cent of general programmes in upper secondary education, and 54 per cent of vocational programmes in upper secondary education.

Annex 3 – Sources, methods and technical notes

France: Starting salaries refer to third level of the salary scale, salaries at 15 years of experience to the eighth level, and salaries at top of the scale to the last level ("*hors-classe*"). Residence allowances (on average 1.3 per cent of salary) are *included*. Certified teachers receive also overtime compensation for 1.5 hours (average of extra hours taught by secondary teachers) and a fixed amount of the special allowance for follow-up and guidance of students.

Additional bonuses refer to maximum bonus which can be received by teachers employed full-time. For primary teachers, it includes a starting allowance, the *Zone d'Education Prioritaire* allowance, and the allowance for headteachers with 5 grades (except at the beginning of the career). For secondary teachers, it includes the starting allowance, the *Zone d'Education Prioritaire* allowance, and the main teacher allowance (flexible amount).

Germany: For the school year 1993/94, the annual pay increase took place rather late in 1994, so the scales for 1993 were valid for the whole period concerned. It was not necessary to calculate averages from two scales.

At the lower secondary level, there are at least three types of teachers with three different salaries. The recorded salaries are weighted means, with roughly estimated weights.

Spain: Figures refer to January 1994. Salaries are extrapolated to one full year.

Switzerland: Salaries vary considerably by category of teacher and canton. The data represent a mean weighted by the number of teachers in each category and canton. The number of years from starting to top salary varies among cantons: from 11 to 40 years in primary education and from 10 to 40 years in lower secondary education. Data represent a mean weighted by the number of teachers in each canton.

Turkey: The salaries of teachers working in independent private schools do not depend on the number of years of service but on the qualifications of the teachers.

Sources

Austria: Salaries Act, Austrian School Statistics.

Belgium: Flemish Community: *Afdeling Begroting en Gegevensbeheer*, Departement Onderwijs.

Denmark, Ireland, Norway, Switzerland, United States: See notes on Indicator P33.

Finland: Teachers' Wage & Salary Agreement of Municipalities, and Wage Statistics of Finland, 1991; Statistics Finland, October 1993.

France: Statutory texts; Budget of the Ministry of National Education.

Germany: Laws, salary tables, decrees.

Greece: Ministry of Education, data for 1992 (national legislation established in 1985).

Italy: National legislation: DPR 399/88 - DPR 13/86 art. 16 - DL 384/92 ext. 7 (converted L 438/92).

Netherlands: For early childhood and primary education: *Rechtspositie besluit Basisonderwijs*; for secondary education: *Rechtspositiebesluit Onderwijspersoneel*.

New Zealand: Primary and Secondary Teachers' Collective Employment Contracts, award settlement statement, 1994; National Survey, Ministry of Education, Data Management and Analysis, Policy Division, Nov./Dec. 1995.

Portugal: Teaching Career Statute; the collective work contract for private school teaching; System of Payments Act - *Portaria* 409/89.

Spain: For public institutions: General State Budget Act 1994; for government-dependent private institutions: General Agreement of Private Educational Establishments partially or wholly supported by public funds (April 1994); for private institutions independent of government: 4th National Collective Agreement of Private Education Centres not subject to control or receiving public support (1994).

Sweden: National agreements, 1 April 1992.

INDICATORS R6: STUDENT ACHIEVEMENT IN MATHEMATICS AND SCIENCE; R7: STUDENT DIFFERENCES IN MATHEMATICS AND SCIENCE ACHIEVEMENT; R9: DIFFERENCE IN ACHIEVEMENT BETWEEN TWO GRADES IN MATHEMATICS AND SCIENCE; AND R10: GENDER DIFFERENCES IN MATHEMATICS AND SCIENCE

General notes

Notes on methodology

The Third International Mathematics and Science Study (TIMSS) collected data on mathematics and science achievement of students in 44 countries at five grade levels. The data on which Indicators R6, R7, R9 and R10 are based concern achievement outcomes in the two adjacent grades in each country in which 13 year-olds are most likely to be enrolled (for the average age of the students tested in each country, see Chart R6.1). For most countries, the two grades tested refer to the seventh and eighth years of formal schooling (see Table R9.1). By convention, these two target grades are referred to as the "seventh" and "eighth" grade in this edition of *Education at a Glance*. The reporting of data on a sub-national level for Belgium and the United Kingdom is based on data availability from the International Association for the Evaluation of Educational Achievement (IEA) and does not

Annex 3 – Sources, methods and technical notes

represent a policy decision by the OECD. The term "country" refers to all entities for which data are reported as a convention.

The TIMSS achievement tests in mathematics and science are based on curriculum frameworks developed to cover the diverse topics and approaches common in the countries tested. The frameworks pertain to three aspects of teaching and learning in mathematics and science: curriculum content, performance expectations (e.g. routine procedures, reasoning skills, and non-routine problem-solving strategies), and perspectives (e.g. attitudes and beliefs about mathematics and science). For a description of the TIMSS frameworks, see D. F. Robitaille, W. H. Schmidt, S. Raizen, C. McKnight, E. Britton, and C. Nicol. *Curriculum Frameworks for Mathematics and Science: TIMSS Monograph Number 1.* Vancouver: Pacific Educational Press, 1993.

- Scaling

The tests in mathematics and science are scored using models based on item response theory. The scale scores in mathematics and science (i.e., the combined grade seven and eight scores) were standardised to produce an overall mean of 500 and a standard deviation of 100 for grades seven and eight combined, with each of the 44 participants in the TIMSS study weighted equally.

- Sampling and response rates

Multi-stage samples were drawn for each participating country. IEA established a set of standards to ensure that the samples obtained in all participating countries were of high quality. (See M. O. Martin and I. V. S. Mullis. *Third International Mathematics and Science Study: Quality Assurance in Data Collection.* Chestnut Hill, MA: Boston College, 1996.) The sample for a country was classified as fully meeting the IEA/TIMSS standards if it met four conditions:

1. the national sampling frame for the country (the "national desired population") included the full national population of students at the two grades tested;
2. no more than 10 per cent of sampled students were excluded from testing for special reasons (i.e., due to special education status);
3. the response rate for schools exceeded 85 per cent (or the combined school and student response rate exceeded 75 per cent) prior to the inclusion of any replacement schools; and
4. the classroom and student samples within schools were selected using a procedure that guaranteed that all classrooms and students at the designated grades had a chance of being drawn.

Fourteen of the countries included in R6, R7, R9 and R10 met all four of these conditions. These countries are: Canada, the Czech Republic, France, Hungary, Iceland, Ireland, Japan, Korea, New Zealand, Norway, Portugal, the Russian Federation, Spain and Sweden.

Countries that did not meet the guidelines are marked with one asterisk or with two, depending on the criteria they failed to meet: countries that did not meet all four criteria, but achieved a school response rate of at least 50 per cent before including replacement schools, met criterion 3 after replacement schools were included in the sample, and met criterion 4, are marked with one asterisk. All other countries that did not meet the four sampling criteria are marked with two asterisks.

- Calculation of OECD percentiles and OECD means

The OECD percentiles and means appearing in Indicators R6, R7, R9 and R10 are based on all OECD Member countries which participated in the survey. For purposes of computing the OECD means, a weighted average of the scores for Belgium (Flemish Community) and Belgium (French Community) was calculated and the resulting average was treated as a single country. The scores for England and Scotland were treated similarly. While the data for Mexico are not presented in the tables, they were used for the calculation of OECD means and percentiles.

Sources

These indicators are computed from data collected for the Third International Mathematics and Science Study (TIMSS), conducted by the International Association for the Evaluation of Educational Achievement (IEA). For a description of TIMSS, see D. F. Robitaille, W. H. Schmidt, S. Raizen, C. McKnight, E. Britton, and C. Nicol. *Curriculum Frameworks for Mathematics and Science: TIMSS Monograph Number 1.* Vancouver: Pacific Educational Press, 1993.

Notes on specific countries

Notes on methodology

- Countries/systems partially meeting sampling guidelines

Belgium (Flemish Community), **United States**: Achieved required response rate of 75 per cent only after including replacement schools.

England: Achieved required response rate of 75 per cent only after including replacement schools; and more than 10 per cent of the students were excluded from sampling.

Switzerland: Omitted four cantons from national sampling plan (sample includes 22 of 26 cantons).

- Countries/systems not meeting sampling guidelines

Australia, **Belgium** (French Community), **Netherlands**, **Scotland**: Did not achieve required response rate of 75 per cent. For **Belgium** (French Community): auxiliary data was provided that would suggest that the likely bias introduced by the low response rate would not significantly affect the means in Indicators R6, R7, R9 and R10.

Annex 3 – Sources, methods and technical notes

Austria: Did not achieve a 50 per cent school response rate before including replacement schools.

Denmark, Greece: Did not meet sampling criteria at classroom and/or student level.

Germany: Achieved required response rate of 75 per cent only after including replacement schools; omitted one region from national sampling frame (Baden-Wüerttemberg); and did not meet age/grade specifications in classroom/student sample (high proportion older than 13).

School and student-level sample sizes and combined school and student-level response rates

	% of population covered	% of students excluded	Number of schools sampled	Number of students sampled	Response rate before replacing schools (%)	Response rate after replacing schools (%)
Australia	100	0.8	161	7 253	69	70
Austria	100	3.1	124	2 773	39	80
Belgium (Flemish Community)	100	3.8	141	2 894	59	91
Belgium (French Community)	100	4.5	119	2 591	52	72
Canada	100	4.5	364	8 362	84	84
Czech Republic	100	4.9	149	3 327	89	92
Denmark	100	0.0	135	2 168	83	83
England	100	11.3	121	1 776	51	77
France	100	2.0	127	2 998	82	82
Germany	88	9.7	134	2 870	63	81
Greece	100	2.8	156	3 990	84	84
Hungary	100	3.8	150	2 912	87	87
Iceland	100	4.5	129	1 769	88	88
Ireland	100	0.4	132	3 076	76	81
Japan	100	0.6	151	5 141	87	90
Korea	100	3.8	150	2 920	95	95
Netherlands	100	1.2	95	1 987	23	60
New Zealand	100	1.7	149	3 683	86	94
Norway	100	2.2	146	3 267	87	93
Portugal	100	0.3	142	3 391	92	92
Russian Federation	100	6.3	174	4 022	93	95
Scotland	100	2.2	127	2 863	69	73
Spain	100	8.7	153	3 855	90	93
Sweden	100	0.9	116	4 075	90	90
Switzerland	86	5.3	250	4 855	92	94
United States	100	2.1	183	7 087	71	78

Annex 3 – Sources, methods and technical notes

INDICATOR R11: GRADUATES AT UPPER SECONDARY LEVEL

General notes

Notes on methodology

Statistics which relate data on enrolments to population statistics are published for the reference date that was used by national authorities for these statistics. The assumption is made that age references in the enrolment data refer to 1 January of the reference year. Population data are, where necessary, linearly interpolated to 1 January as the reference date (which for most countries is a good proxy for the mid-point of the school year) except for **Australia**, **Korea** and **New Zealand** where 1 July is used as the reference date for both enrolments and population data.

Graduation rates from general and vocational programmes do sometimes not exactly add up to the total, mostly due to differences in the underlying typical ages of graduation.

Typical graduation ages are shown in *Annex 1*.

Notes on specific countries

Coverage

Spain: For graduates from vocational programmes, adult education is *excluded*.

Sweden: For graduates from vocational programmes, only the *gymnasium* is *included*: adult and special education are excluded.

Notes on interpretation

Belgium: Graduation rates obtained are subject to bias for three reasons: *a)* presence of double counting, particularly for part-time programmes; *b)* diplomas in part-time programmes are awarded to students whose age is much higher than the typical age; and *c)* many diplomas are awarded to students aged over 18 or 19 years.

Czech Republic: Some programmes that were classified as general education in the 1995 edition of *Education at a Glance*, are now considered vocational education.

Ireland: Students graduating from vocational programmes receive only a certificate of participation, not a formal qualification; however, there are changes underway in this regard. Students of first educational programmes at this level have usually completed 12 years of education, and students in second educational programmes have usually completed 14-15 years of education.

Italy: For the first time, graduates from vocational programmes organised by the Regions have now been included.

Spain: There are considerable differences from data published in the 1995 edition of *Education at a Glance*, due to the new inclusion of *Escuelas, Taller y Casas de Oficios* (15 498 graduates).

Notes on methodology

Finland: For graduates from combined school- and work-based programmes, the age distribution is estimated. Graduates from second educational programmes are included in first educational programmes. Their number is insignificant.

Switzerland: Figures for graduates from final programmes are estimated.

Sources

1995 UNESCO/OECD/EUROSTAT (UOE) data collection on education statistics. For details, see sources for *Indicator F1*.

INDICATOR R12: GRADUATES AT THE TERTIARY LEVEL

General notes

Notes on methodology

By comparison with the 1995 edition of *Education at a Glance*, results are more detailed. They are now shown for each type of tertiary programme: non-university tertiary education and university-level education, short programmes, long programmes, second programmes (e.g. U.S. Master's), Ph.D. or equivalent programmes.

Typical graduation ages are shown in *Annex 1*.

Notes on specific countries

Coverage

Canada: Data on graduates at the non-university tertiary level of education *include* diplomas from very short programmes that in most other countries are not covered by the data. At ISCED 6, graduates from long programmes are *included* in short programmes.

Ireland: The following are *excluded*: full-time accountancy students who receive qualifications from professional associations; a significant number of part-time students in non-university tertiary education who receive professional qualifications from professional bodies (accountancy, marketing, secretarial); about 1 500 student nurses, who obtain a nursing qualification after completing 3-4 years of on-the-job training in hospitals; and graduates from independent private colleges. Only first-time graduates are *included* (unduplicated counts).

Annex 3 – Sources, methods and technical notes

National tertiary degree structures in selected countries

Degree or qualification	Entry requirement	Duration	Cumulative duration	Equivalent to a university degree?	Notes	Category in Table R12.1
Czech Republic						
Bakalár (Bak.)	Maturitní vysvedcení (12 years, secondary school leaving exam, entrance exam)	3	3	Yes	Not required in many institutions for graduate study. Considered equivalent to a Bachelor's	B
Magister (Mgr.)	Maturitní vysvedcení (12 years, secondary school leaving exam, entrance exam)	4, 5 (typical)	4, 5 (typical)	Yes	Considered equivalent to a Master's	C
Inzenyr (Ing.)	Maturitní vysvedcení (12 years, secondary school leaving exam, entrance exam)	4, 5 (typical)	4, 5 (typical)	Yes	Agriculture, Economics, Engineering. Considered equivalent to a Master's	C
Doktor vseobecné medicíny (MUDR) or Doctor veterinarní medicíny (MVDr), Inzenyr architekt (Ing. Arch)	Maturitní vysvedcení (12 years, secondary school leaving exam, entrance exam)	6	6	Yes	Medicine, Dentistry, Veterinary Medicine, Architecture	C
Doktor (Ph.D.)	Magister and an entrance exam	3	8 to 9	Yes	Considered equivalent to a Ph.D.	E
France						
Brevet de technicien supérieur (BTS)	Baccalauréat or Brevet de technicien	2	2		Holders of a BTS may, in certain conditions, continue their studies at university or higher schools	A
Diplôme universitaire de technologie (DUT)	Baccalauréat equivalent	2	2		Short course in technology offered by a university institute of technology. Holders of a DUT may, under certain conditions, continues their studies in a university programme	A
Diplôme des écoles supérieures spécialisées (eg. Social work)	Baccalauréat equivalent	2 or 3	2 or 3		Final qualification	A
Diplôme d'études universitaires scientifiques et techniques (DEUST)	Baccalauréat equivalent	2	2		Final qualification	N*
Diplôme d'études universitaires générales (DEUG)	Baccalauréat equivalent	2	2		First cycle of a university programme	N*
Licence	DEUG or DUT	1	3	Yes		N*
Maîtrise	Licence	1	4	Yes		C
Diplôme des écoles supérieures spécialisées (e.g. Architecture, law (notary), journalism)	Baccalauréat equivalent	5	5	Yes	Award often serves as a professional qualification	C
Diplôme de grande école (in a particular subject, e.g. commerce, engineering)	Baccalauréat equivalent, entrance examination taken after 1 to 3 years of post-baccalauréat preparatory classes	3	5	Yes	Award often serves as a professional qualification	C
Magistère	DEUG or DUT	3	5	Yes	University diploma, pluri-disciplinary in content	C
Diplôme d'études supérieures spécialisées (DESS)	Maîtrise	1	5	Yes	Professionally-oriented final qualification awarded after a year of research work	E
Diplôme d'études approfondies (DEA)	Maîtrise	1	5	Yes	First year of a 3-year programme involving a high degree of specialisation and training in research	E
Docteur en chirurgie dentaire, Docteur en pharmacie, Docteur en médecine	Baccalauréat equivalent	5 to 8	5 to 8	Yes	Dentistry (5 years), pharmacy (6 years), veterinary medicine, (6 years), medicine (8 years). Awarded at the end of professional training and the submission of a thesis (*thèse de doctorat d'exercice de la profession*)	C
Certificat d'études supérieures spécialisées (CESS) and Diplôme d'études supérieures spécialisées (DESS)	Docteur en chirurgie dentaire, pharmacie, or médecine	1	6 to 9	Yes	Post-graduate specialised training	E
Doctorat	Diplôme d'études approfondies (DEA)	3	8	Yes	Awarded after the submission of a thesis based on original research	E

* N = not included
Source: OECD Database. See Annex 3 for notes

Annex 3 – Sources, methods and technical notes

National tertiary degree structures in selected countries *(continued)*

Degree or qualification	Entry requirement	Duration	Cumulative duration	Equivalent to a university degree?	Notes	Category in Table R12.1
Germany						
Meister/Techniker, qualification of Trade and Technical Schools	Successful completion of vocational upper secondary (dual system)	1 to 4	1 to 4		Most programmes require prior work experience. 3- and 4-year programmes are mainly part-time	A
Qualification of Specialised Academies	Realschulabschluß	2	2		Only in Bavaria. Mainly kindergarten teaching, business administration, language translation	A
Qualification of Vocational Academies	Hochschulreife	3	3		Only in Lower Saxony and Schleswig-Holstein	A
Qualification of Health Schools	Completion of lower secondary general + prior vocational training/ experience + minimum age 18	1 to 3	1 to 3		Non-academic medical training. Duration varies by specialisation: 1 year: Auxiliary medical professions; 2 years: Medical assistants; 3 years: Nurses	A
Diplom (Fachhochschule)	Fachhochschulreife	4 to 5	4 to 5	Yes		C
Diplom (University) and similar degrees	Hochschulreife	5 to 7	5 to 7	Yes	Includes Magister, Staatsprüfung, Künstlerischer Abschluß, Kirchlicher Abschluß	C
Lehramtsprüfung	Hochschulreife	5 to 7	5 to 7	Yes	Teaching qualification, degree for teachers	C
Promotion	First university degree	2 to 3	7 to 10	Yes		E
Japan						
Jungakushi (Associate)	Upper secondary	2 to 3	2 to 3			A
Gakushi (Bachelor's)	Upper secondary	4	4	Yes		B
Gakushi (Bachelor's – Medicine, Veterinary Medicine, and Dentistry)	Upper secondary	6	6	Yes		C
Shushi (Master's)	Gakushi (Bachelor's)	2	6	Yes		D
Hakushi (Ph.D)	Shushi (Master's)	3	9	Yes		E
Netherlands						
Baccalaureus	11 years plus HAVO diploma	4	4	Yes	Degrees in teacher training, technical and commercial fields, social work, community education, health care, arts awarded by hogescholen (HBOs) Equivalent to U.S. Bachelor's degree	B
Ingenieur (ing).	11 years plus HAVO diploma	4	4	Yes	Degrees in engineering/agriculture awarded by hogescholen (HBOs) Equivalent to U.S. Bachelor's degree	B
Doctorandus (drs.)	12 years plus VHO diploma or 13 years plus HBO propaedeuse	5	5	Yes	Equivalent to U.S. Master's degree	C
Ingenieur (ir.)	13 years plus VHO diploma or 13 years plus HBO propaedeuse	5	5	Yes	Degrees in engineering/agriculture. Equivalent to U.S. Master's degree	C
Meester in de rechten (law)	14 years plus VHO diploma or 13 years plus HBO propaedeuse	5	5	Yes		C
Doctoraat	University or HBO degree	3	8	Yes		E

* N = not included
Source: OECD Database. See Annex 3 for notes

Annex 3 – Sources, methods and technical notes

National tertiary degree structures in selected countries *(continued)*

Degree or qualification	Entry requirement	Duration	Cumulative duration	Equivalent to a university degree?	Notes	Category in Table R12.1
United Kingdom						
Higher National Certificate	13 years, General Certificate of Education	1	1		Advanced technical training	A
Higher National Diploma	13 years, General Certificate of Education	2	2		Advanced technical training	A
Bachelor's degree	13 years, General Certificate of Education	3	3	Yes	An *honours degree* is at a higher level than an *ordinary* or *pass degree*. May include a sandwich course which incorporates periods of industrial training or professional experience outside the university	B
Bachelor's degree (MB, BDS, BV, etc.)	13 years, General Certificate of Education	5 to 7	5 to 7	Yes	Medicine, Veterinary Medicine and Dentistry	B
Post-graduate Certificate of Education (PGCE)	Bachelor's degree	1	4	Yes		B or D
Post-graduate Diplomas and Certificates (e.g. DipSW, PDA (Scotland only))	Bachelor's degree	1	4	Yes		B or D
Many professional qualifications in various fields (accountancy, law, audit, etc.) e.g. CIMA, Articles, Architecture	Bachelor's degree	1 to 3	4	Yes	Training takes place "on the job", but certification usually involves taking an examination and certification is through a professional body	D or N*
Master's degree (Taught, e.g. MA, MSc, MBA)	Bachelor's degree (honours)	1 to 2	4 to 5	Yes	Award based on a written examination and requires a memoir or short thesis	D
Master's degree (Research, e.g. MPhil)	Bachelor's degree (honours)	1 to 2	4 to 5	Yes	Award based on research and presentation of a thesis	D
Doctorate of philosophy (Ph.D.)	Bachelor's degree (honours)	4	7 to 9	Yes		E
United States						
Post-secondary awards, certificates and diplomas	Typically 12 years, High School diploma or equivalent (not always required)	1 to 4	1 to 4		Certificate is usually a final qualification for technicians	A
Associate of Arts or Associate of Science Degree (A.A. or A.S.)	Typically 12 years, High School diploma or equivalent (not always required)	2	2		Possible to receive credit for first 2 years of a Bachelor's degree programme	A
Bachelor of Arts or Bachelor of Science Degree (B.A. or B.S.)	12 years, High School diploma or equivalent	4	4	Yes	Two components: general education (humanities, social sciences, applied or natural sciences and fine arts) and an area of specialisation or major	B
Post-graduate certificates (e.g. Teaching Credential)	Bachelor's degree	1	5	Yes		N*
Master of Arts, Science, Fine Arts, etc. (M.A., M.S., M.F.A.)	Bachelor's degree	1 to 2	5 to 6	Yes	Duration varies by field and institution	D
Master of Business Administration, Public Administration, Public Health etc.	Bachelor's degree	1 to 2	5 to 6	Yes	Awarded for the completion of a professionally oriented programme	D
First professional degrees: Juris Doctorate (J.D.—Law), Pharm.D. (Pharmacy), Master of Divinity Degree	Bachelor's degree	3	7	Yes	Signifies both completion of the academic requirements for beginning practice in a given profession and a level of professional skill beyond that normally required for a Bachelor's degree	D
First professional degrees: Doctor of Medicine (M.D.), Doctor of Dentistry (D.D.S.), Doctor of Veterinary Medicine	Bachelor's degree	4	8	Yes		D
Doctorate	Master's degree	3 to 5	9 to 11	Yes	If a Master's degree is not required, then duration of programme is longer	E

* N = not included
Source: OECD Database. See Annex 3 for notes

Annex 3 – Sources, methods and technical notes

New Zealand, **United Kingdom**: At ISCED 6, graduates from long programmes are *included* in short programmes.

Portugal: Doctorates are not included: the graduation rate at ISCED 7 is therefore *underestimated*.

Spain: Master's or equivalent degrees at ISCED 7 are *included* in long programmes at ISCED 6.

Sweden: Second degrees awarded at ISCED 6 are *included* in ISCED 7 as Master's or equivalent (programmes of 3 to 5.5 years' duration).

Notes on interpretation

Canada: *See notes on Indicator P6.*

Czech Republic: A Bachelor's degree has been introduced. In some universities it is awarded after three years of study, which can be followed by a Master's degree (after an additional two or three years). In others, the first degree is the Master's degree, typically awarded after 5 years of study. Both types of Master's degrees are classified as a first degree for the purpose of this indicator (there is no distinction between the two types: neither in the length of study, nor in the amount of knowledge attained).

Denmark: There are no Bachelor's degrees in some fields of study (e.g. medicine and law), so that the first university degree obtainable is the Master's degree. The new classifications of university graduates vary therefore according to subjects.

Greece: First-degree programmes in medicine last six years. Engineering studies last five years and lead to a diploma which is a first degree but equivalent to a Master's. Post-graduate studies do not set limits to starting or ending ages and their minimum duration is two years for the equivalent of a Master's and three years for the equivalent of a Ph.D.

Iceland: In 1994, only four out of the five degree-granting institutions at the university level graduated students. One institution grants degrees only every other year, and 1994 was not a graduation year.

Netherlands: Short first university degree programmes refer to Higher Professional Education (HBO). Long first university degree programmes refer to the normal first university programmes leading to titles such as Drs., Mr. or Ir. (WO).

Norway: Some programmes at the non-university tertiary level of education last one year, while others last two years.

Notes on methodology

Ireland: Figures on full-time and part-time graduates are estimates, based on data from the first destination survey of full-time students only.

Sources

1995 UNESCO/OECD/EUROSTAT (UOE) data collection on education statistics. For details, see sources for *Indicator F1*.

INDICATOR R14: TERTIARY QUALIFICATIONS BY FIELD OF STUDY

General notes

Notes on methodology

By comparison with the 1995 edition of *Education at a Glance*, results are more detailed. Furthermore, the classification of subject categories has been changed in order to conform with ISCED. Data are therefore not comparable to the 1995 edition.

"Medical science" includes "Medical science and health related" (ISC50).

"Natural science" includes "Natural science" (ISC42), "Agriculture, forestry and fishery" (ISC62) and "Home economics (domestic science)" (ISC66).

"Mathematics and Computer Science" is defined in accordance with (ISC46).

"Humanities" includes "Education, science and teacher training" (ISC14), "Fine and applied arts" (ISC18), "Humanities, religion and theology" (ISC20), "Social and behavioural science" (ISC30) and "Other fields of study" (ISC89).

"Law and business" includes "Commercial and business administration" (ISC34), "Law" (ISC38), "Trade, craft and industrial programmes" (ISC52), "Transport and communications" (ISC70), "Service trades" (ISC78), and "Mass communication and documentation" (ISC84).

"Engineering and architecture" includes "Engineering" (ISC54) and "Architecture and town planning" (ISC58).

Notes on specific countries

Coverage

France: "Mathematics and computer science" *includes* "Natural science". "Engineering and architecture" *includes* "Trade, craft and industrial programmes" and "Transport and communications". "Humanities" *includes* "Agriculture, forestry and fishery", "Home economics", "Service trades" and "Mass communication and documentation".

Hungary: "Natural science" *includes* "Mathematics and computer science". "Humanities" only *includes* "Law and business".

Ireland: Not only first-time graduates, but all graduations are *included* (unduplicated counts are not available).

Japan: "Natural science" and "Engineering and architecture" *include* "Mathematics and computer science". "Law and business" *includes* "Social and behavioural science". "Engineering and architecture" *includes* "Trade, craft and industrial programmes".

Annex 3 – Sources, methods and technical notes

Korea: For university-level education only, "Natural science" *includes* "Mathematics and computer science". The category "Law and business" is *partly included* in "Humanities" and partly in "Engineering and architecture": "Humanities" *includes* "Commercial and business administration" (ISC34), "Law" (ISC38), "Service trades" (ISC78) and "Mass communication and documentation" (ISC84); "Engineering and architecture" *includes* "Trade, craft and industrial programmes" (ISC52) and "Transport and communications" (ISC70).

Notes on interpretation

Belgium, Canada, Japan, Korea, Netherlands, New Zealand, Norway, Spain, United States: The sum of all categories does not always equal 100 because the category "field of study unknown" (ISC99) is not taken into account in the calculations and is sometimes not negligible.

Canada: See notes on Indicator P6.

Czech Republic: The number of degrees in "Law and business" has increased significantly in recent years.

Spain: See notes on Indicator R12.

Sources

1995 UNESCO/OECD/EUROSTAT (UOE) data collection on education statistics. For details, see sources for *Indicator F1*.

INDICATOR R15: SUPPLY OF HIGH LEVEL QUALIFICATIONS IN SCIENCE RELATED FIELDS

General notes

Notes on methodology

The "Science" category takes into account the following fields of study: "Natural science" (ISC42), "Mathematics and computer science" (ISC46), "Engineering" (ISC54), "Architecture and town planning" (ISC58), "Agriculture, forestry and fishery" (ISC62) and "Home economics (domestic science)" (ISC66). Since the classification of the fields of study has changed, the new results cannot be compared with the results published in previous editions of *Education at a Glance*.

Notes on specific countries

Coverage

Japan: "Science" *includes* "Trade, craft and industrial programmes".

Notes on interpretation

Finland: By comparison with the 1995 edition of *Education at a Glance*, there is a growth in the proportion of scientific graduates: this is due to the increase in leaving certificates and degrees (13 per cent) and the decrease in the labour force aged 25-34 (0.9 per cent).

Sources

1995 UNESCO/OECD/EUROSTAT (UOE) data collection on education statistics. For details, see sources for *Indicator F1*.

INDICATORS R21(A): UNEMPLOYMENT AND EDUCATION; AND R21(B): YOUTH UNEMPLOYMENT AND EDUCATION

See notes on Indicator C1.

General Notes

In some countries the age group 20-24 includes a significant number of persons who are working while at school.

Notes on specific countries

Coverage

France: Apprentices are not included in the labour force.

INDICATOR R22: EDUCATION AND EARNINGS FROM EMPLOYMENT

Notes on specific countries

Coverage

Australia: The income data refer to "usual earnings with employees' main employer" over the reference period (weekly earnings). The data *exclude* income earned from own business.

Belgium: Data refer to monthly income after taxes, recalculated to gross yearly income using general tax percentages.

Denmark: The total population is *included*.

France: The self-employed are not *included* (e.g. liberal professions, artisans, etc.). Data refer to monthly income after taxes (month of the survey).

Italy: Data refer to earnings after taxes.

Netherlands: Earnings from work are defined here as the gross annual earnings from the work of individuals, excluding employers' contributions to social security and similar schemes.

New Zealand: Estimates relate to income of persons living in private households only (i.e. *excluding* those living in boarding houses, hotels, army camps, old people's homes, etc.).

Norway: Compared to the 1995 edition of *Education at a Glance*, employers' contributions to social security schemes

Annex 3 – Sources, methods and technical notes

are *no longer included*. These benefits accounted for about 1 per cent of the total income in 1992.

Spain: Data refer to monthly earnings of people who have worked 15 hours or more per week.

Sweden: Data refer to annual earnings from work before taxes.

Switzerland: Data refer to monthly income (month prior to the interview). Early childhood primary and primary education is *included* in lower secondary education.

United Kingdom: Estimates of gross yearly income are based on usual weekly earnings.

Notes on interpretation

Denmark: The total educational attainment of the population is underestimated because the category "unknown" has been included in lower secondary education. A part of this category (e.g. some immigrants) may have higher educational attainment.

Notes on methodology

Australia: The data were generated from a household survey.

Belgium: The data are based on a sample of 4 000 persons.

Finland: The results reflect the situation at the end of 1993. Data on earnings are annual data.

New Zealand: The data are based on a sample of 2 953 households (out of an estimated 1 166 700 eligible households).

Switzerland: The original sample was 21 500, and the number of interviews achieved 17 900.

United Kingdom: The General Household Survey is an annual survey of approximately 12 000 households.

Sources

Australia: Australian Bureau of Statistics, Survey on Education and Training, April/May 1993.

Belgium: Survey on poverty, within the framework of the Second Community Action Programme to combat poverty, 1992.

Canada: Statistics Canada, Survey of Consumer Finance, 1995 (supplement to the April Labour Force Survey).

Denmark: Register-based personal income statistics, end of 1993, and register on education, October 1993.

Finland: Regional Employment Statistics, 1993.

France: *Enquête Emploi* (Labour Force Survey), March 1994.

Germany: German Socio-economic Panel, Spring 1994.

Ireland: The European Community Household Panel Survey, June-Sept. 1994.

Italy: Sample survey carried out by Central Bank, 1993.

Netherlands: Socio-economic Panel, 1994.

New Zealand: Household Economic Survey, throughout the year ended March 1995.

Norway: Register of salaries and taxes, and register of educational attainment, second quarter 1993.

Spain: Household European Panel, 1994.

Sweden: Income register, and register of the educational attainment of the population, reference year 1993.

Switzerland: ESPA: *Enquête Suisse sur la population active* (Swiss Labour Force Survey), April/June 1994.

United Kingdom: General Household Survey, 1994.

United States: U.S. Department of Commerce, Bureau of the Census, Current Population Survey, March 1994.

INDICATOR R24: UNEMPLOYMENT RATES OF PERSONS LEAVING EDUCATION

Notes on specific countries

Coverage

Australia: Persons aged 15 to 64 are *included* if they attended an educational institution in 1993 for at least one semester, but were not attending in May 1994. Leavers from part-time education are also included.

Primary education cannot be identified separately from lower secondary education.

Canada: Only graduates from formal educational programmes in public institutions are *included*.

Denmark: Figures refer to all leavers 1 year and 3 months after leaving and 5 years and 3 months after leaving. Leavers before completion are also *included*. Continuing training and adult education are *excluded*.

Finland: Only ordinary school and university-level education which is pursued with the view of obtaining a general or vocational qualification is *included*. "Leavers one year after completion" and "leavers five years after completion" are not the same group.

France: Persons who have completed their apprenticeship are also *included* as leavers. Conversely, persons who start an apprenticeship after completing lower secondary education are *not included* as leavers. Apprentices are considered employed according to the norms of the International Labour Organisation (ILO). Unemployment rates of leavers at lower secondary level are therefore high. Apprentices are not included in the labour force.

Annex 3 – Sources, methods and technical notes

Ireland: At the secondary level of education, leavers before completion are also *included*.

Switzerland: For non-university tertiary education, only two types of school are *included*: they represent approximately 20 per cent of all graduates at that level.

For university-level education, only graduates at ISCED 6 are *included*.

United Kingdom: Data cover only England and Wales. They refer to people 16-17 years of age.

United States: Leavers before completion are also *included*.

Notes on methodology

Australia: The sample size varies between 1 in 277 in the larger states and 1 in 75 in the Territories. The rate of non-response is low.

Canada: A sample survey was conducted on persons from trade/vocational and career programmes at community colleges (ISCED 5) and first-degree programmes at universities (ISCED 6). For university graduates at ISCED 7, a complete enumeration was undertaken. The sample was drawn from administrative information provided by institutions.

The total sample of the 1992 National Graduates Survey was 53 500 graduates (trade/vocational programmes: 14 000; career/technical programmes: 12 800; Bachelor's level university: 14 700; university beyond Bachelor's: 12 000). Rate of non-response: 29 per cent.

Denmark: A total enumeration was undertaken (administrative data source).

Finland: An administrative data source was used.

France: The sample size was 100 000 households. Rate of non-response: 5 per cent.

Ireland: For secondary education, a stratified random cluster sample was used (1/4 of all schools, 1/8 of leavers within schools). Target: 2 462; Achieved: 1 950. Rate of non-response: 20.8 per cent.

A total mail survey was conducted for tertiary education. Rate of non-response: 29 per cent for non-university tertiary education, 16 per cent for university-level education.

Spain: The sample size was 7 206 households. Rate of non-response: 33 per cent.

Sweden: For upper secondary education, the sample size was 7 600 (out of 91 000). Rate of non-response: 17 per cent. For university-level education, the sample size was 7 800 (out of 33 400). Rate of non-response: 11 per cent.

Switzerland: A total enumeration was undertaken.

United Kingdom: The sample size was 1 per cent: approximately 24 000 individuals. Rate of non-response: approximately 30 per cent.

United States: The Current Population Survey is a sample survey which covers 729 sample areas consisting of 1 973 counties, independent cities, and minor civil divisions throughout the 50 states and the District of Columbia. The sample size was 59 000 households (with 110 000 persons aged 15 or older). Rate of non-response: 5 per cent.

Sources

Australia: Australian Bureau of Statistics, Transition from Education to Work, May 1994.

Canada: Statistics Canada (on behalf of Human Resources Development Canada), National Graduates Survey and Follow-up of Graduates Survey.

Denmark: Statistics Denmark, individualised statistical registers of education and of the labour force.

Finland: Statistics Finland.

France: *Enquête Emploi* (Labour Force Survey), INSEE.

Ireland: For secondary education: Annual School Leavers' Survey.

For tertiary education: First Destination of Award Recipients in Higher Education, commissioned by Higher Education Authority.

Spain: First wave of the European Household Survey.

Sweden: For upper secondary education: *Elevuppföljning våren 1994 bland examinerade från gymnasieskolans linjer, 1991/92*.

For university-level education: Activity after graduation.

Switzerland: For non-university tertiary education: *Office fédéral de l'industrie, des arts et métiers et du travail* (OFIAMT).

For university-level education: *Schweizerische Arbeitsgemeinschaft für akademische Berufs- und Studienberatung* (AGAB); *Conférence universitaire suisse* (CUS); *Office fédéral de l'industrie, des arts et métiers et du travail* (OFIAMT).

United Kingdom: Youth Cohort Study, Department for Education and Employment.

United States: U. S. Department of Commerce, Bureau of the Census, Current Population Survey, March 1994.

INDICATORS R30: LITERACY AND THE ADULT POPULATION;

R31: ADULT LITERACY BY LEVEL OF EDUCATIONAL ATTAINMENT;

R32: LITERACY LEVELS OF YOUNGER VERSUS OLDER PERSONS; AND

R33: ADULT LITERACY BY GENDER

General notes

Notes on methodology

For the International Adult Literacy Survey (IALS), literacy skills were defined in terms of three domains – prose, document, and quantitative literacy. Prose literacy is defined as the knowledge and skills needed to understand and use information from texts including editorials, news stories,

Annex 3 – Sources, methods and technical notes

poems, and fiction. Document literacy is defined as the knowledge and skills required to locate and use information contained in various formats, including job applications, payroll forms, public transport timetables, maps, tables and graphics. Quantitative literacy is defined as the knowledge and skills required to apply arithmetic operations, either alone or sequentially, to numbers embedded in printed materials, such as balancing a cheque book, working out a tip, completing an order form, or determining the amount of interest on a loan from an advertisement.

Data were collected for five levels of literacy skills, but for reporting purposes, levels 4 and 5 are collapsed due to insufficient percentages of respondents within each level. Item response theory (IRT) scaling procedures were used to establish scale scores for each type of literacy. The scale scores ranged from 0 to 500. These scale scores were translated into literacy levels as follows: Level 1(0 to 225); Level 2 (226 to 275); Level 3 (276 to 325); Level 4 (326 to 375); and Level 5 (376 to 500).

Sample coverage, language of tests, and sample yield were as follows:

	Language of test	Population covered (ages 16-65)	Sample yield (ages 16-65)	Population covered (ages 16-24)	Sample yield (ages 16-24)
Canada	English French	13 676 612 4 773 648	3 130 1 370	2 564 051 805 853	905 288
Germany	German	53 826 289	2 062	7 982 838	296
Netherlands	Dutch	10 460 359	2 837	1 924 325	325
Poland	Polish	24 475 649	3 000	5 035 156	637
Sweden	Swedish	5 361 942	2 645	1 088 062	524
Switzerland	French German	1 008 275 3 144 912	1 435 1 393	172 045 454 940	176 150
United States	English	161 121 972	3 053	34 764 503	4 300

To measure adult literacy skills, it was necessary to go to people's homes. Thus, IALS used household-based survey research. In general, household surveys tend to achieve somewhat lower response rates than do surveys conducted in schools. The structured group setting in which school-based surveys are conducted both encourages participation and facilitates the administration of questionnaires and tests. In household surveys, on the other hand, efforts to secure participation must be made individually for each sampled household, and the time, date, and location of administration must be negotiated. Although a response rate of 80 per cent or higher is desirable, it is not uncommon for well-designed and properly implemented household surveys to achieve final response rates as low as 60 per cent.

Each country was obliged to draw a probability sample that would be representative of the civilian, non-institutionalised population of 16-65 year-olds. In six countries, the survey was conducted in the national language (see table above); Canada's respondents were given a choice of English or French; and in Switzerland, respondents drawn from French-speaking and German-speaking cantons were required to respond in those respective languages (Italian and Rhaeto-Romanic-speaking cantons were excluded). When respondents could not speak the designated language, attempts were made to complete the background questionnaire to allow estimates of their literacy level.

The International Adult Literacy Survey (IALS) consisted of three parts: a "Background Questionnaire" providing demographic information about respondents; a "Core Tasks" booklet screening out respondents with low levels of literacy; and a "Main Tasks" booklet containing the main literacy items.

All sample members who completed at least the Background Questionnaire were considered to be respondents, for purposes of calculating response rates. Response rates for the Background Questionnaire and for the Core and Main booklets (as a percentage of respondents to the Background Questionnaire) are provided in the following table.

Annex 3 – Sources, methods and technical notes

Response rate for International Adult Literacy Survey

	Response rate for Background Questionnaire (%)	Response rate for Core booklet (as a percentage of sample completing Background Questionnaire) (%)	Response rate for Main booklets (as a percentage of sample completing Background Questionnaire) (%)
Canada	69	97	93
Germany	69	99	97
Netherlands	45	99	99
Poland	75	96	89
Sweden	60	100	97
Switzerland	55	97	95
United States	60	88	84

Several procedures were used to impute literacy levels for individuals who did not complete the full set of IALS booklets. Respondents who failed to pass the Core booklet were assigned a literacy level of 1. Respondents who completed the Background Questionnaire but did not complete the Core and Main booklets were assigned literacy levels as a function of their background characteristics, on the basis of a statistical model estimated using the sample of respondents with complete data.

- Estimation of proportions and standard errors

The procedures based on item response theory that were used to estimate IALS scale scores produce five "plausible values" for each respondent. The estimated proportions at each literacy level appearing in the tables are based on the first plausible value only. The estimated standard errors are based on all five plausible values and take into account both sampling error and measurement error.

Information on the percentage of the population that has attained a specific ISCED level of education may differ between IALS data and Labour Force Survey data because of non-response and response errors.

Sources

The indicators are computed from data collected for the First International Adult Literacy Survey (IALS). Data were collected during the autumn of 1994 for adults between the ages of 16 and 65. For further information consult: *Literacy, Economy and Society: Results from the first International Adult Literacy Survey*. Paris, OECD and Statistics Canada, 1995.

Notes on specific countries

Notes on methodology

United States: The data reported for the 16-24 year-olds are taken from the United States' National Adult Literacy Survey. (See I. S. Kirsch, A. Jungeblut, L. Jenkins, and A. Kolstad. *Adult Literacy in America: A First Look at the Results of the National Adult Literacy Survey*. Washington, DC: National Center for Education Statistics, U.S. Department of Education, 1993.). The IALS data for the United States for this age group are not used because of a sampling anomaly, whereby students attending college were inadvertently omitted from the IALS sample. The impact of the omission is substantial for the sample of young adults (ages 16-24), since a high proportion of young adults are in college. But since college students comprise only about 6 per cent of the adult population, their omission has little impact on the literacy results for the overall sample (ages 16-65), and thus the United States IALS data are used for all tables pertaining to the population as a whole.

Glossary

CONTINUING EDUCATION AND TRAINING FOR ADULTS

Continuing education and training for adults refers to all kinds of general and job-related education and training organised, financed or sponsored by authorities, provided by employers or self-financed. Job-related continuing education and training, as used in Indicator P8, refers to all organised, systematic education and training activities in which people take part in order to obtain knowledge and/or learn new skills for a current or a future job, to increase ⊃ earnings and to improve job and/or career opportunities in current or other fields.

CURRICULUM: INTENDED AND IMPLEMENTED CURRICULUM

The *intended curriculum* as referred to in the indicators is the subject-matter content to be taught as defined at the national level or within the education system. It is embodied in textbooks, curriculum guides, the content of examinations, and in policies, regulations and other official statements produced by the education system.

The *implemented curriculum* is the intended curriculum as interpreted by ⊃ teachers and made available to students. It is set in a pedagogical context that includes teaching practices, aspects of classroom management, use of resources, teacher attitudes and teacher background.

EARNINGS

Earnings from work

Earnings from work refer to annual money earnings, i.e. direct pay for work before taxes. Income from other sources, such as government aid programmes, interest on capital, etc., is not taken into account. Mean earnings are calculated on the basis of data for all people with income from work, including the self-employed.

Relative earnings from work

Relative earnings from work are defined as the mean annual ⊃ earnings from work of individuals with a certain level of ⊃ educational attainment divided by the mean annual earnings from work of individuals whose highest level of education is the upper secondary level.

EDUCATIONAL ATTAINMENT

Educational attainment is expressed by the highest completed level of education, defined according to the ⊃ International Standard Classification of Education (ISCED).

EDUCATIONAL EXPENDITURE

Current and capital

Current expenditure is expenditure on goods and services consumed within the current year, which needs to be made recurrently to sustain the production of educational services. Minor expenditure on items of equipment, below a certain cost threshold, are also reported as current spending. *Capital expenditure* represents the value of educational capital acquired or created during the year in question — that is, the amount of capital formation — regardless of whether the capital outlay was financed from current revenue or by borrowing. Capital expenditure includes outlays on construction, renovation, and major repair of buildings and expenditure for new or replacement equipment.

Debt servicing expenditure

The stock of educational debt is the cumulative amount of funds borrowed for educational purposes by educational service providers or funding sources and not yet repaid to the lenders. Such debt is usually incurred to finance ⊃ capital expenditure but may also be incurred, on occasion, to finance portions of ⊃ current expenditure. The term educational debt does not include any funds borrowed by students or households (student loans) to help finance students' educational costs or living expenses. Expenditure on debt servicing consists of i) payment of interest on the amounts borrowed for educational purposes; and ii) repayment of loan principal. Neither component of expenditure on debt servicing is included as ⊃ capital or ⊃ current expenditure.

Direct expenditure on educational institutions

Direct expenditure on ⊃ educational institutions may take one of two forms: *i)* purchases by the government agency itself of educational resources to be used by educational institutions (e.g. direct payments of ⊃ teachers' salaries by a central or regional education ministry); *ii)* payments by the government agency to educational institutions that have responsibility for purchasing educational resources themselves (e.g. a government appropriation or block grant to a university, which the university then uses to compensate staff and to buy other resources). Direct expenditure by a government agency does not include tuition payments received from students (or the families) enrolled in public schools under that agency's jurisdiction, even if the tuition payments flow, in the first instance, to the government agency rather than to the institution in question.

Financial aid to students

Financial aid to students comprises: *i) Government scholarships and other government grants to students* or *households*. These include, in addition to scholarships and similar grants (fellowships, awards, bourses, etc.), the follow-

Glossary

ing items: the value of special subsidies provided to students, either in cash or in kind, such as free or reduced-price travel on public transport systems; and family allowances or child allowances *that are contingent on student status*. Any benefits provided to students or households in the form of tax reductions, tax subsidies, or other special tax provisions are not included; *ii) Student loans,* which are reported on a gross basis – that is, without subtracting or netting out repayments or interest payments from the borrowers (students or households).

Intergovernmental transfers

Intergovernmental transfers are transfers of funds designated for education from one level of government to another. The restriction to funds earmarked for education is very important in order to avoid ambiguity about funding sources. General-purpose intergovernmental transfers are not included (e.g. revenue sharing grants, general fiscal equalisation grants, or distributions of shared taxes from a national government to provinces, states, or *Länder*), even where such transfers provide the funds that regional or local authorities draw on to finance education.

Public and private sources

Public expenditure refers to the spending of public authorities at all levels. Expenditure that is not directly related to education (e.g. culture, sports, youth activities, etc.) is, in principle, not included. Expenditure on education by other ministries or equivalent institutions, for example Health and Agriculture, is included.

Private expenditure refers to expenditure funded by private sources, i.e. households and other private entities. "*Households*" means students and their families. "*Other private entities*" include private business firms and non-profit organisations, including religious organisations, charitable organisations, and business and labour associations. Private expenditure comprises school fees; materials such as textbooks and teaching equipment; transport to school (if organised by the school); meals (if provided by the school); boarding fees; and expenditure by employers on initial ⊃ vocational training. Note that ⊃ private educational institutions are considered service providers, not funding sources.

Staff compensation

Expenditure on staff compensation includes gross salaries plus non-salary compensation (fringe benefits). *Gross salary* means the total salary earned by employees (including any bonuses, extra allowances, etc.) before subtracting any taxes or employee's contributions for pensions, social security, or other purposes. *Non-salary compensation* includes expenditure by employers or public authorities on retirement programmes, health care or health insurance, unemployment compensation, disability insurance, other forms of social insurance, non-cash supplements (e.g. free or subsidised housing), maternity benefits, free or subsidised child care, and such other fringe benefits as each country may provide. This expenditure does not include contributions made by the employees themselves, or deducted from their gross salaries.

Transfers and payments to other private entities

Government transfers and certain other payments (mainly subsidies) to other private entities (firms and non-profit organisations) can take diverse forms – for example, transfers to business or labour associations that provide adult education; subsidies to firms or labour organisations (or associations of such entities) that operate ⊃ apprenticeship programmes; subsidies to non-profit organisations that provide student housing or student meals; and interest rate subsidies to private financial institutions that make ⊃ student loans.

EDUCATIONAL INSTITUTIONS

Educational institutions are defined as decision-making centres which provide educational services to individuals and/or other institutions. The definition is based on the point of view of management and control, which are normally carried out by a Director, Principal, or President and/or a Governing Board, (or similar titles such as Management Committee, etc.). In general, if a centre has a Director, Principal, or President and a Governing Board then it is classified as an institution. If it lacks these, however, and is controlled by an Instructional Educational Institution (see next paragraph), then it is not a separate institution but rather an off-campus centre of an institution. Where a centre is not managed by a Governing Board but is administered directly by a public education authority, the centre is classified as an institution in its own right.

Instructional Educational Institutions are educational institutions which directly provide instructional programmes to individuals in an organised group setting or at a distance. This definition is sufficiently broad to include a Distance Education Centre as well as a pre-primary child-care centre providing some element of education. The generic term "*school*" is often used to refer to both instructional institutions at primary and secondary levels as well as universities at the tertiary level. Business enterprises, individuals operating on their own account, or other institutions providing short-term courses of training or instruction to individuals on a one-to-one basis are not included in the definition.

Non-instructional Educational Institutions are educational institutions which provide administrative, advisory or professional services to other educational institutions.

Public and private educational institutions

⊃ Educational institutions are classified as either public or private according to whether a public agency or a

Glossary

private entity has the ultimate power to make decisions concerning the institution's affairs.

An institution is classified as *public* if it is: *i)* controlled and managed directly by a public education authority or agency; or *ii)* controlled and managed either by a government agency directly or by a governing body (Council, Committee, etc.), most of whose members are either appointed by a public authority or elected by public franchise.

An institution is classified as *private* if it is controlled and managed by a non-governmental organisation (e.g. a Church, a Trade Union or a business enterprise), or if its Governing Board consists mostly of members not selected by a public agency.

In general, the question of who has the ultimate management control over an institution is decided with reference to the power to determine the general activity of the institution and to appoint the officers managing it. The extent to which an institution receives its funding from public or ⊃ private sources does *not* determine the classification status of the institution.

A distinction is made between "government-dependent" and "independent" private institutions on the basis of the degree of a private institution's dependence on funding from government sources. A government-dependent private institution is one that receives more than 50 per cent of its core funding from government agencies. An independent private institution is one that receives less than 50 per cent of its core funding from government agencies. "Core funding" refers to the funds that support the basic educational services of the institution. It does not include funds provided specifically for research projects, payments for services purchased or contracted by private organisations, or fees and subsidies received for ancillary services, such as lodging and meals. Additionally, institutions should be classified as government-dependent if their teaching staff are paid by a government agency – either directly or through government.

EDUCATIONAL PERSONNEL: FULL-TIME, PART-TIME AND FULL-TIME EQUIVALENT

The classification of educational personnel as *"full-time"* and *"part-time"* is based on a concept of statutory working time (as opposed to actual or total working time or actual teaching time). A ⊃ teacher who is employed for at least 90 per cent of the normal or statutory number of hours of work of a full-time teacher over the period of a complete school year is classified as a full-time teacher for the reporting of head-count data. A teacher who is employed for less than 90 per cent of the normal or statutory number of hours of work of a full-time teacher over the period of a complete school year is classified as a part-time teacher. *Full-time equivalents* are generally calculated in person years. The unit for the measurement of full-time equivalents is full-time employment, i.e. a full-time teacher equals one FTE. The full-time equivalence of part-time educational staff is then determined by calculating the ratio of hours worked over the statutory hours worked by a full-time employee during the school year.

EDUCATIONAL SUPPORT PERSONNEL

Educational, administrative and professional staff covers non-teaching staff providing educational, administrative, and professional support to ⊃ teachers and students. Examples are: principals, headteachers, supervisors, counsellors, librarians or educational media specialists, psychologists, curriculum developers, inspectors, and former teachers who no longer have active teaching duties. *Other support staff* covers personnel providing indirect support in areas such as: secretarial and clerical services, building and maintenance, security, transportation, catering, etc.

EMPLOYED POPULATION

The *employed population* is defined, in accordance with ILO guidelines, as all persons above a specific age who during a specified brief period, either one week or one day, were in paid employment or self-employment. It includes both those in civilian employment and in the armed forces.

FIRST AND SECOND (OR FURTHER) EDUCATIONAL PROGRAMMES

A *first upper secondary programme* is any educational programme selected by a student in the ordinary cycle of upper secondary education that leads to a first qualification or certification at that level. A student is counted as enrolled in a *second (or further) upper secondary programme* if he or she has completed a normal or ordinary cycle of upper secondary education and has graduated from that sequence and then enrols in upper secondary education again, in order to pursue another upper secondary education programme. If the student then completes that programme (by obtaining the corresponding certification) he or she is considered a graduate of a second (or subsequent) upper secondary education programme. However, those students who enrol only in a partial programme, or repeaters who did not graduate from an ordinary cycle of upper secondary education but nevertheless repeat a cycle, are not counted as enrolled in a second or further educational programme.

GRADUATES

Graduates are those who were enrolled in the final year of a level of education and completed it successfully during the reference year. However, there are exceptions (especially at the university tertiary level of education) where graduation can also be recognised by the awarding of a certifi-

Glossary

cate without the requirement that the participants are enrolled. *Completion* is defined by each country: in some countries, completion occurs as a result of passing an examination or a series of examinations. In other countries, completion occurs after a requisite number of course hours have been accumulated (although completion of some or all of the course hours may also involve examinations). *Success* is also defined by each country: in some countries it is associated with the obtaining of a degree, certificate, or diploma after a final examination; while in other countries, it is defined by the completion of programmes without a final examination.

GROSS DOMESTIC PRODUCT

Gross Domestic Product (GDP) refers to the producers' value of the gross outputs of resident producers, including distributive trades and transport, less the value of purchasers' intermediate consumption plus import duties. GDP is expressed in local money (in millions). Data for GDP are provided in Annex 2.

GROSS SALARY

Gross salary is the sum of wages (total sum of money that is paid by the employer for the labour supplied) minus employer's contributions for social security and pension (according to existing salary scales). Bonuses that constitute a regular part of the wages – such as a thirteenth month or a holiday or regional bonus – are included in the gross salary.

ISCED LEVELS OF EDUCATION

The levels of education used in this publication are defined with reference to the *International Standard Classification of Education* (ISCED). However, some further elaboration of the ISCED definitions has been undertaken to enhance international comparability of the indicators.

Early childhood education (ISCED 0)

Early childhood education serves the dual purpose of giving the child daily care while the parents are at work and contributing to the child's social and intellectual development in keeping with the rules and guidelines of the pre-primary ⊃ curriculum. It covers all forms of organised and sustained centre-based activities designed to foster learning, and emotional and social development of children. The term *centre-based* distinguishes between activities in institutional settings (such as primary schools, pre-schools, kindergartens, day-care centres) and services provided in households or family settings. The *standard starting age* at this level is *age 3*. Children aged 2 years or older are, however, also included in the statistics if they are enrolled in programmes that are considered educational by the country concerned.

Primary level of education (ISCED 1)

Primary education usually begins at age 5, 6, or 7 and lasts for four to six years (the mode of the OECD countries is six years). Programmes at the primary level generally require no previous formal education. Coverage at the primary level corresponds to ISCED 1, except that an upper threshold is specified as follows: in countries where basic education covers the entire compulsory school period (i.e. where there is no break in the system between primary and lower secondary education) and where in such cases basic education lasts for more than six years, only the first six years following early childhood education are counted as primary education.

Lower secondary level of education (ISCED 2)

The core of *lower secondary education* continues the basic programmes of the primary level but usually in a more subject-oriented manner. This usually consists of two to six years of schooling (the mode of OECD countries is three years). The common feature of lower secondary programmes is their entrance requirement, i.e. a minimum of primary education completed or demonstrable ability to benefit from participation in the programme. Coverage at the lower secondary level corresponds to ISCED 2, except that an upper threshold is specified as follows: in countries with no break in the system between lower secondary and upper secondary education and where lower secondary education lasts for more than three years, only the first three years following primary education are counted as lower secondary education. Lower secondary education may either be *terminal* (i.e. preparing the students for entry directly into working life) or *preparatory* (i.e. preparing students for upper secondary education).

Upper secondary level of education (ISCED 3)

Coverage at the *upper secondary level* corresponds to ISCED 3. This level usually consists of two to five years of schooling. Admission into educational programmes at the upper secondary level requires the completion of the lower secondary level of education, or a combination of basic education and ⊃ vocational experience that demonstrates an ability to handle the subject matter. Upper secondary education may either be *terminal* (i.e. preparing the students for entry directly into working life) or *preparatory* (i.e. preparing students for tertiary education).

Non-university tertiary level of education (ISCED 5)

The *non-university tertiary level* corresponds to ISCED 5. Programmes at this level generally do not lead to the awarding of a university degree or equivalent. A minimum condition of admission into a programme at this level is usually the successful completion of a programme at the upper secondary level. In some countries, evidence of the attainment

Glossary

of an equivalent level of knowledge, or the fulfilment of specific conditions (such as a combination of age and/or work experience) permits admission. In terms of subject matter, the core programmes at this level often tend to parallel those for which university degrees are granted. They are usually shorter, however, and more practical in orientation. Programmes of a level equivalent to this core vary widely in most countries and are provided through many organisations of very different types.

University tertiary level of education (ISCED 6 and 7)

This level of education refers to any programme classified that leads to a university degree or equivalent. Programmes at ISCED 6 are intended for students who have successfully completed prerequisite programmes at the upper secondary level and who continue their education in a programme that generally leads to the award of a first university degree or a recognised equivalent qualification. University programmes at ISCED 7 are intended for students who have completed a first university programme. Some countries do not distinguish, for purposes of international reporting, between ISCED 6 and 7.

NEW ENTRANTS TO A LEVEL OF EDUCATION

New entrants to a level of education are students who are entering any programme leading to a recognised qualification at this level of education for the first time, irrespective of whether students enter the programme at the beginning or at an advanced stage of the programme. Individuals who are returning to study at a level following a period of absence from studying at that same level are not considered new entrants. *New entrants to the tertiary level of education* are students who have never entered any tertiary level before. In particular, students who complete tertiary-level non-degree programmes (ISCED 5) and transfer to degree programmes (ISCED 6) are not considered new entrants. On the other hand, foreign students who enrol in a country's education system for the first time in a post-graduate programme are considered new entrants to the tertiary level. *Entrants to a level of education* are all students enrolled at that level who were not enrolled at that level during the previous reference period.

PURCHASING POWER PARITIES

Purchasing Power Parities (PPP) are the currency exchange rates that equalise the purchasing power of different currencies. This means that a given sum of money, when converted into different currencies at the PPP rates, will buy the same basket of goods and services in all countries. In other words, PPPs are the rates of currency conversion which eliminate the differences in price levels among countries. Thus, when expenditure on GDP for different countries is converted into a common currency by means of PPPs, it is, in effect, expressed at the same set of international prices so that comparisons among countries reflect only differences in the volume of goods and services purchased. The purchasing power parities used in this publication are given in Annex 2.

STUDENTS

A *student* is defined as any individual participating in educational services covered by the data collection. The *number of students enrolled* refers to the number of individuals (head count) who are enrolled within the reference period and not necessarily to the number of registrations. Each student enrolled is counted only once.

STUDENTS ENROLLED: FULL-TIME, PART-TIME AND FULL-TIME EQUIVALENT

Students are classified by their pattern of attendance, i.e., full-time or part-time. The part-time/full-time classification is regarded as an *attribute of student participation* rather than as an attribute of the educational programmes or the provision of education in general. Four elements are used to decide whether a student is full-time or part-time: the units of measurement for course load; a normal full-time course load which is used as the criterion for establishing full-time participation; the student's actual course load; and the period of time over which the course loads are measured. In general, students enrolled in *primary and secondary level* educational programmes are considered to participate full-time if they attend school for at least 75 per cent of the school day or week (as locally defined) and would normally be expected to be in the programme for the entire academic year. Otherwise, they are considered part-time. When determining full-time/part-time status, the work-based component in combined school- and work-based programmes is included. At the *tertiary level*, an individual is considered full-time if he or she is taking a course load or educational programme considered to require at least 75 per cent of a full-time commitment of time and resources. Additionally, it is expected that the student will remain in the programme for the entire year.

The *full-time equivalent* (FTE) *measure* attempts to standardise a student's actual course load against the normal load. For the reduction of head-count data to FTEs, where data and norms on individual participation are available, course load is measured as the product of the fraction of the normal course load for a full-time student and the fraction of the school/academic year. [FTE = (actual course load/normal course load) * (actual duration of study during reference period/normal duration of study during reference period).] When actual course load information is not available, a full-time student is considered equal to one FTE.

Glossary

STUDENT STOCK AND FLOW DATA

Stock data refer to the characteristics and attributes of a specified pool of students for the reference period under consideration. *Flow data* refer to individuals who join the pool at the beginning or during the reference period and to students who leave the pool during or at the end of the reference period. The *inflow* is the number of students who do not fulfil any of the conditions for inclusion in the stock data before the beginning of the reference period but gain at least one of them during this time. The *outflow* refers to the number of individuals who fulfil at least one of the conditions for inclusion in the stock of a group of students at the beginning of the reference period and who lose them all during or at the end of the reference period.

TEACHERS

A *teacher* is defined as a person whose professional activity involves the transmission of knowledge, attitudes and skills that are stipulated in a formal ⊃ curriculum to students enrolled in an educational programme. The teacher category includes only personnel who participate directly in instructing students.

This definition does not depend on the qualification held by the teacher or on the delivery mechanism. It is based on three concepts: *activity*, thus excluding those without active teaching duties – although teachers temporarily not at work (e.g. for reasons of illness or injury, maternity or parental leave, holiday or vacation) are included; *profession*, thus excluding people who work occasionally or in a voluntary capacity in ⊃ educational institutions; and *educational programme*, thus excluding people who provide services other than formal instruction to students (e.g. supervisors, activity organisers, etc.), whether the programme is established at the national or school level.

In ⊃ vocational education, teachers of the "school element" of apprenticeships in a dual system are included in the definition, and trainers of the "in-company element" of a dual system are excluded.

Headteachers without teaching responsibilities are not defined as teachers, but classified separately. Headteachers who do have teaching responsibilities are defined as (part-time) teachers, even if they only teach for 10 per cent of their time.

Former teachers, people who work occasionally or in a voluntary capacity in schools, people who provide services other than formal instruction, e.g., supervisors or activity organisers, are also excluded.

TYPICAL AGES

Typical ages refer to the ages that normally correspond to the age at entry and ending of a cycle of education. These ages relate to the theoretical duration of a cycle assuming ⊃ full-time attendance and no repetition of a year. The assumption is made that, at least in the ordinary education system, a student can proceed through the educational programme in a standard number of years, which is referred to as the theoretical duration of the programme. The *typical starting age* is the age at the *beginning* of the *first* school/academic year of the relevant level and programme. The *typical ending age* is the age at the *beginning* of the *last* school/academic year of the relevant level and programme. The *typical graduation age* is the age at the *end* of the *last* school/academic year of the relevant level and programme when the qualification is obtained. Using a transformation key that relates the levels of a school system to ISCED, the typical age range for each ISCED level can be derived.

TOTAL LABOUR FORCE

The *total labour force* or currently active population comprises all persons who fulfil the requirements for inclusion among the employed or the unemployed as defined in *OECD Labour Force Statistics*.

TOTAL POPULATION

The *total population* comprises all nationals present in or temporarily absent from the country and aliens permanently settled in the country. For further details, see *OECD Labour Force Statistics*.

UNEMPLOYED

The *unemployed* are defined, in accordance with the ILO guidelines on unemployment statistics, as persons who are without work, actively seeking employment and currently available to start work. The unemployment rate is defined as the number of unemployed persons as a percentage of the labour force.

VOCATIONAL AND TECHNICAL EDUCATION

Some indicators distinguish between "general and academic" and "vocational and technical" education. *Vocational and technical education* comprises educational programmes, generally offered by countries at the secondary and non-university tertiary level of education, that prepare participants for a specific trade or occupation or a range of

Glossary

trades and occupations within an industry or group of industries. Completion of a vocational or technical programme can result in direct entry into the labour force or prepare students for entry into technical and vocational tertiary programmes and institutions. Graduates of vocational schools often attend further educational programmes at the same or higher level.

School-based and combined school and work-based programmes

Some indicators divide vocational and technical programmes into school-based programmes and combined school- and work-based programmes on the basis of the amount of training that is provided in school as opposed to training in the workplace. In *school-based* vocational and technical programmes, instruction takes place (either partly or exclusively) in ⊃ educational institutions. These include special training centres for vocational education run by public or ⊃ private authorities or enterprise-based special training centres if these qualify as educational institutions. These programmes can have an on-the-job training component, i.e. a component of some practical experience in the workplace. In *combined school- and work-based programmes,* instruction is shared between school and the workplace, although instruction may take place primarily in the workplace. Programmes are classified as combined school- and work-based if less than 75 per cent of the ⊃ curriculum is presented in the school environment or through distance education. Programmes that are more than 90 per cent work-based are excluded.

Dual-system apprenticeship programmes

Dual-system apprenticeship programmes are examples of combined school- and work-based educational programmes. They typically involve alternating between learning in an ⊃ educational institution (ordinary or specialised) and learning through work experience programmes, which may include highly organised training in a firm or with a craftsperson. Even though only a part of the training occurs in schools, it is considered as a ⊃ full-time activity, because it covers both theoretical and practical training. The objectives of dual-system apprenticeship programmes are: a full vocational qualification, through training in practical and technical skills, and through theoretical instruction; an enhancement of general knowledge; the promotion of the students' personalities and their sense of responsibility; and a basis for modular technical and general education and for ⊃ continuing education and training.

Participants in the INES Project

As mentioned in the Foreword, many people have contributed to the CERI project on the development of international **IN**dicators of **E**ducation **S**ystems (INES). This annex lists the names of the country representatives, policy-makers, researchers and experts on educational measurement and statistics who have actively taken part in the preparatory work leading to the publication of this edition of *Education at a Glance - Indicators*. The OECD wishes to thank them all for their valuable efforts.

I. Policy Review and Advisory Group

Mr. Tom ALEXANDER (OECD)
Mr. Alan GIBSON (United Kingdom)
Ms. Jeanne GRIFFITH (United States)
Mr. Walo HUTMACHER (Switzerland)
Mr. Ulf LUNDGREN (Sweden)
Mr. Alan RUBY (Australia)
Mr. Claude THÉLOT (France)
Mr. Alejandro TIANA (Spain)

II. National Co-ordinators

Mr. Masashi AKIBA (Japan)
Mr. Dan ANDERSSON (Sweden)
Mr. Antonio AUGENTI (Italy)
Ms. Monique BÉLANGER (Canada)
Ms. Virginia BERKELEY (United Kingdom)
Ms. Birgitte BOVIN (Denmark)
Ms. Karina BUTLAGINA (Russian Federation)
Mr. Se Yeoung CHUN (Korea)
Mr. Nicolaas DERSJANT (Netherlands)
Mr. Antonio FAZENDEIRO (Portugal)
Mr. Heinz GILOMEN (Switzerland)
Mr. Sean GLENNANE (Ireland)
Mr. Gregory KAFETZOPOULOS (Greece)
Mr. Reijo LAUKKANEN (Finland)
Mr. Dieter MAGERKURTH (Germany)
Ms. Dawn NELSON (United States)
Mr. Friedrich PLANK (Austria)
Mr. Nicholas POLE (New Zealand)
Mr. Miroslav PROCHAZKA (Czech Republic)
Mr. Johan RAAUM (Norway)
Mr. Jean-Claude ROUCLOUX (Belgium)
Mr. Ingo RUß (Germany)
Mr. Claude SAUVAGEOT (France)
Mr. Paul Inge SEVEREIDE (Norway)
Mr. Thorolfur THORLINDSSON (Iceland)
Mr. Alejandro TIANA (Spain)
Ms. Ann Van DRIESSCHE (Belgium)
Mr. Victor VELAZQUEZ CASTANEDA (Mexico)
Mr. Paul VOLKER (Australia)
Mr. Ziya YEDIYILDIZ (Turkey)
Mr. Pavel ZELENY (Czech Republic)

Participants in the INES Project

III. Technical Group on Education Statistics and Indicators

Mr. Ruud ABELN (Netherlands)
Mr. Paul AMACHER (Switzerland)
Ms. Birgitta ANDRÉN (Sweden)
Mr. Michele BARBATO (Italy)
Ms. Birgitte BOVIN (Denmark)
Mr. Fernando CELESTIONO (Spain)
Mr. Se Yeoung CHUN (Korea)
Ms. Maria DE GRAÇA PACHECO (Portugal)
Ms. Gemma DE SANCTIS (Italy)
Ms. Mary DUNNE (Ireland)
Mr. Timo ERTOLA (Finland)
Mr. Paul ESQUIEU (France)
Mr. Carlos GUTIERREZ (Mexico)
Mr. Heikki HAVEN (Finland)
Mr. Max van HERPEN (Netherlands)
Mr. Walter HÖRNER (Germany)
Mr. Per ISRAELSSON (Norway)
Ms. Vladimira JELINKOVA (Czech Republic)
Mr. Stefan JENSEN (Denmark)
Mr. Gregory KAFETZOPOULOS (Greece)
Ms. Alison KENNEDY (United Kingdom)
Mr. Dong-ok KIM (Korea)
Mr. Felix KOSCHIN (Czech Republic)
Mr. Johan LASUY (Belgium)
Ms. Emel LATIFAOGLU (Turkey)
Mr. Joseph LAUTER (Luxembourg)
Ms. Ema LEANDRO (Portugal)
Mr. Laszlo LIMBACHER (Hungary)

Mr. Douglas LYND (Canada)
Mr. Dieter MAGERKURTH (Germany)
Mr. Robert MAHEU (Canada)
Ms. Maria MASTORAKI (Greece)
Ms. Aurca MICALI (Italy)
Ms. Inger MUNKHAMMAR (Sweden)
Ms. Isabel MUÑOZ (Spain)
Mr. Hironori NAGASHIMA (Japan)
Mr. Friedrich ONDRASCH (Austria)
Mr. Cesar ORTIZ PEÑA (Mexico)
Mr. Wolfgang PAULI (Austria)
Mr. Nicholas POLE (New Zealand)
Mr. Johan RAAUM (Norway)
Mr. Jean-Paul REEFF (Luxembourg)
Ms. Olga REMENETS (Russian Federation)
Mr. Ron ROSS (New Zealand)
Mr. Jean-Claude ROUCLOUX (Belgium)
Mr. Ingo RUß (Germany)
Mr. Philippe SCAILLET (Belgium)
Mr. Paul Inge SEVEREIDE (Norway)
Mr. Joel SHERMAN (United States)
Mr. Thomas SNYDER (United States)
Mr. Matti VÄISÄNEN (Finland)
Ms. Annick VANBEVEREN (Belgium)
Mr. Paul VOLKER (Australia)
Mr. Jean-Pierre WITSCHARD (Switzerland)
Mr. Hiroshi YAMAMOTO (Japan)

Participants in the INES Project

IV. Network A on Educational Outcomes

Lead country: United States

Network leader: Mr. Eugene OWEN

Ms. Gertrudes AMARO (Portugal)
Ms. Jean BRITTON (Canada)
Ms. Chiara CROCE (Italy)
Mr. Bernard ERNST (France)
Mr. Guillermo GIL (Spain)
Ms. Marit GRANHEIM (Norway)
Ms. Aletta GRISAY (Belgium)
Mr. Carlos GUTIERREZ (Mexico)
Ms. Judit KÁDÁR-FÜLÖP (Hungary)
Mr. Thomas KELLAGHAN (Ireland)
Mr. Gerbo KOREVAAR (Netherlands)
Mr. Kimmo LEIMU (Finland)
Ms. Jacqueline LEVASSEUR (France)
Mr. Niels PLISCHEZSKI (Denmark)
Mr. Jules PESCHAR (Netherlands)
Mr. Sten PETTERSSON (Sweden)
Mr. Friedrich PLANK (Austria)
Mr. Dominique PORTANTE (Luxembourg)
Ms. Rosemary RENWICK (New Zealand)
Mr. Dieter SCHWEDT (Germany)
Ms. Jana STRAKOVÁ (Czech Republic)
Mr. Erich SVECNIK (Austria)
Mr. Uri Peter TRIER (Switzerland)
Mr. Luc Van de POELE (Belgium)
Mr. Robert WOOD (United Kingdom)
Mr. Michael RICHARDSON (United Kingdom)

V. Network B on Student Destinations

Lead country: Sweden

Network leader: Mr. Allan NORDIN

Mr. Nabeel ALSALAM (United States)
Ms. Regina BARTH (Austria)
Mr. Kenneth BENNETT (Canada)
Ms. Anna BORKOWSKY (Switzerland)
Ms. Birgitte BOVIN (Denmark)
Mr. Vassilios CHARISMIADIS (Greece)
Mr. Fayik DEMIRTAS (Turkey)
Ms. Eveline von GÄSSLER (Germany)
Mr. Michel-Henri GENSBITTEL (France)
Ms. Kjersti GRINDAL (Norway)
Mr. Damian F. HANNON (Ireland)
Mr. Maurice van der HEIDEN (Netherlands)
Mr. Max van HERPEN (Netherlands)
Ms. Carmen HIGUERA TORRON (Spain)
Mr. Graham JONES (United Kingdom)
Mr. Pavel KUCHAR (Czech Republic)
Mr. Joseph LAUTER (Luxembourg)
Mr. Colin MacLEAN (United Kingdom)
Ms. Christine MAINGUET (Belgium)
Ms. Aurea MICALI (Italy)
Ms. Marion NORRIS (New Zealand)
Mr. Alf RASMUSSEN (Norway)
Ms. Aila REPO (Finland)
Ms. Emilia SAO PEDRO (Portugal)
Mr. Michail SKALIOTIS (Eurostat)
Mr. Luc Van de POELE (Belgium)
Mr. Paul VOLKER (Australia)

Participants in the INES Project

VI. Network C on School Features and Processes

Lead country: Netherlands

Network leader: Mr. Jaap SCHEERENS

Ms. Bodhild BAASLAND (Norway)
Ms. Giovanna BARZANO (Italy)
Ms. Maria do CARMO CLIMACO (Portugal)
Mr. Vassilios CHARISMIADIS (Greece)
Mr. Alan CLARKE (United Kingdom)
Mr. Philippe DELOOZ (Belgium)
Mr. Pol DUPONT (Belgium)
Mr. Jean-Claude EMIN (France)
Mr. Rainer FANKHAUSER (Austria)
Ms. Flora GIL TRAVER (Spain)
Mr. Alan GIBSON (United Kingdom)
Mr. Steen HARBILD (Denmark)
Ms. Heidi HENKELS (Germany)
Mr. Sean HUNT (Ireland)
Mr. Erkki KANGASNIEMI (Finland)
Mr. Arno LIBOTTON (Belgium)
Mr. Heikki LYYTINEN (Finland)
Ms. Marilyn McMILLEN (United States)
Mr. Ramon PAJARES BOX (Spain)
Mr. Nicholas POLE (New Zealand)
Mr. Ferry de RIJCKE (Netherlands)
Ms. Laura SALGANIK (United States)
Mr. Walter SCHWAB (Eurostat)
Ms. Jana SVECOVA (Czech Republic)
Mr. Eugen STOCKER (Switzerland)
Mr. Erik WALLIN (Sweden)
Mr. Ziya YEDIYILDIZ (Turkey)

VII. Network D on Expectations and Attitudes to Education

Lead country: United Kingdom

Network leader: Mr. Archie McGLYNN

Ms. Anna BORKOWSKY (Switzerland)
Mr. Roel BOSKER (Netherlands)
Ms. Birgitte BOVIN (Denmark)
Ms. Carmen CASTANHEIRA (Portugal)
Mr. Frans DAEMS (Belgium)
Mr. Heinz GILOMEN (Switzerland)
Mr. Kauko HÄMÄLÄINEN (Finland)
Mr. François JEGER (France)
Ms. Agnes LEYSEN (Belgium)
Ms. Marcella MAZZOCCHI (Italy)
Mr. Alain MICHEL (France)
Mr. Paul PLANCHON (United States)
Ms. Petra PRUSOVÁ (Czech Republic)
Mr. John MacBEATH (United Kingdom)
Mr. Roland RENARD (Belgium)
Ms. Laura SALGANIK (United States)
Mr. Claude SAUVAGEOT (France)
Mr. Sten SÖDERBERG (Sweden)
Mr. Erich SVECNIK (Austria)
Mr. Alejandro TIANA (Spain)
Mr. Endre UDVARDI-LAKOS (Hungary)
Ms. Consuelo VELAZ DE MEDRANO (Spain)
Mr. Ziya YEDIYILDIZ (Turkey)
Ms. Athanassia ZANALATOU (Greece)

Participants in the INES Project

VIII. Other Experts and Consultants to INES

Ms. Giorgina BROWN
Mr. Alfons Ten BRUMMELHUIS
Mr. Nicolaas DERSJANT
Mr. Walter HÖRNER
Ms. Alison KENNEDY
Mr. Douglas LYND
Mr. Jay MOSKOWITZ

Mr. Walter NONNEMAN
Mr. Kenny PETERSSON
Mr. T. Neville POSTLETHWAITE
Mr. Ingo RUß
Mr. Joel SHERMAN
Mr. Tom SMITH
Ms. Gonnie VAN AMELSVOORT

IX. OECD

Ms. Véronique BIRR
Mr. Norberto BOTTANI
Ms. Jocelyne CARVALLO
Ms. Valérie CISSE
Ms. Catherine DUCHÊNE
Mr. Tom HEALY
Mr. Georges LEMAÎTRE

Ms. Anne-Marie LÉVÊQUE
Mr. Philip McKENZIE
Ms. Carline PIETRASZEWSKI
Ms. Wendy SIMPSON
Mr. Andreas SCHLEICHER
Ms. Jean YIP

MAIN SALES OUTLETS OF OECD PUBLICATIONS
PRINCIPAUX POINTS DE VENTE DES PUBLICATIONS DE L'OCDE

AUSTRALIA – AUSTRALIE
D.A. Information Services
648 Whitehorse Road, P.O.B 163
Mitcham, Victoria 3132 Tel. (03) 9210.7777
 Fax: (03) 9210.7788

AUSTRIA – AUTRICHE
Gerold & Co.
Graben 31
Wien I Tel. (0222) 533.50.14
 Fax: (0222) 512.47.31.29

BELGIUM – BELGIQUE
Jean De Lannoy
Avenue du Roi, Koningslaan 202
B-1060 Bruxelles Tel. (02) 538.51.69/538.08.41
 Fax: (02) 538.08.41

CANADA
Renouf Publishing Company Ltd.
1294 Algoma Road
Ottawa, ON K1B 3W8 Tel. (613) 741.4333
 Fax: (613) 741.5439

Stores:
61 Sparks Street
Ottawa, ON K1P 5R1 Tel. (613) 238.8985

12 Adelaide Street West
Toronto, ON M5H 1L6 Tel. (416) 363.3171
 Fax: (416)363.59.63

Les Éditions La Liberté Inc.
3020 Chemin Sainte-Foy
Sainte-Foy, PQ G1X 3V6 Tel. (418) 658.3763
 Fax: (418) 658.3763

Federal Publications Inc.
165 University Avenue, Suite 701
Toronto, ON M5H 3B8 Tel. (416) 860.1611
 Fax: (416) 860.1608

Les Publications Fédérales
1185 Université
Montréal, QC H3B 3A7 Tel. (514) 954.1633
 Fax: (514) 954.1635

CHINA – CHINE
China National Publications Import
Export Corporation (CNPIEC)
16 Gongti E. Road, Chaoyang District
P.O. Box 88 or 50
Beijing 100704 PR Tel. (01) 506.6688
 Fax: (01) 506.3101

CHINESE TAIPEI – TAIPEI CHINOIS
Good Faith Worldwide Int'l. Co. Ltd.
9th Floor, No. 118, Sec. 2
Chung Hsiao E. Road
Taipei Tel. (02) 391.7396/391.7397
 Fax: (02) 394.9176

CZECH REPUBLIC – RÉPUBLIQUE TCHÈQUE
National Information Centre
NIS – prodejna
Konviktská 5
Praha 1 – 113 57 Tel. (02) 24.23.09.07
 Fax: (02) 24.22.94.33
(*Contact* Ms Jana Pospisilova, nkposp@dec.niz.cz)

DENMARK – DANEMARK
Munksgaard Book and Subscription Service
35, Nørre Søgade, P.O. Box 2148
DK-1016 København K Tel. (33) 12.85.70
 Fax: (33) 12.93.87

J. H. Schultz Information A/S,
Herstedvang 12,
DK – 2620 Albertslung Tel. 43 63 23 00
 Fax: 43 63 19 69
Internet: s-info@inet.uni-c.dk

EGYPT – ÉGYPTE
The Middle East Observer
41 Sherif Street
Cairo Tel. 392.6919
 Fax: 360-6804

FINLAND – FINLANDE
Akateeminen Kirjakauppa
Keskuskatu 1, P.O. Box 128
00100 Helsinki

Subscription Services/Agence d'abonnements :
P.O. Box 23
00371 Helsinki Tel. (358 0) 121 4416
 Fax: (358 0) 121.4450

FRANCE
OECD/OCDE
Mail Orders/Commandes par correspondance :
2, rue André-Pascal
75775 Paris Cedex 16 Tel. (33-1) 45.24.82.00
 Fax: (33-1) 49.10.42.76
 Telex: 640048 OCDE
Internet: Compte.PUBSINQ@oecd.org

Orders via Minitel, France only/
Commandes par Minitel, France exclusivement :
36 15 OCDE

OECD Bookshop/Librairie de l'OCDE :
33, rue Octave-Feuillet
75016 Paris Tél. (33-1) 45.24.81.81
 (33-1) 45.24.81.67

Dawson
B.P. 40
91121 Palaiseau Cedex Tel. 69.10.47.00
 Fax: 64.54.83.26

Documentation Française
29, quai Voltaire
75007 Paris Tel. 40.15.70.00

Economica
49, rue Héricart
75015 Paris Tel. 45.75.05.67
 Fax: 40.58.15.70

Gibert Jeune (Droit-Économie)
6, place Saint-Michel
75006 Paris Tel. 43.25.91.19

Librairie du Commerce International
10, avenue d'Iéna
75016 Paris Tel. 40.73.34.60

Librairie Dunod
Université Paris-Dauphine
Place du Maréchal-de-Lattre-de-Tassigny
75016 Paris Tel. 44.05.40.13

Librairie Lavoisier
11, rue Lavoisier
75008 Paris Tel. 42.65.39.95

Librairie des Sciences Politiques
30, rue Saint-Guillaume
75007 Paris Tel. 45.48.36.02

P.U.F.
49, boulevard Saint-Michel
75005 Paris Tel. 43.25.83.40

Librairie de l'Université
12a, rue Nazareth
13100 Aix-en-Provence Tel. (16) 42.26.18.08

Documentation Française
165, rue Garibaldi
69003 Lyon Tel. (16) 78.63.32.23

Librairie Decitre
29, place Bellecour
69002 Lyon Tel. (16) 72.40.54.54

Librairie Sauramps
Le Triangle
34967 Montpellier Cedex 2 Tel. (16) 67.58.85.15
 Fax: (16) 67.58.27.36

A la Sorbonne Actual
23, rue de l'Hôtel-des-Postes
06000 Nice Tel. (16) 93.13.77.75
 Fax: (16) 93.80.75.69

GERMANY – ALLEMAGNE
OECD Bonn Centre
August-Bebel-Allee 6
D-53175 Bonn Tel. (0228) 959.120
 Fax: (0228) 959.12.17

GREECE – GRÈCE
Librairie Kauffmann
Stadiou 28
10564 Athens Tel. (01) 32.55.321
 Fax: (01) 32.30.320

HONG-KONG
Swindon Book Co. Ltd.
Astoria Bldg. 3F
34 Ashley Road, Tsimshatsui
Kowloon, Hong Kong Tel. 2376.2062
 Fax: 2376.0685

HUNGARY – HONGRIE
Euro Info Service
Margitsziget, Európa Ház
1138 Budapest Tel. (1) 111.62.16
 Fax: (1) 111.60.61

ICELAND – ISLANDE
Mál Mog Menning
Laugavegi 18, Pósthólf 392
121 Reykjavik Tel. (1) 552.4240
 Fax: (1) 562.3523

INDIA – INDE
Oxford Book and Stationery Co.
Scindia House
New Delhi 110001 Tel. (11) 331.5896/5308
 Fax: (11) 371.8275

17 Park Street
Calcutta 700016 Tel. 240832

INDONESIA – INDONÉSIE
Pdii-Lipi
P.O. Box 4298
Jakarta 12042 Tel. (21) 573.34.67
 Fax: (21) 573.34.67

IRELAND – IRLANDE
Government Supplies Agency
Publications Section
4/5 Harcourt Road
Dublin 2 Tel. 661.31.11
 Fax: 475.27.60

ISRAEL – ISRAËL
Praedicta
5 Shatner Street
P.O. Box 34030
Jerusalem 91430 Tel. (2) 52.84.90/1/2
 Fax: (2) 52.84.93

R.O.Y. International
P.O. Box 13056
Tel Aviv 61130 Tel. (3) 546 1423
 Fax: (3) 546 1442

Palestinian Authority/Middle East:
INDEX Information Services
P.O.B. 19502
Jerusalem Tel. (2) 27.12.19
 Fax: (2) 27.16.34

ITALY – ITALIE
Libreria Commissionaria Sansoni
Via Duca di Calabria 1/1
50125 Firenze Tel. (055) 64.54.15
 Fax: (055) 64.12.57

Via Bartolini 29
20155 Milano Tel. (02) 36.50.83

Editrice e Libreria Herder
Piazza Montecitorio 120
00186 Roma Tel. 679.46.28
 Fax: 678.47.51

Libreria Hoepli
Via Hoepli 5
20121 Milano Tel. (02) 86.54.46
 Fax: (02) 805.28.86

Libreria Scientifica
Dott. Lucio de Biasio 'Aeiou'
Via Coronelli, 6
20146 Milano Tel. (02) 48.95.45.52
 Fax: (02) 48.95.45.48

JAPAN – JAPON
OECD Tokyo Centre
Landic Akasaka Building
2-3-4 Akasaka, Minato-ku
Tokyo 107 Tel. (81.3) 3586.2016
 Fax: (81.3) 3584.7929

KOREA – CORÉE
Kyobo Book Centre Co. Ltd.
P.O. Box 1658, Kwang Hwa Moon
Seoul Tel. 730.78.91
 Fax: 735.00.30

MALAYSIA – MALAISIE
University of Malaya Bookshop
University of Malaya
P.O. Box 1127, Jalan Pantai Baru
59700 Kuala Lumpur
Malaysia Tel. 756.5000/756.5425
 Fax: 756.3246

MEXICO – MEXIQUE
OECD Mexico Centre
Edificio INFOTEC
Av. San Fernando no. 37
Col. Toriello Guerra
Tlalpan C.P. 14050
Mexico D.F. Tel. (525) 665 47 99
 Fax: (525) 606 13 07

NETHERLANDS – PAYS-BAS
SDU Uitgeverij Plantijnstraat
Externe Fondsen
Postbus 20014
2500 EA's-Gravenhage Tel. (070) 37.89.880
Voor bestellingen: Fax: (070) 34.75.778

Subscription Agency/
Agence d'abonnements :
SWETS & ZEITLINGER BV
Heereweg 347B
P.O. Box 830
2160 SZ Lisse Tel. 252.435.111
 Fax: 252.415.888

NEW ZEALAND – NOUVELLE-ZÉLANDE
GPLegislation Services
P.O. Box 12418
Thorndon, Wellington Tel. (04) 496.5655
 Fax: (04) 496.5698

NORWAY – NORVÈGE
NIC INFO A/S
Ostensjoveien 18
P.O. Box 6512 Etterstad
0606 Oslo Tel. (22) 97.45.00
 Fax: (22) 97.45.45

PAKISTAN
Mirza Book Agency
65 Shahrah Quaid-E-Azam
Lahore 54000 Tel. (42) 735.36.01
 Fax: (42) 576.37.14

PHILIPPINE – PHILIPPINES
International Booksource Center Inc.
Rm 179/920 Cityland 10 Condo Tower 2
HV dela Costa Ext cor Valero St.
Makati Metro Manila Tel. (632) 817 9676
 Fax: (632) 817 1741

POLAND – POLOGNE
Ars Polona
00-950 Warszawa
Krakowskie Prezdmiescie 7 Tel. (22) 264760
 Fax: (22) 265334

PORTUGAL
Livraria Portugal
Rua do Carmo 70-74
Apart. 2681
1200 Lisboa Tel. (01) 347.49.82/5
 Fax: (01) 347.02.64

SINGAPORE – SINGAPOUR
Ashgate Publishing
Asia Pacific Pte. Ltd
Golden Wheel Building, 04-03
41, Kallang Pudding Road
Singapore 349316 Tel. 741.5166
 Fax: 742.9356

SPAIN – ESPAGNE
Mundi-Prensa Libros S.A.
Castelló 37, Apartado 1223
Madrid 28001 Tel. (91) 431.33.99
 Fax: (91) 575.39.98

Mundi-Prensa Barcelona
Consell de Cent No. 391
08009 – Barcelona Tel. (93) 488.34.92
 Fax: (93) 487.76.59

Llibreria de la Generalitat
Palau Moja
Rambla dels Estudis, 118
08002 – Barcelona
 (Subscripcions) Tel. (93) 318.80.12
 (Publicacions) Tel. (93) 302.67.23
 Fax: (93) 412.18.54

SRI LANKA
Centre for Policy Research
c/o Colombo Agencies Ltd.
No. 300-304, Galle Road
Colombo 3 Tel. (1) 574240, 573551-2
 Fax: (1) 575394, 510711

SWEDEN – SUÈDE
CE Fritzes AB
S–106 47 Stockholm Tel. (08) 690.90.90
 Fax: (08) 20.50.21

For electronic publications only/
Publications électroniques seulement
STATISTICS SWEDEN
Informationsservice
S-115 81 Stockholm Tel. 8 783 5066
 Fax: 8 783 4045

Subscription Agency/Agence d'abonnements :
Wennergren-Williams Info AB
P.O. Box 1305
171 25 Solna Tel. (08) 705.97.50
 Fax: (08) 27.00.71

SWITZERLAND – SUISSE
Maditec S.A. (Books and Periodicals/Livres
et périodiques)
Chemin des Palettes 4
Case postale 266
1020 Renens VD 1 Tel. (021) 635.08.65
 Fax: (021) 635.07.80

Librairie Payot S.A.
4, place Pépinet
CP 3212
1002 Lausanne Tel. (021) 320.25.11
 Fax: (021) 320.25.14

Librairie Unilivres
6, rue de Candolle
1205 Genève Tel. (022) 320.26.23
 Fax: (022) 329.73.18

Subscription Agency/Agence d'abonnements :
Dynapresse Marketing S.A.
38, avenue Vibert
1227 Carouge Tel. (022) 308.08.70
 Fax: (022) 308.07.99

See also – Voir aussi :
OECD Bonn Centre
August-Bebel-Allee 6
D-53175 Bonn (Germany) Tel. (0228) 959.120
 Fax: (0228) 959.12.17

THAILAND – THAÏLANDE
Suksit Siam Co. Ltd.
113, 115 Fuang Nakhon Rd.
Opp. Wat Rajbopith
Bangkok 10200 Tel. (662) 225.9531/2
 Fax: (662) 222.5188

TRINIDAD & TOBAGO, CARIBBEAN
TRINITÉ-ET-TOBAGO, CARAÏBES
SSL Systematics Studies Limited
9 Watts Street
Curepe
Trinadad & Tobago, W.I. Tel. (1809) 645.3475
 Fax: (1809) 662.5654

TUNISIA – TUNISIE
Grande Librairie Spécialisée
Fendri Ali
Avenue Haffouz Imm El-Intilaka
Bloc B 1 Sfax 3000 Tel. (216-4) 296 855
 Fax: (216-4) 298.270

TURKEY – TURQUIE
Kültür Yayinlari Is-Türk Ltd. Sti.
Atatürk Bulvari No. 191/Kat 13
06684 Kavaklidere/Ankara
 Tél. (312) 428.11.40 Ext. 2458
 Fax : (312) 417.24.90
 et 425.07.50-51-52-53

Dolmabahce Cad. No. 29
Besiktas/Istanbul Tel. (212) 260 7188

UNITED KINGDOM – ROYAUME-UNI
HMSO
Gen. enquiries Tel. (0171) 873 0011
Postal orders only:
P.O. Box 276, London SW8 5DT
Personal Callers HMSO Bookshop
49 High Holborn, London WC1V 6HB
 Fax: (0171) 873 8463
Branches at: Belfast, Birmingham, Bristol,
Edinburgh, Manchester

UNITED STATES – ÉTATS-UNIS
OECD Washington Center
2001 L Street N.W., Suite 650
Washington, D.C. 20036-4922 Tel. (202) 785.6323
 Fax: (202) 785.0350
Internet: washcont@oecd.org
Subscriptions to OECD periodicals may also be
placed through main subscription agencies.

Les abonnements aux publications périodiques de
l'OCDE peuvent être souscrits auprès des
principales agences d'abonnement.

Orders and inquiries from countries where Distributors have not yet been appointed should be sent to:
OECD Publications, 2, rue André-Pascal, 75775
Paris Cedex 16, France.

Les commandes provenant de pays où l'OCDE n'a
pas encore désigné de distributeur peuvent être
adressées aux Éditions de l'OCDE, 2, rue André-
Pascal, 75775 Paris Cedex 16, France.

8-1996

OECD PUBLICATIONS, 2, rue André-Pascal, 75775 PARIS CEDEX 16
PRINTED IN FRANCE
(96 96 11 1) ISBN 92-64-15356-X – No. 48863 1996